Preface x
About the Authors xv

For product information and technology assistance, contact us at
Cengage Learning Customer & Sales Support, 1-800-354-9706.
For permission to use material from this text or product,
submit all requests online at **www.cengage.com/permissions.**
Further permissions questions can be e-mailed to
permissionrequest@cengage.com.

Library of Congress Control Number: 2011940463

ISBN-13: 978-1-111-83306-0

ISBN-10: 1-111-83306-0

Wadsworth
20 Channel Center Street
Boston, MA 02210
USA

Cengage Learning is a leading provider of customized learning solutions with office locations around the globe, including Singapore, the United Kingdom, Australia, Mexico, Brazil, and Japan. Locate your local office at **international.cengage.com/region.**

Cengage Learning products are represented in Canada by Nelson Education, Ltd.

For your course and learning solutions, visit **www.cengage.com.**

Purchase any of our products at your local college store or at our preferred online store **www.ichapters.com.**

Printed in Canada
1 2 3 4 5 6 7 14 13 12 11 10

Texas Politics

Twelfth Edition

Charldean Newell
Regents Professor Emerita of Public Administration
University of North Texas

David F. Prindle
Professor of Government
University of Texas at Austin

James W. Riddlesperger, Jr.
Professor of Political Science
Texas Christian University

WADSWORTH ❖ CENGAGE Learning

Australia • Brazil • Japan • Korea • Mexico • Singapore • Spain • United Kingdom • United States

Texas Politics has now been published for more years than most of its readers have lived. Since 1979, the government and politics of Texas have changed a great deal. The state now has over 25 million people—more than double the 1980 figure—and is second only to California in population. The Republicans have evolved from a decidedly minority political party into the dominant party, especially in statewide politics. What appeared to be a Democratic comeback in the House of Representatives in the 2008 elections was negated by the overwhelming Republican victories of 2010. Oil and gas revenues now fuel less than 6 percent of the state budget, which has increased more than tenfold from the first to the current edition of this book. Citizens find it easier to register to vote and cast their ballots. One elective office—that of state treasurer—has disappeared, and the legislature attacked the powerful Texas Railroad Commission in 2011.

Other aspects of government and politics have not changed appreciably. The Texas Constitution is still a patchwork of detailed provisions and numerous amendments—in fact, more each year—rather than a streamlined document. The judicial system still consists of a hodgepodge of courts with overlapping jurisdictions. The governor continues to use public opinion as an ally in differences with the legislature, and business and economic interests continue to be the dominant influence on the legislature. The executive branch remains confusing because of the myriad boards and commissions that dominate state administration. Local governments continue to be well managed but are facing daunting financial challenges. Spending to address social problems remains a low priority in Texas. Change and the lack of it are part of what makes studying Texas politics interesting. The fascinating dynamics inspire us to continue this book.

The reader will encounter three basic themes in *Texas Politics*, Twelfth Edition. In each case, the authors are describing reality and challenging the readers to make their own assessment. In doing so, we often rub against long-held political notions and biases. First, the overriding theme is a comparison of the reality of Texas government and politics to the democratic ideals of participation, majority rule, minority rights, and equality before the law. Throughout, the authors raise the question of whether a particular political decision meets the test of being good for society as a whole or whether only special interests are served. This discussion is set in the context of the state's traditionalistic/individualistic political culture. As political scientists, the authors are trained to be analysts, not merely observers, of politics. Our mission is not to offer a defense or an apology for the present system, but to identify the differences between governmental practices and the sense of fair play and equity expected in a democratic system. Thus, we point out where the system often works well, but we also examine the faults of the system and suggest needed changes. The "You Decide" feature incorporated into each chapter outlines a debate in which the reader can engage with other students.

A second theme is persistent but not unchallenged conservatism. The Democrats have long been divided into liberal and conservative wings, with the term *conservative* mainly meaning protection of business interests and a paternal attitude toward ethnic minorities and the poor. The Republicans have split between economic conservatives and social conservatives.

Third, because political ideologies are so different among the various political factions and because the ethnic and racial composition of the state is changing rapidly, we introduce a theme of conflict. We particularly call attention to conflicts among the rich, the poor, and the middle class; among and between Anglos, Mexican Americans, and African Americans; between ideologies; and between religious traditions. Additionally, the state now displays sharp distinctions between the two major political parties, a secondary indication of racial, ethnic, and cultural differences.

New to This Edition

The Twelfth Edition reflects a substantial reorganization from previous editions. Coverage of the Texas legislature has been streamlined from two chapters in the previous edition (Chapters 6 and 7) to one (Chapter 6, The Texas Legislature), allowing for more efficient delivery of this critical coverage. The new chapter emphasizes the following: the absolute majority held by Republicans in the Eighty-second Legislature and their internal struggles between Tea Party and orthodox members; efforts to end the "two-thirds rule" in the Senate; the wrangling over issues such as redistricting and social programs; and the ultimate accomplishments, or lack thereof, in the 2011 session.

Two policy chapters (versus one in the last edition) provide even more complete coverage of what is happening in the legislature regarding key policy issues and the impact for the future in these areas. The first (Chapter 13) has been refocused to concentrate on people—health care, education, and social welfare. The second and new policy chapter (Chapter 14) focuses on policies affecting resources—water supply, energy supply, environment (especially air quality), and transportation. We have deleted the "futures" chapter from the new edition (formerly Chapter 15).

A new box in each chapter, "Lone Star Media," discusses the role of media—old and new—and media consumption in Texas politics. For example, "The Missing Ingredient?" (Chapter 1) stresses the importance of a dynamic, involved public consuming the news that the media supply; "Rights versus Rights" (Chapter 2) discusses how the right of freedom of the press is tested; "To Tell the Truth—Or Not" (Chapter 5) talks about *Politifact*, an effort to evaluate the truthfulness of politicians; and "How Do I Tell Thee?" (Chapter 11) considers the means of emergency communication.

Several new editorial cartoons from Pulitzer Prize winner Ben Sargent, recently retired from a 35-year career at the *Austin American-Statesman*, call out the bumblings of Texas politics and both entertain and challenge students.

We have eliminated the Study Questions and Surfing the Web sections from the end of each chapter in favor of offering Learning Objectives in each chapter's opener, which orient students to the major concepts that will be presented.

Chapter-by-Chapter Changes

Content and data have been thoroughly updated for the new edition. Major updates and changes in this edition include the following:

- **Chapter 1:** Discussion of the results of the 2010 census and their implications for Texas politics, and of the conflict between the federal Environmental Protection Agency and Texas politicians over air-pollution rules; updated coverage of how Texas ranks among the fifty states (plus the District of Columbia) in expenditures and taxation and in both objective and subjective measures of quality of life; new box, "Lone Star Media: The Missing Ingredient?"

- **Chapter 2:** Coverage of constitutional amendments through mid-2011; updated comparison of the Texas constitution with those of other states; new box, "Lone Star Media: Rights versus Rights"

- **Chapter 3:** Updated discussions of campaign contributions from special interest groups during the 2010 campaigns, the number of lobbyists in Austin, the activities of selected interest groups during the 2011 legislative session, and the activities of specific organizations ranging from Public Citizen to the Texas Trial Lawyers Association to the Christian Right; new box, "Lone Star Media: How about a Game Called 'Influencing Government?'"; new Table 3-1, Campaign Contributions to Texas Politicians from Credit-Service Businesses, 2010 Election Cycle; new Table 3-2, The "Revolving Door" at the Texas Commission on Environmental Quality

- **Chapter 4:** Discussion and analysis of Tea Party activity during the 2010 campaigns; discussion of possible impact of the "new media"—Facebook, Twitter, texting—on Texas politics; new box, "Lone Star Media: The *Texas Tribune* Comes to the Party"

- **Chapter 5**: Update on voting choice and turnout in the 2010 election; on similarities and differences concerning issue opinions among Anglos, Hispanics, and Blacks; on costs of campaigning in mainstream media; and on electronic voting; new box, "Lone Star Media: To Tell the Truth—Or Not"

- **Chapter 6**: Consolidation of the former legislative chapters into one chapter, with emphasis on the Republican domination, the difficulty the party leaders had in controlling the members, the use of parliamentary maneuvering to accomplish legislative objectives, and the policy outcomes of the Eighty-second Legislature; new boxes, including "Party, Party," "Let the Good Times Roll," "Public Policy Legislative Style: A 2011 Sampler," and "Lone Star Media: Techno-Savvy Legislators"

- **Chapter 7:** Update on Governor Rick Perry's leadership as the longest-serving governor of Texas; new box, "Lone Star Media: Perry and the Press"

- **Chapter 8:** Updated information on major changes in state agencies, including the recommendations of the Sunset Commission; new box, "Lone Star Media: Hi, Ho Silver"

- **Chapter 9:** Update on the structure of the court system and issues in Texas judicial fairness as well as enhanced coverage of "too much crime, too many criminals"; new box, "Lone Star Media: Misleading Court System Images"

- **Chapter 10:** General update of the chapter, plus additional material on civil rights for convicted criminals; new box, "Lone Star Media: Civil Liberties Bills and the 2011 Legislative Session"

- **Chapter 11:** Updated information about types of local governments and the fiscal problems of local governments faced with lowered revenues and more federal and state mandates; new box, "Lone Star Media: How Do I Tell Thee?"

- **Chapter 12:** Analysis of the fiscal year 2012–2013 budget, including the struggle to cope with major revenue shortfalls without raising revenues; new box, "Lone Star Media: How to Spend Money in a Fiscal Crisis"

- **Chapter 13:** Refocusing of chapter to concentrate on education, social welfare, and health care policies; new box, "Lone Star Media: New Media Reduce the Role of Texas Schoolbook Adoptions Nationwide"

- **Chapter 14:** A brand-new chapter on policies affecting resources, including water supply, oil and gas, environment (especially air quality), the clash of economic development and environmentalism, and transportation; chapter features include Table 14-1, Estimated Cost of New Electrical Generation by Resource, 2016; Table 14-2, U.S. Public Opinion about Environmentalism, 2000–2010; and boxes, including "Lone Star Media: Exposé or Propaganda?" "You Decide: Which Energy Source for Texas?" "Alien Invaders!" and "Distinctive but Not Unique"

Supplements

Cengage's new online **Texas Politics CourseReader** gives instructors the flexibility to select as many readings as they want from a selection of 200 primary courses, readings, articles, and videos. Instructors can add their own notes to selections within a reading, highlight sections within a reading, publish notes, edit the introductions to the readings, and assign due dates using the pop-up calendar. Assembling and making changes to selections is easy using the drag-and-drop feature. Learn more and view a demo of CourseReader at www.cengage.com/coursereader.

WebTutor Toolbox is a Web-based teaching and learning tool that integrates with a school's learning management system. It offers access to the ExamView test bank and online study tools including learning objectives, flashcards, weblinks, and practice quizzes.

Readers are invited to visit the companion site for this book: www.cengage.com/politicalscience/newell/texaspolitics12e. Here, the reader can gain access to many helpful learning aids, including tutorial quizzes, flashcards, glossaries, crossword puzzles, and learning objectives for each chapter.

Faculty members can use the Web site to access the Instructor's Manual, PowerPoint presentations, and other teaching aids. These resources and a well-crafted Test Bank in Microsoft Word® and ExamView® can also be found on the PowerLecture CD-ROM for *Texas Politics*, Twelfth Edition. Adopters may also request a copy of *Texas Political Theatre 2.0* on DVD, which offers a collection of important news stories, interviews, and other video clips to stimulate class discussion and students' interest in Texas politics.

A 32-page supplement on Mexican American politics, which can be bundled with the text, uses real examples to detail politics related to Mexican Americans.

Because the Dallas County Community College District has adopted *Texas Politics* for its telecourses, individuals with access to DCCCD programming on public television may find the content familiar.

Acknowledgments

Many people have helped in the preparation of the Twelfth Edition of this book. The authors would like to thank the instructors who reviewed the text for their careful reading of the Eleventh Edition and the useful suggestions they made: Lawrence Christopher, Texas A&M International University; Henry Esparza, University of Texas at San Antonio and Northeast Lakeview College; Brian Farmer, Amarillo College; and Jeffrey Key, Hardin-Simmons University.

Our colleagues also offered constructive criticism and helpful hints. Sometimes we agreed with the reviewers but were unable to comply with their suggestions because of page limitations. Nevertheless, many changes in this edition are due to their comments and the comments of colleagues across the state who called our attention to points deserving coverage or correction. We are similarly indebted to students who raised provocative questions and pointed out places where greater clarity would be appreciated.

Additionally, many other individuals offered valuable assistance in helping us find specific information or documents. They include librarians and other faculty members, graduate students, legislative and state agency staff members, and journalists. We are especially grateful to two people who have been endlessly helpful to us over the course of the many editions of this textbook: Ben Sargent, who makes his editorial cartoons from the *Austin American-Statesman* and *Texas Observer* available to us, and Anne Cook, librarian of the photo library at the Texas Department of Transportation, who has helped choose the photographs that have adorned the covers of these books. His co-authors also gratefully acknowledge the work of Jim Riddlesperger in preparing the instructor's materials for this edition of *Texas Politics*.

Of course, any errors of fact or interpretation are ours alone.

Charldean Newell
Regents Professor Emerita of Public Administration
University of North Texas

David F. Prindle
Professor of Government
University of Texas at Austin

James W. Riddlesperger, Jr.
Professor of Political Science
Texas Christian University

Charldean Newell

Charldean Newell, a Fort Worth native (Ph.D., University of Texas at Austin), is also the co-author of *The Effective Local Government Manager* (ICMA Press, 2004) and *City Executives* (SUNY Press, 1989), and recently edited *Managing Local Government: Cases in Local Government Effectiveness* (ICMA Press, 2009). She has received four national awards: honorary lifetime membership in the International City/County Management Association, the Staats Career Public Service Award from the National Association of Schools of Public Affairs and Administration, the Donald C. Stone Award in intergovernmental relations from the American Society for Public Administration, and elective membership in the National Academy of Public Administration. Her thirty-seven years at the University of North Texas included awards from students, colleagues, and alumni. Her hobbies include reading mysteries, playing with her terrier, and watching sports.

David F. Prindle

David F. Prindle was born in Los Angeles and raised in Hermosa Beach, California. He earned a B.A. at UC Santa Cruz, an M.A. at UCLA, and a Ph.D. at MIT, and was hired by the Government Department at the University of Texas at Austin in 1976. His first scholarly book was *Petroleum Politics and the Texas Railroad Commission* (University of Texas Press, 1981). His wide-ranging interests have also resulted in a scholarly book on the Screen Actors Guild and the political economy of Hollywood. His fifth and most recent scholarly book is *Stephen Jay Gould and the Politics of Evolution* (Prometheus Books, 2009). He has won three teaching awards at UT. His hobbies are fly fishing, reading mystery novels, and getting lost in beautiful places.

James W. Riddlesperger, Jr.

James W. Riddlesperger, Jr. (Ph.D., University of Missouri) is Professor of Political Science at Texas Christian University. A native of Denton, he has taught American politics, with interests in Texas politics, Congress, and the presidency, at TCU since 1982. An award-winning teacher, his publications include the co-edited *Presidential Leadership and Civil Rights Policy* (Greenwood Press, 1995), winner of the Aaron Wildavsky book award, and the co-authored *The Austin-Boston Connection: Five Decades of House Democratic Leadership, 1937–1989* (Texas A&M University Press, 2009). A frequent consultant to the news media concerning politics and elections, he serves also as a question leader and a faculty consultant to the College Board's AP U.S. Government exam. He enjoys reading, baseball, and walking his dogs.

1

The San Jacinto
Monument near
Beaumont commemorates
the 1836 battle in which
Texans won their
independence from
Mexico.

iStockphoto.com/shivasingh

The Context
of Texas Politics

If I owned Hell and Texas, I'd rent out Texas and live in Hell.

GENERAL PHILIP H. SHERIDAN, FORT CLARK, 1855

So what is Texas? The simplest answer is that it is America on steroids.

THE ECONOMIST, A BRITISH NEWSWEEKLY, 2003

All government is bad, including good government.

EDWARD ABBEY, THE JOURNEY HOME, 1977

INTRODUCTION

Much changed in Texas between the era in which General Sheridan made his oft-quoted evaluation of the state and the era in which the editors of *The Economist* made theirs. In 1855, Texas was poor and sparsely settled and offered few civilized comforts to a soldier assigned to garrison an outpost against Native American raids. Today, Texas is the nation's second most populous state, with four-fifths of the population living in cities or suburbs. The state leads the country in consuming energy and producing semiconductors, among other distinctions. Yet, as we shall see, in some ways, the state has changed little since Sheridan's time. Texas is a constantly developing mix of old and new.

Old habits of thought and behavior evolved to meet the problems of the nineteenth century, when Texas was settled by Americans of western European background. These habits persist today, despite serious new problems created in the latter decades of the twentieth and the first decade of the twenty-first centuries. As Texans prepare themselves to meet the challenges of the future, they have to ask themselves if the habits and institutions they have inherited are up to the job.

This chapter begins with a summary of the history of Texas, with an emphasis on important political events and the development of the economy. Next some of the basic principles of democratic theory are discussed, along with an explanation of why it is vital to understand them, and a brief look at one of the problems in a democracy is provided. Two discussions then situate Texas within the American federal system and the international arena, after which the focus shifts to the political culture of Texas with examination of some historically crucial social and political attitudes. The economy of Texas is covered next, including the way it interacts with the state's political system. Then, as an introduction to some discussions later in the book, the origin and distribution of the state's population are considered. Finally, the chapter ends with a brief outline of the agenda for the rest of the book.

OBJECTIVES

After reading this chapter, you should be able to

Give a brief account of the major events and realities of Texas history.

Summarize democratic theory and the standards that it supplies so that we can judge the democratic legitimacy of any state or country.

Explain the political difficulties caused by the fact that Texas is a state within a larger federal system.

Discuss whether Texas should have a "foreign policy."

Describe the three political cultures, and explain how they apply to Texas.

Summarize the overall pattern of the relationship of Texas government to the Texas economy, and decide whether you think Texas is a good place to live.

Discuss the ratios of Anglos, Latinos, and African Americans in the Texas population, and explain their political importance.

Texas History: A Chronology

Like a human being, a state is partly what it is because of what it has experienced. A review of Texas history will highlight the background and context of the themes, institutions, behaviors, and events we discuss in this book.[1]

The Earliest Days

Humans have inhabited Texas for much longer than there has been such a thing as a state. Skull fragments found near Midland (dubbed "Midland Minnie") and a complete female skeleton discovered near Leander have been dated at 10,000 to 13,000 years old; a larger Clovis period (10,000–9,000 B.C.) site has been excavated in Denton County.

At the time of the first European exploration in the sixteenth century, perhaps 30,000 to 40,000 Native Americans inhabited what is now Texas, and some estimates run as high as 130,000. Among the major groups were the Caddo tribes of North and East Texas, Tonkawas in Central Texas, Karankawas along the coast, Coahuiltecans from the Rio Grande to what is now San Antonio, Lipan Apaches and Comanches in West Texas, and Jumanos in the Trans Pecos region. Determined to keep their lands, they violently resisted European settlement. Westward advancement in Texas cost seventeen White lives per mile. One can only guess at the cost to the Native Americans, although it was probably much higher.

As early as 1519, just twenty-seven years after the European discovery of the New World and a century before the English Pilgrims landed at Plymouth Rock, Spanish explorer Alonzo Alvarez de Pineda mapped the entire Gulf Coast. Several expeditions followed, but Spanish activity was not extensive until 1685, when the French explorer Rene Robert Cavaliere de Sieur La Salle built a small fort in what is now South Texas. This threat of competition from their imperial rivals spurred the Spanish to establish a series of missions beginning in 1690. The purposes of these missions were to extend the sphere of Spanish domination and civil law and to convert Native Americans to Christianity. Spanish influence extended across South Texas from Louisiana to New Mexico, and by the time of the American Revolution in 1776, about 2,300 Native Americans had been baptized.

However, by the early nineteenth century, Spanish power was already waning as a result of economic and military factors. After one abortive attempt, Mexico achieved independence from Spain in 1821. By that year, despite the centuries of Spanish influence, there were only three permanent European settlements in Texas—San Antonio, Nacogdoches, and Goliad—and the European population had declined to 7,000 during the previous thirty years. Although their numbers were relatively small, Spaniards and Mexicans left rich and indelible influences on Texas through their language, law, religion, and culture.

Anglo-American Colonization

Colonization from the south did not succeed in Texas because of shortsighted economic policies. The Spanish government exploited the few settlers by paying poor prices for their cattle and other products and, at the same time, by

charging them high prices for trade goods. As a result, few settlers moved to the giant province.

Texas was potentially much more attractive to settlers from the neighboring United States. There, frontier land was sold to would-be settlers, but in Texas, land was free if one could get a government grant. Because the Spanish government had failed to persuade Mexican citizens to colonize the area, it was nervous about expansionist impulses in the United States. Spain decided to gamble that it could acculturate Anglo settlers and use them to protect Mexican interests against the growing, rambunctious democracy to the north.

Moses Austin, a native of Connecticut, abandoned his unsuccessful business activities in Missouri and turned his attention to Texas. Moses died after filing a formal application for settlement with the viceroy of Mexico in 1819. He was succeeded by his son, Stephen F. Austin, who received a generous land grant, as well as permission to bring in 300 families for colonization. The first settlements were at Columbus on the Colorado River and at Washington-on-the-Brazos. As **impresario**, or agent, Austin had wide powers over his colony to establish commercial activity, organize a militia, and dispense justice.

Other colonies quickly followed, and the non-Native American population jumped from 7,000 to more than 35,000 between 1821 and 1836. The great majority of the settlers came in good faith, intending to take the oath of allegiance to Mexico and be good Mexican citizens. However, the cultural differences they encountered made this difficult. Not only was Spanish the official language, but also the colonists, mostly Protestant, were required to accept Roman Catholicism. In addition, some colonists continued to keep Black slaves, although this practice was illegal in Mexico.

Furthermore, the new Mexican nation was suffering from violent political instability, and policy toward Texas was both inconsistent and made 900 miles away in Mexico City by men who knew little about conditions in the area. Moreover, Anglos tended to regard themselves as culturally superior to Mexicans and vice versa. Alienation between Texas and Mexico grew, much as alienation between the colonists and the British had grown prior to the American Revolution two generations earlier.

An Ideal, but Unpaid, Job

In 2005 the Texas legislature established the position of official state historian. The job of the person holding the title, which comes with considerable prestige but no pay, consists of advising government leaders and promoting the understanding of and teaching of Texas history. The current state historian, appointed by Governor Perry in 2009, is Light Cummins, professor of history at Austin College in Sherman. Cummins, who describes himself as a "native Texan born in Connecticut," has just finished his eighth book, a biography of Stephen F. Austin's sister, Emily.

Source: Michael Graczyk, "State Historian Revels in Role as Propagator of the Myth of Texas," *Austin American-Statesman*, June 6, 2009, B1.

The Alamo in San Antonio symbolizes the state's colorful political history.

© Dennis Flaherty/Getty Images

Revolution

The Mexican government now feared further Anglo-American settlement and acted to curtail it. The settlers responded with demands for concessions, including the right to use the English language in public business and the separation of Texas from the state of Coahuila. Austin was imprisoned in Mexico City for a time, and conditions degenerated. What followed is known to virtually every schoolchild in the state: Texas's war for independence.

The most celebrated engagement during the war was the battle in San Antonio in March 1836 in which a few Anglos and Mexican Texans held the Alamo against a much larger Mexican force for eleven days before being massacred. Nevertheless, although it makes a stirring story, the Alamo was not a decisive engagement. That distinction belongs to the Battle of San Jacinto, which took place between the new Texas army, led by Sam Houston, and the Mexican army, led by General Antonio Lopez de Santa Anna, on April 21 of that year. Surprising the Mexicans while they took a siesta in the afternoon, the Texans routed them in a mere eighteen minutes, captured Santa Anna, and ordered him to sign a document agreeing to their independence or be executed. Santa Anna signed, but repudiated the treaty as soon as he was safely across the border. Texans, however, considered themselves independent, and the Republic of Texas became a reality.

The history of the republic, though eventful, was short. Independence brought sudden growth, and the population rose rapidly to about 140,000. The new nation struggled, however. The Mexicans invaded twice, capturing San Antonio both times before being repulsed. Resistant Native Americans continued to cause severe problems as well. Soon the nation found itself in debt and with a depreciating currency.

Sentiment for annexation by the United States had always been strong, and on December 29, 1845, the U.S. Congress voted to admit Texas into the Union as the twenty-eighth state. This was one of those rare events in history: an independent nation voluntarily gave up its sovereignty to become part of another nation. Unlike other states, Texas retained the title to all of its public lands when it accepted statehood.

How Many Heroes?

Although Texans are certain that the men who gave their lives at the Alamo were heroes, they are not quite sure how many of them there were. For most of the twentieth century, the Daughters of the Republic of Texas maintained a roster of "Heroes of the Battle of the Alamo" that contained 183 names, mainly Anglo. Over the decades, a few Spanish-surnamed defenders were added, so that by the early 1990s the "official" number of heroes was 189.

Recent scholarly research, however, has suggested that the victorious Mexican army counted as many as 257 Texan bodies after the battle. Because of the incomplete nature of the Mexican records, it may be impossible to come up with a definitive number.

Source: David McLemore, "160 Years Later, Historians Ask: Who Died at the Alamo?," *Austin American-Statesman*, March 12, 1996, B6.

Early Statehood

At the time Texas became a state, a final peace treaty with Mexico had never been signed, and the Mexican government still considered Texas a rebellious province. The annexation of the area by the United States precipitated the Mexican War. This conflict was relatively short and decisive. The first engagement took place at Palo Alto, near present-day Brownsville, on May 8, 1846, and Mexico City fell a year and four months later on September 14, 1847. Under the Treaty of Guadalupe Hidalgo, signed in early 1848, the defeated nation relinquished all claim to Texas and, in return for $15 million, ceded all territory west of Texas and south of Oregon to the United States. One can only wonder what the value of this vast tract is today.

At the time Texas became independent in 1836, the republic was home to about 5,000 Black slaves.[2] No political parties, as such, existed in the Republic of Texas. Sam Houston, the hero of the Battle of San Jacinto, was the dominant political figure, and political debate generally divided along pro-Houston and anti-Houston lines. By joining the United States, however, the Lone Star State was plunged into the political controversy over slavery. That issue simmered at higher and higher temperatures until it boiled over with the election of an antislavery Republican, Abraham Lincoln, as president in 1860.

To the extent that Texans thought about national politics, most were Democrats. Fearful that Republican control would mean a federal effort to emancipate their slaves, the southern states withdrew from the Union. Texas seceded in February 1861 and joined the new Confederacy in March.

During the Civil War, Texans fought at home, on an expedition into New Mexico, and in large numbers in West Virginia, Tennessee, and elsewhere. Southern troops and southern generals were usually superior to their northern counterparts and won many battles. The agricultural South, however, was outgunned, outmanned, and outsupplied by the industrial North,

and southern political leadership was inferior to Lincoln's. The U.S. president issued the Emancipation Proclamation, freeing the slaves, on January 1, 1863—an act that persuaded European powers not to enter the war on the South's behalf.

The North ground down the South's ability to wage war over four years until the Confederacy fell apart in the spring of 1865. With the defeat of the rebellion, federal troops landed at Galveston on June 19, 1865, proclaiming the freedom of the state's 250,000 slaves. "Juneteenth" is still celebrated by African American Texans as Emancipation Day.

Post–Civil War Texas

Confusion and bitterness followed the Civil War. Despite President Lincoln's stated policy of "with malice toward none, with charity for all," the reaction in Texas, as in other parts of the South, was to continue to oppose national policy even though the war was over. Confederate officials and sympathizers were elected to state and local office, and Black Codes that severely restricted the activities of the former slaves were passed by state legislatures.

This defiance by the defeated South strengthened the position of the Radical Republicans in Congress and caused a hardening of policy, and Lincoln's assassination prevented him from moderating their desire to punish the states of the defunct Confederacy for their rebellion. During the period known as Reconstruction, military government was imposed on the South, and former Confederate officials and soldiers were largely excluded from voting and from holding public office. These actions by the federal government intensified the hostility with which most White Texans viewed the Republican Party. African Americans, as one might expect, voted for the Republicans, giving White Texans even more reason to support the Democrats.

Political activity by the freed slaves also gave rise to the Ku Klux Klan in Texas and throughout the South. Klan members met in secret, bound themselves by oath, and frequently wore hoods to conceal their identities. Their purpose was to keep African Americans in a position of great inferiority. Their methods included intimidation, violence, and sometimes murder.

The best remembered governorship of this Reconstruction period was that of E. J. Davis, one of a number of Texans who had fought for the Union during the war. A Republican, Davis held office from 1870 to 1874. Using the substantial powers granted by the state's Constitution of 1869, Davis acted like a true chief executive and implemented policies consistent with the philosophy of the Radical Republicans in Washington. To his credit, Davis reformed the penal system and greatly improved public education. To his discredit, during his tenure, state indebtedness increased considerably, and there were allegations of financial impropriety. But whatever the merits of his administration, to White Texans he was a traitorous agent of the hated Yankees.

In 1873, after political restrictions against former Confederate officials and soldiers were removed, a Democrat, Richard Coke, defeated Davis in his reelection bid by a two-to-one margin. Just as important as the return of the Democratic Party to power was the repudiation of the Constitution of 1869 and its replacement with Texas's current basic law, the Constitution of 1876. The adoption of this document represented the end of Reconstruction and a substantial return to the traditional principles of the Jeffersonian Democrats, including very limited government and low taxes.

The Late Nineteenth Century

Texas did not suffer the physical destruction that burdened other Confederate states, and economic recovery and development came quickly after the Civil War. The Hollywood version of this era in Texas is one of cowboys, cattle drives, and range wars. There is some basis for the mythical view of post–Civil War Texas as a land of ranches and trail drives, for between 1866 and 1880 four million cattle were driven "north to the rails."[3] Nevertheless, the actual foundation of the state's economy was King Cotton. In East Texas, the fields were worked largely by African Americans, and in West Texas, by Mexican Americans. Cotton remained the cash crop and principal export well into the twentieth century. However, in terms of the self-image of Texans, the myth of cow culture has been far more important than the reality of cotton farming.

Texas has few navigable rivers, and therefore transportation was a major problem. Because of the size of the state, thousands of miles of railroad track were laid. In 1881, embarrassed officials discovered that the state legislature had given the railroads a million more acres of land for rights-of-way than were available, and the land-grant laws were repealed. Nevertheless, in 1888, railroad construction in Texas exceeded the total for all of the other states and territories combined. In all, more than 32 million acres of land were given to the railroads, thus establishing early on the easy relationship between the state government and large corporations.

Race relations were difficult statewide, but particularly in East Texas. "Jim Crow laws" severely limiting the civil rights of African Americans began to make their appearance, and violence against the former slaves was common and often fatal. Between 1870 and 1900, an estimated 500 African Americans died as a result of mob violence, much of it led by the Ku Klux Klan. Although citizenship is much more equal today than it was in the late nineteenth and early twentieth centuries, there is still ethnic conflict in Texas, and some parts of the state continue to display "Old South" racist patterns of behavior.

Throughout most of the final quarter of the nineteenth century, conservative Democrats maintained control of the state. Their rule was based on White supremacy and the violent emotional reaction to the Radical Republican Reconstruction era. But other political parties and interest groups rose to challenge them.

With the penetration of the state by railroads and the increase in manufacturing came organized labor. Most notable were the militant Knights of

What Happens in Galveston Stays in Galveston?

For many years, Galveston permitted gambling and the sale of mixed drinks, despite state laws prohibiting these practices. State and local authorities looked the other way—probably because they were bribed—until the 1950s. The common explanation in Texas was that "Galveston was discovered by pirates and has been run by them ever since."

Labor, which struck the Texas & Pacific Railroad in 1885 and won concessions. Another strike a year later, however, turned violent. Governor John Ireland used troops, ostensibly to protect railroad property, and the strike was broken.

In the optimistic and growing economy of the 1880s, labor unions were less acceptable in the South than elsewhere. In Texas, they were viewed as "Yankee innovations" and "abominations." Although a combination of capital was called a corporation and given approval by the state to operate under a charter, combinations of labor, called unions, were frequently labeled restraints of trade by the courts and forbidden to operate. Laws and executive actions also restricted union activities. These biases in favor of capital and against organized labor are still common in Texas.

More important than early labor unions was the agrarian movement. By the 1870s and 1880s, many of those who worked the land in Texas—whether White, African American, or Mexican American—were tenant farmers. Having to borrow money for seed and supplies, they worked all year to pay back what they owed and rarely broke even. Money and credit were scarce even for those who owned land, and railroad rates were artificially high.

The National Grange, or Patrons of Husbandry, was founded in 1867 in Washington, D.C., to try to defend farmers against this sort of economic hardship. The first chapter was established in Texas in 1872 and the organization grew quickly. Grangers were active in local politics, and the state organization lobbied the legislature on issues relevant to farmers. The Grange not only was influential in establishing Texas Agricultural & Mechanical College (now A&M University) and other educational endeavors but also played a significant role in writing the Constitution of 1876.

James S. Hogg, representing a new breed of Texas politician, was elected governor in 1890 and 1892. The first native Texan to hold the state's highest office, Hogg was not a Confederate veteran. He presided over a brief period of reform that saw the establishment of the Railroad Commission, regulation of monopolies, limitations on alien ownership of land, and attempts to protect the public by regulating stocks and bonds. Unfortunately, it was also an era that saw the enactment of additional Jim Crow laws, including the requirement for segregation of African Americans from Whites on railroads.

Jim Hogg left the governorship in 1895, and the brief period of agrarian reform waned, due in large measure to changes in the membership of the legislature. In 1890, about half the representatives were farmers, but by 1901, two-thirds were lawyers and businessmen. The representation of these professions is similarly high today.

Both major political parties were in turmoil in the late nineteenth century, and in the 1890s, opposition to the Democrats in southern states was most effectively provided by the new People's, or Populist, Party. Populists represented the belief that ordinary people had lost control of their government to rich corporations, especially the banks and railroads. This new party advocated monetary reform, railroad regulation, control of corporations, and other programs aimed at making government responsible to the citizens.

Populists reached their peak strength in Texas in 1894 and 1896, but failed to unseat the Democrats in statewide elections. The dominant party adopted some Populist programs, and most farmers returned to the Democratic fold. Although not the majority sentiment, Populism is still influential in Texas. Texans who are usually political conservatives can sometimes be roused to vote for candidates who argue that government is making policy at the behest of

wealthy insiders rather than ordinary people. The Populist streak makes Texas politics less predictable than it otherwise might be.

The Early Twentieth Century

Seldom has a new century brought such sudden and important changes as the beginning of the twentieth century brought to Texas. On January 10, 1901, an oil well came in at Spindletop, near Beaumont. Oil had been produced in Texas earlier, but not on such a scale. In 1900, the state had supplied 836,000 barrels of oil—about 6 percent of the nation's production. The Spindletop field exceeded that total in a few weeks and, in its first year, gushed out 3.2 million barrels. At first, Texas competed with Oklahoma and California for oil production leadership; however, with the discovery of the huge (6 billion barrels) East Texas field in 1930, the Lone Star State became not only the nation's, but also the world's, leading oil producer.

The abundance and low price of oil in Texas led steamship lines and railroads around the country to abandon the burning of coal and convert to oil. The petroleum business also created secondary industries, such as petrochemicals and the well-service business. Thousands of farm boys left home and took jobs as manual labor "roughnecks." A few became "wildcatters" (independent explorers), and some of those earned fortunes.

In time, more large fields were discovered in every part of the state, except the far western deserts and the central hill country. Oil, combined later with natural gas, replaced cotton and cattle as the most important industry in the state. Severance (production) taxes became the foundation for state government revenue.

The rise of the oil industry created considerable conflict, as well as prosperity. Through shrewd and ruthless means, the Standard Oil Company had made itself into a monopoly in the northeastern states. Texans were determined to prevent the expansion of this giant corporation into their state. Beginning in 1889, the Texas attorney general began bringing "antitrust" suits against local companies affiliated with Standard Oil. After Spindletop, attorneys general were

A cluster of oil derricks close together in the Spindletop oil field during the boom of the early 1900s near Beaumont.

AP-Photo/HO

even more energetic in trying to repel the expansion of the monopoly. By 1939, the state had brought fourteen antitrust actions against oil companies.[4] People in other states often see Texas as dominated by the oil industry when in reality, as this brief summary illustrates, the state has had an ambivalent relationship with the industry. Texans generally celebrate small, independent firms, especially wildcatters. They are suspicious of the major corporations, and state politicians sometimes reflect that suspicion. This is one expression of the Populist tradition in state politics.

Oil was not the only topic to bring conflict to Texas. Even though the agrarian movement had ended in the late nineteenth century, the spirit of progressivism was not completely dead in the early twentieth century. In 1903, the legislature passed the Terrell Election Law, which provided for a system of primary elections rather than the hodgepodge of practices then in use. The legislature also curtailed child labor by setting minimum ages for working in certain industries. National child labor legislation was not passed until thirteen years later. Antitrust laws were strengthened, and a pioneer pure food and drug law was enacted. Farm credit was eased, and the legislature approved a bank deposit insurance plan—a program not adopted by Washington until the 1930s.

Running counter to this progressive spirit, however, was the requirement that a poll tax be paid as a prerequisite for voting. Authorities differ as to whether African Americans, Mexican Americans, or poor Anglos were the primary target of the law, but African Americans were hit especially hard. Their voter turnout, estimated to be 100,000 in the 1890s, dropped to about 5,000 by 1906. Even this small number, however, was too high for the advocates of White supremacy. In 1904, the legislature permitted, and in 1923 it required, counties to institute the "White primary," which forbade African Americans and Latinos to participate in the party contest to nominate candidates for the general election. Because in that era Texas was a one-party Democratic state (see Chapter 4), the winner of the Democratic primary was always the winner in the general election. Thus, even if minority citizens managed to cast a ballot in November, they could only choose among candidates who had been designated by an all-White electorate in April.[5]

The environment was another area where progress came slowly. Early efforts to ensure conservation of the state's natural resources enjoyed little success. Few attempts were made to extract oil from the ground efficiently. A large majority of the oil in most reservoirs was never extracted, and some of the recovered oil was improperly stored so that it ran down the creeks or evaporated. Many improperly drilled wells polluted groundwater. The "flaring" (burning) of natural gas was commonplace into the 1940s. Fifteen million acres of virgin pine trees in East Texas were clear-cut, leading to severe soil erosion. By 1932, only a million acres of forest remained, and wood products had to be imported into the state. Conservation and environmental protection are still uphill battles in Texas.

Wars and Depression

World War I, which the United States entered in 1917, brought major changes to Texas. The state became an important military training base, and almost 200,000 Texans volunteered for military service. Five thousand lost their lives, many dying from influenza rather than enemy action.

America's native hatemongering organization, the Ku Klux Klan, flourished in the early 1920s. Originally founded to keep African Americans subjugated, after the war, the Klan expanded its list of despised peoples to include immigrants and Catholics. Between 1922 and 1924, the Klan controlled every elective office in Dallas, in both city and county government. In 1922, the Klan's candidate, Earle Mayfield, was elected to the U.S. Senate. Hiram Evans of Dallas was elected imperial wizard of the national Klan, and Texas was the center of Klan power nationwide.

When Alfred E. Smith, a New Yorker, a Roman Catholic, and an antiprohibitionist, was nominated for the presidency by the Democrats in 1928, Texas party loyalty frayed for the first time since Reconstruction. Texans voted for the Republican candidate, Herbert Hoover, a Protestant and a prohibitionist. Because of such defections from the formerly Democratic "Solid South" and because of the general national prosperity under a Republican administration, Hoover won.

Partly because the state was still substantially rural and agricultural, the Great Depression that began with the stock market crash of 1929 was less severe in Texas than in more industrialized states. Furthermore, a year later C. M. "Dad" Joiner struck oil near Kilgore, discovering the supergiant East Texas oil field. This bonanza directly and indirectly created jobs for thousands of people. Houston became so prosperous because of the oil boom that it became known as "the city the Depression forgot."

The liquid wealth pouring from the earth in East Texas, however, also created major problems. So much oil came from that one field so fast that it flooded the market, driving prices down. The price of oil in the middle part of the country dropped from $1.10 per barrel in 1930 to $0.25 a year later, and some lots sold for as little as $0.05 per barrel. With their inexpensive overhead, the small independent producers who dominated the East Texas field could prosper under low prices by simply producing more. However, the major companies, with their enormous investments in pipelines, refineries, and gas stations, faced bankruptcy if the low prices continued. The early 1930s were therefore a period of angry conflict between the large and small producers, with the former arguing for production control, and the latter resisting it.

The Railroad Commission attempted to force the independents to produce less, but the independent producers evaded its orders, and millions of barrels of "hot oil" flowed out of the East Texas field from 1931 to 1935. There was confusion and violence before the state found a solution to the overproduction problem. After much political and legal intrigue, the Railroad Commission devised a formula for "prorating" oil that limited each well to a percentage of its total production capacity. By restricting production, this regulation propped up prices, and the commodity was soon selling for more than $1 per barrel again.

As part of this system of controlling production and prices, in 1935, Texas Senator Tom Connally persuaded Congress to pass a "Hot Oil Act," which made the interstate sale of oil produced in violation of state law a federal crime. The major companies thus received the state-sanctioned production control upon which their survival depended. Meanwhile, the Railroad Commission was mollifying the independents by creating production regulations that favored small producers.

Thus, for four decades, the Railroad Commission was in effect the director of the Texas economy, setting production limits, and therefore price floors, for the most important industry in the state. Because Texas was such an

important producer, the commission's regulations exerted a powerful effect on the world price of oil. The commission's nurturing of the state's major industry was a major reason the Depression did not hit Texas as hard as it did many other states.

Even though most Texans were able to weather the Depression better than people in some other places, there were still many who were distressed. Unemployment figures for the period are incomplete, but in 1932, Governor Ross Sterling estimated that 300,000 citizens were out of work. Private charities and local governments were unprepared to offer aid on this scale, and in Houston, African Americans and Hispanics were warned not to apply for relief because there was only enough money to take care of Anglos. The state defaulted on interest payments on some of its bonds, and many Texas banks and savings and loans failed. A drought so severe as to create a dust bowl in the Southwest made matters even worse. Texans, with their long tradition of rugged individualism and their belief that "that government is best which governs least," were shaken and frustrated by these conditions.

Relief came not from state or local action but from the national administration of the new liberal Democratic president, Franklin D. Roosevelt. Texas Democrats played prominent roles in Roosevelt's New Deal (1933–1945). Vice President John Nance Garner presided over the U.S. Senate for eight years, six Texans chaired key committees in Congress, and Houston banker Jessie Jones, head of the Reconstruction Finance Corporation, was perhaps Roosevelt's most important financial adviser and administrator. The New Deal poured more than $1.5 billion into the state in programs ranging from emergency relief to rural electrification to the Civilian Conservation Corps.

As it had during the first global conflict, Texas contributed greatly to the national effort during World War II from 1941 to 1945. The state was once again a major military training site; several bases and many out-of-state trainees remained after the war. More than 750,000 Texans served in the armed forces, and thirty-two received Congressional Medals of Honor. Secretary of the Navy Frank Knox claimed that Texas contributed a higher percentage of its male population to military service than did any other state.

The Silver Lining

During the Depression, an incident occurred that is of particular interest to students in Texas politics classes. In 1929, the state legislature mandated that all public college students be required to take three course hours studying the American and Texas constitutions. As the Depression wore on, Dr. Caleb Perry Patterson, chairman of the Department of Government at the University of Texas at Austin, was faced with the prospect of a greatly reduced budget and a consequent loss of teaching positions in the department that would force him to fire several of his colleagues. In 1937 Patterson convinced the legislature to double the American-and-Texas-government requirement to six semester-hours. He thus saved the jobs of his colleagues by imposing a degree requirement that accounts for many of the readers of this book. The History Department was not able to convince the legislature to pass a similar requirement for an American history course until twenty years later, in 1957.

Post–World War II Texas

By 1950 profound changes had occurred in Texas society. The state's population had shifted from largely rural to 60 percent urban in the decade of the 1940s; the number of manufacturing workers had doubled; and Texas had continued to attract outside capital and new industry. Aluminum production, defense contracting, and high-technology activities were among the leading industries. In 1959, Jack Kilby, an engineer employed by Texas Instruments, developed and patented the microchip, a tiny piece of technology that was to transform the state, the nation, and the world.

After World War II, state politics in Texas was increasingly controlled by conservative Democrats. As a former member of the Confederacy, Texas was one of twenty-two states that had laws requiring racial segregation. The 1954 U.S. Supreme Court decision (*Brown* v. *Board of Education,* 347 U.S. 483) declaring segregated public schools unconstitutional caused an uproar in Texas. State leaders opposed integration, just as their predecessors had opposed Reconstruction ninety years earlier. Grade-a-year integration of the schools—a simple and effective solution—was rejected. Millions of dollars in school funds were spent in legal battles to delay the inevitable.

Texas politics also continued to be colorful. In 1948, Congressman Lyndon B. Johnson opposed former Governor Coke Stevens for a vacant U.S. Senate seat. The vote count was very close in the primary runoff which, with Texas still being dominated by the Democratic Party, was the only election that mattered. As one candidate would seem to pull ahead, another uncounted ballot box that gave the edge to his opponent would be conveniently discovered in South or East Texas. The suspense continued for three days, until Johnson finally won by a margin of eighty-seven votes.

Historical research has left no doubt that the box that put Johnson over the top was the product of fraud on the part of the political machine that ruled Duval County. Among students of American politics, this is probably the most famous dirty election in the history of the country. The circumstances surrounding the election have attracted so much attention because "Landslide Lyndon" Johnson went on to become majority leader of the U.S. Senate, vice president, and then, in 1963, the first Texas politician to attain the office of president of the United States.

Also in the postwar period, Texas experienced an influx of immigrants. Immigration in the nineteenth century had been primarily from adjacent states, Mexico, and west, central, and southern Europe. Following World War II, immigrants began coming not only from all fifty states, but also from Latin America and a variety of other areas, including those of the Middle East and Asia. This trend continues today.

Gradual Political Change

Since the 1950s, Texas has become increasingly diverse in its politics as well as its population. Politicians such as U.S. Senator Ralph Yarborough (1957–1971), Commissioner of Agriculture Jim Hightower (1987–1991), and Governor Ann Richards (1991–1995) have demonstrated that liberals can win statewide offices. Republicans also have won, beginning with U.S. Senator John Tower (1961–1984) and continuing with Governor Bill Clements (1979–1983 and 1987–1991). Furthermore, candidates from formerly excluded groups have

LONE STAR MEDIA
The Missing Ingredient?

Throughout the nineteenth and most of the twentieth centuries, the printed newspaper was, in Texas as elsewhere, the medium that mattered for serious-minded citizens. Television drew a larger audience, but TV was by nature a superficial, entertainment-oriented arena. Newspapers were not perfect suppliers of relevant information, but they were the best and most accessible way for most Texans to access facts and opinions that were useful to people trying to figure out how to govern themselves.

In the twenty-first century, as the Internet drained revenue and readers from newspapers (see Chapter 4), many older people grew nostalgic for the days when the first thing good citizens did in the morning was "read the paper." As a long-time Capitol reporter worried in the pages of *The Texas Observer* in 2009, the absence of investigative reporters in Austin "increases the power of those with the resources to communicate. It disempowers the people who have to rely on the free press."

Perhaps the decline of newspapers is indeed bad for democracy. But it is also possible that neither Texas newspapers nor Texas citizens were ever as good as nostalgic hindsight would suggest. As an editor of the *Dallas Morning News* once complained to a reporter, "Only one hundred people read our stories. And it's the same one hundred people over and over again."

The comment is a reminder that the most important ingredient in a democratic media culture is not the specific technology that supplies information but, rather, the quality of the citizens who consume the news the media supply. A dynamic, involved public will always find a source of good information, and act on it. An apathetic, dull-witted citizenry will ignore the highest-quality information, and pay attention only to trivia and sensation. It is citizens that will make or break Texas democracy, not media.

SOURCES: Bill Minutaglio, "Failing Grades," *Texas Observer*, February 18, 2011, 31; Bill Minutaglio, "Un-Covered," *Texas Observer*, June 26, 2009, 10.

---

enjoyed increasing success, especially after the passage of the Voting Rights Act of 1965. Morris Overstreet was the first African American elected to statewide office, gaining a seat on the Court of Criminal Appeals in 1990. That same year, Mexican Americans Dan Morales and Raul Gonzalez were elected attorney general and justice of the Supreme Court, respectively. Kay Bailey Hutchison broke the gender barrier in statewide elections to national office by being elected U.S. Senator in 1993.

Late-Twentieth-Century Texas

Texas entered a period of good times in the early 1970s. As worldwide consumption of petroleum increased dramatically, the demand for Texas oil outstripped the supply. The Railroad Commission removed market-demand production restrictions in 1972, permitting every well to produce any amount that would not damage ultimate recovery. The following year, the Organization of Petroleum Exporting Countries (OPEC) more than doubled world oil prices

and boycotted the American market. Severe energy shortages developed, and the price of oil peaked at more than $40 per barrel. Consumers, especially those from the energy-poor Northeast, grumbled about long lines at gas stations and high prices, but the petroleum industry prospered and the state of Texas enjoyed billion-dollar treasury surpluses.

The 1980s, however, were as miserable for Texas as the previous decade had been agreeable. High oil prices stimulated a worldwide search for the black liquid, and by 1981, so many supplies had been found that the price began to fall. The slide was gradual at first, but the glut of oil was so great that in 1985, the price crashed from its peak of over $40 per barrel in the 1970s to under $10. As petroleum prices plunged, so did the economy in Texas: For every $1 drop in world oil prices, 13,500 Texans became unemployed, the state government lost $100 million in revenue from severance taxes, and the gross state product contracted by $2.3 billion.[6] Northern consumers smiled as they filled the gas tanks of their cars, but the oil industry and the state of Texas went into shock.

Economic poverty was only one of the miseries that visited Texas in the 1980s. The state's crime rate shot up 29 percent.[7] Most of the crimes committed were related to property and were probably a consequence of the demand for illegal drugs, which constantly increased despite intense public relations and interdiction efforts at the national level. Texans insisted upon better law enforcement and longer sentences for convicted criminals just as the state's tax base was contracting.

The combination of shrinking revenues and growing demand for services forced Texas politicians to do the very thing they hated most: increase taxes. In 1984, the legislature raised Texas taxes by $4.8 billion. Then, faced with greatly reduced state income, it was forced to act again. First came an increase of almost $1 billion in 1986; and then in 1987, there was a boost of $5.7 billion, the largest state tax increase in the history of the United States up to that time.

This system of raising revenue by raising taxes, and relying even more heavily on the sales tax, became more regressive than ever. To make matters worse, the increases came just as Congress eliminated sales taxes as a deductible item on the federal income tax. By the end of the 1980s, Texans were battered, frazzled, and gloomy.

However, the situation reversed itself again in the 1990s. As the petroleum industry declined, entrepreneurs created other types of businesses to take its place. Computer equipment, aerospace technology, industrial machinery, and scientific instruments became important parts of the economy. The state began to export more goods. Despite the fact that Texas oil production reached a fifty-year low in 1993, by the mid-1990s the economy was booming, even outperforming the nation as a whole. The boom continued to the end of the century, at which point the state had the eleventh largest economy in the world. The entry into a new economic era was underscored by the fact that by 1997, more Texans were employed in high-tech industries than by the oil industry.

Prosperity brought another surge in immigration, and in 1994, the Lone Star State passed New York as the second most populous in the country, with 18.4 million residents.[8] Even the crime rate was down. The election of the state's governor, George W. Bush, to the presidency of the United States in 2000 seemed to guarantee a rosy future for Texas.

The History of Prehistory

Legislators love to proclaim official state symbols—it doesn't cost anything, and it's fun. Thus, Texas has an official bird (mockingbird), an official mammal (armadillo), an official fish (guadalupe bass), and many other nonhuman representatives. Sometimes, however, the definition of a state symbol depends on science, and when science changes, the symbol has to be adjusted.

In 1997, the legislature named a large plant-eating lizard, *Pleurocoelus altus*—extinct for the last 112 million years—as the state dinosaur. Although fossils of that species of dinosaur were much more common on the east coast of the United States than in Texas, it was apparently impressive enough to be nominated as the state symbol. Because the reptile is never coming back to life, that action would seem to have been the end of the story.

However, in 2007, Peter Rose, a graduate student in paleontology at Southern Methodist University in Dallas, began to examine a fossil of the alleged Texas *Pleurocoelus*. He decided that the fossil skeleton in front of him was so different from the ones that had been found in Maryland that it was really a different species. *Pleurocoelus*, he concluded, had never roamed as far west as Texas. He wrote a professional paper reporting his conclusions and suggesting that the new species receive the scientific name *Paluxysaurus jonesi*, after the Paluxy River and Jones Ranch in northern Texas, where the fossil had been found. His suggestions were accepted by the official organization of paleontology. Therefore, *Pleurocoelus*, the dinosaur symbol of Texas, was exposed as never having lived in the state.

Politicians, of course, could not allow Texas to be symbolized by the wrong extinct creature. In 2009, the state legislature removed *Pleurocoelus* as the state dinosaur and substituted *Paluxysaurus*.

Sources: Paul J. Weber, "Imposter Dinosaur May Lose Official State Crown," *Austin American-Statesman*, February 2, 2009, B1; state Web sites.

Modern Times

The new century brought many surprises for Texans, as it did for other Americans, many of which were unpleasant. The national economy began to stagger during the spring of 2001. Soon, the media were full of revelations of gigantic fraud in the accounting practices of many apparently successful corporations, including Enron, an energy-trading company based in Houston. The news sent the stock market into a tailspin, and the high-tech sector so important in Texas was hit particularly hard. As high tech went into a recession, Texas lost thousands of jobs.[9]

Economic troubles were joined by political disaster when, on September 11, radical Muslim terrorists hijacked four jet planes and flew two into, and destroyed, the World Trade Center in New York, as well as flying another into the Pentagon building in Washington, D.C., and crashing another into farmland in Pennsylvania. The national grief and outrage over the 3,000 murders resulting from these attacks were accompanied by many economic problems as the United States struggled to spend money to prevent such attacks in the future.

Although not a direct target of the attacks, Texans were as much involved in their consequences as the residents of other states. Efforts to guard borders and

protect buildings were hugely expensive, and conflicting ideas about the ways to interdict terrorists while protecting the civil liberties of loyal citizens were as intense in Texas as elsewhere. The new era in American history guaranteed a new era in Texas politics.

The 2000s were also fraught with perils created by nature rather than by human action. In August 2005, Hurricane Katrina flooded New Orleans in Louisiana, sending hundreds of thousands of refugees across the state border to Houston. The Texas state government paid for housing many of the storm refugees in the Astrodome. Just two weeks later, Hurricane Rita roared ashore on the Texas-Louisiana border, causing major flooding in East Texas and draining the state government of more funds. Then, in 2008, Hurricane Ike devastated Galveston with a 16-foot storm surge and 110 mile-per-hour winds, and caused destruction and loss of life in Houston and the Beaumont-Port Arthur area. Two years later, the state's insurance bill for Ike's damage had approached $12 billion, on top of more than three dozen deaths.[10]

The consequences for the state of these natural disasters did not just consist of mourning and disruption; even before Ike, many insurance companies had stopped writing policies for homes along the Gulf Coast.[11] In the aftermath of the destruction, the citizens of Texas began to reexamine their opposition to government regulation in the midst of a debate about the wisdom of legal restraints on building in areas of coastline that are vulnerable to major storms.[12]

Moreover, as the nation tried to deal with a threatened economic catastrophe caused by the popping of a real-estate bubble, the consequent crash of the stock market, and a severe recession beginning in 2008, Texans found the values of their homes and their stock portfolios declining with everyone else's. As the private economy contracted, state revenue plunged. In Chapter 12 we will report on the problems caused for the state budget by the "Great Recession."

Meanwhile, Texas continued to face some old problems. About 17 percent of its population lived in poverty in 2009—the sixth highest among the states.[13] Although the overall crime rate had declined, the tide of drugs coming into society showed no signs of abating. Additionally, as will be discussed in this book, Texas still had major social and political conflicts. One of the questions that will be considered in the course of our discussion is whether the traditional political attitudes of Texas will be adequate to deal with the challenges of the new era.

Texas as a Democracy

In this book, one of the major themes revolves around the concept of **democracy** and the extent to which Texas approaches the ideal of a democratic state. A democracy is a system of government resting on the theory that political legitimacy is created by the citizens' participation. **Legitimacy** is the belief people have that their government is founded upon morally right principles and that they should therefore obey its laws. According to the moral theory underlying a democratic system of government, because the people themselves (indirectly, through representatives) make the laws, they are morally obligated to obey them.

Complications of this theory abound, and a number of them are explored in each chapter in this book. Because some means to allow people to participate in the government must exist, free elections, in which candidates or parties compete for the citizens' votes, are necessary. There must be some connection between what a majority of the people want and what the government actually does; how close the connection must be is a matter of some debate. Despite the importance of "majority rule" in a democracy, majorities must not be allowed to take away certain rights from minorities, such as the right to vote, the right to be treated equally under the law, and the right to freedom of expression.

In a well-run democracy, politicians debate questions of public policy honestly, the media report the debate in a fair manner, and the people pay attention to the debate, and then vote their preferences consistently with their understanding of the public interest. Government decisions are made on the basis of law, without anyone having an unearned advantage. In a badly run or corrupt democracy, politicians are dominated by special interests but seek to hide the fact by clouding public debate with irrelevancies and showmanship; the media do not point out the problem because they themselves are either corrupt or lazy; and the people fail to hold either the politicians or the media accountable because they do not participate or because they participate carelessly and selfishly. Government decisions are made on the basis of special influence and inside dealing.

In other words, a good democracy is one in which government policy is arrived at through public participation, debate, and compromise. A bad democracy is one in which mass apathy and private influence are the determining factors.

All political systems that are based on the democratic theory of legitimacy have elements of both good and bad. No human institution—no family, church, or government—is perfect, but it is always useful to compare a real institution to an ideal of it and judge how closely the reality conforms to the ideal. Improvements come through the process of attempting to move the reality ever closer to the ideal.

Although many of them could not state it clearly, the great majority of Americans, and Texans, believe in some version of the theory of democracy. It is therefore possible to judge our state government (as it is also possible to judge our national government) according to the extent to which it approximates the ideal of a democratic society and to indicate the direction that the political system must move to become more democratic. Chapters in this book will frequently compare the reality of state government to the ideal of the democratic polity, and ask readers to judge whether they think there is room for improvement in Texas democracy.

As indicated, one of the major causes of shortcomings in democratic government, in Texas as elsewhere, is *private influence over public policy*. Ideally, government decisions are made to try to maximize the public interest, but too often in reality, they are fashioned at the behest of individuals who are pursuing their own special interests at the expense of the public interests. This book will explore the ways that powerful individuals try to distort the people's institutions into vehicles of their own advantage. It also will examine ways that representatives of the public resist these selfish efforts to influence public policy. Part of the political process in Texas, as in other democracies, is the struggle to ensure that the making of public policy is truly a people's activity rather than a giveaway to the few who are rich, powerful, and well connected.

Texas and American Federalism

This book is about the politics of one state. However, just as it would be impossible to describe the functions of one organ in the human body without reference to the body as a whole, it would be misleading to analyze one state without reference to the nation.

The United States has a **federal system**. This label means that its powers are divided between, and shared among, the national government and the state governments. Because the national and state governments must share responsibility for many policy areas, a great many state responsibilities are strongly influenced by the actions of all three branches of the national government. Further, the states and the federal government frequently disagree, and often their disagreements become connected to larger political conflict.

For example, in 1994 the state's environmental protection agency, then called the Texas Resource Conservation Commission (TRCC), created a set of rules to apply to power plants and refineries.[14] The rules permitted each plant to vary the amount of air pollution created by individual sources within the plant (such as a boiler), as long as the total amount emitted by the plant as a whole stayed below a specified level. Those rules stayed in place for a decade. But in 2005 the federal Environmental Protection Agency (EPA) issued a statement that it believed that the state rules allowed Texas plants to put too much pollution into the air, thus violating the federal Clean Air Act of 1990. As one environmentalist explained the federal position, the flexible permitting program "is like saying, 'As long as you go 55 miles per hour on average, in a month, you can go 100 or 125 some days.'" The EPA indicated that Texas had better start setting limits for each individual source of pollution within every plant, or it would take over the state's program.

Texas Republican politicians viewed this threat as an occasion to expound on one of their favorite themes—that Washington is inept yet power-hungry, and knows less about how to govern Texas than Texans do. As the dispute became

Cartoonist Ben Sargent illustrates the ironic relationship that Texas politicians have with the federal government: while they despise and verbally abuse it often, they also rely upon it for many vital resources.

Courtesy of Ben Sargent

more heated in 2010, Governor Perry wrote a letter to the EPA that it was about to replace a successful state program "with a less effective Washington-based, bureaucratic-led, command and control mandate," while Lieutenant Governor Dewhurst characterized the EPA's action as "politically driven by the increasingly partisan Obama administration in trying to mess with Texas."

In June of 2010, Texas Attorney General Greg Abbott filed a "petition of reconsideration" with the federal courts, asking the judges to put the EPA's action on hold in order to "defend the state's legal rights and challenge improper overreach by the federal government." Meanwhile, several Democratic state legislators accused the Republican politicians of turning a public health issue into a partisan debate, and called on the EPA to do everything in its power to ensure that Texans breathe clean air.

As a general theme, the state-versus-federal government argument arose before there was a state of Texas, during the 1790s, and will no doubt continue in some form long after this particular tiff between the EPA and Texas politicians is forgotten. For the present, the value of the controversy is that it illustrates the type of not-always-easy relationship that Texas experiences with the larger national government.

Environmental protection is only one of the state's policy spheres in which the federal government is a constant and important—though sometimes irritating—influence. Washington makes an impact on Texas government in other areas as well, including the following:

1. **A significant portion of state revenue each year comes from federal grants (see Chapter 12).**

2. **The U.S. Supreme Court oversees the actions of the state government and, historically, has forced Texas to make many changes in its behavior, especially with regard to civil rights and liberties (see Chapter 11).**

3. **Congress allocates many of the "goodies" of government, such as military bases, veterans' hospitals, highways, and so on, which have a crucial impact on the state's economy.**

4. **Congress mandates the state government to take actions, such as making public buildings accessible to people with disabilities or instituting background checks on gun purchasers, that force the Texas legislature to raise and spend money.**

5. **Congressional policymaking and budget decisions shape sensitive state issues, such as the response to poverty (Medicaid policy, for example) and protection of the environment (requirements for clean water and air, for example).**

6. **When Congress declares war or the president sends troops to a foreign conflict without a declaration of war, Texans fight and die. The war on terrorism that began with the 9/11 attacks has imposed particular burdens on Texas. In its efforts to seal national borders from infiltration, the federal government has slowed the traffic between the United States and Mexico, which has inevitably damaged commerce between Texas and Mexico. Efforts to protect buildings, dams, bridges, and water supplies from future attacks have required expenditures of large sums of money by state and**

local authorities. Campaigns to train "first responders" such as police, fire, and medical personnel to react quickly and competently to potential terrorist incidents have put further strain on local and state budgets. Policies by the federal Department of Justice to identify terrorists by gaining access to information about all residents of the United States have raised fears, in Texas as elsewhere, that ordinary citizens will lose many of their civil liberties.

7. The president's many discretionary powers, such as cutting tariffs on imported goods and releasing federal disaster-relief funds, leave their mark, for good or ill, on the state's economy.

8. When the Federal Reserve Board raises or lowers interest rates, it constricts or stimulates Texas's economy, along with the economies of the other forty-nine states. The changes thus created powerfully affect both the amount of money the state legislature has to spend and the demands on its allocation of resources.

Although this brief list may seem to describe a relationship between the states and the national government that is static, in fact the relationship is constantly changing and thus, as the EPA example illustrates, is often the subject of conflict. Given the nature of federalism, how Texas fits into it at any time is the result of an ongoing argument. Texas politics is a subject unto itself, but it is also part of a larger whole; therefore, this book, which focuses on Texas, contains frequent references to actions by national institutions and politicians.

Texas in the International Arena

Despite the fact that the U.S. Constitution forbids the individual states to conduct independent foreign policies, the shared border between Texas and Mexico has long exercised an important effect on the politics of Texas. Not only are many Texas citizens of Mexican (and other Latin) background, but the common border of Texas and Mexico, the Rio Grande, flows for more than 800 miles through an arid countryside, a situation that almost demands cooperation over the use of water. Furthermore, with the passage of the North American Free Trade Agreement (NAFTA) in 1993, Texas became important as an avenue of increased commerce between Mexico and the United States. Interstate Highway 35, which runs from the Mexican border at Laredo through San Antonio, Austin, and the Dallas/Fort Worth Metroplex, and then north to Duluth, Minnesota, has become so important as a passageway of international trade that it is sometimes dubbed "the NAFTA highway." As a result of geographic proximity, Mexico is an important factor in Texas economy and politics, and vice versa.

Many examples could be used to illustrate the interconnections of Texan and Mexican politics, but the following example is one drawn from the criminal justice system. At first glance, it might seem like this case was wholly a matter of internal interest to Texas. On the contrary, however, this case demonstrates that even a subject such as the state's decision to execute a murderer can have an international impact.[15]

YOU ★ ★ DECIDE

Should Texas Have a Foreign Policy?

As the world has become more integrated, and especially as economies have become globalized, Texas leaders have attempted to establish institutions for dealing with foreign governments. Their efforts in this area have been particularly enthusiastic in regard to Mexico. The state opened a trade office in Mexico City in 1971, helped establish the Border Governors' Conference in 1980, began the Texas-Mexico Agricultural Exchange in 1984, has participated in the Border States Attorneys General Conference since 1986, and established the Office of International Coordination to deal with the problem of retrieving child support payments from fugitive fathers in 1993. Texas governors now have special advisors on the economy and politics of foreign countries, and they make trips to visit foreign politicians in hopes of increasing commerce between their state and foreign countries.

In its attempts to establish regular relationships with foreign countries, Texas comes close to having a state "foreign policy." However, is it wise for a state, as opposed to the U.S. national government, to be so deeply involved in foreign affairs?

PRO	CON
▲ The Constitution does not forbid states to enter into voluntary, informal arrangements with foreign governments, and the Tenth Amendment declares that anything not forbidden to the states is permitted.	▼ A major reason for the independent states coming together to form the union in 1787 was so that they could stop working at cross-purposes in foreign policy and present a united front to the world, and that is why Article I, Section 10 of the Constitution says that "No state shall . . . enter into any Agreement or Compact . . . with a foreign Power. . . ."
▲ Most state foreign policy initiatives, such as the Texas trade agreements with Mexico, deal with friendly relations, not disputes.	▼ The Logan Act of 1799 prohibits U.S. citizens from "holding correspondence with a foreign government or its agents, with intent to influence the measures of such government in relations to disputes or controversies with the United States."
▲ Since when is competition a bad thing? If citizens want to keep labor unions strong and the environment clean, they should vote for candidates who will support such policies.	▼ If states (and cities) are allowed to compete for business with foreign countries, their rivalry will cause them to lower standards of labor and environmental protection.
▲ As the example of Javier Suarez Medina illustrates, domestic actions in Texas already have had an impact on relations with foreign countries. It would be better to acknowledge this fact frankly and make state policy with the conscious intent of furthering the state's interests.	▼ If all fifty states have independent relations with foreign countries, it will cause confusion and chaos between the federal government and those countries.

Source: Julie Blase, "Has Globalization Changed U.S. Federalism? The Increasing Role of U.S. States in Foreign Affairs: Texas-Mexico Relations," PhD dissertation, University of Texas at Austin, 2003.

In 1988, Javier Suarez Medina shot to death a Dallas police officer while the officer was conducting an undercover drug sting. There was no doubt about Medina's guilt, as he was immediately apprehended by other police officers—the perfect open-and-shut, smoking-gun-in-the-hand arrest. However, things were not as simple as they first appeared.

Medina, as became clear later, had been born in Mexico. Because of his foreign nationality, under the Vienna Convention of Consular Relations of 1963, ratified by the United States and 169 other countries in 1969, local authorities were supposed to notify the Mexican consul and allow that country to assist Medina with his defense. While Medina was being held after his arrest, however, he gave conflicting and confusing statements as to his nationality, claiming at various times that he came to El Paso when he was three or seven years old and that he was born in that city. Partly because of their confusion as to his nativity, and partly, no doubt, because of their intense desire to punish a cop killer, neither the Dallas police department nor the state ever contacted the Mexican consulate. Medina was tried, convicted of murder, and sentenced to die by lethal injection.

While Medina sat on death row, however, his case came to the attention of Mexican officials. They launched a campaign to persuade the state to retry him, this time complying with the requirements of the consular treaty. Part of the conflict was caused by the fact that except under unusual circumstances, such as crimes under military law or during wartime, Mexico does not execute criminals. The case became a patriotic cause in Mexico, with that country's politicians feeling bound to try to make Texas officials reverse the conviction or at least commute Medina's sentence to life in prison.

In 2002, Mexican President Vicente Fox made a personal crusade of the Medina case. He appealed to the Texas Board of Pardons and Paroles, Governor Rick Perry, and President George W. Bush to stop or postpone the execution. Nevertheless, all national and state individuals and institutions politely ignored Fox. Medina was executed on August 14, 2002.

Fox was scheduled to visit Texas, and President Bush at his ranch in Crawford, in late August of that year. However, the Mexican president's inability to affect the Medina case was, from his point of view and the point of view of his country, an insult that could not be ignored. Fox canceled the visit. His office issued a statement that "it would be inappropriate to carry out this trip to Texas given these lamentable circumstances." Relations between the two countries, on the upswing after decades of hostility, immediately turned around and became tense.

In January 2003, the Mexican government filed a complaint before the International Court of Justice (ICJ, known informally as the World Court) in The Hague, Netherlands, alleging that fifty-four Mexican nationals, several of them in Texas, were currently on death row even though the Mexican consulate had not been notified of their arrests and trials. The next month, the ICJ issued a decision telling Texas and Oklahoma to postpone three executions until it had time to investigate the cases. The ICJ has no authority in the United States, and both states ignored its "order." The Mexican government obviously hoped to use the publicity the World Court's decision generated to bring moral persuasion to bear on American state governments. So far, it has had no success in this area, but the fact that it is trying is an indication of how seriously Mexicans take the issue.

Fox and Perry eventually decided that the interests of their two polities were too important to ignore, and they agreed to disagree. In November 2003, Fox returned to Texas as the governor's guest.

In 2006, the U.S. Supreme Court held in two other cases, one from Oregon and one from Virginia, that foreign-born convicted criminals do not have the right to be retried because their states failed to notify their native countries of their arrest. The Justices did not squarely address the issue of whether individuals are entitled to rights under the Vienna Convention, or whether that treaty refers only to diplomacy between nations. No matter how the Court ruled, of course, it was too late to save Medina, or to undo the damage to relations between Mexico and Texas/United States.

Despite the legal ambiguity and the eventual reconciliation of the two Mexican and Texan leaders, the point had been made that the actions of Texas's criminal justice system can have repercussions on relations between the United States, as a whole, and a foreign country. The political choices of states, such as Texas, have consequences far beyond their own governments.

The Texas Political Culture

Like the other forty-nine states, Texas is part of a well-integrated American civil society. It is also a separate and distinctive society with its own history and present-day political system. Culture is the product of the historical experiences of a people in a particular area. Our political system is the product of our political culture. **Political culture** refers to a shared system of values, beliefs, and habits of behavior with regard to government and politics.

Not everyone in a given political culture accepts all of that culture's assumptions, but everyone is affected by the beliefs and values of the dominant groups in society. Often, the culture of the majority group is imposed on members of a minority who would prefer not to live with it.

Texas's political culture is unusual, partly because of the state's great size, its geographic isolation until the twentieth century, and the historical fact that it was an independent republic before joining the United States. The state's culture is also distinctive because it is a mixture of the cultures of the Old South and the Western frontier.

Texas shares with other Southern states its history as a society that formerly held slaves, and one that was defeated in a civil war and then occupied, in a humiliating fashion, by victorious Northern troops. In common with other White Southerners after the end of Reconstruction, Anglo Texans attempted to deny full citizenship to African Americans. Because of the Lone Star State's proximity to Mexico, the Anglos further tried to suppress the citizenship of Latinos. The historical heritage of White people in Texas is thus one of extreme cultural conservatism. This conservatism has extended not only to attitudes on civil rights for minority citizens, but also to hostility toward labor unions and toward liberal political programs in general.

Mixing with and reinforcing the Old South cultural conservatism has been an intense individualism deriving from the myth of the frontier. Anglo Texans have always seen themselves as ruggedly independent, as self-sufficient pioneers who need no help from anyone and are not obligated to support other people with their taxes. This hostility toward collective action, especially on behalf of the weak, has dovetailed perfectly with southern cultural conservatism to strengthen public opposition to liberal, activist government in Texas.

Political scientist Daniel Elazar and his associates have extensively investigated patterns of political culture across the fifty states. Elazar identifies three broad, historically developed patterns of political culture.[16] Although every state contains some elements of each of the three cultures, politics within states in identifiable regions tend to be dominated by one or a combination of two of the cultures.

In the **moralistic** political culture, citizens understand the state and the nation as commonwealths designed to further the shared interests of everyone. Citizen participation is widely shared value, and governmental activism on behalf of the common good is encouraged. This culture tends to be dominant across the extreme northern tier of American states. The states of Washington and Minnesota approach the "ideal type" of the moralistic culture.

In the **individualistic** political culture, citizens understand the state and nation as marketplaces in which people strive to better their personal welfare. Citizen participation is encouraged as a means of individual achievement, and government activity is encouraged when it attempts to create private opportunity and discouraged when it attempts to redistribute wealth. This culture tends to be dominant across the "middle north" of the country from New Jersey westward. Nevada and Illinois approach the ideal types of the individualistic culture.

In the **traditionalistic** political culture, citizens technically believe in democracy, but emphasize deference to elite rule within a hierarchical society. While formally important, citizen participation is not encouraged and the participation of disfavored ethnic or religious groups may be discouraged. Government activity is generally viewed with suspicion unless its purpose is to reinforce the power of the dominant groups. This culture tends to be dominant in the southern tier of states from the east coast of the continent to New Mexico. The states with ideal types of traditionalistic cultures are Mississippi and Arkansas.

Table 1-1 summarizes the three political cultures as they are expressed across a number of significant political and social dimensions. It is important to understand that the general tendencies displayed in the table permit many exceptions. They represent only broad patterns of human action, that is, the way many people in the groups have often behaved throughout history. They do not describe everyone, nor do they prescribe a manner in which anyone must behave in the future.

The research that has been done on Texas places it at a midpoint between the traditionalistic and individualistic political cultures.[17] Historically, the state's experience as a slave-holding member of the Confederacy tends to embed it firmly in traditionalism, but its strong business orientation, growing more important every decade, infuses its original culture with an increasingly influential individualistic orientation. Many of the political patterns discussed in this book are easier to understand within the context of the Texas blend of cultures.

Not all Texans have shared the beliefs and attitudes that will be described here. In particular, as will be discussed in more detail in Chapter 5, African Americans and Mexican Americans have tended to be somewhat separate from the political culture of the dominant Anglo majority. Nevertheless, both history and present political institutions have imposed clear patterns on the assumptions that most Texans bring to politics.

There is one sense in which Texas has a well-earned reputation for uniqueness. All visitors have testified to the intense state patriotism of Texans. Whatever their education, income, age, race, religion, gender, or political ideology, most Texans seem to love their state passionately. Whether this state patriotism is due to the myth of the Old West as peddled by novels, schools, and Hollywood,

TABLE 1-1

The Three Political Cultures

Type	Moralistic	Individualistic	Traditionalistic
Attitude toward Participation	Encouraging	Encouraging	Supports if on behalf of elite rule; otherwise, opposes
Attitude toward Political Parties	Tolerant	Strong party loyalty	Discouraging
Attitude toward Government Activity	Supports if activity is on behalf of the common good	Supports if on behalf of individual activity; opposes if on behalf of redistribution of wealth	Supports if on behalf of elite rule; otherwise, opposes
Attitude toward Civil Liberties and Civil Rights	Strongly supportive	Ambivalent; supports rights for themselves, but indifferent to rights of others	Indifferent
Religious Groupings Most Commonly Supporting	Congregationalists, Mormons, Jews, Quakers	Lutherans, Roman Catholics, Methodists	Baptists, Presbyterians, Pentecostals
Geographic Area of Strongest Impact	Northernmost tier of states, plus Utah and Colorado	Middle-northern tier of states	Old South, plus New Mexico

NOTE: These are descriptions of general historical patterns only. They do not necessarily apply to the behavior of any specific family, individual, or group.

SOURCES: Daniel J. Elazar, *American Federalism: A View from the States,* 3rd ed. (New York: Harper & Row, 1984), 109–173; Ira Sharkansky, "The Utility of Elazar's Political Culture: A Research Note," in Daniel J. Elazar and Joseph Zikmund II, eds., *The Ecology of American Political Culture: Readings* (New York: Thomas Y. Crowell, 1975), 247–262; Robert L. Savage, "The Distribution and Development of Policy Values in the American States," in ibid., 263–286, and Appendices A, B, and C.

or to the state's size and geographic isolation, or to its unusual history, or to something in the water, is impossible to say. This patriotism, however, has little political relevance because native Texans show no hostility toward non-natives and have elected several non-native governors. But woe to the politician who does not publicly embrace the myth that Texas is the most wonderful place to live that has ever existed on the planet! As scholars rather than politicians, the authors of this book intend to look at the state through a more analytic lens.

Part of the larger American political tradition is a basic attitude toward government and politicians that was most famously expressed in a single sentence attributed to President Thomas Jefferson: "That government is best which governs least." As the quote from Edward Abbey at the beginning of this chapter attests, Jefferson's philosophy has a powerful presence in the United States in contemporary times. The name usually given to that philosophy is **conservatism**, and it has dominated Texas politics since the end of the Civil War.

The term *conservatism* is complex, and its implications change with time and situation. In general, however, it refers to a general hostility toward government activity, especially in the economic sphere. Most of the early White settlers came to Texas to seek their fortunes. They cared little about government and

wanted no interference in their economic affairs. Their attitudes were consistent with the popular values of the Jeffersonian Democrats of the nineteenth century: the less government the better, local control of what little government there was, and freedom from economic regulation, or **"laissez faire"** (a French phrase loosely translated as "leave it alone").

Conservatism is, in general, consistent with the individualistic political culture on economic issues (welfare, for example) and with the traditionalistic political culture on social issues (civil rights, for example). Texas conservatism minimizes the role of government in society, and particularly in the economy. It stresses an individualism that maximizes the role of businesspeople in controlling the economy. To a Texas conservative, a good government is mainly one that keeps taxes low.

Consistent with the emphasis on laissez faire is a type of **social Darwinism**: the belief that individuals who prosper and rise to the top of the socioeconomic ladder are worthy and deserve their riches, while those who sink to the bottom (or having been born there, stay there) are unworthy and deserve their poverty. Social Darwinists argue that people become rich because they are intelligent, energetic, and self-disciplined, whereas those who become or remain poor do so because they are stupid, lazy, and/or given to indulgence in personal vices. Socioeconomic status, they argue, is the result of natural selection.[18]

It is true that a person's success in life frequently results in part from his or her behavior and qualities of character. Success, however, also depends on many other factors, such as education, race and ethnicity, proper diet and medical care, the wealth and education of the person's parents, and luck. Nonetheless, social Darwinism continues to dominate the thinking of many Texans who strongly resist the idea that government has an obligation to come to the aid of the less fortunate in society.

Rhetoric and Reality

In practice, laissez faire in Texas has often been **pseudo** (false) **laissez faire**. Entrepreneurs do not want government to regulate or tax them, and they denounce policies to help society's less fortunate as "socialism." However, when they encounter a business problem that is too big to handle, they do not hesitate to accept government help.

A good example is the city of Houston. Its leaders praise their city as the home of unrestrained, unaided free enterprise. In fact, however, Houston has historically relied on government activity for its economic existence. The ship channel, which connects the city's port to the sea, was dredged and is maintained by the federal government. Much of the oil industry, which was responsible for Houston's twentieth-century boom, was sustained either by state regulation through the Railroad Commission or by the federal government selling facilities to the industry cheaply, as occurred with the Big Inch and Little Inch pipelines. Billions of dollars of federal tax money have flowed into the area to create jobs in the space industry (the Johnson Space Center and NASA).

Houston's business leaders have not resisted such government action on their behalf—quite the contrary. It is only when government tries to help ordinary people that the business community upholds the banner of laissez faire.

Source: Joe R. Feagin, *Free Enterprise City: Houston in Political-Economic Perspective* (New Brunswick, N.J.: Rutgers, 1988).

This resistance to government aid to the needy has resulted in many state policies that mark Texas as a state with an unusually stingy attitude toward the underprivileged. For example, at the end of the first decade of the twenty-first century, among the fifty states, Texas ranked forty-fourth in its weekly payments to the mothers of poor children (TANF) and forty-seventh in its spending on public welfare programs.[19]

Pseudo laissez faire economic doctrine and social Darwinism lead to a **trickle-down theory** of economic and social development. If business flourishes, so the theory goes, prosperity will follow and benefits will trickle down to the majority of Texans. In other words, if government caters to the needs of business rather than attempting to improve the lives of the poor, everyone's economic situation will improve. To a degree, the trickle-down theory does work, but only to a degree, because approximately 17 percent of the state's citizens existed at or below the poverty level in 2009.[20]

Another general attitude toward government, called **liberalism**, accepts or even endorses government activity as often being a good thing. Although conservatives have dominated Texas politics through most of its history, occasionally liberals have been elected to public office, and sometimes liberal ideas have been adopted as state policy. The conflict between liberalism and conservatism underlies much political argument in the United States. Chapter 4 explores the way these two ideologies have formed the basis for much of Texas politics.

Economy, Taxes, and Services

When General Sheridan made his harsh evaluation of Texas in 1855 (see quotation at beginning of chapter), the state was poor, rural, and agricultural. As summarized earlier in this chapter, however, in the twentieth century, its economy was transformed: first by the boom in the oil industry that began at Spindletop in 1901, and then by diversification into petrochemicals, aerospace, computers, and many other industries. Metropolitan areas boomed along with the economy, and the state became the second most populous in the nation.

The state's political culture, however, has not changed as rapidly as its population and economy. Texas's basic conservatism is evident in the way the state government treats business and industry. In 2007, for example, Texas was rated by cable channel CNBC as number one on its ranking of "America's Top States for Business," passing number two Virginia for the first time.[21] Similarly, in 2009 the Small Business and Entrepreneurship Council ranked Texas as having the third best environment for small business.[22]

Other observers are less admiring of the Texas economy and less optimistic about its future. A favorable business climate consisting of low taxes, weak labor unions, and an inactive government may seem attractive in the short run; however, in the long run, these policies may create a fragile economy. The Corporation for Enterprise Development (CED) is a private organization that sometimes grades each state in terms not only of its economic health at any one time, but also its capacity for positive growth in the future. In 2002 and again in 2007, the CED flunked the Texas economy as a whole, giving it Ds in "earnings and job quality," Fs in "equity," Fs in "quality of life," and Ds in "resource efficiency." The CED commented in 2002 that "a theme of inequality throughout the state . . . the disparity between the wealthy and the poor . . ." augured poorly

TABLE 1-2

Texas Rank among States in Expenditure and Taxation

Category	Year	Rank
a. Per-capita personal income	2008	26
b. State government per-capita spending	2007	50
c. Spending per school pupil	2010	38
d. Average teacher salary	2010	33
e. Per-capita Medicaid spending	2005	37
f. Average monthly benefit, Women, Infants and Children (WIC)	2009	48
g. Average monthly payment, Temporary Assistance to Needy Families (TANF)	2007	44
h. State spending on arts agency	2010	43
i. Per-capita spending on water quality	2002	47
j. Regressivity of state and local taxes	2010	5

SOURCES: a, b, c, d, f, g, and h from Kathleen O'Leary Morgan and Scott Morgan, *State Rankings 2010: A Statistical View of America* (Washington, D.C.: CQ Press, 2010), 102, 354, 142, 125, 554, 546, and 161; e from Kendra A. Hovey and Harold A. Hovey, *CQ's State Fact Finder 2007* (Washington, D.C.: CQ Press, 2006), 255 and 170; i from the document "Texas on the Brink: How Texas Ranks Among the 50 States," on the Web site www.bayareanewdemocrats.org/files/texasrankings; j from *Who Pays? A Distributional Analysis of the Tax Systems in All 50 States* (Washington, D.C.: Institute on Taxation and Economic Policy, 2009).

for the future of Texas. In contrast to Texas, the CED reported that its "honor roll" states of Colorado, Connecticut, Maryland, Massachusetts, Minnesota, New Jersey, Virginia, and Wisconsin were pursuing public policies that ensured them a brighter economic outlook.[23]

Because of the Jeffersonian conservative philosophy underlying many of the activities of Texas government, the state generally does little, compared to the governments of other states, to improve the lives of its citizens. As Table 1-2 illustrates, on several measures of state services, Texas ranks near the bottom. The state spends comparatively little on education, health, welfare, the environment, and the arts. Furthermore, it raises the relatively small amount of revenue it does spend in a "regressive" manner, that is, in a manner that falls unusually lightly on the rich and unusually heavily on the poor. The philosophy that dominates Texas politics holds that if government will just keep taxes low—especially on its wealthier citizens—and stay out of the way, society will take care of itself.

Part of the discussion in this book will center on the way Texas politics reflects "a theme of inequality." Some chapters will analyze the sources of unequal politics; some will portray the consequences of it in terms of public policy. Always, the implications of inequality for democratic legitimacy will be a major focus in this discussion.

Liberals, viewing the facts on display in Table 1-2, would argue that Texas's laissez faire ideology has had a pernicious effect on its quality of life. Texans, as a group, are so patriotic that it is difficult for them to believe that their state is a comparatively undesirable place to live, but liberals would point to the sorts of evidence illustrated in Table 1-3. As the table emphasizes, the state ranks

TABLE 1-3

Texas Rank among States in Measures of Quality of Life

Quality-of-Life Measure	Year	Rank
a. Highest violent crime rate	2008	12
b. Highest overall crime rate	2008	9
c. Highest incarceration rate	2008	4
d. Highest poverty rate	2009	6
e. Best "condition of children" index	2009	34
f. Cleanest drinking water	2004	32
g. Highest air pollution emissions	2002	1
h. Best average SAT reading score	2006	48
i. Best average SAT math scores	2006	44
j. Best health care system	2010	49
k. Highest percentage of overweight or obese adults (66.2%)	2008	8
l. Best "chance for success" for children	2010	39
m. Most liveable based on "state livability" index	2008	39

SOURCES: a, b, c, and k from Kathleen O'Leary Morgan and Scott Morgan, *State Rankings 2010: A Statistical View of America* (Washington, D.C.: CQ Press, 2010), 35, 31, 61, and 422; d from Erik Ekholm, "Report: Poverty Hits 1 in 7," *Austin American-Statesman*, September 17, 2010, A1; e from Annie E. Casey foundation Web site, www.aecf.org; f and g from Kendra A. Hovey and Harold A. Hovey, *CQ's State Fact Finder 2007* (Washington, D.C.: CQ Press, 2007), 95, 309; h and i from Public Agenda Web site, www. publicagenda .org; j from *Businessweek* Web site, www.businessweek.com/interactive_reports/state_health-performance.html; l from *Education Week* Web site, www.edweek.org/media/ew/qc/2010; m from the Web site www.statemaster.com.

Don't Worry, Be Happy

The measures of quality of life reported in Table 1-3 are *objective*. That is, they summarize how Texas ranks in the sorts of living situations that can be measured from the outside. On those measures, Texas looks like a comparatively poor place to live. But what about the *subjective*—the way people feel about themselves on the inside?

In 2009, researchers led by Professor Andrew Oswald of the University of Warwick published their conclusions after examining a 2005 survey of 1.3 million Americans' answers to questions about their satisfaction with their lives. On the basis of that subjective measurement, Texas was one of the happiest states, ranking number fifteen. Louisiana scored as the happiest state, while New York was the least happy.

So, is Texas a good place to live? The answer depends on what measurements are used as evidence.

Source: "Louisiana the Happiest State, Study Says," *Austin American-Statesman*, December 18, 2009, A13.

relatively low on measures of air cleanliness, the general health of its population, freedom from crime, the educational status of its citizens, and other measures of civilized living. Liberals would argue that the policies evident in the first table have caused the problems evident in the second table.

Conservatives might argue, in rebuttal, that the rankings are skewed by the large number of very poor undocumented immigrants who live along the Rio Grande, and that if those people were to be removed from the calculations, the state would rank much higher in quality of life. Whether the liberal critique of the state's conservative policies is justified is something that will be explored during the remaining chapters of this book.

The People of Texas

In many ways, Texas is the classic American melting pot of different peoples, although it occasionally seems more like a boiling cauldron. The state was originally populated by various Native American tribes. In the sixteenth and seventeenth centuries, the Spaniards conquered the land, and from the intermingling of the conquerors and the conquered came the "mestizos," persons of mixed Spanish and Native American blood. In the nineteenth century, Anglos wrested the land from the heirs of the Spaniards. They often brought Black slaves with them. Soon waves of immigration arrived from Europe and Asia, and more mestizos came from Mexico. After a brief outflow of population as a result of the oil price depression of the late 1980s, the long-term pattern of immigration resumed and brought many more thousands during the 1990s and beyond.

The Census

At the end of each decade, the national government takes a census of each state's population. Table 1-4 shows the official Texas numbers for 1990 to 2010. The increase in population indicated in the table entitled Texas to three additional seats in the U.S. House in 1990, two more in 2000, and another four in 2010, bringing the state's total to thirty-six.

Besides the overall increase in population of 20.6 percent in the final decade of the twentieth century, the most significant fact revealed by the 2010 census was the rapid increase in Texas's Hispanic population. Whereas Hispanics—the great majority of whom, in Texas, are either Mexican or Mexican American—constituted 21 percent of the state's population in 1980 and 26 percent in 1990, by 2010 they totaled almost 38 percent. The other important minority group, African Americans, comprised 11.8 percent of the state's citizens, a percentage that has not changed appreciably over the last several decades.

The inevitable consequence of the increasing trend-line of the Latino population arrived in 2005 when the Census Bureau announced an estimate that the population of Texas consisted of 50.2 percent Black and Latino people.[24] The 2010 count confirmed that the falling Anglo percentage of the state population had continued, as that group, which used to be a large majority of the population, had dropped to 45.3 percent. In other words, there is now no "majority" ethnic group in the state; every group constitutes a minority of the population. If present population growth rates continue, however, a majority of Texas's population will be Hispanic by 2020.[25]

TABLE 1-4

The Texas Population, 1990–2010

Ethnic Group	1990	2000	2010	2010 Percent of Total	Percent Increase, 2000–2010
Anglo (non-Hispanic White)	10,291,680	10,933,313	11,390,939	45.3	10
African American	2,021,632	2,404,566	2,967,176	11.8	23.4
Hispanic or Latino* (exclusive of Black Spanish-speakers)	4,339,905	6,669,665	9,454,731	37.6	42.7
Other	378,565	844,276	1,332,715	5.3	57
TOTAL	17,031,782	20,851,820	25,145,561		20.6

*The great majority of Hispanics in Texas are Mexican or Mexican American

SOURCES: For 1990, *1992–93 Texas Almanac and State Industrial Guide* (Dallas: A. H. Belo Corp., 1991); for 2000, U.S. Census Web site, www.census/gov; for 2010, the U.S. Census Web site and various interpretive journalistic articles.

The distribution of the population in Texas shows evidence of three things: the initial patterns of migration, the influence of geography and climate, and the location of the cities. The Hispanic migration came first, north from Mexico, and to this day is still concentrated in South and West Texas, especially in the counties that border the Rio Grande. Likewise, African Americans still live predominantly in the eastern half of the state. As one moves from east to west across Texas, annual rainfall drops by about five inches per 100 miles. East Texas has a moist climate and supports intensive farming, while West Texas is dry and requires pumping from underground aquifers to maintain agriculture. The overall distribution of settlement reflects the food production capability of local areas, with East Texas remaining more populous. Cities developed at strategic locations, usually on rivers or the seacoast, and the state's population is heavily concentrated in the urban areas.

The Political Relevance of Population

In this book Anglos, Mexican Americans, and African Americans often will be discussed as groups, without an intent to be unfair to individual exceptions. Our division of the Texas population into Anglos, Mexican Americans, and African Americans reflects political realities. All citizens are individuals, form their own opinions, and have the right to choose to behave as they see fit. No one is a prisoner of his or her group, and every generalization has exceptions. Nevertheless, it is a long-observed fact that people in similar circumstances often see things from similar points of view, and it therefore helps to clarify political conflict to be aware of the shared similarities.

Historically, both of the minority groups, Mexican Americans and African Americans, have been treated badly by the Anglo majority. Today, the members of both groups are, in general, less wealthy than Anglos. For example, according to the 2000 census, the mean household income of both Latinos and Blacks

was about 62 percent of the figure for Anglos in the state. On the one hand, this represented a narrowing of the income gap between minorities and Anglos that existed in 1990. On the other hand, the difference in wealth was still very substantial and large enough to cause economic conflict.[26] At the time of writing, wealth figures were not available from the 2010 census, but when released they will probably show a continuing economic difference between the ethnic groups.

Political differences often accompany economic divisions. As will be discussed in Chapters 4 and 5, Mexican Americans and African Americans tend to hold more liberal political opinions than do Anglos and to vote accordingly. This is not to say that there are no conservative minority citizens and no liberal Anglos. Nevertheless, when looked at as groups, Mexican Americans, African Americans, and Anglos do display general patterns of belief and behavior that can be discussed without being unfair to individual exceptions.

As a result, as the minority population increases in size relative to the Anglo population, its greater liberalism is likely to make itself felt, sooner or later, in the voting booth. Furthermore, Texans of Asian background are a relatively small, but growing proportion of the population. As their population becomes larger, they may exert an independent influence on the political process. Texas's evolving mix of population is therefore constantly changing the state's politics.

The Plan of This Book

The following chapters will examine the ways Texans organize and behave politically to attempt to deal with their social and economic problems. There will also be a cautious attempt to assess the state's future prospects. Every chapter will contain a comparison of the reality of Texas politics to the democratic ideal and a discussion of how defensible the reality is.

The topics to be considered in the following chapters are, in order, the Texas Constitution, the state's important interest groups, the activities of political parties, and the individual voter within the context of campaigns and elections. Next, the focus will shift to the institutions of state government—the legislature, the executive branch, and the judiciary. An examination of local government will follow and then analyses of state public policy; first, a discussion of various policy areas relating to "people," and then an examination of some policy problems pertaining to "resources." In both policy chapters, there will be some cautious attempts to assess future prospects for the relevant policy.

Summary

This chapter began with an overview of the history of Texas, with emphasis on important political events and the development of the economy. The discussion then shifted to the topic of democratic theory, which holds that the legitimacy of a government rests upon the citizens' participation, and to the topic of Texas's place in the American federal system and the international arena. The focus then moved to the state's conservative political culture.

This chapter has explained how, as a result of its political culture, there is a preference in Texas for an individualistic worldview, a less-government-is-better approach, pseudo laissez faire, social Darwinism, and the trickle-down theory of economic and

social development. The twin results are an inactive government and a relatively poor quality of life compared to many other states. Texas has a large and diverse population that is always growing and changing. Insofar as the future can be predicted, it seems that the population will continue to grow, with an increasingly large non-Anglo, and especially Hispanic, component. These changes have affected, and will continue to affect, politics in Texas.

Glossary Terms

conservatism	liberalism
democracy	moralistic political culture
federal system	political culture
impresario	pseudo laissez faire
individualistic political culture	social Darwinism
laissez faire	traditionalistic political culture
legitimacy	trickle-down theory

2

Representative Debbie Riddle sponsored a series of bills in 2011 regarding voter identification, proof of citizenship to enter school, and immigration enforcement. She also proposed a constitutional amendment that would limit local property assessment.
AP Photo/Thomas Terry.

The Constitutional Setting

Constitutions should consist of only general provisions; the reason is that they must necessarily be permanent, and that they cannot calculate for the possible change of things.

ALEXANDER HAMILTON, AMERICAN STATESMAN AND ONE OF THE AUTHORS OF *The Federalist Papers* URGING ADOPTION OF THE U.S. CONSTITUTION

All political power is inherent in the people, and all free governments are founded on their authority, and instituted for their benefit.

ARTICLE I, TEXAS CONSTITUTION

OBJECTIVES

After reading this chapter, you should be able to

Understand the purposes of constitutions as well as the extent to which these are reflected in the Texas Constitution.

Describe the history of Texas constitutions.

Discuss the key aspects of the present Texas Constitution.

Explain why the Texas Constitution is so frequently amended.

Analyze the political process involved in constitutional change.

INTRODUCTION

Since its ratification in 1789, the U.S. Constitution frequently has been used as a model by emerging nations. State constitutions, however, seldom enjoy such admiration. Indeed, the constitution of the state of Texas is more often ridiculed than praised because of its length, its obscurity, and its outdated, unworkable provisions.

Such criticism of state constitutions is common. The political circumstances that surrounded the writing of the national Constitution differed considerably from those that existed at the times when many of the fifty states—especially those of the old Confederacy—were writing their constitutions. State constitutions tend to be very rigid and include too many specific details. They do not follow the advice of Alexander Hamilton cited in the quotation above. As a result, Texas and many other states must resort to frequent **constitutional amendments,** which are formal changes in the basic governing document.

In federal systems, which are systems of government that provide for a division and sharing of powers between a national government and state or regional governments, the constitutions of the states complement the national Constitution. Article VI of the U.S. Constitution provides that the Constitution, laws, and treaties of the national government take precedence over the constitutions and laws of the states. This provision is known as the "supremacy of the laws" clause. Many states, including Texas, have constitutional and statutory provisions that conflict with federal laws, but these are unenforceable because of Article VI. Although the U.S. Constitution is supreme, state constitutions are still important because state governments are responsible for many basic programs and services, such as education, that affect citizens daily.

This chapter examines purposes of constitutions, as well as outlines the development of the several Texas constitutions. It elaborates the principal features of the state's current document, briefly traces the movement for constitutional reform in Texas, and provides an overview of constitutional politics.

Purposes of Constitutions

A **constitution** is the basic law of a state or nation that outlines the primary structure and functions of government. The purposes of all constitutions are the same.

Legitimacy

The first purpose served by a constitution is to give legitimacy to the government. Legitimacy is the most abstract and ambiguous purpose served by constitutions. Legitimacy derives from agreed-upon purposes of government and from government keeping its actions within the guidelines of these purposes. The constitution contributes to this legitimacy by putting it down on paper. A government has legitimacy when the governed accept its acts as moral, fair, and just, and thus believe that they should obey its laws.

This acceptance cuts two ways. On the one hand, citizens will allow government to act in certain ways that are not permitted to private individuals. For example, citizens cannot legally drive down a city street at sixty miles per hour, but police officers may do so when in the act of pursuing wrongdoers. Proprietors of private schools cannot command local residents to make financial contributions to their schools, but these local residents pay taxes to support public schools.

On the other hand, citizens also expect governments not to act arbitrarily; the concept of legitimacy is closely associated with limiting government. If a police officer were to speed down a city street at ninety miles per hour just for the thrill of doing so, or if citizens were burdened with confiscatory school taxes, these acts probably would fall outside the bounds of legitimacy.

What citizens are willing to accept is conditioned by their history and their political culture. In Texas and the remainder of the United States, democratic practices including citizen participation in decision making, and fair processes are a part of that history and culture. Even within that broad acceptance of democratic principles, legitimacy varies from nation to nation and even from state to state. In England, for example, most police do not carry weapons; in California, pedestrians have absolute right of way in crossing streets. The traditionalistic/individualistic political culture that predominates in the South is even more dedicated to limiting government than the moralistic political culture; thus, southern constitutions, as a group, tend to be very restrictive.

Is It Legal?

Public regard for what is legal is dynamic. For example, until the 1995 "right-to-carry" law, Texans were unable to carry a concealed weapon legally, although police detectives could do so. By 2011, the debate was whether students, teachers, and others should be able to carry weapons into the classroom.

Organizing Government

The second purpose of constitutions is to organize government. Governments must be organized in some way that clarifies who the major officials are, how they are selected, and what the relationships are among those charged with basic governmental functions.

Again, to some extent, the American states have been guided by the national model. For example, both levels incorporate **separation of powers**—that is, a division into legislative, executive, and judicial branches. Also following the national Constitution's lead, the states have adopted a system of **checks and balances** to ensure that each separate branch of government can be restrained by the others. In reality, separate institutions and defined lines of authority lead to a sharing of powers. For example, passing bills is thought of as a legislative function, but the governor can veto a bill.

Each state has an elected chief executive. Each state, except Nebraska, has a legislative body composed of two houses, usually a house of representatives and a senate. Each state has a judicial system with some sort of supreme court. Just as the U.S. Constitution includes many provisions that establish the relationship between the nation and the states, state constitutions include similar provisions with respect to local governments.

Specific organizational provisions of state constitutions vary widely, and invariably reflect the political attitudes prevalent at the time the constitutions were adopted and various amendments added. In Texas, the traditionalistic/individualistic political cultures have dominated the constitutional process.

Providing Power

Article I, Section 8 of the U.S. Constitution expressly grants certain powers to the national government and implies a broad range of additional powers through the "necessary and proper" clause. This clause, also known as the "elastic clause," enables Congress to execute all its other powers by giving it broad authority to pass needed legislation. Thus, granting specific powers is the third purpose of constitutions. The Tenth Amendment reserves for the people or for the states powers not explicitly or implicitly granted to the national government.

As the U.S. Constitution has been developed and interpreted, many powers exist concurrently for both the federal and the state levels of government—the power to assess taxes on gasoline, for example. Within this general framework, which continues to evolve, the Texas Constitution sets forth specific functions for which the state maintains primary or concurrent responsibility. Local government, criminal law, and regulation of intrastate commerce illustrate the diversity of the activities over which the state retains principal control.

A combination of factors has reduced the power of state officials, however. For example, the federal government's widespread use of its interstate commerce powers has limited the range of commercial activities still considered strictly intrastate. The **incorporation** of the **Bill of Rights**—the first ten amendments to the U.S. Constitution—has compelled changes in the criminal justice systems of the states. Incorporation means making the national protections, for example, the right to a fair and speedy trial by a jury of one's peers, applicable to state and local governments. In addition, the ability of individual states to deal with many socioeconomic matters such as energy use, civil rights, and urbanism is

now seriously impaired. Thus, they are increasingly viewed as a responsibility of government at the national level.

Nevertheless, the fundamental law of the state spells out many areas for state and local action. Which, if any, of the broad problems the national government addresses depends on the prevailing Washington political philosophy, the party that controls Congress, the national administration, and who sits on the U.S. Supreme Court.[1] Resistance to perceived national power growth prompted Tea Party adherents (see Chapter 4) to urge a strong "states' rights" interpretation of the Tenth Amendment in 2010 and 2011.

Limiting Governmental Power

American insistence on the fourth purpose of constitutions—limiting governmental power—reflects the influence of British political culture, our ancestors' dissatisfaction with colonial rule, and the extraordinary individualism that characterized national development during the eighteenth and nineteenth centuries.

In Texas, the traditionalistic/individualist political culture resulted in a heavy emphasis on limiting government's ability to act. For example, the governor has only restricted power to remove members of state boards and commissions, particularly those appointed by a predecessor, except by informal techniques, such as an aggressive public relations campaign against a board member. This belief in limited government continues to wax strong in the new millennium. Citizens usually want less government regulation and more controls on spending.

Chief among the guarantees against arbitrary governmental action is the national Bill of Rights. It was quickly added to the original U.S. Constitution to ensure both adequate safeguards for the people and ratification of the Constitution. The Texas Bill of Rights, included as Article I in the Texas Constitution, resembles the national Bill of Rights.[2] Later amendments to the national Constitution have extended guarantees in several areas, especially due process and equal protection of the laws, racial equality, and voting rights.

In Texas, reactions to post–Civil War Reconstruction rule were so keen at the time the current constitution was written that the document contains many specific and picayune limitations. The creation of certain hospital districts and the payment of pensions to veterans of the war of independence from Mexico are examples. Such specificities have made frequent amendments necessary and have hamstrung legislative action in many areas.

Texas Constitutions

The United States has had two fundamental laws: the short-lived Articles of Confederation and the present Constitution. Texas is currently governed by its sixth constitution, ratified in 1876.[3] The fact that the 1876 constitution had five predecessors in only forty years illustrates the political turbulence of the mid-1800s. Table 2-1 lists the six Texas state charters.

Having been formally governed by Spain for 131 years and by Mexico for 15 years, Texans issued a declaration of independence on March 2, 1836. This declaration stated that "the people of Texas, do now constitute a Free, Sovereign, and Independent Republic, and are fully invested with all the rights and attributes which properly belong to independent nations." After a brief but bitter war with Mexico, Texas gained independence on April 21 of that year

Some Key Differences in U.S. and Texas Constitutions

■ Powers are reserved to the states in the U.S. Constitution; local governments are regarded as creatures of the state in the Texas Constitution.

■ The national document is considerably more flexible than the state one in ___ng government to act.

___esidency is a very strong office; the governorship is a weak one.

___tional court system is relatively simple; the Texas system is complex ___nfusing.

___S. Constitution is rarely amended; the Texas constitution is ___ntly amended.

___ver, there are also many similarities because both constitutions ___le separation of powers, checks and balances, and provisions for both ___wering and limiting government, and for protecting individual rights.

difference

Battle of San Jacinto. Independence was formalized when the two ___ of Velasco were signed by Mexican President Antonio López de Santa Anna and Texas President David Burnet on May 14, 1836. By September, the Constitution of the Republic of Texas, drafted shortly after independence was declared, had been implemented. Major features of this charter paralleled those of the U.S. Constitution, including a president and a Congress, but the document also guaranteed the continuation of slavery.

TABLE 2-1

Constitutions of Texas

Welcome to Texas
DRIVE FRIENDLY- THE TEXAS WAY

Constitution	Dates
Republic of Texas	1836–1845
Statehood	1845–1861
Civil War	1861–1866
Reconstruction	1866–1869
Radical Reconstruction	1869–1876
State of Texas	1876–Present

The United States had been sympathetic to the Texas struggle for independence. However, admission to the Union was postponed for a decade because of northern opposition to admission of a new slave state. After ten years of nationhood, Texas was finally admitted into the Union. The Constitution of 1845, the Statehood Constitution, was modeled after the constitutions of other southern states. It was regarded as one of the nation's best at the time. The Constitution of 1845, which not only embraced democratic principles of participation but also included many elements later associated with the twentieth-century administrative reform movement, was a very brief, clear document.[4]

The Constitution of 1845 was influenced by Jacksonian democracy, named for President Andrew Jackson. Jacksonians believed in an expansion of participation in government, at least for White males.[5] Jackson's basic beliefs ultimately led to the spoils system of appointing to office those who had supported the winning candidates in the election ("to the victors belong the spoils"). Jacksonian democracy also produced long ballots, with almost every office up for popular vote, short terms of office, and the expansion of voting rights. Thus, while participatory, Jacksonian democracy was not flawless.

When Texas joined the Confederate States of America in 1861, the constitution was modified again. This document, the Civil War Constitution of 1861, merely altered the Constitution of 1845 to ensure greater protection for the institution of slavery and to declare allegiance to the Confederacy.

Texas was on the losing side of the Civil War and was occupied by federal troops. President Andrew Johnson ordered Texas to construct yet another constitution. The 1866 document declared secession illegal, repudiated the war debt to the Confederacy, and abolished slavery—although it did not provide for improving conditions for African Americans. In other words, the state made only those changes that were necessary to gain presidential support for readmission to the Union.

Radical postwar congressional leaders were not satisfied with these minimal changes in the constitutions of the southern states. They insisted on more punitive measures. In 1868–1869, a constitution that centralized power in the Texas state government, provided generous salaries for officials, stipulated appointed judges, and called for annual legislative sessions was drafted. It contained many elements that present-day reformers would like to see in a revised state charter. Because the constitution was forced on the state by outsiders in Washington and by *carpetbaggers*—northerners who came to Texas with their worldly goods in a suitcase made out of carpeting—White southerners never regarded the document as acceptable. They especially resented the strong, centralized state government and the powerful office of governor that were imposed on them. However, because all former rebels were barred from voting, the Constitution of 1869 was adopted by Unionists and African Americans. Ironically, this constitution least accomplished the purpose of legitimacy—acceptance by the people—but was the most forward looking in terms of power and organization.

The popular three-term governor, Elisha Pease, resigned in the fall of 1869 after the radical constitution was adopted. After a vacancy in the state's chief executive office lasting more than three months, Edmund J. (E. J.) Davis was elected governor and took office at the beginning of 1870. The election not only barred the state's Democrats and traditional Republicans, both conservative groups, from voting, but also exhibited a number of irregularities. Davis was an honest man, but the radical state charter, Davis's radical Republican ties, and his subsequent designation as provisional governor by President Ulysses Grant combined to give him dictatorial powers.[6]

The Present Texas Constitution

Traditionally Democratic, as well as conservative, Texans began to chafe for **constitutional revision**—changes to reform or improve the basic document—when the Democrats regained legislative control in 1872. An 1874 reform effort passed in the Texas Senate but failed in the House. This constitution would have provided flexibility in such areas as how tax dollars could be spent and terms of office. It also would have facilitated elite control and a sellout to the powerful railroads, which were hated by ordinary citizens because of their pricing policies and corruption of state legislatures.[7]

The legislature called a constitutional convention, and ninety delegates were elected from all over the state. The convention members were overwhelmingly conservative and reflected the "retrenchment and reform" philosophy of the Grange, which was one of several organizations of farmers.[8] This conservatism included a strong emphasis on the constitutional purpose of limiting government and a tolerance for racial segregation shared with other institutions of the time. As noted in Chapter 1, southern farmers were determined to prevent future state governments from oppressing them as they believed they had been oppressed under Reconstruction.

Accordingly, the new constitution, completed in 1875, curbed the powers of government. The governor's term was limited to two years. A state debt ceiling of $200,000 was established. Salaries of elected state officials were fixed. The legislature was limited to biennial sessions, and the governor was allowed to make very few executive appointments.

When this document went to the people of Texas for a vote in February 1876, it was approved by a margin of 136,606 to 56,652; 130 of the 150 Texas counties registered approval. All the ratifying counties were rural areas committed to the Grange and would benefit from the new constitution. The twenty counties that did not favor the new charter were urban areas that were heavily Republican, where newspaper criticism of the proposed document had been severe.[9]

Independence Now and Then

Because Texas was an independent republic when the United States annexed it, the annexation agreement reflected compromises by both the state and national governments. For example, Texas gave up its military property, but kept its public lands. The national government refused to assume the state's $10 million debt. Texas, however, can carve four additional states out of its territory should the state want such a division.

In the 1990s, a radical group calling itself the Republic of Texas contended that because Texas had been illegally annexed in 1845, it remained a nation. Pursuing this belief, members of the movement harassed state officials in a variety of ways, including filing liens against the assets of public agencies and regularly accusing state officials of illegally using their powers. Several of these individuals are still in prison for their violent actions.

In 2010, Governor Rick Perry suggested that Texas might secede from the United States. Texas did *not* enter the Union with any right of secession.

General Features

The Texas Constitution of today is very much like the original 1876 document in spite of 467 amendments by the middle of 2011 and some major changes in the executive article. It includes a preamble and sixteen articles, with each article divided into subsections (see Table 2-2).[10]

When the Texas Constitution was drafted more than a century ago, it incorporated protection for various private interests. It also included many details of policy and governmental organization to avoid abuse of government powers. The result is a very long, poorly organized document that does not draw clear lines of responsibility for government actions.

As an example of details that might be contained better in legislation than in constitutional law, Article V, Section 18 spells out procedures for electing justices of the peace and constables. These provisions have been amended four times; one amendment is so specific that it allows Chambers County the flexibility to have between two and six justice of the peace precincts. Besides having its own amendment, Chambers County (county seat: Anahuac) is best known for being one-third under water.

TABLE 2-2

Articles of the Texas Constitution

I.	Bill of Rights
II.	The Powers of Government
III.	Legislative Department
IV.	Executive Department
V.	Judicial Department
VI.	Suffrage
VII.	Education [and] the Free Public Schools
VIII.	Taxation and Revenue
IX.	Counties
X.	Railroads
XI.	Municipal Corporations
XII.	Private Corporations
XIII.	Spanish and Mexican Land Titles—deleted by amendment in 1969
XIV.	Public Lands and Land Office
XV.	Impeachment
XVI.	General Provisions
XVII.	Mode of Amending the Constitution of the State

Cartoonist Ben Sargent compares the wisdom of the national founding fathers who produced a constitution requiring few amendments to the limited viewpoint of the writers of the Texas Constitution, which must be amended very frequently.

Courtesy of Ben Sargent.

The Texas Constitution reflects the time of its writing, an era of strong conservative, agrarian interests, and of reaction to carpetbagger rule. Changes in the U.S. Constitution, both by amendment and by judicial interpretation, have required alterations of the state constitution, although provisions remain that conflict with federal law. These unenforceable provisions, along with other provisions that are so outdated that they will never again be enforced, are known as deadwood. Both the Sixty-fifth Legislature in 1977 and the Seventy-sixth Legislature in 1999 undertook to clean up the constitution by removing deadwood provisions through the formal amending process.

The frequent amendments have produced a state charter that is poorly organized and difficult to read, much less interpret, even by the courts.[11] Yet, the amendments are necessary because of the restrictiveness of the constitution. In recent years, voters have tended to approve virtually all proposed amendments. The Lone Star State can almost claim the record for the longest constitution in the nation. Only the constitution of Alabama contains more than the 93,000-plus words in the Texas charter.[12]

Specific Features

The Texas Constitution is similar in many ways to the U.S. Constitution, particularly the way in which the purposes of organizing and limiting government and legitimacy are addressed. Each government has executive, legislative, and judicial branches. Both are separation of powers systems; that is, they have separate institutions that share powers. Both include provisions against unequal or arbitrary government action, such as restricting freedom of religion. The two documents are less alike in terms of the purpose of providing power to government. The national Constitution is much more flexible in allowing government to act than is the state document. Texas legislators, for example, cannot set their own salaries.[13]

Bill of Rights

Like the national Bill of Rights, Article I of the Texas Constitution provides for equality under the law; religious freedom, including separation of church and

state;[14] due process for the criminally accused; and freedom of speech and of the press. Among its thirty protections, it further provides safeguards for the mentally incompetent and provides several specific guarantees, such as prohibition against outlawing an individual from the state. It includes an equal rights amendment for all Texans.

Citizen opinion generally supports the U.S. and Texas Bills of Rights. However, just as the public sometimes gets upset with the U.S. Bill of Rights when constitutional protections are afforded to someone the public wants to "throw the book at"—an accused child molester, for example— Texans sometimes balk at the protections provided in the state constitution. Nevertheless, modern efforts toward constitutional revision have left the provisions intact.[15]

Following the terrorists' attack on the World Trade Center in New York City in 2001, many Americans became willing to sacrifice some protections to help prevent further acts of terrorism, a willingness that has engendered national debate on the conflict between homeland security and civil rights and liberties. Support for such intrusions on basic civil liberties has been dwindling, however.[16] Because homeland security issues involve racial and ethnic profiling, Texas, with its very diverse population, could be affected more than some other states. In a few Texas cities, such as Farmers Branch, efforts to restrict noncitizen immigrants began in 2006. These actions reflect a national concern over illegal immigration and impatience with the lack of a federal immigration bill.

Chapter 10 discusses rights and liberties in greater detail, including interpretations of the right to keep and bear arms. A stress on individual rights can, however, cause problems of its own. In Texas, the legislature has tended toward liberalizing laws on carrying guns, for example, in spite of objections from law enforcement officers.

Separation of Powers

Like the national Constitution, the state charter allocates governmental functions among three branches: the executive, the legislative, and the judicial. Article II outlines the separation of powers, including the "departments"—as the branches are labeled in the state constitution—of government. The national government divides power between the nation and the states, as well as among the three branches. Providing for a sharing of power should keep any one branch from becoming too powerful. Article II outlines the separation of institutions, and the articles dealing with the individual departments develop a system of checks and balances similar to those found in the national Constitution. Often, the same checks found in the U.S. Constitution are established in the state constitution.

A check on power results from assigning a function commonly identified with one branch to another. For example, the House of Representatives may impeach and the Senate may try—a judicial function—elected executive officials and judges at the district court level and above.[17] The governor has a veto over acts of the legislature and an item veto over appropriation bills—a legislative proceeding. The Texas Supreme Court may issue a writ of mandamus ordering an executive official to act—an executive function. These examples are applicable at the national as well as the state level and illustrate that powers are not truly separated, but overlapping and shared.

LONE STAR MEDIA
Rights versus Rights

Article 8 of the Texas Constitution and Article 1 of the United States Constitution guarantee freedom of the press. Article 10 of the state charter and Article 6 of the national one speak to the accused's access to witnesses.* One of the functions of constitutions, and especially of Bills of Rights, is to protect the personal freedom of choice of individual citizens. Yet, what is an important purpose of democratic constitutions in theory sometimes runs up against the unpleasant fact that rights sometimes are in conflict with each other.

For example, in a much-publicized Denton County trial involving the charge of a man murdering his wife, various media were important in the trial. The *Denton Record-Chronicle* covered the story over more than a six-year period from the wife's disappearance on December 29, 2004, through the husband's trial in January and February of 2011, when he was convicted. Internet subscribers to RSS and MyYahoo read some of this coverage. The defense attorney wanted to call Donna Fielder, the reporter who regularly covers the courts and law enforcement, as a witness, believing that she could testify in rebuttal of the testimony of investigating officers.

However, there is a strong tradition in journalism that members of the press resist efforts to involve them in trials, and over the years, a number of reporters have gone to jail for resisting a subpoena to testify. This tradition is based on the belief that the public cannot trust the press to be free and impartial if it also must work on behalf of the courts. Moreover, in 2009 the Eighty-first Legislature passed the Texas Free Flow of Information Act, known informally as the Shield Law, joining thirty-six other states that shield reporters from revealing sources, making testimonials, or producing notes so long as they practice responsible journalism.

Fielder resisted the subpoena from the defense, which compelled her to serve as a defense witness. District Judge Bruce McFarling quashed the subpoena, saying that the reporter was protected by the Shield Law. The newspaper's attorney successfully argued that the defense did not meet the burden under the new law to compel testimony.**

Thus the right of freedom of the press took precedence in this case over the accused's right to compel witnesses to testify. The reporter has a blog site, and her future comments are pending.

*The two constitutions can be found at www.statutes.legis.state.tx.us/ and www.usconstitution.net/const.html.

**See Peggy Heinkle-Wolfe, "Reporter Won't Testify," *Denton Record-Chronicle*, January 27, 2011, 1A–2A.

Legislative Branch

The Texas legislature, like the U.S. Congress, consists of a Senate and a House of Representatives. The legislative article (III) establishes a legislative body, determines its composition, sets the qualifications for membership, provides its basic organization, and fixes its meeting time. All these features are discussed in Chapter 6. The article also sets the salary of state legislators. Although a 1991 constitutional amendment provided an alternative method to recommend

salaries through the Ethics Commission, the commission has never made a salary recommendation, and legislative salaries remain frozen at a surprisingly low $7,200 a year.

Rather than emphasizing the positive powers of the legislature, Article III spells out the specific actions that the legislature cannot take, reflecting reaction to the strong government imposed during Reconstruction. For example, the U.S. Constitution gives Congress broad powers to make any laws that are "necessary and proper." In contrast, rather than allowing lawmaking to be handled through the regular legislative process, the Texas Constitution sometimes forces state government to resort to the constitutional amendment process. For example, an amendment is needed to add to the fund maintained by the state to help veterans adjust to civilian life by giving them good deals on the purchase of land. Another example is the need for an amendment to change the percentage of the state budget that can be spent on public welfare.

The state constitution also provides the following limitations on legislative procedure:

1. **The legislature may meet in regular session only every two years.**

2. **The number of days for introduction of bills, committee work, and floor action is specified. To permit early floor action, the governor can declare an emergency.**

3. **Salaries and the per diem reimbursement rate are described. Historically, this degree of specificity made an amendment necessary for every change in these figures. Although the Ethics Commission has made no recommendations about salaries, it has upgraded the per diem rate.**

4. **The legislature cannot authorize the state to borrow money. Yet, Section 23-A provides for a $75,000 payment to settle a debt to a contractor for a building constructed at the John Tarleton Agricultural College (now State University) in 1937.**

5. **The legislative article, not the municipal corporations article, includes provisions for municipal employees to participate in Social Security programs.**

6. **In spite of a stipulation that the legislature cannot grant public monies to individuals, exceptions are made for Confederate soldiers, sailors, and their widows.**

These examples are taken only from the legislative article. A list of all similar idiosyncratic provisions in the constitution would be massive because limitations on legislative action are scattered throughout the constitution, especially in the General Provisions. Such detailed restrictions tie the hands of legislators and make it necessary for them to take many issues to the voters that are seemingly of little significance. Still, the legislature is the dominant institution in the state.

Executive Branch

Little similarity exists between the provisions for the executive branch in the state charter and those in the national Constitution. The U.S. Constitution provides for a very strong chief executive, the president, and creates only one other

elected official, the vice president, who since 1804 has run on a ticket with the presidential candidate. Tradition is that the presidential candidate selects the running mate, usually in an effort to pick up votes where the top candidate is weak. Article IV provides that the governor will be elected statewide and will be the chief executive of the state. However, the state constitution requires that the following individuals also will be elected statewide:

1. **The lieutenant governor, who presides over the Texas Senate.**

2. **The comptroller (pronounced con-TROL-ler) of public accounts, who collects the state's taxes and determines who keeps the state's money on deposit.**

3. **The commissioner of the General Land Office, who protects the state's environment and administers its vast public lands.**

4. **The attorney general, who is the state's lawyer.**

5. **Members of the Texas Railroad Commission, who regulate intrastate transportation and the oil, gas, and other mining industries.**

Furthermore, statutory laws require that the commissioner of agriculture and members of the State Board of Education be elected. Thus, quite unlike the president, who appoints most other key federal executives, the governor is saddled with five other elected executives and two key elected policy-making boards. He or she has no formal control over these individuals.

Thus, Texas has a **plural executive**, with the result that the executive branch is "disintegrated" or "fragmented." Each elected executive is independent of the other. The governor must contend with a sprawling state bureaucracy, most of which receives policy direction from an administrative board or commission. The governor also has little power to reorganize executive agencies.

Like the legislative one, the executive article is overly specific and creates roadblocks to expeditious governmental action. Government cannot act when faced with too many restrictions, even when citizens need a fast response. More than the other articles, Article IV reflects the period of its writing—the extreme reaction in the 1870s to the excesses of Reconstruction Governor E. J. Davis.

In a 2007 rating of institutional powers of the governor, the Texas governor was rated just slightly below the mean when the number of separately elected officials, tenure, appointments, budget authority, veto power, and control of party were all considered.[18] The governor was weakest on the factors of separately elected officials and statutory budget authority. This ranking is higher than previous ones, which tended to look only at constitutional factors, but slightly lower than the personal power ranking.

Governors, however, have learned how to use what constitutional powers they have. For example, through control of special sessions and through the veto power, the governor retains significant legislative power. Also, there is no restriction on the number of terms that a governor may serve.

Additionally, two modern amendments have strengthened the governor's position. In 1972, the governor's term of office was lengthened from two years to four years. In 1980, gubernatorial removal powers were strengthened by an amendment to Article XV. This amendment allows governors to remove, with the advice and consent of the Senate, individuals they have appointed. Legislation

approved in 1993 further strengthened the office by giving the governor greater control over major policy boards, such as those dealing with insurance regulation and public education.

Judicial Branch

The national judicial system is clear-cut—district courts, appeals courts, the U.S. Supreme Court—but the Texas judicial system is not at all clear. Like so many other articles in the constitution, the judicial article has various specific sections. These range from the requirement for an elected sheriff in each county to the restricted right of the state to appeal in criminal cases.[19]

Article V, the judicial article of the state constitution, has three distinctive features. First, the constitution establishes a rather confusing pattern of six different types of courts. Further complicating the picture is the fact that Texas (along with Oklahoma) has two supreme courts, one each for civil (Supreme Court) and criminal (Court of Criminal Appeals) matters.

Second, each level of trial courts has concurrent, or overlapping, jurisdiction with another level; that is, either level of court may hear the case. Additionally, trial courts established by statute have different jurisdiction from those established by the constitution. For example, in civil matters, constitutional county courts have concurrent jurisdiction with justice of the peace courts in civil cases involving $200 to $5,000. County courts at law overlap district courts in civil matters involving up to $100,000. Although the legislature can adjust the jurisdiction of statutory courts, the authority of constitutional courts can be altered only by constitutional amendment. Furthermore, the minimum dollar amounts stated in the constitution reflect economic values of the nineteenth century. In an era of multimillion-dollar lawsuits, having a district court—the chief trial court of the state—hear a case in which the disputed amount is $1,000 or less hampers the more significant trial work of that court. The courts are fully discussed in Chapter 9.

Third, qualifications for Texas judges are so stated as to allow those with no legal training to be eligible for a trial court bench.[20] The resulting confusion increases the likelihood that someone without legal experience will

The Succession Amendment

Among the seventeen proposed amendments in 1999, the most interesting one was Proposition 1, which established a procedure for succession to the lieutenant governor's office. Amid wide speculation that Governor George W. Bush might be the next U.S. president, the state wanted to ensure an orderly procedure if Lieutenant Governor Rick Perry moved up to the governor's office. The amendment established a procedure whereby the members of the Senate would elect one of their own members as acting lieutenant governor. The individual would remain a member of the Senate. Even before the vote on the amendment, political speculation began about which senator might be catapulted into the very powerful position of lieutenant governor and, thus, presiding officer of the Senate.

be elected as a justice of the peace or county judge. The problem of judicial qualifications is aggravated by the fact that judges are elected in Texas so that, on occasion, vote-getting ability may be more important than the ability to render fair judgments.[21] The tradition of elected judges reflects the nineteenth-century passion for long ballots. In the national government, the president appoints all judges.

Local Government

Local governments in Texas fall into three categories: counties, municipalities (cities and towns), and special districts. The state constitution, through Articles III, IX, and XI, gives these governmental units varying degrees of flexibility.

Counties, which are administrative and judicial arms of the state, are most restricted. They are saddled with a commission form of government that combines executive and legislative authority and is headed by a judge. The powers vested in the county governments and the services they offer are fragmented. An amendment of some 2,000 words was passed in 1933 to allow larger counties to adopt a home-rule charter, but the provisions were so restrictive as to be inoperable.

Home rule allows a government to write its own charter and make changes in it without legislative approval. Had it been workable, this provision would have allowed counties to choose their own form of government and have more flexibility in day-to-day operations. The provision was deleted in 1969.

In contrast, cities enjoy a workable home-rule provision. Those with populations of more than 5,000 may become home-rule units of government. General-law cities, which are those without home-rule charters, must operate under statewide statutes. Cities, towns, and villages, whether operating under a home-rule charter or general law, are fairly free to provide whatever services and create whatever policies the citizens and governing bodies want, as long as there is no conflict with constitutional or statutory law. The major constitutional difficulties for cities are the ceilings imposed on tax rates and debt and limitations on the frequency of charter amendments.

Special districts are limited-purpose local governments that have taxing authority. The legislature generally authorizes the creation of special districts, although constitutional amendments have created some water and hospital districts. School districts are the best-known type of special district, but there are literally dozens of varieties. Because these types of government provide a way around the tax and debt limits imposed on cities and counties, they continue to proliferate.[22] (Chapter 11 discusses local government in detail.)

Suffrage

The provisions on voting and the apportionment of legislative bodies are interesting because many of them have clearly conflicted with federal law, which itself continues to evolve as the legal/political philosophy of federal judges changes. As a result, Article VI has been subject to frequent amendments to catch up with changes, such as the nationally established voting age and to allow participation in bond elections by voters who do not own property. The suffrage section of the constitution is shot through with "temporary transition provisions" to bridge the gap between state and federal law.

TABLE 2-3

Comparison of State Provisions for Amending the Constitution

State(s)	Legislative Proposal	Initiative by Voters	Constitutional Convention
Texas	Yes	No	No
Number of other states	49	18	41

SOURCE: *The Book of the States, 2010 Edition*, vol. 42 (Lexington, Ky.: Council of State Governments, 2010), 13–17.

Amendments

The framers of a constitution cannot possibly anticipate every provision that should be included. Consequently, all constitutions specify a procedure for amendment. Unlike the eighteen other states, most notably California, that allow citizens to initiate constitutional amendment proposals by petition and the forty-one states that provide for a constitutional convention (see Table 2-3), Texas has only one way to propose an amendment.

In Texas, proposals for amendments may be initiated during a regular or special session of the legislature, and an absolute two-thirds majority—that is, one hundred House and twenty-one Senate members—must vote to submit the proposed changes to the voters. The governor cannot veto a proposed amendment. The legislature also specifies the date of the election at which an amendment is voted on by the public. At least three months before the election, a proposed amendment must be published once a week for four weeks in a newspaper in each county. Whenever possible, amendments are placed on the ballot in general elections to avoid the expense of a separate, called election. Only a simple majority—that is, half plus one—of those citizens who choose to vote is needed for ratification, making it rather easy to add amendments. The governor officially proclaims the passage or rejection of amendments.

The public had voted on 646 proposed amendments by the middle of 2011, resulting in the addition of 467. This number is vivid proof that the amendment process in the state has occupied considerable legislative time and that citizens have frequently confronted constitutional propositions at the polls. This number is sure to grow after ten proposals from the 2011 legislature go to the voters.

Table 2-4 illustrates the relentlessness of the amendment phenomenon and the increasing reliance on amendments as a way to get something done in government. Forty-nine percent of the amendments were added between 1980 and 2009. Some streamlining of the state charter ensued from a constitutional amendment passed in November 1997 that called for elimination of duplicate numbers in the Texas Constitution and of obsolete provisions. Most observers, however, thought that the amendment did not provide sufficient clout to take care of the entire needed cleanup, an opinion reinforced by the seventy-seven amendments passed between 2000 and 2010.

TABLE 2-4

Texas Constitutional Amendments, 1879*–2011

Decade	Proposed	Adopted	Cumulative Total
1870s–1880s	16	8	5
1890s	15	9	17
1900s	20	11	28
1910s	36	10	38
1920s	26	15	53
1930s	45	32	85
1940s	35	22	107
1950s	43	37	144
1960s	84	56	200
1970s	67	42	242
1980s	99	84	326
1990s	81	64	390
2000s	79	77	467
Total through June 2011	646	467	467

*The first amendment to the 1876 Texas Constitution was adopted in 1879. Three early proposals never went to the voters.

SOURCE: Compiled by the authors from *Amendments to the Texas Constitution since 1876* (Austin: Texas Legislative Council, 2010), 1–2.

Constitutional Revision

The framers of the U.S. Constitution were wise enough to provide only the essential structure of national government and to consign broad powers to governmental agents. The flexibility inherent in this approach has made possible the country's transition from a nation whose government was mainly concerned with fending off "hostile" Native Americans and delivering the mail to one whose government now shoulders the burdens of world leadership and myriad socioeconomic policies. State constitutions, on the other hand, tend toward an inflexibility that leads to frequent revision.

Overview of the Need for Reform

During the bicentennial celebration of the U.S. Constitution (1987–1989), Americans were proud that their fundamental law had been amended only twenty-six times (a twenty-seventh amendment was added in 1992) and that ten of the amendments—the Bill of Rights—were added almost immediately after ratification. At the national level, the admonition of Alexander Hamilton that opens this chapter has been heeded.

The Texas Secretary of State's office posted this sample ballot on his Web site prior to the May 12, 2007, constitutional amendment election. This site, www.sos.state.tx.us, is always a source of the latest proposed amendments.

Photo of sample ballot. Texas. Public Domain.

No. 0000

CONSTITUTIONAL AMENDMENT ELECTION *(ELECCIÓN SOBRE ENMIENDAS A LA CONSTITUCIÓN)*

(Condado de) SAMPLE COUNTY, TEXAS

MAY 12, 2007 *(12 de mayo de 2007)*

SAMPLE BALLOT *(BOLETA DE MUESTRA)*

INSTRUCTION NOTE: *(NOTA DE INSTRUCCIÓN)*
Place an "X" in the square beside the statement indicating the way you wish to vote. *(Marque con una "X" el cuadro al lado de la frase que indica la manera en que quire usted votar.)*

No. 1   _ **For** *(A Favor)*   .. **Against** *(En Contra)*

"The constitutional amendment authorizing the legislature to provide for a reduction of the limitation on the total amount of ad valorem taxes that may be imposed for public school purposes on the residence homesteads of the elderly or disabled to reflect any reduction in the rate of those taxes for the 2006 and 2007 tax years."
"Enmienda constitucional que autoriza a la legislatura para disponer la reducción del monto total de impuestos al valor que, siendo para fines de las escuelas públicas, puedan establecerse sobre los hogares residenciales de ancianos o discapacitados, de modo que se refleje cualquier reducción de la tasa tributaria correspondiente a los ejercicios fiscales de 2006 y 2007".

At the state level, however, constitutions have not fared as well. State charters tend to reflect the concerns of vested interests. These interests prefer the "security blanket" of constitutional inclusion to being left at the mercy of legislatures with changing party alignments, political persuasions, and political concerns.

By the middle of 2011, the average state constitution had been amended 145 times. The champions of amendments were Alabama (807), California (519), and South Carolina (493). Texas came in fourth with its 467 amendments. The next closest states (Maryland, Nebraska, New York, Oregon, and South Dakota) were all in the lower 200s.

The ratification dates of state constitutions provide a clue as to what to expect in the way of content and, thus, number of amendments. Older state charters, unless they have been updated, tend to be more problematic than newer ones. For example, the two newest states—Alaska and Hawaii—have workable, sound constitutions that were modeled in part on the ideal document proposed by the National Municipal League.[23] These states have clearly profited from the mistakes of others. In 2011, five state constitutions that had been revised in the modern era—those of Illinois (1971), Michigan (1964), Montana (1973), Pennsylvania (1968), and Virginia (1971)—had only 11, 29, 30, 30, and 43 amendments, respectively.

Recent revision, however, does not guarantee fewer amendments. Louisiana, with a 1975 constitution, already had 154 amendments in 2011. That state also has had eleven constitutions, more than any other state. Whatever the primary method of proposing amendments in a given state, the result can be few or many charter changes, depending on how good the basic document is.[24]

Security Blankets Make Constitutional Change Difficult

One Texas example of a "security blanket" in the state constitution is the provision authorizing workers' compensation insurance for state and local government employees. Another example is the section that benefits veterans by providing funds for land purchases. A third example is the benefits given to homeowners, who receive a partial tax exemption for their primary residence (homestead).

Advocates of reform urge Texas to follow Hamilton's prescription by adopting a new document that is general, flexible, and streamlined in place of the specific, rigid, complicated constitution that hampers its government now. Reformers are not all of one mind and frequently differ on the details of their proposals. Nevertheless, reform advocates tend to agree on fundamentally important changes that should be made in the current constitution, as follows:

1. **The biennial legislative session:** As state politics and finance become more complex, the short legislative sessions held only every other year become more of a problem in developing long-range public policy.

2. **The judicial system:** The Texas judicial system, as previously discussed, is characterized by multiple layers of courts with overlapping jurisdictions. Many reform advocates would like to see the establishment of a streamlined, unified judicial system.

3. **The plural executive branch:** The executive branch has many elected officials. Reformers suggest a state executive branch modeled on the national one—that is, a single elected official and a series of executive departments responsible to that official—to avoid the disintegrated, fragmented nature of the present structure.

4. **County government:** Especially in urban counties, the structure of county government and its lack of power to pass ordinances (local laws) mean that the counties cannot respond readily to urban problems. Reform advocates suggest that county government be streamlined and given at least limited ordinance power.

5. **Detailed provisions in the constitution:** For example, each time more funding is needed for welfare payments or the veterans' land program, a constitutional amendment must be passed. Thus, another area for reform is removing from the constitution details that are better left for statutory law, which can be changed more readily as situations demand.

Recent Reform Efforts

Attempts have been made to modernize the Texas Constitution from time to time since its adoption in 1876. Serious interest in constitutional reform/revision was evident in 1957–1961, 1967–1969, 1971–1974, and to some extent, 1991–1993 and 1999. The only reform effort that resulted in an opportunity for the electorate to decide on a new document came in 1975.

1971–1974

The 1971–1974 effort was important for two reasons. First, it clarified a long-standing concern about whether the legislature had the constitutional right to convene itself as a constitutional convention. A 1972 constitutional amendment authorized the Sixty-third Legislature to convene itself as a constitutional convention. This constitutional convention was quickly labeled the "Con-Con." Second, the Texas Constitutional Revision Commission, created by the same amendment, provided a detailed study of

the state constitution that served as the basis for new constitutions proposed in 1974 and 1975.

The proposal drafted by the constitutional convention was defeated when two issues—parimutuel (that is, racetrack) betting and right to work, which is an antiunion provision—were introduced that became the red herrings for foes of reform. (Red herrings are diversions intended to draw attention away from the main issues.) These two issues brought opposition from Bible Belt conservatives and organized labor. The proposal died before ever reaching the voters.

1975

Interest in constitutional reform remained high. When the Sixty-fourth Legislature convened in January 1975, constitutional revision was a principal issue. Senate Joint Resolution (SJR) 11 (with amendments) emerged as the vehicle for accomplishing constitutional change. Although the legislature did not adopt all the changes suggested by the 1973 revision commission, legislators did draw heavily on that work.[25] Highlights of SJR 11 included annual legislative sessions, a streamlined judicial system, and modernization of county government. SJR 11 eliminated such details as the welfare ceiling. It gave more power to the governor coupled with a limit of two terms. It also provided for property tax relief and a tax on petroleum refining.

Powerful interests lined up on both sides of this proposed constitutional reform, with vested economic interests and emotionalism acting as important components of the struggle for ratification of the document. In spite of the efforts of most state officials to convince voters of the worth of the proposed state charter, voters defeated the entire proposal by a two-to-one margin on November 4, 1975. Governor Dolph Briscoe, fearful of higher taxes and government expansion, and county officials, concerned for their jobs, helped to bring about defeat. A combination of interests worried that the "equal educational opportunity" provisions would upset the scheme of funding public schools helped to convince citizens to vote against the proposal. Texans clearly preferred the old, lengthy, familiar document to one they saw as possibly promoting more spending and allowing greater governmental power.

1991–1993

Little interest in constitutional revision was evident in the fifteen years following the defeat of the proposed new state constitution in 1975. Too many problems demanding immediate solutions filled the legislative sessions, and legislators did not have time to consider constitutional change beyond proposing more amendments. Besides, virtually every group with interests protected by the current constitution, from veterans to the University of Texas and Texas A&M systems to county commissioners, was anything but encouraging of constitutional change.

Following the 1991 legislative session, however, Senator John Montford drafted a joint resolution that proposed a new constitution for consideration in 1993. The Montford proposal included features such as these:

- **Six-year terms for senators and four-year terms for House members**
- **A limit of two consecutive terms for a senator and three for a House member**

- A sixty-day budget session of the legislature in even-numbered years

- Empowerment of the legislature to meet to reconsider bills vetoed by the governor

- The only elected executives to be the governor, lieutenant governor, and comptroller, each with a limit of two terms

- Simplification of the court system and provision for nonpartisan elections

- Creation of five regional university systems, each of which would share in the Permanent University Fund (PUF)

- Ordinance power for counties, subject to local voter approval[26]

As is so often the case, immediate problems—such as the budget shortfall, school finance, and a prison system unable to cope with the volume of state prisoners—crowded out constitutional revision in 1993. When Senator Montford prepared the draft constitution, he was one of the most powerful state senators in Texas, but even he had other issues to address between 1993 and 1995. Subsequently, he left the legislature to become head of Texas Tech University. Without a champion, constitutional revision was not considered by the 1997 legislature either.

1999 and Beyond

After the 1997 legislative session, Representative Rob Junell, chairman of the powerful House Appropriations Committee, expressed interest in constitutional reform. Junell liked some of Montford's ideas, particularly reducing the number of elected officials, including making judges subject to gubernatorial appointment. He was joined by Senator Bill Ratliff, chairman of the equally powerful Senate Finance Committee. Their proposal included the following:

- Six-year terms for senators and four-year terms for House members

- Limiting the elected executives to the governor, lieutenant governor, comptroller of public accounts, and attorney general

- Providing for an executive department that would consist of specified department heads, excluding elective officials, and report to the governor

- Simplification of the court system, with judges to be appointed by the governor

- Establishing the possibility of a veto session for the purpose of reconvening to consider whether to override the governor's veto

Known as HJR 1 and SJR 1 in the Seventy-sixth Legislature in 1999, the Junell-Ratliff proposal was withdrawn from committee in late April when the sponsors realized that their resolution had no chance of being considered by the full House or Senate. Opposition was widespread among both the Democratic and Republican state party organizations, the Texas AFL-CIO, and various other interest groups. Longtime political reporter Sam Attlesey characterized the demise of the proposal as due to "a lack of interest, excitement or crisis in state government."[27]

Although three powerful legislators took an interest in constitutional reform in the 1990s, nothing came of their efforts. Neither other legislators nor citizens

Since 1989, the legislature has wrestled with the thorny issue of public school finance, trying various funding schemes to rectify the objections of state courts that the Texas public education system does not provide "efficient and effective" education for all students. At the "eleventh hour" in 2006, the legislature produced a funding scheme to meet a court-ordered deadline; spending cuts for 2012–2013 might land the state back in court again.

Ben Sargent.

had much interest in constitutional revision. Both were more concerned about the issues that regularly beset the Texas political system—education, health care, highways, air quality, and so on.

Moreover, a pressing concern for constitutional reform is more likely to arise from a moralistic political culture than the traditionalistic/individualistic culture that characterizes Texas. Most Texans are politically conservative and prefer the basic governing document that they know to one that could cause social/political/economic changes that they might not like. Consequently, Texas has continued to use a patchwork approach to its basic document, relying on constitutional amendments and statutory law to alleviate some of the short-comings of the constitution. The 1999 amendment that authorizes removal or rewording of outdated and repetitive parts of the state constitution is illustrative of the amendment approach to constitutional patching. Modifying the election code to ensure that the qualifications for voting in Texas conform to national requirements is one example of a statutory fix.

Twenty-nine states have constitutions newer than Texas's, and twelve have state charters written since 1950. Yet, in spite of the occasional difficulty of governing under the present state charter, only the League of Women Voters has shown a long-term concern for constitutional revision, joined by sporadic media interest in reform.[28] Recent sessions of the legislature have faced too many problems demanding immediate solutions to allow legislators to give any consideration to a new constitution. Furthermore, many citizens fear that change may be for the worse rather than for the better, and special interests want to preserve what they already have embodied in the state charter. This conservative stance, reflecting once again the state's traditionalism, is encouraged by the major economic forces in the state.

Constitutional Politics

Making a constitution, like other lawmaking processes, is highly political. Whether the issue is general constitutional reform or an individual amendment, changing a constitution will benefit some groups and disadvantage others. Because the requirements of a two-thirds legislative vote and public approval make constitutional change more difficult than ordinary lawmaking, the political stakes are greater when alteration of a state's fundamental charter is an issue.

Something for Everyone

Various special interest groups attempt to embody their political, social, economic, and/or moral viewpoints in the constitution by either advocating a particular change or working against it. If a group can embed its particular policy concern in the constitution, the issue is likely to remain there, perhaps forever. In other words, it is easier to "amend in" a provision than to "amend it out." The relative ease of amending the state charter contributes to this attitude of using the constitution as a security blanket. The constitution has become a political "goody" store that contains something for everyone.

One strategy used by these groups is to seek an authorizing provision in the constitution that will result in economic gains for the group. For example, a set of 1985 amendments about funding for water supply has given benefits to small cities, farmers, and ranchers, all of whom vigorously advocated passage of the proposals. Similarly, tax relief has been a frequent subject for constitutional amendment since 1978. Almost everyone—including farmers, ranchers, lumber interests, oil and natural gas producers, and residential property taxpayers—has gotten something from the amendments and the accompanying legislation.

Sometimes a group tries to prohibit a state from taking, or being able to take, a particular action. When the foes of parimutuel betting helped to destroy the efforts of the 1974 constitutional convention, their goal was to prevent the constitutional authorization of gambling in Texas. As noted previously, this issue was a political red herring dragged in by general opponents of constitutional reform, and it illustrates tactics that are used to defeat change. The proposed constitution did not specifically provide for parimutuel betting, but it did not prohibit it. Opposition to parimutuel betting has since lessened, and in November 1987, voters approved it in a referendum held at the time of a constitutional amendment election. A 1991 amendment authorized more gambling through a state lottery.

The strategy of getting something for everyone by opposition to particular policies has more recently focused on various proposed amendments that would prohibit a state income tax. In 1993, voters overwhelmingly approved an amendment that mandates a voter referendum if the legislature should ever pass an income tax. The amendment also requires that at least two-thirds of the revenue from an income tax be pledged to reduce property taxes that support public schools, with the remainder to go to support education. The importance of this provision has been evident in recent years when the legislature has been struggling to find funding sources for state programs.

At other times, a group seeks to advance some special interest that is already the subject of a constitutional guarantee. The periodic amendment of the legislative article on the Veterans Land Board is an example. This constitutional

provision authorizes the state to sell bonds both to purchase land for veterans and to underwrite low-cost loans for home purchasers. It must be amended each time an authorization for more bond sales is needed.

Another example of the politics of constitution making concerns branch banking, which the Texas Constitution prohibited before a 1986 constitutional amendment. Larger banks wanted branch banking because they wanted to establish branches in other parts of a city or even in other cities. Smaller, independent banks, fearing the competition that a change would permit, opposed the practice. From 1987 through 1990, Texas banks and savings and loans suffered many failures. Because branch banking had been legalized, finding purchasers for the failed Texas financial institutions was easier. Larger, more stable banks both in Texas and in other states could acquire the troubled banks and make them branches. In 1997, financial institutions were major advocates of a proposal that would allow Texas homeowners, like the citizens of all other states, to take out a second mortgage on their residence. Voters, viewing home equity loans as a type of easy credit, went along with the banks and savings and loans.

Private interests are not always the only ones seeking constitutional change. Sometimes elected officials want changes in the constitution to enhance their power, but such ideas often do not fly with the general public. In 1980 and 1981, for example, the governor tried to gain greater control over the state's budgeting and spending processes through constitutional amendment, but the public defeated both of the proposed amendments. In 1999, voters defeated a proposal that would have allowed state employees who serve on local government boards to be paid the same as other compensated board members.

Public officials also may try to prevent constitutional change through fear of losing powers. Members of the Texas Association of County Officials (TACO) were a potent lobbying force against the proposed 1975 constitution. They were afraid of losing political control if county governments were modernized.

The Political Process

The political process involved in constitutional change is essentially the same as it is in other activities designed to influence public policy. Elected officials, political parties, special interests and their lobbyists, and campaigning are all involved. A brief illustration of the political process is provided by a situation that began in 1979 and initially appeared to be resolved by an amendment approved by the voters in 1984—namely, the issue of building funds for the state's universities. The 1984 amendment, however, was not the end of the story.

The University of Texas at Austin and Texas A&M University at College Station, through provisions in Article VII of the state constitution, were the sole beneficiaries of the Permanent University Fund (PUF). The PUF fund—which can be used for buildings, other permanent improvements, and enrichment activities—represents a large amount of money; it was worth over $11.4 billion in 2008 (the last full inventory of assets). The PUF money comes from the proceeds of the oil and gas leases on a million acres of public land granted to the two universities and from investment of these proceeds.

Seventeen other state universities originally received money for buildings directly from the legislature and then, beginning in 1947, from a dedicated fund fed by the state property tax. Institutions created after 1947 were dependent on legislative appropriations.

In 1979, as part of a general tax-relief movement, the legislature reduced the rate for the state property tax to almost zero. In the 1979 and 1981 sessions of the legislature, a variety of proposals to establish an alternative to financing college building programs were introduced. Neither the legislators nor the universities could agree on a proposal. The legislature subsequently proposed a constitutional amendment to abolish the state property tax altogether, and the voters approved the amendment in late 1982.

The 1983 legislature agreed on a basic plan that provided PUF coverage for other institutions in the UT and A&M systems, and established a separate fund (the Higher Education Fund) to cover the other state institutions. This separate fund would cover repairs and renovations, new construction, library and equipment purchases, and land acquisitions. They also agreed on a special infusion of funds to the two predominately African American institutions in the state, Texas Southern University and Prairie View A&M.

The UT and A&M representatives wanted to ensure that the PUF was not opened to other universities. They feared a significant reduction in the funds available to the two flagship institutions. Their willingness to include their branch campuses in the PUF avoided the need to include these branch campuses in the new construction fund. At the same time, UT and A&M also gained the agreement of the other universities not to seek inclusion in the PUF. In 1984, the issue of university construction was seemingly resolved as part of a broad solution to financing *capital* improvements (those of long-term duration).

In 2001, however, the legislature changed the system to begin reducing the amount of appropriated funds that went into the Higher Education Fund, and the difference was deposited in a new fund called the Texas Excellence Fund to spur research. No appropriation was made to the permanent Higher Education Fund for fiscal years 2004–2005. Then in 2003, a more conservative group of legislators, faced with a $10 billion deficit, pulled back general capital funding in favor of dollars designed to attract outside research funding. The Seventy-eighth Legislature in 2003 dictated that the Texas Excellence Fund and the University Research Fund would be repealed as of September 1, 2005. At that point, yet another fund, the Research Development Fund, was created.

This shift in emphasis to research-only funding had a major effect on every university student outside the University of Texas and Texas A&M systems. Because of the elimination of the special pot of funding for construction, repairs, libraries, equipment, and land that was not specially tied to external research funding, students found themselves saddled with the costs for these items in the form of assessments, such as special library fees and higher tuition that was in part pledged to construction bonds. At the same time, the PUF institutions were pointing out that they did not have adequate dollars to take care of all their building repair needs and that they were under similar pressures to emphasize their research missions.

This issue of capital funding for universities provides a portrait of how many varied interests can become involved in constitutional change. The saga of university construction has involved many people—legislators, universities, taxpayers, the Higher Education Coordinating Board, business and industry, and ethnic minorities. Different constitutional change issues have different casts of characters, but all are fraught with similar complex political relationships.

YOU ★ ★ DECIDE

Should Texas Convene a Constitutional Convention?

The Texas Constitution was ratified in 1876. By mid-2011, it had been amended 467 times and is now more than 93,000 words in length. The average for all fifty states is 145 amendments and 37,871 words. California, the only state with a population larger than that of Texas, has a constitution with 519 amendments and 54,645 words. The constitution of New York, the third largest state, has 220 amendments and 51,700 words.

PRO	CON
▲ Texas should convene a constitutional convention to draft a new state charter. The present state constitution	▼ The state constitution should not be revised to avoid
• is antiquated.	• mistaking newness for quality; the U.S. Constitution is 89 years older than the Texas Constitution.
• conflicts with the national Constitution.	• increasing partisanship that could create a political disaster.
• protects special interests.	• "fixing something that ain't broke."
• reflects agrarian interests.	• giving more authority to counties, which are already inefficient.
• is far too specific.	• giving government, especially the governor, too much power.
• needs frequent interpretation.	• a process likely to be an expensive exercise resulting in stalemates.
• poorly organizes government, thus does not meet the needs of an urban state.	• removing protection against arbitrary governmental action from those groups protected by the charter.

Summary

Constitutions have four purposes: legitimacy, organizing government, providing power, and limiting governmental power. The six Texas constitutions have embodied these purposes in varying degrees.

When the current constitution was drafted and ratified in 1876, Texans were so unhappy with the Reconstruction government that the framers of the new charter concentrated their attention on legitimacy and limiting governmental power. Thus, they largely ignored the importance of assigning sufficient power to government officials, and they subverted the purpose of organizing government by creating a fragmented set of institutions and offices designed to diffuse authority. Although this approach limits government, it also makes citizen participation more difficult because state government is confusing to most people.

Partisans of democracy are frustrated with the state constitution because it makes the people's ability to govern themselves more difficult. Yet the current constitution reflects the traditionalistic and individualistic political culture of the state. Lacking the farsightedness of the framers of the U.S. Constitution, the authors of the Texas charter produced a restrictive document that today sometimes impedes the development and implementation of needed policies and programs. As a result, by the middle of 2011, lawmakers and citizens had resorted to amending the Texas Constitution 467 times to make possible programs that otherwise would have been consigned to legislative dreamland. In addition, the 2011 legislature proposed 175 additional amendments, but only ten will reach the ballot.

In one sense, the element of democratic theory indicating that public input into policy is important is satisfied by such a practice, but policies are very hard to modify once they are written into the constitution. Dynamic public issues such as funding for water quality, welfare, and public education could be handled more smoothly without the necessity of proposing and ratifying a constitutional amendment. Currently, if a policy proves to be ineffective, only another amendment can solve the problem.

The most cumbersome and/or unnecessarily restrictive provisions in the 1876 constitution and their consequences are the following:

1. The governor, although held responsible by the public for overall state leadership and the action of state agencies, in reality has limited direct control over most major policymaking offices, boards, and commissions.

2. The legislature is caught between the proverbial "rock and a hard place." While constantly being criticized by the citizenry for poor legislative performance, it nevertheless must operate within the constraints of poverty-level salaries, short and infrequent sessions, and innumerable restrictions on legislative action.

3. Texas judges are well aware of the lack of cohesiveness in the judicial system, but they are virtually powerless to provide simpler, more uniform justice because of the overlapping and parallel jurisdictions of the state's courts and the lack of effective supervision of the whole judicial system.

4. County governments, even when county commissioners are progressive in attitude, are restricted by their constitutional structure and scope.

5. The 467 amendments exacerbate the poor organization of the charter, making it even more difficult for the layperson to read and comprehend it.

Twice in the 1990s, powerful legislators showed an interest in constitutional revisions. Whether similar efforts will succeed in the future is uncertain. The electorate still lacks sufficient understanding of the shortcomings of the present constitution to be receptive to revisions that involve increases in governmental power. Also, citizens are far too concerned about state taxes, public education, social services, crime and punishment, and many other pressing issues to give constitutional revision much attention. Although the current constitution "creaks and groans," the state still takes care of its business.

In addition, special interests have found it easy to amend the current document by influencing key legislators and then mounting serious campaigns to elicit voter support. They prefer the protection of a constitution to more easily changed statutes. Thus, a successful revision effort may have to wait not only until the citizens of Texas are more aware of the pitfalls of the present document, but also until powerful special interests can be persuaded to work for, not against, constitutional reform.

Article I of the Texas Constitution as quoted at the beginning of this chapter is ironic: The emphasis on the phrase "inherent in the people" has come to be more about "political power" than "the people." For now, "if it ain't broke, don't try to fix it" prevails.

Glossary Terms

Bill of Rights	home rule
checks and balances	incorporation
constitution	plural executive
constitutional amendment	separation of powers
constitutional revision	

3

Interest Groups

As soon as several of the inhabitants of the United States have taken up an opinion or a feeling they wish to promote in the world, they look around for mutual assistance; and as soon as they have found each other out, they combine. From that moment they are no longer isolated men, but a power seen from afar, whose actions serve for an example, and whose language is listened to.

ALEXIS DE TOCQUEVILLE, *DEMOCRACY IN AMERICA*, 1835

Money doesn't talk, it swears.

BOB DYLAN, "IT'S ALRIGHT, MA (I'M ONLY BLEEDING)," 1965

OBJECTIVES

After reading this chapter, you should be able to

Explain why interest groups create a dilemma for democracy and why government cannot outlaw such groups to resolve it.

Define the term *interest group*, and list some types of such groups.

Explain the biases in the formation of interest groups, and give the consequences of those biases.

List the major resources of interest groups.

Provide the reasons why governments sometimes try to regulate lobbying activity, and evaluate the effectiveness of those activities in Texas.

Explain how the activities of the insurance industry, the credit-service industry, the NAACP, Public Citizen Texas, and the video game industry illustrate some general principles about interest groups in Texas.

List the major interest groups in Texas, describe how they influence state politics, and explain why some have risen or declined in influence over the last quarter-century.

INTRODUCTION

Politics is concerned with the making of *public* policy, but a great many of its actions have *private* consequences. When government imposes a tax, begins to regulate an industry, or writes rules about the behavior of individuals, it makes an impact not just on the public in general, but on citizens in particular. Human nature being what it is, people often tend to judge the action not so much on the basis of its value to their community as on the basis of its benefit to themselves. Seeking to obtain more favorable policies, people organize to try to influence government. When they do, they create a problem for democracy. As citizens, we want our government to take account of the impact of its laws on individuals, but we do not want the special wishes of some people to be more important than the shared needs of us all. To the extent that public policy is made or modified at the behest of private interests, democracy is impaired.

In Texas, as elsewhere in the United States, special organized interests are always busy trying to influence what government institutions do. Citizens have to decide whether these groups are merely presenting their point of view to public authorities or whether instead they are attempting to corrupt the process of self-government.

In this chapter, the discussion first focuses on the definition and classification of interest groups. The chapter describes and analyzes their activities, and then moves on to consider some efforts that have been made to regulate lobbying. Finally, there is an examination of the history and recent activities of some of the major interest groups in Texas, and an evaluation of the interest-group system in Texas in the light of democratic theory.

Interest Groups

The self-concept of Americans, and particularly of Texans, tends to be highly individualistic. The image of the lone cowboy riding across the range, cleaning up corrupt towns single-handedly, summarizes the way many Texans think of themselves. But in reality, ordinary human beings do not have much influence on society unless they are organized into groups. When people join together to cooperate in defense of their interests, however, they become part of a powerful force in the politics of the state and the nation.

Definition

An *interest* is something an individual or individuals have that has value and is therefore worth defending. It can be economic, religious, ethnic, or based on almost anything. People who produce oil have an interest, as do Catholics and fans of Harry Potter novels. Interests affect politics in two general ways. One topic of Chapter 4 will be the manner in which interests form the basis for much of the battle between political parties. In this chapter, the subject is the direct effect of interests and interest groups on Texas government.

In the broad sense, an **interest group** is a private organization of individuals who have banded together because of a common cause or role. The focus here, however, is on **political interest groups**, those that try to influence politicians to make public policy in line with their preferences. When people join these groups, they exercise their right guaranteed by the First Amendment to the U.S. Constitution to "assemble" and "petition" the government. They also gain the ability to affect government decisions beyond what they achieve with just their vote.

Interest groups can be usefully contrasted with political parties. The focus of a political party is broad, encompassing many different interests, whereas the focus of an interest group is narrow, comprising just one interest. Parties attempt to gain power by running candidates in elections, whereas groups try to affect power by influencing officeholders. Therefore, while parties are forced to appeal publicly to citizens to marshal support, groups may work entirely behind the scenes.

Classification

Interest groups may be classified according to the types of interests they defend:

1. **Economic groups, such as manufacturers' associations or labor unions. These represent the most common type of interest group and also, in general, the type with the most resources. Within this large category, many specialized groups represent specific types of industries or occupations. An example of the former would be banking and financial organizations, represented by the Texas Bankers Association, among others. Examples of the latter would be professional associations, such as the State Bar of Texas, representing lawyers, or the Texas Medical Association, representing doctors. Like labor unions, these groups represent people who share a type of livelihood. Unlike most labor unions, they are composed of people who are generally well-educated and relatively wealthy.**

2. **Spiritual groups, such as church organizations or pro-life and pro-choice associations. These groups unite people who may be otherwise very different, but who share a faith or a public policy position derived from their faith.**

3. Artistic or recreational organizations, such as the local Symphony League or the Texas Association of Bass Clubs. This type of group includes people who share a hobby or other type of pastime.

4. Ethnic groups, such as the League of United Latin American Citizens (LULAC) or the National Association for the Advancement of Colored People (NAACP).

5. Associations of local governments, such as the Texas Municipal League and the Texas Association of Counties.

6. Public interest groups, such as Common Cause or the League of Women Voters. These groups try to pursue their understanding of interests common to all citizens rather than the individual interests of their members. The members of these groups can disagree about what constitutes the "public interest"—they can have opposed positions on whether school vouchers would be a good thing for education, for example—but those positions are based on their differing understanding of the broad-based needs of all citizens (in other words, on their political ideologies) rather than on their own personal needs.

Interest Groups in the Political Process

The two most important points to understand about interest groups are that not all people who share an interest are organized and that organized interests are much more powerful than unorganized interests.

If they get organized, students such as those shown here can have an impact on Texas public policy.

© *Young America's Foundation.*

Students, Too, Have Interests

Although many Texas public universities include an elected student representative on their governing board, apparently there is no longer a formal organization representing the interests of students as a group, either in the United States in general or in Texas in particular. There are, however, a variety of national student organizations representing the views of conservative students (Young America's Foundation, Young Americans for Freedom), liberal students (Democracy Matters, Young Democrats of America), and students who want to support specific causes (Students for a Free Tibet, Students for Free Culture). Details about these groups, and many others, can be accessed by typing "student organizations" into a search engine on the Internet.

Who Is Organized?

Although the famous quotation from Alexis de Tocqueville at the beginning of this chapter might lead us to believe that every potential interest spawns an interest group, in fact, some interests are far more likely to be organized than others. Those that are organized are relevant to policymaking; those that are not organized are usually irrelevant.

For example, oil and gas producers are well organized and politically powerful in Texas. Oil and gas consumers, however, are not organized, except insofar as general consumers' groups—which theoretically represent everybody, but never have a very large membership—include petroleum among the many products of interest to them. As a result, unless the price of gasoline at the pump rises steeply, as it did in 2008 and again in 2011, thus creating public anger, petroleum consumers usually are not of much concern to policymakers. Under ordinary conditions, government policymakers are likely to pay much more attention to petroleum producers.

There are three general rules of interest-group formation. First, economic producing groups are more likely to be organized than are consuming groups (as in the oil and gas example above). Second, regardless of the type of group, people with more education and income are more likely to join groups than are people with less education and income. (The Texas Medical Association, to be discussed shortly, is an example.) Third, citizens who join groups out of personal involvement as opposed to economic stake tend to feel very strongly about the particular issue that is the group's reason for existence. (Both pro-choice and pro-life groups are examples.) They are therefore much more likely to contribute money, write letters, attend rallies, and engage in other actions that get the attention of government officials. Consequently, because they are more likely to be organized, producers tend to exert more political influence than consumers, the middle and upper classes more influence than the working classes, and passionate believers more influence than citizens who are less emotionally involved.

Functions

Interest groups attempt to persuade both the public and individual government officials to take a particular point of view on specific public policies. In trying to be persuasive, they perform six important functions in the political process:

1. They furnish information to officeholders in all branches of government. This activity includes both communicating their collective opinion on public policy and supplying policymakers with their version of the facts.

2. They politicize and inform members of their groups, as well as others.

3. They mediate conflict within their groups.

4. They engage in electioneering, especially the contribution of money to candidates, and possibly in other interventions in the governing process, such as filing lawsuits.

5. By disseminating information supporting their own policy stands to citizens, they help to form public opinion.

6. By providing institutions other than political parties that help people to participate in the process of governing, they help their members to become more involved democratic citizens.

Activities

Interest groups enhance democratic government by supplying information to citizens, contributing to debates about issues, getting people involved in politics, and shaking up the established order by influencing institutions. But because they often attempt to skew the process of government to benefit themselves, these groups also can be a corrupting influence. A closer look at their activities will show the extent to which they deflect public policymaking into private channels.

Electioneering One of the most common ways interest groups try to ensure that their future efforts at persuasion will be effective is by supporting candidates for public office. Interest groups that have helped to elect a politician can be confident that they will not be forgotten when the politician enters government.

Usually the most effective way to help candidates is to give them money. Because campaigning demands the purchase of advertising in expensive media (see Chapter 5), all candidates, except the few who are personally rich, need to beg wealthy individuals and groups for large amounts of money. In this regard, one of the important developments in recent decades has been the rise of **political action committees** (PACs) and their influence on elections.

A PAC is a committee formed by an organization, industry, or individual for the purpose of collecting money and then contributing that money to selected political candidates and causes. Because PACs coordinate and concentrate the financial clout of multitudes of individuals with a single interest, they can influence public policy far more effectively than can most ordinary, isolated citizens. Some states, such as California, Maine, and Minnesota, limit the amount of money that PACs can contribute in state elections, but in Texas, these groups may give as much as they wish. Both the politicians and the contributors understand, if only tacitly, that what the interest groups expect is an exchange: The groups give the candidates money, and if they win, the candidates give the groups public policy.

The way in which money purchases political influence is illustrated by the actions of the credit-service industry in Texas. Many people, especially poor Texans, want to take out small loans just before their paychecks arrive. The state prohibits interest rates on these loans that are "usurious," or unfairly high. The industry, however, gets around the state's rules by organizing unregulated middlemen who broker the loans and charge high fees for doing so. People who want to protect poor borrowers from these high fees refer to the industry as being composed of "predatory lenders" and "loan sharks." The industry, however, protects itself from further regulation by giving generously to politicians.

During the 2010 election cycle, for example, according to a study by the public interest group Texans for Public Justice, the credit-service industry contributed $1,369,542 to candidates for public office. Table 3-1 lists the ten most generous credit-service contributors to candidates for public office in Texas during 2010. As the table shows, the reelection campaigns of Republican officeholders such as Governor Rick Perry, Lieutenant Governor David Dewhurst, and House Speaker Joe Straus benefited greatly from the industry's generosity. Not surprisingly, although a bill to regulate payday lenders did pass the 2011 legislature, the law was so watered down that it does almost nothing to protect poor people from predatory practices.[1]

There is no point in criticizing the integrity of public officials for being willing to accept large amounts of cash from groups and individuals that are pushing

TABLE 3-1

Campaign Contributions to Texas Politicians from Credit-Service Businesses, 2010 Election Cycle

Contributor/Company	Amount	City	Top Beneficiary
Tex. Consumer Finance Assn.	$378,750	Austin	Lt. Gov. David Dewhurst
Trevor Ahlberg/Cottonwood Finc'l	283,700	Arlington	Lt. Gov. David Dewhurst
Tex. Consumer Lenders PAC	125,500	Arlington	Speaker Joe Straus
Cash America PAC	88,750	Ft. Worth	Gov. Rick Perry
ACE Cash Express PAC	75,250	Irving	Attorney Gen. Greg Abbott
EZCORP PAC	75,000	Austin	Combs/Dewhurst/Perry/Straus
Tex. Assoc. of Pawnbrokers	38,500	Austin	Sen. Jackson; Reps. Solomon, Truitt
Robert I. Reich/Cmty Loans of Am.	37,000	Deerfield, Fla.	Sen. John Carona
Rent-A-Center PAC	35,500	Plano	Gov. Perry, Lt. Gov. Dewhurst
Rod Aycox/Select Mgmt. Resources	21,500	Alpharetta, Ga.	Speaker Straus

SOURCE: Texans for Public Justice, "Loan-Shark-Financed Campaigns Threaten Payday-Loan Reform," March 2011, 3, from www.tpj.org.

a narrow agenda. It is the reality of electoral financing and permissive lobbying laws, not personal dishonesty, that makes politicians overly sensitive to private, as opposed to public, interests.

Persuading the Public Although most interest-group energy is expended in lobbying government directly, some groups also attempt to influence public policy indirectly by "educating" the public. Sometimes they operate by buying television commercial time to argue their public policy case to citizens, who, they hope, will then pressure their representatives to support the groups' agendas. Sometimes they operate by attempting to persuade citizens to vote a certain way on a referendum.

The 2005 legislative sessions were good ones for observing the efforts of interest groups to persuade the public on behalf of their private causes. Especially noteworthy was a public relations battle between giants SBC and Verizon Communications on one side and cable companies in alliance with Texas cities on another.[2]

Not so long ago, the telephone and television industries were separate entities. Telephones transmitted private conversations over lines owned by the phone company. Television sets received entertainment and news that had been broadcast over the airwaves via large transmitters owned by different corporations. Although both industries were partially regulated by government agencies—the Federal Communications Commission in Washington and the Public Utility Commission in Austin—in each case the industry was under the authority of a different set of laws.

YOU ★ ★ DECIDE

Should Corporate Political Action Committees Be Banned?

A political action committee (PAC) is an organization that collects voluntary contributions from citizens—generally, those who are affiliated with a particular organization such as a corporation, church, or labor union, or who believe in a particular cause—and distributes them to candidates. Reformers have often called for government to forbid corporations to form PACs.

PRO	CON
▲ Although "money talks," money is not speech. The First Amendment to the U.S. Constitution should not be interpreted so as to protect the power of money.	▼ The First Amendment protects individual freedom of expression, and citizens should be able to express themselves by contributing money to candidates or organizations.
▲ It is bad enough that individuals are able to corrupt the process of government by renting the allegiance of politicians with campaign contributions; it is much worse that corporate interests are able to do so.	▼ A PAC is merely an organization that permits individuals with a shared interest to coordinate their political activity; shared economic interests are just as worthy of representation as religious, ideological, ethnic, or any other kind of interest.
▲ Corporations already possess a great political advantage over ordinary citizens because of their ability to hire lobbyists and buy media advertising; the presence of PACs makes that advantage even more lopsided and unfair.	▼ The supposed political advantage possessed by corporations is a fiction in the mind of so-called reformers. In fact, corporations are over-taxed and overregulated. They should have more political influence, not less.
▲ The political power of corporations has resulted in public policies that have contributed to the growing inequality of wealth in the United States; in order to permit the reversal of those policies, corporate power must be curtailed.	▼ Growing inequality of wealth has been caused by economic trends that are independent of government policies. Besides, differences in material equality reflect differences in merit, and are therefore good, not bad.

With the advent of personal computers in the 1980s, however, the phone business and the television business began to melt into one telecommunications industry. By 2005, most consumers watched television programs that had not been broadcast, but had arrived at their homes over coaxial cable, and the cable companies were planning to begin offering telephone services. At the same time, telephone companies, having already merged with computer companies, were

planning to get into the video industry, offering phone and television over the Internet. All these plans, however, were often impeded by communications laws that had been written during an earlier era, and which brought the two previously distinct industries into conflict.

During the regular and special 2005 legislative sessions, two phone titans, SBC and Verizon Communications, attempted to persuade politicians to write a new set of regulations that would help them get into video and thereby compete with cable companies. The existing law ordered a cable company to negotiate franchise agreements with each city it served. The cities, for their part, exacted concessions from the cable companies, requiring them to carry a variety of public-access channels and to pay a fee to the city each year. Because the cable companies enjoyed a virtual monopoly in the provision of clear video programming, they could charge high prices for their services. The arrangement was a win-win situation for both the companies and the municipal governments. Verizon and SBC asked the legislature to exempt their Internet video services from the requirement that they negotiate separate deals with each city. These phone companies lobbied legislators to pass a law allowing them to apply for a single statewide franchise that would enable them to pick and choose the cities, or neighborhoods within cities, where they would offer their new services.

The cable companies cried foul and launched their own lobbying effort in alliance with the Texas Municipal League (whose member cities stood to miss out on a fortune in franchise fees if cable lost this battle) to defeat the phone company bill. The two contending coalitions also conducted a sustained public relations campaign, each side trying to convince members of the public that their version of telecommunications policy was in the public interest. At first, cable companies attempted to bar the telephone companies' ads attacking them, but soon gave up that fight. The public was treated to an ill-tempered video brawl, with ads accusing the other side of being selfish, mean-spirited, and untruthful, and extolling their own side as being paladins of consumer interests. Meanwhile, various observers and spokespeople wrote op-ed pieces for the newspapers, arguing with their version of relevant arguments and evidence that one choice or the other should be the pick of good citizens in Texas. For a technical issue involving difficult questions of technology, economics, and law, it was a remarkably loud and unavoidable controversy on the state's television screens.

Cable and the cities prevailed in the regular session of the legislature, but in the second special session, the tide turned. Mired in indecision over school finance, legislators managed to pass a telecommunications bill that handed SBC and Verizon total victory. It is impossible to say whether this outcome was significantly affected by public opinion, was the result of lobbying, or illustrates the triumph of an idea whose time had come.

From the standpoint of democratic theory, the efforts of wealthy special interests to create public support through such public campaigns have both reassuring and troubling aspects. On the one hand, by expending their resources on propaganda aimed at ordinary citizens, interest groups greatly expand the amount of information available to citizens. Many thousands of people who otherwise would not have considered the issue of regulation of telecommunications were moved to think and act by the noisy campaign. Because an informed citizenry is a democratically competent citizenry, such campaigns are worthy additions to public debate. On the other hand, the arguments presented in the ads reflected a private, one-sided viewpoint. The cable and telephone industries

could choose to express their positions on television, but no one can afford to buy television time to speak for the general public interest. On balance, such campaigns probably do more good than harm, but it is a close call.

Influencing Administrators and Co-Opting Agencies The executive branch of government also is an interest-group target. All laws are subject to interpretation, and most laws allow the administrator substantial leeway in determining not only the intent of the lawmakers, but also the very meaning of their words. Interest groups attempt to influence the interpretation of laws that apply to them.

As society has become more complex, each individual has become less and less able to provide for her or his own needs. Where once people grew their own food, most must now buy it from large corporations. How can they be sure that it is pure, honestly labeled, and sold at a fair price? The wave of illness and death that swept the nation in 2006 as a result of the consumption of bagged spinach contaminated with *E. coli* bacteria, similar problems with peanut butter contaminated by *Salmonella* in 2009, and eggs tainted by the same bacterium in 2010, have illustrated the problem of protecting public health in a large, complicated society in which a chain of business activities connects the people who grow food to the people who eat it.

There are such problems in many other areas of life. Where once people traveled by horses or mules raised on the family homestead, they now drive expensive vehicles that are supplied by large corporations. How can they be sure that these are safe and honestly advertised? Where once they drew water from a local well or river, they now hold a glass under a faucet at home and turn the tap. How can they have confidence that there will always be a water supply to their homes?

To protect people's interests in those areas in which they cannot protect themselves, administrative agencies, or bureaus, have been created in the executive branch of government. Although many agencies provide public services, many others are regulatory. Their function is to protect the public interest by regulating various narrow, private interests. The concern here is with the regulatory agencies created to ensure that a particular industry provides good services at fair prices. Unfortunately, the history of these agencies has demonstrated that, over time, they lose their independent role and become dominated by the interests they were created to control. This transition from guardian of the public interest to defender of private interests—called **co-optation**—has several causes.

First, people who serve on regulatory agencies tend to come from the industry being regulated and return to it after their stint in government is over. This oft-observed activity is called the **revolving door.** Because they come from the industry they are regulating and know that they may be employed there again after they leave government, regulators tend to share the perspective of that industry, to sympathize with its problems, and share its values.

The operation of the revolving door in Texas politics is well illustrated by the history of the Texas Commission on Environmental Quality (TCEQ), the state agency that is supposed to be responsible for protecting Texas's air, water, and land from pollution. As shown in Table 3-2, important people in the TCEQ, once they leave the agency, often get jobs as lobbyists or consultants for industries that are regulated by that agency. Human nature being what it is, while they were still in office they were likely aware of the possibility of receiving a lucrative future offer of employment from firms in the industry they were regulating. The assumption must be that they were thus "pre-bribed" to go easy on those firms while in government service. (For more detail on the revolving door and the TCEQ, see Chapter 14.) The future revolving door creates co-optation in the present.

TABLE 3-2

The "Revolving Door" at the Texas Commission on Environmental Quality

Name	Position at TCEQ/Dates	Job after Leaving TCEQ
Anthony Grigsby	Executive Director/1993–1994	Lobbyist representing oil and gas interests through Baker and Botts law firm
Dan Pearson	Executive Director/1994–1998	Lobbyist representing utilities, cities, and energy companies
Jeff Saitas	Executive Director/1998–2002	Lobbyist for oil, gas, and energy companies
Glenn Shankle	Executive Director/2004–2008	Lobbyist for Waste Control Management and garbage companies
John Hall	Chair/1991–1995	Lobbyist for waste management and oil and chemical companies
Rafael Marquez	Commissioner/1994–2006	Lobbyist for chemical and environmental clean-up companies; then consultant for a company that helps other companies minimize environmental penalties and fines
Barry McBee	Chair/1995–1998	Lobbyist for oil and gas companies

SOURCE: Forrest Wilder, "Agency of Destruction," *Texas Observer*, May 28, 2010, 11.

A second cause of the co-optation of regulatory agencies is that, although a serious problem may cause an initial public outcry demanding regulation of a private interest—railroads, meat packers, or insurance companies, for instance—once regulatory legislation is passed, the public tends to lose interest, and the spotlight of publicity moves elsewhere. From that point on, only the regulated industry is intensely interested in the activities of the government agency. Regulators find that representatives of the industry are constantly in front of them in person, bringing information, self-serving arguments, and the force of personality, while no one is there speaking up for the public.

Historically, the insurance industry in Texas has furnished a particularly obvious example of private influence over public policy. Insurance is a mammoth business that produces $3.5 trillion a year in revenue nationwide. In 2008, a group of political scientists ranked insurance as among the most influential interests on the governments of all the states.[3] The need for government to regulate the insurance industry in order to protect consumers is evident from the nature of the business. As J. Robert Hunter, former Texas insurance commissioner, testified before the Committee on Commerce, Science, and Transportation of the U.S. Senate in 2003,

> insurance is not a normal product like a can of peas or even an auto. One cannot "kick the tires" of the complex legal document that is the insurance policy until a claim arises . . . a consumer pays money today for a promise that may not be deliverable for years. That promise must be secured from many threats, including insolvency and dishonesty.[4]

Texas began to regulate the insurance industry in the late 1800s to try to protect consumers from unscrupulous practices. By the late 1980s, however, the Texas State Board of Insurance was notorious among consumer representatives for always taking the side of the insurance industry in any dispute with customers. In 1991, the Travis County grand jury issued a report on its investigation of the insurance industry and the board. The grand jury reported that it was "shocked by the size of the problem, frightened by what it portends for our future economic health, and outraged by the ineffective regulation of the State Board of Insurance. . . . The potential exists for a . . . disaster in the insurance industry . . . we see embezzlement and self-dealing by insurance company insiders and regulators who are asleep at the switch." The report went on to say that "fraud in the insurance industry is widespread and deep, and it is covered by falsified documents filed with the State Board of Insurance."[5]

Partly because of this report, by 1993, the board's practices were so notorious that it had become a political issue. That year, the legislature abolished the three-member board, giving its former powers to a single commissioner, transferring some of its power to other state agencies, and renaming the agency the Texas Department of Insurance. Politicians and citizens hoped that, because the new commissioner would have clear responsibility for promulgating and enforcing rules, he or she would be more easily held accountable to the public. The fact that there was one person, as opposed to three people, responsible for regulating the insurance industry in the public interest, however, did not change the fact that a wealthy special interest still had all the tools necessary to imprint its private desires upon public affairs. The new institutional structure did nothing to reduce the resources the industry could pour into lobbying, nor did it alter the significant number of state legislators with personal financial ties to the industry.[6]

As a result, by 2002 the actions of the insurance industry had again created a political issue.[7] Ninety-five percent of homeowner insurance policies were unregulated by the state. Premiums had been rising steadily, and many people had lost their coverage. Moreover, one huge company, Farmers Insurance, was discovered to have engaged in some creative accounting in regard to the documents it filed with the Texas Insurance Commission. While claiming to the state that it had to raise premiums because it was losing money, Farmers submitted other documents to the federal Securities and Exchange Commission asserting that it was extremely profitable.[8]

With citizens in an uproar over their insurance rates, the state's politicians responded. In August 2002, Attorney General John Cornyn filed suit against Farmers, alleging violations of the Texas Insurance Code and the law against deceptive trade practices. Governor Perry participated in the press conference at which Cornyn announced the suit. Shortly thereafter, Insurance Commissioner Jose Montemayor ordered Farmers to stop a variety of its business practices, although he pulled his punch considerably by giving the company a ninety-day grace period, during which it could continue its behavior undisturbed.[9]

Moreover, despite the amount of lobbying power arrayed to prevent any change in the power of companies to operate unhindered, in 2003 the legislature passed insurance reform bills that required companies to disclose more information, and gave the state insurance commissioner the authority to review homeowners' premiums and order reductions where warranted. Quickly after the end of the legislative session, Insurance Commissioner Montemayor ordered twenty-four of the companies that operate in Texas, including the three biggest,

Allstate, State Farm, and Farmers, to cut their homeowners' rates an average of 13.4 percent. The Department of Insurance estimated that the cuts would save consumers more than $510 million. The companies complained and threatened to leave the state, but Montemayor held firm and the companies backed down. The insurance crisis was over, at least for the moment.[10]

The episode provides two useful lessons in Texas politics. First, even in a state with powerful lobbies, an aroused and attentive public can prevail against concentrated private influence. And second, administrative agencies are not always captured by the industries they regulate.

Nevertheless, by 2010, consumers' representatives had judged the 2003 reforms to be at best a partial success. The rates charged by the companies for home insurance in Texas had inched down, but were still the highest in the nation. "We were all told that our rates would come back down," commented Alex Winslow, director of the consumer advocacy group Texas Watch. "What actually happened was they went up and stayed up."[11]

The problem, as critics saw it, was that the 2003 law had given the state Department of Insurance the authority to judge a company's rate hike as too high only *after* it had gone into effect. In some states, companies must get permission from the state regulatory agency *before* they can charge homeowners more for their insurance. But in Texas, under the "file-and-use" system instituted in 2003, although a company must notify the state of its intention to raise rates, it does not have to wait for permission to do so. If the Department of Insurance thinks the increase is excessive, it must, after the fact, order the company to refund the excessive charges to consumers. The company can protest and take the state to court, all the while collecting the excessive payments from its customers.

In fact, this is what has happened since 2003. In 2009, for example, the state Department of Insurance decided that State Farm Insurance had been overcharging its 1.2 million Texas customers from 2003 to 2008, and ordered the company to refund a billion dollars to them. But State Farm took the order to court, and as this book went to press in 2011, the company and the state were still fighting the legal battle. Meanwhile, Texas homeowners were continuing to pay the rates that the Department of Insurance had judged excessive.[12]

In a sense, the relationship of the insurance industry and the political system is a template for the Texas interest-group system as a whole. The insurance reform surge of 2002 and 2003 underscores the point that the history of industry and politics in Texas is a story of cycles. For long periods, companies are successful in co-opting government regulation, and in the regulatory vacuum they induce, they are free to get away with almost anything. After enough abuses accumulate, the public becomes enraged and demands action. At that point, there is a spasm of political activity that may, for a time, rein in the behavior of the companies. After the short period of reform, however, the public's attention shifts to other outrages, and the quiet, relentless power of money and organization reasserts itself.

These cycles occur in all fifty states, to a greater or lesser degree. Scholars who have compared interest-group power in all the states have classified each state by category (see Table 3-3). These researchers have placed four states in a "dominant" category, indicating that in those states, interest groups are the "overwhelming and consistent influence on policymaking." The fifteen states in the third category, "complementary," are states in which interest groups tend to work in conjunction with other institutions, especially political parties, the

TABLE 3-3

Classification of the Fifty States According to Overall Impact of Interest Groups, 2007

Dominant	Dominant/ Complementary	Complementary	Complementary/ Subordinate	Subordinate
Alabama	Alaska	Colorado	Kentucky	Empty
Florida	Arizona	Connecticut	Michigan	
Hawaii	Arkansas	Indiana	Minnesota	
Nevada	California	Maine	South Dakota	
	Delaware	Massachusetts	Vermont	
	Georgia	Montana		
	Idaho	New Hampshire		
	Illinois	New Jersey		
	Iowa	New York		
	Kansas	North Carolina		
	Louisiana	North Dakota		
	Maryland	Pennsylvania		
	Mississippi	Rhode Island		
	Missouri	Washington		
	Nebraska	Wisconsin		
	New Mexico			
	Ohio			
	Oklahoma			
	Oregon			
	South Carolina			
	Tennessee			
	Texas			
	Utah			
	Virginia			
	West Virginia			
	Wyoming			

SOURCE: Anthony J. Nownes, Clive S. Thomas, and Ronald J. Hrebenar, "Interest Groups in the States," in Virginia Gray and Russell L. Hanson, eds., *Politics in the American States: A Comparative Analysis*, 9th ed. (Washington, D.C.: *Congressional Quarterly*, 2008), 121.

executive branch, or other groups. Because groups representing narrow private interests do not always win in Texas, they have placed the Lone Star State among the twenty-six states in second category between these two, called "dominant/complementary." This means that groups in Texas are very strong, but not completely dominant.[13] Finally, five states have been placed in the fourth

category, "subordinate/complementary," indicating that in those states, interest-group power is present but relatively weak and nondominant. The researchers provided a fifth hypothetical category of "subordinate" for states in which interest groups are very weak and rarely or never influence political institutions and actors, but that column is empty because the political scientists who created the chart could not find a single state in which interest groups are that unimportant.

Acting in the Judicial Arena Like the legislative and executive branches, the judicial branch of government also makes policy by interpreting and applying laws. For this reason, interest groups are active in the judicial arena of politics. Groups representing important economic interests make substantial contributions during judicial campaigns, hire lawyers to influence judges with legal arguments, and file suits. Money talks in courtrooms, as well as in legislatures and the executive branch of government.

Nevertheless, courts also can be an avenue of success for interest groups that have been unsuccessful in pressing their cases either through electoral politics or by lobbying the other two branches of government. An outstanding example is the National Association for the Advancement of Colored People (NAACP). Not only has this organization won such profoundly important national cases as *Brown v. Board of Education* (347 U.S. 483, 1954), in which segregated schools were declared unconstitutional, but it also has won vital victories at the state level. In *Nixon v. Herndon* (273 U.S. 536, 1927), the U.S. Supreme Court held that a Texas law excluding African Americans from the Democratic primary was unconstitutional. The Texas legislature attempted to nullify this decision by writing a new law authorizing party leaders to make rulings to the same effect, but this was struck down in *Nixon v. Condon* (286 U.S. 73, 1932). Later, in *Smith v. Allwright* (321 U.S. 649, 1944), the Texas NAACP won yet another victory when the Court held that racial segregation in party primaries on any basis whatsoever is unconstitutional. Thus, although groups representing dominant interests may win much or most of the time, the history of the NAACP in Texas proves that any interest group can sometimes prevail if it becomes organized and knows how to use the court system.

Lobbying

To **lobby** means to attempt to influence policymakers face-to-face. Everyone has the constitutional right to try to make an impact on what government does, and it is obvious that a personal talk with a government official has more impact than one anonymous vote. Because of the rules of interest-group formation, however, some groups are much more likely than others to be able to afford to lobby. Corporations and trade organizations can afford to hire the most **lobbyists**—people whose profession is trying to influence government. Wealthy special interests may have good or bad arguments for their positions, but in either case, they employ the most people to make sure that their arguments are heard.

Who Are the Lobbyists?

During the 2011 legislative session, 1,766 lobbyists registered with the Texas Ethics Commission (TEC)—almost 10 lobbyists for each of the 181 members of the legislature.[14] Lobbyists vary as much in their experience and competence

as do the legislators they are trying to influence. Top-flight freelance lobbyists can make over $1.5 million per session; there were 36 of these professional stars during the 2009 legislature, according to a study by Texans for Public Justice.[15]

People do not have to be professionals to exercise their rights to freedom of speech and freedom to petition the government. Concerned citizens who want to express their views to government, especially to the legislature, can do so as individuals or as members of a group (see the box "Citizen Lobbying"). Citizens who are willing to get organized, inform themselves, and spend the time talking to politicians can sometimes have an important impact on policy.

This principle is illustrated by the story of Senator Jeff Wentworth (R–San Antonio) and bicyclists during the 2001 legislative session. Wentworth, concerned about traffic safety in rural areas, filed a bill (SB 238) to forbid cyclists from riding in large groups on farm and ranch roads. The law, if passed, would have required all bicyclists on two-lane roads without a shoulder to ride single file and wear a "slow-moving vehicle" triangle sign on their backs.

But it turned out that bicyclists were organized, felt intensely about their hobby, and were willing to play political hardball. Members of the Texas Bicycle Coalition (TBC) were extremely displeased with the proposed statute. They argued that it would stamp out charity rides and hinder tourism. They began a statewide effort to convince Wentworth of the error of his ways. "Oh, I was inundated," Wentworth told journalist Dave McNeely. "I had more emails and letters and phone calls on that bill than on all the other bills I'd filed combined. And nearly all the communication was in opposition to the bill." The TBC also staged a demonstration at the capitol building to remind legislators that there were lots of bicyclists and that they were willing to vote on this issue.

Faced with massive opposition, Wentworth chose the prudent course and backed down gracefully. He agreed to a watered-down version of the bill, which would have left it up to county officials to decide if some of their roads were so dangerous that they required special regulations for cyclists. The weaker version of the proposed law, however, was still not acceptable to the TBC. SB 238 never got out of committee.[16]

Although examples such as the Texas Bicycle Coalition are numerous, most of the time, on most issues, it is wealthy special interests that have the resources to hire the best lobbyists and, thus, have the most influence. Many of the most successful lobbyists are former state legislators or executives. These individuals are able to parlay their knowledge of the governmental process and their friendship with many current officeholders into a personal influence that is rentable.

For example, Arlene Wohlgemuth represented District 58—Bosque and Johnson counties in north-central Texas—in the state House of Representatives from 1995 to 2004. After her defeat in 2004, she became a lobbyist, representing, among other clients, the Texas Optometric Association, Time-Warner Telecom, and the Texas Association for Home Care. During the 2007 session of the legislature, she was able to use her personal acquaintance with Representative Warren Chisum, chair of the House Appropriations Committee, to persuade him to insert a provision into the state budget that would probably steer a contract, to be awarded by the Health and Human Services Commission, to another of her clients, GHT Development Corporation. The contract was likely to be worth millions. Thus, the $10,000 to $25,000 that Wohlgemuth reported being paid by GHT was money very well spent. The

LONE STAR MEDIA

How about a Game Called "Influencing Government"?

As the economy evolves, old industries may decline, and new industries arise. Those that are in decline often try to influence government to save them, while those in ascent hire lobbyists to enable them to have a voice in legislation that is relevant to their functioning. So it is with the video game industry.

Video games became a minor attraction in arcades and bars during the early 1970s, and took off economically during the 1980s when personal computers began to be mass marketed. As the industry became wealthy during the 1990s and 2000s (video software sales earned $10.5 billion nationwide in 2009), it hired lobbyists to defend its interests in, among other venues, Texas government.

The industry, in broad outline, desires two things from state government. First, it asks to be protected from concerned consumer and parents' groups who want regulation or censorship of such extremely violent games as "Grand Theft Auto." Second, it would like to be included in the tax breaks and incentive packages that state government offers through such agencies as the Texas Film Commission, the Emerging Technology Fund, and the Texas Enterprise Fund.

"We are in every state capital, advancing the truth about the video game industry," Mike Gallagher, top lobbyist for the Entertainment Software Industry Association (ESIA), the industry's trade group, told the Austin Chamber of Commerce in 2008. "We are entitled to the economic respect and the social respect that comes with an industry as diverse and exciting and high-energy as ours."

He might have added that the ESIA does not just ask for respect. It has learned to play the political interest-group game. According to Texas Ethics Commission records, the ESIA employed three lobbyists during the 2011 state legislative session, paying them a maximum of $210,000 to convey its message to lawmakers. The strategy had worked well during the 2009 session, when ESIA persuaded the legislature to appropriate, and Governor Perry to sign, a $60 million incentive package (that is, tax rebates) for video game development in Texas. The legislature had also proclaimed February 3, 2009, as Entertainment Software Day in the state.

SOURCE: Lilly Rockwell, "Video Game Makers Lobby for Attention," *Austin American-Statesman,* October 27, 2008, D1; Web site of the Entertainment Software Industry Association, including its *2009 Annual Report,* 4, 7–8, www.thesa.com/; Web site of the Texas Ethics Commission, www.ethics.state.tx.us/.

GHT corporation bought a profitable chunk of Texas public policy for a trifling investment.[17]

Not all lobbyists come from the ranks of the people they are hired to persuade, not all serve special economic interests, and not all earn fortunes from their work. Some "public interest" lobbyists serve their conception of the common good and take home a modest salary for their efforts. (See the box "Representing the Rest of Us" for an example.) But the biases inherent in the interest-group system mean that most of the people doing most of the lobbying will be serving narrow, wealthy interests.

Citizen Lobbying

Ordinary citizens—those not employed by an interest group—who feel the need to influence legislation have every right to journey to the Capitol in Austin to lobby representatives. During the 2003 legislative session, the *Austin American-Statesman* published some rules that amateur lobbyists should remember when trying to make a persuasive argument. During the 2005 session, the *Dallas Morning News* published an article containing similar rules. Here is the combined list:

1. **Be persistent, outgoing, and friendly.**

2. **Be informed about the process of lawmaking and the party and policy position of individual legislators. The Legislature's Web site is a good place to acquire basic facts.**

3. **Forget the form letters. Many lawmakers refuse to read them.**

4. **Explain your position and situation as clearly and briefly as possible.**

5. **Be personal; tell individual stories that help lawmakers understand your perspective.**

6. **Have available brief, clear, written details.**

7. **Be flexible; committee hearings often run long or late.**

8. **Citizens who have a specific new law in mind should approach legislators as much as a year before the start of the next legislative session.**

Source: Dave Harmon, "Texans Mobilize to Fight Cuts in Their Lifelines," *Austin American-Statesman*, March 24, 2003, AB5; Katherine Goodloe, "Capitol Ideas," *Dallas Morning News*, April 10, 2005, E1.

What Lobbyists Do and How They Do It

The best lobbying technique is direct personal contact. Lobbyists try to see as many legislators as possible every day, buying a lunch, chatting for a few minutes, or just shaking a hand. Most lobbyists are able to get on a first-name basis with each legislator they think might be sympathetic to their goals. The Speaker of the House and the Lieutenant Governor are key figures in the legislature, and lobbyists try, above all else, to ingratiate themselves with these two powerful officials.

Contributions or Bribery?

The best way to ensure personal access to politicians is to give them money or the equivalent. This money is contributed in a variety of ways. Groups spend some of it entertaining legislators and executives at parties, taking them to lunch, giving them awards, and attracting them to events that will give lobbyists the chance to cultivate personal relationships and apply the arts of individual persuasion. Another more direct way in which groups funnel money to politicians is by giving them campaign contributions.

Few lobbyists are as brazen as the East Texas chicken magnate Lonnie "Bo" Pilgrim, who, during a fight over a new workers' compensation law in 1989, simply handed out $10,000 checks on the floor of the Senate.[18] Even though the bad publicity from this incident persuaded Mr. Pilgrim to be less visible in his use of money, he still actively attempted to influence legislators for years afterward. According to TEC records, the Pilgrim's Pride Corporation reported spending between $50,000 and $150,000 as the client of six different state lobbyists during the 2007 legislative session, though following that year its activity dropped off. Nevertheless, although most use money in a less public manner, the state capital is thronged at all times, and especially when the legislature is in session, by representatives of interest groups who are eager to funnel money to politicians in the hope that their largesse will be rewarded with favorable laws, rulings, and interpretations.

Not all interest groups are wealthy, however, and not all use money to try to buy influence. Some groups that employ lobbyists to represent them are relatively poor and rely on persistence, information, and the passion they feel for their cause. Sometimes they score important victories. But despite the occasional influence of such public-oriented groups as Public Citizen (see box "Representing the Rest of Us"), the power of money used, day in and day out, to capture the attention of lawmakers makes wealth one of the great resources of politics and ensures that the rich interest groups, over the long run, will tend to prevail over the poor ones.

The power of money in the interest-group system brings up uncomfortable questions about democracy in Texas. Simply giving money to a politician for

Representing the Rest of Us

A small organization with a small budget, Public Citizen has worked to reform state law and practice on consumer safety, pollution, sustainable energy, access to the courts, government ethics, and campaign finance. The organization's rule to not accept contributions from corporations, professional associations, or government agencies has had two consequences. First, it has freedom of action to follow its principles, regardless of whose toes it may step on in the process. Second, it will never be rich. It relies on the dues and contributions of its 5,300 individual members in Texas to keep it running and on the dedication of its staff.

Despite its relative poverty, Public Citizen has had a series of modest successes over the years. Its influence stems from its skill at marshaling publicity. Whenever journalists need to get a quotation expressing the pro-consumer, pro-honesty-in-government, anti–special interest point of view, Public Citizen is one of the organizations they call. Upon occasion, such publicity influences citizens to pressure government policymakers to take some action that they would otherwise have avoided. Thus, Public Citizen was instrumental in the creation of the Texas Ethics Commission, the passage of a new "lemon law" to protect the buyers of used cars, and the imposition of safety improvements by the South Texas and Comanche Peak nuclear power plants.

In 2002, Public Citizen raised such a clamor over Public Utility Commission Chair Max Yzaguirre's conflicts of interest (his ties to the crooked energy-trading corporation Enron, which frequently did business before the commission) that Yzaguirre resigned. In 2010, Public Citizen won a battle in its long-running campaign to stop the White Stallion company from building a coal-burning power plant near Bay City when two judges ruled

(continued)

(continued)

against recommending a permit necessary to build the plant. "Most Texans are surprised at how open our government is to input from our citizens," opined Tom Smith, director—and therefore chief lobbyist—for Public Citizen Texas in 2005. "Too few of them take advantage of it." By devoting a great deal of time and energy to lobbying on behalf of ordinary Texans, Smith and the employees of similar public interest groups hope to make up for the majority's lack of direct influence on state government.

Sources: Information about Public Citizen Texas comes from its Web site, www.citizen.org/texas/, especially several documents: "Public Citizen Celebrates 20 Years in Texas" from October 5, 2004; "Public Citizen Applauds Yzaguirre's Decision to Resign" from January 17, 2002; and "Accomplishments in 2010;" Smith quoted in Katherine Goodloe, "Capitol Ideas," *Dallas Morning News*, April 10, 2005, E1.

---

personal use is bribery and is illegal. Bribery is a danger to democracy because it substitutes money for public discussion in the making of public policy. When policy is made at the behest of a few rich interests working behind the scenes, then government is **plutocratic** (that is, government by the wealthy), not democratic. The disturbing fact is that the line between outright bribery (illegal) and renting the attention of public officials with campaign contributions, entertainment, gifts, and speaking fees (legal) is a very thin one. Money talks, and those with more of it speak in louder voices, especially in a state characterized by low legislative salaries and no public campaign finance measures.

Providing Information

Thousands of bills are introduced in the Texas legislature every session, and legislators can have no more than a passing knowledge of most of the policy areas involved. Even those legislators who may have specialized knowledge need up-to-date, accurate information. Therefore, in Texas as in other states, information is one of the most important lobbying resources. Although the information furnished by an interest group is biased because it represents the group's viewpoint, it also must be accurate. Getting and keeping a reputation for providing solid information is among the most important assets a lobbyist can develop.

Information is a tool of influence not only in relation to the legislature, but also in dealing with bureaucracies. State executive agencies have a constant need for information and sometimes have no independent means of finding it. They may come to rely on lobbying groups to furnish them with facts. For example, since 1996 the state Insurance Commission has relied on the Texas Insurance Checking Office (TICO) to gather the data the commission uses to regulate automobile and residential property insurance rates. TICO is a subsidiary of an insurance industry lobbying group. An industry group is therefore supplying the information used to regulate the industry it represents. Consumers might suspect that such data will not show that the insurance industry is charging too much.[19]

Regulation of Lobbying

It would be a violation of citizens' constitutionally protected rights of expression and association for government to *prevent* individual citizens from organizing to influence the political process. However, government has the authority to *regulate* the manner in which citizens attempt to exercise their rights. This distinction

is especially apt in regard to the use of money, where the proper freedom to state one's case can easily evolve into an improper attempt to corrupt the system.

Aside from laws of general application regarding such crimes as bribery and conspiracy, Texas has made few attempts to regulate the activities of interest groups, except in the area of lobbying. Early attempts at regulation in 1947, 1973, and 1981 were weak and ineffective because no state agencies were empowered to enforce the laws. In 1991, however, the legislature passed a much-publicized Ethics Bill, which limited the amount of food, gifts, and entertainment lobbyists could furnish legislators and required lobbyists to report the name of each legislator on whom they spent more than $50. Most important, it created an Ethics Commission that could hold hearings on complaints of improper behavior, levy fines, and refer violations to the Travis County district attorney for possible prosecution. Texas seemed at last to have a lobbyist regulatory law with teeth.

The 1991 law was less forceful than it appeared, however. It failed to require legislators to disclose sources of their outside income and also neglected to ban the use of campaign contributions for living expenses. In addition, a three-quarters majority is required on the Ethics Commission for some important actions, which limits its activities. Finally, while members of the Commission are appointed by the Governor, Speaker of the House, and chief justice of the Texas Supreme Court, those who are chosen must come from a list of candidates furnished by the legislature.

By 2003, pressure was again building for a reform of the state's ethics laws. That legislature passed a new bill that made a variety of changes. Among the amended ethics law provisions were the following:[20]

1. **Candidates for public office, whether they win or not, must disclose cash balances in their campaign accounts and report the employer and occupation of larger donors.**

2. **Legislators who are lawyers have to disclose when they are being paid to try to delay trials during a legislative session and their referral fees. Also, they are forbidden to represent a paying client in front of a state agency.**

3. **Candidates must file campaign finance reports via the Internet unless they raise or spend less than $2,000 a year and do not use a computer to keep their records.**

4. **Local officials in cities of more than 100,000 population and school districts with more than 5,000 students must file personal financial statements like those filed by other state officials.**

Information is a useful resource in a democracy, and the 2003 Ethics Bill, because it ensures that more information will be available to the public, is a good thing. Furthermore, the provision that forbids legislators/attorneys to practice before state agencies is genuine reform that will make the outright buying of influence more difficult. Nevertheless, the new law does no more than previous "ethics" bills to dilute the impact of private influence on public affairs.

The history of campaign finance reform, in Texas and elsewhere, shows that politicians often devise creative ways to circumvent the laws that are supposed to keep their behavior within ethical boundaries. Without public determination to change the basis of the problem, the political exchange of policy for money, wealth will continue to exercise an exorbitant influence over Texas politics. As long as legislators' salaries remain below the poverty line, as long as private money dominates public elections, and as long as private information is used to make public policy, the prospects for effective control of lobbying are poor.

Major Interest Groups in Texas

Interest groups want publicity for their programs and goals, but they tend to hide their operations. Political scientists have not done extensive research on interest groups in Texas, and the activities of such groups and the precise nature of their influence are difficult to discover. Nevertheless, we will describe some of the major interest groups in the state, explain their general success or weakness, and chart how their influence has changed over time.

Texans for Lawsuit Reform

Scholars who study interest groups have identified "general business organizations" as the most influential types of lobbying groups in state capitols.[21] It is easy to see why business is so powerful: Business is by definition organized and normally has more resources to put into politics than any other sector of society. The effectiveness of business lobbying, however, varies with the situation,

as illustrated by the insurance example from 2002 and 2003. Not every business interest gets what it wants every time. Nevertheless, many business interests dominate policymaking much of the time.

A good example of a business group that has been spectacularly successful in Texas since 1994 is Texans for Lawsuit Reform (TLR). The group was formed by business leaders determined to change what they perceived as a "Wild West litigation environment" in Texas by altering the state's tort laws. Torts are wrongful acts; the loser of a civil lawsuit concerning such an act can be forced to pay an amount of money to compensate a victim and may be required to pay an extra amount as punishment (see the discussion of "tort reform" in Chapter 10).

The TLR proceeded along two paths. First, it forged alliances with other groups attempting to make it harder to file and win "frivolous" lawsuits in the state, most notably the Texas Medical Association. Second, it used its deep pockets to earn the gratitude of lawmakers in the state, most of them Republican.

In 1994, George W. Bush ran for governor partly on a platform stressing tort reform. A law passed the 1995 legislature, but because the institution was then dominated by Democrats, it was a much-compromised, milder version of the bill than that which partisans of TLR had hoped to see. In the years that followed, however, TLR kept spreading the campaign money to Republican candidates. In 2002, TLR contributed a total of $1,208,032 to candidates, most of whom won.

By 2003, with the Republican accession to majority status in both houses of the legislature, as well as the state house, the group's moment had arrived. The 2003 reforms gave the TLR almost everything it wanted. As of that year, it became much harder to sue anybody for anything in Texas. "Texas will be a better place to live," stated TLR president Richard Trabuisi, Jr., triumphantly, "to raise a family, and work for a living once this historic legislation goes into effect."[22] In 2006, TLR bragged on its Web site that a report from the Pacific Research Institute (which, on its own Web site, identifies itself as a "free market think tank") had ranked Texas "best in the nation" on its "U.S. Tort Liability Index."[23]

The TLR has attempted to maintain its influence by sustaining its campaign generosity. During the 2010 election cycle, for example, its PAC distributed $3.3 million to Texas politicians, with most of the money going to candidates for the legislature.[24] The TLR is an important reason why Republicans now control both houses of the state legislature, and members of the party are well aware of it.[25]

But even complete success can apparently be improved upon, and the people who run TLR have not been satisfied. Their goal has been to make the state with the most hostile environment for lawsuits even more hostile. During the 2011 legislature, the organization attempted to persuade the representatives to pass a new "loser-pays" law, mandating that any person who brings a lawsuit and loses must pay the legal costs of the person being sued.[26] The bill that actually passed was not the version of the statute that TLR desired, since it required a plaintiff whose suit had lost to pay the legal costs of the winner only if a judge ruled that the case was groundless, but it was close enough to TLR's ideal to be counted as yet another victory for the organization.[27]

Even though Texans for Lawsuit Reform has occasionally been forced to compromise, as of 2011, it was still "king of the mountain" among Texas interest groups.

A "PUPPET"? I RESENT YOUR INSINUATION, SIR!

Ben Sargent laments the fact that interest groups with many resources, especially those representing business, have disproportionate influence over politicians.

Ben Sargent.

Doctors

Sitting close to the TLR on top of the mountain of business influence on politics is the Texas Medical Association (TMA).[28] Founded in 1853, this major interest group for doctors in Texas paid scant attention to state politics for most of its history. Its attitude changed in 1987 when, in the first battle of what has since become a war, it attempted to persuade the legislature to put a cap on damage awards in medical malpractice cases. Because such a limit would cut into the income of plaintiffs' attorneys, it was opposed by the Texas Trial Lawyers Association (TTLA). Although the TMA had ten times the membership of the TTLA, it was nevertheless soundly whipped during legislative infighting. As a result, doctors decided to pay more attention to politics.

The TMA turned its attention to acquiring political influence with great intelligence. Like other interest groups, one method it uses is contributing large amounts of money to legislative and judicial candidates. One study determined that the organization's PAC contributed almost $600,000 in the two years prior to the 1998 elections; another concluded that "Physicians Associations and Clinics" gave $1,554,017 to politicians during the 2002 election cycle; and a third reported that the association's PAC and another Texas doctors' PAC distributed $1.8 million during the 2007–2008 cycle. During the 2011 legislative session, according to Texas Ethics Commission records, TMA kept twenty-five lobbyists on its payroll, investing a maximum of $1.48 million in them halfway through the session in April.

Campaign contributions are not the only method used by TMA. The organization also suggests to doctors that they lobby their patients on bills the TMA deems important. The TMA Web site offers physicians supplies of political posters, lapel stickers, and cards to pass out to "staff, patients, family and friends."

In addition, the TMA allies itself with other interest groups, joining forces with business tort reformers and even cooperating with its traditional rival, the Texas Trial Lawyers Association, on some lobbying efforts when the interests of doctors and lawyers run parallel, as they did in 2001. Most important, the group has jumped on the bandwagon of historical success, allying itself with the Republican Party just as the GOP was poised to take over Texas politics.

As a result of these various efforts, the TMA is now one of the most effective political interest groups in the Lone Star State. According to the association's figures, it has succeeded in passing as much as 90 percent of the legislative agenda items it has sponsored. In 1999, it successfully persuaded the legislature to pass a law exempting doctors from antitrust laws and permitting them to negotiate fees and policies with health maintenance organizations (HMOs). This accomplishment was particularly noteworthy because the HMO bill was opposed by business and insurance companies, traditional stalwarts of the Republican Party.

Doctors have been similarly effective in exerting their influence over the courts. According to the consumer group Court Watch, doctors and hospitals won 86 percent of their cases before the Texas Supreme Court from 1994 to 1999—the highest success rate of any interest group.

The TMA has not always made perfect political choices, however. After the 2001 legislature, when Governor Perry vetoed a bill requiring HMOs to pay medical claims promptly, doctors were furious. In retaliation, the group endorsed Democratic gubernatorial candidate Tony Sanchez in 2002. Perry's big victory in that election introduced considerable awkwardness between the governor and the association, and the TMA had to mend its fences. It fired its chief political strategist and began giving even more money to Texas politicians, especially the governor. These efforts were successful. When Governor Perry staged a public signing of a new "prompt-pay" bill in June 2003, he was flanked in front of the news cameras by the TMA's board of directors. Perry made it clear he wanted bygones to be bygones. "Whether it's doctors or hospital administrators or any of a host of other individuals who are involved in the delivery of health care in Texas, we are very much open to bringing them back into the tent, so to speak," said the governor.

During the 2006 special session of the legislature, in which elected leaders labored under an ultimatum from the state supreme court (see Chapters 6 and 7), the TMA worked to lessen the impact of the proposed new business tax. As the organization informed its members on its Web site shortly after the close of the session, "The tax bill that is on its way to Governor Perry's desk will impose new taxes on businesses in the service industry, including many physician practices in Texas. Thanks to the efforts of the Texas Medical Association . . . however, those taxes will not be nearly as onerous as they could have been. For many specialists . . . the tax savings will be $1,000 or more."[29] Taxes that doctors do not have to pay, of course, must be paid by someone else, either in a positive sense—other industries must shell out more to make up the difference—or in a negative sense—citizens must do without some government service that otherwise would have been provided. The changes in the 2006 tax bill are thus a measure of the TMA's lobbying clout in relation to other interests.

By 2008, the TMA was celebrating the five-year anniversary of the tort reforms and reported, based on a survey of its members, that "the reforms have worked. Texans now have more doctors available to take care of them, especially the sickest and most badly injured patients," proving that Texas had "reined in the epidemic of lawsuit abuse."[30]

Thus, the Texas Medical Association, having in the past strayed from the majority party coalition, had bought its way back in. It remains a powerful interest group in the state and serves as an example of how many interest groups acquire influence in Texas.

Lawyers

The Texans for Lawsuit Reform and the Texas Medical Association are good examples of interest groups that have risen in importance over the years. The Texas Trial Lawyers Association (TTLA), however, is the premier example of an interest group that has declined.

Like other occupational groups, attorneys have interests.[31] Unlike many other groups, however, lawyers have a great advantage that is not available to members of other occupations: Many legislators and all major court judges share their profession. Lawyers therefore have an automatic advantage in arguing their positions on public policy to legislatures or courts, as frequently they are addressing people with similar values and points of view.

For this reason, combined with the customarily generous political giving of its members, the TTLA was a powerful force in the state's politics for a long time. Until the late 1980s, the association was able to block all legislation that threatened the income of attorneys. As discussed earlier, in 1987 the TTLA dominated efforts to reform the workers' compensation system in Texas against the opposition of doctors, thereby preserving an important source of employment for its members. By the 1990s, however, the TTLA's influence was waning. Attorneys were a traditional part of the Texas Democratic Party's coalition, and their power declined along with their party's. On the other hand, business, the traditional ally of the Republican Party, grew in power as the GOP's star ascended in Texas.

In the 1995 legislature, business made a determined push to overhaul the state's tort system. Tort reform is an excellent example of an issue that pits well-organized, well-funded groups against each other. People in business and doctors hate such lawsuits because of their costs in time, legal fees, and sometimes punitive damages, while lawyers love them because they constitute the stuff of their livelihood. Thus the TTLA, along with many Democratic representatives and many consumer groups, fought tort reform.

But Republican Governor George W. Bush, riding a tremendous national and state victory by his party in the 1994 elections and aided by wealthy pro-business interest groups such as Texans for Lawsuit Reform, pushed through important changes in Texas's tort laws. These changes, among their other effects, made it more difficult to win punitive damages against a business, lowered the maximum amount of damages that could be awarded, decreased the percentage of an award that one company among many defendants could be forced to pay, and limited the ability of attorneys to "shop around" for a sympathetic judge. As Democrats retreated and became an embattled minority, the TTLA fought ineffectively to reverse their fortunes and its own. In 1997 and 2003, the legislature limited lawsuits even more.

The efforts of the TTLA to regain some of its lost influence have been hampered by public prejudice against the profession. As a thousand "lawyer jokes" attest, Americans tend to view attorneys as sleazy sharks, quite willing to behave unethically to make a buck or keep a criminal out of jail. In a survey conducted for the *Texas Tribune* in 2010, for example, 72 percent of Texans responded

that they would be "less likely to vote for a candidate who accepted campaign contributions from personal injury trial lawyers." Democrats reported this bias against lawyers just as often as Republicans.[32] Since 1994, Republican candidates have taken advantage of the profession's poor public image, routinely portraying themselves as running against "greedy trial lawyers" as much as their Democratic opponents.

Lawyers have found themselves so unpopular that for a while in the 2000s they became a stealth interest group, using their money to finance more respectable spokespeople while keeping themselves invisible. For example, during a fight in 2003 over Proposition 12—which capped maximum medical malpractice awards at $750,000—lawyers' contributions financed the "Save Texas Courts" campaign that urged citizens to vote against the proposition, but attorneys were nowhere to be seen or heard in the public controversy. Business in general, and doctors in particular, were just as generous in supporting the "Yes on 12" campaign, but they did not feel the need to conceal their participation. In fact, much of the advertising in support of Proposition 12 consisted of contrasting symbolic images of doctors (who presumably enjoyed high public esteem) with symbolic images of lawyers (portrayed in the ads as shady characters). In the end, Proposition 12 squeaked to passage by a 51-to-49 percent margin.[33]

For more than a decade, then, the Texas Trial Lawyers Association has seemed to be a giant in eclipse. Lawyers know, however, that there are no final verdicts in politics, and they have not given up. They have continued to make massive contributions to Democratic candidates. During the final five months of the 2010 election campaigns, according to Texas Ethics Commission records, the TTLA contributed $941,308 to candidates, and this total does not include the amounts given by individual lawyers. Steve Mostyn, head of the TTLA, was the single largest contributor to Texas campaigns in 2010, spending millions of dollars on, among other causes, negative TV ads attacking Governor Perry. Close to the end of the 2011 legislative session, the organization reported spending a maximum of $1,250,000 on sixteen lobbyists.[34]

Nevertheless, the 2011 legislature proved that the renaissance of the Texas Trial Lawyers Association has not yet arrived. Lawyers fought strenuously against the "loser-pays" bill described earlier. They managed to achieve a tepid compromise, which means that although they gave up ground, theoretically they could have lost much more. Like the Democratic Party with which they ally themselves, lawyers, as an interest group, can only hope that if they keep fighting, the day will come when they emerge again as winners.[35]

The Christian Right

During the late 1970s, a number of national organizations arose that called for a return to "Christian values," as they defined them, in American government and in society.[36] The groups' purposes were to inform religious, politically conservative voters of a candidate's positions on certain issues and to persuade them to participate more actively in local politics. By the 1990s, these groups were a formidable presence at virtually every level of American politics. They have been especially important in the South.

Although Christian Right groups do not all place the same emphasis on each individual issue, they share a cluster of strongly conservative positions on important political issues. As Texan Tom Delay, Republican former majority leader of the U.S. House of Representatives, told an interviewer in 1999, the choices

facing us are, "Will this country accept the worldview of humanism, materialism, sexism, naturalism, postmodernism, or any of the other 'isms'? Or will we march forward with a biblical worldview, a worldview that says God is our creator, that man is a sinner, and that we will save the country by changing the hearts and minds of Americans?"[37] Members of the Christian Right understand that "a biblical worldview" requires them to be pro-life on the abortion issue, to oppose homosexual marriage, to fight against tax policies they view as subversive to families, to support school vouchers allowing public money to fund private schools, and to endorse a constitutional amendment that would permit organized prayers in public schools.

During the 1990s, the Christian Right made a vivid impact on Texas politics and society. Whereas the power of such interest groups as Texans for Lawsuit Reform rests on their ability to provide large quantities of money to campaigns, the power of the Christian Right rests on its ability to strongly influence the voting decisions of millions of citizens and to mobilize thousands of activists to capture control of political organizations at the grassroots level. Members of the Christian Right are concerned citizens in the best sense, organizing to pursue the public interest as they understand it.

The most dramatic flexing of the Texas Christian Right's muscles occurred in its capturing of the state Republican Party machinery in 1994 and its domination of the GOP's conventions through 2010. These events are discussed in detail in the next chapter.

The 2007 legislature offered a good opportunity for observing the reach, and the limits, of Christian Right influence in Texas politics.[38] When Governor Perry issued an executive order providing for public schools to vaccinate young women for HPV, a sexually transmitted virus that sometimes causes cervical cancer, social conservatives objected. They believed that knowing that they were protected against the virus would encourage young women to engage in premarital sexual activity. Christian Rightists persuaded their Republican allies in the legislature to pass a law overturning the governor's order. Another successful bill sponsored by the representatives of the Christian Right doubled the cost of a marriage license, to $60, unless the intending couple took an eight-hour marriage counseling course. In a third victory for the movement, the House and Senate passed rules that would result in posting the motto "In God We Trust" in their chambers.

However, the 2007 legislative session also demonstrated that the Christian Right, while very powerful, is not absolutely dominant in Texas politics. A bill that would have banned funding for stem-cell research—which Christian conservatives believe to be experimentation on an unborn child—did not pass. Its failure suggests that conservative Christians can expect to be the most successful when they advocate symbolic actions that do not attack anyone else's interests— posting "In God We Trust" in the legislative chambers, for example. These groups appear to have more trouble when they try to influence state policy to take a direction that impinges on other interests, especially when those interests are part of the Republican Party coalition. In the case of the stem-cell research bill, business interests often support such research because it brings science-based industry and federal research money into the state. When the Christian Right groups attempted to ban state funding of such research, they came up against another powerful part of their own coalition.

The 2010 elections and the following legislative session help to illustrate these generalizations. On the one hand, although the Republican sweep in the elections

was interpreted mainly as a massive victory for the "Tea Party" faction of the Republican Party (see Chapters 4 and 5), and the Tea Party is best known for its fiscal conservatism, once the Republican majority got into the legislature it proved to be quite socially conservative. In a vote on a bill in the House of Representatives that would require women to have sonograms before being able to have abortions, for example, 100 of the 101 Republican representatives cast their support for the bill. The bill passed the Senate by a similarly large margin, and was signed by Governor Perry. The Tea Partiers in Texas, it would seem, are also Christian Rightists.[39]

On the other hand, Christian Right Texans lost ground on the State Board of Education during the March 2010 primary elections, when two of the most prominent members of that faction were defeated by more moderate Republican candidates. Business-oriented, as opposed to Bible-oriented, Republicans were concerned that some of the changes sponsored by Christian Right representatives on the board, especially those dealing with the science curriculum, would damage the state's ability to educate its children. They ran, and financed, candidates who promised to pay more attention to scientific opinion, and less to biblical literalism, in adopting curriculum standards. As a result of the 2010 voting, instead of a reliable seven-person voting bloc on the fifteen-member board, Christian conservatives could only count on five votes.[40]

The future promises to supply many examples of issues on which Christian conservative Republicans and more business-oriented Republicans disagree. In addition, the state's democratic governing structure offers many different types of election venues in which those disagreements can be fought out. As a result, the Christian Right and its opposition are certain to be active in state politics for many years to come.

Sex, Power, and Money

There was a time within living memory when there were no women in the Texas legislature and the only female who had served as governor—Meriam "Ma" Ferguson during the 1920s and 1930s (see Chapter 8)—was a joke. That era is gone. Ann Richards, who occupied the governor's mansion from 1991 to 1995, was not considered a joke by anyone, and women now routinely serve in statewide offices and the legislature, and co-author Texas government textbooks.

However, many liberal female activists believe that their sex is still not fairly represented within the state's political establishment, and they believe they know why—it takes money to be elected, and women generally do not have access to the serious financing that is usually needed to make a political career successful. Thus, Annie's List was created.

Founded in 2003 and named for Annie Webb Blanton, the first woman to win a statewide office in Texas as the state Superintendent of Instruction in 1918, Annie's List is a political action committee that raises money for female candidates who are pro-choice on the abortion issue. Although the PAC does not make fine discriminations about the ideology of the candidates to whom it contributes, the fact that they are all pro-choice tends to give those who receive its money a liberal cast. "Ultimately," says Bree Buchanan, its executive director, "electing more women is a means to an end. What we really want is to promote a progressive agenda."

(continued)

(continued)

In a rather short time, the organization has proved itself to be quite formidable. Over the past four election cycles, Democrats backed by Annie's List have captured eight Republican seats and sent thirteen new legislators to Austin. During the 2007–2008 election cycle, Annie's List was the eleventh most generous PAC, contributing $1.6 million to its favored candidates. Four of the six Democratic candidates who unseated Republican House members in the 2008 election were backed by the PAC.

Republicans made a big comeback in the 2010 elections, and candidates backed by Annie's List, like all other liberals in Texas, fared poorly. Texas is still a conservative state. But the dominant conservatism is being pushed hard by liberal counterorganization. If Democrats ever do recapture power in Texas, it will be because of such determined groups as Annie's List.

Sources: Bob Moser, "Bye-Bye Boys' Club," *Texas Observer*, January 23, 2009, 10; Jason Embry, "Top-Spending PACs Backed by Lawyers, Businesses, Parties," *Austin American-Statesman*, January 26, 2009, B1; on 2010 elections: Annie's List Web site, www.annieslist.com/.

Organized Labor

Many Texans think of organized labor as a powerful interest group that has great influence on state policy, but there is little evidence to support this assumption. The primary explanation for this lack of power is cultural. As discussed in Chapter 1, the conservative political culture that dominates most of the southern states is hostile to labor unions. Texas is no exception. It is, for example, one of twenty-two "right-to-work" states with laws that forbid making union membership a condition of employment. As a result, whereas the national average for union membership of wage and salary workers in 2010 was 11.9 percent, in Texas it was only 5.1 percent. (New York had the highest unionized workforce percentage at 24.2 percent; North Carolina was lowest at 3.2 percent.)[41]

Politically, unions have traditionally allied themselves with the Democratic Party nationally and with the liberal wing of that party within the state. But the relative weakness of liberals in Texas has meant that labor unions are even less powerful than their membership figures would suggest. Their weakness is reflected in the relatively antilabor nature of Texas's laws. The result for the unions is a vicious circle: because of the antiunion laws, organized labor is able to enroll relatively few workers in its ranks; because it represents few workers, it is unable to exert much influence over elections; and because it cannot influence elections, it is the victim of antiunion laws.

Organized labor would like nothing better than to break out of the vicious circle, but it lacks the political power to do so. Although the political action committee of the state umbrella labor group, the American Federation of Labor–Congress of Industrial Organizations (AFL-CIO), puts money into political races, the rise of the traditionally pro-management, antilabor Republican Party to unchallenged power has given the workers' organization a set of discouraging alternatives: It can continue to give money to Democrats, who lose continuously, or it can give money to Republicans, who will, once elected, vote against its interests anyway.

Nationally, organized labor made a political comeback in 2006. The Democrats narrowly won both houses of Congress with a strong push from the

national AFL-CIO and its allied unions. Democratic gains continued in 2008, resulting in large majorities in both houses of Congress. Union members comprised a high percentage of the victory margins enjoyed by Democratic candidates in both elections. As a result, labor had much more influence over national policymaking. But the Republican takeover of the U.S. House of Representatives halted the growth of labor's influence as it brought the national parties into deadlock. Furthermore, in Texas, Republicans remained in control of the state political machinery no matter how they fared at the national level.

If such organized efforts as those by labor unions and Annie's List (see box "Sex, Power, and Money") ever result in a Democratic takeover of power in Texas, organized labor will once again become influential. Until such a day arrives, however, unions can only anticipate continuing futility.

League of United Latin American Citizens (LULAC)

The most venerable of the Hispanic organizations, the League of United Latin American Citizens (LULAC), was formed in Corpus Christi in 1929.[42] Its founding members were much concerned about discrimination against Mexican Americans, especially in public education.

In its first three decades, LULAC pursued the goal of equal education as both a private charitable organization and a public crusader. Privately, LULAC formed local self-help organizations to advance Latino education. Its "Little School of the 400" program of the 1950s, for example, which taught Spanish-speaking preschoolers the 400 English words they needed to know in order to survive in first grade in public schools, was so successful that it inspired the national program Head Start. Publicly, the organization persuaded the U.S. Supreme Court to forbid Texas to segregate Mexican Americans in public schools in 1948. Branching out to other issues, in 1953, LULAC won another suit against Texas's practice of excluding Mexican Americans from juries. Then, in 1959, it persuaded the state legislature to sponsor its program to teach Latino preschoolers English. Soon the Texas Education Agency was paying up to 80 percent of the program's funding. LULAC may have represented a struggling minority, but it had become part of the state's political establishment; it was a success.

Into the 1970s, LULAC continued to be the standard bearer for Mexican American aspirations for full citizenship in the United States in general, and Texas in particular. But in that decade, it began to falter. As an organization dispensing millions of dollars in foundation grants, it attracted members who were more interested in advancing themselves than in advancing their ethnic group. Beginning in the mid-1970s, LULAC was rocked by a series of financial scandals. The worst of these occurred in 1994 when the president, José Velez, together with three Taiwanese gangsters, was indicted by a federal grand jury on charges of collecting millions of dollars in a scheme to smuggle Asians and Hispanics into the United States illegally.

Not only was the organization troubled by scandal during the 1990s, but it was also racked by internal power struggles. Individuals and different Latino groups fought each other—Mexican Americans versus Puerto Ricans, for example—so that the organization no longer seemed to be a league of *united* Latin American citizens.

The cumulative effect of LULAC's troubles was devastating damage to both its prestige and its membership. Once capable of mobilizing a quarter of a million citizens nationally, by the late 1990s, the organization could count on no

more than 50,000 active members. At its 1999 national convention in Corpus Christi, there were few people in the audience for its workshops and fewer corporate sponsors. Whereas eight national presidential candidates had addressed its delegates in 1987, not a single one showed up in 1999. Younger, better-run organizations such as La Raza and the Mexican-American Legal Defense Fund (MALDEF, created by LULAC itself in 1968) seemed to be on the verge of taking over the mantle of most-respected Hispanic organization.

But LULAC has made a comeback. Even while the leadership was faltering, the grassroots activists who worked in its local chapters comprised a reservoir of good citizenship, available for mobilization. During the late 1990s and early 2000s, several honest and competent presidents put the organization's finances in order and then expanded and reorganized its staff.

Just as important, LULAC's leadership began engaging in creative political activity. It has forged a political alliance with the most-respected African American organization, the NAACP. In July 2002, LULAC's president, Hector Flores, addressed the NAACP's national convention, the first time a person in his position had given a speech to that organization. His remarks cemented an agreement of cooperation that had been working for a year, featuring a joint and bilingual voter mobilization project. LULAC was also exploring alliances with nonminority, but liberal groups. During the early and middle years of the 2000s, the organization attempted to create partnerships with others concerned with the environment, women's issues, and police-community relations.

LULAC also has expanded its area of activity to include lobbying in the nation's capital. After the Democrats regained majorities in both houses of Congress during the 2006 elections, the organization's influence broadened. During the maneuvering that accompanied Congress's consideration of the Comprehensive Immigration Reform Act of 2007, LULAC's representatives exercised "virtual veto power," according to one press report. Latinos objected to the bill's guest worker program, believing that it would create a group of underclass workers without benefits. In alliance with other Hispanic organizations and various politicians from across the political spectrum, LULAC was able to block consideration of the legislation in the U.S. Senate. It never came to a vote.[43]

In conservative Texas, the coalition of liberal minority groups has found the going to be harder. But with Democrats in charge of the administration in Washington in 2011, LULAC, the NAACP, and their allied organizations tried to use the threat of federal intervention as leverage to move Texas policy in their direction. For example, despite the somewhat less socially conservative stance of the State Board of Education (SBOE) after the 2010 voting, social studies and history curriculum standards adopted by the board before the defeat of the Christian conservatives were offensive to many minorities. Arguing that "the SBOE curriculum changes were made with the intent to discriminate," the two organizations filed a formal complaint with the federal Department of Education at the end of 2010, asking that the DOE deny Texas $5 billion of support that would otherwise be coming to it. Although an SBOE member complained that "These activists are never satisfied, and their whining to the federal government is silly and without merit," the minority groups got the attention of the state legislature.[44] Three Texas House Republican leaders expressed sympathy with the minority groups' complaints and criticized the SBOE's standards.[45]

Thus, by broadening its focus, LULAC's leadership seems to have revitalized the organization. Whatever the ultimate success of this strategy, the organization has regained its vigor.

Teachers

In a 2007 ranking of the fifty most successful interest groups in the fifty states, three political scientists judged teachers to be the second most influential group, after business.[46] Unlike business, teachers do not possess the resource of wealth, for nowhere are they paid very well. Instead, teachers resemble the Christian Right in illustrating the power that can come from use of two other resources: participation and organization. In some states, a high percentage of public school teachers belong to a union or some other advocacy organization, and many belong to several. Teachers usually can be counted on to march, rally, write letters, contribute to political action committees, and vote in an informed manner. It is because they are such good citizens, willing to put in the time and trouble to act together, that teachers are generally so effective in advancing their interests.

In Texas, however, the effectiveness of teacher participation is weakened by a number of cultural and political difficulties. The traditionalistic political culture that has been so important in Texas history has never been particularly friendly to public education, and the state generally places in the lower ranks of educational funding. In 2010, for example, it stood 38th among the states in spending per pupil and 33rd in average teacher salary.[47]

Politically, Texas's teachers are marked more by disorganization and competition than by coordination and cooperation. Like Texas's other white-collar workers, many of the state's teachers resist unionization, and many belong to no professional organization. As Table 3-4 illustrates, the membership of two of the largest organizations declined noticeably in the period from 2000 to 2011. Those teachers who are members of organizations are divided among seven statewide and dozens of local groups, all fiercely competitive and sometimes recommending different strategies to their members (see Table 3-4 for a summary of the differing approaches of Texas's four largest teacher organizations).

Moreover, teachers share with lawyers the current disadvantage of being members of the Democratic Party coalition. This problem does not arise only from a mistake in coalition building. A high percentage of teachers are ideologically liberal (see Chapter 4). They have become a favorite rhetorical target of conservatives, who love to blame teachers for the poor quality of some American schools, and blame teachers' unions for opposing some of the conservatives' favorite proposed reforms, especially school vouchers. The teachers' organizations are therefore fundamentally at odds with the state's current power structure. As Eric Hartman, legislative director for the Texas Federation of Teachers, told a reporter after the 2003 legislative session, "We're getting tired of this 'kick-the-teacher' legislation."[48] Similarly, Mary Ann Whiteker, president of the Texas Association of Mid-Size Schools, remarked to another reporter in 2005 that "The difficult thing is not to take this personally. You just walk through the Capitol thinking, 'Why do they hate me so much?'"[49] Therefore, when teachers' lobbyists attempt to persuade Texas legislators to back their policy proposals, they tend to get a mixed reception. They start from a position of weakness, but can manage to make some headway by using information intelligently and by reminding politicians, however tacitly, that teachers are knowledgeable voters.

During the 2011 legislative session, teachers faced a horrendous situation. As explained in Chapters 7 and 12, the 2006 legislature had created a "structural

TABLE 3-4

Comparison of Four Largest Texas Teacher Organizations, 2000 and 2011

TSTA: Texas State Teachers Association (affiliated with National Education Association)

TAFT: Texas American Federation of Teachers (affiliated with AFL-CIO)

TCTA: Texas Classroom Teachers Association

ATPE: Association of Texas Professional Educators

	TSTA	TAFT	TCTA	ATPE
Founded	1880	1974	1927	1980
Membership, 2011	68,000	64,000	50,000	115,000
Membership, 2000	80,000	85,000	40,000	110,000
Endorses candidates?	Yes	Yes*	Yes*	No
Supports pay raises?	Yes	Yes	Yes	Yes
Supports collective bargaining?	Yes	Yes	No	No
Supports publicly funded vouchers for private schools?	No	No	No	No
Lobbies legislature?	Yes	Yes	Yes	Yes

*Indirectly, through a political action committee.

SOURCES: Compiled by David Prindle in August 2000 and May 2011 from organization Web sites and interviews with organization officers.

deficit" in the financing of state government. The deficit had been masked during the 2009 legislative session by federal transfer payments, but those had dried up by 2011, leaving the legislature with the task of dealing with a $27 billion biennial budget shortfall. Further, the "Tea Party" Republican Party politicians who dominated Texas politics in 2011 were committed to cutting, rather than enhancing through taxes, the state's expenditures. Because more than two-fifths of the state's expenditures go to education, most of the inevitable cuts were going to be at the expense of teachers. The teachers, as individuals and organizations, frantically demonstrated, lobbied, wrote letters, made phone calls, and participated in press conferences, attempting to persuade the public and the legislators to avoid destroying public education in Texas. But a massacre was inevitable.[50] As we will recount in Chapter 12, despite the efforts of the pro-education lobby, the legislature cut $4 billion from public-school funding.

Like the lawyers, like organized labor, like the minority defense groups, teachers are thus in a seriously vulnerable position in modern Texas. Despite their willingness to organize and communicate, teachers are one of the groups considered villains by the Texas Republican party. Like the other liberal groups, they can therefore look forward to having their interests reviled and attacked by the politicians in power. Unless Texans change their voting habits, teachers face a hard future.

Conclusion

Political interest groups present a dilemma to partisans of democratic government. By giving people a channel of input to government, in addition to the one vote possessed by each citizen, such groups broaden and intensify the people's participation and are therefore good for democracy. But by creating a means by which some individuals can be much more influential than others, these groups often allow private perspectives to dominate public policymaking and are therefore bad for democracy. In Texas, where interest groups are powerful, the negative qualities of the interest-group system often dominate.

Summary

Interest groups are very influential in American and Texas politics because they provide two indispensable ingredients: money and information. Groups are active in every phase of politics: They engage in electioneering, lobby government officials, co-opt agencies, litigate in the courts, and attempt to persuade the public to support their point of view. Private interests thus frequently dominate the making of Texas public policy.

Although many efforts have been made to regulate lobbying, the results have not been encouraging. The Texas political system provides a friendly setting for maximizing interest-group influence. The most powerful groups tend to be those that represent major economic interests and especially those that have allied themselves with the dominant Republican Party. Groups that are traditional allies of the Democrats have fared less well.

Interest groups are good for democracy in that they enhance debate about public policy and encourage citizens to participate in politics. But they also damage democratic government by substituting private influence for public deliberation in the creation of government policy. In Texas, the power of interest groups often causes problems for democratic government.

Glossary Terms

co-optation	plutocratic
interest group	political action committee
lobby	political interest group
lobbyist	revolving door

4

Political Parties

This urban wired Latina executive and Anglo cowboy in rural Texas symbolize the vast differences in lifestyles that political parties must try to bridge.

(Top) © Terry Vine/ Blend Images/Corbis (Bottom) Courtesy of Texas Department of Transportation

The political parties created democracy and modern democracy is unthinkable save in terms of the parties. . . . The parties are not therefore merely appendages of modern government; they are the center of it and play a determinative and creative role in it.

E. E. SCHATTSCHNEIDER, PARTY GOVERNMENT, 1942

A political party is an organization that takes money from the rich and votes from the poor under the pretext of protecting the one from the other.

ANONYMOUS

INTRODUCTION

Both Schattschneider's favorable assessment of **political parties** and the anonymous cynical disparagement of their value are justified. Parties are, indeed, the only organizations capable of holding together many fractious interests so that governing is possible. At the same time, in Texas and elsewhere, parties frequently serve democracy badly.

This chapter opens with a discussion of ideology and interests, the two bases for much party conflict. It proceeds to a brief history of the state's political parties, an examination of the major functions of parties, and an outline of party organization in Texas. The "four-faction system" that has recently emerged, and which can make the Texas two-party system confusing, is then explained, followed by a discussion of the state's occasional third-party efforts. At several points, the reality of Texas's party politics is contrasted with the democratic ideal.

OBJECTIVES

After reading this chapter, you should be able to

Understand the nature of ideologies, the differences between political conservatism and political liberalism, and the way ideologies relate to the major political parties.

Discuss the way families, schools, churches, and media socialize citizens to adopt certain ideologies.

Define the concept "interest," and discuss how interests reinforce or contradict socialization in persuading people to adopt certain ideologies or vote for certain parties.

Briefly describe the history of the Democratic and Republican parties in Texas, and the importance of some of its third parties.

Sketch the general functions of political parties, and their specific organization in Texas.

Summarize the typical social support for the parties in Texas, and explain why the Democratic Party faces an uncertain future.

Ideology

In Texas as elsewhere, party rivalry is often based on differences in ideology. **Ideology** is a system of beliefs and values about the nature of the good life and the good society, about the relationship of government and the economy, about moral values and the way they should be achieved, and about how government is to conduct itself. The two dominant, and contesting, systems of beliefs and values in American and Texas life today are usually referred to as "liberalism" and "conservatism."

Conservatism

The basic principle underlying **conservatism,** at least in economic policy, is "laissez faire"—or, to loosely translate from the French phrase, "leave it alone." In theory, conservatives prefer to allow free markets, not government, to regulate the economy. In practice, conservative governments often pursue **pseudo laissez faire** in that they claim to cherish free markets, but actually endorse policies that deeply involve government in helping business to overcome problems in the marketplace. The $700 billion "Wall Street bailout" in 2008 sponsored by the Republican Bush administration (and eventually passed by a Democratic Congress) is a vivid example of the way that supposedly conservative politicians often abandon laissez faire in the face of economic difficulties.

Nevertheless, at the level of ideology, and certainly at the level of their argument with liberals, conservatives believe that economies run best if governments leave them alone. When contemplating economic problems such as poverty, pollution, unemployment, or health care, conservatives argue that government has caused most of them through overregulation and that the best way to deal with them is for government to stop meddling and allow the market to work. It is common to speak of conservatives as being on the "right wing" of the political continuum.[1] The "Tea Party" faction of the Republican Party that first nominated, then elected, many of its candidates in the 2010 election is, in theory, even more conservative than the typical Texas Republican, and therefore "farther to the right." Whether Tea Party activists will be able to keep to their ideology when they are actual public officials as opposed to enthusiastic citizens is a subject for the next edition of this textbook.

Liberalism

Liberalism is the contrary ideology. Liberals are suspicious of the workings of unregulated markets and place more faith in the ability of government to direct economic activity. When thinking about economic problems, they are apt to blame "market failure" and suggest government activity as the solution. The 2008 Wall Street bailout was thus not contrary to liberal philosophy, although liberals also advocated a bailout of the unfortunate people who were losing their homes because of the economic crisis. It is common to speak of liberals as being on the "left wing" of the political spectrum.

All this is relatively clear. When dealing with issues of personal belief and behavior, such as religion, sexual activity, or drug use, however, liberals and conservatives often switch sides. Conservatives are generally in favor of more government regulation; liberals are in favor of less. Liberals oppose prayer in public schools, whereas conservatives favor it; liberals oppose laws regulating

sexual behavior, whereas conservatives endorse them; and so on. An exception to this rule would be the issue of private gun ownership. Conservatives generally want less regulation of guns; liberals want more.

Finally, on foreign policy issues, liberals and conservatives tend to follow partisan rather than ideological cues. That is, liberals tend to endorse whatever a Democratic president wants to do and oppose the wishes of a Republican president, while conservatives support Republicans and oppose Democrats.

Since the 1960s, there has been a slight tendency among liberals to emphasize "human rights" in foreign policy and a slight tendency among conservatives to emphasize military force, but these long-term positions are easily scrambled by the short-term partisan struggle. For example, liberals generally supported, and conservatives generally opposed, Democratic President Bill Clinton's air attack on Iraq in 1998; but liberals generally opposed, and conservatives generally supported, Republican President George W. Bush's ground invasion of the same country in 2003.

In summary, American ideological arguments are often confusing because liberals usually favor government activity in the economic sphere, but oppose it in the personal sphere, whereas conservatives usually oppose government activity in the economic sphere, but favor it in the personal sphere. Confusing or not, this ideological split is the basis for a great deal of rhetorical argument and many intense struggles over public policy (see Table 4-1).

Ideology in Texas

As discussed in Chapter 1, Texas has historically been dominated by a combination of the traditionalistic/individualistic political cultures. The particular mix of those cultures within the state has generally produced an ideology that has been hostile to government activity in general, and especially in regard to providing help for society's poorer and less educated citizens. The basic attitudes associated with cultural values have thus translated, in the Texas case, into an ideology of political conservatism.

The distribution of opinion in the present-day population suggests that, when it comes to ideology, not much has changed in Texas since frontier days. A survey conducted in 2010 reported that only 16.7 percent of Texas adults were willing to label themselves liberals, while 36 percent called themselves moderates, and 43.5 percent claimed the label "conservative."[2] The meaning of these simple self-reports is not completely clear because, by calling themselves conservative, people might be referring to economic issues, social issues, foreign policy issues, or all three. Moreover, national public opinion research over many years has shown that a significant percentage of American citizens label themselves conservative in general, but endorse many specific liberal government domestic programs. Still, the self-reported percentages are sufficiently dramatic to emphasize the weakness of the liberal ideological tradition in the Lone Star State.

In Texas as elsewhere, the contradictory nature of political ideologies—sometimes recommending government activity, sometimes opposing it, and not always in a logically coherent manner—often makes the arguments of politicians and journalists difficult to understand. Nevertheless, ideologies form the basis for much of the party battle. In general, the Democratic Party is controlled nationally by liberals, and the Republican Party is controlled by conservatives. In Texas, however, the picture is more complicated. Both common observation and scholarly research lead to the conclusion that, historically, both the Democratic and Republican parties in Texas have been unusually conservative.[3]

TABLE 4-1

Policy Differences between Liberals and Conservatives

Issue	Conservative Position	Liberal Position
Economic Issues		
Taxation	As little as possible, and when necessary, regressive taxes such as sales taxes*	More to cover government spending; progressive preferred*
Government spending	As little as possible, except for military and antiterrorism	Acceptable to provide social services or homeland security
Nature of government regulation	More in personal sphere; less in economic	Less in personal sphere; more in economic
Organized labor	Antiunion	Pro-union
Environment	Favors development over environment	Favors environment over development
Social Issues		
Crime	Supports more prisons and longer sentences; opposes gun control	Favors social policies to attack root causes; favors gun control
Abortion	Pro-life	Pro-choice
Affirmative action	Opposes	Supports
Prayer in public schools	Favors	Opposes
Homosexual marriage	Opposes	Favors
Foreign Policy Issues		
Human rights as large component of foreign policy	No, although the "Bush Doctrine" favored democracy	Yes
Free trade	More likely to favor	Less likely to favor
Military spending	More	Less
U.S. military intervention abroad	More likely to favor**	Less likely to favor**

* A progressive tax is one that increases proportionately with income or benefit derived, such as a progressive income tax. A regressive tax, such as the sales tax, is a flat rate—the same for everyone. It is termed "regressive" because it places proportionately less of a burden on wealthy taxpayers and more of a burden on those with lower incomes.

** However, liberals tended to support the U.S./NATO bombing war against Serbia in 1999, while conservatives tended to oppose it; the ideologies reverted to form in regard to the invasion of Iraq in 2003.

NOTE: Two words of caution are in order. First, this table presents only a brief summary of complex issues, and thus, some distortion is inevitable. Second, it would be inaccurate to assume that every liberal agrees with every liberal position or that every conservative agrees with every conservative position. Even the most devout ideologues have inconsistencies in the beliefs and hitches in their logic, and personal interests (see discussion this chapter) sometimes affect the way ideologies are applied to specific issues.

The Democrats are more liberal because they, unlike the Republicans, harbor a large and active liberal faction. To understand how this situation has come about, it is helpful to have some knowledge of the way ideologies are learned and of the history of Texas as a southern state.

Political Socialization

As analyzed in Chapter 1, the attitudes and values of the traditionalistic/individualistic political culture that dominates Texas result in ideological conservatism: a basic hostility to government action, pseudo laissez faire, social Darwinism, and the trickle-down theory of economics. How is this ideology perpetuated? How is it transmitted from one generation to another?

The process by which we teach and learn our political knowledge, beliefs, attitudes, values, and habits of behavior is called **political socialization.** In this process, we are influenced by many things—peer groups, political leaders, and a variety of experiences—but the basic agents of political socialization seem to be family, schools, churches, and the media. An extensive discussion of the process of socialization is beyond the scope of this book, but some attention should be paid to these four agents, particularly as they operate in Texas.

Family

The family is the most important agent of socialization. The first things a child learns are the basics: attitudes toward authority, others, oneself, and the community outside the family. Some scholars even believe that political ideology is "in the genes," that it is not learned but inherited.[4] Whether the process is learned or inherited, however, it is fair to say that most parents pass along their attitudes and philosophy to their children.

Many Texans can be generous in making personal contributions to private charities, but as heirs to the Texas political culture, the attitudes most parents in the state transmit to their children are opposed to *government* activity on behalf of the poor. By the time other social institutions begin to "teach" children consciously, the children have already learned fundamental values and attitudes. For this reason, basic political orientations are difficult to alter, and the ideas of the population, in Texas as everywhere else, change only slowly.

Schools and Churches

The public school system, and in some cases the churches, can be very influential in shaping political attitudes and beliefs. Again, the influence in Texas is strongly conservative. Many Texans regularly attend religious services, and most houses of worship teach acceptance of religious theology, an acceptance that often spills over to include acceptance of prevailing social and political institutions as well. Among Whites, the religious establishment is probably more conservative than most because the type of Protestantism that dominates Anglo religion in the state stresses the responsibility of individuals for their own fate rather than the communitarian (government) responsibility of everyone for everyone else.

Other religious traditions are also important in Texas, most notably Roman Catholicism among Mexican Americans. The Catholic Church has historically been more encouraging of government activity on behalf of society's underdogs

than have Protestant churches. However, Protestantism, the dominant religion among the historically dominant social group, has been associated with attitudes that reinforce political conservatism. As Latinos, who are almost always Catholic, increase their percentage in the Texas population, they may dilute the dominant conservatism of Texas.

The overall influence of churches, however, may not be as intense or pervasive as that of the public schools, where students spend six or more hours a day, five days a week, for up to twelve years. There is little indication that schools in Texas educate children about politics or encourage them to participate in the political process in any way other than voting. The essence of politics is conflict, but Texas public education does not recognize this. Instead, the schoolchild is taught to value the free enterprise system, but not to be aware of its potential deficiencies, to be patriotic, and to respect authority. The nature of politics is distorted. The child is educated to passivity rather than to democratic participation.

In the most thorough study of socialization by public schools in Texas, anthropologist Douglas Foley spent sixteen months in a small South Texas town (which he called "North Town") during 1973 and 1974; he then returned during the summers and some weekends in 1977, 1985, 1986, and 1987. After interviewing students, teachers, administrators, politicians, and townspeople, and observing many activities, including sporting events, classroom teaching, social dating, and ethnic confrontations, Foley came to definite conclusions about the sorts of ideas passed along by North Town's schools:

The Realities of Change

While Texans continue to be strongly conservative in a political sense, their efforts to teach their children about social attitudes have undergone a major transformation since the 1960s. This evolution of socialization strategy is well illustrated by scholarly investigations of Texas history. As David Montejano documents, inculcating attitudes of Anglo superiority and Mexican American inferiority was an explicit part of the Texas socialization process during the nineteenth and first half of the twentieth centuries, impressed upon young people through laws, words, and political customs. Montejano writes of the system of practices he terms the "catechism of segregation" thusly: "This meaning was taught to them in countless lessons—the Mexican school was physically inferior, Mexican children were issued textbooks discarded by Anglo children, Mexican teams were not admitted to county athletic leagues, Mexican girls could not enter beauty contests, and so on."

Such raw and ugly socialization is almost inconceivable today, except in a few small-town backwaters. Today, the conflicts between Anglos and Hispanics tend to be at the level of economic class. In terms of socialization, Texas schools now attempt to teach human equality; and history textbooks, starting at the elementary level, make a great effort to include all major ethnic groups in their subject matter.

Source: David Montejano, *Anglos and Mexicans in the Making of Texas, 1836–1986* (Austin: University of Texas Press, 1987), 230, passim; an informal survey of Texas history textbooks conducted during the 1990s by David Prindle.

After a year in North Town . . . I came to see that the school simply reflected the general conservatism of the community. The town's social and political environment did not demand or encourage a highly open, imaginative, critical curriculum. North Towners did not want their children reading avant-garde literature or critiques of corporation polluters or revisionist accounts of President Johnson's political corruption. They wanted their schools to discipline and mold their children into hard-working, family-oriented, patriotic, mainstream citizens.[5]

North Town is only one small place in a big state, but Foley's conclusions are consistent with common observations about Texas schools in general. The conservatism he found in North Town, while not found in every classroom or every school district, is generally representative of Texas public education.

Media

As with other institutions in the state, most of the mass media in Texas are conservative. Most newspapers and TV and radio stations are profitable businesses that depend on other economic interests for their advertising revenues. Consequently, there is a tendency among these institutions to echo the business point of view on most issues. As Everett Collier, former editor of the *Houston Chronicle,* used to put it, "We are not here to rock the boat."[6]

As historical forces are constantly modifying Texas society, however, they are also changing the media. Just in the span of years since the first edition of this textbook was published, established patterns of media influence have suffered the shock of new technology. When this book first appeared in the early 1980s, newspapers and television dominated the political media. In the late 1980s, talk radio became important in the public arena. Because most talk radio programs are conservative, they certainly reinforced the traditional Texas pattern of socialization. Beginning in the 1990s, personal computers, and therefore the Internet, offered a new medium of influence over politics. Now, Texans, like other Americans, can encounter a variety of ideological viewpoints on Web sites, on blogs, on Twitter, on Facebook, and, no doubt, soon on new cyber-inventions that do not even exist yet.

As the new media replace the old, they create uncertainty as to their effects. Social scientists have long studied the impact of television and newspapers, but newspapers are in rapid decline and TV is not nearly as important as it used to be. Public intellectuals are just beginning to try to understand the impact of the new media on people's thoughts and habits.

On the one hand, some people believe that the new media such as Twitter and social networking sites are creating a new "bottom-up" democracy in which public officials will have to pay more attention to the opinions of ordinary citizens. "Politics used to be peer-based," asserts J. D. Angle, a Fort Worth political consultant. "Radio and TV made politics top-down and centralized. Social and new media are gradually returning it to a peer-based state."[7] And congressional representative John Culberson concurs. "Social media has allowed me to communicate more effectively with my constituents. It has also made the legislative process more transparent."[8]

On the other hand, some observers fear that the new media are actually strengthening the top-down control that elites use to manipulate citizens. Journalist Malcolm Gladwell contends that "social media increase the efficiency of the existing order rather than empowering dissidents."[9] And another journalist, Frank Rich, agrees, saying that "The Internet in general and social

LONE STAR MEDIA
The *Texas Tribune* Comes to the Party

Independent, more-or-less nonpartisan information about parties, candidates, and elections used to be the province of newspapers. But it has turned out that the financial sources of newspapers have been extremely vulnerable to the new advertising opportunities created by the new media. Before the Internet came along, about 85 percent of a newspaper's revenue came from advertising and only 15 percent from subscriptions. Since the mid-1990s, however, Web-based advertising and other forms of personal selling—Craigslist, eBay, and the like—have been siphoning off the classified and formal advertising that were the lifeblood of printed news.

With their main source of revenue shrinking rapidly, newspapers have been forced to cut back severely on the sort of expensive, investigative journalism that once made them an essential source of political information for concerned citizens. All major Texas newspapers have released or reassigned most of the reporters they used to employ to cover the process of government in Austin. As a result, people with a serious interest in keeping up on Texas politics face a future without enough information.

Into this widening news vacuum, beginning in November 2009, has stepped the *Texas Tribune*. An entirely Web-based "newspaper" (www.texastribune.org), it employs sixteen experienced political reporters and editors, whom it pays good salaries to do good work. As forward-looking in its financial plan as in its media base, the *Tribune* is organized as a nonprofit corporation, and gets its funding from personal donations and foundation grants, apparently, in other words, from concerned citizens who do not want to see political journalism die in Texas.

Whether the *Texas Tribune* will become the model for the future of serious political reporting is impossible to say now. All that can be said for sure is that students who have an interest in learning about parties, politics, and government in Texas would do well to become familiar with its Web site.

SOURCE: *Texas Tribune* Web site; Matt Haber, "Nonprofit *Texas Tribune* Launched," Portfolio.com Web site, November 3, 2009; Bruce Watson, "Making Online Media Pay: Demand Media vs. The *Texas Tribune*," Daily Finance Web site, November 27, 2009; Bill Minutaglio, "Un-Covered: Where Did All the Capitol Reporters Go—And What Happens Without Them?" *Texas Observer*, June 26, 2009, 10.

networking in particular have done little, if anything, to hobble those pursuing power with such traditional means as big lies and big money."[10]

Whether the new computer-based media will, like talk radio, merely supplement the basic Texas politically conservative socialization, or alter it in surprising and radical ways, is a question that cannot be answered now. All that can be said for sure is that the new media are here to stay, and very important. It is significant that the *Austin American-Statesman*, the state capital's only daily newspaper and one that pays close attention to politics, recently created the position of "social media editor." Robert Quigley, who holds the job, believes that he represents the future of journalism, because, "In this new world, listening to the public is as important as telling the story." He assures his readers that "It is a great time to be a journalist."[11]

Perhaps Quigley is right, but the more important question is whether the rapid evolution of media is making the present era a great time for Texas democracy. That question cannot be answered yet. The future, as always, contains the promise of both stability and change, improvement and degeneration.

Evaluation

After reviewing the socializing effects of families, schools, churches, and the media, one might wonder how any view other than the conservative ideology exists in Texas. It does exist, however, for several reasons: Some people adopt a personal point of view that is contrary to the opinion-molding forces around them; liberal families, churches, schoolteachers, and news outlets do exist in Texas, although they are in the minority; the national, as opposed to local, news media often display a liberal slant; and millions of non-Texans have moved to the state in the last few decades, bringing different political cultures with them. Thus, political conservatism continues to dominate, but as both the Texas population and media technology increase and become more diverse, the ideology is being challenged and modified by competing cultural values.

Ideology, however, is not the only basis for political party support. Equally important are people's interests and the way parties attempt to recruit citizen loyalty by endorsing those interests.

Interests

An **interest** is something of value or some personal characteristic that people share and that is affected by government activity—their investments, their race, their jobs, their hobbies, and so on. When there is a question of public policy on which political parties take differing positions, people often line up behind the party favoring their interests, whether or not their political ideology is consistent with that party's. Moreover, parties often take positions that will attract the money and votes of citizens with clashing interests. Thus, parties put together **coalitions** of interests to attract blocs of voters and campaign contributions. Party positions are therefore almost always much more ambiguous and confusing than they would be if they were simply based on ideology.

Not all interests are economic. Since the 1960s, for example, Mexican Americans and African Americans have tended to support the Democratic Party because they have perceived the Republicans as less tolerant of ethnic diversity. Whether an interest arranges people in a politically relevant manner depends on what sorts of questions become issues of public policy.

Interests and ideologies tend to combine in different ways in different people, sometimes opposing and sometimes reinforcing one another. For example, a Latina doctor in Texas would be drawn to the Republicans by her professional interest and drawn to the Democrats by her ethnic interest. She might have had trouble making up her mind about how to vote in the 2010 election. On the other hand, an Anglo oil company executive or a Black labor union president would probably have experienced no such conflict. In each case, the citizen's personal ideology may either reinforce or contradict one or more of his or her interests.

The way interests and ideologies blend and conflict, and interact with candidates and parties, is one of the things that makes politics complicated and interesting to study. Interests thus help structure the party battle. They are politically important for other reasons as well. See Chapter 3 for a detailed discussion of the organizing and lobbying efforts of interest groups.

TABLE 4-2

Interests Generally Supporting the Two Major Parties

Type of Interest	Democrats	Republicans
Economic class	poor, lower middle	wealthy, upper middle
Economic structure	workers, especially labor unions	management
Professions	plaintiffs' attorneys, public employees	physicians, business entrepreneurs
Development vs. environment	environmentalists	developers, rural landowners
Industry	entertainment	oil and gas, computers
Ethnicity	African American, Mexican American	Anglo
Religion	Catholic, Jewish	Protestant, especially evangelical

The partisan coalitions that have characterized recent Texas politics are summarized in Table 4-2. It is important to understand that not every person who has an interest agrees with every other person with the same interest, and so citizens who share interests are not unanimous in their partisan attachments. For example, although most of the people in the computer business who contributed large amounts to a political party during the 1990s and 2000s gave to the Republicans, not all did. Similarly, although the great majority of African Americans voters supported the Democrats, thousands did not. Table 4-2 describes how people with certain interests lean in general, not how every person with that interest behaves.

Politics would be fascinating enough if, once ideologies and interests had arranged themselves into a party coalition, they stayed that way. In fact, however, the party battle evolves as history changes the way people live. A hundred years ago, the Democratic Party was the more conservative party and dominated Texas almost completely. Today, the Republican Party is more conservative and has achieved at least temporary dominance over the Democrats. It is not too much of an exaggeration to say that the history of Texas is written in the story of the two major parties.

Texas Political Parties: A Brief History

The modern division of Texas political parties has its roots in the aftermath of the Civil War, which ended in 1865. The Republican administration of Abraham Lincoln had defeated the Confederacy, of which Texas was a member, and freed the slaves. Reconstruction, or federal government occupation, settled on all the southern states. White southerners found themselves under the rule of northerners, the military, and African Americans. Rightly or wrongly, they believed themselves to be subject to tyranny by a foreign conqueror. They identified this

despotic occupation with the Republican Party. As a result, when Reconstruction ended in 1874, Texas, like the other former members of the Confederacy, was a solid one-party Democratic state. It kept the **one-party system** until the 1970s, with telling effects on politics and public policy.

Because competition between ideas and candidates stimulates interest, citizens are relatively active in a healthy two-party system, and voter turnouts are therefore fairly high. A one-party system is very different, and Texas furnished a good example in the first three quarters of the twentieth century. Without the argument between the two parties to foster debate and spur voter interest, most White citizens (in most areas of the state, minorities were prevented from voting) were apathetic, and voter turnout was very low. Candidates of all ideological persuasions, from Ku Klux Klansmen to liberals, ran as Democrats.

One result of this situation was that when voters elected Democrats to the offices of Governor, Lieutenant Governor, Attorney General, Treasurer, and so on, they were not sending a Democratic "team" to Austin. They were sending independent officials who were frequently rivals and had little in common except personal ambition and a Democratic label. Because there was no unified team, there was no unified program. Each politician went his or her own way. The act of holding together disparate interests, which is the basis for E. E. Schattschneider's praise of parties at the beginning of the chapter, was not performed.

In other words, one-party politics in Texas was really no-party politics. Instead of the vigorous debate and citizen involvement that characterize well-run democracies, confusion and apathy reigned.

The transition to two-party politics in Texas, as in most of the South, occurred gradually. Beginning in 1928, Texans sometimes voted for Republican presidential candidates. In 1961, Republican John Tower cracked the Democratic monopoly at the state level by winning a special election for a U.S. Senate seat. Republicans began to win a few local elections in Dallas and Houston soon thereafter, but conservative Democrats continued to dominate state politics into the 1970s. In 1978, Bill Clements beat John Hill for the governorship and became Texas's first Republican governor in 104 years. But Clements could not win re-election in 1982, in spite of spending a record $13.2 million during his campaign.

Republican President Ronald Reagan's landslide re-election in 1984 seemed to have finally broken the Democrats' hold on Texas. Dozens of Republican candidates rode Reagan's coattails to victory in local elections, as did Phil Gramm, the Republican candidate for U.S. senator. Some of the local officeholders subsequently lost their re-election bids, but by then, Texas could no longer be considered a Democratic monopoly.

Seen against this historical background, the election of 1994 appears to be truly a watershed. Republicans defeated an incumbent Democratic governor, retained a second U.S. Senate seat, pulled almost even in the state Senate, and saw hundreds of local offices fall to their candidates. The last Democratic bastion—the party's slim majority in the state's thirty-two-member delegation to the U.S. House of Representatives—was destroyed by the legislature's redistricting bill in 2003. Democrats began to make inroads on complete Republican rule in local elections in some big cities in 2006 and 2008, but the state as a whole remained staunchly Republican.

By 2012, Texas could just barely be considered a two-party state. Every statewide elective official, including all eighteen members of the two top courts,

TABLE 4-3

Growth of Republican Officeholders in Texas, 1974–2012

Year	U.S. Senate	Other Statewide	U.S. House	Texas Senate	Texas House	Total
1974	1	0	2	3	16	22
1982	1	0	5	5	36	47
1990	1	6	8	8	57	80
1998	2	27	13	16	72	130
2004	2	27	21	19	87	156
2012	2	27	23	19	101	172

NOTE: Neither the Republican Party nor the Texas secretary of state keep track of the total number of electoral offices within Texas. As a result, it is impossible to express the above raw numbers in percentage terms.

SOURCE: Republican Party of Texas, October, 2005; W. Gardner Selby, "Benkiser Seeking a National Perch, Touting GOP Gains," *Austin American-Statesman*, January 29, 2009, B1; various Web sites.

was Republican, as were both U.S. senators and large majorities in both houses of the state legislature. Moreover, Texans had given decisive majorities of their major-party vote to Republican presidential candidates in 1992, 1996, 2000, 2004, and 2008. If the voting trends of the past two decades continue, Texas might become as much a one-party state in the twenty-first century as it was in the twentieth, but with different parties in command.

Table 4-3 displays the growth in the number of Republican officeholders in Texas from 1974 to 2012. Patterns in Texas's voting history over the past two decades are underscored by public opinion research. In a survey taken in 2010, 52 percent of the state's citizens described themselves as more-or-less regular supporters of Republicans. Meanwhile, only 39 percent claimed to be supporters of Democrats.[12] While 2010 was a "Republican year" at the ballot box, these figures are quite close to the results of polls in previous years.

Together, the voting and survey data suggest that, during the last two decades of the twentieth century, Texas went through a political **realignment**—a change in the partisan identification (psychological affiliation resulting in a standing decision to vote for a given party)—of its citizens. Until the 1980s, enough Texans had adopted a standing decision to vote for Democrats that the party's candidates could count on winning most of the time. By the twenty-first century, however, enough Texans had changed their psychological affiliation so that Republicans were normally victorious in statewide, although not necessarily local, elections. Once solidly Democratic, Texas had realigned to be generally Republican.

The growth of two-party competition in Texas has been good for democracy. Instead of the confused jumble that characterized Texas politics when Texas was a one-party state, in recent years, there has been robust debate between the parties on many issues of importance to the citizens. Whether the

democratic dialogue can last if the Republicans continue their statewide dominance is another question.

The public debate is so loud because policy differences between the parties are quite substantial. Table 4-4 displays some summary statements from the state Democratic and Republican party platforms of 2010. As the table illustrates, the differences between the activists who write these platforms are of three kinds. First, on some issues—for instance, abortion, the minimum wage,

TABLE 4-4

2010 Texas State Political Party Platforms

Issue	Republican	Democratic
Abortion	We affirm our support for a human life amendment to the Constitution. . . . We are resolute regarding the reversal of *Roe v. Wade*.	We believe in and support . . . freedom from government interference in our private lives and personal decisions.
Affirmative action	We oppose affirmative action because we believe it is simply racism disguised as a social value.	Texas Democrats support innovative approaches to ensure diversity in every Texas institution of higher education.
Capital punishment	Properly applied capital punishment is legitimate, is an effective deterrent, and should be swift and unencumbered.	Texas Democrats support the establishment of a Texas Capital Punishment Commission to study the Texas death penalty system and a moratorium on executions pending action on the Commission's findings.
Child care	We oppose any government regulations that will adversely affect the availability, affordability, or the right of parents to choose child care.	Texas families should not have to choose between the jobs they need and the children they love. Texas Democrats support child care initiatives that encourage both private and non-profit providers to expand the availability of quality child care.
Church and state	America is a nation under God founded on Judeo-Christian principles. . . . We pledge our influence toward a return to the original intent of the First Amendment and toward dispelling the myth of separation of church and state.	Texas Democrats believe government should scrupulously honor every Texan's right to religious freedom, as guaranteed by the Texas and U.S. Constitutions and protected by the separation of church and state.
Environment	We reaffirm our belief in the constitutional concept of the right to own property without governmental interference. . . . We believe in . . . eliminating the Endangered Species Act.	We must . . . reward those who voluntarily protect endangered species on their lands through Safe Harbor Agreements and similar measures.
Evolution	Realizing that conflict and debate is a proven learning tool in classrooms, we support objective teaching and equal treatment of all sides of scientific theories, including *evolution, Intelligent Design, global warming*, political philosophies, and others. We believe theories of life origins and environmental theories should be taught as challengeable scientific theory subject to change as new data is produced, not scientific law.	Texas Democrats will realign the state curriculum with objective reality and the facts of history and science.
Guns	We urge the Legislature and Congress to repeal all laws that infringe on the right to bear arms, and to reject any monitoring of gun ownership, and all specific taxation or regulation of guns and ammunition.	Not mentioned.

(continued)

TABLE 4-4 (CONTINUED)

2010 Texas State Political Party Platforms

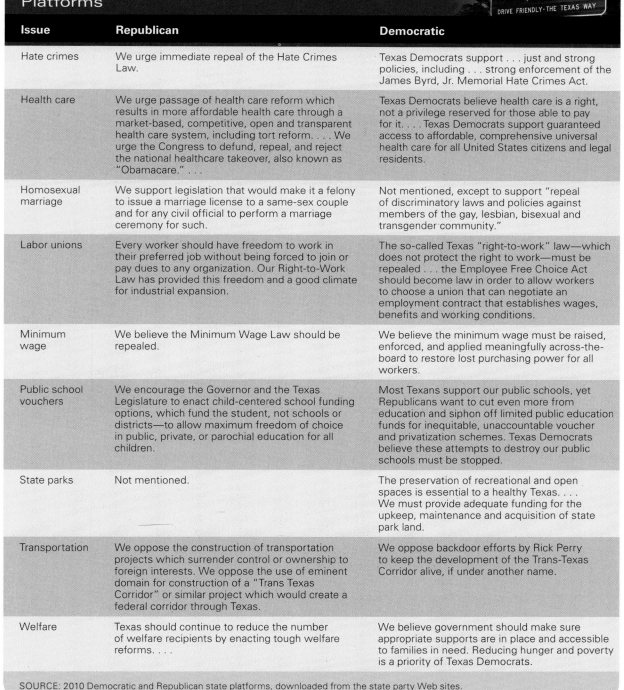

Issue	Republican	Democratic
Hate crimes	We urge immediate repeal of the Hate Crimes Law.	Texas Democrats support . . . just and strong policies, including . . . strong enforcement of the James Byrd, Jr. Memorial Hate Crimes Act.
Health care	We urge passage of health care reform which results in more affordable health care through a market-based, competitive, open and transparent health care system, including tort reform. . . . We urge the Congress to defund, repeal, and reject the national healthcare takeover, also known as "Obamacare." . . .	Texas Democrats believe health care is a right, not a privilege reserved for those able to pay for it. . . . Texas Democrats support guaranteed access to affordable, comprehensive universal health care for all United States citizens and legal residents.
Homosexual marriage	We support legislation that would make it a felony to issue a marriage license to a same-sex couple and for any civil official to perform a marriage ceremony for such.	Not mentioned, except to support "repeal of discriminatory laws and policies against members of the gay, lesbian, bisexual and transgender community."
Labor unions	Every worker should have freedom to work in their preferred job without being forced to join or pay dues to any organization. Our Right-to-Work Law has provided this freedom and a good climate for industrial expansion.	The so-called Texas "right-to-work" law—which does not protect the right to work—must be repealed . . . the Employee Free Choice Act should become law in order to allow workers to choose a union that can negotiate an employment contract that establishes wages, benefits and working conditions.
Minimum wage	We believe the Minimum Wage Law should be repealed.	We believe the minimum wage must be raised, enforced, and applied meaningfully across-the-board to restore lost purchasing power for all workers.
Public school vouchers	We encourage the Governor and the Texas Legislature to enact child-centered school funding options, which fund the student, not schools or districts—to allow maximum freedom of choice in public, private, or parochial education for all children.	Most Texans support our public schools, yet Republicans want to cut even more from education and siphon off limited public education funds for inequitable, unaccountable voucher and privatization schemes. Texas Democrats believe these attempts to destroy our public schools must be stopped.
State parks	Not mentioned.	The preservation of recreational and open spaces is essential to a healthy Texas. . . . We must provide adequate funding for the upkeep, maintenance and acquisition of state park land.
Transportation	We oppose the construction of transportation projects which surrender control or ownership to foreign interests. We oppose the use of eminent domain for construction of a "Trans Texas Corridor" or similar project which would create a federal corridor through Texas.	We oppose backdoor efforts by Rick Perry to keep the development of the Trans-Texas Corridor alive, if under another name.
Welfare	Texas should continue to reduce the number of welfare recipients by enacting tough welfare reforms. . . .	We believe government should make sure appropriate supports are in place and accessible to families in need. Reducing hunger and poverty is a priority of Texas Democrats.

SOURCE: 2010 Democratic and Republican state platforms, downloaded from the state party Web sites.

and labor unions—party activists are clearly and firmly on opposing sides. Second, the parties are concerned about different issues and therefore talk about different subjects. For example, the Republicans, but not the Democrats, talk about the right to gun ownership, whereas the Democrats are the only party to mention the responsibility of government to provide public parks. And third, the parties occasionally agree completely on an issue. Both, for example, clearly oppose the Trans-Texas Corridor (see Chapter 14).

Functions of Political Parties

From the perspective of activists and candidates, the basic purpose of parties is to win elections and thus gain the opportunity to exercise control over public policy. While pursuing this goal, however, political parties often fulfill several functions that make them valuable institutions from the perspective of democratic theory. These functions include the following:

- Involving ordinary people in the political process, especially persuading them to vote and teaching them the formal and informal "rules of the game"

- Recruiting political leaders and persuading them to restrain their individual ambitions so that the party can achieve its collective purposes

- Communicating to the leaders the interests of individuals and groups

- Adding factual information and persuasive argument to the public discussion of policy alternatives

- Structuring the nature of political conflict and debate, including screening out the demands of certain people and groups (usually fringe individuals or groups of very small minorities)

- Moderating differences between groups, both within the party and in the larger society

- Partially overcoming the fragmented nature of the political system so that gridlock can be overcome and coherent policy made and implemented

Political parties in any democracy can be judged according to how well or badly they perform these functions. How do Texas parties measure up?

Party Organization

All parties are organizations, but they follow many different patterns of structure. In general, we can say that American parties, compared to those in foreign democracies, are weakly organized. They are not structured so that they can function easily as a cohesive team. The parties in Texas are especially weak in an organizational sense. As a result, they often do not perform the function of overcoming gridlock and making coherent policy very well, nor do they structure conflict to make it sensible to most ordinary citizens. A review of state party organization will suggest why this is so.

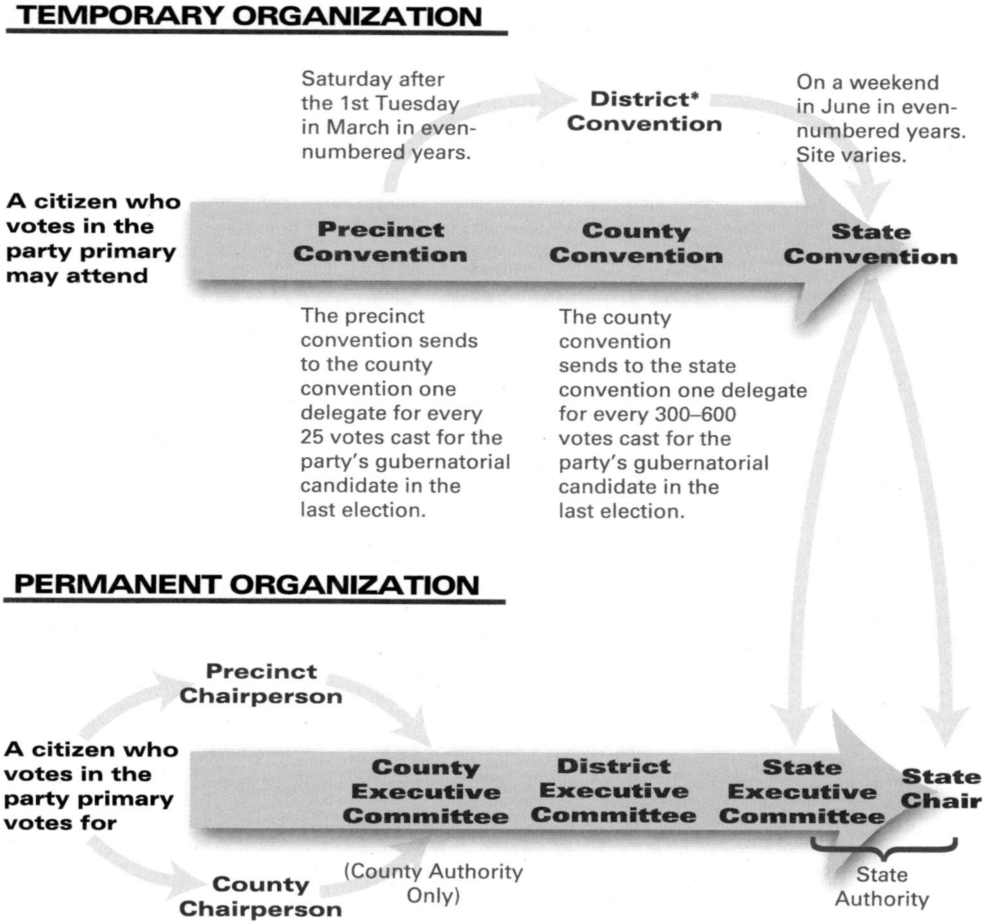

TEMPORARY ORGANIZATION

Saturday after the 1st Tuesday in March in even-numbered years.

District* Convention

On a weekend in June in even-numbered years. Site varies.

A citizen who votes in the party primary may attend

Precinct Convention   **County Convention**   **State Convention**

The precinct convention sends to the county convention one delegate for every 25 votes cast for the party's gubernatorial candidate in the last election.

The county convention sends to the state convention one delegate for every 300–600 votes cast for the party's gubernatorial candidate in the last election.

PERMANENT ORGANIZATION

Precinct Chairperson

A citizen who votes in the party primary votes for

County Executive Committee   **District Executive Committee**   **State Executive Committee**   **State Chair**

County Chairperson

(County Authority Only)

State Authority

FIGURE 4-1 Major Party Organization in Texas.

*District conventions are held in counties with more than one senatorial district.

SOURCE: State Democratic and Republican headquarters.

Figure 4-1 shows that in Texas, as in most states, parties are divided into a permanent organization and a temporary one. The **permanent party organization** consists of little more than a skeleton force of people who conduct the routine, but essential business of the party. The party's primary purpose of winning elections requires far more people and much greater activity. The party comes alive in election years in the form of a **temporary party organization** geared to capturing power.

The Temporary Party Organization

The temporary party organization is focused on the spring primary and the fall general election. It attempts to choose attractive candidates and mobilize voters to support them.

In Texas, party membership is determined by the act of voting; there are no permanent political party rolls. When citizens vote in the Democratic Party

primary, for example, they are considered "affiliated Democrats" until the end of the calendar year. They may vote only in the Democratic runoff, if there is one, and participate only in Democratic conventions. The next year, however, they may legally change their affiliation and participate in Republican Party activities.

Precinct and County Conventions

In the 254 counties of Texas, there are more than 6,000 precincts, each having from 50 to as many as 3,500 voters. Each voter is entitled to have a voice in choosing the precinct chairperson and proposing and voting on resolutions that will establish party policy, but voter participation in party affairs is low. Normally, only a small fraction of those who vote in the primaries—who are themselves only a fraction of the total number of registered voters and a smaller fraction of the citizens of voting age—participate in conventions or other party affairs.

The main function of the precinct convention is to select delegates to the county convention, which is the next level of the temporary party organization. The main function of the county convention is to select delegates to the state convention. Both precinct and county conventions can be either short or long, peaceful or filled with conflict, productive of resolutions or not.

The State Convention

Both major parties hold their state conventions on a weekend in June during even-numbered years. The party State Executive Committee (SEC) decides when and where the convention is to be held. Depending on the year of the election cycle in which it occurs, the June convention performs some or all of the following activities:

1. **It certifies to the secretary of state the party nominees for the general election in November.**

2. **It writes the party platform.**

3. **It selects the members of the SEC.**

4. **It names the Texas committeeman and committeewoman to the national party committee.**

5. **During presidential years, it selects the "at-large" delegates to the national party convention (who are not committed to supporting any particular candidate, as opposed to the "pledged" delegates who are sworn to support specific candidates and whose identity depends on the support candidates received in the March primary election).[13]**

6. **It selects a slate of presidential electors to serve in the national electoral college in the event the party's candidates for president and vice president win in Texas.**

Party conventions have tended, over the past several decades, to travel in opposite directions—the Democrats from argument to harmony and the Republicans from agreement to disharmony. Until the 1980s, the liberal and conservative wings of the Democratic Party often fought viciously over party planks and leadership positions. In the 1990s, however, the party came to be dominated more and more at the organizational level by the liberal faction.

In conventions, the delegates now tend to adopt liberal platforms—at least in regard to social issues—and save their criticisms for the Republicans. In contrast, when the Republicans were a small minority, they rarely argued over policy in their conventions. As their influence in the state grew, however, Republicans generated greater and greater internal disagreement, especially between social and economic conservatives.

The new pattern was set in 1994, when delegates from the Christian Right (see Chapter 3) dominated the convention. The socially conservative platform and the convention's choice of a party chair sparked vigorous, but futile opposition from delegates who were economically conservative, but more moderate on social issues. By 2000, those Republican delegates who were economic conservatives, but social liberals, had stopped making hopeless objections to Christian Right positions at the state convention, although the intra-party battle continued to be waged on other fronts. From 1994 to 2010, the Christian Right dominated Republican state conventions. In 1994, 1996, and 1998, Republican state platforms began with the words, "We believe in you! We believe that you are a sacred being created in the image of God."

By 2002, social conservative delegates to the Republican convention were so frustrated with the economically conservative officeholders they termed "RINOs" (for "Republicans in Name Only'") that they sponsored Rule 43 as a floor amendment to the platform. This "RINO Rule" would have denied party funds to any candidate who refused to swear to endorse and attempt to implement every party plank if elected. Party Chair Susan Weddington, presiding at the convention, managed to squelch the Rule 43 movement, but disappointed Christian Right delegates promised to persevere at future party gatherings.[14]

Although the equivalent of Rule 43 was not adopted from 2004 through 2010, platforms from those years did contain some version of the declaration

Although their candidates had fared poorly in recent elections, delegates to the 2010 Democratic Party state convention were good citizens, participating in politics despite their party's bleak prospects.

AP Photo/Harry Cabluck

Sensing that their candidates would do well in the November general election, delegates to the summer 2010 Republican state convention participated enthusiastically.

© Bob Daemmrich/Corbis

(this specific quotation from 2006) that "We strongly expect the SREC (State Republican Executive Committee) Candidate Resource Committee to consider candidates' support of the Party platform when granting financial or other support."[15] Because candidates raise most of their own campaign funds and thus do not rely on the official party organization, however, such proclamations tend to be empty threats.

Although events in the Democratic and Republican state conventions engender much publicity, their importance should not be exaggerated. Because candidates for public office in Texas are nominated in primaries rather than in caucuses or conventions (see Chapter 5), and because candidates typically raise their own campaign funds independently of the party, the state convention and platform are of little importance to what nominees say and do. Candidates typically run to gather support from the large number of potential voters, not the tiny number of party activists who write the platforms.

In summary, if students want to know what candidates plan to do if elected, they may want to ignore platforms and instead pay attention to the positions of the candidates themselves. The platform positions and rhetoric reproduced in Table 4-4 are good indications of the values and beliefs of the major party activists as groups, but are not reliable guides to the issue positions of candidates as individuals.

Permanent Party Organization

Although the party is not very active between elections, party leaders do not want to have to create a new organization every two years. They therefore maintain a "skeleton" structure that mostly lies dormant between election years, ready to be reactivated as primary time nears. This structure is regulated by the Texas Election Code.

Precinct Chairpersons

The citizen who votes in the primary has an opportunity to participate in the selection of the precinct and county chairpersons of his or her party. The precinct chairperson is the lowest-ranking permanent party official. Elected for a two-year term, he or she is expected to be the party leader at the precinct level, recruiting candidates, arranging for the precinct convention, getting out the vote, and in general, beating the drum for the party.

County Executive Committee

Together, the precinct chairs form the county executive committee, which is charged with two major responsibilities: (1) conducting the party primary elections and (2) conducting the county convention. It is presided over by the county chairperson, the most important official at the local level. Elected for two years to a demanding job, this official is unpaid, although some receive private donations.

County chairs are compensated by the state for the expense of conducting their party's primary elections. After the primary election has been held, the county executive committee canvasses the vote and certifies the results to the state executive committee.

District Executive Committee

The Texas Election Code also provides for district executive committees. Their membership varies according to the number of counties and sections of counties that make up the senatorial district. These committees are supposed to perform party primary duties related to the district. In practice, however, few district executive committees are functional. Most district duties are performed by county executive committees.

State Executive Committee

The highest permanent body in the state party is the state executive committee, and the highest state party official is the party chair. Both are elected by the state convention. If the party controls the governorship, the chair of this party is likely to be a friend and political ally of the governor. Normally, the governor and the party chair work together to advance the party campaign during an election year.

In a similar fashion, the chair of the state committee of the party out of power usually has a close relationship with the party's top leaders. By law, the executive committee of each party is responsible for staging the state convention, for certifying the party's candidates, and for coordinating a general party campaign over and above the efforts made by each individual candidate.

The (Un)Importance of Party Organization

American political parties are not "responsible parties"—that is, they have neither centralized control over nominations and financing nor the power to impose the party platform on members. In Texas, parties are especially weak because it is in fact the primary election, not the party organization, that is important in determining who is nominated to office. Furthermore, candidates normally rely on their own fundraising and organizing ability more than they rely on their party to help them get elected.

As a result, when candidates succeed in capturing an office, they mostly have themselves and the individuals and groups who contributed to their campaign fund to thank for their achievement. They therefore have very little loyalty to the party; they are more likely to feel beholden to some wealthy interest group. Officeholders are often ideologically friendly with others of the same party, but they are not obligated to cooperate with one another. The parties have no discipline over them.

Texas party organizations have some ability to fashion a "party attitude" on public policy because they are centers of information flow and personal interaction, but they are incapable of forging a disciplined governing team. Therefore, the party platforms summarized in Table 4-4 are in fact largely irrelevant to candidates' positions. They are a good indication of the sentiments of the party activists as a group, but they say little about the policy stands of candidates as individuals.

The unimportance of party organization in Texas is illustrated by the fact that the GOP was victorious in elections from 1994 to 2010 despite its internal squabbling. In a similar fashion, the Democratic Party won elections in the Lone Star State in previous decades despite the fact that it was divided into factions.

The consequence of their organizational weakness is that Texas parties often fail to perform many of the functions that make parties elsewhere useful to democracy. By and large, they cannot recruit political leaders or overcome the fragmented nature of the political system by forming officials into disciplined organizations. Instead of thinking of parties in Texas as two stable, cohesive teams, it would be more realistic to imagine them as two (or as discussed in the next section, three or even four) loose confederations of citizens, interest groups, and officeholders that sometimes cooperate because of occasional ideological agreement and temporary parallel interests.

Lack of party cohesiveness also has important consequences in the legislature. Scholarly research has established the importance of party organization in state lawmaking bodies. According to Gerald Wright and Brian Schaffner, when the legislature has parties structured into two teams, political conflict is ordered so that issues tend to fall on either side of a clear, stable, voting cleavage in the legislature. Under such conditions, citizens are able to make sense of the political struggle. When Republicans and Democrats have no institutionalized divisions and organization, however, "It seems almost as though each bill is considered anew rather than in the context of established sides and coalitions."[16] Under

these circumstances, lawmaking is confused and confusing, and citizens have difficulty holding politicians accountable for their actions.

Traditionally, Texas's weak parties have been reflected in the disorganization of its legislature. The presiding officers (see Chapter 6) have normally appointed members of both parties to chair important committees. The parties did not even caucus as separate groups until 1989, and afterward, those caucuses met only rarely during the legislative session.[17] Even in 2005, after the bruising and bitter partisan gerrymander of 2003, Republican Speaker Tom Craddick appointed Democrats to chair ten of forty-three House committees, and Republican Lieutenant Governor David Dewhurst chose Democrats to chair six of the fifteen Senate committees.

Political scientists expect that this lack of partisan organization is likely to change as Texas's parties become more ideologically opposed. Over the past several decades, parties in the United States Congress have become more ideologically polarized and less cooperative.[18] As Texas parties travel in the same direction, the historical pattern of bipartisan cooperation in the state legislature is likely to trace a similar path. Future legislatures will probably witness fewer minority party appointments to committee chairs, stronger legislative party organizations, and much more cohesive party voting. Such changes will undoubtedly produce more stress for legislators, but they might be good for democratic politics because the functioning of state government will be more coherent and responsible.

The new, more party-conscious Texas political environment was on display in the primary election of 2004. Democrat Ron Wilson, an African American from Houston, had been conspicuously independent of his party's organizational needs ever since his election to the state House of Representatives in 1976. His willingness to vote with Republicans had made Wilson one of the few Democrats who retained internal power in the legislature as the party balance changed. He publicly supported the election of the new House speaker, Tom Craddick, and received many favors in return, including being one of the minority-party representatives that Craddick appointed to chair a committee.

Wilson's lack of party loyalty was for many years of no concern to his constituents, who regularly re-elected him by large margins. But by completely deserting the Democrats and endorsing the Republican redistricting plan in

Both Sexes but Only One Profession

As party interests and ideologies evolve through history, so does their leadership. Texas passed some sort of a milestone in the late 1990s when both parties, for the first time, elected women as leaders. Republican Susan Weddington was a former businesswoman from San Antonio. Democrat Molly Beth Malcolm was a former teacher and drug counselor from East Texas. Malcolm was a rarity in modern Texas politics—a former Republican who became an important Democrat.

Weddington and Malcolm each resigned as party chairs in 2003. Since that year the parties have elected several chairs, some male and some female. Clearly, in the twenty-first century, the sex of a politician is of much less importance than it was in earlier times. Recent party chairs do share a profession, however; all have been lawyers.

Source: Texas Republican and Democratic Party Web sites.

2003, he went too far. In the March 2004 Democratic primary, Wilson was challenged by Alma Allen, a professional educator, member of the state board of education, and, incidentally, also a Black candidate. During the primary campaign, Allen pounded Wilson for his support of redistricting, as well as his vote for Republican budget cuts. State Democratic leaders, including party chair Charles Soechting, publicly backed Allen. The voters got the message and nominated Allen by an eleven-point margin. (Because there was no Republican candidate running in this largely African American district, a victory in the primary assured election in November.) The voters had made it clear that, in the new world of Texas politics, party loyalty mattered.[19]

Two Parties, Three Factions (or Perhaps Four)

Although the Republican and Democratic parties dominate Texas and national politics, the fact that candidates and voters participate under one or the other label does not guarantee that they always agree with others who share that label. Each party has **factions**—groups of citizens who differ on some important issues from other groups within the same party. Part of the function of party leadership is to smooth over differences within each party so that its members can concentrate their criticisms on politicians of the other party. Knowledge of the factional makeup of each party can foster a better understanding of the ways that the parties may evolve in the future.

Republicans

Ideologically, the Texas Republican Party tends to be strongly conservative, usually opposing government involvement in the economy, but sometimes endorsing such involvement in personal life. Although the party holds two recognizable factions, the social conservatives (most of whom are members of the Christian Right) and the economic conservatives, it is not quite accurate to speak of two opposed groups within the Republican Party. Many Republican officeholders manage to embody both wings of the party as they endorse social conservatism in their *intangible*, symbolic public statements, but concentrate on passing *tangible* conservative economic policies while in office.

A good example is governor Rick Perry, who took office in 2000 when governor Bush resigned to run for president, and was elected on his own in 2002, then re-elected in 2006 and 2010. In 2006, looking toward another re-election campaign, he publicly endorsed the teaching of Intelligent Design ("ID," a euphemism for Christian creationism) rather than the scientific theory of evolution by natural selection in the state's public-school biology classes. As Table 4-4 illustrates, the Christian Right wing of Perry's party would like to teach ID to students in the state's public-school biology classes. But because "Intelligent Design" is a religious doctrine, it would be unconstitutional to teach it in public schools, as courts have held several times.[20] There is consequently very little chance that such a doctrine could be taught in the state's science classes. Even if such an unlikely event came to pass, the governor would have virtually nothing to do with it because his office does not have the power to set school curriculum for the state. By endorsing the teaching of Intelligent Design, therefore, Perry was not making a genuine proposal for a realistic policy option. He was expressing symbolic solidarity with Christian conservatives.

YOU ★ ★ DECIDE

Should Texas Have Responsible Parties?

In 1950, the American Political Science Association (APSA) sponsored a report entitled "Toward a More Responsible Two-Party System," in which it stated its organizational position that democracy would work better in the United States if the country's parties were more disciplined and coherent. From 2002 to the present, a movement has been present within the ranks of the Texas Republican Party to force its candidates to endorse every plank in the party platform on the theory that democracy would work better if Republicans, at least, were disciplined and coherent. Both APSA in 1950 and many current Republican activists have endorsed the idea that disciplined party teams are better for democratic governance than the disorganized, candidate-centered system that prevails in both Texas and the United States as a whole. Should such disciplined parties be the Texas institutions of the future?

PRO	CON
▲ When different candidates from the same party take differing positions on issues, it confuses the voters. If candidates were all forced to stand for the same things, citizens would be more able to understand the choices available to them, which would make for more intelligent voting.	▼ Election campaigns are often confusing because politics itself is complicated and ambiguous. The solution to confusion is for citizens to better inform themselves, not for parties to impose a false clarity in voting choices.
▲ Many foreign democracies have disciplined, responsible parties. Probably because politics in those countries makes sense, those typically have higher voter turnout than the United States and still higher turnout than Texas.	▼ Almost all those foreign democracies have multiparty systems, so citizens have more choices on election day. There is no evidence that any of those countries is better governed than the United States or Texas.
▲ Disciplined parties would prevent wealthy special interests from secretly buying the loyalty of candidates. Once candidates got into office, there would be no betrayals of the public's trust.	▼ If wealthy special interests were denied access to candidates, they would simply corrupt parties. The problem is the power of money, not the lack of party discipline.
▲ Once candidates were forced to endorse a single set of principles in order to run, they would form a cooperating team when in office, and public policy would be both easier to enact and more self-consistent.	▼ One of the major reasons that candidates vary in their policy positions is that constituencies vary from place to place. Any party that forced its candidates to say the same thing everywhere would soon discover that most of its candidates lost. Losers do not enact public policy.

Source: "Toward a More Responsible Two-Party System: A Report of the Committee on Political Parties. American Political Science Association," *American Political Science Review*, vol. 44 (September 1950), 15; Austin Ranney, *Curing the Mischiefs of Faction: Party Reform in America* (Berkeley: University of California, 1975); Jake Bernstein, "Elephant Wars: The Christian Right Flexes Its Muscles at the Republican Convention," *Texas Observer*, July 5, 2002, 8–9.

Meanwhile, during his tenure in office, Perry concentrated on urging the legislature to pass tangible, business-oriented policies such as tort reform, tax relief, and lightening of regulation. He thus managed to appeal to both halves of his party's coalition, the social conservatives through symbolism and the economic conservatives through policies. As long as Republican politicians such as Perry are able to thus combine both sides of the party in their individual persons, Republicans will not be split into antagonistic factions.

Geographic Distribution

Because the Republicans are the clearly dominant party in Texas, it is easier to describe the areas where they are weak than the areas where they are strong. They are weakest in the areas of the state where Mexican Americans are in the majority or nearly so—along the Rio Grande. They are also less dominant in central Texas, in the "Golden Triangle" of cities in the extreme southeastern part of the state, and in a few counties in the piney woods near the Louisiana border. As a rule, they are less important in the central cities (where minorities are numerous) than in the suburbs or small towns. Everywhere else, their advantage ranges from decisive to overwhelming.

Socioeconomic and Ethnic Distribution

GOP activists come from a relatively narrow socioeconomic and ethnic base. Most candidates and party activists are Anglo, middle or upper class, businesspersons or professionals. Since 1994, they have tended to be evangelical Protestants, although Steve Munisteri, the present state party chair, is Presbyterian. A sprinkling of African Americans and Latinos can be found among active Republicans (such as Railroad Commissioner Michael Williams and Supreme Court Chief Justice Wallace Jefferson, who are Black), but the party has not appealed to significant numbers of minorities at the electoral level since the 1960s. Furthermore, the party's traditional opposition to policies such as welfare and job-training programs aimed at helping the poor has generally ensured that its activists and voters would be fairly wealthy.

Conservative Democrats

Despite the fact that Texas has a "two-party system," it has for several decades actually offered its citizens three voting options, for the Democrats historically have been split into two factions. This "three-faction system" has the advantage of making more choices available to voters and the disadvantage of making Texas politics more confusing and chaotic than it might otherwise be.

Conservative Democrats are the representatives of habits of thought and behavior that survive from when Texas was part of the Old South. This traditionalist culture is very conservative on social issues, but tends to be conflicted and inconsistent on economic issues. Many southerners are normally conservative economically, but can be aroused to a fervent belief in the ability of government to protect the little people of society from wealthy individuals and corporations—an attitude that has historically been known as **populism**. The Populist (People's) Party was strong in Texas during the 1890s, and candidates who make populist-type appeals, such as Jim Ferguson (governor from 1915 to 1917) and W. Lee "Pappy" O'Daniel (1939–1941), have sometimes been elected. This populist streak makes the Old South part of Texas hard to predict on economic issues.

At the level of the party activists and officeholders, the conservative faction of the Democratic Party is slightly less devoted to laissez faire than Republicans, but much more so than the liberal faction. It tends to be conservative on social issues, although conservative Democratic candidates have been known to bend to the left on social issues in an attempt to persuade minority citizens to vote for them.

Geographic Distribution

The historical base of conservative Democrats is the piney woods of East Texas, where the traditionalist political culture is strongest. As Republicans have made major inroads among White conservatives, this base has shrunk considerably.

Small cities and rural areas in other parts of the state sometimes remain conservative Democratic in their affiliation, although they are steadily evolving toward greater Republican strength. Conservative Democratic candidates now have to court Hispanic voters to have any hope of success, a necessity that causes them to moderate their issue positions, especially on social issues.

Socioeconomic and Ethnic Distribution

Representing the historically dominant wing of the party, until the 1980s conservative Democrats drew support from all classes in Texas, but that pattern has changed as Republicans have continued to increase their support among the wealthy. Like the Republicans, they have historically been popular among the Anglo middle and upper classes, business and professional people, and white-collar workers. Unlike the Republicans, they also drew substantial support from workers, especially those in rural areas and small cities. Again, this pattern may be changing as the Republicans grow in popularity.

Liberal Democrats

Liberals usually recommend policies that depend on government's being active in economic affairs, especially on behalf of those who have less wealth and power. They tend, however, to oppose government intervention in personal life. Former Governor Ann Richards (who died in 2006) and former mayor of San Antonio (and also former U.S. Secretary of Housing and Urban Development) Henry Cisneros are good examples of Texas liberal Democrats. The most famous and successful of all Texas Democratic politicians, Lyndon Johnson, was mainly, although somewhat inconsistently, a liberal. While a member of the U.S. House of Representatives from 1937 to 1949, he sided with the left wing of the national party. While U.S. senator from 1949 to 1961, he leaned more toward the conservative side. As president from 1963 to 1969, however, he provided vigorous liberal leadership to the country.

Geographic Distribution

In recent elections, liberal Democrats have been most successful in the areas of Texas where Hispanics are most numerous, in southern and far western areas of the state along and near the border with Mexico. Liberals are also strong where labor unions are a factor: in far East Texas, in East Central Texas, and along some of the Gulf Coast. Liberals can usually rely on doing well in Austin,

the Beaumont–Port Arthur–Orange complex, San Antonio, Corpus Christi, and El Paso. They are few and weak in all of North Texas, the Panhandle, and the south plains; they win very small percentages of the vote in the suburbs around the state's large cities, and they are noticeably absent in the cities of Amarillo, Lubbock, and Midland–Odessa.

Socioeconomic and Ethnic Distribution

Identifying the socioeconomic components of liberal Democratic strength in Texas is more complex than in the case of Republicans or conservative Democrats. Liberals form, at best, an uneasy coalition. While it can be said that liberal strength comes mostly from labor unions, African Americans, Mexican Americans, and certain educated Anglos, the mix is a volatile one that does not make for stable cooperation. White middle- and upper-class liberals can support African Americans and Mexican Americans in their quest for equal treatment, but labor unions have sometimes been cool in this area. African Americans and Mexican Americans usually give little support to reform legislation—of campaign spending and lobbying, for example—or to efforts to protect the natural environment, which energize Anglo liberals. Many Mexican Americans have sometimes been reluctant to vote for African American candidates, and vice versa.

Liberal leadership comes largely, but not exclusively, from the legal, teaching, and other professions. In earlier years, union officials provided leadership for the liberal faction, and in some areas, they still do. But leading the liberal Democrats is an uncertain business, especially after the electoral disasters the party has experienced since 1994.

The Uncertain Future of the Democratic Party

In the surveys reported on pages 107 and 116 of this chapter, we saw that about 17 percent of Texans claim to be liberal, but that 39 percent identify as Democrats. Roughly, then, 22 percent of the state's adult population could be considered to be conservative or moderate Democrats. The problem for the party's leaders in the state is to try to fashion campaign strategies that will appeal to both the liberals (who dominate the party organization) and conservatives (who must form a large chunk of any potential voting majority), as well as to enough moderates to fashion a winning coalition on election days.

This is a very difficult challenge, one that Democrats have not been able to overcome since 1990. During the 2002 campaign, three of the Democrats' major candidates, Tony Sanchez (governor), Ron Kirk (U.S. senator), and John Sharp (lieutenant governor), were so conservative on economic issues that they were virtually indistinguishable from their Republican opponents, differing from the GOP candidates primarily by being more liberal on such social issues as affirmative action and abortion. Chris Bell and Bill White, the party's candidates for governor in 2006 and 2010, however, were clearly liberal on most issues. Yet all these candidates lost.

It might appear, therefore, that the outlook for Democrats of any ideology appears hopeless in Texas. Yet there are facts below the surface that suggest that the party's potential is brighter than it now seems. In the next chapter we will examine the factors that may make for a future Democratic revival.

Third Parties in Texas

Texas has had its share of **third parties**. The Know-Nothing Party, representing those who objected to Roman Catholics and immigrants, made a brief appearance before the Civil War. After the Civil War, the Greenback Party, which advocated inflation of the dollar, made an equally brief visit.

More important was the Populist (People's) Party, which reflected widespread discontent among farmers and other "little people." The Populists advocated an extensive program of government regulation of big business and economic policy reform. In particular, the party's 1892 national platform recommended government ownership and operation of railroads, confiscation of all land owned by corporations "in excess of their actual needs," and an income tax for individuals.[21] The fact that the Populist candidate for president drew 100,000 votes in Texas in 1892—almost 20 percent of the votes cast—illustrates the point that Texas's normal political conservatism can be credibly challenged.

New parties cannot get on Texas ballots by simply announcing their intention to run candidates. To allow every splinter group to call itself a party and thereby grab a line on the ballot would make for confusing, chaotic elections with dozens of candidates running for each office. In addition, of course, the major parties are not eager to make it easy for upstart competitors to grab the attention of voters. As a result, every democratic country, and every American state, has laws that discriminate in some manner against new parties.

Texas has some of the toughest ballot access laws in the nation. A person nominated for statewide office by one of the major parties is automatically accorded a spot on the ballot. But, in the days following the April primary

Anemia is a disease associated with physical weakness. Here cartoonist Ben Sargent uses anemia as a metaphor for the Texas Democratic Party's seeming inability to field strong statewide candidates against the dominant Republicans in the 2006 election year. The Democrats were even more anemic in 2010.

Courtesy of Ben Sargent.

runoffs, an independent candidate must collect signatures totaling 1 percent of all the votes cast in the last gubernatorial election. These signatures must come from registered voters who did not participate in a primary or runoff that year. All signatures must be accompanied by the voter's registration identification number. The rules vary somewhat for candidates for federal offices and local offices, and for parties as opposed to individuals, but none of them are permissive. If a party manages to collect enough signatures to get its candidates on a ballot, it can ensure itself a place for the next election by garnering 5 percent of the vote for any statewide office or 2 percent of the gubernatorial vote. Needless to say, these rules prevent most independent and third-party candidates from ever getting on the ballot.

Nevertheless, Libertarians have qualified for the ballot in every election since 1986. They are the consistent antigovernment party, opposing any regulation of the economy (which makes them more conservative than the Republicans on economic issues) and equally opposing regulation of personal life (disapproving of the war on drugs, for example, which makes them more liberal than the Democrats on social issues). Although their candidates attract only a small percentage of the vote in any given election, the leaders of these parties have hopes of becoming a major force in the future.

Old Tea in a New Package?

The biggest news to come out of the 2010 election was the rise of the Tea Party, which was not, in fact, a political party but a faction within the Republican Party whose members aspired to take it over. Although its name hearkens back to a famous group of colonial Boston patriots who protested the British government's imposition of a tax on tea in 1773, the name is actually misleading. The pre-Revolution protestors were objecting to the fact that they could be taxed without having representation in the British parliament, but today's Tea Partiers have every democratic right and privilege, including representation in Congress.

The Republicans, like the Democrats, are a coalition of many interests. An interest that is nationally important to both major parties, because of its ability to generate campaign contributions, is the community of investors generally known by the catch all nickname "Wall Street." When the entire U.S. economy seemed about to seize up because of the implosion of the "subprime" (high-risk) real estate lending industry in late 2008, the Republican George W. Bush administration sponsored a gigantic $800 billion "bailout" of a small number of banks that were so big and important that their failure might cripple the entire economy. A few months later, the new Democratic Obama administration continued the policy of saving the big banks. The bank bailout may have prevented the coming of a second Great Depression, but it was extremely unpopular with citizens in general, who saw the federal government saving rich people from the consequences of their own foolish behavior, while allowing ordinary people to lose their homes. The wave of anger that swept the country resulted, in 2009, in the founding of the Tea Party movement.

National opinion surveys have shown that Tea Partiers are actually conservative Republicans who are so angry at their own party that they have been inspired to organize, campaign, and vote for candidates in primaries who generally advocate smaller, less active government and lower taxes, and specifically promise to oppose all future bail-

(continued)

(continued)

outs of any industry. In the 2010 Republican primaries, the Tea Party movement was responsible for defeating "establishment" candidates across the country, including Senatorial candidates in Nevada, Delaware, and Alaska. It has thus thrown a major scare into all Republicans in every state, and thereby pushed the party as a whole to the right.

In the Lone Star State, specific Tea Party candidates did not upset any "regular" Republicans in 2010, partly because most Texas Republicans were already very conservative on economic issues, and partly because all of the party's candidates rhetorically endorsed Tea Party values.

Organizationally, the Texas Tea Party, like its national counterpart, is a movement with many different actors and structures. The various Web sites advertising themselves as speaking for the state Tea Party agree on the core objectives of making government smaller, lowering taxes, and slashing spending. Individual groups emphasize other specific goals, such as recognizing that the United States is a Christian nation, defending the right to own guns, opposing the teaching of evolution, and stopping illegal immigration. It is probably the emphasis of some Tea Party groups on advocating socially conservative causes that prevents Tea Partiers from simply becoming Libertarians.

It is unlikely that the Tea Party will become an actual third party in Texas, running candidates independently. It will most likely continue to be a force encouraging an already very conservative state Republican Party to become even more conservative.

Source: Many Web sites and press reports from 2009 to 2011.

African Americans have never established a separate political party in Texas, although their main interest group, the National Association for the Advancement of Colored People (NAACP), often functions as a subfaction of the liberal Democrats.

Mexican Americans have established several well-known political interest groups aimed at improving the lot of Spanish-speaking Texans. In the 1970s, however, Mexican Americans formed their first true political party named La Raza Unida (*la raza* means "the race"), which won some local elections—notably in Crystal City—and even ran candidates for governor and other state offices. But infiltrated by the FBI for alleged radicalism and beset by personal and factional feuds, the party was out of existence by the early 1980s. Mexican Americans in Texas are currently represented by a number of organizations, including LULAC (see Chapter 3) and the Mexican American Legal Defense and Educational Fund (MALDEF), and by two organizations within the Democratic Party, Mexican American Democrats (MAD) and Tejano Democrats. What organizational patterns future Mexican American politics will take is not clear, but it seems certain that Mexican Americans will be of growing importance in Texas politics, as they form an increasingly large percentage of the state's population.

Summary

Ideology is one of the most important bases for political parties everywhere, but in Texas, where parties have historically been weak, ideology has usually been more important than party affiliation. The major ideological conflict has been between conservatives and liberals. Liberals tend to favor government regulation of the economy, but oppose it in personal life, whereas conservatives tend to favor regulation of personal life, but oppose it in the economy. These basic differences lead to differences in many areas of public policy, from taxation to abortion. The Texas Republican Party is consistently strongly conservative, but the Democratic Party is split, at least temporarily, into a conservative and a liberal faction.

Parties appeal to interests, as well as to ideology, to mobilize voter support and campaign contributions. In attempting to form winning coalitions by putting together groups of voters and contributors, they sometimes reinforce their ideological leanings and sometimes violate them.

From 1874 to the 1970s, Texas was a one-party Democratic state. One-party states are characterized by an absence of party competition, inadequate debate about public policy, low voter turnout, and usually conservative public policy. For a while in the 1980s and 1990s, Texas appeared to have established vigorous two-party competition, but in retrospect, those decades witnessed a transition to what may be one-party Republican rule.

Texas's political parties have both temporary and permanent party organizations. Nominations are made in primaries, and party leaders have no control over candidates or officeholders. Thus, party organization is much less important than ideology and interests in explaining the politics of the state. This lack of organizational strength means that Texas's parties are not "responsible" and are incapable of fulfilling some of the functions that they would perform in an ideal democracy. Nevertheless, in today's political situation, there is at least robust and spirited debate of public policy. Furthermore, the increasing partisan intensity in the legislature that accompanied the war over redistricting in 2003 and the Republican electoral sweep of 2010 may be a sign that Texas's parties are about to become more organized, disciplined, and coherent.

Texas has given birth to a number of third parties, none of which have achieved permanence but several of which have influenced public policy in the state.

Glossary Terms

coalition

conservatism

faction

ideology

interest

liberalism

one-party system

permanent party organization

political party

political socialization

populism

pseudo laissez faire

realignment

temporary party organization

third party

5

Voting, Campaigns, and Elections

Governor Rick Perry (top left) and challenger Bill White (below center) are shown campaigning in the gubernatorial contest of 2010. Perry was evidently more persuasive, because the voters chose him for another term.

Suppose they gave an election and nobody came?

Bumper sticker from the 1960s

Politics has got so expensive that it takes lots of money to even get beat with.

Will Rogers, American humorist, 1931

INTRODUCTION

Nothing is more basic to the concept of democratic government than the principle of elected representatives freely chosen by the majority of the people, with each person's vote counting equally. In an ideal democracy, election campaigns are contests conducted by rival candidates for the people's support. Candidates debate public policy rather than engaging in a competition of personal insult and insinuations. On the official voting day, citizens cast their ballots on the basis of their evaluation of the debate, with almost everyone participating. On the other hand, in a bad democracy, election campaigns deal in trivialities, evasions, and slanders, candidates pay more attention to the wants of special-interest contributors than to the needs of the public, and very few citizens bother to participate on election day. Is Texas close to or far from the democratic ideal of campaigns and elections?

The overall purpose of this chapter is to provide readers with information that will allow them to begin to answer this question for themselves. The chapter begins with a consideration of the reasons that voting is important to democracy. The topics that follow include the history of the suffrage (the right to vote) in Texas, the state's registration procedures, and its disturbingly low voter turnout. The focus next turns to election campaigns, with special attention given to the impact of money on the outcome. Afterward, the various types of public elections in Texas are described. Next, the election campaigns and voting results of 1994 through 2010 are chronicled. The chapter concludes with a comparison of the reality of Texas elections with the democratic ideal and an argument that there is much room for improvement.

OBJECTIVES

After reading this chapter, you should be able to

Explain why voting is important to a democratic society.

Discuss types of campaign resources, efforts to restrict the power of money in campaigns, and the issue of negative campaigning.

Describe the types of public elections held in Texas.

Describe voting trends in Texas during the last two decades, and explain their political significance.

Voting

Because voting is such an important activity, it will be helpful to discuss both the relevance of voting to democratic theory and the way voting is practiced in Texas.

Why Vote?

As is the case with many important questions, the answer to "Why vote?" is, "It depends." It depends on whether voting is viewed from the perspective of the individual voter, of the candidates, or of the political system.

From the perspective of the individual voter, there may seem to be no logic in voting, for public elections are almost never won by the margin of a single vote, except perhaps in small towns and special districts. The individual voter has very little hope of affecting the outcome of an election. Why, then, do so many people bother to register and vote?

The main reason people register and vote is that they do not think of voting in completely logical terms. Like other political behavior, voting is governed not only by reason, but also by personal loyalties, ideological fervor, custom, and habit. Most people vote primarily because they have been taught that it is their duty as citizens (as, in fact, it is). And even though a single vote is unlikely to affect the outcome of an election, participation in the governing of the community is important to the self-development of each individual.

From the perspective of the candidate, voting is extremely important. There is a saying among politicians that "votes are counted one by one by one." It expresses the insight that although citizens may seem to be part of a mass, it is a mass of individual personalities, each with their own motivations, ideology, interests, and hopes for the future. Politicians who forget that each potential supporter is an individual soon find themselves forcibly retired.

From the perspective of the political system, elections are crucial. In democratic theory, it is the participation of the citizens that makes government legitimate (that is, morally right and worthy of support). When large numbers of citizens neglect or refuse to vote, this raises questions about the most basic underpinnings of political authority.

Voting also performs other functions in a democratic society. The act of participating in an election decreases alienation and opposition by making people feel that they are part of the system. Further, the electorate does have an effect on public policy when it chooses one set of candidates who endorse one set of policies over another. Although one vote is unlikely to determine the outcome of an election, groups of like-minded citizens who vote the same way can be decisive.

Finally, large-scale voting has the added virtue of helping to prevent corruption. It is relatively easy to rig an election when only a few people bother to go to the polls. One of the best guarantees of honest government is a large turnout on election day.

So, despite the fact that one vote almost never matters, democracy depends on each citizen acting as if it does. When people take their right to vote seriously and act as responsible citizens, the system works. When they refuse to participate and stay home on election day, they abdicate control over government to the elites and special interests who are only too happy to run things. We can at least partly judge the extent to which a country or state has a legitimate government by the level of voter turnout among its citizens.

How does Texas stack up? This question will be addressed shortly. First, however, we must look at the legal context of the voting act. The most important parts of that context are suffrage and the system of registration.

Suffrage

One of the most important historical developments in American politics has been the expansion of the **suffrage**—the right to vote. The writers of the U.S. Constitution in 1787 delegated to the states the power to determine voter eligibility in both national and state elections. At that time, each state decreed the qualifications for voting within its boundaries, and limitations on the suffrage were widespread. Generally, states restricted the suffrage to adult White male property owners who professed a certain religious belief, which varied with the state. As a result of these restrictions, only about 5 percent of the 3,939,214 persons counted in the first national census in 1790 were eligible to vote. An even lower percentage actually went to the polls.

Since that era, a series of democratic reform movements has slowly expanded the suffrage. In the 1820s and 1830s, church membership and property ownership were removed as qualifications for voting in most elections. After the Civil War, the Fourteenth and Fifteenth Amendments to the Constitution were enacted in an attempt to guarantee full political rights to the freed slaves. At first, African Americans voted in substantial numbers. But the southern states, including Texas, retaliated with a series of legal and informal restrictions that succeeded in withdrawing the suffrage from African American citizens in most parts of the old Confederacy by 1900. (It is partly because of persistent southern resistance to Black suffrage that the region is said to have a "traditionalistic" political culture, as discussed in Chapter 1.) It was not until 1965, when Congress passed the Voting Rights Act, that the federal government began to enforce the right of African Americans to vote. In subsequent years, federal court decisions expanded the protection of Black suffrage. Women were enfranchised with the ratification of the Nineteenth Amendment in 1920; and in 1971, the Twenty-sixth Amendment lowered the minimum voting age to eighteen.

Several points stand out in this two-century evolution of the right to vote. First, it is not exclusively Texan, but part of a national, even a worldwide, movement toward expanded suffrage. Within the United States, suffrage has been substantially nationalized. States still enact laws, but they do so within guidelines set down by the Constitution, Congress, and the Supreme Court and enforced by the federal Justice Department.

Second, an important part of the story of the struggle to include all citizens in the suffrage has been the fact that well into the 1970s, Texas and other southern states attempted to evade and obstruct the post–Civil War amendments and, later, the Voting Rights Act. They came up with various gimmicks such as poll taxes, White-only primaries, literacy tests, and more to keep African Americans from exercising the franchise.[1] These obstructions also successfully discouraged many Mexican Americans and poor Whites from voting. As a result, voter turnout in the South was far below the levels prevailing in the North.

Third, however, an equally important part of the story is that the federal government, supported by concerned citizens in both the North and South, gradually defeated these antidemocratic schemes, so that by the mid-1970s, all adult Americans had the legal right to vote. As will be discussed shortly, not all of them exercised that right, but at least state governments were no longer

preventing them from going to the polling booth. The legal battle for democratic suffrage had been won.

Registration

Every democratic political system has a **voter registration** procedure to distinguish qualified voters from those who are ineligible because of immaturity, lack of citizenship, mental incapacity, or other reasons. In most countries, registration is easy; in some nations, the government goes to great lengths to make sure that all citizens are registered before every election.

Like the other former slaveholding states of the old Confederacy, however, for most of its history, Texas used a series of legal devices to deliberately limit registration and thus voting. The most effective and longest lasting of the antiregistration schemes was the poll tax. This was a $1.50 fee that served as the state's system of registration during the first part of the twentieth century. Those who paid it by January 31 were registered to vote in that year's elections. It discouraged less wealthy citizens from registering, for back before inflation had eroded the value of the dollar, the fee represented a substantial portion of a poor person's income. Because people had to be registered in order to vote, this tax was a convenient

Anti-Fraud or Anti-Democrat?

During the 2005, 2007, and 2009 legislative sessions, Republican representatives introduced legislation, which, if it had passed, would have required citizens to show a photo identification, such as a driver's license, before they could be issued a ballot at a polling booth on election day. In the first two sessions, the bills passed the House of Representatives, but were killed by Democratic parliamentary maneuvers in the Senate. In the 2009 session, the reverse occurred, with a Democratic "slowdown" of the legislative process preventing consideration of the voter ID bill in the House, after it had passed the Senate. Before being defeated, however, these proposals sparked heated debate between the parties, both in and out of the legislature.

Republicans argued that under the present system of voter identification, fraud is too easy and has become too common. People need a driver's license to rent a movie or a DVD, they argued, and it is at least as important to prevent dishonest voting as to prevent dishonest film renting. Democrats countered that there was no evidence of widespread voter fakery, and that the real purpose of the measure was to disenfranchise people who tend not to have photo identification—older, minority citizens who tend to vote Democratic. The voter ID bill, they charged, was actually a new form of poll tax.

During the 2011 legislature, Republicans had such large majorities in both houses that Democratic arguments and Democratic maneuvering were both equally futile. The "voter identification" bill passed easily.

Sources: Tim Eaton, "Emotional Voter ID Bill Debate Ends in Passage," *Austin American-Statesman*, March 24, 2011, B1; Jason Embry and Corrie MacLaggan, "Key Bills Left for Dead Amid House Slowdown," *Austin American-Statesman*, May 27, 2009, A1; Mark Lisheron, "A Dewhurst Promise, and Voter ID Bill Dies," *Austin American-Statesman*, May 24, 2007, B7; Tom Aldred and Brent Connett, "ID Rule Will Bolster Integrity of Elections," *Austin American-Statesman*, May 1, 2007, A7; Nathanael Isaacson, "Call ID Rule What It Is— A New Kind of Poll Tax," *Austin American-Statesman*, April 28, 2007, A21; Tina Benkiser, "Democrats Are Blocking a Bill to Halt Voter Fraud," *Austin American-Statesman*, May 16, 2005, A13; Leticia Van de Putte, "Texans Shouldn't Need Driver's Licenses to Vote," *Austin American-Statesman*, May 18, 2005, A11.

The easier it is to vote, the more poor, uneducated citizens are able to exercise their democratic rights, but the easier fraud becomes. The harder it is to vote, the less we must worry about fraud, but the fewer poor and uneducated citizens will vote. In this cartoon, Ben Sargent takes his stand with making voting easy, and against Republican bills that would, if passed, have made it harder in the name of preventing fraud, and against a law, passed by the 2011 legislature, that makes voting more difficult.

Courtesy of Ben Sargent.

way for the more affluent to ensure that they would not have to share power with their fellow citizens. Moreover, because minority citizens were usually poor, this device had the deliberate effect of keeping the ballot box a White preserve.

In 1964, the nation adopted the Twenty-fourth Amendment to the Constitution, outlawing the poll tax. Two years later, the U.S. Supreme Court threw out Texas's tax. The state legislature then devised a new system of voter registration. Although no tax had to be paid, the period of annual registration was identical: October 1 through January 31. Because most poor people (especially minorities) had little education, they were not apt to follow public affairs as closely as those with more education. By the time they became interested in an upcoming election, they had often missed their chance to register. The new law, then, was another ploy to reserve the ballot box for the White and wealthy.

In January 1971, a federal district court struck down this registration law as a violation of the **Equal Protection Clause** of the Fourteenth Amendment to the U.S. Constitution.[2] Declaring two provisions of the law—the annual registration requirement and the very early deadline for registration—to be discriminatory, the court expressed the opinion that 1.2 million Texans were disenfranchised by them. Later that year, the legislature responded with a new law that made registration much easier. Its major provisions, as amended, are as follows:

1. **Initial registration.** The voter may register either in person or by mail. A parent, child, or spouse who is registered may register for the voter.

2. **Permanency.** The voter remains registered as long as he or she remains qualified. A new voter registration card is issued every two years.

3. **Period of registration.** Voters may register at any time and may vote in any election, provided that they are registered thirty days prior to the election.

To vote in Texas today, one must

a. Be a United States citizen eighteen years of age by election day.

b. Be a resident of the state and county for thirty days immediately prior to election day.

c. Be a resident of the election precinct on election day.

d. Have registered to vote at least thirty days prior to election day.

e. Not be a convicted felon or, if convicted, have finished serving one's sentence.

Texas Turnout

It is not just whether voters choose to support a given candidate from a given party that is important. Whether or not citizens actually "turn out" to vote on election day is equally important in a democracy.

Government by the People?

Despite the fact that registration has been relatively easy in Texas for four decades, **voter turnout,** while climbing erratically, is still below national levels. Voter turnout means the proportion of the eligible citizens who actually cast ballots—not the proportion of those registered, but the proportion of adult citizens.

Table 5-1 shows that the percentage of Texans voting in both presidential and off-year congressional elections is considerably lower than the percentage voting nationally. An average of 47.3 percent of eligible Texans turned out for presidential balloting in the three-plus decades since the new registration law went into effect, and an average of 30.8 percent turned out for off-year congressional elections. In the 2008 presidential balloting, Texas voter turnout was about 8 percentage points below the turnout level in the country as a whole, and in the 2010 congressional contest, it was about ten points below. In only the two most recent presidential elections did the state's turnout rise as high as 50 percent—although the trend line is comforting in this regard.

Turnout for state offices is usually even lower than for national elections, and turnout for local offices is lower still. Many mayors have been elected with the votes of fewer than 10 percent of their city's electorate. In other words, government in Texas is never "by the people." At best, it is by a smidgen more than half the people; often, it is by a quarter of the people or even fewer.

TABLE 5-1

Percentage of Voting-Age Population Voting in National Elections, 1972–2010

Presidential Elections										
	1972	1976	1980	1984	1988	1992	1996	2000	2004	2008
U.S.	55.5	54.3	51.8	53.1	50.2	55.2	50.8	52.2	60.3	61.7
TEXAS	45.4	47.3	44.7	47.2	44.2	49.0	43.0	45.0	53.4	53.7

Off-Year Congressional Elections (House of Representatives)										
	1974	1978	1982	1986	1990	1994	1998	2002	2006	2010
U.S.	36.1	35.1	38.0	36.4	35.0	38.9	37.6	39.0	39.5	40.0
TEXAS	18.4	24.0	26.2	29.1	26.8	35.0	28.0	32.0	30.1	30.0

SOURCES: *Statistical Abstract of the United States*, 101st ed. (Washington, D.C.: U.S. Department of Commerce, Bureau of the Census, 1980), 517; 106th ed. (1989), 259; Federal Elections Commission, Washington, D.C., "Political Intelligence," *Texas Observer*, November 27, 1992, 8; "Voter Turnout Higher Than in '98, Survey Says," *Dallas Morning News*, November 7, 2002, A15; for 2004, 2006, and 2008, Walter Dean Burnham, Department of Government, University of Texas at Austin; for 2010, Richard Murray, Professor of Political Science, University of Houston.

Why Don't Texans Vote?

Americans in general are not known for high voter turnouts, but Texans seem to vote even less often than the residents of many other states. Why?

Texas is a rather poor state with a very uneven distribution of wealth. In 2010, the U.S. Census Bureau estimated that it had the sixth-highest rate of poverty among all the states. More than 17 percent of its citizens fell below the threshold of $10,956 for a single adult or $21,954 for a family of four.[3] The poverty rate is important because the poor and less educated, in the absence of strong parties to persuade them to go to the polls on election day, have a tendency to stay home. When the poor don't vote, the overall turnout rate is low.

The differences between rich and poor citizens are strongly related to differences between turnout rates for ethnic groups. Consider, for example, the national voter turnout rates for Hispanics, Anglos, and African Americans in the 2004 and 2008 presidential and 2006 congressional elections (see Table 5-2).[4] As in the nation as a whole, minorities in Texas tend to go to the polls at lower rates than Anglos. (The turnout for African Americans in 2008 was exceptionally high, undoubtedly because of the attraction of Barack Obama, a Black candidate, at the top of the ticket). The low overall state turnout rate is at least partly caused by the tendency of Black and Latino citizens to stay home on election day. Thus, those who vote tend to be richer, better educated, and White; those who abstain tend to be poorer, uneducated, and minority. This does not mean that all Anglos vote, or that all minorities stay home on election day. But in democratic politics, statistical probabilities have major consequences.

TABLE 5-2

Self-Reported Voter Turnout for Federal Elections, 2004, 2006, and 2008

Year	Anglo	Hispanic (any race)	African American
2004	60.3%	28%	56.3%
2006	45.8	19.3	38.6
2008	59.6	31.6	59.6

NOTE: The source for this table is self-reported voter turnout compiled by the U.S. Census Bureau. It has long been known that people tend to exaggerate the extent of their past participation because voting is a socially desirable activity. Thus, these figures inevitably contain an upward bias to an unknown extent.

NOTE: Information for 2010 election not yet available.

The Consequences of Nonvoting

The participation differences among ethnic groups in Texas have an important impact on public policy. Minority citizens tend to have more liberal opinions about what government should be doing, at least partly because they are more likely to be poorer than Anglos. When they fail to go to the polls, however, their views become irrelevant. Because the more conservative White citizens vote at higher rates, their preferences usually determine which candidates win and therefore which policies are pursued by government. Low minority turnout is thus one of the major explanations for conservative public policy in Texas.

For example, minorities as a whole are far more Democratic than are Anglos. According to a 2008 survey, only 28.1 percent of the state's Anglos identified themselves as Democrats, compared to 57.4 percent of Hispanics and 89.7 percent of Blacks.[5] Nothing is permanent in politics, and rising incomes or some other circumstance may change the balance of party identification among ethnic groups in the future. But for the present, when minorities do not vote, it hurts Democrats.

Participation Is Easy

Voting turnout tends to be low among students. Nevertheless, it is very easy for students to register and vote if they want to. Campus political clubs often hand out voter-registration forms, school newspapers frequently list polling areas in advance of election day, and schools themselves commonly provide venues for early voting. Individuals also can access voter registration information by logging on to the state Secretary of State's office. Go on the Web to www.sos.state.tx.us/ and click on the "Vote" icon at the top left of the page, then the "Voter Information" label, and finally the "Request a Voter Registration Application" label.

Furthermore, it is not just any Democrats who suffer from low minority turnout. The liberal wing of the party needs minority support to win. As Tables 5-3 and 5-4 illustrate, African Americans and Hispanics often hold views on public policy that are clearly more liberal than the opinions of Anglos. Once again, the future may differ from the past and present. For now, however, it seems clear that if African American and Hispanic Texans had higher turnout rates, liberal Democrats would win elections much more often. Such an outcome would mean that government policy in Texas would be more liberal. As it is, the liberals rarely go to the polls, so state government remains conservative. Chapters 6, 11, 13, and 14 go into detail about some of the policy consequences of Texas's different turnout patterns among ethnic groups.

The importance of different ethnic turnout rates compels the conclusion that the description of trends in Texas Republican Party success in Chapter 4 must be modified. Chapter 4 presented a portrait of a state that has recently undergone a "realignment" from a normal Democratic majority to a normal Republican majority. Now it can be seen that the realignment scenario depends on a continuation of ethnic differences in voter turnout. Furthermore, Texas's Latino population is rapidly growing (see Chapter 1), and because Mexican Americans generally vote Democratic when they do participate, they present the Democratic Party with a so-far-unrealized potential to resume its majority status among Texans.

Thus, it can be said with some confidence that, in the near future, the Republicans will continue to dominate Texas, *as long as its minority citizens*

TABLE 5-3

White and African American Public Opinion in Texas, 2009–2010

Issue	Percent Agreeing Among	
	White	African American
Teach "Intelligent Design" in public-school biology classes, either along with, or instead of, Darwinism (2009)	62	36
Strongly support an English-only amendment to state constitution (2009)	59	24
Approve "strongly" or "somewhat" of the job that President Obama is doing as president	22.5	79.2
Consider yourself to be a part of the "Tea Party" movement	39.1	12.1
Strongly support blocking the "Obamacare" health care reform law	64.8	23.1
Support increased spending on border security	65.8	36.7
Strongly support Arizona immigration law (which is harsh on illegal immigrants)	67.2	24.2

SOURCE: Texas Polls of March 2009 and September 2010.

TABLE 5-4

Anglo and Hispanic Public Opinion in Texas, 2009–2010

Question	Anglos	Hispanics
Oppose English-only amendment to state constitution (2009)	19	57
Approve "strongly" or "somewhat" of the job President Obama is doing as president	22.5	37.6
Consider yourself to be part of the "Tea Party" movement?	39.1	16.1
Strongly support Arizona immigration law (which is harsh on illegal immigrants)	67.2	28.4
Strongly support blocking "Obamacare" health care reform law	64.8	37.8
Support increased spending on border security	65.8	37.6

Source: UT–Austin Texas Poll, February–March 2009 and September 2010.

continue to stay away from the voting booths. The Republican trend, which seems so solid when viewed from the perspective of election results since 1994, is actually quite fragile and could be easily upset if the Democrats learn how to inspire their partisans to vote.

Election Campaigns

Democracies do not hold elections unannounced. There is a period of time before the voting day in which the candidates attempt to persuade potential voters to support them. This period is the **campaign.** In Texas, would-be officeholders run initially during the spring primary campaign. Those who win nomination in the primary then campaign to win the November general election.

Campaign Resources

Whatever their strategies, candidates must have two essential resources: people and money.

People

The people who are needed to work in campaigns are both professionals and volunteers. The professionals plan, organize, and manage the campaign; write the speeches; and raise the money. Volunteer workers are the active amateurs who distribute literature, register and canvass voters, attend the phone banks, and transport supporters to the polls on election day. No major election can be won without competent people who are brought together early enough to plan,

organize, and conduct an effective campaign or without a sufficient number of volunteers to make the personal contacts and get out the vote.

The act of volunteering to work on a campaign is not only useful to the candidate, but also is of great importance to the volunteers and to the democratic process. People who work on a campaign learn about the stupendous exertions, the difficult choices, and the painful blunders that make up public life in a free society. They learn tolerance for other points of view, how to argue and evaluate the arguments of other people, and why the media are important. Finally, they learn that when they win, the faults of the republic are not all corrected and that, when they lose, civilization does not collapse. They learn, in other words, to be good citizens. In Texas as elsewhere, political campaigns are the most intense means of creating the truly participatory society.

Professional and voluntary participation, the first major resource of campaigns, is thus entirely uncontroversial. Everyone endorses it. But about the second resource, money, there is great controversy.

Money

Except in many municipal elections, where volunteers are most important, money is the most important campaign resource. Politicians need money to publicize their candidacies, especially over television. For example, Tony Sanchez spent more than $67 million (62 percent of it for television advertising) attempting to defeat Rick Perry and win the governorship in 2002. Perry spent almost $40 million to defeat Bill White in 2010. Also in 2010, David Dewhurst spent more than $7.5 million to win the Lieutenant Governorship, and Greg Abbott spent $4.5 million to be re-elected Attorney General.[6] (We are not using figures from 2006 because the Democratic candidates in those campaigns tended to be underfunded.)

It is clear that politicians who run for statewide offices commonly spend millions of dollars on their campaigns. But even candidates for state House seats, which are normally rather small in geographic extent, typically spend in the hundreds of thousands. Why does campaigning cost so much?

Running for office within Texas is commonly very expensive because candidates feel that they must rely on television advertising to get their message across. Although there are many cheaper methods of campaigning—having volunteers go through neighborhoods door-to-door leaving campaign literature, for example—political professionals believe that the most effective way to reach and motivate voters is to advertise on television. Moreover, campaigning via TV is not just a one-shot effort. Campaign organizations must buy ads repeatedly over several months in the many state media markets, because campaigners believe (as do advertisers of commercial products) that citizens must be sent the message many times if it is to have an effect on their thinking and behavior. The need to buy campaign advertising in many such media repeatedly over a period of months makes the cost of running for office in the Lone Star State formidable.

Table 5-5 illustrates the costs of buying advertising in major Texas media markets in terms of buying a single 30- or 60-second spot in selected television stations. The amounts shown are the costs of such a purchase for the stations' most popular prime-time programs during the late winter of 2011. It is obvious from the table that the costs of TV campaigning vary a great deal. Advertising prices change with the size of the media market and the popularity of the program, whether the candidate is running for a state or federal office,

TABLE 5-5

Television Advertising Costs in Selected Texas Cities, 2011

City	Station	Cost of 30-Second Spot	Cost of 60-Second Spot
Houston	KHOU (CBS)	$13,000	$26,000
Dallas/Ft. Worth	WFAA (ABC)	$12,000	$24,000
San Antonio	KABB (Fox)	$4,500	$9,000
Austin	KXAN (NBC)	$4,800	$9,600
El Paso	KDBC (CBS)	$950	$1,900
Brownsville/McAllen	KRGV (ABC)	$950	$1,900
Wichita Falls	KJTL (Fox)	$700	$1,400
Lubbock	KCBD (NBC)	$500	$1,000

NOTE: During the winter of 2011, CBS programs tended to be the most popular, followed closely by those on Fox. NBC and ABC programs lagged far behind. The most popular single program was Fox's "American Idol."

SOURCES: Compiled through telephone conversations with television station advertising managers by David F. Prindle in early March 2011; "Nielsen Scorecard," *Variety*, February 28–March 6, 2011, 13.

and along a variety of other dimensions. Thus, a candidate might have to pay more for time on a very popular show in a smaller market than for a less popular show in a larger market, and more or less at different times of the year (that is, during the spring primary season or the fall general election season). But to put all those complications into the table would prove confusing, without doing much to expand the amount of useful information. Readers should keep in mind that the figures shown in the table should be multiplied by several dozen times each to arrive at a realistic estimate of how much money it takes to run for office in Texas.

The large amounts of money that are necessary to run for office in Texas must come from somewhere. Most candidates—with a few exceptions such as H. Ross Perot, who tried to win the presidency as an independent in 1992 and 1996, and Tony Sanchez—are not so rich that they are able to finance their own campaigns. The great majority of candidates must get their money from a source other than their own pockets.

Except at the presidential level, the United States is one of the few democracies that does not have **publicly funded campaigns.** In many other countries, the government gives the parties tax money to cover part of the expenses of campaigning. This means that the parties, if their candidates are successful, are relatively free of obligation to special interests. In the United States, however, at every level except the presidency, we rely on **privately funded campaigns.** Candidates and parties must persuade private citizens to part with money, or their campaigns will fail.

The candidate with the most money does not win every election. In 1990, for example, Republican gubernatorial candidate Clayton Williams outspent Democratic candidate Ann Richards two to one and still lost;[7] and in 2002, Tony Sanchez paid out more than two-and-a-half times Rick Perry's total, yet failed to defeat him.[8]

But the best financed candidate does win most of the time. And just because a victorious candidate spent less than the loser does not mean that money was unimportant to his or her campaign. Ann Richards's expenditure of more than $10 million in 1990 and Rick Perry's expenditure of $28 million in 2002 are large chunks of cash by anyone's accounting. Furthermore, scholarly research has established that financial share is positively correlated to vote share, or in other words, the more money candidates spend, the more votes they tend to attract, especially in primary elections.[9]

In sum, although money may not be a *sufficient* resource to ensure political victory, it is still a *necessary* resource. People who are willing to contribute large amounts of money to campaigns, therefore, are extremely important to candidates.

Where Does the Money Come From? Most of the money contributed to candidates comes from wealthy donors who represent some sort of special interest. For example, of the four major gubernatorial candidates in 2006, Democrat Chris Bell received a quarter of his contributions from people who contributed $25,000 or more; Kinky Friedman received 30 percent of his contributions from contributions of the same size; Carole Keeton Strayhorn, 45 percent; and Rick Perry, 47 percent.[10] In all state campaigns in 2006, 140 Texans contributed at least $100,000, for a total from those contributors of $52 million.[11]

By employing such large contributions to help fund campaigns, people and organizations with wealth or access to wealth are able to rent the gratitude of candidates. Ordinary people who have to worry about paying their bills are not able to contribute nearly as much and therefore cannot ensure candidates' attention to their concerns. In this way, private funding of campaigns skews public policy in favor of special interests.

Therefore, when it comes to money and political campaigns in Texas, the following summary seems justified: Money is very important, but it is not the only resource. Volunteers, imagination, ideology, partisanship, and personality also play a part, as do such things as the state of the economy and the presence or absence of a scandal. Nevertheless, because economic wealth is so unequally distributed, it seems particularly dangerous to democratic government. It gives a very few citizens access to a very large political resource. For this reason, journalists and textbook authors are always worrying about its potential power.

As a rule, politicians dislike the system of private campaign financing, finding it time consuming and demeaning. Many retired officeholders have written in their autobiographies that they hated having to ask people for money, both because it made them feel humiliated and because they would rather have been working at crafting public policy. When former astronaut John Glenn retired as U.S. Senator from Ohio in 1997, for example, he grumbled to a reporter, "I'd rather wrestle a gorilla than ask anybody for another fifty cents."[12] A survey of Texas candidates taken by Common Cause in 1990 revealed that 65 percent of them supported public financing of campaigns.[13] Yet the opposition of the special interests who benefit from the current system has thus far stymied efforts to introduce reform.

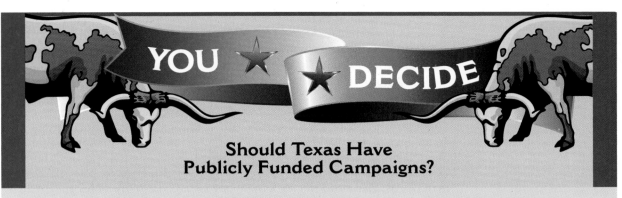

YOU ★ ★ DECIDE

Should Texas Have Publicly Funded Campaigns?

Although there is a system of public financing in place for presidential campaigns, and for state legislative campaigns in Maine and Arizona, most of the states permit their elections to be financed entirely from private sources. In Texas, candidates must either pay their own way or accept contributions from private individuals and organizations. There have been many suggestions, over the years, for some sort of plan (generally modeled on the federal system) for Texas to use tax money to support the campaigns of at least the major-party candidates in whole or in part.

PRO	CON
▲ State support of candidates would free them from dependence on special interests.	▼ Unless all private contributions were outlawed, candidates would still feel beholden to those who contributed. If all private contributions were prohibited, then all candidates would become dependent on state largesse. The state would not be able to resist making "regulations" that would inevitably either favor one party or suppress vigorous debate.
▲ As with the federal income tax check-off system, a state program would devise a means of ensuring that participation in the system was voluntary.	▼ Use of tax money to support candidates would mean that the coerced contributions of citizens were being used to subsidize candidates whose views many of them might abhor.
▲ Granted that the program should be limited to general elections, are we going to refuse to clean up part of Texas politics because we cannot clean up all of it?	▼ State contributions would almost certainly be limited to candidates in the general election. This would leave candidates in primaries still dependent on wealthy special interests. If the program were extended to primaries, then dozens of candidates would have an incentive to enter, and the costs would grow huge.
▲ As with ballot-entry laws, some test of a party's appeal in the previous election could be applied to a party's application for state support. Besides, perhaps a few fringe parties arguing their "extremist" views might be a good thing for Texas politics.	▼ If the program were to be limited to candidates of the two major parties, it would suppress the expression of alternative political opinions. If it were expanded to all parties, it would provide incentives for small fringe parties to claim tax subsidies to publicize their extremist views.

Sources: Elizabeth Daniel, "Public Financing: Making It Work," *The National Voter*, June/July 2001, 8–14; Jim Hightower, "The Hard and the Soft," *Texas Observer*, July 18, 2003, 15; Center for Governmental Studies, *Investing in Democracy: Creating Public Financing of Elections in Your Community* (Los Angeles: Center for Governmental Studies, 2003); Public Campaign Web site, accessed October 2, 2006, www.publicampaign.org/; Cato Institute Web site, accessed October 2, 2006, www.cato.org/campaignfinance/.

Control of Money in Campaigns The power of money in campaigns disturbs partisans of democracy because it seems to create an inequality of citizenship. Everyone has only one vote, but some people are multimillionaires. Those with more money to contribute seem to be "super citizens" who can wield influence denied to the rest. For this reason, many people have for decades been trying to control the impact of money in both state and national races. Their success at both levels is spotty at best.

Both at the federal level and in Texas, several laws have been passed to control the use and disclosure of the money collected by candidates. These laws have been made steadily tougher over the years, but they still allow wealthy individuals to purchase more political influence than is available to their fellow citizens.

Revenue Act of 1971 This federal law was intended to broaden the base of financial support and minimize the dependence of candidates on large donations from a few contributors. It provided that taxpayers may stipulate that $1 of their U.S. income tax ($2 on a joint return) be put into the Presidential Election Campaign Fund to provide for partial public funding of these national campaigns. The amount that taxpayers can contribute has since been raised to $3 for an individual and $6 for a joint return.

Federal Election Campaign Act of 1972 This law applies only to campaigns for federal offices—president, vice president, and members of Congress. It establishes a Federal Election Commission, requires candidates to make periodic reports of contributions and expenses, and places certain limits on contributions. At the time of its passage, individuals were permitted to donate up to $1,000 in each primary or general election and a maximum of $25,000 in a given year, while groups could contribute up to $5,000 per candidate. Over the years since 1972, these limits have been adjusted upward.

Texas Campaign Reporting and Disclosure Act of 1973 As amended, this act outlines procedures for campaign reporting and disclosure. It appears to strengthen the election code in several areas where previously it was deficient. As amended, the act's major provisions are as follows:

1. Every candidate for political office and every political committee within the state must appoint a campaign treasurer before accepting contributions or making expenditures.

2. Contributions exceeding $500 by out-of-state political committees can be made only if the names of contributors of $100 or more are disclosed.

3. Detailed financial reports are required of candidates and managers of campaign committees. They must include a list of all contributions and expenditures over $50.

4. Violators face both civil action and criminal penalties.

The 1973 law sounds like a genuine attempt to force public disclosure of the financial sponsors of candidates. Its great flaw, however, was that it contained no provision for enforcement. Because laws do not enforce themselves, the public reporting of private contributions was at best a haphazard affair. Moreover, the law failed to impose any limits on the amount that individuals or organizations

could contribute to campaigns; as long as they reported the amount, they could attempt to buy as much influence as they could afford.

1991 Ethics Law In 1991, the legislature passed another ethics bill designed to regulate and moderate the impact of private wealth on public policy in campaigns and at other levels of Texas politics. This law created an Ethics Commission that could hold hearings on public complaints, levy fines, and report severe violations to the Travis County (Austin) district attorney for possible prosecution.

Again, however, the law failed to place limits on campaign contributions. Furthermore, it required a "supermajority" of six of eight commissioners for important actions, a provision that was practically guaranteed to prevent the vigorous investigation of violators. As John Steiner, the commission's executive director, stated publicly in 1993, "There's very little in the way of real enforcement . . . in most of the laws we administer. It's just an unenforced statute except that if people don't [obey the law], it gets some bad press."[14]

When the Sunset Commission (SC) began evaluating the Texas Ethics Commission (TEC) in 2002 (see Chapter 7 for a discussion of the SC), the supposed ethics watchdog itself came in for some bad publicity. Journalists reported that in its decade of existence, the TEC had never issued a subpoena, audited a file, or referred a complaint for criminal prosecution. Stung by public criticism, the commissioners began to be more energetic in investigating and punishing candidates who violated the state's campaign finance laws.

For example, in 2008, the TEC fined state representative Rob Eissler (Republican from the Woodlands) $10,600 and ordered him to repay his campaign organization $18,600 for illegally spending donated money for personal use. Eissler had paid his wife from campaign funds to run his legislative office, which violated a law intended to prevent legislators from living off their campaign donors. Then, in 2011, the TEC fined Governor Perry for failing to report rental income from a house in College Station, and for filing incomplete personal finance statements. Neither of these actions attracted much attention, and neither had any noticeable effect on the careers of the two politicians; but these and other such actions showed that the TEC was no longer a completely useless institution.[15]

The evolution of the TEC illustrates the fact that improvement in Texas politics, while it sometimes seems to be very slow, is not at a standstill. Nevertheless, not too much optimism should be extracted from these examples. Despite this small progress, there is still virtually no control over, and very little effort to ensure the public disclosure of, the influence of money in Texas political campaigns. As a consequence, people with money have more influence over politicians than do ordinary citizens. For observers who take democratic theory seriously, this situation is the single most disturbing fact about Texas politics.

Hard versus Soft The Federal Election Campaign Act (FECA) of 1972 originally set limits on the amount of money individual candidates could contribute to their own campaigns. But in the case of *Buckley* v. *Valeo* (424 U.S. 1, 1976), the U.S. Supreme Court held that these limits were unconstitutional suppressions of the freedom of speech guaranteed by the First Amendment. It is this decision that allowed Texas billionaire H. Ross Perot to spend millions of dollars of his own money to finance his independent candidacies for the presidency in 1992 and 1996.

Buckley v. *Valeo* also extended the right of free speech to political action committees (PACs) for "party building" at the national level. PACs were permitted to spend unlimited amounts on political activities, such as get-out-the-vote campaigns, and to contribute as much as they wanted to the party organizations, as long as these contributions were not directly coordinated with an individual candidate's election campaign. In the jargon of campaign financing, contributions that go directly to a candidate are "hard money," while those that go to parties, and therefore presumably benefit candidates only indirectly, are "soft money."

The effect of *Buckley* v. *Valeo* was not limited to federal elections. Shortly after the case was decided, the attorney general of Texas ruled that the decision voided similar provisions in the state's 1973 campaign finance law as well (Texas Attorney General Opinion H864, 1976). As a result, Clayton Williams and Tony Sanchez were able to spend millions of dollars of their own wealth in their runs for governor in 1990 and 2002; and corporate, labor, and trade association PACs were permitted to contribute whatever they wished to state campaigns.

In summary, at the national level, and even more so in Texas, there is very little control over the ability of rich individuals and interests to buy influence over candidates.

Negative Campaigning

In addition to the influence of money, another disturbing characteristic of contemporary campaigning is the use of personal attacks on candidates by their opponents, generally in television spots. Candidates are accused of everything from drug addiction to mental illness to marital infidelity to financial dishonesty to satanism. Mainly, they are accused of being liars.

Cartoonist Ben Sargent points out that there is more than one way to corrupt democratic government.

Courtesy of Ben Sargent.

Personal attacks now dominate the airwaves during election years. According to a study by the Center for Responsive Politics in the Annenburg Public Policy Center at the University of Pennsylvania, 80 percent of the TV campaign spots aired during the fall of 2006 by the Republican and Democratic campaign committees of the U.S. House of Representatives were negative.[16]

LONE STAR MEDIA
To Tell the Truth—Or Not

In most professions—doctors, professors, and attorneys, for example—official codes of conduct require the people who do that job to show ethical behavior, including telling the truth. Not all individuals in those professions obey the rules, of course, but when they are caught behaving unethically they can be disciplined by organizations of their peers, and the penalties are sometimes severe. This professional self-policing functions to punish the worst offenders in the given profession and, more importantly, to either encourage or intimidate the other members of the profession to behave in a responsible manner.

In American democratic politics, however, there is no official body that enforces a code of truth-telling, either on candidates for office or on officials in power. The result has long been a problem for democracy, since it is difficult for the people to make rational choices on election day if they are deceived by candidates. The difficulty is made worse by the fact that until recently the public had no systematic way to detect when politicians were lying to them.

In 2008, however, the St. Petersburg, Florida, *Times* began a project to fact-check statements made by the major presidential candidates. The effort, given the title "Politifact," was quickly picked up by the *Austin America-Statesman* and then by a variety of newspapers around Texas and the rest of the country. Soon it was extended to many other candidates and officials below the presidential level. By looking for the Politifact column in their newspapers or online, scholars, students, and curious citizens can now evaluate the truthfulness of politicians in their state.

The activity of judging truthfulness, of course, can be controversial. Politicians may not like the conclusions that the Politifact truth-checkers make public. For example, over the course of the 2010 Texas gubernatorial campaign, Politifact examined a number of statements by both the Republican incumbent, Rick Perry, and the Democratic candidate, Bill White. It concluded that Perry's public statements had been "False" or "Pants on Fire" (the worst category) 15 percent of the time, and "True" or "Mostly True" only 10 percent of the time. Perry's remaining statements had fallen into one of several ambiguous categories. White's statements had fallen into the two worst categories 6 percent of the time, and into the two best categories 13 percent of the time. In other words, while neither candidate was completely truthful, Perry was a more frequent liar. Perry won anyway, which suggests that the voters were not overly concerned with the truthfulness of their candidates, at least not in Texas in that election.

Naturally, however, whether they win or lose, politicians and their supporters do not enjoy being publicly exposed as liars (although Politifact is careful to not actually use that specific word). Organizations on both the liberal and conservative side of the spectrum

(continued)

(continued)

whose favored candidates have been labeled untruthful have complained that Politifact is biased against them, and that its "fact-checkers" tend to confuse differences of political perspective with efforts to deceive.

"Truth" is a slippery concept, and perhaps the critics have a point. Nevertheless, having an independent organization that attempts to track down and evaluate the accuracy of statements made by politicians, even if it functions imperfectly, is surely in the public interest. To what extent citizens, in Texas and elsewhere, will come to use Politifact's truth-assessments in judging whether or not to support a candidate, however, is yet to be determined.

SOURCES: Bill Adair, "Truth's a Loser in Aggressive Statements of Fall Campaigns," *Austin American-Statesman*, October 31, 2010, D3; W. Gardner Selby, "A Look Back at Perry, White and Flaming Trousers," *Austin American-Statesman*, November 2, 2010, A1; Wikipedia for the general history of Politifact; Politifact's Web site, http://politifact.com/.

Negative campaigning has a corrosive effect on democracy for four reasons. First, some elections are decided on the basis of inaccurate or irrelevant charges. Second, discussions of public policy and how to solve national or state problems are shunted aside in everyone's eagerness to throw mud. Third, many good people may decide not to enter political life so that they can avoid becoming the targets of public attack. Fourth, negative campaigning disheartens citizens, who are thus more apt to stay home on election day. Research by political scientists has concluded that such campaigns may depress voter turnout by as much as 5 percent.[17]

Texas has had its share of negative campaigns and, thus, its share of damage to the democratic ideal. A large part of the gubernatorial race in 1990, during both the Democratic primary and the general election, consisted of accusations of illegal drug use by Ann Richards (who won both races despite the charges). The campaign of 2002, to be discussed shortly, broke all records for viciousness and distortion. Negative campaigning in Texas seems no worse than it is in most states, but that is bad enough.

Public Elections

A public election is the only political activity in which large numbers of Texans (although, as we have seen, usually not a majority) are likely to participate. The state has three types of elections: primary, general, and special elections.

Primary Elections

A **primary** is an election held within a party to nominate candidates for the general election or to choose delegates to a presidential nominating convention. It is because primaries are so important in Texas that parties are weak. Because they do not control nominations, party "leaders" have no control over officeholders and so, in reality, cannot lead.

Under procedures begun in 1988, the primary election in Texas occurs on the second Tuesday in March in even-numbered years, prior to the general

election. The Texas Election Code provides that any political party whose candidate for governor received 20 percent or more of the vote in the most recent general election must hold a primary to choose candidates for upcoming elections. Parties whose candidates polled less than 20 percent may either hold a primary or choose their candidates by the less expensive method of a nominating convention. In effect, Republicans and Democrats must hold primary elections, while smaller third parties may select their candidates in conventions.

Under Texas law, a candidate must win the nomination with a majority vote in the primary. If there is not a majority winner, as there frequently is not if there are more than two candidates, the two leading vote-getters meet thirty days later in a general runoff election.

Texas's "Open" Primary

There are three types of primary elections:

1. **A blanket primary, used in only two states, is like a general election held before the general election. All candidates of all parties run on one list, and any registered voter can participate.**

2. **An *open primary* is one in which any registered voter may participate in any party's primary.**

3. **A *closed primary* is one in which only registered members of a party may participate in that party's primary.**

Technically, Texas laws provide for a closed primary. In practice, however, voters may participate in any primary as long as they have not already voted in the primary of another party during the same year. The only realistic sense in which Texas has a closed primary is that once voters have recorded their party affiliation by voting in one party's primary, they cannot participate in the affairs of the runoff primary or the convention of another party during that year.

Aspiring candidates obtain a place on the primary ballot by applying to the state executive committee for statewide office or to the county chairperson for local office. Drawings are held for position on the ballot, and filing fees (discussed below) must be paid before the ballot is printed.

When Held

For most of the twentieth century, Texas and many of the other southern states held primaries in May. Several small northern states, most famously New Hampshire, held their primaries very early in a presidential year—often in January. Both candidates and the media concentrated on these early primaries, making it seem to the public that the New Hampshire winner was certain to win the party nomination. As a result, candidates who won in the early primaries often had achieved so much "momentum" that they had, in effect, wrapped up their party's nomination before most of the states' primaries had even been held.[18]

Feeling that their own importance was being unfairly neglected, other states, especially in the South, began moving up the dates of their own primaries during presidential years. As all the state primaries began to crowd into the early months of the crucial year, officials of the two major national parties started to make rules about which states could hold primaries in which month. The result

was an ongoing tussle, in which states were always lobbying the parties to be permitted to hold earlier primaries, and party officials were always trying to resist the pressure. The result of this continuous jostling was that Texas held its 2008 presidential primary on March 4th, and in 2010 the primary for state and local office was held March 2nd. The 2012 presidential primary is tentatively scheduled for March 6th, but because of the ongoing maneuvering of the states to try to get permission to hold their presidential-year primaries before the other states, it might very well be held at an earlier date in that year.

Administration and Finance

In Texas, primary elections are administered entirely by political party officials in accordance with the provisions of the Texas Election Code. The process is decentralized. Most of the responsibilities and work fall on the shoulders of the county chairperson and the members of the county executive committee, in cooperation with county clerks.[19] They must arrange for the polling places, provide the voting machines and other equipment, print the ballots, and determine the results. The election is supervised by a presiding judge and an alternate appointed in each precinct by the county chair, subject to approval by the county committee. The presiding judge appoints two or more clerks to actually conduct the election—checking registration rolls, issuing ballots, and settling occasional disputes.

Conducting a primary election is expensive, especially in a state as large as Texas. Clerks are paid a salary, albeit a modest one. Polling places and voting machines must be rented, ballots printed, and other expenses paid. Prior to 1972, the costs were met by charging each aspiring candidate a filing fee. In 1973, the Sixty-third Legislature enacted a permanent primary election finance bill, which provides for a combination of state and private funding. Filing fees are still in use, but the amounts are reasonable, ranging, in 2010, from a high of $3,750 for governor to a low of $75 for county surveyor.[20] Expenses beyond those that are covered by the filing fees are paid by the state. County political party chairs pay the costs of the primary and are then reimbursed by the secretary of state.

General Elections

The purpose of a **general election** is to choose state and national executives and legislators and state judges. General elections are held in even-numbered years on the Tuesday after the first Monday in November. In 1974, Texas joined the group of states that elect their governors and other state officials in the "off year," the even-numbered year between presidential election years. At the same time, the state adopted a constitutional amendment that extended the terms of office for the governor and other state officials from two to four years.

Unlike primary elections, general and special elections are the responsibility of the state. The secretary of state is the principal election officer, although the election organization is decentralized and most of the actual work is performed at the county level. The county commissioners' court appoints election judges, chooses the method of voting—paper ballots or some type of voting machine, and pays the bills. The county clerk conducts absentee balloting and performs many of the functions charged to the commissioners' court.

Nominees of established parties are placed on the ballot when they win a party primary or are chosen by a party convention. New parties and

independent candidates get on the general election ballot by presenting a petition signed by a specified number of qualified voters who have not participated in the primary election of another party. The number of required signatures varies with the office. At the local level, it may be no larger than 500; at the state level, it is 1 percent of the votes cast in the last gubernatorial election.

There is no standard election ballot in Texas. Primary ballots vary from party to party, and general election ballots vary from county to county. Whatever its form, the ballot lists the offices to be filled, beginning with the president (in an appropriate year) and proceeding down to the local positions. Candidates' political party affiliations are listed beside their names, and candidates of the party that polled the most votes in the most recent gubernatorial election are listed first. Other parties' candidates appear in descending order of that party's polling strength in the preceding election. A space is provided for write-in candidates. Constitutional amendments, if any, are listed separately, usually near the bottom of the ballot, followed by local referendum questions.

A somewhat different form of the general election is held in cities. Elections for mayors and city councils are usually held in the spring, and are always technically nonpartisan. Party labels do not appear beside the candidates' names, and no party certification is needed to get on the ballot. It is custom abetted by city charter provisions, not state law, that prevents partisan politics at the local level (see Chapter 12). By denying the voters the guidance provided by a party label, nonpartisan elections are even more confusing for them than are general elections, and voter turnout tends to be even lower.

Special Elections

In Texas, a number of special elections are held in addition to primary and general elections. They may be called at the state level to fill vacancies in Congress or in the state legislature or to vote on proposed constitutional amendments. Because special elections are held at irregular times, they, like municipal contests, generally feature very low voter turnout. A special election held in September 2003 in which the voters were asked if they wished to ratify Proposition 12, which capped medical lawsuit awards at $750,000, generated a barrage of op-ed newspaper columns, and engaged such wealthy interest groups—doctors versus lawyers—that spending on television spots and mailed flyers topped $13 million. Yet all the loud publicity managed to persuade only about 13 percent of the eligible citizens to go to the polls. (Proposition 12 passed narrowly.) Thus do small fractions of the population often determine state policy through special elections.[21]

Absentee or Early Voting

While voters who register their preferences in the conventional manner must get to a polling place between 7 A.M. and 7 P.M. on election day, Texas citizens may vote absentee in any election. Voting may be done for a period of two weeks before the election at the county clerk's office or at a variety of polling places throughout the county. In the past, one needed a reason to vote absentee, such as a planned trip from the county or illness. In 1987, the legislature removed the restrictions, and anyone can now vote early. In the 2008 general election, two-thirds of those who voted cast their ballots prior to the official election day.[22]

An Electronic Fix?

Because there is no standard ballot in Texas, the manner in which voters record their choices varies from place to place, and changes with the evolution of technology. Since 2002, some counties have been experimenting with the eSlate, a minicomputer that permits citizens to record their partisan choices electronically. In theory, voters in the areas where the eSlate is in use can find their preferred candidates on an electronic screen and then record their choices by pressing an "Enter" button at the bottom of the screen. The voters' choices are stored in cyber-memory. After the polls close, the units are delivered to a tabulation center, where the votes are counted. Its advocates argue that this type of voting is more efficient and less subject to fraud than traditional paper balloting.

In practice, the new technology, like the old technology, has proved to be imperfect. In 2002 and 2004, a variety of glitches and mistakes, and perhaps efforts to manufacture results, sparked embarrassment, charges of vote tampering, and threats of lawsuits. Although there were only minor problems with Texas voting in 2006, there was major trouble with the eSlate in Ohio, Pennsylvania, Florida, and Maryland. Moreover, a chorus of criticism of the eSlate by computer scientists has lent authority to skepticism about computer voting. Researchers at Cal Tech, MIT, and Stanford have concluded that the traditional low-tech paper ballots were *less* likely to be lost or fraudulently miscounted than the new e-ballots. Without actual physical ballots that can be observed and stored, electronic ballots offer an opportunity for manipulation of the results through hacking and other means available to cyber-criminals. Few major complaints resulted from the eSlate during the 2008 and 2010 elections. Nevertheless, the co-evolution of computers and computer-crime—SPAM, viruses, and worms, most prominently—suggests that people trying to cheat the system are always just a step ahead or a step behind the people trying to ensure its integrity. If the eSlate has been rendered fraud-proof for now, it is unlikely to remain so in the future.

While paper ballots have never deterred dishonest politicians from attempting to steal elections, the brief history of the eSlate underscores the point that no technology is fool- and fraud-proof. The solution to ballot fraud will remain the same with computer voting as it has been with previous means of recording citizen preferences: eternal vigilance by a suspicious public. There is no technological cure for the ills of democracy.

Sources: Ed Housewright and Victoria Loe Hicks, "County Democrats Say Early Votes Miscounted," *Dallas Morning News*, October 23, 2002, A1; "Votescam in the Electronic Age," *Texas Observer*, December 20, 2002, 12; Erika Jonietz, "Valid Voting?" *Technology Review*, February 2004, 74; Ian Urbana, "Electronic Voting Machines Are Making Officials Wary," *New York Times*, September 24, 2006, A19; Ian Urbina and Christopher R. Drew, "Experts Worry as Poll Problems Resist Overhaul," *New York Times*, November 26, 2006, A1.

Recent Elections in Texas

As is the case with every state, the recent history of elections in Texas displays some clear trends, but also contains hints of possible changes in the future.

Elections of 1994 through 2004

The political realignment toward which Texas had been inching since the 1960s finally arrived in 1994. Republicans successfully defended a U.S. Senate seat, picked up two seats in the U.S. House of Representatives, increased their representation in the Texas legislature, and garnered more than 900 local offices.

They won both vulnerable railroad commission seats and captured minorities on the state supreme court and the state board of education. George W. Bush defeated incumbent Democrat Ann Richards to become Texas's governor. Until 1984, Texas had been a one-party Democratic state. After 1994, it increasingly looked like a one-party Republican state.

The Republican victory was based on a clear pattern of ethnic and economic class cleavages and on differences in voter participation. Democratic candidates drew support from lower-income Anglos, Mexican Americans, and African Americans. Republicans were supported by the wealthy in general and wealthy Anglos in particular. Because voter turnout was higher in the areas and among the people who tend to support Republicans, they were the winners.

The fact that the 1994 results inaugurated a lasting pattern rather than a temporary perturbation was illustrated by the results of 1996, 1998, 2000, and 2004. Republicans continued to win every statewide electoral contest, as well as all of Texas's electoral votes for president.

The only one of these contests in which the state Democratic Party made any credible effort was in 2002. The party, with some difficulties in the primaries, managed to nominate an African American, Ron Kirk, as its candidate for U.S. Senate; a Mexican American, Tony Sanchez, as its standard-bearer for governor; and an Anglo, John Sharp, as its aspirant for lieutenant governor. The Democratic leadership hoped that each candidate would draw voters of his own ethnic group, all of whom would vote for the other candidates of the party. Moreover, by persuading multimillionaire Sanchez to be the nominee, Democrats hoped to overcome the absence of funding that had sunk Gary Mauro, their gubernatorial candidate in 1998.

Sanchez came through with the funding, contributing more than $60 million to his own campaign, but otherwise, the Democratic "dream team" flopped. In fact, although turnout in some Latino and African American districts was up slightly from previous off-year elections, it did not rise nearly enough to offset the overwhelming advantage all Republican candidates enjoyed with Anglo voters. GOP candidates not only won every statewide office—executive, legislative, and judicial—but also captured control of the state House of Representatives for the first time since Reconstruction.

As far as the tone of the 2002 campaign was concerned, all observers agreed that it was the sleaziest, the most vicious, and the least democratically informative contest that anyone could remember. The most deplorable contest among a host of negative campaigns was the one between Sanchez and Perry for the governorship. Sanchez's TV ads were tough, mean, and personal, but at first, they at least dealt with public policy. They blamed Perry for the state's troubled schools, ridiculed him for accepting contributions from energy and insurance interests, and mocked him for being an unelected governor. Toward the end of the contest, however, still behind in the polls, Sanchez made an attack on Perry that was unconnected to any issues before the electorate. Perry's chauffeur had been stopped for a traffic violation by a police officer one day in 2001 as he drove the governor to the capitol building. Not aware that there was a camera and voice recorder on the hood of the police car, Perry had gotten out of the limousine and said to the officer, "Why don't you just let us get on down the road?" Sanchez's campaign got hold of the tapes and played them frequently in television ads, adding: "Rick Perry. Why don't we just let him get on down the road?"

This attack was unfair and unworthy of a hopeful public servant, but it was not the bottom of the barrel. That was supplied by Perry's campaign. For

months, Perry had been running ads informing the electorate that, during the 1980s, one of Sanchez's banks had been discovered to have been knowingly laundering illegal drug money from Mexico. Although the federal judge who had been in charge of the case was happy to tell anyone that he had found that Sanchez had not known about the source of the money, the Perry campaign ignored the facts and kept running the misleading ad.[23]

This was bad enough. But after Sanchez's embarrassing "get on down the road" ad, the Perry campaign retaliated with what was perhaps the most noxious spot in the history of negative advertising. Perry put on camera two former federal Drug Enforcement Administration agents, who insinuated that Sanchez had somehow been involved in the slaying of DEA agent Enrique "Kiki" Camarena in 1985. There was neither evidence nor reasoning to support the charge. If Sanchez had not known about the drug laundering, he certainly could not have known of the drug traffickers' intention to kill an undercover agent. But the Perry campaign played the ad over and over in every media market anyway. Although candidates have asserted many reprehensible things about one another over the years, this was probably the first time that one has accused another of being a murderer. The fact that the charge was a fiction made it all the more indefensible.[24]

Although 2004 did not feature any major statewide races such as that for governor, Republicans continued their domination of the state's elections. Their successful 2003 struggle to redraw the Lone Star State's congressional boundaries resulted in the defeat of four of the five Democratic representatives who had been "targeted." Republicans lost one seat in the state House of Representatives, but retained their majority of 87 to 63. They defended their 19-to-12 advantage in the state Senate, and kept their locks on the railroad commission and court system.

Election of 2006

Since 1994, Texas had generally tracked with the rest of the country in its electoral politics. That is, both the state and the nation moved in a Republican direction. In 2006, however, Texas diverged wildly from the pattern evident in the United States as a whole.

Nationally, 2006 was a "throw the rascals out" election, with citizens furious at the Republican Congress for defending the unpopular war in Iraq and seeming to countenance corrupt governance. Republican President George W. Bush was a particular target of voter ire, as about six in ten respondents in ballot-box exit polls reported that they disapproved of the way he was handling his job. Although Bush himself was not running for anything, independent citizens in particular (those who did not identify with either party) voted against Republican candidates to show their opposition to his foreign policy.[25] The Democrats won both the U.S. House of Representatives and the Senate for the first time in twelve years.

The results in Texas were very different. As they had since 1994, Republican candidates won every statewide office, electing or re-electing candidates to the governorship, lieutenant governorship, railroad commission, attorney general, comptroller, agriculture commissioner, land commissioner, U.S. Senator, and eight judgeships on the supreme court and court of criminal appeals. They kept their majority among the state's 32-member delegation to the U.S. House of Representatives, although Democrat Nick Lampson did defeat a Republican write-in candidate to capture a seat from the 22nd congressional district, previously represented by scandal-tarred Tom DeLay, and Ciro Rodriguez ousted

seven-term Republican representative Henry Bonilla in the 23rd district. Democrats gained five seats in the state House of Representatives, but they still did not come close to commanding a majority in that body.

There were a few local Democratic wrinkles in the statewide Republican triumph. Austin continued to give its votes to the now-minority party. More surprisingly, Dallas County experienced a strong Democratic surge. Democrats won every countywide office they contested, including 42 judgeships. In the most significant contest, Craig Watkins defeated Toby Shook to become the county's first African American district attorney. In Harris County (Houston), Republicans continued to dominate, but their margin of victory was smaller than in the past. The GOP's judicial candidates had won by an average of 9 percentage points in 2002. In 2006, their winning margin was down to 4 points.

Political scientists attributed the trends in the state's two largest cities to continuing demographic changes. Minorities, especially Latinos, had been moving to those cities, while Anglos had been moving to the suburbs in outlying counties. Because minorities tend to vote Democratic, the Democratic vote in the cities was increasing. Observers looked toward the 2008 balloting to see if the partisan trends begun in 2006 in Dallas and Houston would continue.[26]

Election of 2008

Nationally, the 2008 election marked a return to power of the Democrats. Partly because of disgruntlement over the seemingly endless Iraq war and partly because of dismay at an ever-worsening economy touched off by a banking crisis that started on the Republicans' watch, voters turned to the "out" party. Barack Obama, the Democratic nominee for President, defeated Republican John McCain to become the first African American chief executive in American history. In addition, the Democrats, who had won small majorities in the House of Representatives and Senate in 2006, strengthened their grip on both houses.

Governor Rick Perry votes, presumably for himself, in the November 2010 general election.

Ben Sklar/Getty Images.

In Texas, however, Republicans continued as the majority party, although the national Democratic surge made itself felt in some local areas and in the state House of Representatives. It being a presidential year, there was no gubernatorial contest, but the other statewide races showed that Texans had not been persuaded to abandon the Republicans. John McCain took the state's 34 electoral votes by a 55 to 44 percent margin, and John Cornyn was re-elected U.S. Senator by a similar majority. Republican candidates also triumphed in the three seats on the state supreme court that were up for election, in both the seats on the court of criminal appeals, and on five out of the six seats on the state board of education.

In the state Senate, Republicans continued their dominance, winning 19 out of the 30 seats. The Democratic Party showed signs of life in the state House of Representatives races, however, falling just one victory short of forcing a tie in the partisan balance of that body. Meanwhile, Democrats were clearly a growing party in some of the state's large cities and in rural areas with high percentages of Hispanic citizens. Obama garnered majorities in Dallas, Houston, Austin, San Antonio, and El Paso, and won most of the counties along the Rio Grande. And in local balloting, the trends foreshadowed in the 2006 election emerged with even greater force. The Democrats again dominated the voting for local judgeships and administrative positions in Dallas. In Houston, the party completed the rise to dominance that began during the 2006 voting, winning 24 of the 27 local judicial races, as well as the sheriff, county attorney, and district clerk. According to U.S. Census estimates, a large majority of Houston's population is now composed of African Americans and Latinos, and exit-poll interviews on election day showed that the members of both groups voted overwhelmingly Democratic.[27]

Election of 2010

Whereas in 2006 and 2008 Texas had bucked the national Democratic trend, in 2010 the rest of the nation fell in step with the Lone Star state in supporting Republican candidates. Voters across the country, frustrated with the Democratic Obama administraton's inability to get unemployment below 9 percent and, in some cases, alarmed by the huge, expensive, health care reform bill passed by the Democratic Congress, voted overwhelmingly for the "out" party. Republicans took back the U.S. House of Representatives, reduced the Democratic majority in the U.S. Senate, and made large gains in state races across the country.

In Texas, the national Republican surge reinforced the ongoing dominance of the party in state elections. Bill White, mayor of Houston and the Democratic gubernatorial candidate, had hoped that he could leverage the state's looming fiscal crisis and a series of small scandals in the governor's office to defeat Republican Rick Perry's bid for re-election. But Perry wooed the state's economic conservatives with promises to never, ever, raise taxes no matter what budget problems the state faced, and by showing up at "Tea Party" rallies (see Chapter 4) to express solidarity with those who thought that the federal government was spending too much. He courted the social conservatives with rhetoric that suggested he was opposed to the teaching of the scientific theory of evolution in public-school biology classes, and generally proclaiming his Christian faith. He appealed to the Texas state patriots by bashing Washington at every opportunity, even hinting that he was sympathetic to the idea of secession.[28] And, as it had in 2002, Perry's organization produced a sleazy, misleading television ad, this one insinuating that Bill White, as mayor, had somehow allowed a Houston police officer to be murdered.[29] Perhaps because he simply had

the bad luck to run in a year when the voters were furious at the Democrats, White's low-key campaigning style and relatively truthful approach to political argument were not able to overcome the tide of history and Perry's unscrupulous opportunism. The governor was re-elected by a 55 to 42 percent margin.

The gubernatorial race was typical of the state's other races. Not only did Republican candidates win every statewide race, but they achieved such a massacre in the state House of Representatives that, after two Democrats switched party affiliations shortly after the election, they controlled a two-thirds 101-to-49 majority. Their margin in the state Senate was similar.

As usual, however, all was not quite as it seemed in the election of 2010. State voter turnout fell below a third of the eligible population, with the rate of participation following the historically familiar pattern.[30] That is, conservative, middle-class-to-wealthy Anglos, especially those energized by the Tea Party movement, went to the polls in droves, while the more liberal Hispanics and African Americans mostly stayed home. Latino turnout, which was 17 percent in the 2006 election, may have been even lower in 2010. Thus, the fact that 61 percent of Latinos voted Democratic was of no consequence because so few of them went to the polls.[31] If minority citizens had turned out to vote at rates comparable to those of the Anglos, all the races would have been much closer, and Democratic losses would have been less severe. But, as is the usual case in modern Texas, because the liberals did not vote, the state looked to be much more conservative than its citizens actually are.

The era of Republican dominance is thus not over in Texas. But the demographic and political trend lines suggest that, other things being equal, the Democrats can be optimistic about their future. Other things are often not equal in history, so nothing can be predicted with confidence. Texas elections, however, can be expected to be colorful, rough-and-tumble, and surprising.

Conclusion

All in all, a survey of voters, campaigns, and elections in Texas is not very encouraging to people who take democratic theory seriously. If the legitimacy of government in a democracy depends on the participation of citizens, then the very low voter turnout in state elections raises serious questions about the legitimacy of Texas government. Moreover, the great disparity in turnout between ethnic groups most certainly biases public policy away from the patterns that would prevail if all citizens voted. Looking beyond voting, the great impact of money on political campaigns and elections suggests the possibility, if not the certainty, that wealthy elites control the policy process, rendering whatever citizen participation exists irrelevant. A cynical view of democracy finds much support in Texas electoral politics.

There is, however, some cause for optimism. The old barriers to participation that kept people from exercising their citizenship are gone, and in fact, voter turnout has been rising slowly and unsteadily in recent decades. It is possible that time and education will bring more people to fulfill their potential as citizens. Further, the gubernatorial campaigns of 1990 and 2002 proved that money is not the only thing that counts in Texas politics, and the Republican surges of 1994 and 2010, together with the Democratic surges of 2006 and 2008, demonstrated that the electorate is capable of making informed choices in the polling booth.

The system, then, is imperfect, but not completely depraved. F[...]
ing to make a better state, there are both many flaws to try to co[...]
to hope that they may be correctable.

Summary

Voting, campaigning, and elections are important to study because in a democracy the legitimacy of the government depends on the people's participation. Thus, despite the fact that single votes almost never determine the outcome of elections, voting is important to the individual, the candidate, and the political system.

Consistent with its traditionalist history and culture, Texas until recently attempted to suppress voting by all but wealthy Whites. Today, voter turnout is still below the national average, which is itself comparatively low. Turnout of African Americans and Mexican Americans is generally lower than the turnout of Anglos. This disparity makes public policy more conservative than it would be otherwise. Nevertheless, voter turnout has been rising in recent elections, and if the trend line continues, all Texans may, at some point, begin to register their true policy preferences via the voting booth.

In campaigns, candidates attempt to persuade voters to support them. To do so, they are forced to spend large amounts of money, which means that they become dependent on wealthy special interests that contribute to their cause. This dependence has consequences for public policy. Money is not absolutely decisive in campaigns, however, and candidates who are outspent by their opponents sometimes win.

There are three kinds of elections in Texas. Primary elections are held to choose candidates for general elections. In general elections, the electorate determines who will serve in public office. Special elections are held when they are needed between general elections, often to either fill unexpected governmental vacancies or to ratify constitutional amendments.

One of the more disturbing trends in election campaigns is the prevalence of negative personal attacks in television advertising. Recent historical experience is somewhat mixed in regard to negative campaigning. On the one hand, the gubernatorial campaigns of 1990, 2002, and 2010 were paradigms of sleazy viciousness. On the other hand, several of the most important state campaigns in the 1990s and early years of the 2000s were fought cleanly, which gives some reason to hope that future elections may be more issue oriented than those in the past.

A comparison of the reality of Texas electoral politics with the ideal of the democratic polity thus suggests that Texas falls very far below the ideal, but offers some reason for optimism.

Glossary Terms

campaign	privately funded campaigns
closed primary	publicly funded campaigns
Equal Protection Clause	suffrage
general election	voter registration
open primary	voter turnout
primary	

6

The Texas Legislature

> What lobbyists can dream, lobbyists can do.
>
> STEVE WOLENS OF DALLAS, FORMER REPRESENTATIVE, 1995

> Legislative bodies seldom live up to what the public expects of them.
>
> *TEXAS MONTHLY*, 2003

> Why are our leaders in Austin so determined that Texas be a mediocre state?
>
> FORMER LIEUTENANT GOVERNOR BILL HOBBY, *HOW THINGS REALLY WORK*, 2010

OBJECTIVES

After reading this chapter, you should be able to

Understand the functions of legislative bodies.

Discuss the structure of the Texas Legislature, including size, terms, sessions, legislative districts, and compensation.

Know the general qualifications and personal characteristics of legislators.

Understand the presiding officers and committee system.

Perceive the dominance of the legislative leaders.

Trace how a bill becomes a law in Texas.

Understand the complexities of legislative dynamics, including handicaps to thoughtful policymaking, outside influences, and party realignments.

Evaluate the legislature as an institution and consider reforms in its organization and processes.

INTRODUCTION

Legislative bodies are meant to represent the people and to reflect the differing views of a community, state, or nation. However, at the same time, they are meant to enact public policy, to provide funds for government operations, and to perform a host of other functions on behalf of the people who elected them. The legislature is particularly important in democratic theory because it institutionalizes the people's choices and translates the people's wants into public policy. In the second decade of the twenty-first century, the Texas legislature overrepresents the most conservative interests of the state, which are primarily focused on keeping taxes and spending low. As a result, it tends to pass legislation reflecting policies that are so conservative fiscally that some public needs are not met.

Although generally increasing the diversity of its members since the mid-1980s, the Texas legislature is still not completely representative of the state as a whole. In the second decade of the twenty-first century, not only does it overrepresent the most conservative interests and tend toward policies that do not adequately address social needs or the building blocks for future economic success, but it also overly stresses the **privatizing** of public functions, that is, delegating public programs to private service providers. In short, as the Bill Hobby chapter-opening quotation notes, the political leadership has had a recent strong tendency toward mediocrity. The vote is still out on whether the state can meet the most fundamental tests of democratic government: representation, fairness, and transparency.

Texas's **biennial** legislative sessions are the focal point of the state government. Biennial means that the regular legislative sessions occur every other year. In these sessions, legislators must wrestle with important economic and social issues, define public morality and provide methods to enforce it, and also attend to strictly political chores, such as redistricting. They are burdened in these endeavors, however, by a number of structural weaknesses in the legislative system, by a historic lack of public confidence and support, and by the bending of rules and traditions to conform to the desires of the prevailing ideology in any given legislative session.

The Texas legislature is not very easy to understand because it operates under myriad procedural rules as well as informal norms of behavior for its members. Additionally, state services and the quest to find revenue to fund them grow more complex every session. Nevertheless, because the state constitution vests the legislature with considerable power, understanding at the least the basics of legislative operations is important.

This chapter examines the functions of legislative bodies, characteristics of members of the Texas legislature, and legislative compensation. It describes the constitutional, statutory, and informal aspects of legislative structure and the politics of redistricting. The chapter outlines the internal organization of the two houses, including presiding officers, committees, and staff. It then reviews the legislature in action as it goes about the business of making public policy and, finally, evaluates the institution and suggests reforms.

Functions of Legislative Bodies

If asked what legislators do, most people probably would answer, "Make laws." This answer is correct, but incomplete. First, it is incomplete because legislatures don't necessarily pass laws piecemeal. Often, many different laws, over many years, are passed in service to some overall vision, philosophy, or ideology. The unifying philosophy that holds laws together is called *policy*.

Second, legislative bodies have several other functions as well, most of which arise from the separation of political institutions and the system of checks and balances that underlie our system of government. In addition to lawmaking, **reapportionment** and **redistricting**, which refer to the way that a legislative body determines the geographic area any given legislator will represent, and the **constituent function** of proposing constitutional amendments are all activities traditionally associated with legislative bodies. Americans also deem it appropriate for a legislature to help shape the political agenda.

In contrast, activities such as **legislative oversight,** the overseeing of the administration, or doing **casework**—favors—for constituents may at first blush seem to belong to the executive rather than to the legislative branch. Conducting investigations also may seem to be an activity more readily associated with the executive branch, but legislators have broad powers to gather information and hold hearings in order to make informed policy judgments. Similarly, when the activity at hand is accusations and trial (impeachment), the details of court organization or procedures, or the settling of disputes such as those over elections, one may think first of the judiciary. Educating and informing the electorate may seem to be a function well suited to the schools or to private groups. In fact, the legislature is involved in all these functions.

Structure of the Legislature

How legislators are chosen, paid, and organized constitutes legislative structure.

Size, Elections, and Terms

With the exception of Nebraska, which has a unicameral (single-house) legislature, the American states have patterned themselves on the **bicameral** model of the U.S. Congress. Article III of the Texas Constitution stipulates that the legislature is composed of a Senate and a House of Representatives.

The two houses have approximately equal power, but the Senate has more prestige and is considered the upper house. One reason is its smaller size. Another is that each senator represents nearly five times as many citizens as does a member of the House. Still another factor is the Senate's control over executive appointments. In addition, the Senate's presiding officer, the lieutenant governor, is elected by the entire state. The Senate's less formal procedures permit more extended—and sometimes highly publicized—debate than in the House, and a senator's term of office is longer than that of a member of the House. Traditionally, the Senate's national counterpart, the U.S. Senate, has been considered the more prestigious national legislative chamber. At both the state and national levels, when a member of the House seeks and wins a Senate seat, this achievement is regarded as a political promotion.

The average state senate has 40 members; the average lower house, 112. The Texas Constitution fixes the number of state senators at 31 and the maximum number of representatives at 150. The U.S. Congress has 100 senators and 435 representatives.[1] In the national government, the number of senators is determined by the number of states; the number of members of the House, by statute (legislation). Among the 50 state legislatures, only the term *senate* is used consistently; the lower house is known variously as the assembly, house of representatives, and general assembly.[2] While the terms *house* and *senate* are used by both national and state governments, and the term *legislator* refers to a lawmaker at any level, *Congress* and *congressman/woman* are exclusively national.

Key features of the system for electing legislators include the following:

1. **Selection in the November general election in even-numbered years**

2. **Election from *single-member districts***

3. **Two-year terms for House members and four-year staggered terms for senators, without limit as to the number of terms that can be served**[3]

4. **A special election called by the governor to fill a vacancy caused by death, resignation, or expulsion from office**

Newly elected legislators take office in January. Whenever reapportionment to establish districts of approximately equal population size occurs—at intervals of no more than ten years—all senators are elected in the same year. They then draw lots to determine who will serve for two years and who will serve the full four-year term. This phenomenon last occurred in 2011.

If a vacancy occurs because of death, resignation, or expulsion from office, the governor calls a special election to fill it. The most common reason for a vacancy is resignation, usually occurring when a representative runs for higher office or a senator moves to the U.S. Congress or into an executive office. Deaths do occur, but rarely. Often a spouse will be designated to serve as a temporary member if an elected legislator is called to active duty in the armed services.

Term Limits

The issue of term limits—a maximum number of times a representative can be legally or constitutionally re-elected—was hotly debated during the 1990s, although interest seems to have waned in the twenty-first century. Twenty-one states initially set legislative term limits, but by 2007, only fifteen states still had them. The Texas legislature considered but rejected a variety of term limit bills during the 1990s. The U.S. Supreme Court in 1995 struck down efforts by states to limit the terms of members of the U.S. Congress. Many municipal charters in Texas and elsewhere do have limits on the number of terms the mayor and council can serve.

Proponents of term limits see them as a way to try to regain public confidence in legislative bodies that increasingly have been regarded as remote and lacking in understanding of public wishes. Opponents are concerned about such matters as a possible lack of policy expertise on the part of legislative leaders and arbitrarily jettisoning a popular legislator because of artificial term limits. They contend that, "We have term limits now. Just ask any incumbent defeated in the last election." The greatest criticism of term limits, however, is that they are inherently undemocratic because they rob voters of free choice in an election. Thus, democracy today is seeking to limit democracy tomorrow.

Sources: Summary of "Coping with Term Limits: A Practical Guide" (Denver: National Conference of State Legislatures, 2007), available at http://www.ncsl.org/programs/legismgt/ABOUT/Termlimit.htm. For background on this issue, see Keith B. Hamm and Gary F. Moncrief, "Legislative Politics in the States," in Virginia Gray and Russell Hanson, *Politics in the American States*, 8th ed. (Washington, D.C.: Congressional Quarterly Press, 2004), 167–169; B. Drummond Ayres, Jr., "Term Limit Laws Are Transforming More Legislatures," *New York Times,* April 28, 1997, A1, A14; Karen Hansen, "The Third Revolution," *State Legislatures,* September 1997, 20–28; Tim Storey, "2002 State Legislative Elections," *The Book of the States,* 2003, 81.

Sessions

Two types of legislative sessions may be called—regular and special. Regular sessions are legally required.

Regular Session

The constitution provides for regular biennial sessions, beginning on the second Tuesday in January of odd-numbered years. These sessions may run no longer than 140 calendar days. Four other states (Montana, Nevada, North Dakota, and Oregon) also have biennial sessions; the rest have either annual or continuous sessions or the authority to divide a biennial session across two years.

The truncated biennial legislative session accentuates all the formal and informal factors that influence legislation in Texas. For example, insufficient time for careful consideration of bills heightens the power of the presiding officers, the lobbyists, and the governor. Also, the short biennial session prevents issues from being raised in the first place so that the state sometimes delays dealing with problems until a crisis occurs. Although there have been a number of changes in the specifics of the legislative sessions over the years, voters have consistently rejected amendments providing for annual sessions. They fear increased governmental power and spending, in part, a reflection of the antigovernment attitude implicit in a conservative political culture and, in part, an acknowledgment of the $40-plus million price tag for a regular session.

Special Sessions

The governor can call the legislature into special session for a maximum of thirty days. The governor determines the agenda for this session. If a legislator wishes to add items to the agenda for a special session, the governor must agree. Thirty-two other state legislatures have mechanisms for calling themselves into special session. In Texas, only in the extraordinary situation that resulted in the impeachment of Governor Jim "Pa" Ferguson in 1917 for suspected corruption has the legislature ever convened a special session on its own. The Senate, under the 1999 succession amendment to the constitution, can meet as a committee of the whole to elect an acting lieutenant governor.

The governor may call one special session after another if necessary. However, because the voting public has rejected annual sessions several times, Texas governors usually try to avoid calling numerous special sessions that might appear to function as annual sessions. The average price tag—about $9.1 million per special session—is another disincentive. Nevertheless, governors sometimes have little choice about calling a special session because too much legislative business—often including the state budget—is unfinished. It is particularly difficult in a redistricting year to complete both redistricting and the budget.

Legislative Districts

One of the most contentious issues faces the legislature at least once a decade. Disputes over redistricting are strident and partisan.

Mechanics

Only one senator or representative may be elected from a particular district by the people living in that district. Although some districts are 300 times larger than others in geographic size (see http://gis1.tlc.state.tx.us/; the Texas Legislative Council maintains maps of current and proposed districts), each senatorial district should have approximately 811,147 residents, and each house district should have approximately 167,637 as of 2010.[4] Achieving equally populated districts does not come easily, however, because the task is a highly political one carried out by the legislature, and the Texas population continues to grow.

If the legislature fails to redistrict itself, the Legislative Redistricting Board (LRB) comes into play. The LRB is composed of five *ex officio* state officials; that is, they are members by virtue of their holding another office. These five are the lieutenant governor, the speaker of the House, the comptroller of public accounts, the general land commissioner, and the attorney general. If both the legislature and the LRB fail in the reapportionment and redistricting task, the matter goes to the federal courts for resolution. Also, the redistricting handiwork of the legislature and the LRB is always subject to review by the U.S. Department of Justice because Texas, as a state that formerly discriminated against ethnic minorities in the voting process, is subject to the Voting Rights Act of 1965.

History

Prior to the mid-1960s, legislative districts were a hodgepodge based partly on population, partly on geography, and largely on protecting rural interests. Members of the Senate have always been elected in single-member districts, but in the past, those districts reflected land area, not population. Indeed, the Texas

Constitution once prohibited a single county, regardless of population, from having more than one senator. House districts were constitutionally based on population, but with limitations that worked against urban counties.[5] In addition, **gerrymandering**—drawing district lines in such a way as to give one faction or one party an advantage—was the norm. (*Gerrymander* is pronounced with the sound of "g" as in gate, not "g" as in gentry.)

The federal courts changed the ability of the state to artificially limit representation from urban areas and forced the drawing of legislative districts according to population. In 1962, in *Baker* v. *Carr*[6]—the one-person, one-vote case—the U.S. Supreme Court overturned a legislative districting system that gave one group substantial advantages over another. In 1964, in *Reynolds* v. *Sims,*[7] the Court laid down its first guidelines on conditions that would necessitate redrawing district lines, including a mandate that the membership of both houses be based on population. The Texas House of Representatives continued to use multimember legislative districts[8] until the courts forced some counties to abandon them in 1975, and others volunteered to do so.[9]

Citizens in urban areas, Republicans, and ethnic minority groups have all been prominent in redistricting suits. As Table 6-1 shows, the predominant ethnic minorities in Texas—Hispanics and African Americans—have made some gains through population-based districting. Ethnic minority groups made up 21.7 percent of the legislature in 1989; the percentage had risen to 30.9 percent in 2009 before slipping back to 28.1 in the wake of the Republican election landslide of 2010. However, Texas is about 55 percent ethnic minority and only 45 percent Anglo; thus the legislature and the population as a whole are not in alignment. Texas is on the short list of states in which a majority of its population comprises ethnic minorities (the others are Hawaii, California, and New Mexico).[10]

Table 6-2 shows the gains made by Republicans through the 2011 legislative session, with most of these gains coming in urban areas. After the 2002 elections, Republicans held both houses of the legislature, all the executive offices, and all the major judgeships of the state. Democrats briefly kept a slight edge in congressional seats until the 2003 redistricting effects were felt at the polls. Republicans in Texas have benefited not only from reapportionment, but

TABLE 6-1

Ethnicity in the Texas Legislature, Transitional Years since 1989, by Percentage

Year	Anglo	Hispanic/Mexican American	African American	Asian American
1989	77.9%*	14.4%	7.7%	0%
1993	73.5	17.7	8.8	0
2003	69.6	21.0	8.8	0.6
2011	71.8	17.7	9.4	1.1

*Percentages do not always equal 100 due to rounding.

TABLE 6-2

Political Party Membership in the Texas Legislature, 1977–2011, Transitional Years and Most Recent Years, by Percentage

	Senate (N = 31)		House (N = 150)		Both Houses (N = 181)	
Year	Democrat	Republican	Democrat	Republican	Democrat	Republican
1977	90.3%	9.7%	87.3%	12.7%	87.9%	12.1%
1987	80.6	19.4	62.7	37.3	71.3	28.7
1997	45.2	54.8	54.7	45.3	53.0	47.0
2003	38.7	61.3	41.3	58.7	40.9	59.1
2007	35.5	64.5	45	55	44.2	55.8
2009	38.7	61.3	49.3	50.7	47.5	52.5
2011	38.7	61.3	32.7	67.3	33.7	66.3

also from the national trend toward conservative politics and from the steady evolution of the state's politics from one-party Democrat to two-party and then to Republican dominance. However, the strong Democratic showing across the country in 2008 almost led to the Democrats recapturing the Texas House before being overwhelmed by the Republicans in 2010.

In addition to ethnic, party, and urban pressures, legislators have to be concerned with the federal Voting Rights Act of 1965 and with producing redistricting plans that the governor will not veto. Moreover, the federal courts continue to monitor redistricting efforts.[11] With all these competing demands, it is no wonder that the legislature usually fails to produce a plan that pleases everyone. Because redistricting is so controversial, even to the point of dominating the legislative session in which it occurs, the legislature often fails to get the maps drawn or finds that it must do the task more than once.

Redistricting disputes of the 1990s were comparatively mild compared to the disputes following the 2000 census. The legislature failed to agree on a redistricting plan, leading to the Legislative Redistricting Board's coming into play for only the third time since the procedure was established in 1951. The LRB effort subsequently was altered by a three-judge federal court. All of the plans favored the Republicans, who were the majority party, but the GOP was feuding with itself, as well as with Democrats.[12] The biggest redistricting fight of the early 2000s occurred over congressional districts in 2003. The Democrats had already lost all the executive offices and their legislative majority and were focused on holding their U.S. House majority. The result was a nasty, intensely partisan series of special sessions in 2003 that included walkouts by senators to Oklahoma and New Mexico, abandonment of traditional rules, and great rancor.[13] The media branded the walk-out Democrats as the Killer Ds; the Republicans had a less kind name and called the walkers Chicken Ds. Senate efforts to prevent such disputes in the future by establishing a bipartisan commission to oversee congressional redistricting died in the lower house.

Party, Party

How important political party is and how much the Republicans dominated the legislature were evident in the drawing of two adjacent House districts in the Rio Grande Valley in 2011. Aaron Pena, elected as a Democrat, had switched parties before the legislative session began. He was rewarded with a district that packed virtually every conceivable Republican vote into his district. That generosity meant destroying the district of the three-term Democrat Veronica Gonzales, chair of the Border and Intergovernmental Affairs Committee, who retained only 1.5 percent of her former district. In the Senate, Wendy Davis, a first-term Democrat who represented a substantial portion of the minority population of Tarrant County, found her district redrawn to be more heavily Republican. The African American and Latino parts of her district were then disbursed to three other districts and their votes thus diluted.

Source: "There's a Map for That," *Texas Observer*, May 20, 2011, 2; and "Wendy Davis Says Districting Plan an Insult to Her Constituents," *Fort Worth Star-Telegram*, May 12, 2011, available at http://www.star-telegram.com/2011/05/12/3072037/davis-says-redistricting-plan.html on May 19, 2011.

Redistricting was mandatory in 2011, following the 2010 census. Texas gained four new congressional seats. Because Democrats comprised only one-third of the legislature, their say-so was minimal in the drawing of district lines and the determination of which areas would get the new congressional seats. However, the state's population growth that had resulted in the new seats was due mainly to growth in the Hispanic populations of the largest cities. As a consequence, the redistricting plan reflected three concepts, somewhat at odds with one another: (1) consideration of districts that would be safe for Hispanics, (2) some "packing" of districts (that is, creating districts with highly concentrated ethnic populations rather than encouraging minority influence across more districts), and (3) protection of incumbents.[14]

Party and Factional Organization

Historically, until the late 1970s, Texas was a one-party—Democratic—state. In the legislature, unlike the situation in the U.S. Congress and many other state legislatures, political party organization did not exist. As a one-party state, Texas saw factionalism within the Democratic Party replace the party differences that characterized other legislative bodies.

Political party affiliation and party organization have grown in importance as Texas briefly became a two-party state, and then moved into being a Republican-dominant state. As Table 6-2 shows, Republican representation in the legislature has grown from minuscule in 1977 to a super (two-thirds) majority in the Texas House in 2011 and to only one member shy of a super majority in the Texas Senate since 2009. Beginning in 1983, party members in the House designated floor leaders. In the 1989 session, House Republicans formed a formal caucus for the first time since Reconstruction, and today they regularly select a party whip—the person designated to line up votes on behalf of the official party position. House members, particularly, reported more intensely partisan disagreements beginning with the 1997 session when the Democratic majority

Reapportionment and redistricting are always highly partisan, and Texas Democrats were never surer of that fact than after the 2011 redistricting further minimized the likelihood that Democrats would be elected. The dominant Republicans just carved up the state for themselves.

Courtesy of Ben Sargent.

narrowed substantially, and especially with the coming of the Republican majority and the change in the speaker's position in 2003. The 2009 session, with an almost even party split in the House, was more peaceful, but the 2011 session was very divisive. House Tea Party Republicans demanded huge cuts in social services and even challenged their own leaders. Some went so far as to contend that the Democrats should be kept off major committees. Senators of both parties found ways to adopt the rules for their own purposes and to shun traditional procedures.

Although the Senate has been Republican-majority since 1997, most of the time—redistricting notwithstanding—the Senate has continued a long-standing tradition of operating with less partisanship than the House. The Senate presiding officer has continued to deal with members on an individual basis. The Texas House has grown to look more like the U.S. Congress, which is organized strictly along party lines.

Even with the party alignment shifting and with partisanship increasing, the minority party did continue to receive significant committee appointments, and the presiding officers often relied on their assessment of and ties to individual legislators more than party affiliation in working through legislative business. For example, in 2011, eleven (30 percent) of the thirty-six standing House committees were chaired by Democrats, who held 33 percent of the seats. However, there were also three powerful select committees and a joint committee, all chaired by Republicans. In the Senate, where Democrats held 39 percent of the seats, they still held six of the eighteen standing committee chairmanships (33 percent) as well as three of seven major subcommittee chairmanships. Republicans chaired the two select committees.

The liberalism or conservatism of a legislator once was more important than the party label. Liberals versus conservatives and urban versus rural/suburban interests were typical divisions. These differences cut across party lines and were most evident on issues such as taxation, spending, and social welfare programs.

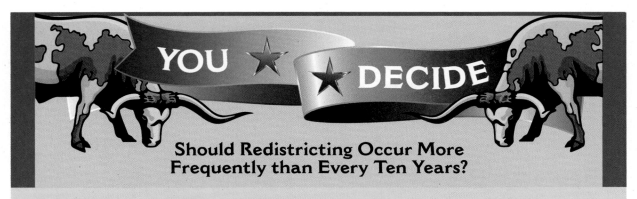

YOU ★ ★ DECIDE

Should Redistricting Occur More Frequently than Every Ten Years?

The redrawing of state legislative and congressional district lines must occur every ten years after each federal census to reflect changes in population. In Texas, congressional lines were redrawn in 2001 and then again in 2003, prompting loud protests from Democrats. In 2011, all state legislative and congressional districts had to be redrawn following the 2010 census. Should redistricting continue to occur more frequently than the year following each decennial census report?

PRO	CON
▲ Districts should be drawn frequently to reflect changes in Texas's growing population.	▼ The population changes daily; it is impossible to "keep up" with the population on a yearly or biennial basis.
▲ Although the law does not require equity in political party distribution, lines should be redrawn to reflect changes in party preference.	▼ The legal requirements are only for equality in population size and for an absence of racial discrimination.
▲ The legislature should always redraw lines to avoid having the district lines established by the courts.	▼ If the courts have drawn the lines, the legislature has already failed once. Why should it change lines that the courts have approved?
▲ The state legislature should be sensitive to the desires of the political party in the majority nationally.	▼ The U.S. Constitution gives state legislatures the power to determine district lines.

When legislators can avoid the pursuit of rigid ideologies of the left or the right, they have more focus on solving public policy problems. However, discussion of legislative procedure will indicate that the minority party sometimes has a hard time being heard, especially in the House.

The long-standing tradition of working across party lines, of allowing the minority adequate voice, and of generally behaving in a civilized manner has been eroding throughout the twenty-first century. Analysts were concerned that parliamentary maneuvering in 2011 to silence the opposition—the Republican majority's tendency to shut off debate prematurely and the Democratic minority's penchant for using technicalities to delay debate—may have permanently altered the tenor of the legislature.[15]

Compensation

Since 1975, members of the Texas legislature have received a salary of $7,200 each year; this figure was established by constitutional amendment. (Texas is one of only six states that set legislative salaries by constitution.) Legislators also receive a per diem (daily) allowance when the legislature is in regular or special session to cover lodging, meals, and other expenses; for the Eighty-second Legislature in 2011–2012, the per diem rate was $168. In contrast to salary, the per diem rate is among the highest in the nation. When they serve on a state board or council or conduct legislative business between sessions, legislators also are entitled to per diem expenses for up to twelve days a month. In addition, they receive a $0.51 mileage allowance. The presiding officers receive the same compensation and are also entitled to apartments provided by the state.

As Figure 6-1 shows, as of 2010, California, the largest state in population, paid legislators $95,300 a year (a reduction from two years earlier), more than thirteen times what Texas, the second largest state, pays.[16] The Texas legislative stipend is not even half the federal minimum for a family of four to be above the poverty level! The low level of Texas salaries, which voters have repeatedly refused to change, makes legislators simultaneously more susceptible to lobbying tactics—at $7,200, a free lunch is important—and more likely to divert their attention to finding ways to earn a decent living. The latter task has become more difficult with the increase in committee work between legislative sessions and occasional special sessions.

Under a 1991 state constitutional amendment, the Ethics Commission can convene a citizen advisory board to recommend changes in legislative salary; the

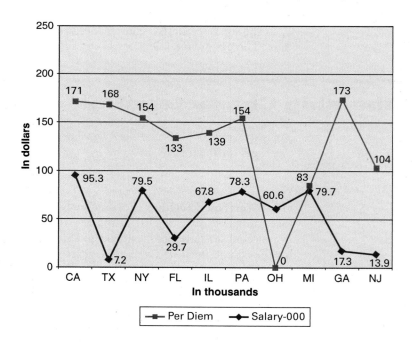

FIGURE 6-1 Legislative Salaries, Per Diem in Ten Largest States, 2010.

The New York and Pennsylvania rates are based on the federal rate. The Michigan rate is calculated.

SOURCE: The Book of the States, 2010 Edition, vol. 42 (Lexington, Ky.: Council of State Governments, 2010), 113–116.

proposal must then be submitted to the voters. However, as of 2011, no such board had been formed. The Ethics Commission also is empowered to increase the per diem expense money and has done so regularly.

The "bottom line" on legislative compensation is that the salary is very low, especially for a high-population state with a complex legislative agenda. The fringe benefits are rather generous, however. Some legislators have manipulated salary, the per diem, and travel reimbursements to bring in more than $75,000 during a regular session year. On average, a legislator receives about five times the stipulated salary when all forms of compensation are considered. The fundamentally undemocratic aspect of legislative compensation is that citizens have authorized only the $7,200 salary and might be surprised at the total compensation package. Nevertheless, the reality that confronts Texans is that only Texas, Alabama, and New Hampshire have not increased legislative salaries for more than thirty years. Although some states, such as California, with long-standing revenue problems have temporarily reduced legislative compensation, the base was generous to begin with.

Legislators also receive an allowance for operating an office both during the session and in the interim between sessions. In 2009, the monthly allowance during the regular legislative session for senators was $37,000; for House members, $13,250. These allowances compare favorably with those granted by other states. Additionally, legislators are entitled to retirement benefits if they serve at least twelve years if the retirement age is under fifty or eight years if the age is sixty or over. Joining the retirement system is optional; participants have 8 percent of their monthly salaries deducted. The retirement is based on the annual salary of a district judge, which was $140,000 in 2009. A major controversy in 2005 was the legislative decision to raise judges' salaries, in effect granting themselves a handsome retirement increase.

The small legislative salaries follow the general principles of a citizen legislature. The per diem allowances, staff budgets, and retirement provisions do not.

Membership Characteristics

As is true with all officeholders, legislators have both formal and informal qualifications for the job.

Formal Qualifications

The **formal qualifications** necessary to become a member of the Texas legislature are stipulated in Article III of the constitution. They are those commonly listed for elected officials: age, residency, U.S. citizenship, and voting status. Members of the Senate must be twenty-six years of age or older, qualified voters for five years, and residents of the senatorial district from which they are elected for one year. Members of the House must be at least twenty-one years old, qualified voters, legal residents of the state for two years, and residents of the district from which they are elected for one year.

Personal Characteristics

The formal qualifications are so broad as to make a substantial portion of the Texas citizenry eligible to run for legislative office. However, individuals with certain types of personal characteristics tend to get elected more readily than

individuals who lack the characteristics. These characteristics reflect political, social, and economic realities and traditions and confirm the state's conservative political tradition. That they exist does not mean that they are desirable. Indeed, they indicate that certain groups may be underrepresented in the Texas legislature.

In general, Texas legislators tend to be middle-aged, White, male Protestant lawyers or businessmen who are married, have college educations, belong to a number of civic organizations, have considerable personal money, as well as access to campaign funds, and have the support of the local media. Not every legislator has all of these personal characteristics, but an individual elected without having any of them would be extraordinary indeed. Trends in ethnicity and party membership were shown in Tables 6-1 and 6-2. Selected characteristics are shown in Table 6-3.

White Male

Race, ethnicity, and gender are all factors in politics. Both ethnic minorities and women are considerably underrepresented in the Texas legislature in terms of numbers, though not necessarily ideologically. Although Texas's total minority population exceeds 50 percent, minority membership in the legislature in 2011 was only 28 percent. The first Asian American member was elected in 2002; no Native American is a member. Although there are about 100 women for every 97 men in society, slightly less than 21 percent of the Eighty-second Texas Legislature were women. An important contextual fact about ethnic representation is that most ethnic minority members are Democrats, and the Democrats have been the minority party in both houses since the 2002 elections. However, the Texas legislature is more diversified than most state legislatures. The national average is 86 percent Caucasian.[17]

TABLE 6-3

Selected Characteristics of Members of the Eighty-Second Texas Legislature, 2011–2012

Category	Senate = 31	House = 150
Republicans/Democrats	19/12 (61.3%–38.7%)	101/49 (67.3%–32.7%)
Ethnicity	7 Hispanic, 2 African American (29% minority)	25 Hispanic, 15 African American, 2 Asian American (28% minority)
Women	25 men, 6 women (19.4% women)	118 men, 32 women (21.36% women)
Median Age	50–59, 60–69	50–59
Professions	16 different ones, led by law, fields of business	*
Tenure	29 returning, 2 freshmen (6.5% turnover)	113 returning, 37 freshman (24.6% turnover)

*The House did not provide summary information on professions. Usually, House members reflect more types of careers than the members of the smaller Senate do.

SOURCE: By count, using official records of the House of Representatives and the Senate and Legislative Reference Library, "Membership Statistics for 82nd Legislature," available at http://www.lrl.state.tx.us/sessions/sessionSnapshot.cfm?legSession=82-0 on May 11, 2011.

Students as Legislative Staffers

House members in particular are always seeking additional staff assistance because their office budgets are often less than those of senators. Students often volunteer and frequently become very responsible members of a legislator's staff, either in Austin or in the home district. Some become paid staffers.

Lawyers and Businesspersons

Legislators tend to be white-collar professionals and businesspersons. Other fields, such as farming and ranching, also have fairly strong representation, given their small numbers in the general population. Law traditionally has been seen as preparation for politics. In fact, aspiring politicians often attend law school as a means of gaining entry into politics. The result is that attorneys, who make up less than 4 percent of the state's total population, hold almost one-third of Texas legislative seats. Their numbers have been slowly waning in recent years, reflecting a national trend away from lawyers as legislators. The most frequent business fields are real estate, insurance, finance, and various forms of consulting.

Fiftyish

The House and Senate no longer list the age of individual members, but instead provide age information by decade. Their Web sites then indicate the median, or middle, group. In 2011, the median age group of members of the Texas House was 50–59; in the Senate, the medians were 50–59 and 60–69 (the same number of members were in each group). These numbers compare to the state median age group of 30–39. Only two House and no Senate members were under 30; thirty-eight House members and fourteen senators were age 60 or older. Thus, the growing numbers of young adults are especially underrepresented, but the statistics are a bit misleading because two-thirds of those under 40 are children. Senior citizens are somewhat overrepresented, a fact that may reflect the reality that the paltry salary of legislators dictates that most individuals wait until they are financially secure to consider running for office.[18]

Other Factors

Education, marital status, religion, organization, money, and the media are additional factors in legislative elections. Since the late 1970s, virtually all members of the legislature have some college education, and slightly over half hold more than one degree—especially in law or business. The preponderance of legislators is married, although each year more members decline to state whether they are married. In 1991, the legislature had its first acknowledged gay man as a member. Legislators no longer include religious preference in their biographical information, and it is increasingly difficult to find current information about the religious preferences of Texas citizens. This reality may reflect a greater sensitivity to religious freedom in the state. The most recent information is from the 1990s, when about two-thirds of both houses were Protestant, a little over a quarter of each house was Roman Catholic, a small number of Jews were

members, and several members provided no information about their religion. Those preferences were roughly in keeping with the preferences of the state's residents as a whole, and one can assume that legislators continue to look a great deal like the general public in their religious preferences. The Texas legislature rarely deals with issues that have a basis in religion, although someone's religious views may influence thinking about issues, such as school vouchers or parental consent for teenage abortions. However, in 2007, the House considered a number of bills that would infuse religion into public policy,[19] one of a number of areas that reflected sharp differences in Senate and House policy preferences.

Legislators also tend to be members of the "right" groups. Memberships in civic associations, business and professional groups, and social clubs all help convince voters that the candidate is a solid citizen. Such memberships also provide contacts with potential campaign donors. Campaigning for office is expensive.

In 2010, the lowest amount of campaign funds raised by a winning candidate for the Texas House of Representatives was $29,466, while the highest amount was $5,265,357. In the Senate, the range of funds raised by winning candidates was $374,334 to $1,299,315.[20] The amounts raised, especially in the House, reflect whether the district is considered "safe," making election/re-election easy, and who the candidate is (the most dollars went to the powerful speaker of the House). Also, unexpended funds can be held over and used for a variety of purposes that must be only vaguely related to the role of state legislator.[21] (See Chapter 5 for a discussion of campaigns and elections.) Generally, candidates with some personal money are better able to attract financial support than those of ordinary means, in part because they move in "money" circles. Favorable media exposure—news coverage and editorial endorsements by newspapers, magazines, radio, and especially television—is of tremendous importance during a campaign. The media decide who the leading candidates are and then give them the lion's share of free news space. Texas media tend to be conservative and to endorse business-oriented candidates.

Experience and Turnover

Seniority has long been of great importance in the committee structure of the U.S. Congress, and Texas voters in many districts were accustomed to re-electing members of the Texas congressional delegation, at least until new district lines were drawn in 2003. Rapid **turnover** of 20 to 25 percent traditionally characterized the Texas legislature, with the result that state legislators have been accused of being inexperienced and amateurish. In 2011, the House turnover rate was 24.6 percent, although the Senate rate was only 6.5 percent. Moreover, a typical freshman senator is likely to have had prior governmental experience in the House, and a typical freshman House member may have served on a county commissioners court, city council, or school board.

What causes legislative turnover? Running for higher office, retirement, moving into the more profitable private sector, and reapportionment/redistricting are among the causes. Other causes of legislative turnover include tough urban re-election races, changing party alignments, and voter perception. Seniority is not as important in the state legislature as it is in the U.S. Congress. Nevertheless, seniority is important. Not only does it increase the probability that a legislator will be knowledgeable about policy issues, but it also means that the legislator will understand how the system works. In the Senate, especially, the more-senior members tend to chair committees.

Legislative Officers and Committees

The presiding officers and committee chairs are the dominant players in the Texas legislature. The presiding officers have an unusual amount of power, a phenomenon described later in this chapter.

Presiding Officers

The presiding officers of any legislative assembly have more power and prestige than do ordinary members. In Texas, however, the lieutenant governor and the speaker of the House have such sweeping procedural, organizational, administrative, and planning authority that they truly dominate the legislative scene.

Although most state legislatures have partisan leadership positions analogous to the majority and minority leaders in the U.S. Congress, this is not yet the case in Texas because of the historical one-party tradition, the tendency to have bipartisan leadership, and the domination of the presiding officers. The committee chairs hold the secondary positions of power, after the presiding officers. Chairs are appointed by the presiding officers and thus do not offer any threat to the power of either the speaker or the lieutenant governor.

Lieutenant Governor

The lieutenant governor is elected independently by the citizenry, serves as president of the Senate, but is not a member of it, and does not run on the ticket with the gubernatorial candidate. The lieutenant governor rarely performs any executive functions and is chiefly a legislative official. The term of the office is four years.

Twenty-seven other states use the lieutenant governor as the presiding officer of the upper house. But these states (usually) also look to the governor for policy recommendations; their chamber rules are such that the lieutenant governor, far from exercising any real power, is generally in a position similar to that of the vice president of the United States—neither an important executive nor a legislative force. Such is not the case in Texas, where the lieutenant governor is a major force in state politics and the dominant figure during legislative sessions.

The lieutenant governor orchestrates the flow of legislation in the upper house. Republican David Dewhurst, a wealthy businessman and former CIA agent who served a single term as commissioner of the General Land Office as his only previous public office, was first elected as lieutenant governor in 2002. His leadership has been hit-or-miss ever since. He was well prepared for the 2003 session and maintained the precedent of bipartisanship among committee chairs begun thirty years earlier by Lieutenant Governor William P. (Bill) Hobby. During the partisan battles over redistricting in the summer of 2003, Dewhurst originally held firm and tried to maintain the neutrality and calm of the Senate. Ultimately, he yielded to party pressures and forced the redistricting issue by setting aside the traditional two-thirds rule. In 2005, Dewhurst apparently tried to seek the high road on issues, such as school finance and child protection legislation, but he and his House counterpart, as well as the governor, seemed to go in different directions.[22] In 2007, his interest in the governorship was apparent, and many senators thought Dewhurst failed as a legislative leader. In 2009, he got the Senate off to a fast start while the House struggled with its

change in leadership. By 2011, Dewhurst was pursuing a U.S. Senate seat and, eager to please the most conservative members of his party, forcing votes to the detriment of the minority Democrats.

Dewhurst's immediate predecessors were both Republicans. Bill Ratliff, a Senate powerhouse, was selected by his colleagues to act as presiding officer for the 2001 session. Lieutenant Governor Rick Perry, who presided over the 1999 session, had moved up to the governor's mansion in late 2000 following Governor George W. Bush's election to the U.S. presidency. Ratliff chose to return to the Senate rather than run for lieutenant governor, and subsequently resigned from office after the rancorous redistricting battles of 2003. Ratliff rued the end of civility in his beloved Senate and thought that it no longer played the important moderating role it long had in tempering the actions of the more passionate and more fractious House.[23] These two short-term presiding officers followed two long-term presiding officers, both Democrats. Bob Bullock ruled the Senate from 1991 until 1999, and Bill Hobby presided over the Senate from 1973 until 1991.[24]

Speaker of the House

The speaker of the Texas House of Representatives is an elected member of the House who is formally chosen as speaker by a majority vote of the House membership at the opening of the legislative session. The results of the election are rarely a surprise; by the time the session opens, everyone usually knows who the speaker will be. Candidates for speaker begin maneuvering for support long before the previous session has ended. And during the session interims, they not only campaign for election to the House in their home districts, but also try to secure from fellow House members written pledges of support in the race for speaker. If an incumbent speaker is seeking re-election, usually no other candidates run.

It is important for legislators to know whether the speaker is seeking re-election because they must decide whether to back the incumbent or take a chance on supporting a challenger. The decision is crucial: The speaker rewards supporters by giving them key committee assignments—perhaps even the opportunity to chair a committee—and by helping them campaign for re-election to the legislature. A House member who throws support in the wrong direction risks legislative oblivion.

Until 1951, speakers traditionally served for one term; between 1951 and 1975, they served either one or two. The House has abandoned the limited-term tradition, however. Billy Clayton served four terms as speaker (1975–1983), and his successor, Gib Lewis, served five (1983–1993). James E. (Pete) Laney, a West Texas cotton farmer, bested eight other House members to become speaker in 1993 and was elected to a fifth term in 2001.

Tom Craddick, known for his partisanship, ideology, and vindictiveness, served as speaker for three terms (2003–2009) until his ousting in January 2009. He was almost overturned in 2007, and by 2009, a movement known as ABC ("anyone but Craddick") made it obvious that the House would have a new speaker. House members had lost confidence in Craddick and wanted someone who could lead through a more peaceful legislative session than Craddick could. However, in 2011, he received an honorary title of Dean of the House.

Although the candidates at one point numbered a dozen, Joe Straus, a San Antonio Republican, emerged as the leading candidate in 2009. The bipartisan ABC proponents actually met to agree on a candidate to ensure that Craddick

did not continue. Straus is sometimes a party maverick in spite of fifty years of family GOP tradition. He replaced many of Craddick's cronies on key committees and tried to steer the House toward a harmonious session.[25] In 2011, the Republicans had a super majority (two-thirds) of the House and could do as they pleased. The far-right of his party tried to oust Straus because he was Jewish, not Christian, but they failed. However, the Democrats who supported him were stunned by Straus's allowing a number of motions to stop debate and expedite the majority viewpoint.[26]

Pro Tempore Positions

Pro tempore ("for the time being") positions are largely honorific in Texas. At the beginning of the session, the Senate elects one member to serve as president pro tempore to preside when the lieutenant governor (president of the Senate) is absent or if the lieutenant governor's office becomes vacant. At the end of the session, another individual is elected to serve as president pro tempore during the legislative interim; this person is usually one of the senior members. House rules also provide for the speaker to appoint someone to preside over the House temporarily or to appoint a speaker pro tempore to serve permanently. Whether to select anyone at all and who the individual will be are options left to the speaker.

Legislative Committees

Legislative bodies in the United States have long relied on committees to expedite their work because the alternative is trying to accomplish detailed legislation, planning, and investigation by the whole house. These committees are critical to the legislative process. The types of committees are discussed below, but the power of the committees is also a significant part of the discussion of legislative process later in this chapter. The five basic types of committees in the state legislature are listed here. Note that these categories are not mutually exclusive.

1. **Standing committees are established by the rules of the two houses as permanent committees. They deal with designated areas of public policy.**

2. **Subcommittees are subdivisions of standing committees. They consider specialized areas of their standing committees' general jurisdiction.**

3. **Conference committees are formed for the purpose of arriving at acceptable compromises on bills that have passed both houses, but in different forms. These temporary committees include members from both houses; a selected number of members of the standing committees that originally had jurisdiction over the bills in question are usually members of the conference committee.**

4. **Ad hoc committees are temporary and are appointed to consider specific issues or problems. Conference committees are a type of ad hoc committee. So are select committees appointed to deal with a specific item of legislation (such as the Senate Select Committee on Redistricting).**

5. **Interim committees continue the work of the legislature after the session ends, to study a particular problem and/or to make recommendations to the next legislature. Interim committees are frequently joint committees—that is, they have members from both houses.**

Standing Committees

One of the thrusts of Speaker Price Daniels's reform legislation of 1973 was to reduce the ever-expanding number of House committees. While the House has not returned to the forty-six standing committees of the Daniels years, it has fluctuated between thirty-four and forty in recent years. In 2011, the House had thirty-six standing committees and three select committees dealing with "hot-button" issues. When there are many committees, the lines of committee jurisdiction are hazy, and determining which committee has jurisdiction over a bill is much like trying to fit together a jigsaw puzzle. Table 6-4 lists the standing and select committees of the Eighty-second Texas Legislature in 2011–2012.

TABLE 6-4

Standing and Select Committees of the Eighty-Second Legislature, 2011–2012

Eighteen Senate Committees (Plus Seven Standing Subcommittees)	Thirty-Six House Committees
Administration	Agriculture & Livestock
Agriculture & Rural Affairs	Appropriations
Business & Commerce	Border & Intergovernmental Affairs
Criminal Justice	Business & Industry
Economic Development	Calendars
Education	Corrections
Finance (six subcommittees)	County Affairs
Government Organization	Criminal Jurisprudence
Health & Human Services	Culture, Recreation, & Tourism
Higher Education	Defense & Veterans' Affairs
Intergovernmental Relations (one subcommittee)	Economic and Small Business Development
International Relations & Trade	Elections
Jurisprudence	Energy Resources
	Environmental Regulation
Natural Resources	General Investigating & Ethics
	Government Efficiency and Reform
Nominations	Higher Education
State Affairs	Homeland Security
Transportation & Homeland Security	House Administration
Veterans Affairs & Military Installations	Human Services
Also: Select Committees on Open Government and Redistricting	Insurance
	Judiciary & Civil Jurisprudence
	Land & Resource Management

(continued)

TABLE 6-4 (CONTINUED)

Standing and Select Committees of the Eighty-Second Legislature, 2011–2012

Eighteen Senate Committees (Plus Seven Standing Subcommittees)	Thirty-Six House Committees
	Licensing & Administrative Procedures
	Local & Consent Calendars
	Natural Resources
	Pensions, Investments, & Financial Services
	Public Education
	Public Health
	Redistricting
	Rules & Resolutions
	State Affairs
	Technology
	Transportation
	Urban Affairs
	Ways & Means
	Also: Select Committees on State Sovereignty, Voter ID and Voter Fraud, and Election Contest and a Joint Committee on Oversight of HHS Eligibility

In 1973, a modified seniority system was introduced in the Texas House of Representatives. Under this system, a representative may ask for appointment to a desired committee slot on the basis of seniority—that is, the number of terms the legislator has served in the House.[27] If less than half the committee's membership has been selected according to seniority, the member's request is granted. The speaker then appoints the remainder of the committee members, including the committee chairperson and vice chairperson.

In the Senate, the presiding officer—the lieutenant governor—appoints all committee members and the committee chairpersons and vice chairpersons. A modified seniority rule applies as follows: For committees of ten or fewer members, three must be persons who have served on that committee in the last session; for committees of more than ten members, four must have served on that committee during the last session. A senator may serve as chairperson of only one standing committee during any one session. Ironically, while reformers at the federal government level have worked hard and with some success to gain a relaxation of the seniority rule in Congress, reformers at the state level have sought to introduce seniority into the Texas legislature. The reason proposed for introducing seniority into the Texas system is the same as that for originally instituting the system in Congress: to mitigate some of the power concentrated in the hands of the presiding officers. Although seniority

can discourage capable young legislators, it does ensure that those who play a significant part in conducting legislative business have experience and possibly some degree of expertise. The experience factor is important. Legislative committees control the flow of legislation in both houses, and the method by which their members are selected generally influences the outcome of public policy in the state.

Other Committees

The standing subcommittees in the Senate are also appointed by the lieutenant governor. Other subcommittees in both houses are named by the committee chairpersons, who are unlikely to act contrary to the wishes of the presiding officers. Ad hoc and conference committees are creatures of the speaker and lieutenant governor.

Interim committees are somewhat different. Their members *may* include a combination of appointees of the presiding officers and the governor, including citizen (nonlegislative) members. The 1961 Legislative Reorganization Act directed standing committees to study matters under their jurisdiction during the legislative interim, but in many cases, special interim committees are appointed instead. Often, these committees are support-building devices for legislation that failed during the previous session. Such committees are not mandated to deliver a report back to the legislature. Of course, if the speaker or lieutenant governor is interested in the study, the likelihood of a full report increases substantially. Although legislative staff is available to assist either standing or special committees between legislative sessions, interim committees often are created without a staff and/or funds.

A modern device is the select committee, which includes legislators and governor's appointees. The Select Committee on Public Education created by the Sixty-eighth Legislature (1983–1984) had the support of the leadership and the governor; consequently, it is an example of a well-funded, highly publicized study committee. Another example is the Select Committee on Tax Equity in 1987–1988, created by the Seventieth Legislature. The Joint Select Committee on Public School Finance, which served in 2003–2004, is an example of a significant interim committee intended to produce recommendations for legislative action on an important topic. Its job was to recommend a way to fund public schools in the state. In 2007, the Select Committee on the Operation and Management of the Texas Youth Commission had the important function of producing legislation that would result in the reorganization of a corrupt, abusive agency. In recent sessions, select committees have also been used during the session to focus on a particularly important legislative concern such as redistricting or voter identification.

Legislative Staff

Although Texas legislators enjoy better office budgets and staff allowances than their counterparts in some other states, they still must rely on information furnished by outside groups. For example, the Texas Research League, a private business-oriented group, performs numerous studies and makes recommendations to the legislature. The Legislative Budget Board (LBB), an internal agency of the legislature, makes recommendations on the same appropriations bills that it helps to prepare. The Legislative Reference Library, while a valuable tool, is limited to maintaining a history of legislation in Texas and furnishing information on comparable legislation in other states.

Legislative committees also have limited budgets and professional staff, although a presiding officer may give his or her favorite committees liberal spending privileges. Accordingly, committees often must rely on assistance from the institutional staff of the legislature, such as the LBB, and from other state agencies, such as the attorney general's office or the comptroller's office. In addition, from time to time, legislators with compatible views form study groups to work on issues.

The lack of adequate staffing is of major importance to Texans. It means that legislators, in committee or individually, cannot easily obtain impartial, accurate information concerning public policy. Nonetheless, citizen interest in supporting larger budgets for legislative operations seems to be nil. Indeed, some Texans see any move on the part of legislators to eliminate their dependence on private groups and state administrators for information as a ploy to "waste" more tax money. This attitude, fully encouraged by lobbyists, keeps staffing low, although the National Conference of State Legislatures notes that the strength of a legislative body rests with its staff.[28]

The creation of the Texas Legislative Council (TLC) in 1949 was a major step toward providing research and technical services to Texas legislators. But the TLC has never been adequately funded to provide full-time bill-drafting and research services, and its small staff receives more requests for information than it can handle. The LBB, composed of the presiding officers and other legislators, prepares the legislative budget. Its staff, heavily influenced by the presiding officers, is in an awkward position to make independent recommendations. And the other auxiliary organization of the legislature, the Legislative Audit Committee, is composed of the presiding officers and certain ex officio legislators. Its professional staff, headed by the state auditor, who serves at the pleasure of the committee, also is heavily influenced by the presiding officers.

House Bill 7, passed during the third called session in 2003, made several changes in these staff agencies. The LBB, the most powerful staff agency, was given even more power at the expense of the state comptroller's office. The online reports that provide performance and budget information on Texas government, the public school reviews, and the state agency efficiency reviews were removed from the comptroller's office and given to the LBB. The comptroller remains the responsible official for certifying that sufficient funds exist to fund

Let the Good Times Roll

Although lobbyists fully expect to pay for many meals and lots of liquor during a legislative session, even they were shocked by the demands of the members of four House legislative committees to contribute $500 apiece so that committee members could "monkey around" [the language on the invitation] at the close of the 2011 regular session. While accustomed to enjoying freewheeling privileges in Austin, even the lobbyists thought the legislators went too far in this out-and-out solicitation of money for a party with the implied exchange of support for legislation.

Source: Christy Hoppe, "Lobbyists Solicited to Pay for House Panels' Bash," *Dallas Morning News*, May 14, 2011, A1, A2.

the state budget. The presiding officers were designated as joint chairs for all three staff agencies, and the membership and quorum for the TLC were changed to give less advantage to House members.

Other political appointees assist members individually, but their major responsibilities are to the House or Senate as a body. These include the secretary of the Senate, the chief clerk of the House, their assistants, the sergeants-at-arms, the pages, and clerical staff.

Powers of the Presiding Officers

Although their powers have been somewhat limited by the modest seniority rules adopted by both houses in 1973 and described previously, the presiding officers basically control the flow of legislation in Texas. Their power over public policy in Texas is tremendous. However, many who are not legislators—a supporting cast that includes the governor, the lobbyists, the state bureaucrats, legislative staffers, and sometimes the public—are also involved in making legislative policy. Representative Wolens's comment at the opening of the chapter expresses his frustration at the brazenness of the business lobby during the 1995 session. As Chapter 3 discusses, nothing that has happened since that year has diminished the influence of business in Texas politics. Presiding officers generally work with, not against, such powerful groups.

By constitutional mandate, the presiding officer in the Senate is the lieutenant governor, and the presiding officer in the House of Representatives is the speaker of the House. The powers that the holder of each of these positions

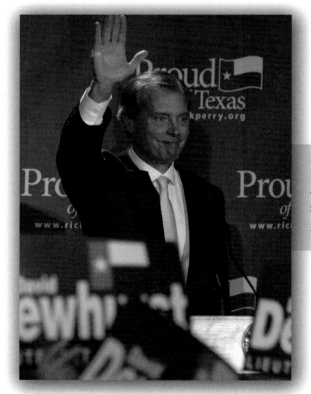

Lieutenant Governor David Dewhurst hoped his third term would lead to the U.S. Senate in 2012.

AP Photo/LM Otero.

enjoys are derived from the rules of the legislative body over which he or she presides and are of two basic sorts. The first has to do with the organization of the legislature and legislative procedure. In varying degrees, all presiding officers exercise this power of the chair. The second sort of power is institutional, and it has to do with the maintenance of the legislature as a vital organ of government.

A reform-oriented House or Senate can limit the powers of the presiding officers. Also, politics can dictate a change anytime when there is a new leader. However, tradition and the realities of politics ordinarily militate against an overthrow of the powerful legislative leadership during the session. So also does the legislative amateurism that results from short sessions, low pay, and high turnover in membership. The Eighty-first Legislature in 2009 proved to be an exception because it featured not only low turnover rate in both houses but also the ouster of a three-term speaker who was replaced by Joe Straus whose approach was more nearly even-handed than that of his predecessor. From time to time, the leaders themselves have a reform bent. One reason for the introduction of modified seniority in 1973 was that one-term reform Speaker Price Daniel, Jr., insisted on some controls over lobbyists. In 1993, Speaker Pete Laney blunted the power of the speaker and made the House more democratic.

Often, though, powerful leaders are a convenience, albeit sometimes a tiresome or costly one. The significance of some of the specific procedural and institutional powers of the lieutenant governor and speaker of the House is discussed in the following sections.

Procedural Powers

The presiding officers' controls over legislative procedure dictate the who, what, and when of the legislative session.

Committee Membership

Legislative committees have life-or-death power over a **bill,** the way in which legislation is introduced. Legislators' appointments to major committees, especially as chairperson or vice chairperson, largely determine their influence with the legislature as a whole. Presiding officers can thus use their powers of appointment to reward friends and supporters with key positions on important committees and to punish opponents with nonleadership positions on minor committees.

Although seniority does play a role in the formation of House committees, the speaker still effectively determines their composition. The seniority appointments are made after the speaker appoints the chairpersons and vice chairpersons of the committees. The speaker always has some choice because several representatives often have the same amount of seniority in the House. The power of an individual speaker is illustrated by the 2003 actions of Speaker Tom Craddick when he eliminated the seniority appointments from the Appropriations Committee to ensure that its makeup would reflect his conservative ideology.

Senate rules stipulate only that a minority of members must have prior service on a particular committee. Thus, the lieutenant governor, as presiding officer of the Senate, dominates those committee selections.

Special interest representatives, as well as legislators, are frequently involved in the bargaining that eventually determines who will fill committee slots. Members of interest groups, wanting friends on committees, frequently make suggestions to the presiding officers about member selection. The only committee appointments not made by the presiding officers are those few appointments

to special interest study committees that the governor might make. And even in these cases, the legislature has the power to approve or disapprove nonlegislative appointments to the interim committee.

Conference Committees

A major bill seldom passes both houses in identical form. Each time one fails to do so, a conference committee may be appointed to resolve the differences. Before 1973, conference committees could, and frequently did, produce virtually new bills. Beginning in 1973, the House adopted a rule effective at the beginning of each session limiting the conference committee to ironing out differences in the two versions of a bill. Resolving these differences often means adding new material to the bill at the conference stage. Five members from each house are appointed to conference committees by their respective presiding officers. Each house has one vote on the conference committee report; in other words, three members on each house's team of five must agree on the conference version of the bill before the bill can be reported back to the House and Senate. The conference report must be accepted or rejected, without change, by each house. This procedure makes conference committee members key figures in the legislative process. Most conference reports, or versions of the bill, are accepted because of time limitations.

Appointees to conference committees usually share the viewpoints of the presiding officers on what should be done with the bill in question. Representatives of special interests often become involved in conference committee deliberations in an attempt to arrange trade-offs, or bargains, with the presiding officers, making one concession in exchange for another. However, sometimes the main proponents of the two versions of the bill are able to work out a compromise without the committee even meeting.

Committee Chairpersons

The standing committees control legislation, and their chairpersons not only specify the committee agenda, subcommittee jurisdiction, and assignments but also control the committees. Lobbyists for special interest groups work hard to influence the selection of chairpersons and vice chairpersons of committees. A lobbyist's year is generally successful if his or her choice is appointed to chair a committee crucial to the lobbyist's special interests. However, if a lobbyist must deal with an unfriendly chairperson, the session may seem long and trying.

The reward-and-punishment aspect of committee appointments is especially evident in the appointment of chairpersons, for it is through them that the presiding officers control legislation. True seniority is relatively unimportant in determining chairmanships, but some experience is useful. Obviously, political enemies of the lieutenant governor or the speaker are not likely to chair standing committees.

As noted in Chapter 5, Democrats and Republicans are increasingly sharing power in the legislature. In 2003, the divisiveness in the legislature was partially along party lines but even more because the extremists in both parties dominated their colleagues. Rather than steering toward the middle, or slightly to the right of the middle, as had been the tradition in the state, the Seventy-eighth Legislature saw clash after clash of right versus left. As a result, ordinary civility was a casualty to the legislative wars.[29] Out-and-out rudeness and hostility were openly displayed, particularly on the floor of the House of Representatives.

Especially in the House, elements of that partisanship have continued, though the Senate has returned to a somewhat less partisan style. The Eighty-second Legislature in 2011 was a virtual repetition of the 2003 session.

Although sessions from 2003 on have been branded as highly partisan, especially during the tenure of Speaker Craddick and the 2011 session, the presiding officers have continued to operate to an extent on a nonpartisan basis by blessing the members of both parties with committee chairmanships. This approach has helped to avoid the gridlock that is common in Congress, where each party has traditionally put up roadblocks against the favored legislation of the other party, and thus has allowed the Texas legislature to set public policy in spite of a very short legislative session. Taking a nonpartisan approach to legislation has worked well, as the partisan alignment in the legislature has gone from Democratic domination to Republican ascendancy to a strong but thwarted Democratic effort to recapture the House.

Referral

Because of the large number of committees, which committee has jurisdiction over a particular legislative proposal is ill defined by the Texas legislature. Unlike the U.S. Congress, where committee jurisdictions are relatively clear, jurisdictional ambiguities are pervasive in the Texas committee system. The large number of standing committees—thirty-six in the House and eighteen in the Senate in 2011—plus the absolute silence of Senate rules on committee jurisdiction, create these ambiguities. The committee system in Texas thus allows the presiding officers to use their referral power to determine the outcome of a bill. In other words, if the speaker or lieutenant governor favors a bill, the bill will be referred to a committee that will act favorably toward it. If the presiding officer opposes the proposed legislation, it will be assigned to an unfriendly committee. However, the referral powers of the Senate's presiding officer were curtailed somewhat by the 1973 reform of the committee system and by Senate rules that can force a change in referral.

Some of the factors considered by the presiding officers when assigning bills to committees include: (1) the positions of their own financial supporters and political backers on the bill; (2) the effect of the bill on other legislation, especially the availability of funding for other programs; (3) their own ideological commitment to the bill; (4) the past record of support or nonsupport of the bill's backers, both legislators and special interests; and (5) the bargaining in which the bill's backers are willing to engage, including promises of desired support of, or opposition to, other bills on which the presiding officers have strong positions, as well as a willingness to modify the bill itself.

Scheduling/Calendar

In all legislative bodies, bills are assigned a time for debate. This scheduling—placing the bill on a legislative calendar—determines the order of the bill's debate and vote. In Congress, the majority leader controls the two Senate calendars, although the informality of the Senate reduces the importance of the calendars; the Rules Committee of the House assigns bills to one of four calendars.

In the Texas House, two calendars committees control placement of bills on the four legislative calendars to establish the order for debate—the Local and Consent Calendars Committee, which handles noncontroversial matters, and the Calendars Committee, which handles the main legislative agenda. Although

appointed by the presiding officers like all standing committees, the House Calendars Committee is quite powerful. Todd Hunter, chair of the Calendars Committee in 2011, noted that only he and the governor could absolutely block a bill. In the Senate, the members control the agenda by being able to take bills out of order with a two-thirds vote. However, the lieutenant governor controls efforts to change the order of debate by making legislators publicly state their intentions.

Scheduling is more important in Texas than in some other states or in Congress because of the short biennial legislative session. A bill placed far down on the schedule may not come to the floor before the session reaches its 140-day mandatory adjournment. In addition, items on the calendars are called in order, and some calendars do not allow debate. For example, in the House, it is highly advantageous to have a bill placed on the Local, Consent, and Resolutions Calendar, which is used for uncontested legislation. The timing of debate may well determine the outcome of the vote. Legislative strategies include trying either to delay the call of a bill until negative votes can be lined up or to rush a bill through before opposition can materialize. Another factor to be considered in Senate scheduling is the possibility of a **filibuster**. It is much easier to shut off attempts to "talk a bill to death" early in the session than when only a few days are left for action. (The filibuster is discussed under "Step Three: Floor Action" later in this chapter.)

A member essentially goes "hat in hand" to one of these gatekeeper committees—usually the Calendars Committee, because it deals with major legislation—to try to get his or her bill on the agenda. However, if any committee member objects to the bill, the bill is never scheduled. Moreover, these committees meet in secret. House members can challenge a ruling by the committee, but because a two-thirds vote is required to pry the bill from committee and

The state struggled with public-school funding, children's health, and other issues from 2003 on, but the legislature often focused on political questions such as immigration and voter identification instead of pressing policy needs. This Ben Sargent cartoon sums up legislative and executive leadership during the period as an empty gas tank.

Courtesy of Ben Sargent.

other members fear reprisals as they try to get their own bills out of committee, attempts to force a scheduling of debate are very rare.

The calendar system in the House is somewhat confusing. There are four calendars (see Table 6-5): the Daily House; the Supplemental House; the Local, Consent, and Resolutions; and the Congratulatory and Memorial. The most significant of these is the Supplemental House Calendar because it incorporates the daily calendar as well as any carryover business. Compounding the confusion is a series of categories—which overlap the names of the calendars—used to group legislation on the calendars and rules about differential treatment of House and Senate resolutions. For example, well-publicized bills will find their way to the Supplemental House Calendar under the category of Major State unless an emergency exists (such as authorizing repairs to the capitol after a fire). The Local, Consent, and Resolutions Calendar deals with business involving one part of the state (for example, the creation of a new special district in a single county) and with noncontroversial proposals. Placement of a bill on that calendar signifies no opposition, although the bill can be withdrawn and placed on a different calendar if opposition develops later.

TABLE 6-5

A Comparison of the Legislative Calendars in the Texas Legislature and the U.S. Congress

Texas Legislative Calendars	
Senate	**House**
Senate	Daily House
Intent	Supplemental House
	Local, Consent, and Resolutions
	Congratulatory and Memorial
	Categories for grouping legislation on the Supplemental House Calendar, which is the major calendar, are: emergency; major state; constitutional amendments; general state; local, consent, and resolutions; resolutions; and congratulatory and memorial resolutions

Congressional Calendars	
Senate	**House**
Senate	House
Executive	Union
	Consent
	Private
	Discharge

No calendars committee exists in the Senate, and technically, the main calendar—the Senate Agenda—is simply called in numerical order. However, bills virtually never come up in order because of motions to take up other bills out of order. A motion to take up a bill out of order requires a two-thirds vote. Moreover, if a senator intends to ask for consideration of a bill out of order, he or she must file an intention to do so with the clerk, stipulating the date on which the motion will be made and asking for a place on the Intent Calendar. When Bill Hobby was lieutenant governor, he formalized the Intent Calendar as a way of forcing the members to reveal their plans in advance to avoid surprising the presiding officer. All other business not on the Intent Calendar can then be placed on the Senate Calendar.

A legislator has two ways to improve the chances that a bill will be placed high enough on a calendar to ensure floor debate on it. First, members may pre-file bills as soon as the November elections are completed. Early filing does

Four Ways to Block a Bill

The Filibuster and Chubbing

Former Senator Bill Meier, who talked for forty-three hours straight in 1977, holds the Texas and world records for filibustering. He successfully blocked consideration of a workers' compensation bill. More recently, in 1993, Senator Gonzalo Barrientos stopped just short of eighteen hours in an unsuccessful effort to protect Austin's Barton Creek and its popular swimming hole. The House does not allow filibusters, but has experienced "chubbing," which is a term that describes minority efforts to block a bill by offering needless amendments to and discussion on other bills in an effort to prevent the offending bill from reaching the floor. It has been a tactic of last resort for House Democrats since 2009.

The Technicality

One of the most bizarre events in the history of the Texas legislature occurred in 1997, when conservative Representative Arlene Wohlgemuth, angry at the blockage of a bill regarding parental notification before girls under eighteen could get an abortion, raised a point of order about the calendar for May 26. The effect was to kill fifty-two bills that were scheduled for debate because the point of order concerned the calendar itself. Her fellow legislators referred to the incident as the "Memorial Day Massacre" and were irate that months of work, including the delicate negotiations between House and Senate members to achieve compromise bills, apparently had been for naught. After tempers cooled, legislators found ways to resurrect some of the bills by tacking them onto other bills that had not been on the calendar for Memorial Day and by using resolutions.

Pocketing

The presiding officers can also block bills by pocketing them; that is, they can decline to send a bill to the floor for debate even though a committee has given it a favorable report. Often, a presiding officer will pocket a bill because it virtually duplicates one already in the legislative pipeline or to keep an unimportant bill from cluttering up the agenda near the end of the session when major legislation is pending.

not ensure that the presiding officer or the chair to whose committee the bill is referred will be favorably disposed toward the proposed legislation, but obtaining a low number because of quick filing may at least ensure that the bill is referred to committee early in the session. Second, if the bill is one in which the governor has a keen interest, the governor can declare an emergency to force speedy consideration of the proposal.

Recognition

One of the prerogatives of the presiding officer of any assembly is the recognition of individuals who wish to speak. In legislative bodies, with the occasional exception of presiding officers who are simply arbitrary, the recognition power is traditionally invoked in a fair and judicious manner. Recent speakers and Senate presidents have mostly followed this tradition, although Speaker Craddick allowed some heckling in 2003 and seemed to lose interest in maintaining control in 2007. In Texas, the Senate procedures for scheduling legislation—that is, the Intent Calendar—give the presiding officer extraordinary power. The lieutenant governor must recognize a bill's sponsor before the sponsor can move the bill for consideration, and the sponsor needs the presiding officer's support to achieve the necessary two-thirds vote on the legislation. Effectively, eleven senators who oppose a bill can block it, because the sponsor cannot then hope to achieve a two-thirds majority.

Rules of Procedure

At the beginning of each regular session of the Texas legislature, each house adopts the rules of procedure that will govern that session's legislative process. Procedures can change considerably, as was evidenced by the 1973 reforms and the 1983 and 2003 House changes giving the speaker more control over appropriations, members' office budgets, and committee jurisdictions. However, many rules are carried over from one session to another or are only slightly modified. Sometimes, significant rules, such as the two-thirds vote required to bring a bill to the floor in the Senate, are cast aside for political expediency.

Numerous precedents determine how the rules will be applied, and of course, all parliamentary rules are subject to interpretation by the chair. Thus, the presiding officers greatly influence the outcome of policy deliberations by their acceptance or rejection of points of order, their decisions as to whether a proposed amendment is germane, their announcement of vote counts, and so forth.

In summary, procedural interpretation, recognition of those wishing to speak, determination of the timetable for debate, referral of bills, and the appointment of committees and their chairpersons all combine to make the presiding officers truly powerful. While none of these powers is unusual for a club president, they take on greater significance when we realize that they are used to determine the outcome of policy struggles within the government of a major state.

Institutional Powers

The presiding officers also appoint the members of three important arms of the legislature: the Legislative Budget Board, the Texas Legislative Council, and the Legislative Audit Committee. Each of these bodies exists to serve the legislature as a whole, providing policy guidelines at the board level and technical assistance at the staff level. The third called session of the legislature in 2003 made a number of changes affecting the organization and jurisdiction of these three agencies. One change was that the presiding officers now serve as joint chairs of each board.

Can Presiding Officers Vote?

The presiding officer of the Senate has limited voting powers because the lieutenant governor is not a member of the Senate. He or she can vote when a tie on a bill occurs and during debate when the Senate sits as a committee of the whole. The speaker is a member of the House and can vote, although he or she rarely does. However, if he or she does vote, and there is a tie, the speaker cannot vote again to break it. A tie is considered a failed vote at that point.

Source: One of the speakers who did occasionally vote was Ben Barnes, whose autobiography is a rich summary of Texas politics in the 1960s. See Ben Barnes, *Barn Burning, Barn Building: Tales of a Political Life, from LBJ to George W. Bush and Beyond* (Albany: Bright Sky Press, 2006).

Legislative Budget Board

At the national level, in most states and even in most cities, the chief executive bears the responsibility for preparing the budget. In Texas, both the governor and the legislature prepare a budget, and state agencies must submit their financial requests to each. The legislative budget is prepared by the Legislative Budget Board (LBB), a ten-member Senate–House joint committee that operates continually, whether the legislature is in session or not. In addition to the presiding officers, there are four members from each house appointed by the presiding officers. By tradition, these include the chairpersons of the committees responsible for appropriations and finance. Because of the importance of these "money" committees, their chairpersons sometimes develop power bases within the legislature that are independent of the presiding officers.

A professional staff assists the board in making its budget recommendations and then often helps defend those recommendations during the session. The staff recommendations on state agency requests are crucial to an agency's appropriations. Executives in administrative agencies therefore work closely with LBB staff in an effort to justify their spending requests. Additionally, the staff assists the legislature in its watchdog function by overseeing state agency expenditures and agency efficiency. This function increased in importance during the long period of budget "crunches" from 1985 through 1995 so that the LBB and the Governor's Office of Budget and Planning now oversee agency planning and monitor agency performance in meeting state goals and objectives.

Texas Legislative Council

The membership of the Texas Legislative Council was modified in 2003 to reduce the domination by the House of Representatives. Today, its fourteen members consist of the speaker and the lieutenant governor, who each appoint six additional members from the House and six members from the Senate.

The council oversees the work of the director and professional staff. During the session, the council provides bill-drafting services for legislators; between sessions, it investigates the operations of state agencies, conducts studies on problems subject to legislative consideration, and drafts recommendations for action in the next session. In short, it is the legislature's research office, similar to the Congressional Research Service.

Legislative Audit Committee

In addition to the presiding officers, the other four members of the Legislative Audit Committee are the chairpersons of the Senate Finance, House Ways and Means, House Appropriations, and Senate State Affairs committees. The state auditor, appointed by the committee for a two-year term subject to two-thirds confirmation of the Senate, heads the professional staff. This committee oversees a very important function of all legislative bodies, namely, checking that agencies properly spent money budgeted to them (the *post-audit*). The auditor and the auditor's staff also check into the quality of services and duplication in services and programs provided by state agencies. The highly detailed work of the professional staff involves a review of the records of financial transactions. In fact, the larger state agencies have an auditor or team of auditors assigned to them practically year-round.

Limits on Presiding Officers

It may seem as if the presiding officers are nearly unrestrained in their exercise of power. There are several personal and political factors, however, that prevent absolute power on the part of the speaker of the House and the lieutenant governor.

Presiding Officers' Powers of the Chair: A Summary

Procedural Powers

1. Appointing half or more of the members of substantive committees and all members of procedural and conference committees (the House reserves half of the positions for seniority appointments; the Senate requires only that some members have prior experience)

2. Appointing the chairs and vice chairs of all committees

3. Determining the jurisdiction of committees through the referral of bills

4. Interpreting procedural rules when conflict arises

5. Scheduling legislation for floor action (especially important in the Senate, which lacks a complex calendar system)

6. Recognizing members who wish to speak or not recognizing them and thus preventing them from speaking

Institutional Powers

1. Appointing the members of the Legislative Budget Board and serving as the cochairs thereof

2. Appointing the members of the Texas Legislative Council and serving as the cochairs thereof

3. Appointing the members of the Legislative Audit Committee and serving as the cochairs thereof

Personality and Ambition

Although there is always the danger that presiding officers may become arbitrary or vindictive and thus abuse their office, they are usually so powerful that they do not need to search for ways to gain influence other than through persuasion, compromise, and accommodation. Arbitrariness is a function of personality, not of the office. Former Lieutenant Governor Bill Hobby of Houston, who served eighteen years and seemed content to play a statesmanlike role rather than seeking higher office, was the epitome of fair play, as was Bill Ratliff, who was elected by his colleagues to serve as presiding officer when Rick Perry became governor. One of the most fascinating lieutenant governors was Bob Bullock, a beloved bully.

Also, speakers or lieutenant governors with political ambitions—at least six have become governor—generally avoid angering special interests and thus cutting themselves off from potential financial campaign support or business credit. They also prefer not to anger other state officials who may be instrumental in furthering their political plans. Not making enemies is also the rule for presiding officers contemplating lucrative business positions when they leave office.

Legislators

State senators and representatives have their own power bases, without which they probably would not have been elected. Longtime members not only have supporters across the state, including influential special interests, but also have the advantage that seniority brings within the legislature itself. If they have served as the chairperson of a major committee for more than one session, legislators are especially likely to have their own power bases as well as the support of the presiding officers.

Furthermore, the presiding officers are limited in their leadership responsibilities to legislators. The speaker of the House, especially, spends considerable time trying to organize and manage 149 colleagues and their pet bills and requests. The lieutenant governor is more of a statewide public figure. He or she is elected independently of the governor and is in demand as a speaker and goodwill ambassador. In addition, the House has more complicated legislative procedures than does the Senate. The president of the Senate can frequently bring about consensus behind the scenes and prevent disruption on the Senate floor.

It may appear that the membership always follows the lead of the presiding officers. In many cases, basic agreement on ideological positions already exists among the majority because the leadership and most legislators are usually conservative. In other instances, members will go along with the leadership in the hope of later being able to act independently on matters of importance to them or to their districts. Finally, the powers of the presiding officers are largely granted by House and Senate rules. A totally arbitrary leader whose abuse of the system has become intolerable can be stripped of much power by changes in those rules, although such action is very rare.

Interest Groups and State Administration

Over the past fifty years, as the number of state governmental agencies and bureaucrats has increased, an alliance has developed between private and public interests. These coalitions and the presiding officers often share the same political viewpoint, making confrontations unlikely. The public is seldom considered

LONE STAR MEDIA
Techno-Savvy Legislators

In the Eighty-first Legislature in 2009, all members used an electronic voting board and had laptop computers available. A few sent out tweets—short 140-character electronic messages. Two years later, members of the Eighty-second Legislature were very electronically savvy.

The most popular device has been the iPad because it allows a representative or a senator to look at a bill, to use a "search" function to find a specific provision, and to avoid the reams of paper that pile up when a bill is printed for legislative consideration. Next most popular has been the BlackBerry because this personal digital assistant (PDA) allows them to send and receive e-mails and text messages even while debate is ongoing in the chamber, and to make quick telephone calls during recesses.

In addition, though only a few legislators have become bloggers, they can all get fast information about what information the public is seeing and what is going on in the other chamber by looking at popular blog sites. *Statesman.com*, *Chron.com*, *TexasTribune.org*, and *Trailblazerblog* are among the most frequently referenced sources.

The Web sites of both the Texas House of Representatives and the Texas Senate now allow the person accessing the site not only to see a picture of the legislator but to click on specific items, including a map of the legislative district and a list of recent media releases the member has made. A few legislators even attach video to their sites, and most have an audio greeting that their constituents can click.

by these alliances, especially when some of the more powerful special interests of the state, such as oil and gas, insurance, banking, and real estate, are involved. An example of a bureaucracy–private interest alliance is the Department of Banking and financial institutions.

Governor

Constitutionally, the governor is a weak chief administrator—hence, the alliance between state bureaucrats and the lobbyists, not the chief executive. Even so, the governor is by no means a weak chief legislator. The governor's veto power is almost absolute because the legislature often adjourns before the governor has had time to act on a bill.

A governor who wants a particular piece of legislation enacted can threaten the legislature with a special session if the legislation seems to be in jeopardy. Because special sessions are costly to state legislators in terms of both time and money, such a threat can be a powerful tool for the governor. The governor must be prepared to make good on such a threat. Rick Perry's three special sessions in 2003 to force redistricting are an example. Such threats, however, do not always work, particularly if the legislature perceives that the governor is usurping legislative authority, as was the case in 2007 when Governor Perry tried to create state policy by executive order, leading to legislative rebellion, and in 2009 when he and the legislature were at odds over federal stimulus money. Perry's chief tactic in 2011 was forcing consideration of bills as emergencies though no true emergency existed. Another of the governor's strengths lies in the strong ties a

Whose Bill Is It, Anyhow?

An Austin lawyer-lobbyist remarked on his twenty years as a legislator by noting, "Here at the legislature, if you ask the question, 'Whose bill is it?' what you mean is, 'Which lobby wrote it?' If you want to know which legislator is sponsoring the bill, you ask, 'Who's carrying the bill?' That'll give you some idea of how influential lobbyists are."

conservative (usually the political orientation of the Texas governor) has to the same interest groups as the legislators. These ties often make it possible for the governor to call on these interests to support a position that is in conflict with that of the legislature.

Electorate/Constituents

Legislative bodies were created to be the people's voice in government, although only about one-third of the eligible voters bother to vote in legislative elections. Citizens are likely to find it challenging and perhaps difficult to exert as much influence over the leadership and members of the Texas legislature as do state officials and private interests. One reason for this situation is the strength of special interests. Another is the lack of knowledge on the part of most citizens in Texas and other states about what goes on in the state capital. Citizens focus on issues affecting them directly, such as drunken driving, but the ordinary day-to-day legislative events do not stir the interest of most Texans. Furthermore, powerful special interests work hard to avoid stirring up the citizens unless they can convert citizen interest to citizen advocacy for their cause. One exception in 1995 involved an impressive show of solidarity by women who believed that symptoms they were experiencing resulted from breast implants as the legislature was debating a measure that would make it difficult to sue for such problems. They were a vocal lobby and deflected the legislation for that session. In 2007, the religious right helped to bring down the governor's proposal to mandate that all sixth-grade girls be inoculated with a vaccine designed to prevent a type of sexually transmitted cervical cancer. Based on the significant number of parent-teacher protest groups outside the Capitol, the aftermath of the 2011 legislative budget cuts in public schools may be seen in the 2012 elections.

How a Bill Becomes a Law in Texas

The Texas Constitution specifies that a bill be used to introduce a law or a change in a law. Bills that pass both houses successfully become acts and are sent to the governor for his or her signature or veto. In addition to bills, there are three types of resolutions in each house:

1. **Simple resolutions are used in each house to take care of housekeeping matters, details of business, and trivia. Examples include procedural rules adopted by each house—serious business, indeed—and trivia, such as birthday greetings to a member.**

2. Concurrent resolutions are similar to simple resolutions but require the action of both houses. An example would be their use for adjournment.

3. Joint resolutions are of major interest to the public because they are the means of introducing proposed constitutional amendments. They require no action by the governor.

Each bill or resolution is designated by an abbreviation that indicates the house of origin, the nature of the legislation, and a number. For example, S.B. 1 is Senate Bill 1; S.J.R. indicates a joint resolution that originated in the Senate.

Bills may originate in either house or in both simultaneously, with the exception of revenue bills, which must originate in the House, according to the Texas Constitution. During a typical session, legislators introduce more than 7,000 bills and joint resolutions, of which only 25 to 30 percent are passed.[30] After each census, when the legislature must also deal with reapportionment and redistricting, the number is reduced by several hundred as a concession to the time redistricting will take. Because lawmakers must consider so many proposals in such a limited time, originators of a bill often mark a bill "By Request" and drop it in the hopper—the traditional legislative "in-basket." This is their way of indicating that they were asked to introduce the legislation but do not expect it to receive serious consideration.

Table 6-6 summarizes the procedural and structural differences in the two houses. These are the major differences in the procedures of the two houses:

1. The House has about twice as many committees as the Senate; therefore, the speaker has a greater choice in determining where to refer a bill.

2. The calendars are different (as explained earlier in this chapter).

3. Debate is unlimited in the Senate, whereas House debate is usually limited to ten minutes per member and twenty minutes for the bill's sponsor.

TABLE 6-6

A Comparison of the Texas House and Senate

Feature	House	Senate
Size	150	31
Term	2 years	4 years
Committees	36	18
Limits on debate	Usually 10 minutes	None
Calendars	4	2
How presiding officer selected	Elected by constituents in a single-member district, then elected by fellow members of the House as speaker	Elected statewide as lieutenant governor of Texas

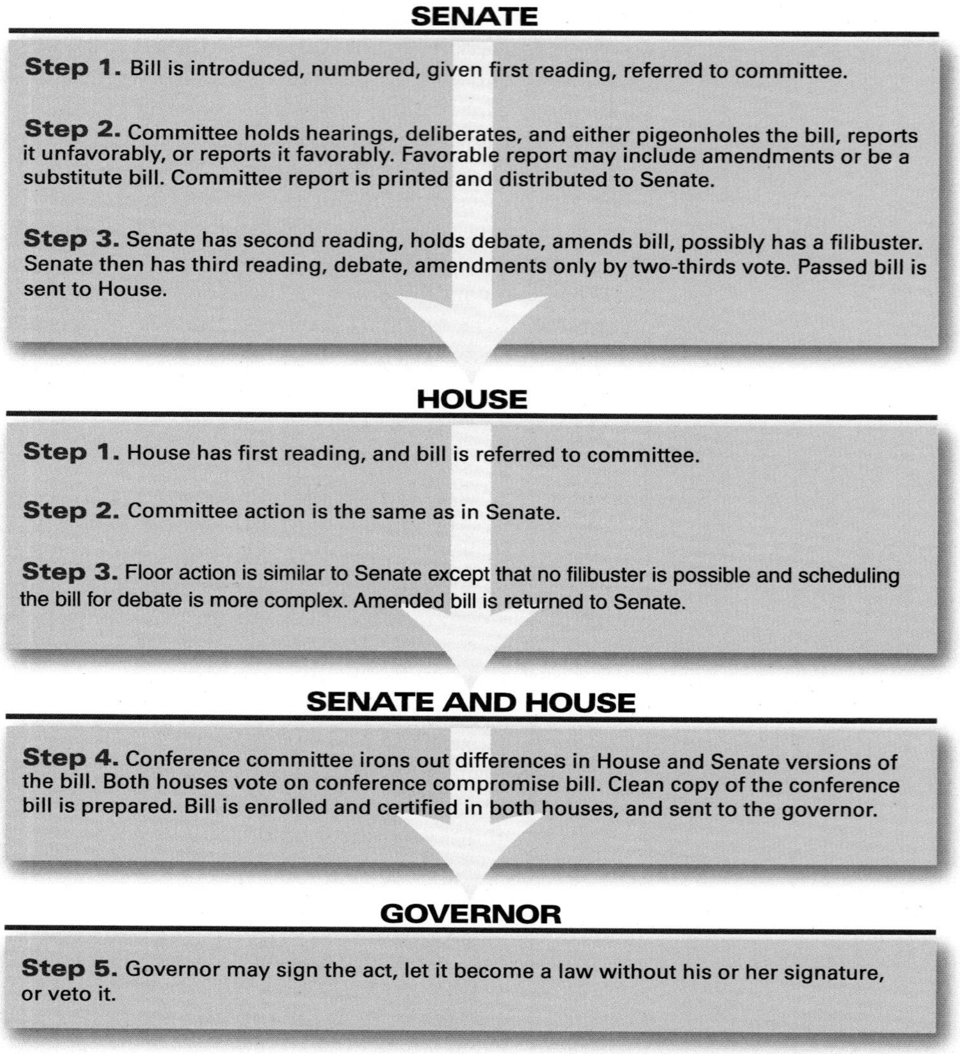

SENATE

Step 1. Bill is introduced, numbered, given first reading, referred to committee.

Step 2. Committee holds hearings, deliberates, and either pigeonholes the bill, reports it unfavorably, or reports it favorably. Favorable report may include amendments or be a substitute bill. Committee report is printed and distributed to Senate.

Step 3. Senate has second reading, holds debate, amends bill, possibly has a filibuster. Senate then has third reading, debate, amendments only by two-thirds vote. Passed bill is sent to House.

HOUSE

Step 1. House has first reading, and bill is referred to committee.

Step 2. Committee action is the same as in Senate.

Step 3. Floor action is similar to Senate except that no filibuster is possible and scheduling the bill for debate is more complex. Amended bill is returned to Senate.

SENATE AND HOUSE

Step 4. Conference committee irons out differences in House and Senate versions of the bill. Both houses vote on conference compromise bill. Clean copy of the conference bill is prepared. Bill is enrolled and certified in both houses, and sent to the governor.

GOVERNOR

Step 5. Governor may sign the act, let it become a law without his or her signature, or veto it.

FIGURE 6-2 How a Bill Becomes a Law in Texas

This figure traces the passage of a bill that originated in the Senate. Steps 1 to 3 for the Senate and House would be reversed if the bill originated in the House. The example presumes the need for a conference committee.

To be enacted into law, a bill must survive as many as four legislative steps and a fifth step in the governor's office (see Figure 6-2). Because the smaller size of the Senate enables it to operate with less formality than the House, we use the Senate to trace the path of a bill through the legislative process.

Step One: Introduction and Referral

Every bill must be introduced by a member of the legislature, who is considered the sponsor. If a bill has several sponsors, its chances of survival are greatly enhanced. There are two ways to introduce bills: (1) the member, after being recognized by the lieutenant governor as president of the Senate, may introduce

it from the floor; or (2) the member may deposit copies of the bill with the secretary of the Senate (in the House, with the clerk), including pre-filing a bill in November. The secretary assigns a number to the bill that reflects the order of submission. The reading clerk then gives the bill the first of the three readings required by the constitution. The first time, only a caption is read, which is a brief summary of the bill's contents. The second method of introducing bills is the one more commonly used. Legislation can only be introduced in the first sixty days of the session; as the deadline draws near, the number of bill filings increases exponentially.

The lieutenant governor (in the House, the speaker) then refers the bill to a committee. If the bill is to survive, it must be assigned to a friendly committee. The bill's sponsor will have been on "good behavior" in the hope that the lieutenant governor will give the bill a favorable referral.

Step Two: Committee Action

Standing committees are really miniature legislatures in which the nitty-gritty of legislation takes place. Legislators are so busy—particularly in Texas, with the short, infrequent sessions—that they seldom have time to study bills in detail and so must rely heavily on the committee reports. A bill's sponsor, well aware of the committee's role, will do everything possible to ensure that the committee's report is favorable. It is particularly important to avoid having the bill *pigeonholed* (put on the bottom of the committee's agenda, with or without discussion, never to be seen again) or totally rewritten, either by the committee or, if the bill is referred to a subcommittee, by the subcommittee. If the bill can escape being pigeonholed, its sponsor will have a chance to bargain with the committee in an effort to avoid too many changes in the bill.

The standing committees hold hearings on proposed legislation. Major bills will generate considerable public, media, and lobbyist interest. The large number of committees and the volume of proposed legislation sometimes mean that these hearings are held at odd hours, such as 11 P.M.

A senator, but not a representative, can **tag** a bill, indicating that the lawmaker must get a forty-eight-hour written notice of the hearing. If the senator does not receive notice or if the bill was not posted publicly seventy-two hours in advance, a senator can use a tag to object to the bill and delay the committee hearing. Tagging is sometimes an effective practice to defeat a bill late in the legislative session.

The committee may report the bill favorably, unfavorably, or not at all. An unfavorable report or none at all will kill it. Unless there is a strong minority report, however, there is little reason for the committee to report a bill unfavorably; it is easier to pigeonhole it and avoid floor action completely.

Step Three: Floor Action

Once reported out of committee, a bill must be scheduled for debate. The Senate Calendar is rarely followed; instead, senators list their bills on the Intent Calendar, which in essence is a declaration of intent to ask for a suspension of the rules to take up a bill out of order. As with any motion to suspend the rules, two-thirds of those present and voting must vote yes on the suspension. Before filing intent to ask for a suspension, the bill's sponsors generally get an assurance from the presiding officer that they will be recognized, and thus given an opportunity to make the motion. The two-thirds rule (really a tradition instead of a rule) allows

legislators to proceed smoothly because most members have agreed to consider it. The lieutenant governor can force a vote without a two-thirds majority by using another rule that allows House bills to be taken up on certain days of the week without the super majority,[31] a tactic that Dewhurst used several times in 2011.

When the bill receives the necessary two-thirds vote, it can proceed to its second reading and debate. If the second reading has not occurred by the time the legislature is within seventy-two hours of adjournment, the bill dies. The sponsor of the bill is relieved because only a simple majority of votes is required for passage. (In the House, the Calendars Committee establishes a schedule for debate.) Senators have unlimited privileges of debate: They may speak as long as they wish about a bill on the floor. Sometimes senators use this privilege to filibuster—that is, to try to kill a bill by talking at length about it and anything else that will use up time. By tying up the floor and preventing other bills from being considered, the senator or group of senators hopes to pressure enough of the membership to lay aside the controversial bill so that other matters can be debated. The filibuster is most effective at the end of the legislative session when time is short and many bills have yet to be debated. Shutting off debate, however, requires a simple majority vote. Despite their potential effectiveness, filibusters do not occur frequently because so much Senate business is conducted off the Senate floor in bargaining sessions. The presiding officer, incidentally, has the power to ask the intention of a member when the member is recognized for debate and thus knows when a filibuster will occur. Tradition also dictates that a member who plans to filibuster notify the press of the forthcoming event.

If a bill is fortunate enough not to become entangled in a filibuster, debate proceeds. During the course of debate, there may be proposed amendments, amendments to amendments, motions to table, or even motions to send the bill back to committee. However, if a bill has succeeded in reaching the floor for discussion, it is usually passed in one form or another. A vote is taken after the third reading, again by caption, of the bill. At this stage, amendments require a two-thirds vote. It is more or less routine for four-fifths of the Senate to vote to suspend the rules and proceed immediately to the third reading.

In the House: Steps One through Three Repeated

If it was not introduced in both houses simultaneously, a bill passed in the Senate must proceed to the House. There, under its original designation (for example, S.B. 341), it must repeat the same three steps, with the exceptions noted earlier. It has little chance of passing if a representative does not shepherd it through. (This situation is true in reverse also, when a bill passes the House and is then sent to the Senate.) In addition, the Laney reforms of 1993 included a series of deadlines concerning the final seventeen days of a legislative session, and a bill must comply with those House rules. For example, after 135 days of a regular session, the House cannot consider a Senate bill except to adopt a conference report, reconsider the bill to remove Senate amendments, or override a veto; the deadlines for various types of House bills are earlier.[32] The following explanation assumes that the bill being followed passes the House, but with one amendment added that was not part of the Senate's version.

Step Four: Conference Committee

Because the Senate and House versions of the bill differ, it must go to a **conference committee,** which consists of ten members: five appointed from each house by

Ghosts in the Capitol

National media have criticized the House for its tradition of allowing a member to vote for one or more absent colleagues. Even $100,000 in fingerprint recognition equipment has not stemmed the legislators' behavior.

Source: Christy Hoppe, "Ghost Voting Haunts Texas Capitol," *Dallas Morning News*, April 25, 2009, 1A, 4A.

the presiding officers. If the House and Senate versions of the bill exhibit substantial differences, the conference committee may attach several amendments or rewrite portions of it. It may even be pigeonholed. On a bill with only one difference between the versions passed by the two houses, the single vote of the committee members from the Senate and the single vote of those from the House may be obtained without too much wrangling.

The bill is then reported back to the Senate and the House for action in each chamber. The report of the conference committee must be voted on as it stands; neither house can amend it. It must be accepted, rejected, or sent back to the conference committee. If it fails at this stage—or indeed, at any stage—it is automatically dead. No bill can be introduced twice during the same session, although a bill can be rewritten and introduced as a new piece of legislation.

If the bill receives a majority of the votes in each house, the engrossing and enrolling clerk prepares a correct copy of it, first for the house where the bill originated, then for the other house. Its caption is read a final time, and it is signed by the presiding officers, the House chief clerk, and the Senate secretary. The vote of passage is certified, and the engrossed (officially printed) bill, now an act, is sent to the governor for action. A record of these steps is printed in the journal of each house.

Step Five: The Governor

The governor has ten days (excluding Sundays) to dispose of enacted legislation. If the legislature adjourns, the ten-day period is extended to twenty days. The governor has three options available to deal with an act. The first is to sign it, thus making it law.

The second is to allow the act to become law without signing it. If the governor does not sign it, an act becomes law in ten days if the legislature is in session, and in twenty days if it is not. By choosing this rather weak course of action, the governor signifies both opposition to the legislation and an unwillingness to risk a veto that could be overridden by a two-thirds vote of both houses or that would incur the disfavor of special interests supporting the bill.

Third, the governor may veto the act. Although it is possible for the legislature to override a veto, the governor often receives legislation so late in the session that the act of vetoing or signing it can be deferred until the session has ended. A veto then is absolute because it must be overridden during the same legislative session in which the act was passed and the legislature cannot call itself into special session. At any time, the legislature may have difficulty mustering the two-thirds vote necessary to override a veto. Because recent legislative sessions have been faced with one crisis after another and have had too little

time to deal with issues, the governor's powers have been strengthened through use of the veto and threats of a veto.

If the governor chooses to veto, the veto applies to the entire act, except in the case of appropriations bills. On an appropriations act, the governor has the power of **item veto**; that is, specific items may be vetoed. This is a powerful gubernatorial tool for limiting state spending, but in recent years, the legislature has blunted this tool by making lump-sum appropriations to agencies, such as colleges and universities.

When the governor signs an act, it becomes one of the few proposals that manage to survive. It is entered in the statute books by the secretary of state. If it contains an emergency clause, it becomes effective as law either immediately or whenever designated in the bill. If it does not, it becomes effective ninety days after the session ends. Again, there are special circumstances for appropriations acts. They always become effective September 1 because the state's **fiscal year** (its budget period) is from September 1 through August 31 of the following year.

Legislative Dynamics

The public often thinks that the legislature accomplishes very little, as the chapter opening quotation from *Texas Monthly* notes. It is in fact amazing that the legislature accomplishes as much as it does, given the limitations under which the institution must labor. The forces influencing legislation are complex and varied: interest groups, the powers of the presiding officers, the governor, constitutional limitations, political parties, the role of committees, short and infrequent sessions, inadequate salaries, and the prerogatives of individual members.

Handicaps

Consideration of thousands of bills and resolutions each session means the legislative workload is very heavy. Very few of these proposals are substantively important, and many are trivial matters that could more easily be left to administrative agencies. Less than one-third of them are passed. Nevertheless, in the short 140-day session, legislators must acquaint themselves with the proposals, try to push their own legislative programs, attend to a heavy burden of casework, spend countless hours in committee work, meet with hometown and interest-group representatives, and hear the professional views of state administrators who implement programs. Although many legislators are personally wealthy, those who are not must also try to avoid going into debt because their salaries are inadequate and their personal businesses or professions cannot be attended to when the legislature is in session.

Lenient lobbying laws, lack of public support for adequate information services for legislators, and the need for continuous campaigning make the average legislator easy prey for special interests. On many issues, the interests of a legislator's district and of special interest groups often overlap and are difficult to distinguish. Even when the interests are not so closely aligned, legislators may have to depend on lobbyists for much of their information. Certainly, they depend on them for campaign help.

The legislators' frustrations are especially evident when the biennial budget is considered. Appropriations are the major battleground of legislative sessions. There are always more programs seeking support than there is money available

to support them. Power struggles over money continue because each individual who promotes a program—be it for highways, public schools, utilities rates, environmental protection, lending rates, tort reform, law enforcement, or welfare administration—believes in either its moral rightness or its economic justification. Who wins the struggles is determined not only by the power and effectiveness of the groups backing a program, but also by the political preferences of the legislators. Furthermore, the winners largely determine public policy for the state because few government programs can operate without substantial amounts of money. Chapter 12 examines the politics of the budgetary process in detail.

Lack of public understanding and support is another handicap for legislators. The public often criticizes politicians for being unprincipled and always willing to compromise. But the role of compromise in the political system, and especially in legislative bodies, is undervalued by the citizens. Caught in all the cross-pressures of the legislative system, members rarely have the opportunity to adhere rigidly to their principles. Those who watch closely what happens in the legislature are not the electorate back home, but campaign supporters, lobbyists, and influential citizens. Members must satisfy these people if they are to have any chance of getting their own proposals through the legislature, or in fact of being re-elected for another term.[33]

Legislators may have to vote for new highways that they view as superfluous to get votes for issues important to them and their home districts. They may have to vote in favor of high interest rates on credit cards to gain support for tighter regulation of nursing homes. They may have to give up a home-district highway patrol office to obtain funds for needy children. Just as legislators who hope to be successful must quickly learn the procedural rules, they also must learn the art of legislative compromise. However, in 2011, the art of compromise seemed to be a lost one, with ideological positions dominating the session. Other states found themselves in the same partisan dogfight.[34]

Changing Alignments

Recent sessions of the legislature have been especially interesting because of the shifting alliances within it. The transitional nature of the state, and thus of the legislature, serves to substantiate the adage that "politics makes strange bedfellows." Thus, an additional difficulty legislators face is adjusting to the shifting trends within the legislature. Long dominated by rural, Democratic conservatives, in recent years, the legislature has become more urban and more Republican. When urban issues are at stake, temporary bipartisan alliances among big-city legislators sometimes are formed. However, the 2003 legislative session brought to the forefront a growing problem for the Texas legislature, namely, its sharp division between liberals and conservatives—effectively, a sharp division between Democrats and Republicans—that threatens the state lawmaking body with the same sort of gridlock that characterizes the U.S. Congress.

Compounding the problem of party and geographic transition is the fact that the two houses have not changed in the same way. Although Republicans are the majority in both houses, the degree of partisanship, the sharpness of the ideological divisions, and the traditions surrounding the operation of the two houses are quite different. The Senate periodically provides glimpses of moralistic thinking; the House appears frozen in the state's individualistic/traditionalistic political culture.

Frivolity Forever

State legislatures are somewhat notorious for wasting time on frivolous matters, and Texas and California are among the worst. Here are several examples of frivolous issues that are not the stuff of major public policy. The first example is from California; the rest are pure Texan.

- An accolade to actor Ed Asner for his television work on the *Mary Tyler Moore Show*

- Naming the *Brachiosaur sauropod, Pleurocoelus* the official state dinosaur, and then changing it to the *Paluxysaurus jonesi*

- Naming the chiltepin as the official pepper; the sweet onion, the official vegetable; the guitar, the official musical instrument; the Guadalupe bass, the state fish; and rodeo, the official sport

- Designating the Texas red grapefruit as the state fruit; the Texas blue topaz, the official gem; the horned lizard, the official reptile: and the Blue Lacy, the state dog breed

- Designating the following "capitals": Waxahachie, crape myrtle; Weslaco, citrus; and Knox City, seedless watermelon

Sources: Charles Mantesian, "The Official Waste of Time," *Governing*, September 1997, 18; http://www.infoplease.com/ipa/A0108277.html; and Peggy Heinkel-Wolfe, "Designation Inspires Donation," *Denton Record-Chronicle*, March 17, 2009, 1A, 3A.

In the Senate, as previously discussed, eleven members can prevent a measure from reaching the floor for debate. Most of the time, the Senate continues to operate as a chamber characterized by civility and a lack of hard-edged partisanship. Only when really partisan issues are at stake does the Senate minority gain its way by preventing consideration of the bill or expediting a vote on an issue that the minority still wants to discuss.

The alliance of conservative Democrats and Republicans gave the House a distinctly conservative flavor beginning in the mid-1980s. Liberal-conservative skirmishes, nevertheless, have been plentiful since the late 1990s and promise to continue regardless of which party is in the majority. The Texas House of Representatives temporarily seemed to draw strength from the Laney reforms, which brought a higher sense of ethics, as well as fairer procedures to the lower chamber. However, splits along party lines have worsened, and blatant partisanship often arises in the House. The 2009 session was especially interesting because of the 76–74 Republican-Democratic alignment in the House. The 2011 session was characterized by an overwhelming majority sufficient to allow the majority to ignore the minority.

Nonlegislative Lawmaking

The responsibility for lawmaking was intended to rest with the legislature; however, executive, administrative, and judicial officials also make public policy that

has the force of law. This overlap of functions, rather than being described as a separation of powers, should more correctly be defined as a separation of roles and institutions with a sharing of powers.

Governor

The governor is involved in lawmaking in two ways. First, by presenting messages to the legislature giving actual recommendations on legislation, the governor influences its outcome. The governor may also rally the support of political cronies and lobbyists for or against a bill. Besides vetoing bills, the governor can threaten to veto and so force changes in appropriations and other bills.

Second, the governor can indirectly influence how, or even if, legislation will be administered through appointments to state boards and commissions. Because the bureaucracy interprets general legislation and thus determines how it is to be applied in specific instances, gubernatorial appointees may have tremendous influence on how the public does (or does not) benefit from state laws. Often, though, the ties between an agency's permanent bureaucracy and legislators are so strong that the board members appointed by the governor have only limited influence.

The governor also influences legislation indirectly by being the major liaison between Texas and other states, and between Texas and the federal executive establishment. In this capacity, the governor can affect interstate and federal-state relationships and policies. This aspect of the governorship was evident in 2009 when Rick Perry did not want to accept all the economic stimulus money available from Washington.

Administration

In addition to the governor and lieutenant governor, the state executive branch includes four other elected executives and two elected state boards. There also are dozens of policymaking boards and their staffs. As noted earlier, the administration (or bureaucracy) has a tremendous effect on how legislation is carried out. Because statutes are written in rather general terms to avoid unnecessary rigidity and specificity, administrative policies, rules, and regulations are a must. Each board policy made and each staff rule or regulation written supplement the statutes enacted by the legislature and constitute lawmaking.

Individual administrators also interpret statutes, an action that is a type of lawmaking. In addition, by functioning as expert advisers to members of the legislature during the session, administrators can directly influence the outcome of bills. Indeed, they often use their bureaucratic skills in conjunction with special interest groups that are concerned with similar issues. Perhaps no executive agency is as influential as the attorney general's office, which can issue opinions on the constitutionality of legislation. These opinions have the force of law unless they are successfully challenged in court.

Courts

The judiciary, too, has a role in lawmaking. The courts are frequently asked to determine whether a statute is in conflict with higher law. Both federal and state courts can review legislative acts that have been challenged on the grounds of unconstitutionality. Federal and state judges also spend considerable time hearing challenges to administrative interpretations of laws. In fact, most of the civil dockets of the courts are taken up with administrative matters—for example, whether an agency has jurisdiction over the matter at hand or whether an administrative interpretation is correct.

Evaluation and Suggested Reforms

How does the Texas legislature stack up in terms of efficiency, effectiveness, and democratic theory? Both the structure of the legislature and its operations warrant criticism, as well as the courtesy of suggested changes.

Legislative Structure

The structure of the Texas legislature is regularly subjected to criticism. These criticisms focus on the poor compensation of legislators and session inefficiencies, most of which are constitutional in nature.

Criticisms

Extensive efforts to revamp state legislative structures have been made by organizations such as the National Legislative Conference, the Council of State Governments, the Citizens Conference on State Legislatures, and the National Municipal League. This last organization even produced a Model State Constitution as a "companion piece" for its Model City Charter. But state legislatures have been universally noninnovative. As Alexander Heard observes, "State legislatures may be our most extreme example of institutional lag. In their formal qualities, they are largely 19th-century organizations, and they must, or should, address themselves to 20th- [and now 21st-] century problems."[35]

The Texas legislature seems caught in the proverbial vicious circle. Low salaries and short terms force legislators to maintain other sources of income, a necessity that leads to inattentiveness to legislative business, especially between sessions. On salary alone, a legislator would be far below the federal poverty line. However, the generous $168 a day allowance, plus mileage, helps raise the total compensation to over $30,000 for the average legislator during a legislative year. That sum is not as munificent as it sounds, as living away from home in Austin for five months consumes most of the per diem allowance. Indeed, legislators often have roommates to share expenses, just like college students.

The electorate, on the other hand, views the legislature as a group whose members work only 140 days every two years (many citizens forget about interim committee assignments), but get paid every month. Most citizens probably do not realize—and may not care—that legislators make only $600 a month in salary. They would probably care more if they realized that most of a legislator's compensation comes from the per diem allowance. In 1984, voters explicitly refused to allow legislators more than $30 a day in expense money. The $168 figure came about through the discovery of a loophole in the statute setting per diem payments.

Yet citizens are not very consistent in their views. While they are reluctant to vote for decent legislative salaries, they seem to find little difficulty in entrusting a multibillion-dollar budget to an inexperienced and poorly paid group of legislators whom they view as amateurs at best and scalawags at worst.[36] Furthermore, they seem oblivious to the detrimental effect on legislation caused by inadequate salaries for both legislators and their staffs and the resulting dependence on special interests or on "gamesmanship" to maximize the per diem payments.

Suggested Structural Reforms

Interest in changing the structure of the Texas legislature has centered on sessions, size and salaries, and terms. In reality, none of these elements is likely to change.

The institution of annual *legislative sessions* has been a major reform proposal in all recent constitutional revision efforts. Annual sessions would allow legislators time to familiarize themselves with complex legislation, permitting them, for example, to bring a little more knowledge to the chaotic guessing game that produces the state's biennial budget. Annual sessions would virtually eliminate the need for special sessions when a crisis arises between regular sessions. They would allow time for the continual introduction of all those special resolutions, such as declaring chili the official state dish, that have negligible importance for the general public, but take up so much valuable legislative time. They also would provide an opportunity for legislative oversight of the state bureaucracy. Coupled with adequate staff support, annual sessions would allow legislators to engage in more long-range planning of public policy.

The legislature also needs to be empowered to call itself into special session. At present, if legislative leaders see the need for a special session and the governor is reluctant to call it, the legislature is helpless. In thirty-two other states, legislators can initiate a special session either independently or in conjunction with the governor, and efforts to gain that privilege for Texas legislators continue to be pressed. At a minimum, legislators need more freedom to add to the agenda of special sessions. Even though a session is called for a specific purpose, other significant items could be entered on the agenda and dispensed with, thus reducing the clutter of the next regular session's agenda.

The restrictions on both regular and special legislative sessions result in a high concentration of political power. The presiding officers dictate the flow of business during regular sessions, and the governor dominates special sessions.

Some advocates of reform have recommended that the Texas House be reduced in *size* to 100 members. Others have suggested that, because both houses are now elected on the basis of population distribution, one house should be eliminated altogether and a unicameral legislature adopted. But tradition strongly militates against such a change. The physical size of the state poses another risk to reducing the size of the legislature. As population and thus district size continue to grow, citizens will increasingly lose contact with their representatives. A reduction in the number of legislators would be a trade-off between legislative efficiency and representativeness. Although efficiency is important to citizens, so is being represented by someone from a small enough geographic and population area to understand the needs of the people in the district.

More serious are recommendations for salary increases. The $7,200 salary is insufficient to allow legislators to devote their full energies to state business. A salary in the range of the average among the nine other largest states—$58,000—would not, of course, guarantee that legislators would be honest and conscientious and devote all of their working time to the business of the state. A decent salary level, however, would ensure that those who wished to could spend most of their time on state business. Moreover, it might also eliminate the retainer fees, consultant fees, and legal fees now paid to many legislators. In addition, it would guard against only the rich being able to run for public office. However, a livable wage for legislators also flies in the face of the fiction that the state has a citizen legislature filled with individuals serving only because of their civic-minded nature.

If Senate members had staggered six-year *terms* and House members had staggered four-year terms, legislators could be assured of having time to develop

expertise in both procedures and substantive policy. Moreover, the virtually continuous campaigning that is required of legislators who represent highly competitive urban districts would be greatly reduced, leaving them more time to spend on legislative functions. Less campaigning also might serve to weaken the tie between legislators and the lobbyists who furnish both financial support for campaigning and bill-drafting services.

Legislative Process

At the close of each legislative session, a number of organizations assess the session and evaluate the membership. These evaluations help citizens determine whether the legislature was effective.

Assessing the Legislature in Action

Many of the rankings merely reflect how closely the members adhered to the position favored by the organization, so it is difficult to use these lists except as measures of, say, pro-business or pro-labor votes. The press also joins in the rating game, but reflects publishers' viewpoints—for example, the liberal viewpoint of the *Texas Observer*'s annual legislative assessment. One effort to judge legislators on grounds other than political philosophy, however, is that of *Texas Monthly*, which includes both liberals and conservatives of both urban and rural persuasions in its biennial list of ten best and ten worst legislators.[37] The criteria used by *Texas Monthly* are also suitable for use by the public in its evaluation, as follows:

> Our criteria are those that members apply to one another: Who is trustworthy? Who gets things done? Who brings credit upon the Legislature and who brings shame? Who does his homework? Who looks for ways to solve problems and who looks for ways to create them? Who is hamstrung by ideology and partisanship and who can rise above them? Politics is not just about conservatives and liberals and Republicans and Democrats. It is and always will be about personality and relationships and comportment—not that there's anything wrong with that.[38]

The session as a whole is even more difficult to evaluate. One's own political viewpoint and interest in specific issues can bias one's view of the actions of legislators. It is necessary to consider the bills and the votes, as well as the people. A sample of general criteria for such an assessment would include these questions:

1. **Did the legislature deal with major issues facing the state or mainly with trivial issues?**

2. **Did the appropriations bill reflect genuine statewide concerns or only the interests of the large lobbies?**

3. **Did the leadership operate effectively, forcing the legislature to give attention to major issues and arranging compromises on stalled bills, or did it cater to the lobbyists or the personal agendas of the presiding officers?**

4. **Was the effect of current legislation on future social, economic, and physical resources considered, or did the legislature live for today?**

5. **Were basic tests of democracy—representation, transparency, fairness—met?**

A brief evaluation of the legislatures in the 2000s reveals changes in that branch of government over time.

In 2001–2002, the Seventy-seventh Legislature was dominated by increasing partisanship tied to the decennial redistricting battle and the need to undo some of the legislation of the previous session that made Governor George Bush look good for his presidential run, but created problems for state government.

In 2003–2004, the Seventy-eighth Legislature consolidated health and human services agencies, focused on redistricting through three special sessions, and gave more power to legislative staff agencies at the expense of the comptroller.

In 2005–2006, the Seventy-ninth Legislature finally dealt with school finance, but only after a last-minute special session, stabilized teacher retirement, and overhauled the workers' compensation system.

In 2007–2008, the Eightieth Legislature was almost overwhelmed by the rancor in the House of Representatives, but did manage to overhaul the Texas Youth Commission, pass a miscellany of bills affecting senior citizens and children, and produce a $152.5 billion budget.

In 2009–2010, the Eighty-first Legislature ended the session in acrimony, with Republicans blaming Democrats for failure to pass legislation sought by the right such as voter identification and the Democrats blaming the Republicans for failure to consider expansion of human services programs such as better children's health care.

Suggested Procedural Changes

Ways to improve the formal structure for the legislature were suggested in the previous section. Improvements are also needed in legislative organization and procedures, especially in the areas of committees and ties to lobbyists.

The twenty-one House standing committees of 1973 had grown to thirty-six for the 2011 session. The Senate managed to operate with only nine standing committees from 1973 until 1985, but has had eighteen since 2009 (for only thirty-one members). These numbers do not count subcommittees or select committees in either house. Thus, both houses need to be wary of further committee expansion.

Public Policy, Legislative Style: A 2011 Sampler

The Eighty-first Legislature's 2011 regular session was characterized by acrimony, ideology, a willingness to have among the worst state programs in the country to avoid revenue increases, and further efforts to control human behavior. The Republican speaker tried to remain moderate, but was pushed hard from

the Tea Party wing of his own party. The Republican lieutenant governor did not want to offend the right because he was intent on running for the U.S. Senate, and left the "heavy lifting" to Finance Committee Chair Steve Ogden. The governor, who planned a run for president, also catered to the right and even suggested secession from the Union. In short, there was a dearth of leadership. Former Lieutenant Governor Bill Hobby's lament in the chapter-opening quote that the state's leaders seem to be seeking mediocrity was all too accurate. For the first time, the legislature slashed funds to public education as well as making its usual intrusions on social programs when the budget is tight.

The Eighty-second Legislature in regular and special sessions passed bills that included the following:

- **Voter identification, requiring not only a voter registration certification but also a photo identification to cast a ballot**

- **Redistricting both congressional and legislative seats (see Figures 6-3 and 6-4 for an example of rural and urban districts)**

- **Stringent $172.3 billion budget achieved through cuts in education and health care spending**

- **Ten proposed constitutional amendments**

- **Emergency legislation the governor wanted such as requiring a vaginal sonogram of a woman seeking an abortion and "loser pays," which requires the loser in a civil lawsuit to pay all costs of the suit**

- **"State's rights" resolution seeking state control, including a cap on spending for the federal Medicaid and Medicare programs**

- **Prohibiting texting while driving (vetoed by the governor)**

The failures of the 2011 legislative session included the following legislation that was considered but not passed:

- **Criminalizing the act of a federal Transportation Safety Authority employee who gropes a passenger during screening checks**

- **Numerous immigration bills, including elimination of "sanctuary cities"**

- **Restrictions on legislators becoming lobbyists immediately after leaving the House or Senate**

- **Stronger penalties for drunk-driving convictions**

- **Requirements for restaurants to post nutritional information**

- **Internet sales tax (left in legal limbo)**

Sources: Karen Brooks, "Time Runs Out for Ethics, Immigration, Other Bills," *Dallas Morning News*, May 14, 2011, 3A; Christy Hoppe, "25 Likely New Texas Laws," *Dallas Morning News*, May 31, 2011, 6A; Wayne Slater, "Perry Hits a Bump on the Road to the Presidency," *Dallas Morning News*, May 31, 2011, 6A; "Winners, Losers, and In-betweeners," *Dallas Morning News*, May 31, 2011, 7A; Thanh Tan, "Sine Die Report: What Survived, What Died," *Texas Tribune*, posted June 30, 2011, at http://www.texastribune.org/texas-legislature/82nd-legislative-session/sine-die-report-what-survived-what-died-/?utm_source=texastribune.org&utm_medium=rss&utm_campaign=Tribune%20Feed:%20Main%20Feed

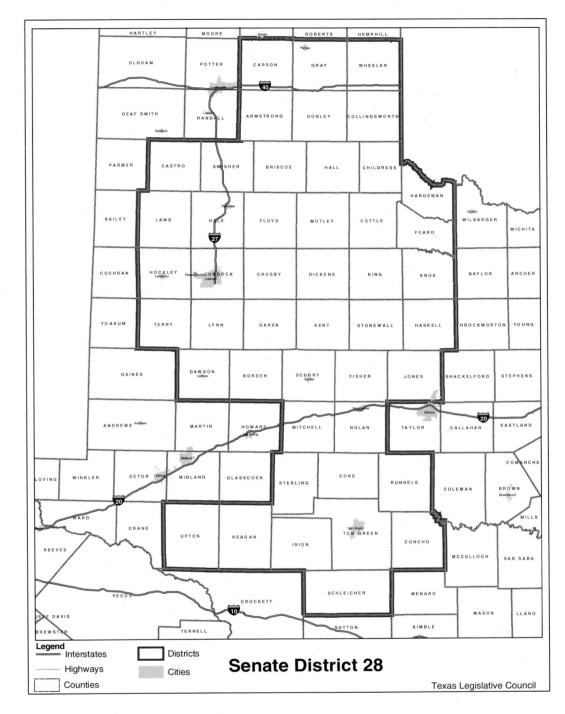

FIGURE 6-3 Example of a Texas Senate District

Although it includes two metropolitan areas, San Angelo and Lubbock, Senator Robert Duncan's district nevertheless encompasses forty-six counties, as of 2011.

SOURCE: *Courtesy of the Texas Legislative Council.*

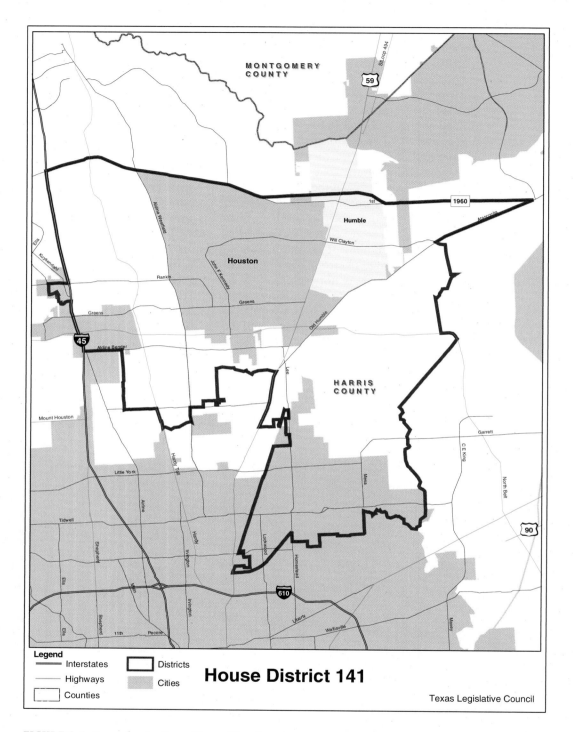

House District 141

Legend

— Interstates　☐ Districts
— Highways　▨ Cities
☐ Counties

Texas Legislative Council

FIGURE 6-4　Example of a Texas House District

Representative Senfronia Thompson's district includes both part of Houston and part of unincorporated Harris County, as of 2011.

SOURCE: *Courtesy of the Texas Legislative Council.*

Having substantially fewer committees would result in less ambiguity over committee jurisdiction. In addition, both houses could make more use of joint committees instead of submitting every issue for separate study and hearings. A joint budget committee is particularly needed. Fewer committee meetings would give legislators more time to familiarize themselves with the issues and the contents of specific bills. Fewer committees also might increase the chance for adoption of uniform committee rules throughout the two houses. Better meeting facilities for committees and more professional committee staff also are needed. Currently, chairs can hire staff or elect to use their own, so that independence is also a political issue.

Until legislators are able to declare their independence from *lobbyists and state administrators,* it will be impossible for the legislature to be truly independent of all interests but the public interest. Such a change depends on many factors: citizen attitudes, such as public willingness to allow adequate legislative sessions, pay, and staff support for legislators; public financing of election campaigns; and a commitment on the part of legislators to give up the social and economic advantages of strong ties to the lobby. The likelihood of total independence from the lobby is not high: All legislative groups everywhere have some ties to special interests. At a minimum, however, Texas needs to abandon such blatant practices as allowing lawyer-legislators to accept retainer fees from corporations that subsequently send lobbyists to Austin to influence these same legislators. A starting point in reform was Speaker Laney's rule prohibiting members of his own staff from accepting a job as a lobbyist for a year after leaving the speaker's office. That rule, however, is not binding on the staff members hired by other speakers, and the legislature has failed to pass a bill institutionalizing restrictions.

The 2011 legislature slashed funding for public and higher education, Medicaid, and many other programs that helped ordinary people, leading Ben Sargent to draw this cartoon saying Texans had been mugged.

Courtesy of Ben Sargent.

Conclusion

The Texas legislature has lost some minority members, reflecting the increasing Republicanism of the state. In this century, the strident ideology and partisanship displayed over issues such as redistricting and social programs has made the legislature more nearly resemble the U.S. Congress. Such a resemblance is not a good thing because fragmentation of power makes coherent public policy virtually impossible at the national level. In Texas, the tone is set by the powerful presiding officers in Texas, who can seek to bring about consensus and make the development of coherent public policy highly likely or who can opt to push their own personal agendas. Thus, for all its problems, the Texas legislature can be highly effective if the leadership is so inclined. Because the Texas legislature is centralized, it is capable of translating public preferences into policy.

Because so few Texans vote, however, the preferences of the richer and more educated minority are often translated into policy. The most evident case is that in Texas, only 37 percent of Hispanics vote, compared to 57 percent in California.[39] Although liberals criticize the content of public policy, they cannot deny that the process is effective and that it is rational from the standpoint of most Texas voters, if not of all citizens.

Summary

In many ways, the Texas legislature is typical of state lawmaking bodies, including its large size (181 members), its domination by Anglo males, its somewhat limited professional staff, its relatively short terms of office for its members (two years in the House and four in the Senate), and its reliance on legislative committees as the workhorses of the legislative process. Nevertheless, the following distinctive features of the Texas legislature are atypical, especially when it is compared with the legislatures of other large urban states:

1. **The legislature is restricted to one regular session of 140 days every two years.**

2. **Legislators are paid only $7,200 a year, although they receive a generous per diem payment for expenses.**

3. **The presiding officers—the speaker of the House and the lieutenant governor in the Senate—are preeminent in the legislative process. If either presiding officer is inclined to be arbitrary, democracy suffers.**

4. **A sometimes high turnover rate and the shifting memberships of the large number of committees make it difficult for legislators to develop expertise in specific areas of legislation.**

5. **Special interests have an extraordinary influence on both the election and the performance of legislators. This dominance raises the issue of when and how constituent voices are heard.**

Texas legislators face the biennial task of developing sound public policy for a major state without jeopardizing the support of the presiding officers or the special interests crucial to their re-election. Moreover, they operate in the highly constrained

environment of both structural handicaps and lack of public confidence. They must spend much of their time tending to casework, sitting in committee meetings, or running for office. Nevertheless, changes in legislative organization would help promote legislative independence and allow more time for planning and policy development. Recommendations for reform include the following:

1. **Annual sessions**

2. **Higher salaries, approximately $60,000**

3. **Four-year terms for House members and six-year terms for senators**

4. **Reduction in the number of legislative committees**

Understanding the legislative process in Texas involves some knowledge of parliamentary procedure and an appreciation for the role of the presiding officers. To become a law, a bill must survive numerous parliamentary and political obstacles. Most bills never become laws. Here are some important features of the Texas system:

1. **The presiding officers control both the composition of legislative committees and the appointment of committee chairpersons.**

2. **The speaker of the House and the lieutenant governor in the Senate—the presiding officers—decide whether a friendly or unfriendly committee will consider a bill.**

3. **The presiding officers indirectly determine when and if a bill will be debated.**

4. **The presiding officers decide who will speak for and against a bill once it reaches the floor, and the lieutenant governor can even use this power of recognition to allow a filibuster to develop.**

5. **The staff agencies designed to assist the legislature have relatively low budgets and are dominated by the presiding officers.**

6. **Even if a bill passes both houses, it may still be killed by a conference committee or a governor's veto.**

Legislators face many pressures, and evaluating their work is more difficult than it might seem. Sometimes they are blamed for lawmaking that is really the handiwork of the governor, the state bureaucracy, or the courts. Changes in legislative organization and procedure would help improve legislative efficiency and independence. Recommendations for reform include the following:

1. **Reducing the number of committees, especially in the House, and then in turn providing adequate funds for a professional and independent committee staff**

2. **Evaluating continually the method of selecting committee chairpersons**

3. **Reducing the influence of the lobby**

Reforms in the day-to-day operation of the legislature are unlikely, however, unless some of the structural changes, such as higher pay, better staff support, and annual sessions, are instituted.

Despite its obstacles, the Texas legislature has traditionally been able to produce laws that are in keeping with the political sentiments of a majority of Texas voters. Legislative bodies are the manifestation of representative government. While elected executives must represent the whole, diverse state of Texas, individual legislators represent smaller and presumably more homogeneous districts. Thus, they can more easily discern the wishes of their constituents and try to enact those wishes into law. Even though any given individual may not like the public policy developed by the legislature, careful observers must admire the legislature's ability to conduct business under the pressure of a short session.

However, since 1993, the legislature has been moving toward the partisan and ideological gridlock for which the U.S. Congress has been criticized. Initially, only occasional, truly partisan issues such as redistricting produced stand-offs, but other legislation was enacted with bipartisan support. By 2009, the efforts of each party to defeat the other, come-what-may with the citizens, meant that there was keen disagreement with much of the legislative output. The old bipartisan civility and ability to expedite important legislation seem to have eroded considerably. Nevertheless, one can conclude that the Texas legislature serves its democratic purpose of enacting the will of the majority—or at least, the will of the fraction of the public that votes—into statutory law. The following chapters turn to an examination of the executive branch.

Glossary Terms

bicameral	item veto
biennial	legislative oversight
bill	privatizing
casework	reapportionment
conference committee	redistricting
constituent function	seniority
filibuster	single-member districts
fiscal year	tag
formal qualifications	turnover
gerrymandering	

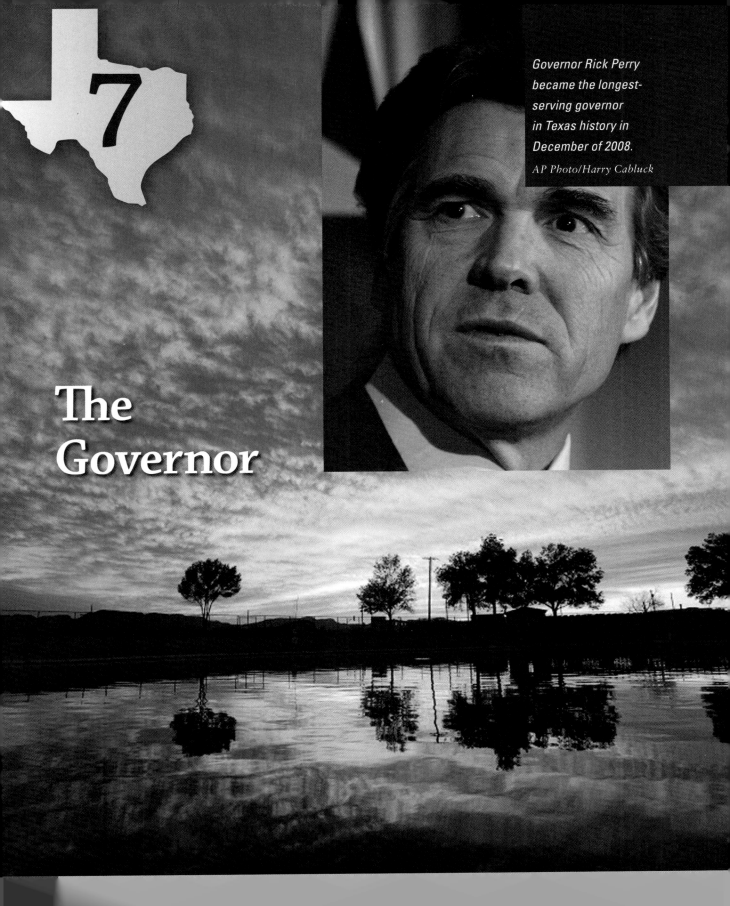

7

The
Governor

Governor Rick Perry became the longest-serving governor in Texas history in December of 2008.

AP Photo/Harry Cabluck

Why does anyone want to be governor of Texas? The governorship is like the super-super gift in the Neiman-Marcus Christmas catalog—something for the man who has everything and absolutely unique!

ANONYMOUS POLITICAL SCIENTIST

It is widely reported that the governorship of Texas is by design a weak office. However, the strength of an individual governor's personality can overcome many of the limitations imposed on the office.

BRIAN McCALL, TEXAS HOUSE OF REPRESENTATIVES, 2009

OBJECTIVES

After reading this chapter, you should be able to

Describe the structure of the Texas governorship, including how the governor is selected, the term of office and tenure possibility, the process of impeachment, compensation, and staffing.

Discuss the personal characteristics that might lead to gubernatorial success.

Assess the formal and informal roles that the governor plays.

Understand the limitations on gubernatorial power.

INTRODUCTION

Though democratic theory may pay more attention to the legislature than to the executive, chief executives and administrative agencies are important components of government, so they too deserve to be measured against the ideal of democracy. In Texas, the legislature has been the dominant branch of state government through most of the state's history. Indeed, since the governor's office in Texas is weak in formal powers, bargaining skills and persuasive ability are the keys to gubernatorial leadership.

This chapter examines the basic structure of the governor's office, the formal qualifications for the office and personal characteristics of those who are typically elected to it, the roles that the governor plays, and the limitations on those roles, including the **plural executive** system. It is a portrait of a well-paid, prestigious state office hampered by a restrictive state constitution and a state administration that is largely independent of the governor's control. It is also a portrait of individuals who have overcome the constitutional weaknesses of the office through their political skills and personal magnetism. The governor's powers have been enhanced in recent years, but they remain among the weakest of governors in the United States.

Basic Structure of the Governor's Office

This chapter first examines how the governor is selected, the length of the term, and the usual number of years served.

Election

In Texas, the governor and all statewide elected executives are chosen in statewide elections held in even-numbered years when there is no presidential election. The candidates are selected in party primaries held earlier the same year (see Chapter 5). Gubernatorial elections are held in the "off year" so that national issues won't overshadow state issues, but election contests for the Texas governor's office often focus on personalities and not issues. As a result, these off-year elections attract fewer voters absent the presidential election as a drawing card. In fact, voter turnout reached a modern low of 16 percent of registered

LONE STAR MEDIA

Perry and the Press

Governor Perry is one of the most successful politicians in Texas in recent history. Traditionally, one becomes successful, especially in a state like Texas, with such large population and geography, by successfully cultivating the media—newspapers and television stations—that can spread your message across the state without direct cost and who, by tradition, can destroy you if they oppose your candidacy. A political adage is "Never pick a fight with a man who buys ink by the barrel." The message is clear: in order to have success in politics, one must openly court the media.

In 2010, however, Governor Perry followed a different tact. He mostly ignored the media. He refused to meet with the editorial boards of newspapers in the state, and none of the major newspapers in the state endorsed his candidacy. He refused to take questions after a speech at the National Conference of Editorial Writers meeting in Dallas during the campaign. His spokesperson said that "a better use of the governor's time is to talk directly to Texans and reporters throughout the state."

Editorial endorsements have normally been highly coveted by candidates for office, so Perry's tactic was clearly a departure from tradition. Perry's pollster said that their research showed that only 6 percent of Texans would be more likely to vote for a candidate endorsed by the media, while 37 percent said they would be less likely to support such a candidate. So in the year of the Tea Party and suspicion of the "liberal" media, Perry clearly struck the correct chord, winning the election by 13 percent.

Instead of concentrating on traditional newspaper endorsements, Perry used social media extensively.

Perry announced his candidacy for the U.S. Presidency on August 12, 2011, in Charleston, South Carolina. His announcement came before an audience of bloggers hosted by the conservative RedState blog.

SOURCES: Jay, Root, "Updated: Perry Announces 2012 Run, Attacks Obama," Texas Tribune, August 13, 2011. http://www.texastribune.org/texas-politics/2012-presidential-election/rick-perry-announces-president/. Accessed August 18, 2011; Ross Ramsey, "Rick Perry's Love-Hate Relationship with the Press," *Texas Tribune*, November 5, 2010; Jason Embry, "Perry Will Skip Editorial Boards," *Austin American-Statesman*, August 12, 2010.

TABLE 7-1

The Texas Governor's Institutional Powers among the States

Texas Provision	Number of Other States with the Provision	Beyle's Ranking of Institutional Power
Four-year term without restrictions on number of terms or number of consecutive terms*	12	5 (high)
Public election of six or fewer state executives	29	2 (fairly low)
Governor's appointment power**		1.0 (low)
Shares responsibility for budget preparation	14	2 (fairly low)
Gubernatorial party control		4 (fairly high)
Item veto over appropriations	42	5*** (high)
Overall ranking among the states		Tied for 40th

*Only Vermont and New Hampshire have a two-year term.
**Beyle's ranking was of appointment power over major functional areas of state government.
***Beyle's ranking was of the whole veto power, including the Texas governor's advantage because of the short legislative session.

SOURCES: *The Book of the States, 2010*, vol. 42 (Lexington, Ky.: Council of State Governments, 2010), 196–197; 201–206; Thad Beyle, "The Governors," in Virginia Gray and Russell L. Hanson, eds., *Politics in the American States: A Comparative Analysis*, 9th ed. (Washington, D.C.: CQ Press, 2008), 212–213.

voters (roughly 10 percent of eligible citizens) during the 1994 primaries, though turnout has improved slightly since then. The lieutenant governor is selected in the same manner, but runs independently of the governor.

Term of Office

In 1974, the governor's term of office was extended from two to four years. No constitutional provision limits the number of terms a governor may serve in Texas. Table 7-1 summarizes some institutional characteristics of the governor's office compared with those of other states. The table shows the number of other states that share a particular characteristic with Texas, as well as the ranking of the Texas governor on a national scale of institutional power. The Texas governor, overall, ranks well below average in overall powers—tied for fortieth among the states.

Tenure

Until World War II, Texas governors were routinely elected for two two-year terms.[1] During and after the war, this precedent was supplanted by a trend to three terms, as indicated in Table 7-2. The precedent was broken when Governor Preston Smith, trying for a third term in 1972, was among the many state politicians who were swept out of office on the wave of public reaction to the Sharpstown Bank scandal, an event in which a number of public officials,

TABLE 7-2

Texas Governors and Their Terms of Office, under 1876 Constitution

Richard Coke*	1874–1876	Miriam A. Ferguson	1933–1935
Richard B. Hubbard	1876–1879	James V. Allred	1935–1939
Oran M. Roberts	1879–1883	W. Lee O' Daniel*	1939–1941
John Ireland	1883–1887	Coke R. Stevenson	1941–1947
Lawrence S. Ross	1887–1891	Beauford H. Jester*	1947–1949
James S. Hogg	1891–1895	Allan Shivers	1949–1957
Charles A. Culberson	1895–1899	Price Daniel	1957–1963
Joseph D. Sayers	1899–1903	John Connally	1963–1969
S. W. T. Lanham	1903–1907	Preston Smith	1969–1973
Thomas M. Campbell	1907–1911	Dolph Briscoe	1973–1979
Oscar B. Colquitt	1911–1915	William (Bill) Clements	1979–1983
James E. Ferguson**	1915–1917	Mark White	1983–1987
William P. Hobby	1917–1921	William (Bill) Clements	1987–1991
Pat M. Neff	1921–1925	Ann Richards	1991–1995
Miriam A. Ferguson	1925–1927	George W. Bush	1995–2000
Dan Moody	1927–1931	Rick Perry	2000–
Ross Sterling	1931–1933		

*Coke and O'Daniel resigned from the governorship to enter the U.S. Senate. Jester died in office.
**James Ferguson was impeached and convicted.

SOURCE: Adapted from "Governors of Texas," prepared by the Texas Legislative Council and available at http:www.lrl.state.tx.us/legeLeaders/governors/govBrowse.cfm.

including the governor, were alleged to have taken a profit on buying, and then selling stock at a great profit in exchange for passing a bill benefiting the Sharpstown Bank.

Modern governors serving four-year terms have had mixed results in being re-elected, in part due to the shifting party preferences of Texans. Bill Clements (Republican) lost to Mark White (Democrat) in 1982, but White lost to Clements in 1986. Ann Richards (Democrat) then served a single term after her 1990 election. On the other hand, George W. Bush (Republican) won a second term by an overwhelming majority, although he resigned to become president of the United States. Rick Perry (Republican) has been elected to three full terms after serving out Bush's unexpired term, and he became Texas's longest-serving governor in December of 2008.

In recent decades, because Texas is the second most populous state in the Union, Texas governors have often been in the spotlight as future presidential or vice presidential candidates. Such was the case with Bush, who became president in 2001, and Perry has had a high national profile in the last few years.

Impeachment and Succession

If the legislature believes a governor has misused the office, it may begin action to remove him or her. The state's succession plan then goes into effect.

Impeachment

In Texas, a governor may be removed from office only through an **impeachment** proceeding. Impeachment is similar to a grand jury indictment; that is, it is a formal accusation. The state constitution does not define what constitutes an impeachable offense. By implication and by the precedents set in the impeachment of Governor James E. Ferguson in 1917, however, the grounds are *malfeasance, misfeasance,* or *nonfeasance* in office—in other words, official misconduct, incompetence, or failure to perform.[2]

The impeachment procedure in Texas is similar to that at the national level, and has been successfully used only in the case of James Ferguson, just mentioned. The House of Representatives, by a majority vote of those present, must first impeach the executive. Once the formal accusation is made, the Senate acts as a trial court; a two-thirds vote of the senators present is necessary to convict. Penalties for conviction are removal from office and disqualification from holding future governmental offices in the state.

Gubernatorial Succession

The last governor to die in office was Beauford Jester in 1949, who was succeeded by Allan Shivers. The 1999 amendment ensured a smooth transition when Governor George W. Bush, whose term was to expire in 2002, was elected president in 2000.

Succession

If a governor is removed from office by impeachment and conviction, dies in office or before taking office, or resigns, the constitution provides that the lieutenant governor shall become governor. When Governor Bush resigned to assume the presidency following the 2000 election, Rick Perry rose to the governorship from his position as Lieutenant Governor.

A 1999 constitutional amendment further stipulates that, should the governor become disabled, the lieutenant governor will carry out the duties of the office; should the governor die or otherwise be unable to return, the lieutenant governor will become governor for the rest of the term. If the lieutenant governor is unable to serve, the president pro tempore of the Senate will carry out the duties. Once the lieutenant governor becomes governor, the lieutenant

governor's position is vacant. Within thirty days, the Senate will elect one of its members to fulfill all of the duties of lieutenant governor until the next general election. The amendment clarifies that no one can be governor and lieutenant governor simultaneously, but also leaves some ambiguity in the wording. The executive article states that the senator who is elected as presiding officer is also the lieutenant governor, but the legislative article is more ambiguous, stating only that he or she will "perform the duties of the Lieutenant Governor."

Compensation

A 1954 amendment allows the legislature to determine the salary of the governor and other elected executives. The legislature provided generous increments for many years, raising the governor's salary from $12,000 in 1954 to $150,000 in 2009, ranking 11th among all governors. Interestingly, the highest paid state officials are often not governors, but instead the head football coaches at state universities.[3] The lieutenant governor is paid as a legislator—$7,200 a year plus a per diem—although he or she receives a salary supplementation for acting as governor whenever the governor leaves the state.

The governor also receives numerous fringe benefits. The constitution provides an official mansion, and other benefits include a travel and operating budget, a car, the use of state-owned aircraft, bodyguards furnished by the Texas Department of Public Safety, and offices and professional staff. Since 2007, Governor Perry has lived in a rental apartment while the Governor's Mansion is being repaired after being burned down in a fire started by an arsonist. Critics have charged that the $10,000 per month fee for his rent is excessive during tough economic times.[4] These benefits compare favorably with those of other governors.

Staff and Organization

Like other chief executives, the governor must rely on staff to carry out his or her functions, including a personal staff and help from the professional staffs of the divisions that make up the Office of the Governor. Certain staff members are assigned to act as legislative liaisons—in effect, to lobby for the governor's programs—and often it is through them that the governor makes known an impending threat to veto a particular piece of legislation. Other staff members are involved in recommending candidates for the hundreds of appointments the governor must make to state boards, commissions, and executive agencies. The governor's aides also prepare the executive budget, coordinate the various departments and activities of the governor's office, and schedule appointments and activities. Overall, in addition to handling routine duties and occasional

Governor's Office Staffing

How do the big-population states compare in the number of gubernatorial staff members? Florida leads with 325; Texas has 266; California, 185; New York, 180; Illinois, 130; and Pennsylvania, only 68. Whether the state has a cabinet and how many functions have been temporarily assigned to the governor's office both play a role in determining staff size.

Show Me the Money

Although well paid, particularly in comparison to legislators with their $7,200 salaries, the Texas governor is by no means the best-paid executive on the state payroll. The chancellors of the major university systems and the presidents of the largest institutions often receive compensation packages of $500,000 or more. University of Texas Chancellor Francisco Cigarroa led Texans in 2010 with base pay of $750,000 and another $37,258 in retirement pay. In addition, some large institutions pay bonuses for successful fundraising, and some chancellors receive supplemental pay from individual institutions in the system—particularly medical schools.

However, even these salaries pale when compared to those of the football and basketball coaches at UT-Austin and Texas Tech. Coach Mack Brown at the University of Texas has a compensation package of $5,000,000 per year, leading to a Faculty Council resolution that such a salary at an institution of higher learning was "unseemly and inappropriate." In 2011, Coach Tommy Tuberville was given a $500,000 per year raise to more than $2,000,000 per year at the same time as faculty salaries remained frozen.

Sources: Jeanne Kever, "Recession Hits the Top Ranks of Colleges, Too," *Houston Chronicle*, January 18, 2010; Ralph K. M. Haurwitz, "Mack Brown's Salary Deemed 'Unseemly,'" *Austin American-Statesman*, December 14, 2009; Matthew McGowen, "Tuberville Raise Rankles Tech Faculty," *Lubbock Avalanche-Journal*, February 21, 2011.

emergency situations, the governor's staff must provide assistance in performing the specific tasks assigned to the office by law and in formulating political moves to promote the enactment of the governor's programs.

As of 2006, Governor Rick Perry's office had 266 staff members, more than any governor other than Florida's.[5] This number appears low when one considers that Governor Ann Richards had a staff of almost 400. The comparison is somewhat deceiving because the Richards payroll was significantly less than the Perry payroll.

Each governor organizes the office somewhat differently. Commonly, new program initiatives begin under the governor's auspices and then become independent or move to other agencies. More than anything else, the configuration of programs makes the difference in organization. As of 2011, the governor's office consisted of the following elements:[6]

Advisory Council on Physical Fitness—charged with improving the state's overall fitness through sports, health and nutrition education, and exercise

Appointments Office—charged with assisting the governor in appointing more than 3,000 people to lead boards, commissions, and other oversight groups in Texas

Budget, Planning, and Policy—advises the governor on key policy issues, especially those regarding his or her role as chief budget officer

Commission for Women—promotes opportunities for Texas women

Committee on People with Disabilities—intended to help people with disabilities enjoy full and equal access to lives of independence, productivity, and self-determination

Constituent Communication—provides the link between the governor and the people of Texas by reviewing and responding to letters, faxes, e-mails, and phone calls

Criminal Justice Division—designed to contribute to public safety and the reduction of crime in Texas

Economic Development and Tourism—promotes Texas to expanding companies and visitors worldwide

Financial Services—assists in making the governor's financial transactions according to law and state ethical standards

General Counsel—provides legal advice to the governor

Human Resources—assists applicants seeking employment and governor's office employees with policy and program support

Press Office—works closely with the news media to convey the governor's political perspective and vision

Scheduling and Advance—responsible for responding to requests for the governor's time and organizing the logistics of the governor's schedule

Texas Criminal Justice Statistical Analysis Center—collects, analyzes, and reports statewide criminal justice statistics; evaluates the effectiveness of state-funded initiatives; and disseminates analysis results in order to enhance the quality of criminal justice and crime prevention

Texas Film Commission—informs filmmakers of the state's complete range of film-related services, locations, and facilities

Texas Health Care Policy Council—studies and recommends changes to the health care system in Texas

Texas Homeland Security—coordinates the resources and responses necessary to prepare for and respond to all threats of terrorism and disaster

Texas Music Office—promotes the Texas music industry

Texas Workforce Investment Council—works to improve the overall quality of the state's workforce, emphasizing education and training to meet the needs of modern economic growth

As is evident from this list offices, the governor has a wide range of responsibilities that include making recommendations regarding public policy, applying the laws according to the law, promoting the Texas economy, providing opportunity for people who have traditionally not had equal chances, and even providing for the state's homeland security.

Qualifications for Governor

Both legally mandated criteria and informal standards set by political interests and voters shape who is eligible to serve as governor.

Formal Qualifications

As is true of the qualifications for members of the legislature, the formal qualifications for governor are minimal. Article IV of the constitution stipulates that the governor must be at least thirty years old, be a citizen of the United States, and have been a resident of Texas for the five years immediately preceding the election. These qualifications also pertain to the lieutenant governor. Article IV also mandates that the governor "shall be installed on the first Tuesday after the

Texas Version of Foreign Affairs

One of the surprising consequences of the end of the Cold War between the United States and the former Soviet Union has been the assertion of American state activity in international affairs. Although Article I, Section 10 of the U.S. Constitution forbids the states to enter into any agreement or compact with a foreign power, many states have begun to do so rather explicitly. For example, on the Texas governor's Web site, the Department of Economic Development and Tourism "promotes Texas domestically and internationally as a premier tourist destination to generate tourism revenues and jobs for Texas communities" while the International Business and Recruitment Program helps Texas companies expand into foreign markets and assists them with recruiting foreign companies to Texas.

California has opened ten trade offices in foreign capitals, including Mexico City, London, and Tokyo. In the period of 2004 to 2010, Governor Perry made twenty-three trips abroad in his role as governor, including trips to the Bahamas, Italy, the United Arab Emirates, Qatar, Grand Cayman, Israel, Jordan, Sweden, China, Turkey, Taiwan, Korea, Slovakia, Japan, Germany, Malta, France, the Czech Republic, Azerbaijan, Canada, Spain, Brazil, and Argentina. While no doubt the trips included time for tourism and relaxation, their primary purpose in most instances was to recruit business, promote increased trade with other nations, encourage investment in Texas business, and attend official functions, such as the inauguration of the Mexican president. Costs of these trips approached a million dollars in public funds, but most neutral political observers thought those costs reasonable and necessary in the modern state leadership environment.

Sources: Julie Blase, "The Evolution of State Influence on U.S. Foreign Policy as Illustrated by Texas-Mexico Relations," unpublished paper, Department of Government, University of Texas at Austin, December 1, 1997; Dave Lesher, "Golden and Global California," *Los Angeles Times*, January 8, 1998, A1; Peggy Fikac, "$1 Million for Perry's Security over 7 Years," *Houston Chronicle*, October 15, 2010.

organization of the Legislature, or as soon thereafter as practicable." Article III gives the legislature the responsibility for settling any election disputes that might arise concerning the governor.

Personal Characteristics

Formally qualifying for the governorship and actually having a chance at being considered seriously as a candidate are two very different matters. The social, political, and economic realities of the state dictate that personal characteristics, not stated in law, help determine who will be the victors in gubernatorial elections. Some of these personal characteristics are based on accomplishments, or at least positive involvement, of the gubernatorial aspirant. Others are innate traits that are beyond the control of the individual.

These characteristics are similar to, but even more stringent than, those for members of the legislature. In short, unless something unusual occurs in the campaign, tradition dictates that the successful candidate for governor will be a White Anglo-Saxon Protestant (WASP) male who is politically conservative, involved in civic affairs, and a millionaire. More than likely, but less inevitably, this individual will have held some other office, often that of attorney general or lieutenant governor, although being a professional politician is sometimes a liability among voters with a penchant for electing "good ol' boys."

The most atypical governor in more than a half-century was Ann Richards (1991–1995), a populist Democratic female (see Chapter 4 for a discussion of populism in Texas). Richards took strong stands against concealed weapons and environmental destruction, and urged reform of selected state agencies, such as the Insurance Commission and Department of Commerce, that had strong ties to business. Rick Perry, a Republican, is very much in the conservative mainstream of Texas political belief and served as a member of the Texas House, as agriculture commissioner, and as lieutenant governor before ascending to the governorship in late 2000. He is distinguished perhaps by representing rural West Texas rather than an urban area. His re-election in 2010 was highlighted by defeating popular U.S. Senator Kay Bailey Hutchison and Tea Party candidate Debra Medina for the Republican nomination and easily outdistancing Democratic nominee Bill White in the general election. In his 2011 State of the State address, he confronted economic hard times, with a projected shortfall of as much as $27 million over the 2011–2012 budget years, by saying that he wanted the legislature to trim agency budgets and be in the business of "doing more with less."

Conservative

Traditionally, a gubernatorial candidate had to be a conservative Democrat. E. J. Davis, a much-maligned Republican governor during Reconstruction, was the only Republican governor until Bill Clements was elected in 1978. Since 1978, Republicans have held the office most of the time. Though the demography of Texas continues to change, the governor is likely to be a conservative Republican for the immediate future.

In the 1990 Ann Richards–Clayton Williams race, Richards's self-proclaimed Democratic populism did not win the race for her. Rather, Clayton Williams's "open-mouth-put-foot-in" rhetoric lost the election for him. He seemed particularly adept at insulting women and ordinary taxpayers. In the first instance, he opined that rape was like bad weather so that, "If it's inevitable, [a woman should] just relax and enjoy it." In the second, Williams, a multimillionaire who financed much of his own campaign, bragged about not paying federal income taxes. Richards was the most recent Democratic governor.

In the previous race, between Clements and Mark White in 1986, White—the conservative Democrat—lost because of a faltering economy that he neither caused nor could fix and because of the education funding issue. White had taken a strong stand for school reform and the tax increase necessary to finance it, noting at the time that he probably had forfeited his own second term. Indeed, during the 1986 campaign, White was portrayed as a high-tax, free-spending liberal.

George W. Bush entered the race in 1994 as a mainstream Republican, concerned with state control over state policy, the integrity of the family, the quality of education, and the rising incidence of juvenile crime. He and Richards differed little on those issues. He reflected more of a national Republican position in wanting to cut welfare and in openly advocating a freer operating climate for business, especially by placing many restrictions on lawsuits for such activities as professional malpractice and faulty products. Significantly, however, he talked about his conservatism, not his party affiliation. Because of the growth of the Republican Party, Bush won that election even though Richards remained personally popular among voters even at the time of the election.

George W. Bush served as governor from 1995 until 2000, when he resigned after being elected president of the United States.

AP Photo/Harry Cabluck

The Tony Sanchez–Rick Perry gubernatorial race in 2002 was costly and mean spirited, a signal of the 2003 legislative session yet to come. Perry claimed education, health care, transportation, water, and border affairs as priorities, but focused on pro-business legislation rather than problem solving. He was successful in reducing the power of Comptroller Carole Keeton Strayhorn, who had tested the waters for a possible run against Perry in the next Republican primary by lambasting the lack of concern for poor children and their health care needs, and in augmenting the power of the governor's office.

Perry continued to earn his conservative credentials in the subsequent legislative sessions, pushing business interests, emphasizing tax cuts over solutions to the knotty school finance problem (see Chapter 12), and even enduring criticism from fellow Republicans for letting his industry ties dominate public policy. His major speeches often addressed the concerns of poor people, but his legislative agenda tended to address the desires of business. He ran against Senator Kay Bailey Hutchison in the Republican primary and Democrat Bill White in the general election of 2010 as a conservative alternative to each. Since Hutchison votes conservatively around 80 percent of the time in the U.S. Senate, and Bill White had been seen as a pro-business mayor of Houston, Perry's conservative credentials were impressive.

Most state officeholders in Texas are conservative, and a candidate for governor needs not only their support, but also access to the big campaign money waiting in the pockets of conservative businesspersons, bankers, and attorneys (these last two often have state agencies as customers and clients). Although

Good Ol' Girl

Ann Richards wanted to ensure that Texans understood the difference between her people's campaign (populism) and run-of-the-mill liberalism. She went to some lengths to look like a good ol' girl, including joining the boys for the opening of bird-hunting season. She also posed for the cover of *Texas Monthly* wearing a black leather jacket and sitting on a Harley-Davidson motorcycle.

Ann Richards served as governor from 1991 until 1995.

AP Photo/Eric Miller, File

unanimity does not exist in either party, and while urban-rural differences increase yearly, the nominee generally can count on all factions of the party for support in the general election.

WASP, Middle-Aged Male

Texas has not had a non-Anglo governor since it became independent of Spain and Mexico. Only two Roman Catholics—Frances (Sissy) Farenthold in the 1972 Democratic primary and Tony Sanchez in 2002—have been serious contenders for the governor's office; Kinky Friedman in 2006 was the only serious

Jewish candidate, but he drew only 12 percent of the vote. The religious preferences of the governors elected in the Lone Star State have been confined to the mainstream Protestant churches, such as Methodist and Baptist.

Texas governors have tended to reach the top office shortly after their fiftieth birthday. Of the thirty-one individuals who have served as governor of Texas under the 1876 Constitution, only two—Ann Richards and Miriam A. Ferguson—were female. However, across the United States, among the twenty-five women who had been elected as governors by 2007, only Texas, Arizona, Kansas, and New Hampshire had elected two different women.

Attorney/Businessperson, Community Pillar

Governors, as well as legislators, are often attorneys. Since 1876, sixteen of the thirty-one Texas governors have been lawyers. However, of the five most recent governors in the state, only Mark White was a lawyer. Bill Clements and George W. Bush were businesspeople. Ann Richards, although she had been a public school teacher, was essentially a professional politician who went to work as a lobbyist for a Washington-based law firm when she left office. Rick Perry is a fifth-generation Texas farmer-rancher with more than twenty years spent as an elected official.

The final personal characteristic that candidates must have is being a "pillar of the community." Governors are members of civic, social, fraternal, and business organizations and seem to be the epitome of stable family life. Richards, being divorced, was something of an exception, but she was frequently photographed with her children and grandchildren.

Roles of the Governor and Limits on Those Roles

The office of governor consists of a repertoire of at least seven roles that the incumbent must play. Five are formal; that is, they are prescribed by the constitution and supplementing statutes. Two are informal and symbolic; that is, they derive from the Texas political setting (see Table 7-3). Governors of all states play similar roles, as does the president, who also has added responsibilities in the areas of diplomacy and economics.

TABLE 7-3

Roles of the Governor

Constitutional and Statutory Roles	Informal and Symbolic Roles
Chief Executive	Chief of Party
Chief Legislator	Leader of the People
Commander in Chief/Top Cop	
Chief of State	
Chief Intergovernmental Diplomat	

The personality of the governor and the political and economic circumstances that prevail during a governor's administration largely determine which roles are emphasized. As the first opening quotation in this chapter indicates, the governorship is a unique office, with its distinctive qualities further highlighted by the varied approaches taken by different governors.[7] How a governor goes about trying to get policy preferences enacted by the legislature and implemented by the bureaucracy constitutes leadership style. Leadership style is crucial in Texas because the governor so often has to depend on persuasive skills to offset the limitations of the office. Democratic theory dictates that the elected executive be accountable for the executive branch. In Texas, the governor has to rely heavily on informal means to gain the expected control over the state bureaucracy and to achieve his or her policy agenda.

To view the governor in action, this chapter looks briefly at the styles of the governors of the state during the modern era. These brief biographical sketches may help the reader understand the diverse personalities and operating styles of recent Texas governors.

Mark White (1983–1987) inherited a deteriorating economy and emphasized education and economic development as ways to shore up the state financial picture. He oversaw comprehensive reform of the public school system and pushed for vigorous regulation of public utilities in Texas. His accomplishments could not overcome the faltering Texas economy and the growing Republican Party.[8] Bill Clements (1979–1983, 1987–1991) emphasized tax reform, a war on drugs and crime, long-range planning, and better ties to neighboring states and Mexico during his first term. During his second term, out of necessity, he emphasized economic diversification. Clements had a reputation as an obstructionist, making it difficult for public policy to develop, but his legacy was bringing "business principles and discipline to the state budget and government."[9]

The governor acknowledged to be atypical, Ann Richards (1991–1995), was grounded in Travis County politics and got high marks for the quality and diversity of her appointments; for forcing changes in the controversial boards governing some state agencies, especially the State Insurance Board and the Board of Pardons and Paroles; and for exerting executive control over other agencies, such as the Texas Department of Commerce. Richards insisted on high ethical standards, although some of her staff members stumbled later on. She also worked hard at economic diversification. However, Richards's approach to legislative relations was partisan and heavy handed, and, although she was appreciated for her salty sense of humor and her reputation as "the thorny rose of Texas,"[10] she sometimes had difficulty pushing her policy agenda through the legislature. Her 1994 bid for re-election was inept, and she also faced the national Republican sweep. Though she was popular among Texans even at the end of her term, Richards lost handily to George W. Bush.[11]

George W. Bush (1995–2000), son of a former president,[12] operated very differently from Richards. The Bush approach to legislators was nonpartisan, low-key, and consensus building. Bush saw himself as a deal maker. He campaigned on four issues: reform of the juvenile justice system, setting limits on civil lawsuits (tort reform), more flexible and better public education, and restrictions on welfare. These issues were common throughout the country in 1994. Once elected, Bush stuck with those issues and pushed each through the 1995 legislature. While he was successful in further expanding public school flexibility in the 1997 legislative session, his push for major changes in the Texas tax system was rebuffed. He had to settle for a proposed constitutional amendment to increase

the tax exemptions for homesteads. He was an immensely popular governor in part due to his bipartisan approach to governing, working well with Democratic leadership in the legislature. He gained re-election in 1998 by 69 percent of the vote.[13]

By the time the Seventy-sixth Legislature met in January 1999, no doubt existed about the Governor Bush's political plans. The *Wall Street Journal*, whose political philosophy is closely aligned to that of Bush's "compassionate conservatism," summarized the year by noting the total dominance of the capitol complex by a governor who was out of the state campaigning much of the time. The *Journal* staff noted the Bush "'Yellow Rose Garden' strategy of having potential presidential supporters and advisers, along with world leaders, come to Austin" as overshadowing "anything that was happening across the street at the state Capitol,"[14] including the partial resolution of the state's public school funding issue.

Rick Perry's tenure as governor began on such a low key that *Texas Monthly* magazine rated him as "furniture" after the 2001 session. That designation indicated that he had little effect on the outcome of the session until after it was over. Then Perry surpassed even Preston Smith's and Bill Clements's penchant for using the veto, killing eighty-two bills—some of vital concern to his own party. In 2003, Perry let congressional redistricting (see Chapter 6) come to dominate his thinking and expressed more concern about not raising taxes than about resolving the knotty problem of school finance. In 2005, Perry's plan to solve the state's most pressing problem, school finance, was unanimously rejected by the legislature, which finally produced a school finance bill in a special session in 2006. In 2007, Perry used a variety of techniques in an effort to appear as an

Governor Rick Perry was criticized during 2011 for being entirely too willing to cut essential programs during the budget-challenged legislative session.

Courtesy of Ben Sargent.

effective executive suitable for national office, but found great resistance from the legislature, the attorney general, and the public.[15]

Perry was re-elected to an unprecedented third four-year term in 2010, advocating a conservative agenda and lambasting the national government. He even suggested that national politics, and especially the national health care reform law of 2009, were such an anathema that Texas could secede from the Union if it wanted to. He quickly added that he thought we had a great union and that "there is absolutely no reason to dissolve it." But the secession talk was unprecedented since the Civil War and belied overwhelming constitutional precedent to the contrary. As early as 1869, in the case of *Texas v. White*, the U.S. Supreme Court clearly declared that, regarding the Civil War, "the ordinance of secession . . . of Texas, and all the acts of her legislature intended to give effect to that ordinance, were absolutely null."[16] Perry's strong leadership and his suspicion of a dominant national government made him popular among conservatives within the Republican Party. Building on his nationwide following, he declared as a candidate for the 2012 Republican presidential nomination on August 12, 2011.

Formal Roles and Limitations

The Texas Constitution was written at a time when concentrated power in the hands of a single state official was viewed with great apprehension. E. J. Davis, the last Republican governor before Clements, held office from 1870 to 1874, and his administration was characterized by corruption and repression. Consequently, when the 1876 Constitution was drafted, the framers reacted against the Davis administration by creating a constitutionally weak governor's office (see Chapter 2).

Today, the governor must still cope with a highly fragmented executive branch that results in a plural executive. The executive branch includes not only the governor, but also five other elected executives, two elected boards, and a complex system of powerful policymaking boards and commissions. Recent governors have sought greater institutional power with modest success, and Rick Perry made substantial progress toward modernization of the Texas governor's office with a series of bills passed by the Seventy-eighth Legislature in 2003. These bills resulted in control of economic development, health and human services, and the chairmanship of many state boards.[17]

Chief Executive

News stories frequently describe the governor as the "chief executive," referring to gubernatorial control over the state bureaucracy and **appointment and removal,** budgeting, planning, and supervisory and clemency powers. Although this is one of the governor's most time-consuming roles, it traditionally has been one of the weakest, as the following discussion illustrates.

Appointment

Texas uses a long ballot, indicating that a large number of state officials are elected by the people rather than appointed by the governor. The list of officials elected on a statewide basis includes the lieutenant governor, whose major role is legislative; the attorney general; the comptroller of public accounts; the

How a Governor Can Get Things Done

George W. Bush, elected in 1994, observed that "the way to forge good public policy amongst the leadership of the legislative branch and executive branch is to air our differences in private meetings that happen all the time. . . . The way to ruin a relationship is to leak things and to be disrespectful of meeting in private."

Source: R. G. Ratcliffe, "Away from the Spotlight, Governor Makes His Mark," *Houston Chronicle*, April 15, 1995, 10A.

commissioner of the General Land Office; and the agriculture commissioner. In addition, members of the Texas Railroad Commission and the State Board of Education are elected. They are elected independently, so they feel no obligation to the governor, and because they may want the governor's job, they may even wish to make the incumbent look bad. Absent direct influence on these elected officeholders, the governor must be highly skilled in the art of persuasion. One important consequence of these independently elected officials is that often the governor's most likely competitors have held statewide elective office, such as when Attorney General Mark White defeated Bill Clements in 1982 and when Comptroller Carole Keeton Strayhorn challenged Governor Perry in 2006.

The most visible executive appointments that the governor makes are those of secretary of state, commissioner of education, commissioner of insurance, commissioner of health and human services, and the executive director of the Economic Development and Tourism Division. The governor also appoints the director of the Office of State-Federal Relations and the adjutant general, who heads the state militia. He or she also fills any vacancy that occurs in one of the major elected executive positions, such as railroad commissioner. In the event of a vacancy, the governor appoints someone to fill the office until the next election. She or he also appoints all or some of the members of about two dozen advisory councils and committees that coordinate the work of two or more state agencies.

Most state agencies are not headed up by a single executive making policy decisions. The result is a highly fragmented executive branch; power is divided among both elected executives and appointed boards. Nevertheless, the governor has a major effect on state policy through approximately 3,000 appointments to about 125 policymaking, multimember boards and commissions. Examples include the University of Texas System board of regents, the Public Utility Commission, and the Texas Youth Commission. In 2003, the legislature gave Governor Rick Perry greater control over the chairs of state boards, allowing him to be able to appoint the presiding officer, as long as the appointee had received Senate confirmation.[18]

The members of these boards are usually appointed for a six-year term, but with the following limitations:

1. **The terms of board and commission members are overlapping and staggered to prevent the governor from appointing a majority of the members until late in his or her first term of office.**

2. **The statutes establishing the various boards and commissions are highly prescriptive and often specify both a certain geographic representation and occupational or other background characteristics of the members.**

3. **Appointments to some boards and commissions must be made from lists supplied by members of professional organizations and associations.**[19]

One other important use of the appointment power is filling vacancies in the judiciary. Although Texas has an elected judiciary, every legislature creates some new courts, and vacancies occur in other courts. The governor makes appointments to these benches until the next election. Indeed, many district court judges in the state are first appointed and subsequently stand for election.

The governor must obtain a two-thirds confirmation vote from the Texas Senate for appointments; the president needs only a simple majority from the U.S. Senate. As in national politics, there is the practice of "senatorial courtesy": The Senate will usually honor the objection of a senator from the same district as the nominee for appointment by refusing to approve confirmation.

Texas's short biennial legislative session, however, permits the governor to make many interim appointments when the legislature is not in session. This practice gives these appointees a "free ride" for as long as nineteen months. These recess appointments must be presented to the Senate within the first ten days of the next session, whether regular or special.

Another aid to the governor is incumbency. If a governor is re-elected, he or she will be able to appoint all members of the board or commission by the middle of the second term, perhaps earlier if some members resign. The governor may then have considerable influence over policy development within the agency, albeit with little time left in office. With Governor Perry's long tenure in office, he has appointed all members of all state boards.

Removal

The governor has only limited removal power in Texas. The governor can remove political officials he or she has appointed, with the consent of the Senate, a power in effect only since a 1980 constitutional amendment. He also can remove personal staff members and a few executive directors, such as the one in the Department of Housing and Community Affairs. However, the governor cannot remove members of boards and commissions whom he did not appoint and obviously cannot remove state executives who were elected in their own right. This lack of removal power deprives the governor of significant control over the bureaucrats who make and administer policy on a daily basis. In turn, the governor's job of implementing policies through the state bureaucracy is made more difficult.

There are three general methods for removing state officeholders:

1. **Impeachment, which involves a formal accusation—the impeachment—by a House majority and requires a two-thirds vote for conviction by the Senate.**

2. **Address, a procedure whereby the legislature requests the governor to remove a district or appellate judge from office (a two-thirds vote of both houses is required).**

3. **Quo warranto proceedings, a legal procedure whereby an official may be removed by a court.**

Because Article XV of the Texas Constitution stipulates the right to a trial before removal from office, impeachment is likely to remain the chief formal removal procedure because it does involve a trial by the Senate. However, even its use is quite rare.

Budgeting

By law, the governor must submit a biennial budget message to the legislature within five days after that body convenes in regular session. This budget is prepared by the governor's Budget, Planning, and Policy Division. The executive budget indicates to the legislature the governor's priorities and signals items likely to be vetoed. With the exception of the item veto, the Texas governor lacks the strong formal budgetary powers not only of the president, but also of many state executives (see Chapter 12). The governor has one additional financial power, that of approving deficiency warrants of no more than $200,000 for the biennium for agencies that encounter emergencies and/or run out of funds.

Traditionally, the Legislative Budget Board (LBB), which also prepares a budget for the legislature to consider, has dominated the budget process. The legislature always has been guided more by the legislative budget than by the governor's. A significant exception occurred in the regular 2003 legislative session when the governor's staff was heavily involved in developing the final budget for floor consideration. This concession by legislative leaders, along with reorganization measures, was one of several signals that the Republicans—usually known as the party opposed to strong government powers—were willing to consider greater executive authority in Texas.[20] In addition, the legislature gave the governor $224.4 million to spend on economic development in fiscal years (FY) 2008–2009 and another $203 million for 2010–2011.

Planning

Both modern management and the requirements of many federal grants-in-aid emphasize substate regional planning, and the governor directs planning efforts for the state through the Budget, Planning, and Policy Division. When combined with budgeting, the governor's planning power allows a stronger gubernatorial hand in the development of new programs and policy alternatives. Although still without adequate control over the programs of the state, the governor has had a greater voice in suggesting future programs over the past two decades, mainly because many federal statutes have designated the governor as having approval power for federal grants.

During Ann Richards's administration, Comptroller John Sharp—in part at the request of the governor to allow a more rational appropriations act for fiscal years 1992–1993—developed an elaborate system for monitoring the performance of state agencies. This system, known as the Texas Performance Review (TPR), requires state agencies to engage in strategic planning. The TPR has continued as a vital part of state government. In 2003, Governor Rick Perry and the legislative leaders, following disputes over the budget process, removed this function from the office of Comptroller Carole Keeton Strayhorn and moved it into legislative staff agencies.

Supervising

The state constitution charges the governor with the responsibility for seeing that the laws of the state are "faithfully executed," but provides few tools for fulfilling this function. The governor's greatest supervisory and directive powers occur

Budget Growth in a Conservative Era

Although Governor Rick Perry frequently called for conservative revenue measures and restrictions on state spending, he saw the budget continue to grow during his administration, including a 10.3 percent increase from FY 2006–2007 to $152.5 billion for FY 2008–2009. This period also saw the state swing from a deep shortage to a generous surplus. Per-person spending actually declined in terms of national rankings. The budget shortfall estimated for the 2011–2012 years threatened to change that trend, with an initial proposal to cut spending by $31 billion over that biennium compared to the previous one, a cut of 16.6 percent. Although that level of cuts will not occur, the recession of 2008–2011 has taken a toll on state revenues.

Source: "Texas House Proposes Sweeping Cuts," *Texas Tribune*, January 19, 2011.

in the role of commander in chief (see "Commander in Chief/Top Cop" section). Governors can request reports from state agencies, appoint board chairs, remove their own appointees, and use political influence to force hiring reductions or other economies. But lack of appointment power over the professional staffs of state agencies and lack of removal power over a predecessor's appointees limit the governor's ability to ensure that the state bureaucracy performs its job.

The governor thus must fall back on informal tactics to exercise any control over the administration. In this respect, the governor's staff is of supreme importance: If staff members can establish good rapport with state agencies, they may extend the governor's influence to areas where the governor does not have formal authority. They are aided in this task by two factors of which agency personnel are well aware: the governor's leadership of the party and veto powers (both discussed in the "Chief Legislator" section).

Clemency

The governor's power with regard to acts of clemency (mercy) is restricted to one thirty-day reprieve for an individual sentenced to death. In cases of treason against the state (a rare crime), the governor may grant pardons, reprieves, and commutations of sentences with legislative consent. The governor also may remit fines or bond forfeitures and restore driver's licenses and hunting privileges. In addition, the governor has the discretionary right to revoke a parole or conditional pardon. Beyond these limited acts, the state's chief executive officer must make recommendations to the Board of Pardons and Paroles, which is part of the Department of Criminal Justice. Although empowered to refuse an act of clemency recommended by the board, the governor cannot act without its recommendation in such matters as full and conditional pardons, commutations, reprieves, and emergency reprieves.

Chief Legislator

Although the legislature tends to dominate Texas politics, the governor is a strong chief legislator who relies on three formal powers in carrying out this role: **message power**, **session power**, and **veto power**.

Message Power

The governor may give messages to the legislature at any time, but the constitution requires a gubernatorial message when legislative sessions open and when a governor retires. By statute, the governor must also deliver a biennial budget message. Other messages the governor may choose to send or deliver in person are often "emergency" messages when the legislature is in session; these messages are a formal means of expressing policy preferences. They also attract the attention of the media and set the agenda for state government. Coupled with able staff work, message power can be an effective and persuasive tool. In both 2003 and 2007, Governor Perry declared insurance rates and medical malpractice reform as emergency measures, an indication that he had not achieved his policy objectives. A governor also often delivers informal messages at meetings and social gatherings or through the media.

Session Power

As discussed in Chapter 6, the legislature is constitutionally forbidden to call itself into special session; only the governor may do so. Efforts to modify this power via constitutional amendment did not survive in the 2007 legislative session. Called sessions are limited to a maximum duration of thirty days, but a governor who wants to force consideration of an issue can continue calling one special session after another.

The governor also sets the agenda for these sessions, although the legislature, once called, may consider other matters on a limited basis, such as impeachment or approval of executive appointments. As the complexity of state government has grown, legislators sometimes have been unable to complete their work in the short biennial regular sessions. When they fail to complete enough of the agenda, they know they can expect a special session. However, any governor contemplating a special session must consider whether she or he has the votes lined up to accomplish the purpose of the session.

Special sessions offer a way around the restricted biennial legislative session of 140 days. The eight governors before Bush called a total of thirty-four

Ma Ferguson and Clemency

The governor's clemency power was not always so restricted. Under the Constitution of 1876, it was actually quite extensive. During the 1920s and 1930s, however, Governor Miriam "Ma" Ferguson was suspected of selling pardons, in combination with other financial shenanigans. Critics complained that "Ma pardons criminals before they're indicted." In response to this perceived abuse of the governor's power, in 1936, the state adopted a constitutional amendment establishing the Board of Pardons and Paroles and severely limiting the governor's authority to pardon, especially in the area of prisoners condemned to die. Now, the only action the governor can take without the written recommendation of the board is to give a death row inmate one thirty-day reprieve.

Source: Dave McNeely, "What Bush Could and Couldn't Have Done," *Austin American-Statesman*, June 24, 2000, A15.

special sessions. Bill Clements called six; Ann Richards called only two. Bush called none, a reflection on the one hand of his ability to get along with the legislative leadership, and on the other hand of budget surpluses. Rick Perry, in part because of his party's dominance of state government, used the session power extensively, calling eight special sessions in the 2003–2009 time period, including three in 2003 to deal with congressional redistricting and government reorganization and four (2003, two in 2005, and 2006) to address the state's method of funding public schools.[21]

Veto Power

The governor's strongest legislative power is the veto. Every bill that passes both houses of the legislature in regular and special sessions is sent to the governor, who has the option of signing it, letting it become law without signing it, or vetoing it.[22] If the legislature is still in session, the governor has ten days—Sundays excluded—in which to act. If the bill is sent to the governor in the last ten days of a session or after the legislature has adjourned, the governor has twenty days—including Sundays—in which to act. If the governor vetoes a bill while the legislature is still in session, that body may override the veto by a two-thirds vote of both houses.

Because of the short legislative session, many important bills are often sent to the governor so late that the legislature has adjourned before the governor has had to act on them. In such instances, the veto power is absolute. The legislature cannot override if it is not in session, and consideration of the same bill cannot be carried over into the next session. Short biennial sessions thus make the governor's threat of a veto an extremely powerful political tool. Also, the override of a veto takes a two-thirds vote in both houses of the legislature, a majority that is not easy to get. As an indication of how rare an override is, thirty-eight years separated the last two: W. Lee O' Daniel had twelve vetoes overridden in 1939–1941, and Bill Clements had a veto of a local bill overridden in 1979. Some observers have argued that when a governor uses his or her veto power frequently, it is actually a sign of gubernatorial weakness. The reasoning for such a claim is that a powerful governor actually is able to negotiate with legislative leaders, thus ironing out compromises over legislation, while a weak governor, not having such persuasive abilities, is left only with the veto pen to exert his or her influence. Governors often use the veto pen after their first legislative session, while using negotiation as a leadership tool in subsequent years.

The Veto Record Book

Governor Rick Perry holds the record for the most bills vetoed in a single session—82—and for the most bills vetoed in the shortest time—132 in three years. Bill Clements holds the overall record for the most bills vetoed—190 in eight years. Perry is a Republican governor with a Republican legislature; thus, he vetoed the bills of his own party. He also used the veto to discipline wayward legislators—for example, his annulment of four noncontroversial bills sponsored by fellow Republican Charlie Geren, who failed to support his reorganization efforts. Clements was a Republican governor with a Democratic legislature who was trying to transform the state in terms of both policy and procedure.

Governor Rick Perry vetoed a record 82 bills passed by the legislature in 2001, including several important to his own Republican Party. In 2003, he vetoed 50, and in 2005, another 19. Perry vetoed 49 bills in 2007 and 37 in 2009.

Courtesy of Ben Sargent

The governor has one other check over appropriations bills: the item veto.[23] The governors in forty-three other states have a similar power. This device permits the governor to delete individual items from a bill without having to veto it in its entirety. The item veto, however, may be used only to strike a particular line of funding; it cannot be used to reduce or increase an appropriation.

The item veto illustrates a reality of gubernatorial power in Texas. The governor's power over legislation is largely negative—he or she often finds it easier to say no than to get his or her own legislative agenda adopted. This truism particularly describes the budget process. Yet the timing of the appropriations act and the number of items that the legislature can cram into one line item are factors that affect the governor's use of the item veto as a fiscal tool to control spending.[24]

The line-item veto power has been blunted somewhat since the first term of Bill Clements. Reacting to a Clements veto of special appropriations for higher education in 1983, the legislature passed lump-sum appropriations for each higher educational institution when Clements returned to office in 1987 to prevent use of the item veto on special line items. Clements still vetoed several other bills favoring higher education. The legislature has continued to pass lump-sum appropriations acts.

Commander in Chief/Top Cop

The state of Texas does not independently engage in warfare with other nations and thus would seem to have no need for a commander in chief. However, the governor does have the power to declare martial law—that is, to suspend civil government temporarily and replace it with government by the state militia and/ or law enforcement agencies. Although seldom used, this power was invoked

to quell an oil field riot in East Texas in 1931, and to gain control of explosive racial situations in East Texas in 1919 and on the Gulf Coast in 1943.

Additionally, the governor is commander in chief of the military forces of the state (Army and Air National Guard), except when they have been called into service by the national government. The head of these forces, the adjutant general, is one of the governor's important appointees. The governor also has the power to assume command of the Texas Rangers and the Department of Public Safety to maintain law and order. These powers become important during disasters, such as floods or tornadoes, when danger from the aftermath of the storm or from unscrupulous individuals, such as looters, may be present.

Furthermore, following the national tragedy of terrorist attacks on the United States on September 11, 2001, the national government created a Department of Homeland Security and mandated security responsibilities for state and local governments in addition to their traditional function of disaster management. The Texas homeland security office, the Division of Emergency Management, reports to the governor, but is operationally attached to the Texas Department of Public Safety. Chapter 15 discusses the consequences and implications of the terrorist threat.

In routine situations, the governor is almost wholly dependent on local law enforcement and prosecuting agencies to see that the laws of the state are faithfully executed. When there is evidence of wrongdoing, the state's chief executive often brings the informal powers of the gubernatorial office to bear on the protection problem, appealing to the media to focus public attention on errant agencies and officeholders. Such was the case in 1992, when Governor Richards received considerable media coverage for joining nursing home inspectors in on-site visits to both poorly run and well-run nursing homes.

Chief of State

Pomp and circumstance are a part of being the top elected official of the state. Just as presidents use their ceremonial role to augment other roles, so also do governors. Whether cutting a ribbon to open a new highway, leading a parade, or serving as host to a visiting dignitary, the governor's performance as chief of state yields visibility and the appearance of leadership, which enhance the more important executive and legislative roles of the office. In the modern era, the governor is often the chief television personality of the state and sets the policy agenda through publicity. Ann Richards, for example, was a national TV celebrity, sometimes more popular outside the state than inside. George W. Bush was a presidential candidate and in demand outside the state, too.

Ranger Bush

Before George W. Bush ran for public office, he was the managing owner of the Texas Rangers baseball team. When he was sworn in as governor, he became the commander of the Texas Rangers state police force. He is thus the only human being in history to go from being the head of the Texas Rangers to being the head of the Texas Rangers.

The Governor in Command

In 1985, Governor Mark White used the commander-in-chief powers in a controversial way. First, he authorized the state militia to participate in a military training exercise in Honduras, which borders on the politically volatile countries of Nicaragua and El Salvador. Then White joined the troops and oversaw the delivery of Texas barbecue to the militia over the Easter weekend—just as the legislature began to discuss the state budget.

In 1999–2000, Governor George W. Bush also used the commander-in-chief powers in an unusual way. In his bid for the Republican nomination for president, he traveled across the United States. During these campaign tours, he was protected by the Texas Department of Public Safety, which always guards the governor. Thus, for a change, a few state troopers and Texas Rangers got to see much of the country.

In 2005, Governor Rick Perry announced that Texas would need to guard its own borders because the federal government had failed to do so. He emphasized reducing crime along the Texas-Mexico border, training the National Guard to respond to emergencies, and generally relying on law enforcement for safety. Like President George W. Bush at the national level, he endorsed a sponsored immigrant worker program. With increased drug-related violence along the Texas-Mexico border in 2011 and a very tight state budget, Perry asked for 3,000 additional federal officials to patrol the border. In 2006, Perry used the commander-in-chief powers again to mobilize the evacuation of Texas coastal cities threatened by Hurricane Rita.

More and more, Texas governors are using the ceremonial role of chief of state, sometimes coupled with the role of chief intergovernmental diplomat, to become actively involved in economic negotiations, such as plant locations. Efforts are directed toward both foreign and domestic investments and finding new markets for Texas goods. In such negotiations, the governor uses the power and prestige of the office to become the state's salesperson. Mark White and Bill Clements both made significant use of this role to attract businesses to the state, and Rick Perry traveled from Austin to New York to Italy touting the benefits of business relocation to Texas. Ann Richards strongly pushed for U.S. Senate approval of the North American Free Trade Agreement (NAFTA) because of the likelihood of expanded Texas-Mexico trade.

A savvy governor uses the chief of state role to maximize publicity for him/herself and his/her program. Because Texas is the second largest state in the country, the actions of the Texas governor often make national, as well as state, headlines.

Chief Intergovernmental Diplomat

The Texas Constitution provides that the governor, or someone designated by the governor, will be the state's representative in all dealings with other states and with the national government. This role of intergovernmental representative has increased in importance for three reasons. First, federal statutes now designate the governor as the official who has the planning and grant-approval authority for the state. This designation has given the governor's budgeting, planning, and supervising powers much more clout in recent years, and federal budget philosophy (see Chapter 12) further enhances the governor's role.

Second, some state problems, such as water and energy development, often require the cooperation of several states. For example, in 1981–1982, Governor Clements and five other governors tried to plan solutions for the water problems of the High Plains area. Additionally, although the U.S. Constitution precludes a governor from conducting diplomatic relations with other nations, Texas's location as a border state gives rise to occasional social and economic exchanges with the governors of Mexican border states on matters such as immigration and energy. The box entitled "Texas Version of Foreign Affairs" earlier in this chapter outlines the aggressive international role of the two largest American states in the lower 48, California and Texas.

Third, acquiring federal funds is essential in modern times. Not only might they relieve the pressure on state and local government revenue sources, but states and localities alone do not have nearly the resources necessary to provide the wide array of governmental services in a modern state. In 2009, during the economic downturn, the federal government offered states money to help stimulate the economy. Governor Perry, believing such stimulus might hurt the state in the long run, rejected $556 million in federal unemployment funds because they might have required Texas to expand the program to cover different kinds of workers, but accepted other stimulus funds.[25] Often, the governor works in concert with other governors to try to secure favorable national legislation, including both funding and limits on unfunded federal mandates (see Chapter 11). Thus, the governor is active in the National Governors Association, the National Governors Conference, and in regional and political party groups. Texas governors, like their counterparts in other states, are proactive representatives.

A more traditional use of the governor's intergovernmental role is mandated by Article IV of the U.S. Constitution, which provides for the rendition (surrender) of fugitives from justice who flee across state lines. The Texas governor, like other governors, signs the rendition papers and transmits them to the appropriate law enforcement officials. Law officers are then in charge of picking up the fugitives and returning them to the appropriate state.

Informal Roles and Limitations

In addition to the five "hats" just described, there are at least two others that the governor must wear. They have no basis in law, but they are nevertheless important to the job. The degree of success with which the governor handles these informal roles can greatly affect the execution of the formal roles.

Chief of Party

As the symbolic head of the Democratic or Republican Party in the state, the governor is a key figure at the state party conventions and usually is the leader of the party's delegation to national conventions. A governor may, however, have to compete with his or her party's U.S. senator. Governors are able to use their influence with the party's state executive committee and at party conventions to gain a subsidiary influence over candidates seeking other state offices. An active, skilled governor can thus create a power relationship with state legislators and bureaucrats that the more formal roles of the office do not permit. The governor also wins some political influence by campaigning for other party candidates who are seeking state or national offices.

Governor Bill Clements, the first modern Republican governor of Texas, used the party role extensively to extend Republican influence through the appointment power. He appointed enough Democrats to maintain the goodwill of the majority leadership at the time. Governor Ann Richards made key executive and judicial appointments from her Democratic Party colleagues, but worked with the minority party on other issues. For example, she showed some willingness to deal with the Republicans on redistricting in exchange for GOP support for legislation, such as a state lottery, that she and the Democrats wanted.

One of the most interesting contrasts is that between the state's two most recent Republican governors. In 1995, George W. Bush operated on a nonpartisan basis and secured the support of both members and leaders of the Democratic majority legislature for his legislative program. He also made his own Republican Party angry by cooperating with the Democrats and by having a moderate position on a number of issues. For example, Governor Bush and Speaker of the House Pete Laney worked especially well together, and Bush told the state party bigwigs to back off from trying to defeat Laney in his 1996 re-election bid. He also battled the party establishment to insist on the inclusion of Senator Kay Bailey Hutchison in the delegation to the presidential nominating convention in 1996 (social conservatives wanted to exclude her because of her moderate position on the abortion issue). In 1997, he fared somewhat less well with the legislature even though the Senate had become Republican, in part because of resistance to his tax plan by conservative members of the GOP. He had also become staunch friends with Democratic Lieutenant Governor Bob Bullock. By the time the delegation was formed for the 2000 national convention, Bush was the assured presidential nominee of the party. Even with the obvious presidential bid, Bush continued to work well with Democrats, who realized the advantages that having a Texas president could bring.

Rick Perry's approach was more combative, both with members of his own party and with the state's Democrats. In 2001, the legislature was split between a Republican Senate and a Democratic House, and Perry had come to office by succession when Bush ran for president. Perry was not a significant factor in the legislative session until he angered his GOP colleagues by vetoing some of their pet bills after the session had ended. In 2003, Perry was emboldened by having been elected to office and by the Republican control of all branches of government. He took a particularly partisan approach by forcing congressional redistricting and continued to demonstrate that Republicans were sparring among themselves, especially when he led the attack on the comptroller to reduce her power—and thus her possible vantage point as a contender against him in 2006. In 2007, Perry stormed into the legislative session with policy positions at variance not only from those of Democrats, but also his fellow Republicans; and in 2010, in part because of the conservative swing in the political mood of the United States, Perry continued to reiterate his conservative approach to governance.

Leader of the People

Most Texans, unaware of the limitations on formal gubernatorial powers, look to the chief executive of the state for the leadership necessary to solve the state's problems and to serve as their principal spokesperson on major issues. A skilled governor can turn this role to substantial advantage when bargaining with other key figures in the policymaking process, such as the presiding

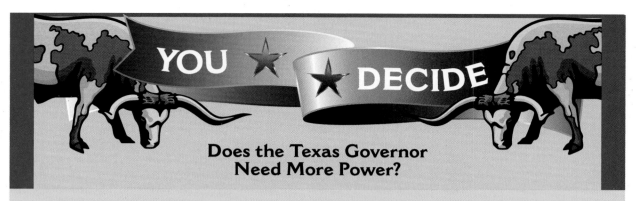

YOU ★ ★ DECIDE

Does the Texas Governor Need More Power?

The powers of the Texas governor used to be ranked almost at the bottom of gubernatorial powers in the fifty American states. More recently, the Texas governor's institutional powers—those established by constitution and statute—rank just about in the middle. Indeed, the powers of the governor of California are considered less than those of the Texas governor, although the New York governor has greater power. Thus, even among the very largest states, Texas stands in the middle.

PRO	CON
▲ Texas should, by statute or constitutional amendment, increase the power of the governor because:	▼ Texas should not, by statute or constitutional amendment, increase the power of the governor because:
▲ Bureaucrats have far too much discretion to act when there is no clear executive authority.	▼ The personal power of the governor—based on margin of electoral victory and personal persuasion—is already great.
▲ The public is confused by the number of elected officials in Texas (the long ballot).	▼ The veto power is virtually absolute.
▲ Texas needs someone with greater authority to show mercy to convicted felons facing the death penalty.	▼ Dispersion of power is a good way to keep one person from gaining too much control.
▲ A governor needs to be able to control all boards and commissions soon after election to implement policies he or she favors.	▼ The governor's clout is obvious when one considers the salary, the size of the staff, and the lack of effort over the years to remove the governor from office.
▲ A more powerful governor would mean that the legislature's power could be reduced.	▼ Democracy is better served when the legislature is the more powerful institution because the people are closer to their elected representatives than to the governor.
▲ Texas needs its governor to have meaningful budget authority.	▼ The dual budgeting system encourages fiscal control.

officers, legislators, and top bureaucrats in the state's administration. For example, through the media, the governor can rally public support for programs and policies. Choosing to accept invitations to speak is another way a governor can gain public exposure and thus support for programs and plans, including the budget. Public appearances usually serve as occasions for emphasizing gubernatorial accomplishments. They also allow a governor to show concern for ordinary citizens with extraordinary problems, such as visits to areas damaged by tornadoes or floods. In keeping with the traditionalistic tenor of the state, some governors use this role to show that they are "active conservatives."

Coupled with the strong legislative role, this informal role is critical to a governor's success. Leadership has been depicted as consisting of two parts: the ability to "transact" (that is, to make things happen) and the ability to "transform" (that is, to decide what things should happen).[26] The successful Texas governor is one who can both make things happen and decide what policies ought to happen.

A **populist** approach is consistent with the values of democracy. So also is a more conservative approach that addresses issues that the public reiterates with each opinion poll. Thus, although Ann Richards and George W. Bush held different positions—except that both wanted to improve public education—and used different styles, they both demonstrated leadership, which is extremely important in a plural executive system. Perry has pushed to strengthen the office of governor while at the same time limiting the powers of government in general; thus, his leadership skills seem more dedicated to a personal agenda than to a public one.[27]

Summary

The governor of Texas shares many of the characteristics attributed to members of the legislature in Chapter 6. Generally, the governor is a conservative White male attorney or businessman. Since 1974, the Texas governor has had the advantage of a four-year term and is paid fairly well. Nevertheless, the office is constitutionally weak, and the approval and successful implementation of gubernatorial budgetary and programmatic policies depend more on the governor's adroitness in developing leadership skills than on formal powers. Some movement toward increasing gubernatorial powers by legislative action has taken place in recent years.

The Texas governor has many important functions to perform, which are embodied in the various roles that make up the office of chief executive for the state. These roles, however, are restricted in the following major ways:

1. There are five other elected executives, an elected state policy board, and an elected regulatory commission. Thus, the state has a plural executive.

2. The state bureaucracy is largely controlled by multimember boards and commissions, with the result that the state administration is fragmented.

3. Senatorial confirmation of appointees requires a two-thirds vote.

4. The governor's power to remove appointed officials other than personal staff is still restricted in spite of recent statutory increases in the removal power.

5. The state has both a legislative and an executive budget.

On the other hand, the governor does have some constitutional and statutory strengths, and gubernatorial powers have increased substantially with the New Federalism concept of federal funding for state programs and the subsequent prominence of the governor's role in planning and interstate problem solving. The major strengths of the governor's office are the following:

1. Effective control over regional planning and federal grant applications.

2. An item veto over appropriations and a general veto over legislation that, because of timing, is often absolute.

3. Command over the militia and law enforcement agencies in time of crisis.

4. Party, personal, and ceremonial leadership opportunities.

5. Control over the presiding officers of appointed boards and commissions.

The description of state bureaucracy in the next chapter should help the reader gain a greater understanding of the governor's difficulties when trying to control state agencies.

Glossary Terms

appointment and removal

impeachment

message power

plural executive

populist

session power

veto power

8

The Administrative State

Many people consider the things which government does for them to be social progress, but they consider the things government does for others to be socialism.

EARL WARREN, CHIEF JUSTICE OF THE UNITED STATES, 1953–1969

The public's right to know is essential to accountability in government. We have the right to know what occurs in government meetings and what is contained in public records.

INTRODUCTION TO THE OPEN MEETINGS ACT TRAINING VIDEO, TEXAS ATTORNEY GENERAL'S OFFICE, 2006

INTRODUCTION

Few of us need an introduction to the administrative state because public administration is part of our daily lives. Traffic police, public school principals, highway workers, college registrars, clerks in state and federal offices—we all have seen, or been involved with, public employees who apply and enforce public policy.

All of us have also heard considerable criticism of government policies and administration. Earl Warren's observation in the opening quote summarizes the dilemma of democratic government. As citizens seek more programs, any given individual's preferred program is social progress, but a contrary preference by someone else is suspect. Given the conservative mood of the United States since the last years of the twentieth century, calling attention to this dilemma is particularly appropriate. We simultaneously want less government, but more programs that benefit us.

The political culture of a state directly affects what government programs the state provides. In states with a moralistic culture, greater emphasis is placed on programs for the common good, such as environmental protection, education, and social services, and state policy is more forward-looking. In states such as Texas, with a heritage of individualistic/traditionalistic political culture, policymakers focus more on cost avoidance and its corollary, tax cutting, and on providing a business environment with minimum regulations and impediments. In turn, the state administration reflects those policy preferences.

This chapter begins with a description of the state administrative agencies. To help the reader gain a clearer understanding of the complexities of modern **bureaucracy** and how our state public administration works, this chapter then discusses why and how "big government"—the administrative state—became so big. Bureaucracy is a type of organization associated with red tape, specialization, and **hierarchy**. Hierarchy refers to an arrangement that puts few people but maximum power at the top of the organization, and many people with little power at the bottom of the organization. Finally, the chapter examines efforts to control the bureaucracy and ensure that it performs as the public and elected officials intend.

OBJECTIVES

After reading this chapter, you should be able to

Understand the complexity of the administrative organization in Texas, including the plural executive.

Trace the growth of big government.

Describe the characteristics of bureaucracy and bureaucratic survival techniques.

Evaluate bureaucratic orientation and its effect on the public interest.

Assess the bureaucracy's accountability to the governor, the legislature, and the public.

A few definitions are in order at the outset. *Public policy* is the strategy or philosophy behind individual government decisions. These decisions come to us in forms such as laws, judicial rulings, and federal and state programs. Public policies are carried out, or implemented, by public administrators. Legislators determine what is to be done in general. Bureaucrats determine what is to be done specifically because it is their job to *implement* policy—that is, to translate policy into action. Thus, some bureaucratic decisions are in themselves operational public policy—for example, determining the college tuition rate on a campus in pursuit of a broader statewide policy that those who benefit from higher education should have a substantial role in paying for it. Policy is not always implemented successfully. For example, Texas state government coupled with local school districts run a large establishment, the purpose of which is to educate young people; yet, tests show that many of the state's young people never learn to read above a very rudimentary level. The budget cuts described in Chapter 12 have worsened the already-bad situation.

Public administration has several different, but related meanings. It refers not only to the activities necessary to carry out public policy, but also to the various agencies, boards, commissions, bureaus, and departments that are responsible for these activities and, collectively, to the employees who work in the various agencies. The term *agency* itself refers to any department, agency, commission, board, bureau, or other public administrative organization. Both *administrator* and *executive* refer to top-level individuals in public administration. Any state employee may be a *bureaucrat,* but the term most commonly is limited to administrators, executives, and lower-echelon white-collar office employees who are appointed politically or, especially, selected because of some test of their merit. Members of the traditional professions and also of the professions peculiar to government are more usually referred to by their professional titles, such as teacher, nurse, attorney, or game warden.

Implementing or executing the law is formally the responsibility of the executive branch of government; thus, the bureaucracy is nominally headed by the chief executive—in Texas, the governor. This chapter shows, however, that the bureaucracy permeates all branches and that its interests and powers crisscross the entire fabric of governmental structure. Furthermore, as the previous chapter demonstrated, the governor is a constitutionally weak chief executive who lacks the full set of tools required to control the bureaucracy in spite of significant recent increases in statutory power. In fact, many politicians and political scientists consider the administrative state so powerful as to constitute a fourth branch of government.

Woven throughout this chapter is a concern for the democratic legitimacy of the administrative state. In a democracy, the participation of the citizens legitimates government action. However, administrators, or "bureaucrats" as they are frequently called, are not elected. Often, they cannot be removed by the governor, who is, of course, elected by the people. Yet, they often wield great power in Texas politics. What can justify such power?

State Administrative Agencies

Although we must concede that a state bureaucracy is necessary to carry out government policy, we might be happier if the Texas administration were easier to understand. Even for the experienced observer, state administration in Texas is

confusing; for the novice, it is perplexing indeed. Three essential characteristics of the state administration cause this confusion.

1. **No single, uniform organizational pattern exists.**

2. **Texas administration features numerous exceptions to the traditional bureaucratic characteristic of hierarchy.**

3. **The number of state agencies depends on one's method of counting.**

There are at least five different types of top policymakers in state agencies: (1) elected executives, (2) appointed executives, (3) an elected commission and an elected board, (4) ex officio boards and commissions, and (5) appointed boards and commissions (see Table 8-1). Agencies headed by an elected or appointed executive follow traditional hierarchical principles in that a single individual clearly is the "boss" and thus is ultimately responsible for the

TABLE 8-1

Types of Administrative Agencies in Texas

Agencies Headed by Elected Executives

Office of the Attorney General

Department of Agriculture

Office of the Comptroller of Public Accounts

General Land Office

Agencies Headed by Appointed Executives

Office of the Secretary of State

Health and Human Services Commission (see Chapter 13)

Multimember Boards and Commissions

Elected Board and Commission

*State Board of Education

*Texas Railroad Commission

Ex Officio Board

*Bond Review Board

Appointed Boards and Commissions

*Texas Higher Education Coordinating Board

*Public Utility Commission

operation of a particular department or office. But the agencies that are headed by a multimember board or commission have three or six or even nineteen bosses—whatever the number of members on the board. Although there also is a hierarchical organization in these agencies, it begins with the professional staff of the agency, the level below that of the policy-setting board.

Another complication is that one office, board, or commission may be responsible for the general policies of a number of separate agencies. For example, the Board of Regents of the University of Texas is the policymaking board for the entire University of Texas System, which includes fifteen agencies that are separately funded. As of fiscal years 2010–2011, about 200 agencies, institutions, and independent programs are funded by general appropriations.[1] This list is not all-inclusive, however, because not all agencies appear individually in the state budget. For example, the fifty community college systems are listed as a single entity, but not as individual systems or campuses. Only the four state technical schools and three lower-division Lamar University campuses are listed separately. A rough count of just the *budgeted* policymaking boards, commissions, departments, institutions, and offices—excluding the courts and related agencies, the legislature and its staff agencies, and the offices of elected executives—yields a count of about 145 agencies, most of which are governed by a multimember board. Community/junior colleges are excluded from this number because they have locally appointed boards.

Perhaps the reader is beginning to see why the number of state agencies is usually expressed in approximate terms. In the space allotted here, there is no way to name, much less describe, even those agencies with which the authors are very familiar. Therefore, a few of the most important state agencies are used to illustrate the various bureaucratic arrangements in the state.

Agencies with Elected Executives

Five state officials, in addition to the governor, are elected on partisan ballots for four-year terms. They are, in theory at least, directly accountable to the citizenry for their performance and their integrity in office. One of these, the lieutenant governor, David Dewhurst, who was profiled in Chapter 6, presides over the Texas Senate and does not head any executive office. Dewhurst was one of several state executives contemplating running for a different office should Governor Rick Perry make a presidential run for 2012. The lieutenant governor performs as an executive only when the governor is away from the state or upon succession to the governorship. The other four are department heads.

Attorney General

Along with the governor, the lieutenant governor, and the speaker of the House, the attorney general is one of the most powerful officers in Texas government. Although candidates for the position often run on an anticrime platform, the work of the office is primarily civil. As the attorney for the state, the attorney general and staff represent the state and its agencies in court when the state is a party to a case. The Office of the Attorney General also is responsible for such varied legal matters as consumer protection, antitrust litigation, workers' compensation insurance, organized-crime control, and environmental protection.

The attorney general's greatest power, however, is that of issuing opinions on questions concerning the constitutionality or legality of existing or proposed

legislation and administrative actions. These opinions are not legally binding, but they are rarely challenged in court and thus effectively have the same importance as a ruling by the state's Supreme Court. Because the attorney general's opinions often make the headlines, and because the attorney general works with all state agencies, the office is second only to the governor's office in the public recognition it receives, a situation common in other states.[2] Because the position is regarded as one of the stepping-stones to the governor's office, attorneys general often encourage publicity about themselves, their agency, and their support groups with an eye to possible future election campaigns. Republican Greg Abbott, a former Texas Supreme Court justice, was first elected in 2002, and then re-elected in 2006 and 2010.

Comptroller of Public Accounts

The comptroller (pronounced con-TROL-ler) is responsible for the administration of the state tax system and for performing pre-audits of expenditures by state agencies. In addition, as part of the budget process, the comptroller certifies to the legislature the approximate biennial income for the state. The Texas Constitution precludes the legislature from appropriating more funds than are anticipated in state revenues for any biennial period. Texas, like most other states, must have a balanced budget. Since the phase-out of the treasurer's office in 1996, the comptroller is also the state's banker. As such, the comptroller is the custodian of all public monies and of the securities that the state invests in or holds in trust. The comptroller's office also issues the excise tax stamps used to indicate the collection of taxes on the sale of alcoholic beverages and cigarettes in the state. In short, the comptroller takes in the state's revenues, safeguards them, and invests them. In 2003, the Legislature limited the power of the comptroller somewhat by placing primary responsibility for performance evaluations in the hands of the Legislative Budget Board.

Susan Combs, who previously served as commissioner of agriculture, was elected as comptroller in 2006, and then re-elected in 2010. One of the hallmarks of her campaign was transparency in government; she immediately began to post the expenditures of state agencies on her Web site to keep the public

The highest-paid state employees in Texas are major college coaches, followed by university presidents.

Courtesy of Ben Sargent.

informed. Combs had a rough beginning to her second term both because of the magnitude of the budget shortfall she had to predict before the 2011 legislative session and a huge mistake made by her office that exposed vital information such as Social Security numbers of 3.5 million Texans, including most state employees and public school teachers, when these data were inadvertently posted on the Internet.

Commissioner of the General Land Office

Only Texas and Alaska entered the Union with large amounts of public lands, and only they have land offices. About 22.5 million Texas acres are administered by the commissioner of the General Land Office. This acreage includes 4 million acres of bays, inlets, and other submerged land from the shoreline to the three-league marine limit (10.36 miles out). The land commissioner's land-management responsibilities include the following:

1. Supervising the leasing of all state-owned lands for such purposes as oil and gas production, mineral development, and grazing (more than 14,000 leases).

2. Administering the veterans' land program, by which veterans may buy land with loans that are backed by state bonds.

3. Maintaining the environmental quality of public lands and waters, especially coastal lands.

Republican Jerry Patterson was first elected as commissioner in 1998, and then re-elected in 2002, 2006, and 2010. Like all land commissioners, he must try to balance environmental interests with land and mineral interests. Patterson is a former state senator.

Commissioner of Agriculture

Farming and ranching are still important industries in the state, even though only about 1 percent of the population is engaged in agriculture. The Texas Department of Agriculture, like its national counterpart, is responsible both for the regulation and promotion (through research and education) of the agribusiness industry and for consumer protection, even though these functions may sometimes be in conflict. Departmental activities are diverse—for example, enforcing weights and measures standards, licensing egg handlers, determining the relative safety of pesticides, and locating export markets for Texas agricultural products. Pesticides illustrate the conflicting nature of the roles assigned to this office: Requiring that pesticides be safe for workers, consumers, and the environment may be detrimental to the profits of farmers.

Election to this office is specified by statute rather than by the state constitution. Republican Todd Staples, whose experience cuts across many functions of the department he now heads, has been a cattleman, owned a plant and landscape business, owned a real-estate company, and served three terms as a state representative. He was elected as commissioner for the first time in 2006, and then re-elected in 2010.

Agencies with Appointed Executives

One example of an agency headed by an appointed executive is the Office of the Secretary of State. The state constitution stipulates that the governor shall appoint the secretary of state, whose functions include safeguarding the great

Elected bureaucrats in 2011: Commissioner of Agriculture Todd Staples takes a strong stance against watered gas.

AP Photo/Tony Gutierrez.

seal of the state of Texas and affixing it to the governor's signature on proclamations, commissions, and certificates. In addition to this somewhat ceremonial duty, the duties of the secretary include certifying elections (verifying the validity of the returns), maintaining records on campaign expenditures, keeping the list of lobbyists who register with the state, administering the Uniform Commercial Code, issuing corporate charters, and publishing the *Texas Register*—the official record of administrative decisions, rules, regulations, and announcements of hearings and pending actions. The newest duty of the secretary is to serve as the state's international protocol officer. Governor Rick Perry appointed Esperanza (Hope) Andrade, a successful San Antonio businesswoman and former Texas Transportation Commission member, to the office in July 2008.

The secretary of state's office, though appointive, can sometimes be a springboard to elective office. Former Lieutenant Governor Bob Bullock and former Governor Mark White both held the position, as did former Comptroller John Sharp and former Mayor Ron Kirk of Dallas, appointed by President Barack Obama as his trade negotiator. Antonio (Tony) Garza continued in their footsteps by being elected to the Texas Railroad Commission in 1998; President George W. Bush then appointed him as ambassador to Mexico in 2002. Roger Williams, a former Perry appointee, was a candidate for the U.S. Senate in 2012.

Boards and Commissions

Multimember boards or commissions head most state administrative agencies and make overall policy for them. These boards appoint chief administrators to handle the day-to-day responsibilities of the agencies, including the budget, personnel, and the administration of state laws and those federal laws that are carried out through state governments. Two of these boards and commissions have elected members. The others have appointed or ex officio members.

Elected Boards and Commissions

The Texas Railroad Commission (TRC) is one of the most influential agencies in the state, and its three members are powerful indeed. The commission has tremendous political clout in the state because of its regulation of all mining and extractive industries, including oil, gas, coal, and uranium. Of growing importance is its control of intrastate road transportation—buses, moving vans, and trucks, including tow trucks—because of the importance of trucking rates to economic development. (Trucking is the number-one method by which goods are conveyed to market.) The TRC also regulates intrastate railroads. Its members are chosen in statewide elections for staggered six-year terms. In 1995, the TRC became all Republican for the first time and has remained so. The commissioners are Elizabeth Jones, chair, first appointed in 2005 and then elected in 2006; David Porter, elected in 2010; and Barry Smitherman, appointed in 2011 to fill out the term of Michael Williams, who announced plans to run for the U.S. Congress.

The fifteen-member State Board of Education (SBOE) was originally created as an elected body. As part of the public school reforms of 1984, it was made an appointive board. In 1987, the voters overwhelmingly approved returning it to elective status. Its fifteen members are chosen by the voters from districts across the state. A majority of the board's members are conservative Republicans, a fact that has reintroduced a long-standing controversy about the board's selection of textbooks for public schools.

The State Board of Education, which oversees the Texas public schools, is an elected board that is well known for its ultraconservatism and lack of enlightenment. The SBOE has been particularly controversial when selecting science and social science textbooks.

Courtesy of Ben Sargent.

Ex Officio Boards and Commissions

There are many boards in the state administration whose members are all ex officio; that is, they are members because of another office they hold in the administration. When these boards were created, two purposes were served by ex officio memberships: The members usually were already in Austin (no small matter in pre-freeway days), and they were assumed to have some expertise in the subject at hand. An example is the Bond Review Board, which includes the governor, lieutenant governor, comptroller, and speaker of the House and ensures that debt financing is used prudently by the state.

Appointed Boards and Commissions

Administration of most of the state's laws is carried out by boards and commissions whose members are appointed rather than elected and by the administrators the boards then appoint. The members of many boards are appointed by the governor, but some other boards have a combination of gubernatorial appointees, appointees of other state officials, and/or ex officio members. These boards vary in size and, as a rule, have general policy authority for their agencies. Members serve six-year overlapping terms without pay.

There are three broad categories of appointed boards and commissions: (1) health, welfare, and rehabilitation; (2) education; and (3) general executive and administrative departments. Examples of each category are: (1) the Health and Human Services Council, (2) the Texas Higher Education Coordinating Board, and (3) the Parks and Wildlife Department and the Public Utility Commission, respectively.

Appointed Boards and Citizens

How do the 125 or so policymaking boards, which oversee some 145 agencies, affect the ordinary citizen? Three examples give one an idea.

The Case of the Public Utility Commission One example is the Public Utility Commission of Texas (PUC), which fosters competition and promotes a utility *infrastructure* (the basic physical structure for delivery of public utilities, such as pipelines, cables, and transformers). The PUC has been very busy since the legislature deregulated the

electric industry in 1999, both overseeing procedures for deregulation and trying to ensure the availability of adequate and reliable electric power. A second focus is overseeing the telecommunications industry. Any Texas citizen can contact PUC's Office of Customer Protection to complain about unreliable electric or telecommunications service, or seeming misdeeds on the part of providers of those utilities. For example, if a Texas college student has been "slammed" (had her telephone service switched without authorization from one carrier to the next), "crammed" (had unauthorized charges on his telephone bill), or is unable to resolve a dispute with the manager of an apartment complex due to the submetering of electric service, the PUC represents a possible solution to the problem.

The Case of the College Governing Board Whether one is in a public community college, a private university, or a public university, that institution has a board of trustees or a board of regents. These board members set policy for the college and appoint the president. In the case of a university system, such as University of Texas or Texas A&M, the board is responsible for all institutions in the system. At one typical board of regents meeting, the board members (1) renewed the president's contract, (2) approved a resolution increasing tuition, (3) granted tenure to twenty faculty members, (4) approved the hiring of a new liberal arts dean, and (5) approved a contract for construction of additional classrooms in the environmental sciences building. Each of these actions affected students—directly in the case of tuition increases and classroom space, and indirectly in the case of the three types of personnel actions.

The Case of the Parks and Wildlife Commission If a person is "outdoorsy" and likes to camp, fish, or hunt, the annual decisions of the Texas Parks and Wildlife Commission (TPWC) on what fees will be levied for each of these activities are of interest. Texas traditionally has had very low parks and wildlife fees compared with other states. If a fishing license suddenly costs $100 instead of $30, the outdoors person might have second thoughts about this form of recreation. Sports people also are affected by decisions of this board as to what type of fish it will release into the lakes of the state, and how well state and sometimes local parks are managed. (The TPWC through the Parks and Wildlife Department often operates local parks, such as a lakeside recreational area, by agreement with the local government.) It has been controversial since 2006–2007 when the sorry condition of most state parks became a frequent topic in the media; both underfunding and poor spending habits have led to the decline of the parks system.

Big Government: How Did It Happen?

Our country changed from an individualistic society that depended on government for very little to an urban, interdependent nation supporting a massive governmental structure. How did this change come about? And why?

The many, and complex, answers to these questions involve the Industrial Revolution, the mechanization of farms and ranches, and the technological revolution. These changes in turn led to urbanization. When workers followed job opportunities from farms to factories, much of the nation's population shifted from rural to urban areas. The American business philosophy was *pseudo laissez faire*—that is, commerce and industry should be allowed to develop without

government restraint but with governmental aid, and government's responsibility for the well-being of its citizens was minimal. The American social philosophy was social Darwinism, which holds that the poor are poor because they are "supposed" to be that way due to their "naturally" inferior abilities, and that the rich are rich due to their "naturally" superior abilities. American barons of industry—individuals earlier in our history and now usually corporate owners—grew rich and powerful, controlling not only the economy, but also the politics of the nation.

Eventually, the conditions resulting from these two philosophies, principally an unpredictable boom-and-bust economy and widespread poverty, caused a number of political developments. The expansion of voting rights, big-city ward politics, and a Populist movement that insisted on protection for workers and farmers are only a few examples. The outcry against the economic conditions brought about by pseudo laissez faire finally became so great that the national government stepped in to curb the worst excesses of big business and to attempt to protect citizens who could not protect themselves. For example, the railroads so controlled state legislatures in the last quarter of the nineteenth century that state governments were powerless to protect their citizens. The Interstate Commerce Commission (ICC) was created in 1887 to regulate the railroads, which had been pricing small farmers out of business by charging exorbitant freight rates.

The creation of the ICC illustrates the beginning of an activist national government. During the thirty years just before and just after the turn of the twentieth century, the focus was on regulation of the economy. The second growth thrust came in response to the Great Depression of the 1930s, with the expansion of both government services and the administration necessary to implement them. For example, the Social Security, farm price support, and rural electrification programs all began in the 1930s. This expansion represented a major shift in political ideology from a conservatism that held, in the words attributed to Thomas Jefferson, that "that government is best which governs the least, because its people discipline themselves," to a liberalism that held government intervention to be the best route to the betterment of the individual.

Postwar Growth

After World War II, government continued to expand in scope. There were social concerns such as civil rights, newly recognized industrial problems such as environmental pollution, and technologies such as nuclear power, all requiring oversight. The federal government not only entered areas that traditionally had been left to state and local governments—education and health care, for example—but also fostered social change through such policies as equal opportunity and affirmative-action employment. By channeling funds for new programs at the state and local levels through state agencies, the federal government has served as the major catalyst for the increased role of the public sector. An expanding electorate and a more complex society both contributed to government growth.

The national government continued to expand its programs and their associated costs throughout the 1970s. State and local governments grew rapidly to take advantage of available federal dollars for new programs, to respond to mandatory federal initiatives, to promote economic expansion, and to develop new programs and services brought about by citizens' demands for an improvement in the quality of life. Each new service increased the number of people necessary

to keep the wheels of government turning. In a state such as Texas, with a high population growth rate, it is inevitable that the combination of more programs and increased population would cause an increase in the size and scope of state and local governments.

Figure 8-1 shows the largest program areas in Texas as compared with all of the fifteen most populous states. Texas has the same or fewer employees per 10,000 populations than the other states, except in the category of corrections and public welfare. Because these numbers already take into account the difference in population among the states, one is left to conclude that either Texas has proportionately more criminals than other states or more of a lock-'em-up attitude. The following two chapters help to explain that the reason for the large number of corrections employees is the lock-'em-up attitude. The lower numbers in the other major categories do not signal greater efficiency. Rather, they signal that Texans receive proportionately fewer government services than citizens in the other large states and that the state has a significant number of poor people requiring public hospital and public welfare services.

1980 On

The election of Ronald Reagan to the presidency in 1980 signaled a shift away from liberal ideology and a new stress on the role of the states in the American federal system. Along with an erratic economy in the modern era, the new conservatism also brought about cuts in funding for federal programs, forcing reductions in state and local social programs that had previously been funded by the national government.

Moreover, citizens across the nation were beginning to doubt what liberal ideology had wrought. As early as the 1970s, a taxpayers' revolt had begun,

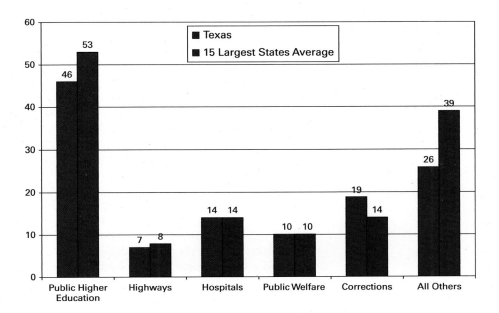

FIGURE 8-1 State Employment in Texas and Fifteen Largest States, per 10,000 Population, by Function.

SOURCE: Fiscal Size-Up, 2010–2011 Biennium (Austin: Legislative Budget Board, 2009), 58.

CHAPTER EIGHT: THE ADMINISTRATIVE STATE

and was manifest across the country by the 1980s. Demands for accountability, transparency, and greater productivity were popular campaign themes. At the national level, programs such as education and social welfare were cut back or capped, and "tax reform" meant lower income taxes, particularly for the affluent. At the same time, defense spending went up significantly. The gap between government spending and government revenue was filled by borrowing. By the end of the decade, the United States had become the world's largest debtor nation while its domestic programs largely fell into disarray.

During the early 1990s and again in 2007–2009, the economy faltered all across the country. The largely Anglo middle class was more concerned about the economy and its role in it than about social issues. Economic and political distance between the mainly White suburbanites and the basically minority lower economic class in the central cities increased. Because the lower economic class tends not to vote, governments at all levels tended to listen to the suburbanites, a phenomenon that meant even more emphasis on accountability, greater demands for tax ceilings and spending cutbacks, and more emphasis on economic development and less on the welfare state. However, major problems that only government could address remained—crime, environmental pollution, and the deteriorating educational system, for example. Moreover, the national government began to impose requirements such as clean air and water upon the states in the form of mandates. The states then passed problems and mandates such as the need for better education to the local governments.

Therefore, state and local governments continued to grow in size, programs, and expenditures, much to the regret of many taxpayers, who preferred less government and an end to state and local tax increases. Texans have always had a strong antigovernment streak, but the state has the additional burden of high population growth. A bias against government spending and growth and a burgeoning population do not mix well, as Chapter 12 will discuss.

Figure 8-2 shows relatively steady growth in state and local government since 1980, with a higher growth rate for local government, which includes public schools. Even when the economy is in the doldrums, government employment often holds steady or even grows as government responds to the needs of the people. The best example of this phenomenon is the Great Depression of the 1930s; a contrary example is the number of public jobs lost as a result of the Texas budget cuts for the 2012–2013 fiscal years.

In Texas and many other states, a review of bureaucratic performance began, especially on the criterion of efficiency—the least expenditure of dollars and other resources per unit of output—in the early 1990s. President Bill Clinton assigned Vice President Al Gore to begin a similar initiative in the national government based on the models set by Texas and a half-dozen other states. These activities are known as *reinventing* or *reengineering government.*

However, in 2000 nationally and in 2002 in Texas, the Republican Party captured the executive branch and a majority of both houses of the legislative branch. As a result, policy preferences shifted again. At the national level, domestic programs were secondary to defense, and the budget deficit was allowed to balloon. At the state level, policymakers showed more concern for reducing taxes and constraining social programs than for addressing citizen needs, especially when dollars were short.

Nationally, the Democrats took control of Congress in 2007 and the presidency in 2009. By 2009, they faced an existing deficit, international turmoil, and

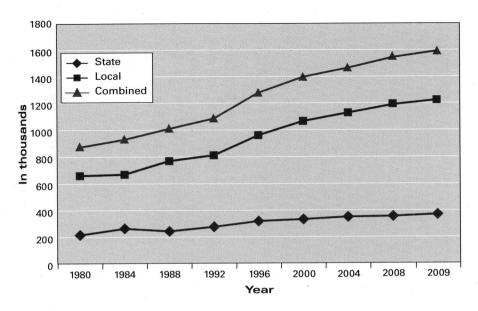

FIGURE 8-2 State and Local Government Employment in Texas, 1980–2009.

SOURCES: Texas Almanac, 1982–1983, 1986–1987, 1990–1991, 1994–1995, 1998–1999, 2002–2003, 2006–2007, 2008–2009 (Dallas: *Dallas Morning News*, 1981, 1986, 1989, 1993, 1997, 2001, 2006, 2008), 410, 597, 502, 467, 548, 548, 578, 603, respectively, and *Texas Almanac, 2010–2011* (Denton: Texas State Historical Association, 2010), 607.

especially domestic economic woes that were addressed with massive expenditures, further increasing the national debt (see Chapter 12). The Democrats then lost control of the House in 2010. In the elections of 2010, the emergence of the Tea Party movement made it clear that voters thought there was too much government, at least in programs that did not benefit them. Moreover, because the Republicans still control Texas, awkwardness exists in the relationship between Texas and the national government.

Characteristics of Bureaucracy

Of the many ways to organize human activities—committees, commissions, task forces, and so forth—the form most often used is bureaucracy, not only in government, but also in businesses, clubs, churches, and many other organizations. The bureaucratic structure is traditionally viewed as the most efficient way to organize human endeavors so as to ensure competent, quick, and expert problem solving. As so often happens, however, the ideal differs considerably from the reality. Indeed, experts on governmental organization and management frequently suggest alternatives to a strict bureaucratic organization.[3]

Traditional Characteristics

Early in the 1900s, Max Weber, considered the father of modern sociology, listed the main characteristics of a bureaucratic organization as part of his examination of the phenomenon of authority. Weber's list is important because it has been the starting point for subsequent discussions of bureaucratic structures.

1. **Authority is hierarchical; an organization chart of a bureaucracy looks like a pyramid. At the top, there are the fewest people but with the greatest authority. At the base of the pyramid are the most people but with the least authority.**

2. **Individuals are assigned specific tasks to perform, and a combination of training and the continual performance of these tasks results in expertise in the specific area.**

3. **Bureaucracies have defined jurisdictions; that is, they are created to accomplish definite and limited goals.**

4. **There are extensive rules and regulations to ensure that policy is implemented uniformly and consistently.**

5. **Bureaucrats, because they follow comprehensive and detailed rules that depersonalize administration, are politically neutral.[4]**

Modern Characteristics

Today's American bureaucracies deviate considerably from the classic European organizations that Weber observed. Boards and commissions, rather than a single chief executive, are often at the power peak of agencies; authority (and accountability) is thus diffused. Jurisdictions are so broadly defined (as in the national Department of Health and Human Services) that limits on goals and authority are obscured; confusion and competition result from overlapping jurisdictions and authority. Agency staffers, especially executives and sometimes minor bureaucrats, far from being politically neutral, are very much involved in political processes. Moreover, bureaucracies hire, fire, and promote from within.

Pushing the Cost of Government Downward

Citizens see the cost of government as rising even when one level of government brags about tax cutting. Examples of what happens when a higher-level government begins to retrench are seen all over Texas in the very practical matters of water runoff and solid waste (garbage) disposal. At one point, the national government provided considerable assistance with the costs of laying new sewer lines and acquiring landfill sites. The assistance is no longer forthcoming, but environmental standards have risen higher and higher. Small cities can ill afford the costs of disposing of their own wastes under the new standards and are dependent on contracts with larger communities to provide all or some of these services, as is the case, for example, with Graham and Fort Worth or Krum and Denton. While the higher-level government can boast of budget slashing and program reduction, citizens don't pay any less; they just transfer their dollars from one government to another. The situation for small cities and their residents has not changed.

It is often very difficult even for bureau managers to fire someone and usually impossible for the chief executive to dismiss an employee. This feature of modern bureaucracies means that they are largely divorced from outside control.

The public interest sometimes becomes lost in the shuffle. We seemingly are overwhelmed by the administrative state, which Emmette Redford defines as a society in which "we are affected intimately and extensively by decisions in numerous organizations, public and private, allocating advantages and disadvantages to us."[5] The cumulative effect of these deviations from Weber's model is that the bureaucracy is relatively free from outside control. Administrators enjoy a substantial amount of independence. Politicians in most democracies complain about the difficulty of getting bureaucrats to do anything they don't want to do. When administrators do not fear being fired for refusing to cooperate with politicians, they may evade and even disobey the orders of the people they are supposedly working for. In the twenty-first century, we must consider how the power of government agencies that are not accountable to the people's representatives can be considered legitimate. Conversely, we have to consider that bureaucrats may be dedicated to professional standards that transcend the politics of the moment; thus, the recipients of public services may continue to receive benefits even while politicians running for office call for an end to various social programs.

The rules designed to ensure consistency and fairness sometimes contradict one another. Equal opportunity requires absolutely equal treatment of all candidates for a job, for example, but affirmative action requires special measures for protected classes of citizens. Other rules create problems while trying to solve them. For example, regulations of the federal Occupational Safety and Health Administration (OSHA) require roofers to be tethered to the roof to avoid falling, but roofers contend that many injuries can occur because of tethering. However, rules or "red tape" have been a nuisance to citizens throughout much of history. In fact, the term *red tape* goes back to the sixteenth century when orders from the English king were bound in packets by red ribbons.

Today, we also are unsure of what the role of the expert should be. Traditionally, the expert was to carry out detailed functions—whether issuing a driver's license or testing water purity in the city's laboratory. But increasingly, experts, who often disagree with one another or have narrow views, dominate

Up a Tree

Why do citizens rail against bureaucracy so often? One answer is that bureaucrats often have to enforce laws that elected officials poorly conceived. In Highland Village, northwest of Dallas, one family tangled with the city because of their children's tree house for which they had not sought a zoning variance or building permit. A city ordinance placed a number of restrictions on structures that were not part of the main house. Although the city manager and the public works director worked with the family, helping whenever they could, they still had to enforce the law and insist on relocation of the tree house.

Source: "Bird House Dwellers, You're Next," an item in *Select List*, May 4, 2000, published for subscribers by Lewis F. McClain.

our organizations. Lawyers and accountants are prime examples in both business and government.

Another characteristic of modern bureaucracies is their reliance on managers not only to oversee policy implementation, but also to serve as brokers between citizens and elected officials. In both business and government, layers of management isolate the citizen-customer from key decision makers.

In the United States, size also is of concern, especially the relationship between the number of government employees and the number of citizens served. The number of federal civilian employees—about 195,000 of whom work in Texas—has changed little since the 1960s. In fact, state and local governments, contract employees, nonprofit organizations, and consultants administer many national programs. Major shifts in the numbers of federal government personnel have occurred only when the military was engaged in a buildup or during a downsizing. In the 1990s, for example, government reorganization and the quest for a balanced budget resulted in the elimination of about 300,000 federal jobs. Even new federal spending initiatives often mean that state and local government workers will increase in number as implementation of national policy falls to these governments.

An economy of scale exists in the states. Generally, the larger the state, the lower is the ratio of state employees to citizens. As Figure 8-3 shows, this relationship is approximate. California, the most populous state, has the third

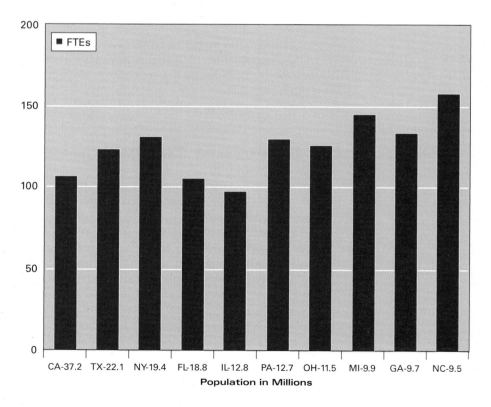

FIGURE 8-3 Number of Full-Time Equivalent (FTE) Employees per 10,000 Population, Ten Largest States.

SOURCE: *Fiscal Size-Up, 2010–2011 Biennium* (Austin: Texas Legislative Budget Board, 2009), 57.

lowest number of full-time equivalent (FTE) employees per 10,000 population (106) and is ranked forty-eighth. Illinois, the fifth largest state, has 97 employees per 10,000 population and ranks fiftieth in per capita employment. However, Texas and New York, the second and third largest states, respectively, seem to have some inefficiencies, because they rank only forty-fourth and forty-first, respectively, with 122 and 130 employees per 10,000 population. Still, they look very efficient indeed when compared with the 448 and 377 employees per 10,000 population of Hawaii and Alaska, respectively. Hawaii is a series of islands and Alaska is huge in land mass but sparsely populated, making service delivery difficult for both states. Texas may appear slightly inefficient because it has a similar problem of vast distances in the western part of the state. The number of FTEs in Texas has been relatively constant.

A final characteristic of modern bureaucracy is frequent reorganization. In trying to find the most efficient means of carrying out policies and, at the same time, coping with increased numbers of employees and the proliferation of programs, governments keep shuffling their internal organization. President Jimmy Carter drew up a major reorganization plan for the federal bureaucracy that was approved by Congress in 1978. In the 1990s, President Bill Clinton assigned Vice President Al Gore the task of government reorganization. Many states, Texas among them, have enacted legislation that calls for periodic evaluations of state agencies. An example is the Sunset Act, discussed later in this chapter. Some major agencies in Texas, such as those dealing with health, welfare, and water, have been reorganized, with an emphasis on consolidating fragmented services. Other agencies have initiated their own reorganizations. Many students have seen examples of such reorganization on their own campuses as departments have been combined or moved from one dean to another.

Bureaucratic Survival Techniques

Bureaucratic agencies share one characteristic with the rest of us: They need money. In the push and scramble of overlapping jurisdictions, authorities, and programs, agency staffers must fight for funds if they want their agency to continue. Agency people seek first survival and then growth for three principal reasons: (1) personal—their jobs; (2) programmatic—genuine commitment to the program administered by the organization; and (3) clientele—a sincere concern for the people who benefit from the agency's programs. Because the administrators operate in the arena of political activities, they use political tactics to achieve their goals, just as state legislators and the governor do. Administrators must develop their own sources of political power if they want policies favorable to them enacted into law, and they have done so.[6]

Sources of Bureaucratic Power

The principal sources of bureaucratic power are clientele group(s), the legislature, the chief executive, the public, the agency's own expertise and information, its leadership, and the strength of its internal organization. Each of these categories is explored in the following sections.

Employee Turnover

In addition to greater efficiency that results in fewer full-time equivalent employees per 10,000 population, the number of state workers has been affected both by program cuts (some of which are described in Chapters 12 through 14) and a number of factors leading to higher turnover among Texas public employees. Chief among those factors are low pay and modest retirement and other benefits.

Sources: Jason Embry, "Turnover Among State Workers Has Inched Up in '05," *Austin American-Statesman*, December 24, 2005, B1; Mark Lisheron, "Texas Ranks Last in Benefits for Public Employees," *Texas Watchdog*, March 5, 2011, accessed at http://www.texaswatchdog.org/2011/03/tune-in-to-ktsa-550-in-san-antonio-texas-watchdogs-mark-lisheron/1299529105.column.

Clientele Groups

The cornerstone of an agency's political clout is its relationship with its **clientele** (interest) **group** or groups. This relationship is mutually beneficial. The agency and its clientele have similar goals, are interested in the same programs, and work together in a number of ways, including sharing personnel, information, and lobbying strategies. The greater the economic power of the clientele groups, the stronger the political ties between them and "their" agencies—so strong in fact that "regulation" often becomes promotion of the clientele group's interests.

Among the better-known agency-clientele relationships are those between the oil, gas, and transportation industries and the Texas Railroad Commission; the Texas Good Roads and Transportation Association (an interest group) and the Texas Department of Transportation; and the banking industry and the State Banking and State Depository Boards. The ties are not always economically motivated, however, as, for example, in the case of the support given to the Parks and Wildlife Department by local chapters of the National Rifle Association or to Texas Tech University by its alumni. During a legislative session, the competition for as large a share as possible of the state's financial resources can be fierce indeed, with phalanxes of agency-clientele group coalitions lined up against one another.

The Legislature

Agencies' relationships with legislators are of two types: direct and indirect. First, agencies directly attempt to influence legislation and their budgets by furnishing information in writing and through testimony to legislative committees. In addition, agency executives work hard to get to know the speaker of the House, the lieutenant governor, and the members of the Legislative Budget Board and the Legislative Council, all of whom operate year-round, even when committee chairs and other legislators have gone home. Second, agencies use their clientele groups to try to influence legislation, budgets, and the selection of legislative leaders. During budget shortfalls in recent years, a number of state agencies—including higher education—became adept at finding powerful groups, such as chambers of commerce and specially formed support groups, to help them try to ward off agency budget cuts.

The Chief Executive

As previously noted, the governor's power over state agencies has been strengthened, but bureaucrats also want gubernatorial support. The governor usually appoints the agency head or members of the board or commission that oversees the agency, and for many agencies, he or she appoints the board chair. A governor who is a skillful chief legislator can help an agency get its budget increased or add a new program. The chief executive can also referee when an agency does not have the support of its clientele group and give an agency visibility when it might otherwise languish in obscurity. The governor's legislative and party roles can be used to influence neutral legislators to look favorably on an agency, and the governor can greatly affect an agency's success or failure through appointments to the policy board or commission that oversees it. To state administrators, the chief executive is more powerful than the formal roles of the gubernatorial office would suggest.

For example, in 1991, Governor Ann Richards forced the reorganization of the Texas Department of Commerce. Four years later, Governor George W. Bush pushed legislation that would benefit insurance companies by making it harder to sue and to gain large dollar amounts from a suit, but he also insisted that the companies find ways to lower rates. In 2003, Governor Rick Perry gained control of the economic development function while seeing to the end of the Department of Economic Development. Although that move may seem hostile, in reality, he rescued an important state function from a corrupt agency, and immediately began to push for more international trade. In 2007, he had to contend with a corrupt Texas Youth Commission, which, by a combination of gubernatorial and legislative actions, was essentially reconstituted. In 2011, he was influencing higher education by appointing board members more focused on undergraduate education and less on research.

The Public

Some bureaucratic agencies enjoy considerable public recognition and support. Among these are the Texas Rangers (perhaps the most romanticized bureaucracy in the state), the Texas Department of Transportation, and the Parks and Wildlife Department. The Rangers are well known, of course, because of many dramatic incidents in the early days of bringing "law and order" to the state. The latter two agencies use the technique of news and information for gaining public attention: road maps, carefully labeled highway projects, mapped-out camping tours, and colorful signs. In fact, the photograph on the cover of this book was supplied without charge after having been chosen from the many hundreds available in the photographic library of the Department of Transportation in Austin. However, generally favorable opinion toward Parks and Wildlife has not saved the agency from disastrous budget reductions that have resulted in the closing of some state parks and related facilities.

Usually, however, agencies have little, if any, public support to help them gain legislative or gubernatorial cooperation. The public, diverse and unorganized, often is unaware of the very existence of many agencies, much less able to give them the concerted support necessary to influence top-level elected administrators. Such support, when forthcoming, depends largely on the public's awareness of the importance of the agency's programs to the general welfare.

LONE STAR MEDIA
Hi, Ho Silver

One Texas state agency has been romanticized not only more than any other Texas bureaucracy but also more than most agencies other than the Federal Bureau of Investigation. The Texas Rangers, now a division of the Department of Public Safety, have been popularized in various entertainment media. Perhaps best known was the popular radio and television series, *The Lone Ranger*, which was developed from a 1930s movie serial. This tale depicted the story of John Reid, a Ranger who was the last man left after Butch Cavendish and the Hole in the Wall Gang ambushed a troop of Rangers. Long after the series left the air, Clayton Moore, the last TV Lone Ranger, made personal appearances as the famous "masked man" at fairs and rodeos.

The Rangers have been depicted in other popular radio and television series, including *Tales of the Texas Rangers*, *True Tales of the Texas Rangers*, and *Walker, Texas Ranger*. They also have been the subject of songs (both a lament and a farewell) and movies such as *The Hole in the Wall Gang* and *The Legend of the Texas Rangers*. Even the American League baseball team, the Texas Rangers, bears the name of these fabled law enforcers.

"One Riot, One Ranger" is a phrase that depicts the allure of the Texas Rangers. Those words were never a Ranger motto but stem from an incident when a single ranger was sent to break up any riots that might have occurred as a result of a prize fight in 1896. Because the Rangers have been so romanticized, many people forget that their early days were violent and that their apprehension of alleged criminals was with total disregard for any rights lawbreakers might have.

SOURCES: "The Great Terquasquicentennial Road Trip: No, 11, One Riot, One Ranger," *Texas Monthly*, March 2011, 130; the Internet Movie Data Base, with a search for Texas Rangers, at http://www.imdb.com/; "Texas Ranger Division," *Wikipedia*, at http://en.wikipedia.org/wiki/Texas_Ranger_Division; and "The Lone Ranger,'" *Wikipedia*, at http://en.wikipedia.org/wiki//The_Lone_Ranger, all accessed March 13, 2011.

Expertise and Information

Expert information is a political commodity peculiar to bureaucrats, who enjoy a unique position in state government through their control of the technical information that the governor and legislators must have to develop statewide policies. Although all bureaucracies have this advantage, it is particularly strong in Texas because the state's legislative committee system does not produce the same degree of legislative expertise as do the seniority system and continuous sessions of the U.S. Congress. Usually, the only alternative source for the legislator who does not want to use the information from an agency is the agency's clientele group. However, the more technical an agency's specialty, the greater is that agency's advantage in controlling vital information. For example, if the legislature is trying to determine whether the state is producing enough physicians, the Board of Medical Examiners and the Department of State Health Services, as well as the Texas Medical Association and the Texas Osteopathic Medical Association, are all ready to furnish the information. The public's ideas on the subject are seldom considered.

Leadership

Another factor that determines the political power of bureaucracies is the caliber of leadership within the agency. Agency heads must be able to spark enthusiasm in their employees, encourage them toward a high level of performance, and convince elected officials and clientele groups that their agencies are performing effectively. A competent chief administrator will usually be retained by the members of the agency's governing board or commission, even though the board or commission membership changes over the years. The department benefits from continuity and stability at the top, and there is minimal disruption in the agency's relationship with clientele groups and legislators.

Internal Organization

Some agencies have a **civil service system** that protects agency workers from outside influence. In a civil service system, workers are hired on merit—that is, their performance on written tests and other forms of examination—and are evaluated on job performance. Agencies with a merit-based personnel system can resist the influence of, for example, a legislator trying to get his nephew hired for the summer or an aide to the governor who wants an agency employee fired because the two had a disagreement.

The adoption of a civil service system for hiring and promoting state workers introduces a paradox into the democratic nature of Texas government. The point of the "merit system" is to insulate agency workers from undue interference by politicians and from having to make decisions on a partisan basis. Yet those politicians are the people's representatives. When they cannot control state administrators, the people's will is obstructed. Part of the hostility that private citizens often express against bureaucrats may be due to the recognition on their part that "civil servants" are paid with taxes, yet are at best imperfectly accountable to the people. At the same time, we must consider the consequences if every administrative agency was forced to bend to the partisan will of elected officials.

Bureaucratic Involvement in the Policymaking Process

Bureaucrats cannot directly lobby, but they have other ways of influencing public policy. These include the use of discretion and the way in which information is provided to the legislature.

Implementation of the Laws

The primary task of state bureaucrats is to implement the laws of Texas. In carrying out this task, however, they have considerable **administrative discretion;** that is, they are relatively free to use their own judgment as to how the laws will be carried out. Regulatory boards illustrate most clearly the power of administrative agencies. When the Texas Railroad Commission (even if efforts to reorganize it should ever be successful) determines the monthly oil allowable (the number of barrels of oil that can be pumped during a particular month), it is making (administrative) rules that, like legislative statutes, have the force of law. It is, therefore, performing a quasi-legislative function. When the Alcoholic Beverage Commission decides who will be issued a license to sell beer, wine, and distilled spirits, it is performing a quasi-judicial function by determining whether a person has the right to go into business.

Often, a statute passed by the legislature creates a general framework for implementing a service or regulatory program, but state agencies have considerable discretion in interpreting statutes. Consequently, the 125 or so policymaking boards, commissions, and authorities are very important in determining what government actually does. Especially in a state like Texas, which lacks a cabinet system and an integrated executive branch, the average citizen is affected on a daily basis by what these boards do, but that citizen may have little understanding of how they work or how to approach them. Recent changes that resulted in making the board chairs accountable to the governor may help because the public can more nearly determine "who's in charge here." The board and commission structure makes public participation more difficult.

Moreover, these boards usually appoint an executive director or college president to carry out their policies, and that executive officer has considerable influence over board policies. For example, a Texas State University student may wish to protest the abolition of a popular major. Determining how to make a protest requires information about how the decision was made. Was the change made by the system's board of regents on its own or upon recommendation of the president, or was it forced by policies of the Texas Higher Education Coordinating Board in Austin? Were the students consulted before the decision was made?

Although it can obscure how a decision was made, administrative discretion can be a positive factor in effective government. A common example is the decision of a Department of Public Safety law enforcement officer to allow one suspect to go free in the hope that he will lead criminal-intelligence agents to a more important suspect. Another example is that of professors at state universities, who have considerable freedom to design their classes. Each professor decides on the balance between lecture and discussion, textbooks, whether to use a CD or DVD, what the mix of multiple-choice and essay tests will be, whether to require work on the World Wide Web, and the basis of grading. Thus, by interpreting laws, making rules, and making judgments, administrators make public policy.

Influencing Legislation

Bureaucrats directly influence the content and meaning of statutes that are passed by the legislature, and they do so in three principal ways: by drafting bills, furnishing information to legislators, and lobbying.

Reorganization, Texas Style

In 2003, Governor Rick Perry sought legislative approval of a major state reorganization that would move Texas toward a cabinet-style government by giving him power over the heads of state agencies. The legislature responded by reorganizing the comptroller's office, eleven health and human services agencies, the pardons and paroles board, and economic development, and by giving the governor control over the heads of appointed state boards and commissions. In 2011, Perry began a campaign to collapse other agencies.

During its short session, the Texas legislature is under great pressure to draft, consider, and dispose of needed legislation. State bureaucrats are eager to aid the lawmakers, and two ways in which they do so are mutually beneficial: furnishing specialized information to legislative committees and drafting bills that individual legislators may then present as their own. Legislators thus gain needed assistance, and administrators are able to protect their agencies by helping to write their own budgets and develop their own programs.

Bureaucrats also influence legislation by lobbying legislators for or against proposed bills. State employees cannot legally act as lobbyists, but they can furnish information. For the average citizen, it's splitting hairs to make that distinction. Agencies usually work closely with their clientele group or groups in the lobbying endeavor. The governor is also lobbied not only for support of legislation that is favored by agencies and their clients, but also for agency appointments that are acceptable to them and their clients. If successful, both of these lobbying activities can greatly influence the decisions of legislators, as well as the policies set by boards and commissions. Furthermore, more than 366,000 state employees, through such organizations as the Texas Public Employees Association, are an active lobby at budget time on matters of salary and fringe benefits.

What Happens to the Public Interest?

Public administration originally was created to serve and protect the public interest. Sometimes, however, the public interest can be forgotten in the shifting, complex kaleidoscope of hundreds of agencies, bureaus, departments, and commissions constantly striving for more money, more personnel, more programs, and more power. Bureaucrats are no more evil, incompetent, or venal than employees of privately owned companies. However, the bureaucracy is funded with public money—tax dollars—so people naturally are a little more concerned with the honesty and efficiency of the state's administration than with that of Texas Instruments or Tenneco, for example.

Administrative scandals, such as the mistreatment of people with intellectual disabilities at state schools or public employees benefiting from state travel in the name of economic development, heighten that interest. Sixty years ago, Paul Appleby drew the distinction between government and private administration by noting that the public administrator is continually subject to "public scrutiny and outcry" by "press and public interest in every detail of his life, personality, and conduct."[7] In short, public administrators live in the proverbial goldfish bowl. For people who are worried about democratic accountability, of course, it is a good thing to put administrators into a goldfish bowl. Constant publicity may not be as effective in instilling democratic accountability into administrators as it is with elected politicians, but it is better than nothing.

Bureaucratic Orientation

It is a fact of organizational life that the longer one remains in one agency or company, the more one's perspectives narrow to those of the organization. After a while, one begins to support that organization's way of doing things. In a public agency, this orientation often leads to a loss of concern for more general public

goals and an inability to see different points of view. This shifting of bureaucratic orientation is known as *goal displacement*—that is, the replacement of one goal by another. In this case, the public interest is forgotten and the agencies' interests and those of their clientele groups become paramount. Many complex factors are involved in the displacement of publicly stated goals in agency priorities: (1) the rapid, piecemeal creation of new agencies that have overlapping jurisdictions and authorities; (2) the co-optation of regulatory agencies by their clientele groups; (3) the fact that most top-level administrators are appointed by an executive who has no power to remove them from office and that most career bureaucrats are protected in their jobs by tenure; (4) the fact that the public is generally bewildered about which government official or body is responsible for what governmental action or program; and (5) the fact that the publicly stated goals may not have been the "real" goals to begin with.

The vast majority of public managers and bureaucrats are conscientious, and many of them have a keen sense of public interest. Nevertheless, the authors share with democratic theorists a concern about reconciling bureaucracy and democracy. The growth in the size and scope of government brings with it a need for adequate controls. Even if the controls are not needed all the time, citizen participation in government requires their presence.

Overstepping the Law

In addition to the bureaucratic orientation that develops over time, some state administrators are further tempted toward inappropriate bureaucratic activities. In Texas, these temptations are due to (1) extremely strong special interest groups, (2) weaknesses in the governor's office, and (3) the handicapped

One agency that overstepped the law was the Texas Youth Commission, which underwent a considerable overhaul in 2007 after sexual abuse and physical violence against the young inmates in its charge were revealed. It was a merger target in 2011.

Courtesy of Ben Sargent.

legislature. State agencies and bureaucrats have run afoul of the law in a variety of ways, such as using state funds for personal travel, assigning contracts without bids, awarding six-figure consulting contracts as a means of hiring "unseen" staff, and causing injuries and deaths through failure to enforce safety regulations. These incidents involved irregularities, not simply inefficiencies.

How, then, do we go about the job of ensuring that the state bureaucracy performs honestly, efficiently, and effectively? How do we ensure that public trust is warranted and that legislative intent is satisfied? In short, how do we ensure accountability on the part of the state administration?

Harnessing the Administrative State

As part of the state's system of checks and balances, the governor has a veto over legislative acts, and the legislature can impeach a governor or refuse to confirm gubernatorial appointments. As well as controlling various offices and agencies that report directly to them, all three traditional branches of government—executive, legislative, and judicial—have means of holding the bureaucracy, sometimes called the "fourth branch of government," in check. Democratic theory posits that government should be elected by the people, but most administrators are not. The governor and other elected officials have legitimacy (popular acceptance). State administrators must derive as much legitimacy as they can from these elected officials.

During the 1980s, the issue of bureaucratic accountability to the people through their elected representatives became increasingly important at both the state and the national levels because of tight budgets, public desire to maximize each tax dollar, and a strong, conservative, antigovernment trend. The importance of accountability was brought home in 1991 when the governor and the legislature agreed that a budget would not be forthcoming for the 1992–1993 biennium until all state functions were audited to determine if money was being wasted. From that agreement sprang the nationally recognized Texas Performance Review (TPR) system administered first by John Sharp, later by Carole Keeton Strayhorn, and then by the Legislative Budget Board. TPR requires that, before agencies can submit their budget proposals, they must prepare strategic plans that emphasize quality of service, access to programs, and measures of agency performance. Citizen demand for accountability and government's response to it illustrate that both citizens and elective officials play a role in harnessing the administrative state. The budget shortfalls of 2011 led to considerable outcry for bureaucratic accountability.

How Much Accountability to the Chief Executive?

It would seem logical to make the bureaucracy accountable to the governor, who is the chief executive and nominal head of the state administration. But the governor's powers were limited intentionally to avoid centralizing government power in any one office.

1. **Appointment powers are restricted and removal powers are limited.**

2. **There is no true executive budget.**

3. **The executive branch is fragmented:** Four departments, a major commission, and a major board are headed by elected officials, and many separate agencies deal with related functional areas—more than 30 policymaking boards are involved in the area of education alone. Instead of single-headed agencies, about 125 multimember boards and commissions officially make policy for their 145 or so agencies. In reality, the executive director of the agency, who administers the affairs of the agency, is usually the most powerful person connected with the organization—and is partially insulated from elected officials by the board.

Even if there were a complete reorganization of the executive branch, including consolidated departments headed by officials who constituted a governor's cabinet—such as thirty-nine other states have—the sheer size and diversity of the bureaucracy, coupled with other demands on the governor's time and staff, would make executive control loose and indirect. Just as it is difficult to hold a president responsible for the actions of a Social Security clerk in Laramie, Wyoming, it would be difficult to hold a governor responsible for the actions of a college professor in Canyon or a welfare caseworker in El Paso. Some agencies have responded to the governor's urging to use an *ombudsman*—grievance person—to hear public complaints against administrative agencies in an effort to increase executive responsiveness to citizen problems.

Stronger supervisory control would allow the governor to exercise greater influence over major policy decisions. With a consolidated executive branch, unencumbered by other elected administrators, and with managerial control over the state budget, the chief executive would have more hope of implementing policy. The advantage of having a strong chief executive as the head of a more truly hierarchical administration would be having overall responsibility vested in a highly visible elected official who could not be so easily dominated by special interests.

Texas has been moving slowly toward a more integrated executive branch, at least with regard to agencies headed by appointed executives or appointed boards. Nevertheless, the governor relies heavily on the roles of chief legislator, chief of state, and leader of the people to influence state agencies. However, all the modern governors have succeeded in adding some clout to their chief executive role—more removal power, more appointments to the executive director positions in state agencies and to the chairmanships of boards, more budget clout, and mandatory strategic planning. They are aided by the Budget, Planning, and Policy Division.

How Much Accountability to the Legislature?

To what extent can the legislature oversee the bureaucracy? It has two main tools: legislative oversight and the Texas Sunset Act.

Legislative Oversight

Legislatures traditionally have been guardians of the public interest, with powers to oversee administrative agencies. These powers include budgetary control, the post-audit of agency expenditures to ensure legality, programmatic control through the statutes, investigation of alleged wrongdoing, and impeachment of officials.

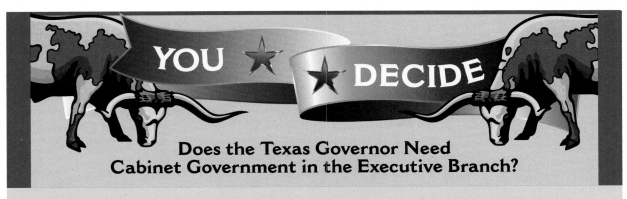

YOU ★ ★ DECIDE

Does the Texas Governor Need Cabinet Government in the Executive Branch?

Thirty-nine other states have an executive branch that is organized like that of the U.S. government—that is, a chief executive who heads a cabinet made up of directors or secretaries of a limited number of broad-based departments. Possible departments include Public and Higher Education, Public Safety and Criminal Justice, and Health and Human Services, for example.

PRO	CON
▲ Texas should pass the necessary statutory and constitutional provisions to establish a cabinet system because:	▼ Texas should not pass the necessary statutory and constitutional provisions to establish a cabinet system because:
▲ Citizens could more easily understand a government that was organized like that of the United States.	▼ "Supersized" departments would concentrate power in the hands of too few people.
▲ Greater economy and efficiency could be achieved with broad-based departments that could operate with economy of scale.	▼ Many smaller programs that serve useful purposes—for example, medical help for children with kidney disease—would get lost in the bureaucracy of large departments.
▲ The heads of the broad-based departments would be clearly associated with their agencies, could more easily be held accountable, and would more likely carry out the governor's policy preferences.	▼ The governor already has enough to do without directly supervising a cabinet.
▲ The fact that a majority of states have a cabinet system is evidence in and of itself of the value of this type of organization.	▼ There is almost no chance that voters would approve a constitutional amendment supporting cabinet government; thus, efforts to make this major change would be better aimed at improving state programs.

Although traditional legislative oversight is somewhat effective in Texas, several factors militate against its total success. One is the tripartite relationship among legislators, bureaucrats, and special interest groups. Legislators may be reluctant to ruffle the feathers of groups that supply them with campaign contributions by pressing their oversight vigorously. These groups in turn often have strong connections to the bureaucracy. Another is the high turnover of legislative committee personnel. A third is the lack of ongoing supervision because legislators are on the job only part-time as a result of Texas's short biennial legislative sessions. Much of the burden of oversight falls on the Legislative Budget Board, the Legislative Council, and the Legislative Audit Committee, although historically none of these has adequate staff or time for a thorough job, and none is well known to the general public.

A substitute for direct legislative oversight is legislation that micromanages an agency or set of agencies and requires some other agency to be the control force. A good example is the highly specific legislation passed in the 1997 session that dictates the core curriculum, the admission standards, and the maximum number of credit hours at publicly assisted colleges and universities. The Texas Higher Education Coordinating Board was put in charge of enforcing these statutes, which affect every student at a public college or university in the state.

Texas Sunset Act

With the passage of the Texas Sunset Act by the Sixty-fifth Legislature in 1977, Texas established a procedure for reviewing the existence of all statutory boards, commissions, and departments—except colleges and universities—on a periodic basis. More than 150 agencies and advisory committees are included, and new ones are added as they are created. These **sunset reviews** are conducted by a twelve-member Sunset Advisory Commission composed of five senators and five representatives appointed by their respective presiding officers, who also appoint two citizen members. The chairmanship rotates between the House and the Senate every two years. The Sunset Commission can determine the list of agencies to be reviewed before the beginning of each regular legislative session as long as all agencies are evaluated within a twelve-year period. The agencies must submit self-evaluation reports, and the Sunset Commission coordinates its information gathering with other agencies that monitor state agencies on a regular basis, such as the Legislative Budget Board, legislative committees, and the offices of the state auditor, governor, and comptroller. Following sunset review, the legislature must explicitly vote to continue an agency, and may reorganize it or force it to modify its administrative rules and procedures.

By the time of the 2011 legislative session, the sunset process had resulted in the following:

- **Creating a new structure for workers' compensation**
- **Strengthening of the Public Utility Commission's authority to oversee the Electric Reliability Council of Texas**
- **Public membership on most state boards and more public participation**
- **Stronger prohibitions against conflicts of interest**
- **Improved enforcement processes**

- Elimination of overlap and duplication by abolishing twenty-three agencies and transferring their functions
- Outright abolition of thirty-five agencies
- Consolidation of twelve agencies
- About $784 million in savings and increased revenues to the state since the inception of the process[8]

The Sunset Commission's 2010–2011 agenda included a mixed bag of twenty-eight agencies cutting across the functional areas of government. The most significant recommendations were elimination of the Texas Railroad Commission and the creation of a Texas Oil and Gas Commission, with a single elected commissioner, and strong recommendations to strengthen the Texas Commission on Environmental Quality's enforcement practices. The twenty-five reviews scheduled for 2012–2013 include the Health and Human Services Commission, the Lottery Commission, the Board of Pardons and Paroles, and the Public Utility Commission.

How Much Accountability to the Public?

One might easily assume that the general public has no control over bureaucrats. However, a citizen can take measures to ensure effective and honest bureaucratic performance.

Elective Accountability

American government is based on the premise that it will be accountable to the people it governs. If accountability cannot be achieved directly—all citizens of a political division meeting to vote directly on laws and policies—theoretically, it can be achieved through elected representatives who meet in government and report back to their citizen-constituents. But voters encounter difficulty when they try to make intelligent decisions regarding the multitude of names on the long ballot in Texas. Long ballots tend to lead to confusion, not accountability. Additionally, the vastness of the bureaucracy and the reality that incumbents can usually count on being re-elected simply because the voters recognize their names mean that the elective process has become an unsatisfactory method of ensuring responsible administrative action. In view of these problems, Texas citizens need some way to check on the activities of particular administrators and agencies on which public attention, for whatever reason, is focused. Until recently, however, there has been no easy way to do this.

Open Records and Meetings

Under the Texas Open Records Act, originally passed in 1973, the public, including the media, has access to a wide variety of official records and to most public meetings of state and local agencies. The importance of this access in a democracy is reinforced by the second quotation opening this chapter. Sometimes called the **Sunshine Law** because it forces agencies to shed light on their deliberations and procedures, this act is seen as a way to prevent or expose bureaucratic ineptitude, corruption, and unnecessary secrecy. An agency that denies access to

information that is listed as an open record in the statute may have to defend its actions to the attorney general, and even in court.

The 1987 Open Meetings Act strengthened public access to information by requiring government bodies to certify that discussions held in executive sessions were legal or to tape-record closed meetings. Closed meetings are permitted when sensitive issues, such as real-estate transactions or personnel actions, are under consideration, but the agency must post an agenda in advance and submit it to the secretary of state, including what items will be discussed in closed session. Since 1981, the legislature has also required state agencies to write rules and regulations in understandable language. In recent years, the Texas Open Records Act has been frequently amended to permit exceptions. For example, many search committees looking for city managers, executive directors of agencies, and college presidents were being foiled by premature disclosure of the names of individuals under consideration and sought some protection from the act.

In 1999, the legislature strengthened open meetings provisions by placing firm restrictions on staff briefings that could be made before governing bodies at the state and local level. Two new types of exceptions emerged from the Seventy-sixth Legislature—economic development and utilities deregulation—but these were seen as protections on behalf of the public when a government was in a competitive situation.[9] That is, while Texas government became even more open following the 1999 session, governments were allowed to have closed meetings when competitive issues were the topic of discussion.

In 2005, the Seventy-ninth Legislature mandated that not only public officials but also members of all boards, including local ones, receive training in open government. The second quotation at the beginning of this chapter is drawn from the materials made available to those required to receive training. The formats include online instruction, DVDs, and organized classes. In 2011, the legislature tinkered with the Sunshine Law, restricting some information and opening other information to the public.[10]

Whistle-Blower Protection

The 1983 legislature passed an act affording job security to state employees who spot illegal or unethical conduct in their agencies and report it to appropriate officials. The national government established the precedent for whistle-blower legislation in 1978. The term *whistle-blower* comes from the fact that employees who report illegal acts are "blowing the whistle" on someone. The implementation of this act has not been promising. Even settlements mandated by the courts have tended to be delayed as long as a decade.

Is There Accountability?

The passage of sunshine and sunset laws in recent years has enabled the public, the press, and the legislature to harness the worst excesses of bureaucracy more successfully. In addition, routine audits often turn up minor violations, a forceful governor or attorney general can "shake up" a state agency, and the state budget can be a means of putting a damper on any agency that seems to be getting out of hand. Top-level officials also have to file financial disclosure forms as a check on potential conflicts of interest. These devices help guard against serious wrongdoing on the part of state officials and help ensure accountability.

Serious wrongdoing is not usually the problem. Much more frequently, we see indifference or occasional incompetence. How can we minimize the

indifference and incompetence that citizens sometimes encounter in state, federal, or local agencies? How can we reduce the amount of time-consuming red tape? There seem to be few formal means of ensuring that bureaucratic dealings with citizens are competent, polite, and thorough—until citizen reaction demands them. What little political attention is given to the administrative state is aimed primarily at the federal bureaucracy rather than at state or local bureaucracies. Yet, public managers may have come up with their own solution: the Citizens as Customers Movement. This approach requires that public employees treat citizens as customers in the same way that a business treats its customers as valuable resources. State and local governments also have implemented Raising the Bar campaigns to signify a commitment to higher standards of service. Their ability to meet those standards may be hampered severely by the budget slashes for 2012 and 2013.

Thus, we find that elected officials, with the assistance of the media, can ensure a fair measure of bureaucratic accountability and that they continue to seek ways to control the appointed bureaucracy. The current emphasis on government performance is merely the latest of these ways.

Suggested Reforms

The Texas administrative structure is difficult for the average individual to understand. Overhauling it is not easy because a major package of constitutional amendments and statutes would be required. Perhaps the most important suggestion is also the most obvious: to create a cabinet-type government. The 200-plus total agencies could be consolidated into a series of executive departments reporting to the governor. The only elected executives would be the governor and the lieutenant governor. The new departments might include the following:

- **Public and Higher Education**
- **Health and Human Services**
- **Natural Resources**
- **Highways and Public Transportation**
- **Public Safety and Criminal Justice**
- **Commerce and Economic Development**
- **Administrative Services**
- **Professional and Occupational Licensing**

This scheme, similar to the organization of the national government, would still leave the biggest regulatory commissions as independent agencies—the Texas Railroad Commission and the Public Utility Commission, for example.

The likelihood of such a sweeping change is almost zero. However, minor steps toward consolidation have occurred, most noticeably in the creation of a single office responsible to the governor to oversee health and human service activities. Ironically, a cabinet system was advocated by liberals for many years, but their enthusiasm has waned during the administration of Governor Rick Perry, who has served longer than any other governor.

Summary

A combination of the Industrial Revolution, public reaction against a pseudo laissez faire philosophy and social Darwinism, urbanization and the development of a mass society, and the enormous amount of federal funds that have been made available to the states in the past few decades have contributed to the rise of big government. Big government means big bureaucracy: the administrative state. The Texas bureaucracy, like administrations everywhere, has had to develop its own sources of political support and power. Having done so, it influences the development of state policy not only in the day-to-day execution of the state's laws, but also through providing information and influencing legislation.

A major problem, then, is to harness the powerful state administration, a task that is far from easy. Two measures, however—the Open Records Act and the Sunset Act—have made strides in the direction of giving Texas citizens a responsible bureaucracy. Since 1991, the combined efforts of the governor, the comptroller, and the legislative leadership to insist on a budget based on planning and on quantitative measures of agency performance—the Texas Performance Review—have been another important step. Traditional controls, such as the legislative audit and the legislature's power to investigate agency activities also help promote accountability on the part of the administration.

Nevertheless, major problems continue. The fragmented structure of the state's administration—200 agencies, including four department heads and a commission and a board that are completely independent of the governor—permits the bureaucracy considerable flexibility in carrying out legislative mandates according to its own priorities. It also makes controversial programs easier to attack if they are housed in small agencies.

For the present, the growth of government—prompted by public demand for services, business demands for programs, and bureaucratic survival tactics—seems destined to continue in a hodgepodge fashion. On the one hand, such a system means that citizens can gain access to their government through many points. On the other hand, it means that it is very difficult to tell "who's in charge here" and to place responsibility.

To some extent, then, the state's bureaucracy represents the proverbial twin horns of a dilemma. The goal of representativeness may be achieved by the administrative state in Texas; the goal of responsiveness may not be. Yet democratic theory demands that government not only represent its many constituents, but also respond to their needs.

Chapters 12 through 14 cover the state budget and major policy issues in Texas. Together they provide a picture of state-elected officials and state administration in action.

Glossary Terms

administrative discretion

bureaucracy

civil service system

clientele groups

hierarchy

sunset review

Sunshine Law

9

The Judiciary

Nothing can contribute so much to [the judges'] firmness and independence as permanency in office.

ALEXANDER HAMILTON, *FEDERALIST* 78, 1787

If I asked you to design a criminal justice system and you came up with one like we have here in Texas, we'd have to commit you to Austin State Hospital because you'd be a danger to yourself and society.

JIM MATTOX, ATTORNEY GENERAL OF TEXAS, 1988

The law, in its majestic impartiality, forbids the rich as well as the poor to sleep under bridges, to beg in the streets, and to steal bread.

ANATOLE FRANCE (JACQUES THIBAULT), FRENCH NOBEL PRIZE WINNING AUTHOR, *LE LYS ROUGE*, 1894

OBJECTIVES

After reading this chapter, you should be able to

Discuss the judiciary as a political branch of government.

Describe the major players in the judicial system, including the central roles of the attorney general, the bar, and lawyers in the process.

Understand the structure of the Texas court system from the lowest courts to the two "supreme" courts.

Compare the roles of grand juries and trial juries.

Evaluate major issues in the Texas judiciary, including problems with crime, problems with judicial selection, and issues of equality in the administration of justice.

INTRODUCTION

A discussion of the **judiciary**—the system of courts, judges, lawyers, and other actors in the institutions of justice—brings up several problems for democratic theory. Judges are the arbiters of conflicts within society and the interpreters of the rules by which we govern ourselves. Many people think that judges should be able to hold themselves above the dirty struggles of the political process. As a consequence, there have always been those who followed Alexander Hamilton in arguing that judges should be as independent as possible from the democratic necessities of elections, interest groups, and money. Many other people have pointed out, however, that democracy requires important decision makers to be accountable to the public and therefore made to stand for election.

As a consequence, a democratic political system faces troubling questions: Are judges part of the political process or not? If they are, how can they be installed in office in a manner that ensures they will be fair and impartial but still accountable to the public? In Texas, the customary answer has been to come down firmly on the side of democracy and to make judges answerable to the people. It turns out, however, that when judges are treated like other politicians, they become vulnerable to the same suspicion that they are allowing private interests to corrupt their views on public affairs.

Furthermore, the importance of money in the judicial system has another disquieting aspect: It creates doubts as to whether the courts are fulfilling the democratic ideal that they provide equal justice to all. If access to legal representation is expensive, and if the outcome of trials depends on adequate representation, do poor people have a fair chance in a courtroom?

Also complicating the election of judges is that judicial elections are numerous—including judges from the supreme court all the way down to the Justice of the Peace—and they are "down ballot" elections that often draw little attention among average voters. As a result, when people come to the polls to vote on judicial elections, the judicial candidates are largely unknown to them, making informed voting much less frequent in judicial elections compared to higher-profile elected offices. Because of these issues, the Texas judiciary is a troubled democratic institution.

The first subject of this chapter is an examination of the political nature of judges, followed by a summary of the important features of the judicial branch of government in Texas. The focus then shifts to a consideration of the players in the state system of justice. The remainder of the chapter is devoted to discussions of some of the vexing problems facing the state judiciary from the perspective of democratic theory. The output of the judicial system—the substance of justice—is discussed in the next chapter.

The Myth of the Nonpolitical Judiciary

"There ought to be a law . . ."

This expression is sometimes heard in America and reflects the faith many of our citizens have in laws as solutions to social problems. When a law is enacted, Americans tend to believe that the problem has been solved and promptly forget about it. The fact that the many laws already on the books have not solved our society's problems does not seem to shake our faith that a few more will do the trick.

Hand in hand with this faith goes the American perception of **judges**—the government officials who preside over a courtroom and rule on the application of the laws—as men and women who are somehow "above" the political process. Professor Geoffrey C. Hazard, Jr., of Yale Law School describes this perception: "Scratch the average person's idea of what a judge should be and it's basically Solomon. If you had a benign father, that's probably what you envision. We demand more from them, we look for miracles from them. . . . It's romantic, emotional, unexamined, unadmitted, and almost undiscussable."[1]

Over the centuries, most judges in Texas and elsewhere have attempted to live up to the romantic ideal of the wise rule giver. They do so because they know that people are more likely to comply with the decisions of judges if those judges are perceived as nonpolitical. Judges wear black robes, are addressed as "Your Honor" in the courtroom, write opinions in a specialized language that is beyond the understanding of most citizens, and in general try to speak and act in a way that indicates they are not part of the messy business of governing.

This performance is not entirely insincere. In the long history of the development of our legal system, great jurists in England and the United States have developed—and are developing—neutral, impersonal criteria to use in making decisions. The hope is that a judge can become like a surgeon operating on a patient or a scientist examining evidence to support or contradict a hypothesis: impartial and incorruptible, above passion and prejudice. The ideal judge will rule purely on the basis of fairness and established principles. Common observation suggests that this ideal has some basis in reality and that judges are less moved by personal idiosyncrasy and outside influence than are legislators or governors.

But the notion that what judges do is not political is a well-polished myth. Whenever judges apply a statute, and especially when they interpret a constitution, they make choices among competing rules, individuals, and groups. Even deciding not to decide a case is a decision. When a judge makes a decision, somebody wins and somebody loses. Those somebodies can be very large groups of people who win or lose a great deal and care intensely about the outcome of the decision. As a result, the coalitions of interests that tend to oppose each other in political parties also tend to adopt differing philosophies of judicial interpretation. Republican judges, in perfectly good faith, usually interpret words so as to favor the interests displayed in Table 4-2 in Chapter 4. Democratic judges, also in good faith, generally interpret words so as to favor a conflicting set of interests. Therefore, judges make laws, and the constitution, in the process of interpretation. This crucial activity of interpretation makes Texas judges, and especially members of the supreme court and court of criminal appeals, central components of the state's political system.

Former Texas Judge W. A. Morrison, a justice of the Texas Court of Criminal Appeals, made no bones about his personal contribution to the state's system of laws. "I have engrafted into the law of this great state my own personal philosophy," he stated. Claiming that every appellate judge does much the same thing, he explained that during his first day on the bench as a young man, the other two judges—both of whom were "at least seventy years old"—could not agree on more than a dozen cases, and so Morrison cast the deciding vote in each one. He attributed his having "engrafted" his personal philosophy into the state's law to a greater degree than most other judges to the fact that he came to the bench early in life and remained longer than most.[2] More recently, Texas District Judge John Dietz clarified the political aspect of his job: "I redistribute wealth. I decide whether someone can keep theirs or [must] give it to someone else."[3]

The fact that Texas judges are elected makes the political nature of their work even more obvious. As one state jurist proclaimed in the early 1970s, "This job is more politics than law; there's no two ways about it. Hell, you can have all kinds of dandy ideas, but if you don't get yourself elected, you can sell your ideas on a corner somewhere. Politics isn't a dirty word in my mouth."[4]

Although judges from the rival political parties frequently split in judicial philosophy, they can also strongly disagree with others of the same party in their analysis of individual cases. A case in point is a verbal brawl that erupted in the Texas Supreme Court in 2000 over the proper interpretation of a law requiring a doctor to notify the parents of a girl under the age of eighteen before performing an abortion on her.[5] All nine of the justices were Republicans, but the case reveals the important differences over judicial principles that can exist between nominal allies.

In 1999, a law requiring "parental notification" was enacted and signed by Republican Governor George W. Bush. Mindful of federal courts' history of voiding state antiabortion laws, however, the legislature had put in a "judicial bypass" clause, allowing an underage girl to get an abortion without informing her parents if she could convince a state judge that she met certain criteria. Among the criteria were that she was mature and well informed. In early 2000, a pregnant teenager ("Jane Doe" in court discussions) had asked a judge to give her a judicial bypass and had been turned down. She appealed, and the problem quickly landed on the docket of the state's highest civil court.

The case brought up important questions of interpretation. What did "mature" and "well informed" mean when applied to a teenager? Had the

legislature intended to make judicial bypass a relatively easy and common process or something difficult and rare? By a six-to-three vote, in March 2000, the Court ruled that the legislature had intended the criteria to be relatively easy to meet and, overruling the lower appeals court, granted permission to "Jane Doe" to have an abortion.

Although all nine justices were members of the same party, the partisan unanimity masked an ideological divide. The three dissenters expressed their outrage. "The plain fact is that the statute was enacted to protect parents' right to involve themselves in their children's decisions and to encourage that involvement, as well as to discourage teen-age pregnancy and abortion," fumed Justice Nathan Hecht. "The court not only ignores these purposes, it has done what it can to defeat them." The majority's "utter disregard" for legislative intent was "an insult to those legislators personally, to the office they hold, and to the separation of powers between the two branches of government." No less annoyed, Justice Priscilla Owen charged that the majority had "manufactured reasons to justify its action" and "acted irresponsibly." (A year later, after President Bush had nominated her to be a federal judge, this allegedly "extremist" antiabortion opinion caused Democrats in the U.S. Senate to filibuster against Owen's confirmation. She was not finally confirmed until 2005.) Justice Gregg Abbott accused the majority of practicing "interpretive hand-wringing."

In response, several members of the majority criticized Hecht's "explosive rhetoric," accusing him of having "succumbed to passion." To interpret the law as the dissenters urged, argued Justice Alberto Gonzales (later to be appointed U.S. Attorney General by President Bush), would be to misunderstand the new law and "would be an unconscionable act of judicial activism."

In this one episode, the true nature of the judiciary stood revealed. Fair-minded or not, judges bring as many ideological commitments to their work as do legislators or executives. They have no Olympian detachment from the issues they decide. They are politicians in black robes. Similar questions will doubtless arise regarding the 2011 legislative law requiring women to receive a sonogram of their fetus and then wait at least a day before an abortion can be performed. So the challenges of judicial interpretation continue.

The Players in the System of Justice

The judiciary is part of an entire system that attempts to interpret and apply society's laws. A summary of the parts of this system, and some of its subject matter, follows.

The Attorney General (AG)

The attorney general is an independently elected executive (see Chapter 8) who has important functions within the judicial system. Indeed, although the governor may be the most important single politician in Texas, the attorney general is more directly relevant to the judicial functions of the state. As Texas's chief lawyer, the attorney general (helped by many assistant AGs) represents state agencies when they sue a private individual or another agency or when they are sued. The AG also represents the state as a whole when it becomes involved in the federal courts.

In addition, the AG has a highly significant, if somewhat informal, power: the authority to issue **advisory opinions.** The constitution established the attorney general not only as Texas's chief legal officer, but also as legal adviser to the governor and other state officials. The legislature later expanded the scope of the AG's advisory activity. Out of this expansion has arisen the now firmly established practice that the legislature, agencies of the executive branch, and local governments will seek advice on the constitutionality of proposals, rules, procedures, and statutes. In 2010, Greg Abbott handed down seventy-five "Attorney General's Opinions" dealing with the constitutionality of proposed government laws or actions, and his office supplied various state and local governments with 19,592 Open Record Letter Rulings, answering their requests for advice on whether to release specific information.[6] Rather than filing a court action that is expensive and time consuming, Texas officials who go to the attorney general obtain a ruling on disputed constitutional issues in a relatively brief period of time and at almost no expense. The Texas judiciary and virtually everyone else in the state have come to accept these rulings, albeit sometimes with a good deal of grumbling.

The most publicized attorney general's ruling of modern times, and perhaps in history, dealt with the divisive subject of affirmative action. For some years prior to 1996, the University of Texas Law School had been favoring African American and Latino applicants in its admissions process; that is, minority applicants were judged by a lower set of standards than were Anglo applicants. An Anglo woman, Cheryl Hopwood, had been turned down for admission to the law school despite the fact that her qualifications (grades and Law School Aptitude Test scores) were higher than those of some minority applicants who had been admitted. Hopwood sued in federal court. In 1996, the fifth circuit federal appeals court ruled in Hopwood's favor, deciding that such "reverse discrimination" against Anglos was unconstitutional.[7]

The federal fifth circuit court's decision was significant as it stood because it applied to the state's premier law school. Nevertheless, its scope did not extend to other schools. On February 5, 1997, however, Attorney General Dan Morales dismayed Texas's university community by issuing Letter Opinion 97-001, in which he decreed that the federal court's ruling had outlawed race as a consideration in any admissions process or financial aid decision at any public school. Affirmative action was therefore forbidden in all Texas public colleges.[8]

In 1999, Morales's successor as attorney general, John Cornyn, rescinded Morales's ruling, stating that colleges should wait and see how an appeal of the Hopwood decision to the U.S. Supreme Court turned out.[9] Although the Supreme Court declined to hear Texas's appeal, in 2003, it in effect reversed the Hopwood decision when it upheld the affirmative-action program at the University of Michigan. After seven years, therefore, Texas universities were again free to consider race in their admissions policies.[10]

While the issue of affirmative action has not been finally settled, the important point here is that in one of the most important and intensely conflict-ridden issues in Texas, policy has been set neither by the state legislature nor the governor, but by the attorney general. Such is the power of this institution in state government.

Lawyers

Law is a "profession," meaning that not just anyone can claim to be an attorney. Everyone who practices law for money must have passed the state bar examination and received a license; the overwhelming majority of licensed lawyers

have also attended law school. In 2010–2011, the state was home to 78,844 licensed attorneys. Although most lawyers are White males, the bar is rapidly becoming more diverse in ethnic and gender background. In 2010, 33 percent of Texas lawyers were women, 5 percent were African American, and 8 percent were Latino/Hispanic.[11]

The State Bar of Texas

All lawyers who practice within the state are required to maintain membership in the State Bar and pay annual dues. The State Bar occupies a unique position: It is an agency of government, a professional organization, and an influential interest group active in state politics.

The Court System

The structure of the Texas court system is essentially the same today as it was under the republic of Texas. The rigidity of the structure, prescribed by the Constitution, has led to the development, out of necessity, of one of the most complex and fragmented judicial systems of all the states.[12]

In 1991, the Texas Research League opened its study of the state's court system with the words, "The Texas judiciary is in disarray with the courts in varying parts of the state going their own way at their own pace. . . . Texas does not have a court *system* in the real sense of the word."[13] This league has not been the only reformers' panel to be dismayed by the Texas court system. As the chapter-opening quotation from former Attorney General Jim Mattox suggests, almost anyone who has looked closely at the state judicial system has concluded that its tangled organization prevents it from functioning efficiently. Critics complain about the duplication of jurisdiction between types of courts, about the fact that not all courts keep records of their proceedings, about the fact that a single court may both try cases and hear appeals, and about the lack of standardization within the system, so that the jurisdiction of the sundry types of courts varies from county to county. Whether it functions well or badly, however, the court system does function.

The following sections present a brief description of the activities of Texas's 3,378 judges from its lowest to its highest levels (see Figure 9-1).[14]

Municipal Courts

City courts are authorized by the state constitution and by state laws to handle minor criminal matters involving a fine of no more than $500 with no possibility of imprisonment (Class C misdemeanors), where they have **concurrent jurisdiction** with justice courts. They also have **exclusive jurisdiction** over municipal ordinances and can impose fines of up to $2,500. Municipal courts have no **civil jurisdiction** and deal mainly with violations of traffic laws. They generally do not keep records of trials. In fiscal 2010, there were 1,500 municipal court judges in 917 cities, who disposed of 6,852,239 cases, a decline of 1.4 percent from the previous year.

Qualifications for municipal judges are decreed by the governing body of the city. Most municipal judges are appointed by the governing body, although

COURT STRUCTURE OF TEXAS

SEPTEMBER 1, 2010

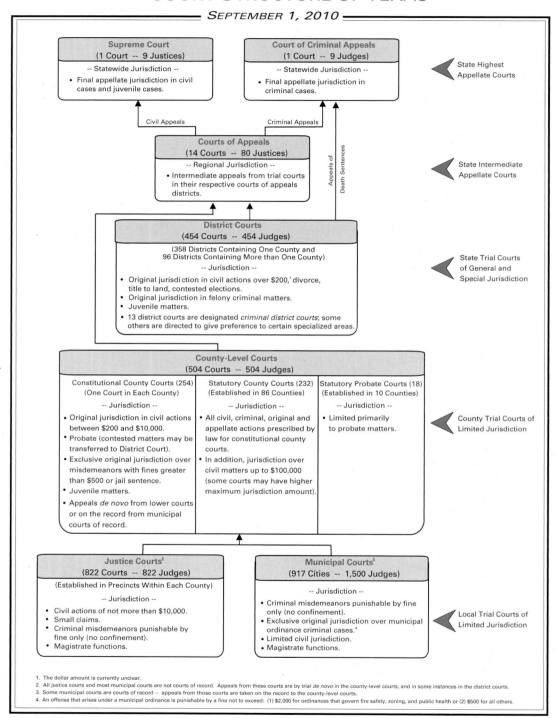

FIGURE 9-1 Court Structure of Texas

SOURCE: http://www.courts.state.tx.us/pubs/AR2010/jud_branch/1-court-structure-chart.pdf.

in a few cities, they are chosen in nonpartisan elections. Terms of office are usually two years. Their salaries are paid entirely by the city and are highly variable.

Justice Courts

Until recently known as "Justice of the Peace" (JP) courts, these are **original trial courts** with both civil and **criminal jurisdiction.** The JP courts deal with misdemeanor criminal cases when the potential punishment is only a fine. They have exclusive jurisdiction over civil cases where the amount in controversy is $200 or less and concurrent jurisdiction with both county and district courts when the amount in controversy is between $200 and $5,000. Their judges preside over small claims courts, act as notaries public, and, like other Texas judges, are authorized to perform marriages. In all but the largest counties, they may function as coroners, and in this role, they may be required to certify cause of death, despite the fact that few if any justices have any medical training. In fact, there are no constitutional or statutory qualifications for justice court judges, who may therefore come from any background. As a result, only about 6 percent of Texas's justice court judges are lawyers.

Justice court judges are elected by the voters of the precinct and, like other county officials, serve for four years. Salaries are set by county commissioners, and can range from practically nothing to more than $60,000 per year depending on the size of the precinct and the volume of activity. Texas's 821 justice courts disposed of 2,810,369 cases in 2010, nearly two-thirds of which were traffic tickets.

County Courts

The Texas Constitution requires each county to have a *court of record*—that is, a court where a complete transcript is made of each case. Judges of these 254 "constitutional" courts need not be lawyers, but only "well-informed in the law of the state." They are elected for four-year terms, and their salaries are paid by the counties and are highly variable. County court judges in urban areas can be paid more than $100,000 per year. At the other end of the scale, judges in rural counties can bring home closer to $10,000. Vacancies are filled by appointments made by the county commissioners' court. Not all constitutional county courts exercise judicial functions. In large counties, the constitutional county judge may devote full time to the administration of county government.

When county courts do exercise judicial functions, they have both original and **appellate jurisdiction** in civil and criminal cases. Their **original jurisdiction** extends to all criminal misdemeanors where the fine allowed exceeds $500 or a jail term may be imposed. County courts also hear appeals in criminal cases from justice and municipal courts. In civil matters, constitutional county courts have concurrent jurisdiction with justice courts when the amount in controversy is between $200 and $5,000.

The volume of cases in approximately thirty of the state's larger counties has moved the legislature to establish a number of specialized county courts, with jurisdiction that varies according to the statute under which they were created. Some exercise jurisdiction in only civil, criminal, probate, or appellate matters, while others are in effect extra, generalist county courts. Judges for these 250 "statutory county courts" and "statutory probate courts" must

be attorneys. They are paid the same amount as the judges in the constitutional county courts.

Appellate jurisdiction from the decisions of county courts rests with the courts of appeals. County courts disposed of 769,348 criminal, civil, and juvenile cases in fiscal year 2010, a decline of 2.2 percent from the previous year.

State Trial Courts: The District Courts

In Texas, district courts are the principal trial courts. There were 454 of these busy courts as of 2010. Each has a numerical designation—for example, the 353rd District Court—and each court has one judge. Most district courts have both criminal and civil jurisdiction, but in the metropolitan areas, there is a tendency for each court to specialize in criminal, civil, or family law cases.

District court judges must be attorneys who are licensed to practice in the state and who have at least four years' experience as lawyers or judges prior to being elected to the district court bench. The basic salary of $125,000 paid by the state is supplemented by an additional sum in most counties. Terms are for four years, with all midterm vacancies filled by gubernatorial appointment.

Cases handled by district court judges are varied. The district courts usually have jurisdiction over felony criminal trials, divorce cases, suits over titles to land, election contests, and civil suits in which the amount in controversy is at least $200. They share some of their civil jurisdiction with county courts depending on the relevant state statute and the amount of money at issue. An additional complication for the allocation of jurisdiction is that at least one court in each county must be designated as the **juvenile court** to handle Texans younger than seventeen who are accused of crimes. These courts can be district, county courts at law, or constitutional county courts.

District court cases are appealed to a court of appeals, except for death-penalty criminal cases, where appeal is made directly to the court of criminal appeals. In fiscal year 2010, district courts disposed of 547,355 civil, 277,201 criminal, and 31,514 juvenile cases.

Intermediate State Appellate Courts: The Courts of Appeals

The courts of appeals have intermediate civil and criminal appellate jurisdiction. Unlike the lower courts, appellate courts—the courts of appeals, the court of criminal appeals, and the supreme court—are multi-judge courts that operate without juries. Appellate courts consider only the written records of lower court proceedings and the arguments of counsel representing the parties involved.

Texas's fourteen courts of appeals, each of which is responsible for a geographical district, have from three to thirteen justices per court, for a total of eighty judges statewide. In each court, the justices may hear cases *en banc* (together) or in panels of three. All decisions are by majority vote. Justices are elected for staggered six-year terms and must have the same qualifications as justices of the state's supreme court: Each must be at least thirty-five years of age and have ten years' legal experience either as a practicing attorney or as a practicing attorney and judge of a court of record. Associate justices receive an annual salary of $145,000, and the chief justice, elected as such, receives $147,500.

Jurisdiction of the courts of appeals consists of civil cases appealed from district courts, county courts, and county courts at law and of criminal cases, except for capital murder, appealed from lower courts. These appeals courts both review

the decisions of lower court judges and evaluate the constitutionality of the statutes or ordinances on which the convictions are based. Decisions of the courts of appeals are usually final, but some may be reviewed by the court of criminal appeals or the Texas Supreme Court. The courts of appeals disposed of 11,201 criminal cases in fiscal year 2010, of which 49.4 percent were civil cases and 50.6 percent were criminal cases.

Highest State Appellate Courts

Texas and Oklahoma are the only states to have split their highest appellate jurisdiction between two courts: a **supreme court** that hears only civil cases and a **court of criminal appeals** for criminal cases. Each has responsibility not only for reviewing the decisions made by lower court trial judges, but also for interpreting and applying the state constitution. It is this last power of constitutional interpretation that makes these courts of vital political importance.

The Court of Criminal Appeals

This is the state's final appeals court in criminal matters, although in rare instances, its decisions may be appealed to the U.S. Supreme Court. It considers *writs of error,* filed by losing attorneys who contend that their trial judge made a mistake in applying Texas law and who wish to have the verdict overturned, and *writs of habeus corpus,* in which attorneys claim that a certain person has been unlawfully detained and should be released. In fiscal year 2010, this court disposed of 211 direct appeals, in the process writing 433 opinions. Those dispositions included a review of 19 death-penalty appeals, all of which affirmed the lower court sentences.

Qualifications for judges of the court of criminal appeals and the justices of the supreme court are the same as those for justices of the courts of appeals. The nine judges of the court of criminal appeals are elected on a statewide basis for six-year staggered terms, and the presiding judge runs for that position. Vacancies are filled by gubernatorial appointment. Cases are normally heard by a three-judge panel. The salary is $150,000 per year, and the presiding judge receives $152,500.

The Supreme Court

Like its counterpart at the national level, the Texas Supreme Court is the most prestigious court in the system. Unlike its national counterpart, it hears only appeals from civil and juvenile cases.

Qualifications for supreme court justices are the same as those for the judges of the courts of appeals and the court of criminal appeals. There are nine justices on the bench, including a chief justice who campaigns for election as such. All are elected for six-year staggered terms, with three justices elected every two years. Salaries are the same as those for the judges of the court of criminal appeals.

The supreme court has no authority in criminal cases. Its original jurisdiction is limited, and most cases that it hears are on appeal from the courts of appeals. Its caseload is somewhat lighter than the caseloads of other state courts; it disposed of only 110 cases in fiscal year 2010, writing 118 opinions in the process.

However, the supreme court also performs other important functions. It is empowered to issue *writs of mandamus*—orders to corporations or persons, including judges and state officials other than the governor, to perform certain acts. Like the court of criminal appeals, it spends much of its time considering

applications for *writs of error*, which allege that the courts of appeals have ruled wrongfully on a point of law. It conducts proceedings for removal of judges and makes administrative rules for all civil courts in the state. Thus, the court "acted upon" 2,418 matters in fiscal 2010.

The supreme court also plays a unique role within the legal profession in Texas. It holds the power of approval for new schools of law; it appoints the Board of Law Examiners, which prepares the bar examination; it determines who has passed the examination; and it certifies the successful applicants as being entitled to practice law in Texas.

Juries

Ordinary citizens have an important part to play in the judicial system. There are two institutions that temporarily recruit Texans from their jobs and pastimes to participate in the functioning of the courts.

Grand Juries

Grand juries meet in the seat of each county and are convened as needed. Grand jurors are chosen from a list prepared by a panel of jury commissioners—three to five persons appointed by the district judge. From this list, the judge selects twelve persons who sit for a term, usually of three months' duration. Grand jurors consider the material submitted by prosecutors to determine whether sufficient evidence exists to issue a formal **indictment,** that is, an official accusation.

Normally, the cases considered are alleged **felonies**—serious crimes. Occasionally, persons are indicted for **misdemeanors**—minor crimes—as was Speaker of the House of Representatives Gib Lewis in December 1990. In

Citizenship Pays Better Now

Although it is the duty of every citizen to help run the state judicial system by serving on juries, the government recognizes that time is money, and that therefore it is appropriate to pay jurors for their participation. Nevertheless, until 2005, jurors were reimbursed at the rate of only $6 a day, an amount that often could not even compensate them for the price of their lunches. A 2003 study on jury participation rates reported that only 19 percent of those summoned to jury duty in Dallas and Houston actually showed up, and it argued that the low pay was a major reason for the cities' inability to motivate those called to serve.

Spurred by the report, and urged to action by some of the state's prominent judges and attorneys, the 2005 state legislature upped jurors' pay for the first time since 1954. As of January 1, 2006, jurors still receive $6 for the first day of work but are paid $40 for each subsequent day.

Source: Steve Quinn, "Texas Jurors Getting $34-a-Day Raise," *Denton Record-Chronicle,* December 30, 2005, A2.

Texas, grand juries are frequently used to investigate such problems as drug trafficking within the community, increasing crime rates, alleged misconduct by public officials, and other subjects. Former U.S. House majority leader Tom DeLay was convicted of a felony in a money-laundering campaign finance scheme in violation of Texas law on November 24, 2010.

Trial Juries

Trial juries make actual decisions about truth and falsehood, guilt and innocence. Under Texas law, defendants in civil cases and anyone charged with a crime may demand a jury trial. Although this right is frequently waived, thousands of such trials take place within the state every year. Lower court juries consist of six people, and district court juries have twelve members. The call to duty on a trial jury is determined through the use of a jury wheel, a list generated from the county voter registration, and driver's license and state identification card lists.

Police

The state maintains an extensive organization primarily for the enforcement of criminal law. In addition to the judiciary and various planning and policy-making bodies, Texas has about 55,000 law enforcement officers staffing state and local police agencies. Principal among these is the Texas Department of Public Safety (DPS). The DPS, with headquarters in Austin, employed 37,603 commissioned officers in 2009.[15] It is one of only eight state police agencies across the nation empowered to conduct criminal investigations. The other law enforcement officers are employees of the 254 county sheriff's departments and more than 1,000 local police departments. With so many law enforcement officials working for various agencies, the coordination and cooperation among agencies is complex. Modern technology has helped coordinate law enforcement, but challenges remain.

Removal and Reprimand of Lawyers and Judges

The Texas State Bar is authorized by the legislature to reprimand or disbar any practicing attorney in the state for fraudulent, dishonest, or unethical conduct. Grievance committees have been established in each congressional district to hear complaints and to act against offending attorneys. In practice, however, reprimand and disbarment are uncommon and usually occur only after the offending lawyer has been convicted on some serious charge.

District and appellate court judges may be removed from the bench by impeachment after a vote of two-thirds majority of the legislature. District judges may also be removed by the Texas Supreme Court, and lower court judges may be removed by action of a district court. A 1965 constitutional amendment established the Texas State Commission on Judicial Conduct to hear complaints against any judge in the state and to censure, reprimand, or recommend removal by the Texas Supreme Court. But again, as with the disbarment of lawyers, punishment of judges is a rare occurrence.

Issues Facing the Texas Judiciary

Too much crime, problems with the methods of selecting judges, and persistent issues of equality in the justice system remain as concerns for the Texas judicial system.

Too Much Crime, Too Many Criminals

Even if the Texas court system were perfectly organized, it would still be having major problems. There are simply too many accused criminals being arrested for any system to handle. From 1982 to 1992, the state's crime rate increased 12 percent so that its citizens suffered 44,583 reported robberies, 9,424 reported rapes, 86,196 reported aggravated assaults, and 2,239 reported murders in the last of those years.[16] In the early 1990s, however, the crime rate began to decline and continued to fall through the decade. It remained essentially level through the first decade of the new millennium, and remained below its 1992 level. Nevertheless, even with the dramatically lowered crime rate, the police still made 1,205,202 arrests in 2009.[17]

Further, while the crime rate as a whole was moderating, the number of offenses by juveniles—especially of a violent nature—remained dismayingly high. Although the growth in juvenile violence seems to have leveled off after the mid-1990s, the number of juvenile arrests remains alarmingly high, with 128,654 juvenile arrests in 2009, including 55 for murder.

The high levels of street crime, leading to large numbers of arrests, have swamped the courts, making Texas's 3,378 judges, the most of any state, still not enough. Not only are the courts dangerously overcrowded, but so also are the prisons. On January 1, 2010, Texas prisons held 171,249 inmates. This actually represented a decline of 1,257 prisoners from the previous year. After considering spending more than $2 billion to build more prisons to accommodate rising populations of inmates, Texas opted instead to develop residential and community-based treatment programs at a fraction of the cost. With heavy financial pressure on state finances, it appears likely that Texas, like other states, may seek to find ways to lower prison populations to achieve cost savings.[18] This new strategy reflects a change from the "lock 'em up and throw away the key" view that has often dominated Texas politics, but Texas still has the largest prison population of any state, including California, which has a population of 12 million more people than does Texas.

Given the impossible prison situation, judges do what they can to keep the system functioning by accepting **plea bargains.** A defendant pleads guilty to a lesser charge—say, manslaughter instead of murder—and receives a lesser penalty (less time in prison or a probated sentence), and a trial is avoided. More than nine of ten criminal trials in Texas end in a plea bargain.[19] Because a plea bargain puts the criminal back on the streets quickly, it does almost nothing to make society safer. Ordinary citizens are often appalled at the swiftness with which violent criminals are recycled into their neighborhoods, but the courts cannot handle the twin problems of a crushing caseload and overstuffed prisons in any other way.

And so, despite the somewhat lower crime rate it has enjoyed over the past decade, Texas still suffers from a plague of criminals. As a result, its judicial system continues to deal unsuccessfully with an impossibly large workload.

LONE STAR MEDIA
Misleading Court System Images

Oftentimes citizens are misled regarding the normal process for disposing of a court case. Media images suggest that most cases that are brought end up in trial. If one watches tru-TV (formerly Court TV), one can see high-profile criminal cases and civil trials (such as celebrity divorces) on television virtually twenty-four hours a day. And legal dramas from the classic *Perry Mason* series through more recent series such as *Boston Legal* or *Law and Order* suggest that most lawyers spend a great deal of their time arguing cases before juries. These media images are at nearly complete variance with the reality of Texas court procedures. Trials are time consuming, expensive, and risky. Lawyers, judges, and clients cannot predict the outcome of a trial. As a result, they have great incentives to *negotiate* the outcomes of their cases.

In criminal cases, as a result, those charged with crimes often will "cop a plea" so that they can be assured of their punishment rather than risking a harsher sentence that they might receive in a trial. This process might be to negotiate a long sentence rather than risking the death penalty such as that negotiated by Virginia Youngblood in a double homicide case where she agreed to serve twenty-five years in prison in exchange for a plea of guilty. Or it might be for settling a minor misdemeanor such as marijuana possession, as singer Willie Nelson negotiated in Hudspeth County in March 2011 when Nelson agreed to pay a $100 fine.

In civil cases, most cases are "settled" by attorneys for the two sides ultimately agreeing on terms before a trial takes place. Sometimes settlements are to simply agree on a "fair" settlement, as when an insurance company agrees to pay the costs of a traffic accident that may involve hospital costs in addition to the damages to an automobile. Other times, settlements are to end a long process and to avoid additional negative publicity, as when a clergy member has been charged with sexual assault.

In any case, the sensational trials that gain headlines and dramatic media coverage are the exception to the outcomes of legal cases rather than the rule.

While media portrayals depict criminal cases as being settled in trials, most cases are settled by plea bargains. Here, a lawyer discusses a plea offer with his client.

© 2011 Halfdark/Jupiterimages Corporation.

SOURCES: Matt Peterson, "Woman Pleads Guilty in 2009 Murders of Addison Mom, Her 10-Year-Old Daughter," *Dallas Morning News*, April 7, 2011; Pete Mongillo, "Willie Nelson Offered a Plea Deal in Pot Case," *Austin American-Statesman*, March 25, 2011; Abe Levy, "Three Catholic Groups Settle Case," *San Antonio Express-News*, January 11, 2011.

Judicial Selection

The job of a judge is an inherently ambiguous one in a democratic society. Many people believe, with Alexander Hamilton, that judges serve society best if they are *independent*—that is, if they are at least partly insulated from outside pressures. The best way to insulate judges is to have them appointed for life. Yet democratic theory requires that all public officials be *accountable* to the public, which would seem to demand that they all be subject to frequent review through regularly scheduled elections. Although some scholars have tried to argue that judges should be both independent and accountable, the two concepts are inherently contradictory.[20]

In practice, various levels of government have tried to compromise the two desirable but incompatible goals in different ways. At the federal level, judges are appointed by the president and serve for life, whereas in many states, including Texas, their jobs must be periodically ratified by the voters in partisan elections. Whatever compromise is chosen, it is never satisfying to everyone. National politicians frequently argue that federal judges must be made more accountable, but in Texas, there are always some prominent people arguing that state judges should be granted more independence. There is no easy answer to the dilemma of accountability versus independence; citizens must make up their own minds. Here is a discussion about two of the ways the argument has surfaced in Texas.

Partisan Elections?

In the fifty states, six methods are used to select judges:[21]

1. **Partisan elections. Judges are chosen in elections in which their party affiliation is listed on the ballot. This is the system employed in Texas and fourteen other states.**

2. **Nonpartisan election. Judges are chosen in elections, but no party labels appear on the ballot (nineteen states).**

3. **Appointment by legislatures. The state legislature chooses the judges, although the governor often influences its choices (four states).**

4. **Appointment by the governor. The chief executive appoints judges, sometimes with the consent of the legislature. Various interest groups—legal, political, and economic—attempt to influence the governor's choice (seven states).**

5. **Merit plan. The governor makes the appointments from a list submitted by a nominating commission. At regular intervals, judges must be approved by the voters in a referendum. If they fail to win a majority of the votes, they must leave office, and the governor appoints someone else (twenty-two states).**

6. **Combination. There are various combinations of the first five methods, meaning that judges at different levels in the same state may be chosen by different methods. Because a state may thus fall under more than one category, the sum of the numbers listed for each method of selection is sixty-seven rather than fifty.**

In Texas, all judges except municipal judges are popularly elected in a partisan contest. Trial court judges serve for four years before having to face the voters again, and appellate judges enjoy a six-year term. The consequence of the state's system is that judges are like other politicians in that, although they do not campaign all the time, they must always be thinking about the next election. Like other politicians, they are aware that what they do or say today may affect their chances for re-election tomorrow. Unlike other politicians, however, judges are supposed to be fair and impartial when trying cases and to pay no attention to the possible partisan consequences of their decisions.

This task is too difficult for imperfect humans. With the next election always just over the horizon, partisanship comes to permeate a courthouse, and the struggle for advantage may taint the quest for impartial decisions. After her defeat in the 1994 Republican landslide, Democratic District Judge Eileen O'Neill wrote a sad analysis of the impact of Texas's judicial electoral processes on its justice system:

> As the campaign season approaches at the courthouse, lines get drawn. Sitting judges join in the search for contenders for open, and sometimes occupied, benches. Judges become guarded in their comments to colleagues and suspicious of their staffs. . . . By November, most everyone belongs to a side, willingly or otherwise, with some perceived stake in the outcome.[22]

It would be placing too much faith in human self-restraint to expect justice to be blind under such circumstances.

People who want to change the way Texas chooses its judges argue that circumstances such as the one sketched by Judge O'Neill are unavoidable in a selection system that rests upon partisan elections. But others are less eager to throw out the democratic baby with the partisan bathwater. All systems have flaws, and the democratic appeal of partisan elections is strong. As David Willis, an adjunct law professor at the University of Houston, wrote in a defense of Texas's system:

> Judicial candidates, like everyone, have philosophical preferences. Choosing a partisan label suggests a whole cluster of attitudes toward the role of government in addressing social challenge. It is an inexact science, but why deprive us of this crucial information about a candidate?[23]

Scholarly research supports Professor Willis's point. Studies show that the most important factor in allowing citizens to predict how judges will decide cases is their political party. Republican judges tend to favor business and people with power and wealth; Democrats tend to favor labor unions, the poor, and social underdogs in general. In other words, Texas has the perfect system for allowing its citizens to select judges who share their ideologies.[24]

Moreover, as the findings summarized in the "Is Reform Needed?" box illustrate, there is no good evidence that a different system of choosing judges would produce a more honest system than the one Texas has now. An appointive or nonpartisan system might not create a better judiciary and would be less democratic.

Robed Debaters?

While some reformers are trying to make Texas judges less like other politicians, federal courts have been issuing rulings that must make them more like the others. Until July 2002, state judicial candidates were required to follow Canon 5(I) of the Texas Code of Judicial Conduct, which stated, "A judge or judicial candidate shall not make statements that indicate an opinion on any issue that may be subject to judicial interpretation by the office which is being sought or held. . . ." In other words, judicial candidates were forbidden to discuss the issues they might be required to decide.

In *Republican Party v. Minnesota*, however, the U.S. Supreme Court struck down a state restriction almost identical to the one in Texas. Writing for the five-to-four majority, Justice Antonin Scalia enunciated the principle that "We have never allowed the government to prohibit candidates from communicating relevant information to voters during an election." Two months later, the Texas Supreme Court issued a new code, which still prevents candidates from promising to decide a specific case in a specific manner but permits them to indicate a general attitude on a question that might come before their court.

In January 2006, the U.S. Supreme Court affirmed its *Minnesota* ruling. Later the same year, a federal appeals court issued another ruling about judicial campaigns, in which it held that the state of Kentucky could neither forbid candidates for judgeships to personally solicit campaign funds, nor prevent them from advertising their partisan affiliations.

The result of these federal court rulings will certainly be that judicial candidates will campaign on issues, personally ask for donations, and advertise their party membership more than ever. One can anticipate a future campaign in which candidates for the supreme court or court of criminal appeals debate each other on television.

Sources: David Rottman, "The State Courts in 2005: A Year of Living Dangerously," *The Book of the States*, vol. 38 (Lexington, Ky.: Council of State Governments, 2006), 238; Christy Hoppe, "Ruling Likely to Change Texas Judicial Elections," *Dallas Morning News*, June 28, 2002, A20; "Texas Judges Can Now Opine Publicly," *Austin American-Statesman*, August 23, 2002, B7; Adam Liptak, "Judges Can Solicit Election Funds, Court Rules," *Austin American-Statesman*, October 12, 2006, A19.

Is Justice for Sale?

The practice of electing judges is thus in line with democratic theory. When judges must run for office at periodic intervals, they are kept accountable to the people's wishes. However, there is a problem with elections, a problem common to all offices, but particularly troubling in regard to the judiciary. When judges have to run for office like other politicians, they also have to raise money like other politicians. When lawyers who practice in judges' courtrooms or others with a direct interest in the outcome of legal cases give judges campaign contributions, it raises the uncomfortable suspicion that those judges' court rulings might be affected by the money. Wealthy special interests may taint the administration of justice just as they deform the public policy made by other institutions.

Is Reform Needed?

I n 2001, political scientist Melinda Gann Hall published a systematic evaluation of the consequences of supreme court selection processes in the fifty states. Her conclusion was, "Court reformers underestimate the extent to which partisan elections have a tangible substantive component and overestimate the extent to which nonpartisan and retention races are insulated from partisan politics." In simpler language, state high court judges who are appointed are not, as a group, more independent from the political process than are judges who are elected in partisan races.

In short, the available evidence suggests that the way Texas chooses its judges is not an unusually bad way, and there is no reason to think that some other way would be better.

Sources: Melinda Gann Hall, "State Supreme Courts in American Democracy: Probing the Myths of Judicial Reform," *American Political Science Review*, vol. 95, no. 3 (June 2001), 326.

James Andrew Wynne, Jr., is a judge in the North Carolina Court of Appeals. The North Carolina judicial system is similar to the one in Texas, with partisan elections for almost all levels. In 2002, Judge Wynne used a vivid metaphor to summarize the uneasiness of those who suspect that justice may be for sale in such judicial systems. Suppose, he mused, that major-league baseball umpires had to run for office, and the players were allowed to contribute money to their campaigns: "Under that scenario, how can anyone have the confidence in the strike calls of an umpire if you know the pitcher contributed $10,000 to select that umpire to call the game?"[25] It is a fair question. Wealthy private interests may taint the administration of justice just as they deform the public policy made by other institutions. (Perhaps Judge Wynne's argument had some effect. Before the 2004 election, North Carolina instituted partial public financing of state judicial campaigns.)[26]

Texas, however, continues to require its judicial candidates to finance their election campaigns with private funds. Not surprisingly, one of the chief sources of campaign contributions to judicial candidates is the very lawyers who will be practicing in their courts if they win office. In 2003, for example, Texans for Public Justice (TPJ) analyzed the campaign finances of eighty-seven winning candidates for the intermediate courts of appeals. TPJ concluded that attorneys contributed 72 percent of the total funding for those successful races.[27] In a preliminary analysis of the funding of the re-election races of the five justices on the supreme court running for re-election in 2006, TPJ concluded that 51 percent of their total funding had come from attorneys and law firms.[28] It is difficult to imagine that judges would be able to forget the source of their campaign resources when arbitrating the cases of attorneys and groups that have supported them.

In an analysis of the decisions of the Ohio Supreme Court aimed at addressing this very question, reporters for the *New York Times* compared the behavior of those justices to the sources of the funds for their campaigns. They came to two conclusions. First, Ohio Supreme Court justices almost always failed to withdraw from hearing cases in which lawyers and interests who had contributed

Money and Justice

I t is not only in raising campaign funds that judges become beholden to attorneys who may practice in front of them. In 2005, the state Commission on Judicial Conduct rebuked Texas Supreme Court Justice Nathan Hecht for his vocal advocacy of Harriet Miers, President Bush's nominee to the U.S. Supreme Court. (Miers later withdrew her name from consideration.) Hecht objected to the official criticism and filed suit against the Commission, which meant, of course, that he had to hire lawyers. Hecht won his case, and the rebuke was withdrawn, but meanwhile he had amassed a debt of $340,000.

Not a wealthy man, Hecht could not pay his debt himself. Instead, he turned to his list of campaign contributors and asked for financial assistance. In 2007, the same lawyers who had helped get him into office gave him enough cash to pay his legal bills. Hecht would be superhumanly virtuous if he did not feel very grateful to his benefactors, both in and out of the courtroom.

Source: Chuck Lindell, "Proposals to Reimburse Justice Moot," *Austin American-Statesman*, March 21, 2007, B1.

to their campaigns appeared. Second, over the course of twelve years, supreme court justices voted in favor of those contributors 70 percent of the time.[29] There is no reason to think that Texas judges behave any differently.

Responding to the public perception that justice might be for sale, in 1995, the legislature passed the Judicial Campaign Fairness Act (JCFA). This legislation limited individual contributions to statewide judicial candidates to $5,000 each election and prohibited law firms from contributing more than $30,000 to individual supreme court candidates. Judicial candidates were also forbidden to accept more than a total of $300,000 from all political action committees.

Although the intent of the JCFA was clearly to stop the contamination of the Texas judiciary by money, events almost immediately proved it to be ineffective. In 1996, Texas Supreme Court Justice James A. Baker allowed an attorney with a case pending before him to participate in his fundraising efforts.[30] When journalists reported this obvious conflict of interest, the bad publicity forced Baker to withdraw from the case. His withdrawal solved the immediate concern about one questionable case, but it did not address the basic problem. As long as attorneys are allowed to raise campaign funds for judges and to contribute money themselves, there will be public doubts about the impartiality of the judiciary. The JCFA, while it was well intentioned, does not address this fundamental problem.

In 2000, two consumer-advocacy groups filed suit in federal court, arguing that when Texas allows judges to solicit campaign contributions from lawyers who may appear in their courts, the state violates its citizens' constitutional rights to fair trials. They lost the case, with U.S. District Judge James Nowlin writing, "The issue of limiting campaign contributions and/or potential contributions are questions for the citizens of Texas and their state representatives, not a federal court." Given this decision, if the Texas system of financing judicial elections is to be changed, the impetus must come from inside the state.[31]

As with elections to other offices, the suggestion is sometimes made that both the appearance and the reality of impropriety could be avoided if judicial

campaigns were publicly, as opposed to privately, financed (see Chapter 5). Public financing, it is argued, would permit judges to be held democratically accountable, yet would soften the impact of special interests. Former Chief Justice Tom Phillips of the Texas Supreme Court, for one, has advocated this change in the state's judicial elections. Phillips points out that no additional tax money need be used for this reform because judicial campaigns could be bankrolled using an existing $200 lawyer occupation tax that raises $10 million annually.[32] So far, however, this suggestion has found no support among lawmakers.

Equal Justice?

The dilemmas of too much crime and of judicial selection are not the only serious problems facing the Texas system of justice. The state has for some time been in the midst of another argument over the way it affords legal representation to poor people accused of crimes.

Before people are put in prison, they must be tried and convicted. Because one of the most important ideals of democracy is that everyone is equal before the law, Texans would like to think that all accused persons are treated fairly and impartially in this process. A well-functioning democracy features a judiciary that rigorously but fairly judges the guilt of everyone brought to trial. Nevertheless, there is substantial evidence that the Texas criminal justice system does not affect all citizens equally. It imposes severe burdens on the poor and, particularly, on

In this cartoon, Ben Sargent satirizes the fact that elected judges bow to the popular will of voters, and especially those who donate money to their campaigns, even when justice is compromised.

Courtesy of Ben Sargent.

members of ethnic minorities—the same groups who are at a disadvantage in other areas of politics. Legal fees are expensive—in 2007, the standard lawyer's fee was $300 per hour—and the system is so complex that accused people cannot defend themselves without extensive and expensive legal help.

The result is that the prisons, and death row, are full of poor people. Wealthier defendants can afford to hire attorneys to help them try to "beat the rap," and in any case, they are often offered plea bargains that allow them to stay out of prison. But until recently, Texas lacked a system of *public defenders* to provide free legal assistance to accused criminals who were too poor to pay a lawyer, except in the case of defendants who had been convicted of capital murder and sentenced to death. Judges, using county rather than state funds, appointed private attorneys to represent indigent defendants. Frequently, they were inexperienced or already busy with paying clients.

In 1999, journalist Debbie Nathan spent time observing the way county-appointed attorneys interacted with their indigent clients. Her summary had to be troubling to citizens who thought that the poor, too, should be entitled to competent legal counsel when they are accused of a crime:

> What I witnessed was low-grade pandemonium. Attorneys rushed into court, grabbed a file or two, and sat down for a quick read; this was their first and often most lengthy exposure to their new client's case. Confused-looking defendants, mostly Hispanic or African American, met their counsel amid a hubbub of other defendants, defendants' spouses, and defendants' squalling babies.[33]

Reformers argued that if justice was to be done, Texas should have a system of public defenders equal in number and experience to the public prosecutors. Without such procedures, the system inevitably discriminated against poor defendants, who tended to be minority citizens. For example, in 1993, the Texas Bar Foundation sponsored a study by the Spangenberg Group of the state's system of appointing attorneys for indigents accused of murder. The group's conclusions about Texas justice were consistent and unambiguous:

> In almost every county, the rate of compensation provided to court-appointed attorneys in capital cases is absurdly low . . . the quality of representation in these cases is uneven and . . . in some cases, the performance of counsel is extremely poor.[34]

If such deficient legal representation was common for citizens accused of murder, which is a high-profile crime, then the representation afforded people accused of lesser crimes must have been even worse. It stood to reason that defendants who received inferior public legal representation would be convicted more often, and be given harsher sentences, than defendants who could afford to hire private attorneys. Indeed, a study in the early 1990s concluded that a White person convicted of assault had a 30 percent chance of drawing a prison sentence, while a Hispanic with a similar record had a 66 percent chance and an African American had a 76 percent chance.[35]

In short, the reality of unequal justice was a challenge to the democratic ideal of the Texas judicial system. Responding to such persistent criticism of the way the state's legal system treated the poor, the 2001 legislature moved to make it more equitable. The Texas Fair Defense Act, sponsored by Senator Rodney Ellis

YOU ★ ★ DECIDE

At-Large or Single-Member District Elections?

State district judges in Texas are selected in **at-large elections.** All candidates receive their votes from the whole district, which, in a metropolitan area, is typically a county. Such elections tend to make it difficult for minorities to be elected. If, for example, a quarter of the population of a county is Hispanic, and there is more-or-less bloc voting by each ethnic group, then Hispanic candidates will be outvoted three to one every time. Although Hispanics represent 25 percent of the population in a given county, they will have 0 percent of the judges in that county.

Consequently, minority representatives almost always prefer single-member **district elections** to at-large elections. If the county is carved into a number of geographic districts, with each district electing a single judge, then (assuming that people of different ethnic groups tend to live in different areas) the proportion of judges from each group should be roughly proportional to that group's representation in the population of that county. Minority leaders, therefore, often argue that Texas should adopt a system of electing county judges in which all candidates run from single-member districts.

PRO	CON
▲ The 1965 Voting Rights Act forbids systematic discrimination against the voting rights of minorities. Because at-large districts make minority candidates unelectable, they are illegal.	▼ The Voting Rights Act forbids discrimination against *voters*. It does not guarantee that minority *candidates* must win.
▲ In many counties, the proportion of minority judges is far below the proportion of minority citizens in the county.	▼ The lack of minority judges is mainly caused by the lack of qualified minority attorneys. It is therefore not evidence of discrimination.
▲ Ever since 1994, very few minority judges have been elected in Texas. This fact is evidence that Anglo citizens refuse to vote for minority candidates.	▼ The lack of minority success at the polls is caused by the fact that almost all minority candidates are Democrats. Where Democrats do well, as in Dallas County in 2006, minority candidates do well.
▲ When minority citizens see that there are no minority judges, it undermines their faith in the justice system; such a lack of faith cannot be good for society as a whole.	▼ Granted, this is a problem. The solution is for minorities to become Republicans, thereby increasing their chance to be elected.
▲ Minorities should be guaranteed some representation on the bench by the deliberate creation of some "minority-majority" districts.	▼ Such a plan would amount to a "Democrat-protection scheme," which the Constitution does not oblige Republicans to endorse.

(continued)

(continued)

▲ Putting aside questions of minority politics, single-member districts provide better representation for discrete areas of a city or county.

▼ At-large election plans ensure that each candidate must consider the welfare of the entire county, whereas district plans create a system of jealous, quarreling pieces.

▲ Minorities should keep suing in federal court until Texas is forced to create a single-member district judicial election system.

▼ In *Houston Lawyers' Assoc. et al. v. Attorney General of Texas et al.* (501 U.S. 419, 1994), the federal courts already settled this question; more lawsuits would be futile.

Sources: James Cullen, "Lawyers Protect Their Own," *Texas Observer,* September 17, 1993, 4; Suzanne Gamboa, "Judicial Elections Proposal Rejected," *Austin American-Statesman,* August 25, 1993, A1; Lani Guinere, *The Tyranny of the Majority: Fundamental Fairness in Representative Democracy* (New York: Free Press, 1994); David Lubin, *The Paradox of Representation: Racial Gerrymandering and Minority Interests in Congress* (Princeton, N.J.: Princeton University, 1997); David T. Canon, *Race, Redistricting, and Representation: The Unintended Consequences of Black Majority Districts* (Chicago: University of Chicago, 1999).

of Houston, was designed to standardize and better fund indigent defense in felony cases. Although the law left counties, not the state, with primary responsibility for providing lawyers for poor defendants, it required prompt appointment of counsel, mandated quick attorney-client contact, ordered the counties to create a standard of qualification for attorneys, charged them with setting a fee schedule for defense attorneys, and imposed other requirements. Just as important, it appropriated $19.7 million in state funds each year to supplement the $90 million the counties typically spend on indigent defense.

The democratic ideal of equal justice for all citizens faces a severe test when poor people are accused of crimes. If they cannot pay a private attorney, and the state refuses to provide them with competent counsel, they stand little chance of receiving an adequate defense.

Courtesy of Ben Sargent.

In 2003, the Texas Defender Service and the Equal Justice Center cooperated to study how the Fair Defense Act was being implemented. Their conclusions were disturbing. Studying the thirty-three counties that had accounted for 87 percent of those sent to death row since 1976, they reported that only Lubbock and Brazoria Counties were fully complying with the law. The thirty-one others were failing in their obligation to provide adequate counsel to indigent defendants for various reasons, including insufficient compensation for attorneys, low standards, or unsatisfactory or complete lack of standards for defense lawyers. Implementation of the law was haphazard and not systematic. A follow-up report by National Public Radio reported that counties claimed to be implementing the law but had not made complete reports of their activities to authorities in Austin. The best that can be said, therefore, is that troubling questions remain about the adequacy of the defense that the state provides to its accused indigent citizens.[36]

The problem of unequal justice is especially acute because Texas is a state with the death penalty. From the year 1982, when Texas resumed executions following a hiatus ordered by the U.S. Supreme Court, through early 2011, the state executed 475 people, including three women.[37] In Chapter 10, the issue of whether capital punishment is defensible will be examined. Whether the death penalty is justifiable, however, it would seem to be inflicted unequally on poorer and wealthier defendants. The problems of unequal justice for the poor continue up the judicial ladder to the most serious crime. A troubling case came in 2007, when the presiding judge of the Texas Court of Criminal Appeals, Sharon Keller, turned away the last appeal of a death row inmate because the rushed filing was delayed past the court's 5 P.M. closing time. Keller was reprimanded by the State Commission on Judicial Conduct for action that was inconsistent with the proper performance of her judicial duties which cast "public discredit on the judiciary."[38]

The fact that poor defendants probably have a greater chance of being incarcerated, and executed, would not be so worrisome if there were reasons to have confidence in the fact that they were all guilty. However, recent history is not reassuring to partisans of the state's criminal justice system on that issue. As detailed in the box entitled "Does Texas Execute the Innocent?," there is good reason to think that some of the people convicted of capital crimes in Texas have actually been innocent, the victims of a criminal justice system that often fails to ensure them an adequate trial.

Furthermore, there are numerous examples of people who have been convicted of crimes and sentenced to prison, only to have later advances in investigative science prove them innocent. The ability of geneticists to analyze DNA, in particular, has led to the overturning of a remarkable number of convictions. From 1989 to May 2007, 200 people nationwide were released from prison after DNA tests led to the nullification of their sentences, 28 of them in Texas.[39] The Dallas County district attorney has been especially dedicated to righting DNA wrongs, establishing a separate unit in his office to ferret out the errors from that county.

A remarkably large number of these wrongfully convicted people have been in Texas. In 1997, Governor Bush pardoned Ben Salazar, who had spent five years in prison, and Kevin Byrd, who had been incarcerated for twelve years, both for rape. In 2000, Roy Wayne Criner was also pardoned on the basis of new DNA evidence. He had served ten years of a life sentence for a rape and murder he did not commit. In 2003, Josiah Sutton, serving twenty-five years for a 1998 rape, was freed when the Houston Police Department crime lab admitted

Does Texas Execute the Innocent?

Theoretically, the state maintains an elaborate system of safeguards to ensure that defendants who have been convicted of murder and sentenced to die for their crime are actually guilty. There is an automatic appeal filed by the defendant's lawyer and reviewed by the staff and justices of the court of criminal appeals. At the same time, the original trial judge appoints a second attorney to investigate the conditions of the trial, try to find additional evidence or indications of official misconduct, and then file a "writ of habeas corpus" asking the court of criminal appeals to overturn the conviction or the death sentence.

In practice, as Chuck Lindell discovered when he reviewed eleven years of writs for the *Austin American-Statesman* in 2006, the court of criminal appeals tolerates such shoddy work from its habeas corpus lawyers that the system is often a fraudulent substitute for real justice. "Lawyers appointed to handle appeals for death row inmates routinely bungled the job," Lindell wrote in a series of articles, "submitting work that falls far below professional standards. Some appeals are incomplete, incomprehensible or improperly argued. Others are duplicated poorly from previous appeals." Lindell found examples of cases in which "[w]itnesses lied, prosecutors hid evidence or scientists flubbed their analyses." His articles described an underfunded system that routinely had to employ the worst lawyers in the state to provide a sham review of the convictions of the state's poorest defendants.

Although Lindell did not state the implied conclusion directly, others made the obvious deduction from his investigation. "Texas has sent a number of innocent people to death row and has executed several with strong claims of innocence . . . , " wrote Dave Atwood shortly after the series ran in the paper. And indeed, Atwood's conclusion from Lindell's evidence is inescapable. It only remained to point out that those who have been wrongly put to death have tended to be the state's poor and minority citizens.

Sources: Chuck Lindell, "Sloppy Lawyers Failing Clients on Death Row," *Austin American-Statesman*, October 29, 2006, A1; Chuck Lindell, "When $25,000 Is the Limit on a Life," *Austin American-Statesman*, October 30, 2006, A1; Dave Atwood, "We Are All Guilty of Homicide," *Austin American-Statesman*, November 27, 2006, A9.

that it had botched his DNA test.[40] In 2006, Governor Perry pardoned Greg Wallis and Billy Wayne Miller for similar reasons. They had been in prison eighteen and twenty-two years, respectively, and if the ability to analyze DNA had not come along, they would be there still.[41]

Perhaps the most unsettling of cases in recent years concerned Cameron Todd Willingham who was put to death in 2004. Willingham was charged with starting a fire in his home in Corsicana, Texas, purposely to kill his three young children in 1991. He was convicted of murder in the case in a trial that took place in 1992. Willingham was defended by court-appointed attorneys, one of whom, at least, thought Willingham guilty of the crime. Willingham rejected a plea deal that would have allowed him to have a life term in prison but would have spared him from lethal injection. He refused the offer, saying, "I ain't gonna plead to something I didn't do." Willingham persistently claimed innocence even to his final words before being put to death.

Cameron Todd Willingham, shown here, was put to death after being convicted of murdering his children. Some have questioned whether the conviction was based upon good evidence and whether Willingham was actually an innocent man.

© Lara Solt/Dallas Morning News/Corbis.

The case against Willingham was circumstantial. As motive for the crime, the prosecutors claimed that Willingham was a sociopathic personality whose children were "an impediment to his lifestyle." And there was a life insurance policy for the children, though the children's maternal great-grandfather was the beneficiary, not Willingham. It was charged that Willingham had used an accelerant to start a fire that killed the children, and the state had testimony from two fire experts who claimed the evidence pointed clearly to Willingham. A former jail mate in prison claimed that Willingham had confessed to the murders while in prison. And several witnesses thought Willingham had behaved unusually during the fire. Finally, Willingham had had a volatile relationship with the mother of his children, had occasionally abused her, and had had some minor arrests during his teenage years in Oklahoma.

During trial, some of the evidence was rebutted, but a jury found Willingham guilty of murder and sentenced him to death. While on death row, Willingham found an advocate named Elizabeth Gilbert who had become his pen pal. Gilbert began to examine the evidence and to challenge its validity. Over the course of time, it became obvious that the testimony about Willingham's personality and state of mind had changed over time as witnesses thought about the charges against him. Such changing perceptions are not unusual, as people assume that someone charged with a crime is probably guilty of it. The jailhouse witness, Johnny Webb, who said Willingham had confessed, was a drug addict and had been convicted of several crimes. In 2000, Webb recanted his testimony, declaring "Mr. Willingham is innocent of all charges." But most importantly, the testimony about a fire being set by an accelerant was discredited by a highly credentialed arson expert who concluded that the fire had not been set at all and that of the twenty arson indicators identified by experts during trial, only one

had any validity. Indeed, there was sign of lighter fluid found on the house's front porch, but pictures taken before the fire showed that the front porch had been used for a grill and that lighter fluid had been used with the grill. The new expert concluded that the fire had been accidental, that there was no evidence of arson, and that Willingham had been convicted based upon "junk science."

The capital conviction was appealed by Willingham several times, and once, in 1997, a federal court granted him a temporary stay of his execution. But all other appeals were denied, and eventually the stay expired. Four days before his execution, Willingham's petition for a stay was denied by the Texas Board of Pardons and Paroles, and at 4:00 P.M. on the day of his execution, Governor Rick Perry refused to grant a stay. A spokesman for the governor stated that the decision was made "on the facts of the case." After eating his last meal, Willingham was put to death by lethal injection on February 17, 2004. Among his last words: "I am an innocent man convicted of a crime I did not commit."

Of course, one cannot make final statements about Willingham's guilt or innocence based upon the limited information in this short recounting of the facts. However, the case does point to the uncertainties of many convictions and to the finality of the death penalty. In the words of one columnist, remembering the case: "The ghost of Cameron Todd Willingham is still haunting us, as well it should."[42]

Such examples of possible miscarriages of justice must make observers wonder how many other people are in prison or on death row in Texas because they were too poor to pay a lawyer, were in the wrong place at the wrong time, made an enemy of some county prosecutor, or happened to be assigned an indifferent or incompetent defense attorney. After an execution, of course, it is too late to help the person who has been wrongly convicted.

Summary

The judiciary is an uncomfortable part of the political system. There is a sense in which what judges do is neutral and nonpolitical, and jurists play up this aspect of their job. It is a myth, however, that the judiciary handles every problem in a nonpolitical manner. Especially in the higher appellate courts, which are responsible for interpreting the state constitution, the act of judging is an intensely political process. The conflict between functioning as neutral arbiters and functioning as political adjudicators creates problems for all judges, and it does so especially in Texas, where judges are part of the partisan system of state governance.

Many individuals function together to make the state judicial system what it is. The most important single official is the attorney general, but judges, attorneys, the State Bar, the police, and members of juries also play important roles. The state's judicial system is inadequately organized, which makes its other problems worse.

Over the last quarter-century, many observers have concluded that the Texas judiciary does not function well. Besides its inefficient organization, its problems are caused, first, by the fact that there is simply too much crime for the system to process effectively. Second, the system of partisan elections runs the risk of forcing judges to worry about the next campaign instead of applying themselves to impartial evaluation. Third, the system forces judges to rely on campaign contributions from people affected by judicial decisions, which creates many opportunities for impropriety. There is controversy over whether there is a fourth problem: At-large districts have the effect of making the election of minority judges less likely.

The disadvantage that poor people experience when dealing with the judicial system mirrors their disadvantages in the rest of the political system, but the problem is particularly troublesome because equal justice under law is one of the most cherished ideals of democracy. Unequal justice, which appears to result in the conviction of innocent people in Texas, is especially disturbing because the state enforces capital punishment on many of its convicted murderers.

Glossary Terms

appellate jurisdiction

at-large election

attorney general's advisory opinion

civil jurisdiction

concurrent jurisdiction

Court of Criminal Appeals

criminal jurisdiction

district election

exclusive jurisdiction

felony

grand jury

indictment

judge

judiciary

juvenile court

misdemeanor

original jurisdiction

original trial courts

plea bargain

Supreme Court

trial jury

10

The Substance of Justice

The majority, in that country [the United States], exercise a prodigious actual authority, and a power of opinion which is nearly as great; no obstacles exist which can impede or even retard its progress, so as to make it heed the complaints of those whom it crushes in its path. . . . I know of no country in which there is so little independence of mind and real freedom of discussion as in America.

ALEXIS DE TOCQUEVILLE, FRENCH VISITOR TO THE UNITED STATES, *DEMOCRACY IN AMERICA*, 1835

Every person shall be at liberty to speak, write or publish his opinions on any subject, being responsible for the abuse of that privilege; and no law shall ever be passed curtailing the liberty of speech or of the press.

TEXAS CONSTITUTION BILL OF RIGHTS, ARTICLE 1, SECTION 8, 1876

OBJECTIVES

After reading this chapter, you should be able to

Define civil rights and civil liberties.

Discuss issues in civil liberties in Texas, including freedom of expression, freedom of religion, the right to bear arms, and abortion.

Describe issues in civil rights in Texas, including school segregation, education, and civil rights for convicted criminals.

Discuss the way recent episodes in Jaspar and Tulia illustrate both progress and continuing problems with civil rights in Texas.

Assess capital punishment in Texas.

Evaluate tort laws in Texas.

INTRODUCTION

The output of the judicial system is extraordinarily important to all of us. The system protects—or fails to protect—our rights in a democratic society and processes our case in the event we are accused of a crime. It also allocates large amounts of money and power by arbitrating between various conflicting interests, especially those of a business nature.

The subject of the previous chapter was the structure and behavior of the Texas judiciary. On the whole, it has earned rather low marks for democratic virtue. That being so, it might be expected that the products of the system—the substance of justice—would similarly fail to stand up under scrutiny. However, justice in Texas is a good deal more complicated, and, in some cases, more admirable than a knowledge of the judiciary's institutional weaknesses might lead us to believe.

The first topic of this chapter is an examination of the Texas judiciary's record on civil liberties and civil rights, followed by an evaluation of the manner in which it deals with accused criminals, and then a discussion of some of the issues surrounding the cry for "tort reform" in the area of lawsuits against business. The system's record is uneven; in some areas, such as civil rights and liberties, it is dishearteningly backward. In other areas, especially the manner in which it has forced the state to equalize education, it is surprisingly progressive, though funding issues in 2011 challenged the education system. When measured against the standards of democratic theory, Texas justice provides cause for both pessimism and optimism.

Civil Liberties

The phrase **civil liberties** refers to the basic individual freedom from government interference that is crucial to sustaining a democratic government. Democracy requires that citizens be free to speak, read, and assemble so that they may choose in an independent and informed manner among competing ideas, candidates, and parties. In addition, because a democratic society must respect individual autonomy of thought and conscience, government must not be allowed to interfere with freedom of religious choice.

The First Amendment to the U.S. Constitution declares that Congress may neither abridge the people's freedom of speech or of the press, nor their right to assemble peaceably, nor to petition the government for a redress of grievances. It also forbids Congress to "establish" religion—that is, support it with money and coercive laws—or prohibit its free exercise. The Fourteenth Amendment, passed after the Civil War in the 1860s, has gradually been held by the U.S. Supreme Court to apply most of these protections to the states—a process known as "incorporation."

In addition, the states have similar guarantees in their constitutions. As the quotation at the beginning of the chapter shows, the Texas Constitution ensures freedom of speech and press. Beyond that, Section 27 promises that the state's citizens may assemble "in a peaceable manner" and petition the government "for redress of grievances or other purposes." Individual liberties are thus acknowledged in Texas, as in the federal government, to be of fundamental importance to a democratic society.

Given this apparent unanimity, we might think that there would be little disagreement about how these freedoms were to be protected. If so, we would be mistaken. The words in both constitutions seem to protect individual freedoms, but the history of the documents teaches us that no political guarantee can be taken for granted. In the South, especially, the traditionalist political culture has never been eager to grant the individual freedoms promised by constitutions. Majorities in the South have been especially resistant to the idea that African Americans and Mexican Americans should enjoy the same personal liberties as Anglos. For all of the nineteenth and most of the twentieth century, Texas was quite reluctant to give its citizens the freedom its constitution guarantees. Even in the twenty-first century, there are hot disagreements about which exercises of government authority are legitimate and which violate someone's civil liberty.

Furthermore, some politicians and private citizens either do not understand the importance of civil liberties or do not value them, placing individual rights frequently under siege somewhere, in Texas or other states. The aftermath of the terrorist attacks of September 11, 2001, and the challenges of immigration into Texas have sharpened disagreements about the balance between government authority and personal freedom. Sometimes the battle over civil liberties is fought in the legislature. Just as frequently, however, the struggle takes place in court.

Freedom of Expression

Although "freedom of speech and press" seems to be an unambiguous phrase, only a little thought can create a variety of difficult problems of interpretation. Do constitutional guarantees of freedom of speech protect those who would incite a mob to lynch a prisoner? Teach terrorist recruits to make bombs? Tell malicious

lies about public officials? Wear a T-shirt lettered with obscenities to high school? Spout racist propaganda on a local cable TV access program? Publicly burn an American flag? Falsely advertise a patent medicine? These questions and others like them have sparked intense political and intellectual conflict.

In 1925, in *Gitlow v. New York*, the U.S. Supreme Court for the first time held that the freedom of speech and press guarantees of the First Amendment to the federal Constitution were binding on state and local governments through the "due process of law" clause of the Fourteenth Amendment.[1] In the more than eight decades since the *Gitlow* decision, the Court's interpretation of the meaning of "freedom of speech and press" has constantly evolved so that American liberties are never quite the same from year to year. Since the 1960s, the First Amendment has come to contain protection for a "freedom of expression" that is larger than mere speech and press. Citizens may engage in nonspeech acts that are intended to convey a political communication.

For example, at the 1984 Republican National Convention in Dallas, Gregory Lee Johnson and others protested the Reagan administration's policies by burning an American flag while chanting, "America the red, white, and blue, we spit on you." Johnson was arrested and charged with violating a Texas law against flag desecration. Johnson's attorneys argued that his act was "symbolic speech" protected by the First Amendment. The U.S. Supreme Court agreed. In its 1989 decision in *Texas v. Johnson*, the majority held that "Johnson's burning of the flag was conduct sufficiently imbued with elements of communication to implicate the First Amendment,"[2] thus overturning the Texas law and freeing Johnson from the threat of jail time.

This decision caused a national furor. A large majority of Americans, while they supported freedom of expression in the abstract, were not willing to grant it to someone whose ideas they found so obnoxious. In this way, they showed the inconsistency that people sometimes display when they discover that they dislike the specific consequences of general principles they otherwise endorse.

First Amendment freedoms are not designed to protect conventional or conformist views; rather they protect the expression of despised views such as Johnson's. Democracy requires not only majority rule, but also minority rights. Fashionable opinion does not need protection because its very popularity renders it immune from suppression. But the expression of a political idea that the great majority finds agreeable is not "freedom of expression" at all. Freedom comes into play only when there is some danger to the speaker for expressing his or her thought—that is, when the thought is disagreeable to the majority. The American—and Texas—public missed this point. The clamor to outlaw flag burning was an example of the "tyranny of the majority" that Alexis de Tocqueville, quoted at the beginning of this chapter, warned would be the dark side of American democracy.

The public being so aroused, the U.S. Congress was not about to stand in its way. Congress quickly passed the Flag Protection Act of 1989, mandating a one-year jail sentence and $1,000 fine for anyone who "knowingly mutilates, defaces, physically defiles, burns, maintains on the floor or ground, or tramples upon, any flag of the United States." A federal court quickly struck down this law for the same reason that the Supreme Court had invalidated the Texas statute. Because federal judges could not be removed, they were free to protect the liberty of an unpopular person such as Gregory Lee Johnson.

An antiwar protest in Austin on March 20, 2003, the day after the United States invaded Iraq, created a superficially similar question of the right to protest. Reacting against President Bush's attack on that Middle Eastern country, several

hundred peace activists marched from the University of Texas campus down Congress Avenue to the bridge crossing the Colorado River, where they stopped in a mass and sat down in a circle, blocking all traffic. After warning the sitters to disperse, police arrested about fifty.

The protestors seemed to see themselves as latter-day Gregory Lee Johnsons. One claimed to a reporter that by obstructing the city's transportation, they were exercising their "right to civil disobedience."[3] But the differences between Johnson and the antiwar activists are instructive. Although Johnson had deliberately chosen to express his opinions in a manner that was offensive to most Texans in 1984, he had not interfered with the rights of other people to go about their business. In contrast, the 2003 protestors had intentionally blocked the bridge precisely because such an action would hinder the activities of thousands of city residents. In arresting Johnson, Dallas police had done nothing but squelch his political statement. In arresting the antiwar protestors, Austin police had protected the city's residents from disruption of their lives. While Johnson did have a right to express his unpopular opinion, the more recent protestors were mistaken when they thought that they had a "right to civil disobedience." Argument is one thing; imposition on other people is another.

Similar confrontations everywhere often call for such subtle distinctions. Always, protestors are apt to exaggerate their rights to self-assertion while government officials are apt to exaggerate their authority to protect the public peace. In these disputes, judges are often needed to decide where the rights of individuals end and the rights of the community begin.

Freedom of Religion

The First Amendment provision that forbids Congress to pass laws "respecting an establishment of religion" has been interpreted to mean either (1) that there should be a "wall of separation" between church and state, and that government

As Ben Sargent dramatizes in this cartoon, preventing people from expressing their opinion by burning the flag violates the freedom for which the flag stands.

Courtesy of Ben Sargent.

may not help or even acknowledge religion in any way, or (2) that government may aid religion, at least indirectly, as long as it shows "no preference" among the various religious beliefs. Although the U.S. Supreme Court frequently talks "wall of separation," in practice it has allowed the states to provide a variety of aids to religion—for example, school lunches and public facilities for church-run schools and tuition grants for church-run colleges—as long as government agencies do not show a preference for one church over another.

A First Amendment provision regarding religion that is frequently misunderstood forbids Congress to prohibit the "free exercise" of faith. The freedom to believe in a supreme being necessarily involves the freedom to disbelieve. The freedom to worship requires the freedom not to worship. As U.S. Supreme Court Justice David Souter wrote for the majority of the court in 2005, "the touchstone for our analysis is the principle that the First Amendment mandates government neutrality between religion and religion, and between religion and nonreligion."[4] Under the U.S. Constitution, therefore, the atheist and the believer are equally protected. Thus, the provision of the Texas Constitution—Article I, Section 4—that requires persons holding public office to "acknowledge the existence of a Supreme Being" is contradicted by the nation's fundamental law and is no longer enforced.

Because of the passion and prejudice that surround the subject of faith, government officials sometimes follow momentary convenience rather than timeless principles when making decisions about religious questions. As a result, the politics of religious freedom is often characterized by inconsistency and hypocrisy.

A Conflict of Good Causes

Conflicts over religion involve more than the civil rights of individuals. They also impinge upon such profane subjects as city zoning ordinances.

In 1999, the Texas legislature passed the Religious Freedom Restoration Act. Under that law, local governments must show that they have a compelling interest, such as protection of public health or safety, before they can limit the practice of religion.

Also in 1999, Rick Barr, pastor of Grace Christian Fellowship in Sinton, near Corpus Christi, set up a faith-based rehabilitation center for nonviolent parolees across the street from his church. Shortly afterward, Sinton officials passed an ordinance prohibiting parolees from living within 1,000 feet of a church or school, thus effectively outlawing the program. Barr sued, arguing that the law was specifically intended to prevent him from operating his faith-based program, and was therefore a violation of the Religious Freedom Restoration Act. City attorneys argued that the zoning change did not limit the Grace Christian Fellowship's religious practice, and that they had the authority to protect the community from parolees.

In 2009, the Texas Supreme Court ruled that the city violated the state law when it shut down the halfway houses. Writing for the court, Justice Nathan Hecht said that laws require governments to tread carefully when they may interfere with religious practices. He did note, in deference to the city, that the decision "in no way suggests that the government never has a compelling interest in zoning for religious use of property or in regulating halfway houses operated for religious purposes."

Source: *Pastor Rick Barr v. City of Sinton*, No. 06–0074 (Tex. Sup. Ct., June 19, 2009).

Nevertheless, courts have devised some tests with which to bring a measure of rationality to their decisions. On the one hand, the courts usually do not permit a general law protecting the public welfare to be violated in the name of religious freedom. For example, early in the twentieth century, Texas courts ruled that parents could not refuse to have their children vaccinated against smallpox on the grounds that it was contrary to their religious convictions.[5] In a similar vein, Texas courts ruled that members of a church were not denied their freedom of religion by a zoning ordinance that restricted use of property surrounding the church to single-family dwellings.[6] (This particular principle may be due for a rethinking—see the box entitled "A Conflict of Good Causes.")

On the other hand, laws conflicting with religious beliefs may sometimes be overturned if the public interest is not seriously threatened. For example, in 1938, a Texas appellate court, anticipating a similar U.S. Supreme Court ruling five years later, held that a parent who refused to salute the flag as a matter of religious conviction could not be deprived of custody of his or her child.[7]

In Texas as in other states, religious belief can be intense, and religious people can sometimes be intolerant of others who do not share their particular doctrinal enthusiasm. Politicians responding to their constituencies sometimes take actions that threaten the religious rights of people whose views happen to be in the minority. When they do so, they come into conflict with the federal Constitution, and religious fervor is translated into political tension.

A major issue of this sort is the question of religious recitation in public schools. In 1962 and 1963, the U.S. Supreme Court ruled that a nondenominational prayer used in public schools[8] and the reading of the Bible and the recitation of the Lord's Prayer[9] were unconstitutional. The basis of the decisions was that the prayer was a Christian ritual imposed upon all children of a school, many of whom might be non-Christian. Because the prayer takes place in a public school, it is an example of the "establishment" of religion outlawed by the First Amendment.

Although the reasoning of these decisions is difficult to refute, they nevertheless caused a great public outcry, and even today, a large majority of Americans would support a constitutional amendment to permit prayer in the schools.[10] In the absence of such an amendment, local politicians and school boards in many areas try to evade the Court's pronouncements by sneaking in prayer under some other name. As a result, the courts still deal with school prayer cases.

A good example is the situation in Santa Fe, on the Texas mainland north of Galveston. The population of this small town is about 90 percent Protestant, and mainly Baptist, with a significant representation of fundamentalists (who believe that every word of the Bible is literally true). In the 1990s, encouraged by the Santa Fe school board, teachers and students began pushing their variety of religion in the classrooms. Among other instances of official advocacy of a particular faith, a teacher handed out flyers advertising a revival, schools invited representatives of the Gideon Bible society to campus to proselytize, and a Protestant chaplain was recruited to read Protestant prayers at school ceremonies.

Two sets of parents, one Catholic and the other Mormon, objected to such spiritual propaganda aimed at their children and in 1995 filed suit. Realizing the legal threat, the Santa Fe school board forbade most of the objectionable activities. It retained, however, the practice of allowing one student, elected by majority vote of the student body, to recite a "brief invocation and/or message"

over the stadium's public address system before each high school football game. The parents sued again, pointing out that a majority of the student body would always pick a Protestant to speak the "message" and that the chosen person would invariably select a prayer as the message. Moreover, because the district's public address system was employed to broadcast the prayer, this state institution was being used to subject their children to a religious message they did not want to hear. In other words, the parents argued, the Texas government was imposing an establishment of religion on their children, an action that violated the First Amendment. They were victims of the tyranny of the majority.

Texas's Republican establishment, part of a political coalition that includes the Christian Right (see Chapters 3 and 4), supported the school board. The fact that a public opinion survey showed that 82 percent of Texans agreed that students should be allowed to lead prayers over public address systems before sporting events no doubt encouraged the politicians to endorse the Santa Fe majority.[11]

"Have we actually reached the point as a society where saying a prayer for the health and well-being of the players and the safe return home of the visiting team is no longer acceptable in Texas?" asked party chair Susan Weddington. Attorney General John Cornyn and Governor George W. Bush filed a "friend of the court" brief supporting Santa Fe's position. "The Santa Fe district's students have a constitutionally protected right to free speech, including the right to offer a prayer before football games," wrote Cornyn.[12]

Because it dealt with a First Amendment issue, the Santa Fe lawsuit was decided by federal rather than Texas courts. And federal judges, not subject to the same pressure to cater to majority values as are Texas politicians, did not think that the majority in Santa Fe had a right to impose its particular religious beliefs on the minority. In June 2000, the U.S. Supreme Court upheld a lower appeals court ruling that the Santa Fe pregame "message" was unconstitutional. At their next meeting, the school board eliminated the policy, and that particular squabble over civil liberties was over.[13]

The general issue, however, showed no sign of exiting from Texas politics. In 2003, the Texas legislature passed a law requiring that all the state's school-children must begin the day with a quasi-religious ritual. First they must recite the Pledge of Allegiance to the American flag, then the Texas Pledge, and then observe a minute of silence (during which, presumably, most of them would pray, although that activity was not required in the statute). The law was certainly intended to instill patriotism in children; it may have been intended as a first step in the reintroduction of prayer in the state's schools.[14] In 2007, the words "under God" were added to the Texas Pledge by the legislature. The bill's sponsor said that it was simply a "common sense" move to bring the Pledge into conformity with the United States Pledge of Allegiance.[15] On October 13, 2010, the federal Fifth Circuit Court ruled that the Pledge did not constitute an Establishment Clause issue. There was no violation of separation of church and state. The court concluded that there was a **secular** justification for the addition of "under God," writing, "There can be no doubt that mirroring the national pledge and acknowledging the state's religious heritage are permissible secular purposes."[16]

Without question, however, the general issue remains unsettled. The future of Texas holds many more laws, and many more lawsuits, on the subject of church and state.

A Right to Keep and Bear Arms?

Crime has become one of the most important political issues in the United States in general, and Texas in particular, and arguments about how to control it are part of contemporary political discussion. One of the suggested ways of reducing the number of homicides is to restrict access to guns. On the one hand, because firearms kill about 30,000 people in the United States each year, including about 14,000 homicides (1,328 of them Texans in 2009) annually, it is not implausible to argue that crime would be less of a problem if fewer people had guns.[17]

On the other hand, there are about 14 million hunters in the country and millions more who own firearms for target practice or self-defense, so there is also a great resistance to the idea of gun control. Many people agree with the opposite of the gun-control argument; they believe that law-abiding citizens would be safer from crime if they were allowed to carry concealed weapons for self-defense. Although there were only 163 justifiable homicides (defense of persons or property) by private citizens in the United States in 2003, *protective* uses of guns against burglary, assault, and robbery have been estimated to be as high as 2 million a year.[18] Thus rational arguments exist both for and against an armed citizenry.

The purpose of this chapter is not to examine the entire political issue of whether government should attempt stricter control over firearms. As part of a discussion of civil rights and liberties, however, it will be useful to evaluate one important part of the argument: the claim that Americans have a personal right, guaranteed by both the United States and Texas Constitutions, to own guns.

The Second Amendment to the U.S. document reads in its entirety, "A well regulated Militia, being necessary to the security of a free State, the right of the people to keep and bear Arms, shall not be infringed."[19] Millions of Americans believe that this part of the Bill of Rights prohibits government from interfering with their gun ownership. The National Rifle Association, an organization with

In Texas, hunting is a popular pastime. Texans cling to their tradition and to their shared lore of cherishing the right to own guns. Here a hunter poses after a successful hunt, with his shotgun and his trophy.

Milwaukee Journal Sentinel/MCT/ Landov.

a 2010 membership of nearly 4 million, is particularly tireless in arguing this position. Any issue of the NRA's magazine, *The American Rifleman*, contains numerous assertions of an individual "right to keep and bear arms" as promised by the Second Amendment. Although public opinion surveys consistently show that two thirds of the American people, and depending on the question, from three fifths to three quarters of Texans, favor stricter gun control, many politicians echo the claim that the Second Amendment prohibits all regulation of firearms.[20]

Furthermore, a significant proportion of Texans evidently believe that they have a constitutional guarantee to own anything from a purse pistol to an assault rifle and that government does not have the legitimate authority to do anything about it. They agree with former Republican State Representative Rick Green, who wrote in 2000 that "The Second Amendment prevents federal interference with the citizen's right to keep and bear arms for personal defense."[21] (This is an argument about "rights," but it falls under the category of civil "liberties" because its subject is individual freedom from government intrusion.)

The amendment was created in 1789 to protect state militias—that is, official state military organizations, not private clubs or vigilante groups—from being disbanded by the federal government. It was not explicitly intended to guarantee the right to firearm ownership to private citizens.

In June 2008, the U.S. Supreme Court established a new view of the meaning of the Second Amendment, finding for the first time in history that it protected the rights of individuals to own firearms. This decision was extended in 2010 to apply the Second Amendment protections directly to the states in the case of *McDonald v. Chicago.*[22] The court's reasoning in these cases clarified some issues, while leaving others open for future litigation. Both were 5–4 decisions. The reasoning of the decisions rested on three grounds: (1) that the second clause of the Amendment ("the right to keep and bear arms") is controlling, and is meant to ensure the right of self-defense, as well as protection against tyranny; (2) that the first clause (calling for a "well-regulated militia") originally referred to "all males physically capable of acting in concert for the common defense" rather than an organized military force; and (3) that state constitutions in existence at the same time justify this interpretation (because there is evidence that the Bill of Rights was intended to extend provisions of state constitutions to the national government). This decision, while clear on the right to bear arms, does not settle a lingering set of questions about *which kinds of arms* will ultimately be deemed to be protected.

The Texas Constitution, in Section 23 of the Bill of Rights (Article I), guarantees that "Every citizen shall have the right to keep and bear arms in the lawful defense of himself or the State, but the Legislature shall have power, by law, to regulate the wearing of arms, with a view to prevent crime." Although the wording of the guarantee evidently establishes the right to keep a gun in the home, the right to any other use of firearms is highly ambiguous. Because the legislature can regulate the "wearing" of a gun, it can in effect prevent citizens from "bearing arms" outside their homes. Therefore, private citizens have no constitutional *right*, in a realistic sense, to carry weapons. Their ability to do so is subject to the decisions of the legislature. Although the section on bearing arms is placed in the Bill of Rights, as a practical matter the subject is not about rights, but about ordinary law and, thus, ordinary politics. In other words, the question of citizen ownership and use of firearms, under both the American and Texas Constitutions, is a question of public policy, not a question of civil liberties.

Because the opinion articulated by Representative Green is strong in Texas, the state's public policy has long been permissive of private gun ownership.[23] In 1995, the armed-citizen attitude carried the day in the state legislature, which passed a law allowing Texans who have undergone ten hours of training to carry concealed handguns, and affirming the right of a citizen to defend his or her home against intrusion (this is known as the "castle doctrine"). Many local governments, however, continued to ban firearms from various areas within their jurisdiction, such as city buses, libraries, and senior citizen centers. In 2003, pro-gun groups persuaded the legislature to pass a law preempting local authority to regulate concealed weapons. Under this law, only the state can designate areas where weapons are banned.[24] (It may be of interest to students that schools and colleges are among the places designated by the state as areas where handguns are not permitted.)

The 1995 law was explicit in permitting citizens to defend their homes with deadly force. It was ambiguous, however, about the extent to which they might defend their property outside the home. In 2007, the legislature clarified this point. It passed a law extending the castle doctrine to defense against unlawful entry of a vehicle or workplace.[25] During the 2011 session, the legislature considered laws that would have allowed guns on college campuses and in the workplace in hopes of deterring crime, but those bills were not passed. However, Governor Perry did sign legislation blocking those adjudged mentally ill from passing background checks necessary to purchase guns.

Abortion

Today, in Texas and in the United States as a whole, abortion joins the race for the top position in the list of divisive and inflammatory political issues. People do not even agree on what they are arguing about. Supporters of legal abortion maintain that the issue is whether a woman should have the right to control her own body. Opponents insist that the issue is whether the born should be allowed to kill the unborn. Because those on each side feel deeply, discussion of the issue never produces agreement; it only creates division and anger. Sometimes it results in violence.

Until 1973, there was no national abortion policy. For the first two thirds of the twentieth century, most states either discouraged or forbade private citizens to have abortions. In that year, however, the situation was radically changed by the U.S. Supreme Court's decision in the case of *Roe v. Wade,* a case arising from the Texas courts.[26] Building on the notion of a personal right to be free of government intrusion that it had been expanding since the mid-1960s—a right grounded in the freedoms granted by the First, Third, Fourth, and Fifth Amendments to the Constitution—the Court wrote that the Bill of Rights protected sexual privacy, including the right to have an abortion. All state antiabortion laws were overturned.

After the *Roe v. Wade* decision, abortion became a common medical procedure, in Texas as elsewhere. About 82,056 legal abortions were performed in the state in 2006.[27]

The case also, however, ignited an emotional national political debate that continues today. People who support the Court, who call themselves "pro-choice," argue that the decision to terminate a pregnancy should be made by the woman and her doctor; government has no business interfering. Those who disagree, styling themselves "pro-life," argue that to terminate a

pregnancy is to commit homicide and that government has every obligation to prevent such a crime.

One of the arguments of the pro-choice forces is that no court, federal or otherwise, should have the authority to intervene in an area of public policy that impinges on such deeply held personal values as the nature and beginning of human life. Pro-life activists make the opposite argument from Alexander Hamilton's, quoted at the beginning of Chapter 9. They say that an "independent" judiciary that preempts the legislature—the people's representatives—from creating policy in an area of passionately felt moral opinions is short-circuiting democracy. Pro-life citizens therefore believe that in this area, unelected judges have no legitimacy. Pro-choice advocates, looking to the courts to protect what has become, to them, an important civil liberty, agree with Hamilton and support the concept of an independent judiciary.

The abortion debate is as fierce in Texas as in any other state. The Christian Right, in particular, is fervently antiabortion. In 1994, it captured the state's Republican Party and wrote an uncompromising "pro-life" plank into the platform at the state convention. (The state Republican platforms have commonly repeated this call for a "Human Rights Amendment" to the U.S. Constitution— see Chapter 4.) Although statewide Republican candidates have sometimes tried to distance themselves from the party's official position on this issue, the pro-life position is endorsed by most members of the majority Republican delegations in both houses of the state legislature. Meanwhile, most members of the Democratic Party are liberal on social issues, as exemplified by former Governor Ann Richards and 2010 gubernatorial candidate Bill White. Democrats, as a whole, have many different views on this topic.

The 1999 legislature passed a "parental notification law," which required that, before a girl under the age of eighteen could get an abortion, her physician must inform her parents. Although the parents could not stop the operation, they would have forty-eight hours to counsel the girl about her choices. In 2010, the legislature added a sonogram requirement, meaning that any woman seeking an abortion would first have to view a sonogram of her fetus before the procedure could be done. The bill had 62 percent support among Texans.[28] Pro-choice groups immediately filed suit in federal court to block the new sonogram law. If a single lesson can be learned from the history of the abortion debate, it is that political conflicts that derive from strongly held, clashing moral convictions cannot be resolved by judges. Perhaps they cannot be resolved at all.

For the present, the tenor of state policy is strongly pro-life. The 2003 legislature passed three laws that were intended to discourage or obstruct women from having abortions. First, the Women's Right to Know Act's main provision required that any woman must sign a statement at least twenty-four hours before the termination of her pregnancy affirming that she had been given access to photos of fetal development and information regarding the risks of abortion and pregnancy. Second, an amendment to the state's general appropriations bill cut off all public funding to any organization that provides abortions—a provision that applied mainly to Planned Parenthood. (This organization immediately sued, and federal Judge Sam Sparks quickly suspended the law on the grounds that much family planning money that the state administers comes from the federal government, and the state does not have the legal authority to cut off such funding.) Third, the Prenatal Protection Act amended the state's penal code to define an "individual" as beginning at the moment of fertilization and allowing criminal charges or civil lawsuits to be filed when an unborn child is killed.[29]

In 2005, the legislature passed a law that severely restricted the ability of doctors to perform abortions during the last three months of pregnancy, and required them to get the written permission of a girl's parents before performing an abortion on her at any stage of her pregnancy. The representatives who voted for this law appear not to have realized that, when combined with the Prenatal Protection Act, it created the possibility of criminal charges against doctors.

But the Texas District and County Attorneys Association immediately perceived the implication in the intersection of the two laws, worrying that if a doctor performed such a procedure on a girl without her parents' permission, or performed the procedure during the third trimester on even an adult woman, the doctor could be charged with murder. Although this consequence had not been the intention of the 2005 law, it did seem that such a doctor could potentially be facing capital punishment. Moreover, it was not hard to imagine that some county attorney, ambitious for higher political office, might seek to enhance his or her reputation as an antiabortion crusader by putting a doctor on trial for capital murder. Mindful of this potential development, in 2006, David Swinford, chair of the House State Affairs Committee, formally asked Greg Abbott for an Attorney General's Opinion (see Chapter 10) exploring the possibilities in the combination of the two laws.[30]

In early 2007, Abbott rendered his opinion, stating that a doctor could not be charged with a capital crime for violating the state's abortion laws. Such an action would make a doctor subject to the state Occupations Code, not the Penal Code. The OC provides for civil and administrative penalties—that is, a fine or the revocation of a license to practice—but does not permit jail time or execution.[31] Although this opinion prevented the state courts from having to render an opinion that would surely have made a large proportion of the state's population unhappy no matter how the issue was decided, the episode illustrated the passions underlying the abortion debate, and the way they can generate unintended consequences for citizens and the judiciary.

Whether pro-life or pro-choice positions dominate Texas government in the future, the state's judges will have their hands full attempting to apply the law in an impartial manner.

Civil Rights

Broadly speaking, *civil liberties* refers to citizens' rights to be free of government regulation of their personal conduct, whereas **civil rights** refers to the claim that the members of all groups have to be treated equally with the members of other groups. Generally, if government harasses individual people because of something they have said or done, it may have taken away a civil liberty. If government oppresses groups of people because of some ethnic, gender, or other category to which they belong, it has violated their civil rights.

Historically, the domination of Texas by the traditionalist political culture inhibited state courts from actively protecting the civil rights of Blacks and Mexican Americans. Jim Crow laws, Black Codes, poll taxes, and other infringements on rights and liberties existed undisturbed by the state judicial system for decades. These blights on democracy were overturned by federal, not state, courts.

School Segregation

In 1954, the U.S. Supreme Court rendered one of the landmark decisions of its history. In a unanimous verdict, the Court ruled in *Brown v. Board of Education* that public schools that were segregated on the basis of race were in violation of the "equal protection of the laws" clause of the Fourteenth Amendment.[32] This decision was intensely disagreeable to the ruling Anglos in Texas and the sixteen other states that had segregated schools, and, at first, sparked a great deal of obstruction and evasion.

In 1970, for example, Sam Tasby, an African American, sued the Dallas Independent School District (DISD) in federal court because his son was unable to attend a White school near his home. The DISD was in almost continuous litigation for more than thirty years thereafter, spending millions of tax dollars to draw up unsatisfactory desegregation plans and then contest the adverse rulings of the courts. In 2000, long after Mr. Tasby's son was grown and out of school, DISD officials decided that compliance was a better strategy than resistance and hired Mike Moses, deputy chancellor of Texas Tech University, to lead the district toward integration. In 2003, U.S. District Judge Barefoot Sanders decided that "the segregation prohibited by the United States Constitution, the United States Supreme Court and federal statutes no longer exists in the DISD" and ended federal court supervision. By that time, the composition of the district's students had declined from 59 percent White to 7 percent, the percentage of Hispanic students had risen to 59 percent, and the percentage of African Americans had held steady at a third of the population.[33]

As with school prayers and Bible reading, schools occasionally still attempt to defy the federal courts by segregating their students by ethnicity. For example, although North Dallas's Preston Hollow Elementary School was officially integrated, in practice the principal assigned White students to one set of classes, and minority students to another set. In 2006, a Hispanic parent sued, and federal judge Sam Lindsay found for the parent. Preston Hollow's principal, wrote Lindsay in his opinion, was "in effect, operating at taxpayers' expense, a private school for Anglo children within a public school that was predominantly minority." The judge ordered the school district to pay the Hispanic parent $20,200, and immediately stop segregating the students.[34]

Despite such attempts to bring back the Old South, the great majority of school districts, the great majority of the time, are now legally integrated. The major problem today is not that school districts deliberately separate students, but that economic class separates them. Because poor people and middle-class people tend to live in different areas, and especially because the poorer tend to make their homes in the cities while the wealthier often live in the suburbs (Dallas and its environs are a good example), citizens of different economic classes are served by different school districts. And because poorer districts cannot afford to supply adequate schooling, economic disparity is turned into educational inequality. This is one of the major civil rights problems of the twenty-first century. For many states, Texas included, it has raised the question of whether education should be considered a civil right.

Education: A Basic Right?

In 1987, Texas District Judge Harley Clark shocked and outraged the Texas political establishment by ruling in the case of *Edgewood v. Kirby* that the state's system of financing its public schools violated its own constitution and laws.

Clark's ruling referred to Article VII, Section 1, which requires the "Legislature of the state to establish an efficient system of public free schools," and part of Article I, which asserts that "All free men . . . have equal rights." Additionally, Section 16.001 of the Texas Education Code states that "public education is a state responsibility," that "a thorough and efficient system [is to] be provided," and that "each student enrolled in the public school system shall have access to programs and services that are appropriate to his or her needs and that are substantially equal to those available to any similar student, notwithstanding varying local economic factors."

At the time of that ruling, the state's educational system did not begin to offer equal services to every child. During the 1985–1986 school year, when the *Edgewood* case was being prepared, the wealthiest school district in Texas had $14 million in taxable property per student, and the poorest district had $20,000. The Whiteface Independent School District in the Texas Panhandle taxed its property owners at $0.30 per $100 of value and spent $9,646 per student. The Morton ISD, just north of Whiteface, taxed its property owners at $0.96 per $100 evaluation, but because of the lower value of its property was able to spend only $3,959 per student.[35]

Gross disparities such as these made a mockery of the constitutional and statutory requirements, as well as the demands of democratic theory for equal educational funding. An estimated 1 million out of the state's 3 million school-children were receiving inadequate instruction because their local districts could not afford to educate them. Democracy requires only equality of opportunity, not equality of result. But inequality of education must inevitably translate into inequality of opportunity. The courts were following the dictates of democratic theory in attempting to force the rest of the political system to educate all Texas children equally. (It is worth noting that since 1971, twenty state supreme courts have likewise held that their state's school funding system unconstitutionally discriminates against poor districts.)[36]

The appropriate remedy was to transfer some revenue from wealthy to poorer districts. But, given the distribution of power in Texas, and especially the way it is represented in the legislature, this strategy was nearly impossible. As explained in Chapters 4 and 5, because of the lack of voting participation by the state's poorer citizens, its wealthier citizens are overrepresented in the legislature.[37] Despite the fact that a badly educated citizenry was a drag on the state's economy and therefore a problem for everyone, taxpayers in wealthier districts resisted giving up their money to educate the children of the poor in some other district. Their representatives refused to vote for some sort of revenue redistribution, regardless of what the court had said.

In October 1989, the Texas Supreme Court unanimously upheld Clark's ruling that the system was unconstitutional, and told the legislature to fix it. After four years of stalling, blustering, and complaining, the legislature passed a law that would take about $450 million in property taxes from ninety-eight high-wealth districts and distribute the money to poor districts. (The media instantly dubbed this the "Robin Hood Law," after the twelfth-century English bandit who allegedly robbed from the rich and gave to the poor.) In January 1995, the Texas Supreme Court upheld the new law by a bare 5-to-4 majority, but that did not end the issue.

Wealthy citizens continued to complain about the Robin Hood law and to file lawsuits against it. Beginning in 2001, several school districts challenged the plan on the grounds that it violated the state constitution. In order to fulfill

their obligations both to their own and to other districts' children, they argued, they were forced to peg their property-tax rates at the constitutional ceiling of $1.50 per $100 of assessed evaluation. Therefore, by in effect forcing all districts to tax at the same top rate, the Robin Hood law violated the constitution's ban on a statewide property tax. The slow movement toward a state supreme court decision in this case through 2005 undoubtedly encouraged legislatures to adopt a wait-and-see attitude and, thus, not do anything to upset the tax applecart (see Chapters 6 and 13).

In November 2005, the state supreme court declared the Robin Hood law unconstitutional on the narrow grounds that it forced school districts into a statewide property tax. The court did not address the larger issue of whether redistribution of wealth between rich and poor districts was itself constitutional. The justices gave the legislature until June 1, 2006, to reform the system.[38]

In a May 2006 special session, the legislature's task was greatly eased by the state's $10.5 billion surplus. With so much extra money to spread around, the governor, the lieutenant governor, and the speaker of the house were able to give something to both rich and poor school districts (for the financial details, see Chapter 12). Essentially, they increased the amount of money the state would give to poor districts—the state's share of funding public education went up from 38 percent to about half—while cutting property taxes for wealthier citizens and reducing the amount that wealthy districts had to share. The whole agreeable scheme depended on the continued generation of a surplus by a roaring state economy, but the formula proved deficient when the legislature was confronted with decreasing state revenues as a consequence of a deep recession in the 2011 legislative session (see Chapter 12 for a detailed discussion of this issue).[39]

Nevertheless, nearly two decades of litigation and political struggle have made one thing clear. The state judiciary, at least in this one area, has become the champion of the underdog. There never would have been a Robin Hood law in 1993 or a special legislative session in 2006 if the courts had not held the feet of the legislature and the governor to the fire. Although Texas courts are lagging on civil rights and civil liberties, they are ahead of the curve in educational equity. In this one area, Texas judges have somehow risen above the burdens of history and are attempting to force the people of Texas to live up to their democratic ideals.

Civil Rights in Modern Texas: Jasper and Tulia

Even though the civil rights atmosphere in Texas is very different from what it was a few decades ago, there are still problems to overcome before everyone is treated equally under the law. Two of the most intense confrontations between the attitudes of the Old South traditionalist culture and progressive racial policies occurred in the towns of Jasper, in 1998 and 1999, and Tulia, in the first years of the new century.

Jasper is a small city near the Louisiana border in the piney woods of East Texas. In June 1998, three White men chained an African American named James Byrd, Jr., by his ankles to the bumper of a pickup truck and then dragged him three miles down country roads, leaving his mangled corpse by the gate of a traditionally Black cemetery. This horrendous murder, which raised collective memories of the days when dozens of southern Black men were lynched every year, shocked the nation and attracted enormous media attention. For a few distraught hours, it almost seemed to people of goodwill that no progress had been made in Texas race relations in a century.[40]

Soon, however, the differences between the old and new Texas became clear. Only two days after the crime, Jasper County Sheriff Billy Rowles, who is White, arrested three White men. The evidence against them was overwhelming; among other things, Byrd's blood was found on their clothing. All three men were uneducated and had criminal records. Two were avowed racists. By February 1999, one of the men had been tried, convicted, and sentenced to death by an integrated Jasper jury. This was only the second time in Texas history that a White man had been given capital punishment for the murder of an African American. Soon, the other killers had been convicted, one also receiving the death penalty and the other a life sentence. Meanwhile, at James Byrd's funeral, citizens of every color had mourned together.

The Jasper murder and its aftermath underscored that, while racism remains virulent in Texas, it is neither dominant nor respectable. The killers were on the fringes of society; indeed, two were virtually career criminals. Texas officials unanimously expressed outrage at the actions of the criminals, and in Jasper, no one attempted to justify the actions of the three killers. Citizens of the community treated the murder as a shared calamity.

While the Jasper drama was unfolding, a different kind of civil rights outrage was beginning in Tulia, a small town between Amarillo and Lubbock.[41] In January 1998, the Panhandle Regional Narcotics Task Force hired Thomas Coleman, a former law enforcement officer in several cities, as an undercover agent. Regional drug task forces, financed by federal money but answerable to the governor's office, are special law enforcement agencies that span jurisdictional boundaries and traditionally operate without much outside scrutiny. The members of this one evidently did not bother to discover that Coleman had left many of his jobs under an ethical cloud and that he was, as one journalist would later summarize, "a racist, a liar, and a thief."[42] Working with the

John William King, front, and Lawrence Russell Brewer are escorted from the Jasper County courthouse on June 9, 1998, in Jasper, Texas. King, Brewer, and Shawn Allen Berry were convicted of first-degree murder in the death of James Byrd, Jr., who was tied to a truck and dragged to his death along a rural East Texas road.

AP Photo/David J. Phillip.

Swisher County prosecutor's office (which was also apparently uncurious about his background), Coleman began conducting undercover "sting" operations in Tulia, looking for drug pushers.

In July 1999, police and sheriff's officers arrested forty-six people, most of them African American, but a few Hispanic, whom Coleman accused of having sold him illegal drugs. In a series of trials and plea bargains, by the spring of 2000, thirty-eight of these people had been convicted of various drug charges. Several later explained that they had accepted plea bargains because, having seen the sentences handed down after the first convictions—60, 99, and 434 years—they were convinced by their lawyers that their best strategy was to plead guilty and accept a lesser sentence, even though they were innocent. Coleman's testimony was the only evidence against any of these people. He never produced any drugs or drug paraphernalia to substantiate his accusations, and no drugs were found when any of the defendants were arrested. Nevertheless, Coleman was named "Outstanding Lawman of the Year" by the Texas Narcotics Control Program.

But soon after the Tulia defendants went to prison, journalists and the NAACP began to raise public doubts. For one thing, it did not seem to make sense that Tulia, a town of about 5,000 residents, could support so many

Thought-Crime or Emotion-Crime?

In the 1999 legislature, Senator Rodney Ellis, an African American from Houston, sponsored a bill that attempted to clarify Texas's 1993 hate crime law. Because of its vagueness, this law had been employed to prosecute criminals only twice since it had been passed, despite the occurrence of more than 300 hate crimes a year in Texas.

Supporters of the bill contended that the Byrd murder highlighted the need for additional measures to protect people from being assaulted because they happened to belong to an unpopular group. The bill passed the House, but failed in the Senate. Several arguments were made against the measure. Some critics pointed out that, without a new law, Byrd's killers had been swiftly brought to justice and given the ultimate penalty—why was another law necessary? Others expressed discomfort with the idea of punishing criminals for the thought behind their crime rather than for the crime itself. Still others argued that to punish criminals based on the identity of their victim would be to deny the equal protection of the laws to victims who were not included under the law's protection. Finally, some politicians refused to vote for a law extending special protection to homosexuals, asserting that such a consideration would be tantamount to endorsing their behavior.

By 2001, however, the temper of the state had changed. The legislature passed, and Governor Perry signed into law, the "James Byrd Jr. Hate Crimes Act" in May. It increased penalties for crimes that were motivated by hostility to race, color, disability, religion, national origin or ancestry, age, and gender and sexual orientation.

Sources: Nathan A. Kracklauer, "The Crusade Against Hate: A Critical Review of Bias Crime Legislation," Plan II honors thesis, University of Texas at Austin, May 1, 2000; *Crime in Texas 1998* (Austin: Department of Public Safety, 1999), 61; Terence Stutz, "Hate Crimes Bill Fails," *Dallas Morning News*, May 14, 1999, A1; The Power of One Web site: www.powerofone.org/.

Better Late than Never?

Sometimes, efforts to rectify past injustices take strange turns. In 1921, the City of Denton condemned an entire African American neighborhood, called "Quakertown," to create Civic Center Park, and moved the residents to another part of town. In 2007, the city council voted to rename the park Quakertown Park as a sort of perpetual apology to its former residents.

drug pushers. For another, investigations into Coleman's past turned up plenty of people willing to testify to his habitual disregard for the truth, his tendency to take things that did not belong to him, and his hostility toward Black citizens.

Further, solid evidence surfaced as to the unreliable nature of Coleman's testimony in these specific cases. One woman produced bank records proving that she was in Oklahoma at the time Coleman testified he was buying drugs from her. A man had a timecard showing that he was at work when Coleman claimed that the two of them were engaging in a transaction. Another man, who was short and bald, pointed out that Coleman had identified him in testimony as tall and bushy-haired. As the evidence mounted of something rotten in Tulia, the state's judicial system was persuaded to act.

In early 2003, the Texas Court of Criminal Appeals assigned retired state judge Ron Chapman to investigate the case. After hearing from a variety of witnesses, including Coleman, the judge, prosecutors, and defense attorneys agreed that, in the words of Chapman's opinion, "Coleman's repeated instances of verifiably perjurious testimony render him entirely unbelievable under oath."

By the end of 2003, all the Tulia defendants had been released from prison and pardoned by Governor Perry. In March 2004, the city of Amarillo agreed to pay $6 million to the forty-five Tulia defendants in return for their agreement to drop lawsuits (an average of $133,000 each). By the end of 2004, Tom Coleman had been convicted of aggravated perjury and imprisoned, and Swisher County district attorney Terry McEachern had lost his bid for reelection and had been sanctioned by the state bar association.[43]

From a civil rights perspective, the Tulia case is both different from and similar to the Jasper case. In Jasper, three White individuals inflicted a terrible crime on another individual because he was Black, but the community responded as one civilized entity. In Tulia, the community power structure itself—the county district attorney's office, in league with the drug task force—was so indifferent to the civil rights of the local minority citizens that it was virtually an accomplice in a crime against them. Nevertheless, in both cases, eventually justice was done. For much of the history of Texas, crimes against minorities, official and individual, were everyday occurrences in the state. Texas officials did not concern themselves with injustices to African Americans or Latinos, and did not respond to accusations that their rights had been violated. In that sense, Jasper and Tulia, for all the residual racism they revealed, also show us how far Texas has progressed in granting equal rights to all its citizens.

When the Texas Legislature considered passing the "sanctuary cities" bill during the 2011 legislative sessions, critics of the bill charged that passage would lead to racial profiling, harkening back to the ugly days of discrimination against African Americans prior to passage of civil rights legislation at the national level in the mid-1960s. The bill did not pass.

Courtesy of Ben Sargent.

Civil Rights for Convicted Criminals

People convicted of crimes are still citizens, and although they lose many of their civil rights, they retain others. The Eighth Amendment to the U.S. Constitution forbids "cruel and unusual punishments," and most people probably agree that however much they fear and dislike criminals, there is something unseemly about subjecting them to torture or bestial conditions while they are incarcerated.

For most of the twentieth century, however, state prison systems, especially in the South, were places where criminals were subjected to treatment that, if not unusual, was certainly cruel. A number of states even passed laws declaring the inmates of correctional institutions to be legally dead during their confinement. They might sue the state for violation of their rights after being released—being returned to life—but the chances of receiving justice months or years after the fact were remote.[44]

In the 1960s, however, as federal courts became more receptive to civil rights cases, literally hundreds of suits were brought in areas such as access to courts, mail censorship, medical care, solitary confinement, racial discrimination, work programs, staff standards and training, and a host of other aspects of a prisoner's existence. A glance at the legal record indicates that more cases were being filed against Texas jails and prisons than against those of any other state.[45]

The most important case of this type, and one that attracted national attention, began in 1972. An inmate brought suit against the Texas Department of Corrections (TDC), alleging cruel and unusual punishment of the 15,700 inmates

LONE STAR MEDIA

Civil Liberties Bills and the 2011 Legislative Session

Two of the most publicized issues in the 2011 Texas Legislative session were issues of civil liberties—a "sanctuary cities" bill and a bill regarding screenings of passengers at Texas airports. Ultimately each failed in the legislature. However, due to their inflammatory nature, they each received wide coverage from the media.

The sanctuary cities bill would have barred local governments from implementing policies prohibiting law enforcement officers from asking the immigration status of people they detain. The bill was passed in the House during the regular session and by the Senate during the special session, but never passed by both chambers at the same time. Proponents argued that this was a necessary step for stemming illegal immigration to the state while opponents focused on the racial profiling that would result from passage, a threat to the civil liberties of Texas citizens of Latino heritage. Law enforcement officials also were concerned that the law would make it less likely that people living in immigrant communities would report crime because they would fear invasive police interrogation. Perhaps the turning point of the debate came when Houston builder Bob Perry and Texas grocery magnate Charles Butt testified against the bill in part because of its potential negative effect on business.

The other major issue of civil liberties was the concern about invasive screening procedures at airports for passengers. The invasive procedures, including full body scanning procedures and thorough pat-downs, were enacted to screen against potential terrorists boarding airplanes, but had the effect of making potential passengers feel that their privacy was being violated. The bill would have faced challenges from the Transportation Security Administration as an overstepping of state power in a federal matter.

SOURCES: Peggy Fikac and Susan Carroll, "Critics Raise Doubt over 'Sanctuary Cities' Bill," *Houston Chronicle*, June 16, 2011; Patricia Kilday Hart, *Houston Chronicle*, June 24, 2011; Dave Montgomery, "TSA Pat Down Law Dies in State Legislature," *Fort Worth Star Telegram*, June 29, 2011.

---

in Texas prisons. In *Ruiz v. Estelle*, David Ruiz accused the TDC of violating prisoners' constitutional rights in the following five areas:

1. **The physical security of prisoners**

2. **Living and working conditions**

3. **Medical care**

4. **Internal punishment administered by the TDC**

5. **Access to courts of law**

Testimony in the case revealed horrific differences between the ideal system portrayed by top TDC officials and the actual conditions that existed within the prisons. Among the more chilling revelations was the fact that guards rarely entered the prisoners' cell blocks. Internal security was maintained by "building tenders"—privileged prisoners—who maintained order by terrorizing other inmates with lead pipes and other weapons.

Federal Judge William Wayne Justice, now deceased, ruled in favor of Ruiz, finding the TDC guilty of violating the Eighth Amendment. He ordered the organization to make a series of changes in its housing and treatment of prisoners. State officials reacted by "stonewalling"—denying that poor conditions existed, criticizing Judge Justice's "interference," and stalling on reform. The case dragged on for years before Governor Clements and other officials finally agreed to spend the money to make an effort to bring the TDC up to minimum standards.[46]

In 1992, Judge Justice approved a partial settlement of the Ruiz case, and the state was put back in charge of most of its prison functions. He warned Texas authorities, however, that the federal government would be monitoring its treatment of prisoners. In 2002, when David Ruiz was sixty years old, and the state prison system housed 145,000 inmates, Justice approved an agreement ending the lawsuit.[47]

As with any social change, the recognition that prisoners and others in state custody are human beings and have constitutional rights came about only with difficulty. The state resisted, and the federal courts had to step in. But much progress has been made. Official attitudes and programs today are more enlightened than those of three decades ago.

Capital Punishment

Texas is one of thirty-eight states that imposes **capital punishment**—the death penalty—for specific types of murder. The state reserves the ultimate punishment of lethal injection for "capital felony"—criminal homicide associated with one or more of eight aggravating circumstances.[48] Some examples of those circumstances would be murder of a peace officer or firefighter, murder for hire, and murder of a child under six.[49]

Capital punishment is a highly controversial issue in Texas, in the United States, and internationally (see the "You Decide" box). The great majority of Texans approve of imposing the death penalty for criminals who have been convicted of a capital felony (see Table 10-1). An ancient Greek definition of justice is

TABLE 10-1

Texas Public Opinion about Capital Punishment, 2010

Welcome to Texas
DRIVE FRIENDLY - THE TEXAS WAY

Percentage Who Somewhat Support or Strongly Support Capital Punishment	
Overall	78%
Anglo-American	89%
African-American	57%
Hispanic/Latino	76%
Democrats	66%
Republicans	90%

SOURCE: *Texas Politics*, University of Texas at Austin, August 25, 2011, http://texaspolitics.laits.utexas.edu/11_5_4.html.

YOU ★ ★ DECIDE

Is Capital Punishment Justified?

Large majorities of citizens in the United States as a whole and Texas in particular support capital punishment, but a vocal minority strongly opposes the practice. The arguments for and against capital punishment are both moral and practical:

PRO	CON
▲ Executions are expensive because they are delayed by frivolous appeals. Eliminate those appeals and the cost will fall.	▼ It costs more than $2 million to execute a criminal, about three times the cost of imprisoning someone for forty years.
▲ Not executing people costs lives. Convicts escape and kill, and they kill while in prison. No executed person has ever committed murder again. New scientific techniques, such as DNA testing, make the system less mistake-prone.	▼ No matter how careful the judicial system, some innocent people are bound to be executed.
▲ Social science studies are inconclusive as to whether capital punishment deters crime. Besides, a main purpose of capital punishment is retribution, not deterrence.	▼ The death penalty does not deter criminal behavior.
▲ Forcing a murderer to pay for his or her crimes with his or her life is not wrong; it is justice.	▼ Two wrongs do not make a right.
▲ The great majority of Americans believe that killing is sometimes justified, as in defense of the country or to punish murderers.	▼ Killing is always wrong, whether done by an individual or the state.
▲ Statistical studies show that Black murderers are no more likely to be executed than White murderers.	▼ The system of capital punishment is racially biased.

Sources: Thomas R. Dye, *Understanding Public Policy*, 8th ed. (Upper Saddle River, N.J.: Prentice Hall, 2008), 86–87; Hugo Adam Bedau, ed., *The Death Penalty in America: Current Controversies* (New York: Oxford University, 1997), passim; Audrey Duff, "The Deadly D.A.," *Texas Monthly*, February 1994, 38; Jim Mattox, "Texas' Death Penalty Dilemma," *Dallas Morning News*, August 25, 1993, A23; Thomas Sowell, "The Trade-Offs of the Death Penalty," *Austin American-Statesman*, June 15, 2001, A15; "Death No More," editorial in *Dallas Morning News*, April 15, 2007, P1.

"getting what one deserves." The majority of citizens believe that some people have committed crimes so terrible that they "deserve to die." Yet, many scholars and people of conscience argue that the death penalty does not deter crime and only adds a public, official murder to the private, unauthorized murder committed by the criminal. Both sides in the debate feel strongly. As with other emotional social issues such as abortion, the courts are not able to resolve the dispute.

In 1972, the U.S. Supreme Court stopped the states from carrying out capital punishment because, it ruled, the death penalty was capriciously applied and, especially, racially biased.[50] In 1976, after the states had taken steps to meet the Court's objections, it allowed executions again, subject to a number of rather stringent rules. The state must ensure that whoever imposes the penalty—judge or jury—does so after careful consideration of the character and record of the defendant and the circumstances of the particular crime. States are not allowed to automatically impose capital punishment upon conviction for certain crimes, such as murder of a peace officer. The capital sentencing decision must allow for consideration of whatever mitigating circumstances may be relevant. Capital punishment may be imposed only for crimes resulting in the death of the victim, so no one may be executed for rape, for example.[51]

Texas resumed executions in 1982. Of the states that now allow capital punishment, it has been by far the most active in killing convicted criminals. The Lone Star State executed 470 people convicted of murder from 1982 through the middle of 2011, far more than its share of those who were put to death nationally. Like the national trend, the number of executions per year in Texas seems to be declining, from 24 in 2009, to 17 in 2010, to 6 by mid-year 2011.[52]

Although capital punishment draws persistent criticism (see the "You Decide" box and the story of Cameron Todd Willingham in Chapter 9), its overwhelming popularity virtually ensures that it will remain the law of the state. Within that overall truth are smaller issues that confront the state's policymakers. Until recently, one of these was the question of whether Texas should create a sentencing category of "life without parole." Until 2005, there were two possible sentences for those convicted of murder: life and the death penalty. Those sentenced to life were eligible for parole after having served forty years. Opponents of the death penalty believed that juries would sentence more killers to life if they could be assured that the criminal would never be paroled; consequently, they supported the addition of the new sentencing category. Supporters of capital punishment shared that analysis of the situation, and consequently, they opposed the reform.

A related issue is whether a "life-without-parole" option should replace the death penalty. In each legislative session in the recent past, civil liberties groups, anticapital punishment organizations, and some prosecutors endorsed a bill that would make the change in the state's laws. In each session, however, the bill also was strongly opposed by some big-city prosecutors and victims-rights groups, and failed.

Nevertheless, in 2005, the tide was running against the hard-line position on the death penalty. An awareness of the results of DNA testing, already discussed in Chapter 9, had tended to take the wind out of the sails of those who argued that states do not make mistakes in their judicial processes. Moreover, a series of Supreme Court decisions had made it clear that the justices were losing patience with state judiciaries that seemed too ready to ratify the results of sloppy court processes.[53]

As a result, in 2005 a bill filed by Eddie Lucio, a Democrat from Brownsville, passed the House and Senate and was signed by Governor Perry. In order to persuade enough legislators to back his measure, Lucio was forced to drop a provision in the bill that retained the old "life-with-parole-after-forty-years" possibility. Now, a "life" sentence in Texas means just that; convicted murderers cannot expect to ever get out of prison. But they will probably be less likely to be sentenced to the ultimate penalty.[54]

Another recent issue associated with the death penalty debate is the question of how young a killer must be before he or she is too young to execute. In the history of crime, people as young as six years old have purposefully killed other people, but no one argues that children who become murderers that young should be executed. Yet, if not at six, then at what age does a criminal become executable by the state? Traditionally, the official Texas answer was that people who become murderers at seventeen are mature enough to pay the ultimate penalty, and the state put its policy into practice. In 2002, for example, three men who had committed murder at the age of seventeen were given lethal injections in Huntsville.[55]

Nevertheless, even many people who support capital punishment in general are given pause by the thought of holding seventeen-year-olds to a mortal standard. In virtually every other area, state law has considered someone of that age to be a child and too immature to be trusted with the responsibilities of adulthood. In Texas, people of seventeen years have been too young to vote, to buy alcohol, or to enter into a contract. To consider them mature enough to forfeit their lives for a crime seems to many people to be a large contradiction.

One controversial issue regarding capital punishment concerns the execution of juveniles. While Texans might support such executions in particular cases, there is less support than for capital punishment of adults. The American Bar Association, which took no position on the issue of capital punishment itself, opposed the execution of juvenile offenders. The Inter-American Commission on Human Rights, a judicial committee of the Organization of American States, periodically appealed to Texas and other states to end the execution of those who committed their crimes while they were children.[56]

Texas lawmakers and judges, fearing campaign criticism, seemed content to leave the seventeen-year-old minimum alone. The question of the execution of underage murderers was seldom even discussed in the legislature. No doubt this lack of interest in the question was caused by most politicians' determination to be known as "tough on crime," and their fear that, if they voted for any leniency toward murderers, their opponent in the next electoral campaign would label them "soft on crime." The justices of the U.S. Supreme Court, however, not being under the necessity of defending themselves during election campaigns, had no such fear. In 2005, they struck down the execution of criminals who were younger than eighteen when they committed their crimes. The ruling in effect commuted the sentences of seventy-two convicted murderers nationwide—twenty-eight of whom were in Texas—to life imprisonment, and forbade the capital sentencing of others in the future.[57]

In these two important issues surrounding capital punishment, therefore, Texas policy changed significantly in 2005. One remaining issue regarding the death penalty involves how the appeals are handled by the Texas Court of Criminal Appeals. In 2007, presiding Judge Sharon Keller decided to close the court at 5 P.M. rather than allow a last-minute appeal in the case of a man executed later that night. Judge Keller was reprimanded for her inaction. That reprimand was later overturned, though Keller's actions were deemed "not exemplary of a public servant."[58]

Torts and Tort Reform

A **tort** is a private or civil wrong or injury resulting from a breach of a legal duty that exists by reason of society's expectations about appropriate behavior rather than a contract. The allegedly injured party sues the alleged wrongdoer to receive compensation for his or her losses. Because tort actions are civil, not criminal, the losing party does not go to jail, but must pay money to the injured party. The loser may also sometimes have to pay "punitive damages," compensation in excess of the actual damages. These are awarded in the case of willful and malicious misconduct. A doctor whose negligence causes health problems to a patient may be the object of a tort action, as may a company whose defective product causes injury to its customers, a business whose unsafe premises cause an accident among its shoppers, a city that fails to warn of a washed-out road, and so on.

Up to 1995, business in Texas had been complaining for years that it was being stifled by unjustified litigation. Doctors joined business leaders in asserting that "pain-and-suffering" awards in malpractice suits had gotten so out of hand that many physicians were being forced to stop treating patients. The tort reform movement thus originated in the opinion of important, wealthy interests that the Texas judicial system was dominated by the wrong values and had to be reined in. "Tort reform" is really "court system reform," in that it consists largely of taking power out of the hands of judges and juries, limiting their discretion, and denying them jurisdiction.

Meanwhile, lawyers and many consumers' groups argued that there was no "litigation crisis" and that the whole tort reform movement was the result of

Hurry Up and Go Out of Business

At the same time that state lawmakers severely restricted the ability of patients to sue their doctors for malpractice in 2003, they created an institution that was supposed to protect and inform consumers about the behavior of health professionals. The Office of Patient Protection was supposed to monitor thirty-five boards that oversee and regulate more than a half-million doctors, nurses, dentists, dietitians, and others.

But the OPP never got off the ground. By the time its first chair, Harry Whittington, had been appointed by the governor, rented an office, purchased furniture, hired a staff, created a Web site, developed a complaint form, and visited with the heads of the thirty-five boards under his authority, it was time for the 2005 legislature. Searching for ways to save the state money, and perhaps responding to the health professionals' doubts about regulation of their behavior by a state office, senators refused to fund the commission. It folded up and went out of business in August 2005, without having acted on a single consumer complaint. The extra five dollars that health professionals were made to pay for licensing fees, which was supposed to fund the OPP, now goes into general state revenue.

Source: Mary Ann Roser, "Patient Protection Office Shut; Fee Goes On," *Austin American-Statesman*, October 13, 2005, A1.

a business-physician political alliance that was misleading the public in order to get away with abuse of consumers. Tim Curtis, executive director of the Texas Citizen Action Network, argued, "Remember that these defendants include: insurance companies who cheat their policyholders; manufacturers of dangerous and defective products that have killed and maimed children; inexperienced, careless, or drug impaired doctors who commit medical malpractice on trusting patients; even unscrupulous lawyers.... Legal concepts like joint and several liability and punitive damages have removed countless dangerous products from store shelves. Professionals who abuse their trust have been forced to change their practices or leave the profession."[59] The antitort reform coalition is thus pro-courts. Its purpose is to defend the power and discretion of judges and juries by endorsing the intelligence and justice of their actions in regard to civil litigation.

Whatever was the reality behind the clashing perceptions of the American, and Texas, litigation systems in the early 1990s, business (especially the insurance industry) and doctors launched a massive and well-financed campaign to persuade both state legislatures and Congress to enact comprehensive tort law reform. In Texas, the trend of history was on their side in this endeavor. Traditionally, business and doctors are part of the coalition of the Republican Party, while lawyers and consumer groups are part of the Democratic coalition (see Chapter 4). As Republicans partially took over Texas government in the 1994 election, and then wholly took it over in 2002, they became increasingly able to enact legislation that pleased their core constituency.

Tort reformers wanted to change several aspects of Texas's laws regulating civil suits.

1. **Punitive damages.** Reformers wanted to change the law to make a litigant prove that not just "gross negligence"—the wording under the state's statute until 1995—but actual malice was involved before punitive damages could be awarded. Also, they wanted to limit the amount of punitive damages. Doctors were particularly determined to cap the size of any amounts that a jury could award a plaintiff beyond actual medical damages.

2. **Joint and several liability.** Under the law prevailing to 1995, anyone who participated in as little as 11 percent of the cause of the injury could be held liable for the actions of others. This meant that if company A was found to be 11 percent at fault, and the other companies were bankrupt or otherwise unreachable, company A had to pay 100 percent of the award to the plaintiff. Reformers hoped to eliminate this responsibility of the richest, most available company.

3. **Venue.** Attorneys filing tort cases had been able to "shop around" for a judge who was known to be sympathetic to plaintiffs. Reformers wanted to restrict filings to the geographical area where the injury occurred.

4. **Deceptive Trade Practices Act.** Texas's consumer protection act provided triple damages for things such as deceptive real estate or stock deals. Reformers wanted to make a consumer prove that a deceptive act occurred knowingly.

In 1995, with Republican Governor George W. Bush lobbying hard for tort reform, but Democrats holding on to shrinking majorities in both houses of the legislature, the result was a compromise. Highlights of new laws passed that year include the following:

1. **Punitive damages were limited to the greater of $200,000 or the sum of two times economic damages, plus $75,000.**

2. **The joint and several liability rule was changed so that a defendant would have to be more than 50 percent responsible to be held liable for all damages.**

3. **To eliminate venue shopping, the legislature decreed that a business can be sued only in the county in which an injury occurred or in a county in which it has a principal office.**

4. **Judges were given more power to punish plaintiffs who file frivolous suits.**

5. **Plaintiffs who sue doctors or hospitals were required to post a $5,000 bond; if the claim proved baseless, the plaintiff was made to forfeit the bond.**

In 2003, after achieving majorities in both houses of the legislature, Republicans finished the job of revamping Texas's tort laws. They limited citizens' ability to file class-action suits, conferred immunity from suits on companies whose products meet government standards, limited the fees of trial lawyers in some cases, established penalties for plaintiffs who rejected settlements before trial (even if they won the case), and capped "pain-and-suffering" awards in medical malpractice suits at $250,000.[60]

As a result of the tort reform movement, therefore, Texas civil courts are markedly less important, and have much less freedom of choice than they enjoyed prior to 1995.

Reactions to the legal changes have been predictably different from different sides of the political fence. Supporters of the 1995 and 2003 reforms argue that patients now have more access to health care because doctors who were leaving the state or retiring due to increasing insurance costs are staying in practice now that insurance rates have moderated.[61] Opponents of the reforms counter that malpractice insurance rates rose in the late 1990s and early 2000s, and fell after 2003, because of changes in the insurance market, and had nothing to do with tort reform. Meanwhile, patients who have been the victim of negligent doctors or dishonest hospitals have no recourse because they have been frozen out of the legal system.[62] Likewise, the pro-reformers boast that the "New Era of Pro-Business Leadership Is Good for Texas,"[63] while antireformers lament that the members of Texans for Lawsuit Reform "have remade the world in their image, one in which there is no recourse for wrongdoing, one in which the powerful simply get their way."[64] (For a discussion of the politics of tort reform during the 2011 legislature, see Chapter 3.)

Like the arguments over abortion, capital punishment, and other controversies discussed in this chapter, the disagreement over the value of tort reform will never die because, on the issue of lawsuits, there is a permanent conflict between people who are likely to sue and those who are likely to be sued. Unlike those other issues, however, torts do not involve constitutionally protected rights. As

a result, on this subject, federal courts are reluctant to intervene in the Texas political process. Whatever the legislature, the governor, and the state Supreme Court endorse will be Texas law. Given the Republican alliance with antitort interests, and that party's ascendancy in state politics, Texas policymakers can be expected to remain hostile to "frivolous" lawsuits. For the time being, tort reformers have won, and as a result, the Texas civil justice system is greatly diminished in authority.

Conclusion

Overall, a survey of the products of the state court system suggests that it works better than its chaotic organization and controversial system of judicial selection might lead us to expect. Although Texas courts are not perfect examples of democracy in action, they have sometimes been ahead of the rest of the state's political system in dealing with the substance of justice. The state's judicial system, troubled as it is, gives some hope that it will be able to cope with the challenges of the future. Meanwhile, courts will continue to be asked to resolve the unresolvable social conflicts of our time.

Summary

The output of the Texas system of justice has improved, in some ways, in recent years. Whereas Texas courts used to be inhospitable to claims that people's civil rights and liberties had been violated, they are now more open to such claims. As the incidents in Jasper and Tulia illustrate, Texas still contains hard-core racism, but the state judicial system is working to mitigate its effects.

Although there is an argument about whether citizens have a right to keep and bear arms, the frame of that issue has changed recently. The U.S. Supreme Court now has ruled gun ownership an individual right, though questions concerning which kinds of guns are protected remain unanswered. The Texas courts have courageously taken on the rest of the political establishment, especially the legislature, in ordering a more equitable distribution of school revenues. They have not completely succeeded in introducing educational equality into Texas public schools, but they have forced the legislature to make the educational system at least somewhat more equitable.

Arguments are ongoing over some questions of rights and liberties. Although the national and state courts participate in social struggles over abortion, prayer in the schools, and personal expression, these issues provoke so much disagreement that they cannot be settled judicially. In two areas, however—the rights of criminals in Texas prisons and school segregation—the federal courts have been very active over the past three decades in forcing the reform of the system.

In recent years, many businesses became convinced that the outcome of Texas's tort laws was damaging the state's economy. They complained that the courts were too tolerant of frivolous suits that sometimes cost businesses so much money that they were forced to close down. In 1995 and 2003, the legislature, at the urging of Governors Bush and Perry, rewrote many of the tort laws so as to take discretion

away from the civil judiciary. It is now much more difficult to file, and to win, a civil lawsuit in Texas. This change made consumer representatives unhappy, but as long as the Republican Party controls most state offices, the changes are not likely to be undone.

Glossary Terms

capital punishment

civil liberties

civil rights

secular

tort

11

Solid waste collection is a basic local government service, whether it is provided by the city, as this photo of Denton depicts, or by a private agency with which the city or county contracts.

Courtesy of Denton Municipal Utilities.

Local Government

All politics is local.

ADAGE IN AMERICAN POLITICS

The average city portion of your property tax bill often costs less per month than a subscription to cable . . . television. For that amount, the local police keep you safe from crime, emergency medical workers respond to your emergencies, clean water flows from your faucets, and much more.

WE NEED: SAFE COMMUNITIES, ESSENTIAL INFRASTRUCTURE, VITAL SERVICES

TEXAS MUNICIPAL LEAGUE 2011 LEGISLATIVE THEME

INTRODUCTION

When the Texas Constitution was being written in 1875, only 8 percent of the state's population lived in urban areas. By the 2010 federal census estimates, Texas's 25.1 million population was 87 percent urban based on the proportion of the people living in places with a population of 2,500 or more. From 2000 to 2010, more than 5 million people were added to the state's population, with most of the increase in the Houston-Galveston, Dallas-Fort Worth, Austin-San Antonio, and Lower Rio Grande Valley areas. Much of this population growth has been among people who have specific problems—Hispanics and the elderly in particular. Much of the state's history and many of its problems are linked to urbanization and population growth.

Once one of the most rural states, Texas is now one of the most urban. Most of the change has taken place since 1950, when the development of such industries as petrochemicals and defense began luring rural residents into cities. Like most American cities, Texas cities have been unplanned until very recently. Growth patterns have been determined by developers, who give little thought to the long-range effects of their projects on the total community. Only in the past forty years has community planning come to be taken seriously. In Texas and elsewhere, the nation's domestic problems—racial strife, unemployment, inflation, storm damage, delinquency, crime, substance abuse, inadequate health care, pollution, inadequate transportation, taxation, and the shortage of energy—seem to be focused in the cities. But before examining city government and its problems, this chapter steps back in time and looks at the first unit of local government: the county.

Local government is an especially rich field for exploring whether the tests of democratic government outlined in Chapter 1 have been passed. Americans have long viewed local government as the government that is closest and most responsive to them. As one of the opening quotations notes, "All politics is local." Political careers begin at the local level; even

OBJECTIVES

After reading this chapter, you should be able to

Describe the nature of county government in Texas and the relationship of counties to state government.

Discuss the nature of city government in Texas and the distinctions between home rule and general-law cities and among forms of government (especially council-manager and mayor-council).

Understand both the advantages and disadvantages of special district government.

Realize the fiscal and other issues facing all local governments in Texas.

Understand leadership in local governments.

national issues are translated into their prospective effect on the local community; the local paper—whether daily or weekly—provides in-depth information about local government doings. Local government in Texas reflects more of a moralistic culture than does the Texas state government, in that local government traditionally offers an array of tools for general citizen involvement and control. In looking at the organization, politics, and finance of Texas's local governments, this chapter closely examines whether citizens take advantage of the opportunity for involvement at the local level and whether differences exist between general-purpose local governments (cities and counties) and special-purpose local governments (special districts).

Counties: One Size Fits All?

The county is the oldest form of local government in America. Today, 3,043 counties in 47 states have this unit of government. Texas has the largest number of counties—254—of any state in the nation.

Historical and Legal Background

In rural Texas, the county is still the most important local government.[1] Across the nation, counties vary enormously in size and importance. The largest in area is San Bernardino County in California, with 20,131 square miles. Arlington County, Virginia, is the smallest, with only 2 square miles. The largest county in Texas is Brewster, with 6,028 square miles; the smallest is Rockwall, with 147 square miles. Even more striking contrasts exist in population size. The 2010 population of Loving County in West Texas was a grand total of 82 people, while Harris County, which includes Houston, had 4.1 million—a figure that represented continuing growth.[2] (Long regarded as the U.S. county with the smallest population, Loving County came in second in the 2010 census to Maloka'i County, Hawaii, the site of a former leper colony.)

In Texas, as in other states, the county is a creation of state government. In the days before automobiles, citizens could not be expected to travel to the capital to conduct whatever business they had with the state; therefore, counties were designed to serve as units of state government that would be geographically accessible to citizens. Indeed, county size was limited so that a citizen could ride to the county seat on horseback in a single day. Until city police departments assumed much of the role, the county sheriff and the sheriff's deputies were the primary agents for enforcement of state law.

County courts still handle much of the judicial business of the state, and they remain integral to the state judicial system. Many state records, such as titles, deeds, and court records, are kept by the county; many state taxes are collected by the county, and counties handle state elections. Counties also distribute large portions of the federal funds that pass through the state government en route to individuals, such as welfare recipients.

Thus, most dealings that citizens have with the state are handled through the county. Yet, strangely, state government exercises virtually no supervisory authority over county governments. They are left to enforce the state's laws and administer the state's programs pretty much as they choose.

County officials are elected by the people of the county and have substantial discretion in a number of areas. For example, they can appoint some other county officials and set the tax rate. The result is a peculiar situation in which the county is a creation of state government, administering state laws and programs—with some discretion on the part of its officers—but county officials are elected by the people of the county and are in no real way accountable to the state government for the performance of their duties. Not surprisingly, county officials view themselves not as agents of the state, but rather as local officials. One result is that enforcement of state law varies considerably from county to county.

Organization and Operation of County Government

The Constitution of 1876, which established the state government, also set out the organization and operation of county government. The same concerns and styles are manifest for both governments, and there are close parallels in their organization and operation. For example, the decentralized executive found at the state level is reproduced at the county level in the county **commissioners court,**[3] the governing body in all Texas counties, and in semi-independent county agencies.

Structure

Another distinctive feature of Texas counties is the absence of **home rule,** which allows local governments to adopt their own charters, design their organizations, and enact laws within limits set by the state. Texas had a county home-rule provision of sorts between 1933 and 1969, but it was unworkable and was finally amended out of the constitution.

Because the county is the creation of the state and has no home-rule authority, the organization and structure of county government are uniform throughout Texas. Tiny Loving County and enormous Harris County have substantially the same governmental structure. Unlike counties in many other states, Texas counties do not have the option of having a form of government with an appointed professional administrator, such as the council-manager type described later in this chapter. Nor can they choose a form of government with an elected chief executive similar to the strong mayor-council form of city government. Counties have often found themselves saddled with unnecessary offices, such as treasurer, school superintendent, or surveyor. In November 1993, Texas voters amended the constitution so that only residents of the county involved would need to vote to abolish an office.

Figure 11-1 illustrates the organization of Texas county government. The county is divided into four precincts, each of which elects a commissioner to the commissioners court. The presiding officer of the commissioners court is the county judge. The county commissioners and the administrative agencies constitute the executive branch of county government, but the commissioners court performs as a legislature as well. Figure 11-1 also illustrates that counties have a large number of elected officials, ranging from a sheriff to constables to an attorney.

Each of the four commissioners is elected from a precinct, but the county judge is chosen in an **at-large election**—that is, one in which all registered voters in the county are eligible to participate. County officials are chosen in partisan elections; that is, candidates run as Democrats, Republicans, or minor-party candidates.

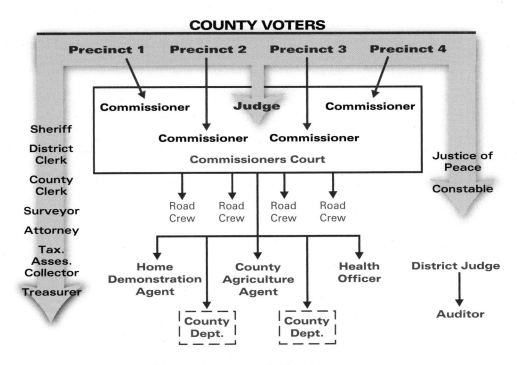

Figure 11-1 **Organization of County Government in Texas**

SOURCE: *Citizens' Guide to the Texas Constitution*, prepared for the Texas Advisory Commission on Intergovernmental Relations by the Institute of Urban Studies, University of Houston (Austin, 1972), 51.

Apportionment

In the past, when county commissioners drew county precinct lines, they drew those lines on some basis other than population. Unlike **gerrymandering**, where the objective is to perpetuate the position of the dominant party or faction, county precinct apportionment was for the purpose of re-electing incumbent commissioners and dividing the county road mileage on an equal basis. Roads, a major county function, were often more important than people. Not only were roads the lifeline for the state's rural population, which was once in the majority, but also contracts for roadwork represented the best opportunity for individual commissioners to wheel and deal. As a result, county commissioners often created precincts with great disparities in population.

In 1968, the U.S. Supreme Court, acting in a case against Midland County, ruled that all counties had to abide by the *one-person, one-vote* rule that had been applied earlier to the U.S. House of Representatives and to state legislatures (*Avery* v. *Midland County*, 88 S. Ct. 1114, 1968) (see Chapter 6). This rule requires that electoral districts must be roughly equal in population. After this ruling, some commissioners courts voluntarily redistricted on the basis of population; in other counties, federal judges ordered population-based redistricting. County apportionment has resurfaced as an issue in recent years in disputes over adequate opportunities for ethnic minorities to contend for county offices, in counties with substantial political party competition, and in urban counties with fast-growing suburbs.

Commissioners Court

The term *commissioners court* is a misnomer. It is not a judicial body, but an executive (policy-administering) and legislative (policymaking) body for the county.

Although technically the county is nothing more than an administrative arm of the state, the commissioners court does have functional latitude in several areas. In addition to setting the tax rate for the county (a legislative function), it exercises discretion in the administration of state programs (an executive function). Some of these state programs are mandatory, but the county may choose among others and may determine the amount of money allocated to each. For example, the state and counties are responsible for health care for the indigent, including care for individuals who are not qualified for the federally funded Medicaid program, and counties must ensure that hospital service is provided. An individual county, however, may elect to operate a public hospital, pay a public hospital in an adjacent county for services, or pay a private hospital for care of the indigent. Counties also are responsible for building and maintaining county jails, generally for providing health and safety services in rural areas, and for subdivision regulation in unincorporated areas.

Perhaps the most important power of the commissioners court is that of controlling the county budget in most areas of county government. If it chooses, it can institute a variety of different programs, many of which are major undertakings, such as county hospitals, libraries, and various welfare programs. Counties are also active in economic development activity.

The county commissioners court has the responsibility for conducting general and special elections. The court also has the power to determine the precinct lines for the justice of the peace precincts, as well as for the precincts of the four commissioners themselves. This power is a potent political weapon that can be used to advance the cause of some individuals and groups, and to discriminate against others. When these lines are not drawn fairly and equitably, malapportionment results, as was the case in the Midland situation noted earlier.

County Officials

The *county commissioners* also perform important functions as individuals. Each is responsible for his or her own precinct, including the establishment of road- and bridge-building programs, which represent a major expenditure of county funds. Since 1947, counties have had the authority to consolidate the functions of building and maintaining roads and bridges. About 10 percent of Texas's 254 counties have established a countywide unit system, enabling commissioners in those counties to take advantage of volume purchasing, share heavy road equipment, and so on. When she was a Travis County commissioner, former Governor Ann Richards led an unsuccessful campaign for statewide adoption of the unit system. In the other 90 percent of Texas's counties, individual commissioners still tend to roads and bridges in their individual precincts. One reason is the importance of these transportation facilities to residents in outlying areas, and thus the potential effect on re-electing the commissioner. Another reason is that individual commissioners simply like the power implicit in hiring personnel and letting contracts for road and bridge work. They also like the political advantage to be gained from determining the locations of new roads and which existing roads and bridges will be improved.

The *county judge* performs many functions. As a member of the commissioners court, the judge presides over and participates fully in that body's decision making. As a member of the county election board, the county judge receives the election returns from the election judges throughout the county, presents the returns to the commissioners court for canvassing, and then forwards the final results to the secretary of state. In counties with a population of fewer than 225,000, county judges also serve in an administrative capacity as county budget officer. They have the authority to fill vacancies that occur on commissioners courts. They are notaries public, can perform marriages, and issue beer, wine, and liquor licenses in "wet" counties. Many citizens see the county judge as a representative of the people and ask him or her to intervene with other elected officials and county bureaucrats. Many county judges have strong countywide power bases and are influential politicians.

The county judge also presides over the county court, although the position does not require legal credentials other than "being well informed in the law." County judges devote time to such matters as probate of wills, settlement of estates, appointment of guardians, and in many counties, hearing lawsuits and minor criminal cases. However, in larger counties, the county commission usually relieves the judge of courtroom responsibilities by creating one or more county courts at law.

One of the most visible legal officers is the *county sheriff*, who is elected at large. The sheriff has jurisdiction throughout the county, but often also makes informal agreements involving a division of labor with the police of the municipalities in the county. Particularly where large cities are involved, the sheriff's office usually confines itself to the area of the county outside the city limits. A major exception is that the sheriff is sometimes in charge of a joint crime task force, for example, a specialized group created to address illegal drug manufacturing and sales. The county sheriff has comprehensive control of departmental operations and appoints all deputies, jailers, and administrative personnel. In fact, the principal function of the sheriff is to serve as administrator of the county jail system. County jails house defendants awaiting criminal trial, individuals convicted of a misdemeanor and sentenced for a term up to a year, and felony (serious crime) convicts waiting to be transported to a state prison.

Corralling Sheriffs

Sheriffs and county commissioners often tangle. Although the sheriff is elected independently of the commissioners court, the county's chief law enforcement agent still must depend on the governing body for a budget. Sheriffs tend to view the law enforcement and jail budgets as sacrosanct, but the commissioners have to fund the budgets and tend to pare down sheriffs' requests for dollars.

Sometimes the conflicts are more colorful. In one North Texas county, the sheriff decided to "encourage" a high level of participation in local elections by requiring that all employees of the sheriff's department vote in the party primaries. The requirement was even included in the departmental personnel manual. Following widespread negative publicity, the sheriff recanted. Employees were allowed to decide for themselves whether to vote.

Some counties have found it profitable to build larger jails than they require and rent space to the state and to other counties. Depending on the size of the county, the sheriff's department may be quite complex and may have a substantial annual budget. A 1993 amendment to the state constitution authorizes the legislature to impose qualifications on sheriffs, such as mandatory training as a peace officer.

Another prominent county official is the *county attorney,* also elected at large. As the head of the county's legal department, the county attorney provides legal counsel and representation of the county. The attorney also prosecutes misdemeanors in the justice of the peace and county courts.

Another of the important elective offices in the county is that of *county clerk,* who is also elected at large. The county clerk is the recorder of all legal documents (such as deeds, contracts, and mortgages), issues all marriage licenses, and is the clerk of both the county court and the commissioners court. Many of the responsibilities for the conduct of elections, which formally rest with the commissioners court, actually are performed by the county clerk. For example, absentee voting is handled by the county clerk.

The *assessor-collector of taxes* collects the ad valorem (general property) tax for the county—and, often, by contract, for other local governments in the county; collects fees for license plates, license renewal stickers, and certificates of title for motor vehicles; and serves as the registrar of voters. This last duty is a holdover from the days of the poll tax, which was a fee paid to register to vote. The assessor-collector's job has been changed in recent years by the creation of the uniform appraisal system, to be discussed later in this chapter. In counties of 10,000 or more population, a separate assessor-collector is elected at large; in smaller counties, the sheriff serves as assessor-collector.

Other legal officers of the county are the *justices of the peace* (JPs) and the *constables.* In most but not all counties, there is at least one justice of the peace and one constable for each of the four precincts. Larger counties may have as many as eight JP districts. In the largest counties, numerous deputy constables assist the elected constables. The justice of the peace is at the bottom of the judicial ladder, having jurisdiction over only minor criminal cases and civil suits. The constable has the duty of executing judgments, serving subpoenas, and performing other duties for the justice of the peace court. Like the commissioners, the constables and JPs are elected for four years on a partisan basis by district.

Another elected official is the *county treasurer,* who is the custodian of public funds. Some counties have a *county school superintendent* to oversee rural schools.

The county has a number of other officers, some of whom perform important functions. In larger counties, a *county elections coordinator* is appointed to supervise elections. In counties with a population of more than 35,000, the state law requires that an *auditor* be appointed by the district judge having jurisdiction in the county for the purpose of overseeing the financial activities of the county and assuring that they are performed in accordance with the law. State law requires a *county health officer* to direct the public health program, and in most counties, the commissioners court appoints a *county agricultural agent* and a *home demonstration agent* for the purpose of assisting (primarily) rural people with agriculture and homemaking. The last two officers are appointed in conjunction with Texas A&M University, which administers the agriculture and home demonstration extension programs.

County Politics

County politics is characterized by three interrelated qualities: partisanship, precincts, and a long ballot. With the exception of the professional appointments noted earlier, such as a home demonstration agent and health officer, all the county officials discussed earlier in this chapter are elected. The key electoral units are the four commissioners' precincts, which also serve as the electoral base for constables and JPs. All contenders run under a political party banner and are elected during general elections when major officials such as president, governor, and members of Congress are elected. Because the form of government is the same in all counties, so also are the electoral arrangements. Thus, to a great extent, a description of state parties and elections also describes county politics (see Chapters 4 and 5).

An Evaluation of County Government

When industrial firms experience problems, they call in teams of management consultants, who make a searching examination and a critical evaluation of the firm's operation. If one could arrange for a management consulting firm to make a thorough examination of county government in Texas, its report would very likely include the following topics.

Structure and Partisanship

The county in Texas is a nineteenth-century political organization struggling to cope with the twenty-first century—hence, the "one size fits all" title of this main section. In many states, counties have the same flexibility as cities to choose a *form of government* that is appropriate for the size and complexity of that particular jurisdiction. In Texas, all county governments have the same structure, and the emphasis is on *party politics* because all officials are elected on a partisan basis. The positive aspect of partisanship is that the average voter can understand more clearly what a candidate's approximate political position is when the candidate bears the label Republican or Democrat than when there is no identifying tag.

Nationally, although most counties operate with a commission, urban counties serving the majority of the nation's citizens operate with a county manager or appointed administrator.[4] California, Florida, and North Carolina are examples of states in which counties are professionally managed. Texas, of course, does not provide formal authority for counties to vary the form of government, but the county judges in the largest Texas counties increasingly are hiring experienced local government managers to tend to administrative functions. Although the current structure is uniform and simple, it also makes it difficult to produce decisions for the benefit of all or most county residents because of the emphasis on precincts. Commissioners tend to see themselves as representing their precinct rather than the county as a whole. In turn, the precinct focus makes it difficult to enjoy economies of scale, such as purchasing all road-paving materials at one time.

The partisanship and restrictive structure can lead to governance problems. Commissioners often squabble over petty matters. Citizens have difficulty deciding whom to blame if they are dissatisfied with county government, because the commissioners serve as a collective board of directors for the county. For example, a troublesome sheriff or constable may be re-elected while the voters blame the county commissioners for the law officer's behavior. Similarly, the voters may focus on the county judge, who has one vote on the commissioners court just

PRESIDIO COUNTY COURTHOUSE

TARRANT COUNTY COURTHOUSE

VAL VERDE COUNTY COURTHOUSE

LLANO COUNTY COURTHOUSE

Texans enjoy roaming through historic Texas county courthouses, many of which have been restored to their nineteenth- and early-twentieth-century glory.

(top left) © Panaormaic Image/Getty Images. (top right) © Walter Bibikow/The Image Bank/Getty Images. (bottom left & right) © Bob Daemmrich Photography.

like the other members, when other members of the court should be the object of attention. Such confusion can happen in any government, but the large number of elected officials—mirroring the state pattern—compounds the problem.

A plus for counties is that they are less bureaucratic than other governments; thus, the average citizen can more easily deal with a county office. One reason may be that, unlike the state government, county government does not have a clear-cut separation between legislative and executive branches and functions. The merger of executive and legislative functions, which is called a unitary system, also is found in some city and special district governments. It can sometimes produce a rapid response to a citizen problem or request.

One county judge assessed county government by noting that many county officials are highly responsive to public demands when they must face competitive elections. In fact, he argued that counties are the last true bastions of *grassroots politics,* whereby government is close to all the people in the county. Although the court sets much of the policy and the tone for the conduct of county operations, it lacks the authority to give explicit orders to subordinate officials. Nevertheless, this county judge pointed out, by controlling the budget, the commissioners court can often dictate the behavior of other elected officials. Additionally, counties have the lowest tax rates of all the governments in Texas.[5] Another county judge put it this way: "We do meat-and-potatoes government . . . not flashy, press-release government, but good government."[6]

Thus, the evaluation of county organization and politics is mixed. The public often shows little interest in county government. Voter turnout is low, and even the media tend to ignore county government and focus instead on big city, state, and national political events. The county is a horse-drawn buggy in structure. It is often highly democratic, especially when it advocates the interests of groups ignored by other governments, because the commissioners must secure support for re-election. However, the willingness of commissioners and other elected officials to attend to the needs of individuals and to deal with details can easily lead to corruption.

Management Practices

County government in Texas is one of the last bastions of the **spoils system** in which people are appointed to government jobs on the basis of whom they supported in the last election and how much money they contributed. A spoils system may help to ensure the involvement of ordinary citizens in government by allowing a highly diverse group of people to hold government jobs. When such a dispersion of jobs occurs, the result is *pluralism*—that is, a reflection in public employment and public policy of the cultural diversity in society.

However, a spoils system can also lead to the appointment of unqualified people, especially in jobs requiring specialized training. It can contribute to a high turnover rate if the county tends to usher new elected officials into office on a regular basis. For example, a common practice is for a newly elected sheriff to fire several deputies and bring in his or her own people. Finally, a spoils system may create not pluralism but *elitism;* those persons appointed to public office may represent only a narrow spectrum of society and reflect only the upper crust of the dominant political party.

Democratic government demands that citizens not only be willing to obey the law, but also be able to count on public officials being scrupulous in their own behavior, and not merely partisan. Also, political appointees may not be

Consequences of No County Ordinance Power

In unincorporated areas, the lack of county ordinance power manifests itself in many ways. Fireworks stands inevitably are erected a few feet outside a city's jurisdiction; contractors frequently take more liberties with sound construction principles in rural areas; and controversial establishments such as topless bars, noisy gun ranges, and polluting cement plants find homes in unincorporated county areas. In Williamson County, just north of Austin, a property management company even erected a 120-foot-high billboard that violated both state signage regulations and the rules of the homeowners' association for the apartments themselves. In all of these cases, counties are powerless to act.

current on modern management practices; for example, an elected commissioner of Travis County (fifth largest in the state) complained that the computer system is still based on DOS, a computer language that is now obsolete almost everywhere else. As one might expect, most experts think a spoils system has more risks than advantages.

From a management standpoint, a *civil service* or a *merit system* of recruitment, evaluation, promotion, and termination based on qualifications and a pay scale that would attract and hold competent personnel would help improve governmental performance. Such practices also would be fair to employees as recognition for their labors and to taxpayers as a return on their dollars. Some larger counties have made significant strides toward developing professional personnel practices, such as competitive hiring, merit raises, and grievance processes, but 90 percent of the counties have a long way to go. In a larger county, commissioners also appoint a wide array of professionals, such as a budget officer, personnel director, and economic development coordinator.

Two other features of county government illustrate its tendency toward inefficient management: decentralized purchasing and the road and bridge system. *Decentralized purchasing* means that each department and each commissioner make separate purchases, whether for office supplies or heavy road equipment. Quantity discounts, which might be obtained with a centralized purchasing agent, are unavailable on small-lot purchases. Also, the opportunity for graft and corruption is real. To make sure that they will get county business, sellers may find themselves obligated—or at least feel that they are—to do a variety of favors for individual officials in county government. This situation is not unknown in the other governmental units, but becomes more widespread in highly decentralized organizations.

Unless a Texas county belongs to the elite 10 percent that have a *unit system for countywide administration of the roads and bridges*, individual commissioners may plan and execute their own programs for highway and bridge construction and maintenance at the precinct level. The obvious result is poor planning and coordination and also duplication of expensive heavy equipment. These inefficiencies are important because counties, like other local governments, must cope with taxpayer resistance to providing more funding for government. Thus, efficient performance is a must.

Lack of Ordinance Power

Texas counties have no general power to pass ordinances—that is, laws pertaining to the county. They do have authority to protect the health and welfare of citizens, and through that power, they can regulate the operation of a sanitary landfill and mandate inoculations in the midst of an epidemic. They can regulate subdivision development in unincorporated areas, sometimes sharing power with municipalities and, for flood control, the federal government. However, the lack of general ordinance power means that, for example, they cannot zone land to ensure appropriate and similar usage in a given area, and they have trouble guarding against rutted roads and polluted water supplies when land developers or gas drillers start to work.[7]

Recommendations

Having reviewed Texas county government, our mythical management consultants probably would recommend the following:

- ■ **Greater flexibility in this form of government, particularly in heavily populated areas, to encourage more professional management of personnel, services, purchasing, and all other aspects of county government**

- ■ **Taking advantage of economies of scale by centralizing purchasing and adopting a unit system of road and bridge construction and maintenance**

- ■ **Cooperative delivery of services**

Texas counties have no authority to pass general ordinances that could, for example, regulate land use in rural areas. The *colonias* on the outskirts of Texas cities along the Mexican border are an example of unregulated growth.

Courtesy of Ben Sargent

However, they probably would not yet explore any of the forms of city-county cooperation that exist in areas such as San Francisco, Honolulu, or Nashville because counties in Texas are not yet ready to function as cities. The exceptions are El Paso County, where the county and city have explored consolidation, and Bexar County, where the county judge has advocated merger. The *Austin American-Statesman* has also urged some consideration of "government modernization" on the Travis County commissioners.[8]

Prospects for Reform

Given the obvious disadvantages of the current structure, what are the prospects for changing county government in Texas? County commissioners, judges, sheriffs, and other county officers, acting individually, as well as through such interest groups as TACO (Texas Association of County Officials), are potent political figures who can and do exercise substantial influence over their state legislators. Unfortunately for the taxpayers, most county officials have shown little willingness to accept change in the structure and function of county government. The exceptions are usually county commissioners in more heavily populated counties, who have taken a number of steps to professionalize government, including the appointment of personnel and budget experts. They are outnumbered ten to one by commissioners in less populous areas. Thus, substantially more citizen participation will be necessary if change is to occur. If city residents, who tend to ignore county politics, were to play a much more active role, reform might be possible because of the sheer numbers they represent when approaching legislators.

Cities: Managed Environments

Unlike the county, the city has a long history of independence and self-government. The power of ancient Greece was concentrated in city-states such as Athens and Sparta, which as early as 700 B.C. were centers of culture and military might. In the Middle Ages, European cities received crown charters that established them as separate and independent entities. One of their major functions was to protect their citizens from external danger; for this reason, the cities of the period were surrounded by high walls, and the citizens paid taxes for this protection. In America, this tradition continued, and early American cities sought charters initially from the British crown and later from the state legislatures. In Texas, San Fernando de Béxar (now San Antonio) was the first city. Its settlement was ordered by the king of Spain and began with fifteen families in 1731.

State legislatures traditionally have been less than sympathetic to the problems of the cities, partly because of rural bias and partly because they wished to avoid being caught in the quagmires of city politics. Therefore, in the nineteenth century, the states (including Texas) established **general laws**—statutes that pertained to all municipalities—for the organization of the city governments, to which municipalities were required to conform. But these general laws were too inflexible to meet the growing problems of the cities, and around the turn of the century, there was a movement toward *municipal home rule*. The home-rule laws permitted the cities, within limits, to organize as they saw fit.[9]

In Texas, the municipal home-rule amendment to the constitution was adopted in 1912. It provides that a city with a population of more than 5,000 is allowed—within certain procedural and financial limitations—to write its own constitution in the form of a city charter, which would be effective when approved by a majority vote of the citizens. A city charter is the local equivalent of a constitution. Home-rule cities may choose any organizational form or policies as long as they do not conflict with the state constitution or the state laws. General-law cities may organize according to any of the traditional forms of municipal government discussed later in this chapter, but with a number of restrictions due to the complex statutory categorization of general-law cities based on combinations of population and land area.

Traditionally, municipalities were organized into one of three types of governments: *mayor-council*, *commission*, and *council-manager*. Within these categories were a variety of subtypes. In the modern era, the commission form is rarely used, but hybrid forms of government that combine mayor-council and council-manager are growing in popularity; at least seven modern forms of municipal government have been identified.[10] Thus, it is sometimes difficult to slot an individual city into a particular category. This chapter looks at the three basic types, noting the most frequent variations on each.

In addition to home rule, two other legal aspects of city government in Texas are *extraterritorial jurisdiction* (ETJ) and *annexation*. ETJ gives cities limited control over unincorporated territory contiguous to their boundaries; that is, cities get some control over what kind of development occurs just outside the city limits. The zone ranges from a half-mile in distance for cities under 1,500 in population to five miles for those over 100,000. Within these zones, municipalities can require developers and others to conform to city regulations regarding construction, sanitation, utilities, and similar matters. In this way, cities can exercise some positive influence on the quality of life in the immediate area around them.

Socially irresponsible individuals and businesses sometimes locate outside both city limits and a city's extraterritorial jurisdiction for the dual purposes of avoiding city taxes—usually higher than the county's—and city regulation, such

Life Downtown: A View of Five Cities

Although Easterners have long seen the advantages of living downtown rather than in the suburbs, Texans are only recently coming to realize pluses such as elimination of rush hour traffic woes and proximity to sports venues and entertainment centers. Austin, Dallas, Fort Worth, Houston, and San Antonio have paid special attention to downtown redevelopment and to attracting residents to the downtown area. One of the biggest drawbacks has been the lack of grocery stores. Indeed, early in 2004, when a major grocery chain announced plans to build a store in downtown Dallas, the news received prominent coverage in both the print press and the broadcast media; ultimately, by 2006, the grocery store required almost $600,000 in subsidies from the city to stay open.

Sources: Dave Harmon, "Livable, Workable, Playable: Five Texas Cities Have Seen the Future, and It's an Urban Center That Is Livable, Workable, Playable," *Austin American-Statesman*, January 1, 2004, A5, A12–13; Dave Levinthal, "Grocery for City's Center," *Dallas Morning News*, January 6, 2004, 1A, 9A.

as building codes. The lack of county ordinance power encourages such behavior, while ETJ helps to correct it.

Annexation power allows cities to bring adjacent unincorporated areas inside the municipal boundaries. Doing so helps prevent suburban developments from incorporating and blocking a large city's otherwise natural development. It also allows a city to expand its tax base. In the 1950s and 1960s, municipalities could make great land grabs without any commitment to providing services, but over the years, annexation powers have been curbed. The legislature in 1999 considerably tightened requirements for notice and provision of service with the passage of SB 89. Exceptions are areas with fewer than 100 residents and areas that have asked for annexation.

Annexation laws in Texas help prevent a phenomenon that is very common in other states' cities, such as Cleveland and Denver. There, more affluent residents have fled to upscale suburbs in what is often called "White flight" because most of the people who leave are Anglos. They leave the inner cities with inadequate tax revenues and decaying facilities. They no longer pay city taxes, but continue to use and enjoy such services as airports, libraries, utilities, and museums, which city residents pay taxes to support. When a city exercises its annexation powers, it can protect its tax base somewhat, as well as preserve space for future development. Although Texas's larger cities are surrounded by suburbs, many of which are upscale, they have been somewhat successful in counteracting White flight and the erosion of their tax bases, and are even experiencing new development in downtown areas. Houston is the best (or worst) example of a city using annexation to protect itself. In 1995, Houston, along with Austin, Nederland, and Longview, was the target of special legislation advocated by suburbanites to limit annexation power. Again, the cities prevailed.

A Zoning-Free City

Houston has long been known as the only major American city without zoning ordinances that dictate what can be built where—homes, offices, factories. In the past, city leaders have used such terms as "Communist plot" and "socialized real estate" to describe zoning. Voters have explicitly and repeatedly rejected it, most recently in 1993. As a result, a church, an office tower, and a home can be found adjacent to one another.

Houston, with more than 2.2 million people, is the fourth largest city in population in the United States. It is the second largest city in terms of land area, behind Anchorage, Alaska, which has only 300,000 people. Nevertheless, a growing, sprawling American megacity without zoning is rare.

Sources: See, for example, Sam Howe Verhovek, "'Anything Goes' Houston May Go the Limit: Zoning," *New York Times*, October 27, 1993, 1; Patrick Barta, "To Limit Growth, Houston Turns to Deed Restrictions," *Wall Street Journal*, May 12, 1999, T1, T3. See also "United States Cities by Population," Wikipedia, accessed at http://en.wikipedia.org/wiki/List_of_United_States_cities_by_population#Incorporated_places_over_100.2C000_population, for comparative population data.

Organization of City Government

Home-rule cities have overwhelmingly opted for the council-manager plan of government. Of the 389 cities for which information was available, [11] approximately 368 (94.6 percent) used the council-manager form, and only 20 operated under the mayor-council plan, including 12 with a mayor-appointed administrator. None used a commission form, although some city councils still call themselves "commissions." Among the 821 general-law cities, some 335 (40.5 percent) were recognized council-manager or mayor-administrator cities. The basic forms of municipal government are described next, with emphasis on the two most popular forms—council-manager and mayor-council—followed by a look at a hybrid form and a historical note on the commission form.

The Council-Manager Form

San Antonio and Dallas are two of the largest cities in the country—along with Phoenix and San Jose—using this organizational model (Figure 11-2), but smaller cities such as Beeville, Gainesville, and Yoakum also operate with the *council-manager* form of government. Under this system, a city council of five to fifteen members is elected at large or by districts and, in turn, appoints a city manager who is responsible for the hiring and firing of department heads and for the preparation of the budget. A mayor, elected at large or by the council, is a member of the council and presides over it, but otherwise has only the same powers as any other council member.

Proponents of council-manager government, including many political scientists, traditionally have argued that this form of government allows at least some separation of politics and administration. They believe that the council makes

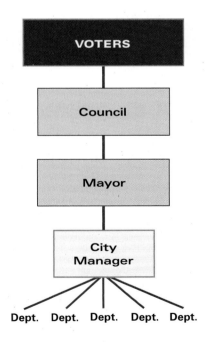

Figure 11-2 Council-Manager Form

SOURCE: Adapted from *Forms of City Government* (Austin: Institute of Public Affairs, University of Texas, 1959), 23.

public policy and that, once a decision is made, the manager is charged with administering it. In reality, however, politics and administration cannot be separated: The city manager must make recommendations to the council on such highly political matters as tax and utility rates and zoning.[12] Nevertheless, some citizens claim to perceive a distinction in this type of government between politics and policymaking on the one hand and administration on the other, and many are convinced that it is the most efficient form of city government. States with a large number of council-manager cities include Texas, California, Florida, Maine, and Michigan, among others.

For all its efficiency and professionalism, council-manager government does have some problems. First, because council members are part time and often serve short tenures, they may rely heavily on the manager for policy guidance. Because the manager is not directly responsible to the voters, this practice makes it more difficult for the average citizen to influence city hall, and many citizens react negatively to reading in the local newspaper about the city manager's policy recommendations, even though the council must approve them. Second, the comparison is frequently drawn between council-manager government and the business corporation because both involve policymaking "boards" and professional managers. When coupled with the emphasis on efficiency, this image of a professionally trained "business manager" also tends to promote the values of the business community. The result is that festering political problems, especially those involving ethnic minorities and the poor, may not be addressed in a timely manner. However, district elections and direct election of the mayor in council-manager cities have reduced this problem somewhat, as representation on city councils has become more diversified. Also, city managers are now trained to be sensitive to all citizens. As the former executive director of the International City/County Management Association put it, "For nearly 90 years, the council-manager form has successfully adapted to American community needs."[13]

On Becoming a City Manager

How does one become a city manager? A city manager usually has a master's degree in public administration, public policy, or public affairs. The most common route is an internship in a city while still in school, followed by a series of increasingly responsible general management positions: administrative assistant, assistant to the city manager, assistant city manager, and then city manager. Alternatively, an individual may begin in a key staff area—for example, as a budget analyst, then budget director, and then director of finance—or in a major operating department—for example, as an administrative assistant in the public works department, then as an assistant director, and then director. Usually, the individual must move up through these positions in several municipalities to reach the top job. The Web site of the International City/County Management Association (www.icma.org) provides other information for the individual seeking a local government career, as does the Web site of the National Association of Schools of Public Affairs and Administration (http://www.naspaa.org/students/careers/careers.asp).

The Mayor-Council Form

In the *mayor-council* form of municipal government, council members are elected at large or by geographic districts, and the mayor is elected at large. "At large" means citywide. The mayor-council form has two variants: the *weak mayor-council* form and the *strong mayor-council* form. The words *strong* and *weak* are used in reference to a mayor's powers in the same way that the word *weak* is applied to the Texas governorship. The terms have to do with the amount of formal power given to the chief executive by the city charter. An individual mayor, by dint of personality, political savvy, and leadership skills, can heavily influence local politics regardless of restrictions in the city charter.

In the weak mayor-council form, other executives such as the city attorney and treasurer also are elected, whereas in the strong mayor-council form, the mayor has the power to appoint and remove other city executives. In the strong mayor-council form, the mayor also prepares the budget, subject to council approval. In both mayor-council forms, the mayor can veto acts of the city council, but typically fewer council votes are needed to override the mayor's veto in a weak mayor-council city than in a strong mayor-council city. An individual city charter may combine elements of both strong mayor-council and weak mayor-council government—for example, giving the mayor budget control while also allowing for some other elected positions.

Figure 11-3 illustrates the strong mayor-council form. A diagram of a weak mayor-council form would be very similar, except that a series of other elected officials would be specified, such as the city attorney, police chief, and parks and recreation director.

The strong mayor-council form is most common among the nation's largest cities, whereas the weak form prevails in smaller communities. In Texas, the only large city with mayor-council government is Houston, which also has an elected controller to run the city's finances. Small-city examples include Hitchcock and Quinlan.

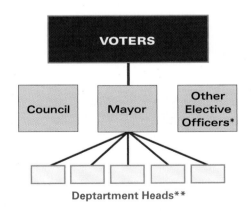

Figure 11-3 Strong Mayor-Council Form

SOURCE: *Forms of City Government* (Austin: Institute of Public Affairs, University of Texas, 1959), 10.
* In a number of strong mayor-council cities, the chief of police and some other department heads are elected, although that is not the case in Texas.
** Common departments are fire, police, streets and sanitation, utilities, and parks and recreation.

Because mayor-council government is what is called an "unreformed" or a "political" model,[14] it may experience more efficiency problems than a professionally managed city, and have less ability to arrive at consensus on policy. To overcome some of its problems, mayor-council cities—particularly larger ones—often have a deputy mayor or chief administrative officer appointed by the mayor who tends to the internal business of the city, while the mayor tends to political matters.[15]

Many political scientists favor the strong mayor-council form of government because they think it seems most likely to provide the kind of leadership needed to cope with the growing problems of major urban areas, and it focuses on an elected, not an appointed, official. Another reason for this opinion is that the mayor and council members, especially in larger cities, are full-time paid officials who can devote their time to the development of public policy and oversight of government services. Thus, policy proposals come directly from elected officials. If these officials represent a broad public interest, as opposed to narrow interest groups, democracy is well served.

The Mayor-Manager Form

The *mayor-manager* form of government, also called the *chief administrative officer* (CAO) form, is growing in popularity nationwide.[16] This plan has generated interest because it combines the overt political leadership of a mayor-council plan with the professional management skills identified with council-manager government. Typically, it arises when the mayor recognizes a need for managerial assistance. In this form of government, the city manager reports only to the mayor, not to the council as a whole, and focuses on fiscal/administrative policy implementation. The mayor provides broad policy leadership in addressing major problems, such as crime and economic development.

In Texas, some smaller cities, such as Argyle and Mathis use a city administrator plan, but often the smaller communities use the hybrid only until a charter election can be held to adopt council-manager government. Elsewhere, mayor-manager government is often practiced in consolidated city-county governments, such as Lexington-Fayette County, Kentucky, and some cities, such as San Ramon, California.

A variant of mayor-manager government is arising in larger municipalities. In Texas and across the country, large cities using the council-manager plan have seen disputes develop among the mayor, council members, and managers as assertive mayors try to carve out a larger role for themselves. The growing interest of big-city mayors in controlling both the political and the administrative aspects of city government is illustrated by events in Dallas. In 1987–1991, Mayor Annette Strauss imposed strong political leadership on the city with her "Honey, do it for Dallas" approach that masked behavior at times more reminiscent of a strong mayor than the mayor of a council-manager city. Then, in 1992–1993, Mayor Steve Bartlett, a former U.S. congressman, and City Manager Jan Hart struggled for control, with Hart ultimately leaving in 1993 to enter the private sector. In 1997, Mayor Ron Kirk struggled more with the Dallas City Council, which resisted his bid for greater power, than he did with City Manager John Ware, but his intent was the same as Bartlett's: to gain control of the city's executive establishment. In 2002, a charter review commission initiated by Dallas Mayor Laura Miller began studying stronger formal powers

for the mayor and perhaps the possibility of eliminating the city manager position. Two different elections on the issue of a strong mayor-manager form for Dallas were held in 2005; both resulted in retention of the traditional council-manager form. More cooperative mayor-manager relationships *can* exist in large cities, as, for example, in Fort Worth.

Table 11-1 summarizes the form of government used in the nation's and the state's largest cities. It also provides information on population size, the percentage of population change between the 2000 census and the 2009 census estimates, and the physical size of the cities.

The Commission Form

The *commission* form of city government is said to have originated in Galveston. In 1900, the city lost 7,200 persons in a disastrous storm surge that swept the Texas coast in the wake of a fierce hurricane. The city then applied for and received permission from the state legislature to adopt a commission form of government to meet its emergency needs.

TABLE 11-1

Basic Facts about America's Ten Largest and Texas's Seven Largest Cities, as of the 2009 Census Estimate

City with Rank in Population	2009 Population	% Population Change 2000–2009	Land Area in Square Miles	Type of Governance
1. New York City	8,391,881	+4.8	303.3	Mayor-Council
2. Los Angeles	3,831,868	+3.7	469.1	Mayor-Council
3. Chicago	2,851,268	−1.5	227.1	Mayor-Council
4. Houston, TX	2,257,926	+15.6	579.4	Mayor-Council with elected Controller
5. Phoenix	1,601,587	+10.7	474.9	Council-Manager
6. Philadelphia	1,547,297	+1.9	135.1	Mayor-Council
7. San Antonio, TX	1,373,668	+16.1	407.6	Council-Manager
8. San Diego	1,306,301	+6.8	324.3	Mayor-Council with Chief Operating Officer (COO)
9. Dallas, TX	1,299,543	+9.3	342.5	Council-Manager
10. San Jose	964,695	+7.8	175	Council-Manager
15. Austin, TX	786,382	+19.8	251.5	Council-Manager
17. Fort Worth, TX	727,575	+36.1	292.5	Council-Manager
22. El Paso, TX	620,447	+10.1	249.1	Council-Manager
49. Arlington, TX	380,084	+14.1	99.5	Council-Manager

NOTE: This information is for the city alone, not the metropolitan area, which may be double or triple the population size and several times the land area of the central city. The land area is as of 2005.

SOURCES: "Top 50 Cities in the U.S. by Population and Rank," *Infoplease.com*, found at http://www.infoplease.com/ipa/A0763098.html, plus individual city Web pages.

Under this type of organization, the elected commissioners collectively compose the policymaking board and, as individuals, are administrators of various departments, such as public safety, streets and transportation, finance, and so on. They are usually elected at large. Although widely copied initially, the commission system has more recently lost favor because many think that the commissioners tend to become advocates for their own departments rather than public interest advocates who act on behalf of the entire city. Also, the city commission is subject to many of the same problems as the county commission, including corruption and unclear lines of responsibility.

Although some cities still call their city councils commissions and some cities in other states still use the form, Texas home-rule cities have abandoned the commission form. Galveston itself was recognized by the International City/County Management Association as a council-manager city in 1961, and worked to recover from the devastation of Hurricane Ike in 2008 using that form. Some general-law cities still have commission government.

Forms Used in General-Law Cities

Texas has about 821 general-law cities—cities whose population is fewer than 5,000 or somewhat larger cities that, for one reason or another, have not opted for home rule. These cities can organize under any of three basic forms of government: aldermanic (a variant of the mayor-council type), council-manager, or commission. However, state law limits the size of the council, specifies other municipal officials, spells out the power of the mayor, and places other restrictions on matters that home-rule cities can decide for themselves.[17]

Because of their small size, most of the general-law cities have chosen the aldermanic model—basically, mayor-council government. The council-manager form, calling for the hiring of a professional city manager, is thought to be too expensive and unnecessary in a small city. There is also the problem of finding a trained city manager who is knowledgeable about small-town issues. However, some smaller cities, such as Morton, have designated the city clerk as the chief administrative officer without bothering to adopt council-manager government formally. A few have hired a part-time manager—usually a graduate student in a nearby public administration program—or have banded with other small communities to hire a "circuit-riding" city manager. Whatever their official title—city manager, city clerk, city secretary, or assistant to the mayor—administrators in smaller cities more than earn their salaries. They usually serve as general managers, personnel directors, tax assessor-collectors, and so forth because they are often the only full-time professional in the city's government.

What Form Is Preferable?

The only clear answer is that city size seems to have some effect on the type of municipal government that works best. For small cities, the type of government does not seem to matter much. Smaller cities that can afford a city manager often do well with that form, but most use a mayor-council form, often relying on the city secretary to coordinate administrative affairs. Mid-size cities (from 25,000 to 250,000 in population) can afford to hire a manager, and because they tend to be suburban and relatively homogeneous in terms of class and ethnicity, they experience fewer intense political conflicts than larger cities.

San Antonio, with its River Walk, is often considered Texas's most distinctive city.

Brandon Seidel/Shutterstock.com.

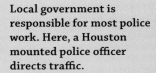

Local government is responsible for most police work. Here, a Houston mounted police officer directs traffic.

© James Nielsen/AFP/Getty.

A shrimper unloads the *Lady E* at the Port of Brownsville. The sea is an important part of the economy of Texas.

© *Eric Gay/Associated Press Images.*

Sports are important in Texas, but especially in a small town like Pilot Point where G. A. Moore became Texas's winningest high school football coach.

© *Paul Buck/Associated Press Images.*

YOU ★ ★ DECIDE

Should the Largest Cities (Dallas, San Antonio, Austin, Fort Worth, for example) Abandon Council-Manager Government in Favor of a Strong Mayor-Council Form?

It is not uncommon across the country for cities to switch from council-manager government to mayor-council or mayor-manager (mayor-administrator) government once they near or exceed a half-million people in size. In Texas, Dallas has struggled bitterly with the issue of possible change, while El Paso moved from mayor-council to council-manager government. What do you think the very large cities in the state should do?

PRO	CON
▲ Any large city should adopt a new municipal charter calling for a strong mayor-council form because:	▼ A large city that has council-manager government should keep its present governmental form because:
▲ It needs a strong chief executive as leader, someone elected to provide political and policy direction for the city.	▼ A strong mayor would just divide the community because mayors must spend more time tending their electoral bases, to ensure that their friends win and their enemies lose, than focusing on making city government work efficiently and effectively for all citizens.
▲ The mayor and the manager disagree publicly too much.	▼ The mayor can provide leadership even in a city manager form of government.
▲ The city has district council elections. Only the mayor can represent the whole city (except in Austin, which has at-large elections).	▼ The city manager is bound by a national code of ethics that requires him/her to stay out of politics and focus on making sure things run properly.
▲ City managers tend to favor business interests.	▼ The mayor and individual council members would be more likely to jockey for political position in a different form of government.
▲ It is too easy for the city manager and the rest of the bureaucracy to perform poorly without anyone knowing.	▼ Day-to-day operations are so complicated in a big city that a professional manager needs to be in charge of them.
▲ More citizens would vote if the mayor's race mattered more.	▼ A strong mayor is more likely to "break the bank" in giving away political favors.
▲ The city could address its out-and-out political problems better.	▼ Large cities with mayor-council or mayor-manager government still have major political problems.

As a result, they often adopt the council-manager form of government because it allows for relatively efficient operation, and permits the city administration to maintain a distance from party politics and from state and national political issues. In big cities, however, where it is impossible to escape from class and ethnic tension, the overtly political mayor-council or mayor-manager form is often a better choice because of the need for the political focus provided by the elected mayor.[18]

City Politics

The discussion of forms of city government has provided a framework for understanding the operations of the city, but has said little about how city government really works. Who gets the rewards, and who is deprived? Which individuals and groups benefit most from city government, and which groups bear the burdens?

The electoral system used by Texas cities is an indication of how the rewards and deprivations are distributed. Although the partisanship of candidates is well known in cities such as Beaumont and El Paso, all Texas cities hold **nonpartisan elections.** The irony is that the municipalities are surrounded by counties with highly partisan elections. In most Texas cities, municipal elections are held during the spring in a further attempt to separate city government from party politics.

In this electoral setting, a private interest group such as a local realtors' association or homeowners may sponsor a slate of candidates for municipal office, just as a political party would, under the guise of a civic organization that purportedly has no goals of its own, except efficient and responsive government. Such a claim is misleading, however. These groups do have goals and are highly effective in achieving them. In some cities, a charter association or good government league exists; these organizations inevitably reflect the interests of

Urban Diversity

Changes in Texas politics are most evident in the major cities where leaders and interest groups reflect newer interests and where the sacrosanct principle of nonpartisanship is sometimes violated.

Austin, San Antonio, Houston, Dallas, El Paso, Fort Worth, and Galveston have had women mayors, as have more than 200 smaller communities. El Paso and San Antonio have elected Mexican American men as mayors, and Dallas and Houston have elected African American men. Austin, Houston, and Dallas have become the homes of large groups of politically active homosexuals. In all three cities, politicians of many ideological persuasions seek the support of the Gay and Lesbian Political Caucus, and in 2006, Dallas launched a major initiative to attract gay and lesbian tourists.

In the big cities, the importance of neighborhood representation and ethnic representation has intensified to such an extent that it is difficult to gain a workable consensus for establishing public policy. Instead, individual council members sometimes advocate the needs of their districts to the exclusion of concerns about the city as a whole.

conservative business elements in the community. In other cities, environmentalists or neighborhood advocates or antitax groups may launch well-organized single-issue campaigns. In addition, a number of more or less ad hoc groups usually appear at election time to sponsor one or more candidates, and in all Texas cities, independent candidates also come forth with their own campaigns to seek public office.

Closely associated with nonpartisan elections is the system of electing candidates for the city council at large. All voters select all the members of the council and vote for as many candidates as there are positions on the council. In another practice widely followed in Texas cities, the **place system,** the seats on the council are designated as Place One, Place Two, and so on. In this type of election, candidates who file for a particular place run only against other candidates who also file for that place. Voting is still citywide. The at-large, by-place system predominates in smaller cities.

Increasingly, however, Texas cities with populations of 50,000 or more are amending their charters to provide for a **district system,** wherein candidates are required to live in a particular geographic area within the city and run against only those candidates who also live in the district. Voters choose only among candidates within their district, although the mayor is usually elected at large. In other cities, some council members are elected by district and some at large. Austin is the major exception. Although debate over whether to change was evident in 2011, the state capital is one of the largest cities in the country to use an at-large, by-place electoral system.

Often, the change to district elections occurs as the result of a successful court suit alleging discrimination against minorities, who find it difficult to win election in a citywide race. Running in districts costs less money and has the advantage of allowing minority candidates to concentrate their campaigning in neighborhoods with large numbers of individuals who share the candidate's ethnic background. Also, additional council seats are sometimes created when a city switches to district elections.

Advocates of at-large and by-place elections argue that the council focuses on citywide concerns, but district elections result in a fragmented council whose members concentrate on only the problems of their electoral district. They also think district elections are incompatible with council-manager government, which predominates in the state's home-rule cities, because they make local elections "too political."

Advocates of district elections think the council is more representative when members are elected by wards or districts because minorities, spokespersons for citizens' groups, and individuals without personal wealth have a better opportunity to be elected and will be more inclined to address "local district" problems. They believe government by its very nature is political, and so all political viewpoints should be represented.

Questions about the organization of elections and the nature of representation are at the heart of the democratic process. One measure of a city's democratic morality is the extent to which the council represents the city's ethnic, economic, and geographic diversity. Thus, democratic theorists sometimes recommend district over at-large elections, except in small municipalities where all candidates are likely to be known by most voters.[19]

Controversy also exists over whether elections should be nonpartisan. One argument is that nonpartisan elections rob the voters of the most important symbol that they have for making electoral choices: the party label. Without knowing

whether a candidate is a Democrat, a Republican, or a member of some other party, how does the voter decide how to vote?

In answering this question, critics of nonpartisan elections say that voters depend on personalities and extraneous matters. For example, television personalities and athletes frequently win elections simply because they are better known than their opponents. These critics also think that nonpartisan elections rob the community of organized and effective criticism of the government in power. Because most candidates win as individuals rather than as members of an organized political party with common goals and policies, such criticism is sporadic and ineffectual, and meaningful policy alternatives seldom are stated. Texas political parties are not well organized. The blame for weak party organizations is often placed on nonpartisan local elections because the parties have no strong grassroots input. Another criticism is that nonpartisan elections encourage the development of civic organizations that are in essence local political parties whose purposes and policy proposals are not always clear to the voters.

Advocates of nonpartisan elections obviously disagree. They think the absence of a party label allows local elections to focus on local issues, and not on national issues about which the municipal government can do little or nothing—for example, whether President Bush should have invaded Iraq or whether President Obama's economic stimulus package is appropriate. They note that television personalities, athletes, and actors are also elected under party banners. Moreover, they point to the fact that local civic groups clarify, not confuse, local issues. Homeowners, taxpayers, and consumers have become political forces that stand in contrast to the traditional, business-oriented civic associations. As a result, participation is enhanced, although resolving political disagreements has become more difficult.

At-large elections, nonpartisan voting, and holding elections in the spring apparently do contribute to low voter turnout. A municipal election in which as many as 25 percent of the eligible voters participates is unusual. Many local elections are decided on the basis of the preference of only 5 to 10 percent of the eligible voters. Moreover, statistics on voting behavior for all elections show that older, affluent Whites vote more frequently than do the young, the poor, and ethnic minorities. The structure of municipal elections in Texas, particularly when those elections are at large, tends to perpetuate the dominant position of the White middle-class business community. Thus, when one examines municipal government against the criteria for a democratic government, one finds some problems of participation, especially among the less affluent and ethnic minorities.

Special Districts: Our Hidden Governments

Perhaps the best way to introduce the topic of special districts is to look at the changes in Texas local government shown in Table 11-2. The number of counties has been stable for almost a century; the number of school districts has declined as districts have consolidated to gain greater economy and efficiency. The number of municipalities has increased largely because unincorporated suburbs on the edges of central cities have become incorporated cities. In spite of increases in utility and economic development districts, the growth of nonschool special districts appears to be slowing.

TABLE 11-2

Number of Units of Local Government in Texas, 1992–2007

Type of Government	1992	2002	2007	% Change 1992–2007
Counties	254	254	254	0
Municipalities	1,171	1,196	1,209	+3.2
School districts	1,101	1,090	1,090	−1.0
Other special districts	2,266	2,245	2,291	+1.0
TOTAL	4,792	4,835	4,785	−.01

SOURCE: U.S. Department of Commerce, Bureau of the Census, *2007 Census of Governments*, available at http://ftp2.census.gov/govs/cog/2007/tx.pdf. The Census of Governments, like the population census, is taken every ten years. The next one is slated for 2012, with results due in 2013.

What Is a Special District?

A special district is a unit of local government created to perform limited functions. Its authority is narrow rather than broad, as in the case of the city or the county. Any further definition is almost impossible; special districts vary enormously in size, organization, function, and importance. A few early special districts were created by the constitution, but Texas statutes now stipulate that the legislature itself can create special districts, that counties and municipalities can create some types of special districts (especially for utilities, other basic services, and economic development), and that even state agencies can create some special districts (usually involving natural resources).

There are about two dozen different types of special districts in Texas. Approximately one fourth of these are housing and community-development districts, while another fourth are concerned with problems of water—control and improvement, drainage, navigation, supply, and sanitation (see Chapter 14 for additional information on water districts and conservation). Other frequently encountered types of special districts are airport, soil conservation, municipal utilities, hospital, fire prevention, weed control, and community college districts.

No single state or county agency is responsible for supervising the activities or auditing the financial records of all these special districts. Such supervision depends on the type of district involved. For example, community college districts are supervised by the Texas Higher Education Coordinating Board and the Texas Education Agency. Average citizens, however, have a hard time keeping track of the many special districts surrounding them. The lack of uniformity and resulting confusion are caused in part by the various ways in which special districts can be created: through special acts of the legislature or under general laws, by general-purpose governments (cities and counties) in some instances, and even by state agencies.

Why Special Districts?

Why does Texas have so many special districts? Are they really necessary?

Inadequacy of Established Governments

First, our established governments—the cities and counties—are inadequate to solve many of the increasingly diverse problems of government. The problem of flood control can seldom be solved within a single city or county, for example; in fact, it frequently goes beyond state boundaries, thus requiring an interstate authority. Cities and counties may find it difficult to finance needed projects. Hospital and community college districts are sometimes created because the debt limitations on established governmental units make taking on a major new activity all but impossible. Then, too, local units may be incapable of coping with governmental problems for other reasons, such as poor organizational structure and a lack of personnel. Special districts are part of the price paid for governmental institutions, such as counties that were fashioned a century ago and are not always capable of addressing complex modern problems.

These inadequacies make the creation of a new unit of government an attractive solution. Perhaps nowhere does one see the need for, and advantages of, special districts more than in the various water supply districts. The Lower Colorado River Authority, for example, owns and operates six of the seven lakes in the Austin area.

Ease of Organization and Operation

Part of the attraction of special districts is that they are *easy to organize and operate*. Political leaders of cities and counties frequently promote a special district as a solution to what might otherwise become "their problem," and the legislature is willing to go along. Creating a hospital district, for example, means that the city and the county don't have to raise their taxes. Indeed, the cost may be spread over several cities or counties included in the special district. Hunt Memorial Hospital District (Greenville and Commerce areas) is illustrative.

Private Gain

In a few instances, *special districts have been created primarily for private gain*. Land speculators and real estate developers create special districts called municipal utility districts (MUDs) on the outskirts of urban areas to increase the value of their holdings. Once enabling legislation has been obtained from the state, it requires only a handful of votes in the sparsely settled, newly created district to

Central Appraisal Districts

Every county has a central tax appraisal district that is responsible for assessing property and providing up-to-date tax rolls to each taxing jurisdiction—county, municipalities, school districts, and other special districts. This system began in 1982 to eliminate the confusion caused by different taxing jurisdictions setting different values on property.

authorize a bond issue for the development of water, sewer, and other utilities. This development increases the value of the property in the district to the benefit of the developers. Ultimately, of course, the taxpayers pay for the bonds, sometimes through very high utility rates. MUDs are a good example of the consequences of a lack of effective state regulation of special districts.

Economic development districts created by counties have the ability to collect taxes that are used mainly for private benefit. Examples include a district in Bexar County created to establish a golf course resort, one in Smith County that allowed a builder and his employees to constitute the board governing a district created to fund a truck stop, and a Hays County water control and improvement district that benefited only one California-based home builder.[20] Denton County became so profligate in creating special taxing districts to help the developers of luxury housing additions that the attorney general in 2001 announced new rules for approving bond elections affecting such districts. However, a special district was created in 2010 by only two voters, although another district was dismantled.[21]

Flexibility

Special districts offer great flexibility to government organizations and have the added attraction of rarely conflicting with existing units. A two-city airport such as Dallas–Fort Worth International is the result of a flexible airport authority. However, DFW proponents periodically find themselves in conflict with airlines that wanted to expand operations at Dallas's Love Field.

Apolitical Approach

With highly technical problems such as flood control, the *special district offers the opportunity to "get it out of politics."* In other words, it is possible to take a businesslike approach and bring in technical specialists to attack the problem. The Wise County Water Control and Improvement District #1 is an example. Such districts really are not apolitical, but they do allow the focus to remain on the task at hand. Of course, other types of special districts—most notably, those whose purpose is economic development—tend to be highly political.

Assessment of Special Districts

Special districts other than school and appraisal districts are *profoundly undemocratic.* They are "hidden governments," with far less visibility than city or county governments. It is not an exaggeration to say that every reader of this book is under the jurisdiction of at least one special district, yet it will be a very rare reader who knows which districts affect her or him, how much they cost in taxes, who the commissioner or other officials of each special district are, whether they are elected or (as is more frequently the case) appointed, and what policies they follow. Special district government is unseen by and frequently unresponsive to the people. Thus, when one applies the test of democratic morality, one finds that special districts fail to meet the standards of participation and public input. Indeed, they are sometimes an unfortunate reflection of Texas's traditionalistic and individualistic political culture.[22]

Most special districts are small in size and scope. Therefore, they are *uneconomical.* Their financial status is often shaky, and so the interest rates that taxpayers must pay on the bond issues used to finance many types of special district projects are exceptionally high. Economies such as large-scale purchasing are impossible.

Finally, one of the most serious consequences of the proliferation of special districts is that they *greatly complicate the problems of government, particularly in urban areas.* With many separate governments, the likelihood is greater that haphazard development, confusion, and inefficiency will occur. No single government has comprehensive authority, and coordination among so many smaller governments becomes extremely difficult.

Texans have been reluctant to experiment with a comprehensive urban government. Their individualism demands retention of the many local units, although other states' metropolitan areas, such as Miami and Nashville, have succeeded with comprehensive government. Instead, Texans rely on one of the twenty-four *regional planning councils,* also known as *councils of governments* (COGs), to provide coordination in metropolitan areas. These voluntary organizations of local government provide such functions as regional land-use and economic planning, police training, and fact-finding studies on problems such as transportation.

Given the inadequacies of comprehensive planning and periodic revenue shortfalls at the local level, special districts will surely continue to proliferate. Under current conditions, they are too easy to create and operate as short-range solutions to governmental problems. Such continued proliferation, without adequate planning and supervision, will result not in solutions to, but rather in worsening the problems of, local and particularly urban government.

School Districts

School districts are an exception to much of the foregoing discussion of special districts for several reasons. First, school board members are publicly elected, most commonly in an at-large, by-place system. Second, their decisions are usually well publicized, with the local newspapers and broadcast media paying careful attention to education decisions. Third, the public has considerable interest in and knowledge about school-district politics. Indeed, although county or city public hearings sometimes fail to attract a crowd, as soon as a school board

Shiney Hiney: Taxation without Representation

Denton County has been among the worst in the state for the creation of special districts by developers who want to use tax moneys to install utilities. One of the best—and funniest—examples is Shiney Hiney, a one-thousand-acre ranch slated for development in 2011. One voter cast his ballot to create Denton County Municipal Utility District No. 7, with rights to issue $400 million in bonds, assess a $1-per-$100 of valuation property tax, and even use the power of *eminent domain,* a legal procedure for forcing a private property owner to sell to a public entity. The *Denton Record-Chronicle* called the voter "the emperor of Shiney Hiney."

Source: Editorial, "The Emperor of Shiney Hiney," *Denton Record-Chronicle,* online edition of May 5, 2010, available at http://www.dentonrc.com/sharedcontent/dws/drc/opinion/editorials/stories/DRC_Editorial_0505.1a969c3d.html. The Denton paper carried news stories about Shiney Hiney through most of 2010 into early 2011.

School Board Elements

Large urban school districts have had the same struggles over district versus at-large elections as have cities. At-large proponents argue that "children" not "politics" should prevail. District proponents argue for "representation." In Dallas, the board is elected by district and has been sharply divided. Bill Rojas, a new superintendent hired in the fall of 1999, had already grown crosswise with several board members before Thanksgiving. By July, he had been fired after quarreling with the board over everything from bringing in the for-profit Edison Project to pump up the district's low-performing campuses to personality clashes with individual board members to allegations of serious expense account abuses. Amarillo has used an experimental voting procedure to try to find a compromise between district and at-large elections.

agenda includes a topic such as determining attendance districts—basically, who gets bused and who doesn't—or sex education, the public turns out for the debate. Fourth, the number of school districts has been steadily declining for fifty years as smaller districts consolidate into larger ones. Finally, although the local boards have a substantial amount of control over such matters as individual school management, location of schools, and personnel, the state is the ultimate authority for basic school policies and shares in the funding of public schools.

Public school finance has been a dominant issue in Texas politics at several points in the state's history, but particularly since 1987. The fact that almost 1,100 school districts exist is one of the factors contributing to considerable unevenness in the quality of education provided from one district to the next. That unevenness in turn creates inequities in funding public education. School districts depend on two revenue sources: property taxes and state assistance. However, in Texas, state aid pays for only about half the cost of public education, thereby putting considerable pressure on the unpopular tax. The two largest differences in spending in richer versus poorer districts are in facilities (posh buildings, full computerization versus bare bones) and enrichment activities (choir trips to Europe versus a poor-quality field for athletics and band). The issue of school finance, which is addressed throughout this book, was the source of enormous controversy during the budget-slashing 2011 legislative session (see Chapter 12).

The Austin Example

A graphic example of the problem of rapid growth and dealing with a sprawl that even cuts across county lines is the Austin Metropolitan Area, which topped 1.6 million in population in 2010. The city of Austin grew from 254,000 in 1970 to 790,000 by 2010. Two of the authors of this book have lived in Austin, and the third has family ties to the city. They can recall a smooth flow of traffic that always led to arriving within twenty minutes at any destination. Now, it can take twenty minutes to go from the University of Texas at Austin campus just to a main thoroughfare.

LONE STAR MEDIA
How Do I Tell Thee?

The use of many different kinds of communication was nowhere more evident than during the severe winter of 2011 when ice and snow gripped the state and led to the closing of colleges and universities, public and private schools, churches, businesses, city and county governments, and even some Super Bowl events. In addition, some basic services such as solid waste collection had to be delayed. The pattern for notification for local governments seemed to be Facebook first, then Twitter, and then the Internet site of the jurisdiction. In addition, most colleges and universities had assigned an e-mail address to all students, faculty, and staff so that a blanket notice of closing was sent via e-mail. Because of the shortage of electricity, rolling power black-outs occurred across the state on February 2. Many cities, especially those that distribute electric power, used an automated emergency system that warned customers of the impending blackouts by telephone.

The governments and institutions also notified conventional media, particularly major television and radio stations. Although most college students are accustomed to having access to computers and cell phones that have many applications on them, many citizens are dependent on radio and TV for information. Newspapers came into play after the fact, as the sources of detailed information on what havoc the weather had caused. About the only forms of media not invoked were those primarily devoted to data storage or entertainment (compact discs and movies, for example).

Local Government: Prospects for the Future

The trends toward urbanization and suburbanization no doubt will continue, with the result that local government problems will become more acute than they are today. Yet local governments are absolutely vital components of the governance structure, as the chapter-opening quotation from the Texas Municipal League attests. What are the prospects for local governments in Texas under these circumstances?

Finance

Local governments have issues involving both income and spending. Indeed, the long-term economic outlook and resource challenges are two of the mega-issues facing cities nationally.[23]

Revenue

Local government finance closely parallels the state's economic and fiscal condition (see Chapter 12) in that lean times mean tight budgets and boom economies afford greater revenue and spending possibilities. However, local governments are more restricted in the ways they can attain revenue.

Across the country, the backbone of county, municipal, and school district finance is the **ad valorem property tax,** which is assessed against homes

and commercial properties. All of these entities also borrow money to finance government operations, often with **revenue bonds.** For example, to build a new sewer system, a city might issue bonds that are then paid off with the revenue from wastewater collection fees. Municipalities have more flexibility with regard to revenue sources because they can collect sales taxes, but counties and some special districts can also collect a sales tax under limited circumstances.

Governments also collect **user fees.** For example, a county will collect fees associated with court expenses; a water district will collect fees for the water it delivers; an airport district will collect landing fees from airline companies; a school district will collect admissions fees for athletic contents. Municipalities collect a number of fees, especially if they provide electric, water, wastewater, or drainage services or operate recreational facilities such as a golf course.

In addition, local governments receive **intergovernmental transfers**—money from a higher level of government such as the federal and state funds that flow to counties for welfare and indigent health care and the dollars that go to counties and cities to help with road and bridge construction. The most dramatic example is the funding of public schools.

Spending

General-purpose governments, counties and municipalities, provide a wide variety of services to their citizens. Counties spend much of their budgets on roads and bridges, law enforcement, and welfare and indigent health care. Municipalities also provide streets, law enforcement, and some social services, but in addition they provide parks, libraries, transportation, fire protection, and public utilities. Special districts are much more limited in the scope of their spending: the type of district determines the expenditures (schools, water, drainage, airport, utilities, and so on). For all local governments, revenue shortfalls make spending choices difficult.

Fiscal Woes

Local governments gained fiscal support during the first stages of the recovery from the deep recession of 2007–2009 because of federal **stimulus funds** earmarked for local governments, but lost those funds as the national government faced its own financial crises for the 2012 budget year. As the following chapter discusses, the state has significant, long-term problems with revenues, and the 2011 legislative session saw major cuts in support for local governments, including schools. Moreover, both the national and state governments continue to **mandate** spending on certain programs whether or not the local governments want to provide those services.

As a high-growth state, Texas continues to have more and more residents, with proportionately less revenue to provide services. Local governments have sought creative solutions to the budget woes, including cooperating with one another and with the private sector, asking citizens to volunteer, seriously addressing productivity issues, and turning to contracting out services to the private sector (for example, using private solid waste companies to pick up garbage). However, local fiscal problems, like state budget issues, will continue to grow for a number of reasons, such as public aversion to tax increases, the increasing inability of the state and national government to provide relief, and competition with one another, particularly over the property tax.

Other Issues

Several developments are worth noting. As urban problems and local finance problems become more acute, national and state governments are being forced to pay more attention to them. The *legislature is becoming more "citified,"* though its capacity to act may be limited.

Until 1978, Texas had virtually no *mass transit* (trains, subways, buses) to relieve the congestion on the freeways. Beginning in Houston and Harris County, mass transit has developed across the state, especially in the counties of a half-million or more population. It has long been obvious that the practice of virtually every person using his or her own motor vehicle for personal and business travel is incompatible with increasing urbanization. Smog, congestion, and even rush-hour gridlock do not make for a high quality of life. Mass transit systems must be established if the trend toward further urbanization is to continue, especially given the inability of the state to build roadways fast enough to move traffic at peak times or to clean the air sufficiently to meet federal standards. See Chapter 14 for a more complete discussion of transportation issues.

Another development is that of *strategic planning*, a type of planning that focuses on identifying a mission and pursuing it in an opportunistic manner by taking advantage of any favorable situation that comes along. For example, a community that strives to attract high technology might aggressively seek to persuade electronics plants to locate there, perhaps even ignoring some of their environmental problems.

A third area of concern for the future is *interlocal cooperation.* COGs are one example of an arrangement that allows the many kinds of local governments— counties, cities, special districts—to work together to solve their common problems. Cooperative ventures such as city-county ambulance service, city-school playgrounds and libraries, and multiple-city purchasing are other examples. Indeed, interlocal agreements are the most dynamic element of modern intergovernmental relations and can help overcome some of the negative effects of the growing number of governments.

A fourth area of concern is *ordinance-making power for counties.* The lack of ordinance-making power is developing into a serious problem for safety, environmental, and aesthetic standards, as well as other matters. For example, an

Metropolitan Areas

Exactly what constitutes a metropolitan area is confusing because the U.S. Bureau of the Census categorizes metropolitan statistical areas (MSAs) in several ways. Texas has twenty-five metropolitan areas, including two of the largest ten in the United States. The twenty-five recognized metropolitan statistical areas in Texas are, in descending order of population: Dallas–Fort Worth–Arlington (number 4 nationally), Houston–Sugar Land-Baytown (number 6), San Antonio-New Braunfels, Austin–Round Rock–San Marcos, El Paso, McAllen–Edinburg–Mission, Corpus Christi, Brownsville–Harlingen, Killeen–Temple–Fort Hood, Beaumont–Port Arthur, Lubbock, Amarillo, Laredo, Waco, College Station–Bryan, Longview, Tyler, Abilene, Wichita Falls, Texarkana, Odessa, Midland, Sherman–Denison, Victoria, and San Angelo.

Hurricane Force

Texas cities in 2005 and early 2006 were severely impacted by Hurricanes Katrina and Rita. The former resulted in tens of thousands of persons, especially New Orleaneans, fleeing Katrina in favor of Houston, Dallas, and many other Texas cities, creating a long-lasting effect on law enforcement and social services. Rita caused major damage to the Texas Gulf Coast, especially in the Golden Triangle (Beaumont–Port Arthur–Orange and surrounding towns) just as Hurricane Ike devastated Galveston in 2008. Houston hosted more evacuees than any other city. Because of its successful response to the crisis, the city was named "Texan of the Year" for 2005 by the *Dallas Morning News*.

issue of growing concern is the lack of control over adult bookstores and massage parlors that set up shop just outside a municipality, where control of them becomes a problem for the county. Counties want and need ordinance-making power, but have thus far been denied it, primarily because of the opposition of real estate businesses and developers, who can, for example, create developments in unincorporated areas outside the extraterritorial jurisdiction of the cities that do not have to meet rigorous city building codes.

A fifth major problem that will continue to plague local governments is *sprawl*. The demands on and costs of local government are not subject to

How to Get Involved in Local Government

Local government is the logical starting point for exercising your democratic rights and becoming involved as a participant in government. Here are a few suggestions for how to go about getting involved.

■ Go to the party precinct conventions, held immediately after the primary elections (see Chapter 4).

■ Attend a public hearing and speak out.

■ Organize a petition drive on a matter of importance to you—saving the trees along a planned freeway route, for example.

■ Attend a neighborhood meeting.

■ Attend a meeting of the city council, county commission, or school board.

■ Talk to the city clerk or the county clerk to find out how to volunteer for an advisory committee or citizen task force.

■ Volunteer to work for a local candidate during an election.

economies of scale. In manufacturing, for example, producing more cars or soap bars results in a lowered *unit cost*, the cost of one car or bar of soap. This principle doesn't hold true for picking up more bags of garbage or cleaning more streets or teaching more children. Burgeoning populations that move farther and farther away from the central city make delivery of services more costly and more difficult.

Leadership in Local Government

Historically, genuine differences have existed between county leadership and the leadership of other local governments. Elected officials in county government hold full-time positions that pay decent salaries and represent starting points in party politics. In most other local governments, a strong tradition of amateurism prevails: Elected officials are paid parking-and-lunch money and give their time as merely an extension of the same service orientation that leads them to accept office in Kiwanis or Rotary or the Business and Professional Women's Club.

The decentralized nature of county governments has often led to rural fiefdoms of commissioners or sheriffs, but in urban counties, candidates as diverse as ethnic minority candidates with major social agendas and young conservatives contemplating a lifetime in politics are beginning to seek county office. As previously noted, Former Governor Ann Richards began her political career as a county commissioner. In large cities, serving on the city council also can be a step into big-time politics, and mayors have gone on to both the state and national capitols. City councils and school boards are becoming increasingly diversified in terms of gender, ethnicity, and viewpoint.[24]

The Texas Association of County Officials continues to be dominated by rural interests, although there is a block of urban counties interested in more than roads and bridges. Municipalities are more consistently aided by the Texas Municipal League, which has divisions for both elected officials and professional personnel. In addition, a variety of specialized organizations, such as the Texas Public Power Association address other local interests. All of these groups also lobby for local interests with the legislature.

Summary

Local governments are the governments most likely to have a daily impact on citizens, and much of this effect is critical to the quality of life. Will our children get a good public school education, or should we save to send them to private school? Is our neighborhood safe, or will we have to live behind triple-locked doors with a guard dog for a companion? Will we enjoy a reasonably efficient and economical transportation system, or will we have to fight dangerous and congested freeway traffic two or three hours a day to get to and from our jobs?

The answers to these and a hundred other critical questions are given by the units of local government. Texas counties, cities, special districts, and COGs are not fully prepared to provide optimum solutions. County governments must cope with modern problems despite having an inflexible, outmoded organizational structure. City governments are better organized and have more comprehensive powers, yet they too are burdened by a variety of factors, including the rapid increase in urban

population, the proliferation of independent special districts, and the limited and frequently reluctant cooperation of state and national government. COGs, as voluntary organizations, provide only very limited solutions to problems of organized, coordinated planning. All local governments will face serious revenue problems for the foreseeable future.

This chapter has examined how the general units of local government—counties and cities—are organized and financed and what the major political features are. It has looked at the reasons for and the problems created by special districts, singling out school districts as not fitting the pattern of other special districts. It suggests that Texas, like most states, will undoubtedly continue to become more and more urbanized. Consequently, problems such as congestion, poor housing, inadequate schools, and crime will continue to grow, along with issues involving inadequate revenues to solve them. It is imperative that local governments both represent the diversity of the state and govern effectively. Democracy is about both participating and getting things done.

Glossary Terms

ad valorem property tax

at-large elections

commissioners court

district system

general laws

gerrymandering

home rule

intergovernmental transfers

mandate

nonpartisan elections

place system

revenue bonds

spoils system

stimulus funds

user fees

12

The State Economy and the Financing of State Government

Texas has an economy that is the second largest in the nation and the 15th largest in the world based on GDP (PPP) figures. [GDP/PPP are database acronyms.]

WIKIPEDIA: THE FREE ENCYCLOPEDIA, 2007

. . . most officeholders would rather handle rattlesnakes than vote for an income tax.

DAVE MCNEELY, LONG-TIME WRITER ON TEXAS POLITICS, IN *STATE LEGISLATURES*, 2007

We will protect them, support them and empower them, but cannot risk the future of millions of taxpayers in the process. We must cut spending to keep our economic engine on track.

GOVERNOR RICK PERRY, INAUGURAL ADDRESS, 2011

OBJECTIVES

After reading this chapter, you should be able to

Discuss the mainstays of the Texas economy, the growth of lower-paying jobs, and efforts to create a favorable business climate.

Discuss where Texas gets its revenue, including state taxes.

Assess whether the revenue structure is fair and equitable.

Understand how the budget of the state is produced.

Evaluate the results of the spending plan in terms of meeting the needs of Texans by providing an adequate level of state services.

INTRODUCTION

The *ability* of any government to generate the revenues needed to provide the programs and services that citizens want is directly tied to the economy. Are most people working? Are wages good? Are profits high? Is money available for loans to finance business expansion and home ownership? The *willingness* of a government to raise and spend money is dictated by the prevailing political philosophy, previously described in this book as traditionalistic-individualistic. This chapter looks at the Texas economy, how the state gets its revenue, and both its *ability* and its *willingness* to raise and spend money for public purposes.

Texas's political leaders have bragged for years about the state's ability to create jobs and the state's highly favorable (low-tax, few labor unions) economic environment. They have made the arguable assumption that all there is to having a robust economy is to recruit new business investment.[1] However, a sound economy includes helping existing businesses to grow and bringing as much diversity to the economy as possible. Furthermore, in industrialized nations, one expects the government to promote policies that create a good quality of life for all citizens and to manage the state's finances in such a way that the needs of tomorrow, as well as today, are considered.

Texas has a long history of a boom-or-bust economy. When oil and gas prices were high, the state had big surpluses. As the United States began to rely more on foreign oil, the state's revenue picture dimmed because Texas could no long depend on energy sales to citizens in other states to fuel its budget needs even if prices went up. Consequently, it began to find that shortfalls were more common than surpluses. Particularly since a solution

Fiscal Years

All governments and businesses operate on fiscal years, a phrase that refers to the budget year. Sometimes the fiscal year is the same as the calendar year, but often, particularly for governments, the year is different. In Texas, the fiscal year is September 1 until August 31 of the following year. The year in which the fiscal period ends is designated as the fiscal year. Thus, FY 13 covers September 1, 2012, until August 31, 2013. Forty-six states use a fiscal year that runs from July to June. The other exceptions besides Texas are New York (April to March), Alabama, and Michigan. The latter two states have the same fiscal year as the national government, October to September.

to the problems of public-school finance (the largest share of the state budget) was supposedly fixed by changes in the business tax in 2006, the state has had problems because the structure of the tax was inadequate from day one. Not only has the state faced revenue problems since 2006, its population had grown by another 2 million persons by 2011.

Texas is "pay-as-you-go"; it cannot just go into debt to finance government services, and services often suffer, as Chapter 13 particularly points out. The three quotations that open this chapter neatly summarize the dilemmas that the legislature constantly faces—a boom-and-bust economy, big spending needs spurred by high population growth, and a tendency to talk a good game when providing programs to meet ordinary people's needs but simultaneously be unwilling to fund such programs adequately.

Another major issue concerning the revenue system is its fairness. Citizens always seek fairness. Yet, as we shall see, the poor in Texas pay a higher proportion of their incomes in taxes than do the wealthy, and the business tax has so many exclusions and exceptions that it will never meet revenue expectations. These facts raise questions about how democratic the state revenue system is, which constitutes a major theme of this chapter.

The chapter also looks at how the state spends its money, including how elected officials struggle to agree on what the budget will be. Because the budget is the best guide to policy priorities, it is a practical test of how well citizens' interests are accommodated in state spending.

Texas has grown from 17 million people in 1990 to more than 25.8 million people in 2011, an increase of almost 52 percent in just twenty-two years. During that same period, the state budget has increased from $126.6 billion for **fiscal years** (FY) 1990–1991 to $182.2 billion for FY 2010–2011—an increase of only 43.8 percent. Moreover, the FY 2012–2013 budget was reduced to $172.3 billion in spite of continuing population growth. When adjusted for population growth (more people require more services) and for **inflation** (that is, increases in what things cost), the Texas budget has been relatively flat according to the Legislative Budget Board, as Figure 12-1 shows. Budget growth has been only about 1.7 percent a year, less than the population growth and inflation rates for the period as a whole.[2] This figure does not even include the 5.4 percent reduction for FY 2012–2013.

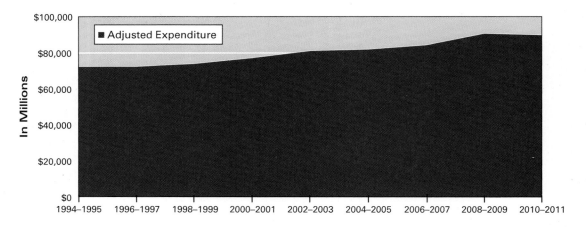

FIGURE 12-1 Trends in Texas Government Expenditures, FY 1994–1995 to FY 2010–2011, Adjusted for Inflation and Population (in 1993 dollars)

SOURCE: Legislative Budget Board, *Fiscal Size-Up 2010–11* (Austin, 2009), 9.

The Texas Economy

The Texas economy is characterized by cycles of boom and bust. The economic uncertainty is made worse by revenue policies that are inflexible.

Heart of the Economy

Historically, the Texas economy has been based on natural resources, chiefly oil, land, and water. Indeed, Texas has been characterized as the state where "money gushes from the ground in the oil fields and grows on the citrus trees in the irrigated orchards."[3] Texas is still an important producer of oil and gas, and listings of its principal products include petroleum, natural gas, and natural gas liquids.[4] Chemicals, cotton, and cattle also contribute their share of wealth, as do construction and manufacturing.

The state's natural resources are bountiful but not endless—that is, once used, they cannot be replaced. Furthermore, the Texas economy is shifting from one based on natural resources to one based on information and technology, including financial management. In 2010, the Texas gross state product was over $1.5 trillion a year, according to the United States Bureau of Economic Analysis, which ranked second only to California in actual dollars but twenty-fourth on a per capita basis.[5] This output made Texas roughly the equivalent of Russia in terms of its economic output.[6] Although the economy has grown and diversified, the percentage of the state economy derived from agriculture still is second only to California. Moreover, Texas remains one of the top ten states for mining, which includes oil and natural gas production.[7] Yet, one cannot ignore that the oil fields no longer represent the chief revenue source for the state. Indeed, gas drilling has shown more promise than oil.

Although the state's recent economy has moved away from one based solely on natural resources, it still has been subject to the ups and downs of resource-based components, such as oil and agriculture. Indeed, the erosion of the natural-resource-based economy has meant that thousands of Texans have

found themselves out of work. In June 1986, the state unemployment rate reached 9.6 percent, compared with a national rate of 7.3 percent. The collapse of financial institutions has made the problem worse. In 1988–1990, Texas led the nation in the number of banks and savings and loans that failed. Also at that time, the defense industry was depressed by the end of the Cold War in the early 1990s.

State government has worked to shore up the shaky economy by consolidating economic development programs, developing aggressive marketing campaigns for farm and ranch products, and selling the high-technology capability of the state through industry-university partnerships. By the turn of the century, Texas was second only to North Carolina in business relocations, and the employment rate was going up, although with some concern that too many of the new jobs were at the lower end of the pay scale. College-educated workers who found jobs in the high-technology and dot.com firms were doing well, but the economic distance between highly skilled and unskilled workers seemed to be growing.

Boom and Bust

In the spring of 2000, the high-tech sector of the U.S. economy began to plummet. The NASDAQ, the index that reflects technology stocks, lost almost three-quarters of its value; and large layoffs in telecommunications, computer, and Internet firms led to prolonged unemployment in "new economy" industries.

On September 11, 2001, terrorists attacked the United States by hijacking four airliners and using them as weapons. Two of these planes brought down the twin World Trade Towers in New York and a third destroyed a section of the Pentagon in Washington, D.C. The horror of lost lives and the surprise of the attack coupled with actual economic damages, particularly to the travel industry, further shook confidence in the U.S. economy. A series of corporate scandals made matters worse, especially because they involved the top corporate officers growing very rich while the pensions, and ultimately the jobs, of ordinary workers were squandered. The largest scandal of all was Houston-based Enron. Military action that began in Afghanistan in 2001 and Iraq in 2003 followed the 9/11 attack. Coupled with two national tax cuts, the costs of war sent the country into significant debt and rattled the economy further.

Texas and other states were in no way immune to these national and international events. Although Texas exports more products for sale than any other state, trade with Mexico was marred by both agricultural drought and fear of crossing the border into areas that were run by drug lords. Texans' confidence in the economy was steadily eroding due to the lack of job growth and the sluggish economy. The state had banked on high technology as an answer to the waning of the old natural-resource-based economy, but the high-technology crash led to tens of thousands of job layoffs and foreclosures on thousands of homes. The feeling of malaise was not improved by national news that some of the "new economy" jobs based on information and technology were being exported permanently to other countries with lower wage scales.[8]

However, some bright spots began to emerge. Houston's low unemployment rate signaled recovery in the oil and petrochemical industries. Texas also profited from heightened military activities because of its many defense contractors, even though individual families lost ground when reservists were called up from better-paying jobs into military service. Generally, however, higher unemployment rates cause a demand for more government services. The "bottom line"

was that the legislature began its 2003 session with a $10 billion deficit, a situation not unfamiliar to those in other state capitals.

The 2005 and 2007 legislatures both began with surpluses as the economy improved. Thus, once again, the boom-and-bust cycle had made its will known. Texas reemerged as the number-one state in the country for corporate relocation and expansion.[9] By 2007, unemployment was down to 4.1 percent, and 239,000 jobs had been created in twelve months, in part due to robust foreign trade. Dallas–Fort Worth, Austin, and Houston ranked in the top thirty global cities in the country, which is a designation given to cities with a strong orientation toward international business. Texas had moved to number two in the country as a desirable retirement spot. Even agriculture was improving because the 2005–2006 drought had ended.[10]

By late 2008, Texans, like other Americans, were finding themselves mired in debt even to the point of losing their homes in foreclosures and lacking in basic protections such as health insurance. This situation was a product of the deep national recession of 2007–2009, although the Texas economy was not as bad as that of other states, and two years of prolonged drought in key agricultural areas of the state. The 2009 legislature had some leftover surplus money and new federal funds, but the economic weakness of the state resulted in little effort to address social needs. Moreover, private sector wages had dropped more than $15 trillion from 2007 to 2009.[11]

The housing market continued to lag, and economy recovery did not include many new well-paying jobs. Although Texas boasted that it had created more new jobs than any other state, it also had the highest percentage (12.6 percent) of workers in the nation earning only the minimum wage.[12] A fully employed individual earning minimum wage would make only $14,616 a year.

In April 2011, the unemployment rate was 8.1 percent, better than the national 8.8 percent but still high, and concerns were growing about prospects for middle-class employment (highly skilled technical workers and minimally skilled service workers).[13] The legislature was forced to cope with a $27 billion shortfall in revenues needed just to maintain the level of service for the previous two years and pay leftover bills from FY 2011.

Creating a Favorable Business Climate

It is often said that the "bidness of Texas is bidness." Chapter 3 discussed the most powerful interest groups in the state, including energy and insurance. State policymakers have tried to create an environment in which business could easily expand and would want to locate in Texas. Indeed, Texas was ranked third among all states in the best place to make a living and thirteenth among the states for a favorable business tax environment.[14]

State politicians like to brag that Texas has the most favorable tax environment for business; however, the Texas Foundation also considers the fairness of state taxes and whether they are adequate to fund state needs. The Texas revenue system, particularly its tax structure, lacks **elasticity;** that is, it is not easily adjusted to ups and downs in the economy, a problem made worse when the national government also cuts back payments to states. Whatever the system's limitations, the Texas tax structure is an overall plus for the business community.

So also are the state's stingy policies toward workers who find themselves unemployed or injured on the job. For a generation, the legislature has tinkered with legislation in these two areas in an effort to minimize costs to businesses

and to provide them flexibility in the ways money must be set aside to pay for unemployment or injury. In Texas, a worker who loses his or her job can receive from $60 to $415 a week, based on previous earnings, for up to 26 weeks unless the federal government extends the time period. A worker who is injured or who develops a job-related illness can receive workers' compensation income and medical assistance. The rate is based on the wage rate of the person's previous thirteen weeks of employment, and the maximum number of weeks of support is 104.

Texas provides the governor with up to $300 million in incentives to lure technology companies and entrepreneurs to the state, although this funding was imperiled by the 2011 budget crisis. The state is loath to cut highway funds, regardless of other budget slashing, because of the importance of the roads to the movement of goods. However, the most serious shortcoming of the state's efforts to spur business development that provides better-than-minimum-wage jobs is its failure to understand the need for adequate support of its public education system. As business leaders noted during the 2011 legislative session, "School cuts are [a] risky business."[15] During that session, Raise Your Hand Texas was developed by well-known politicians, business executives, and entertainers in an effort to address the lack of vision in attacking an already low-ranking education system.

Where Does the Money Come From?

State finance consists of raising and spending money. For most of those involved in government, the budget is the bottom line, as it is for the rest of us. Policy decisions regarding state financing are made in the glaring light of political reality—what political scientist Harold Laswell called "Politics: Who Gets What, When, and How" back in 1911. Whenever money is raised, it comes from someone; whenever it is spent, someone gets it. Struggles over who will pay for the government and who will receive dollars from it are at the heart of politics in Texas, as elsewhere.

Part of the struggle over revenues comes from philosophical disagreements about revenue sources and who should bear the burden of taxation (see the later section on "Ability to Pay"). Both the traditionalistic and individualistic political cultures are antitax overall and in favor of regressive taxes when money must be raised. Figure 12-2 gives an approximate idea of the sources of state revenue for FY 2012–2013. It shows that 43.2 percent of all revenues come from taxes; 39.5 percent from federal grants; and 17.3 percent from all other sources, including fees, fines and penalties, interest, investments, land leases, the lottery, the surplus, and other sources such as lawsuits. Figure 12-2 is best considered in conjunction with Table 12-1, which provides a view of the changing revenue picture since FY 1982–1983—used as baseline because those were the last years when oil ruled the Texas budget. The table emphasizes years when a major revenue source changed significantly, for example, federal funding. However, the federal contribution must be considered in the context of what the funding can be spent for (homeland security, roads, Medicaid, for example) and what it cannot be spent for (little for environmental compliance or education, for example). The table shows further fluctuation in revenue sources over time due largely to economic downtrends and uptrends, as well as the changing federal budget priorities.

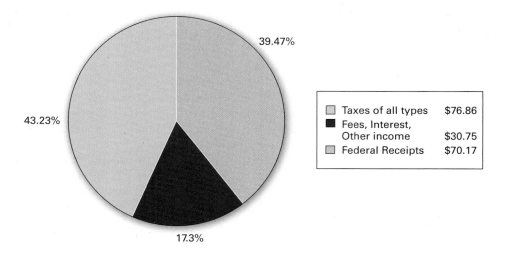

☐	Taxes of all types	$76.86
■	Fees, Interest, Other income	$30.75
☐	Federal Receipts	$70.17

FIGURE 12-2 Projected Texas State Revenues by Source, 2012–2013 Biennium, in Percentages (in Billions)*

SOURCE: "State Revenue . . . All Funds, Excluding Trust Funds," *Biennial Revenue Estimate, 2012–2013 Biennium* (Austin: Texas Comptroller of Public Accounts, 2011), 41.

*TOTAL: $177.78 billion. All numbers are rounded. Only $172.3 billion were available for spending after FY 2011 deficits were covered.

TABLE 12-1

Texas State Revenue Sources over Time, in Percentages, Showing Years of Significant Change and Most Recent Years

SOURCE	1982–1983 Baseline	1990–1991	1994–1995	2006–2007	2008–2009	2010–2011	2012–2013
Taxes	62.2	60.0	50.9	45.7	51.1	45.4	47.3
General sales	24.3	33.5	27.7	26.3	35.1	25.4	30.1
Severance	18.4	4.9	3.2	2.5	3.7	2.7	2.4
Other	19.5	21.6	20.0	16.9	12.3	17.3	14.7
Federal funds	21.4	24.6	30.1	35.5	31.2	34.6	49.2
Licenses, fines, fees, other receipts, surplus	5.2	9.1	10.9	12.1	13.6	13.6	1.0
Leases, interest, investments	11.2	6.3	5.7	4.2	2.5	4.6	1.1
Lottery	—	—	2.3	2.5	1.6	1.8	1.4

NOTES: The "other" category of revenue was calculated differently in earlier years so that the categories of "licenses, etc." and "leases, etc." are directly comparable beginning only in 1990–1991. Numbers do not necessarily equal 100 percent due to rounding. The numbers for FY 2012–2013 are distorted by the fact that $5.139 billion were deducted to cover FY 2010–2011 deficits and to hold back allocations from dedicated funds, such as those for parks, to make the budget appear balanced.

SOURCE: *Fiscal Size-Up, 1982–83, 1990–91, 1994–95, 2006–07, 2008–09, 2010–11* (Austin: Legislative Budget Board), Chapter II on revenue, and "Economic Outlook," "General Revenue-Related Funds by Source," and "Estimated All Fund Revenue, Excluding Trusts," *Biennial Revenue Estimate* (Austin: Office of the Texas Comptroller, 2011), 3–4, 12, 30.

Table 12-1 reflects the rise of the Middle East as a major supplier of petroleum and the decline of the Texas oil industry, both in the relentless loss of revenues from the severance tax—the tax on the production of oil, natural gas, and other minerals—and in the downward trend of leases, interest, and investment income, although gas mining has picked up considerably in recent years, particularly in the northern part of the state. Texans historically enjoyed low taxes because out-of-state consumers, buying gasoline that had originated as oil produced in the Lone Star State, indirectly subsidized Texas state government by paying most of the severance tax.

Seeking to avoid tax increases, the legislature has frequently turned to charges such as the fees paid for professional licenses or college tuition to augment the state treasury. Table 12-1 illustrates that such revenues paid directly by individuals—for example, licenses and fees—showed steady increases as politicians attempted to offset the loss of severance tax dollars. The table also reflects the use of a budget surplus in FY 2008–2009, federal stimulus money in FY 2010–2011, and some Rainy Day Fund (emergency) fund money in FY 2012–2013 to cover deficits from FY 2011. As the table also reveals, however, hoped-for infusions of cash from nontax sources, such as the lottery, were not forthcoming.

Always of importance is the proportion of state revenues generated by the general sales tax—the added cents on every hamburger and spiral notebook—because this tax tends to hit the poor the hardest. The sales tax actually has erratically declined in percentage of revenues generated, although not in dollars, since FY 1982–1983 because of the increase in nontax revenues and federal dollars.

Economic growth, higher and more expensive fees, and requiring local governments to fund some activities previously paid for by the state generated sufficient dollars for the state to operate until FY 2012–2013, when significant budget cuts were necessary to avoid a tax increase. This chapter examines each major source of state income.

Collection and Administration

State revenues are collected in many ways by many people. Monies from federal grants may be sent directly to the state agency responsible for administering the program being funded. The general retail sales tax is collected by retail merchants and then forwarded to the state comptroller. Other taxes, such as the inheritance tax, may be forwarded directly from the individual to the state comptroller. The two officials most concerned with state financial administration are the comptroller, who is responsible for tax collection, investments, and the safeguarding of public funds, and the auditor, who oversees state agencies to ensure the legality of their expenditures.

Once collected, state revenues are channeled into more than 5,000 funds, some of which are designated to supply monies for the general operation of government, while others are dedicated to (reserved for) specific services. Here are the five major funds in Texas:

1. **The General Revenue Fund, which supports the majority of state programs**

2. **The Omnibus Tax Clearance Fund, which is allocated in part to two other funds, the General Revenue Fund and Available School Fund, and in part to such specific functions as the construction of farm-to-market roads, parks, and teachers' retirement**

3. The Available School Fund, which underwrites public school textbooks and part of the Foundation School Program, the major source of state aid for local school districts

4. The Highway Motor Fuel Fund, one-fourth of which is allocated to the Available School Fund and the remainder to highways and roads

5. The State Highway Fund, which is used for highway and road construction and maintenance, right-of-way acquisition, and related purposes

Other funds set aside for particular purposes include those dedicated to federally funded programs, parks and wildlife, roads, and teachers' retirement.

Nontax Sources of Revenue

The state has sources of revenue other than the checks oil producers write to the state comptroller and the pennies, nickels, and dimes that citizens dig out of their pockets to satisfy the sales tax. These revenues include federal grants, borrowing, and several other sources, including fees such as college tuition. Together, these sources account for 56.8 percent of state revenues.

Federal Grants

The largest nontax source of money is federal grants. Beginning in the 1960s, state and local governments became heavily dependent on national budgetary policies that distributed monies to the treasuries of states, cities, and other local governments. Originally, these dollars came to states in the form of **categorical grants-in-aid** that could be used only for specific programs such as community health centers. **General revenue sharing** was then enacted; it was distributed by formula and could be used by state and local governments for whatever projects these governments wanted—police salaries, playground equipment, home care for the elderly. General revenue sharing ended for states in 1979 and for cities in 1986.

In addition, the federal government began to fund **block grants,** which ultimately became the principal vehicle for distributing dollars for general use in broad programs such as community development. States gained more control under block grants because many funds were no longer channeled directly to local governments, but rather "passed through" a state agency. This flexibility came at a price, however, as the amount of funding for many programs, especially those affecting the poor and urban development, was reduced.

Increases in federal funding were attributable initially to interstate highway construction and maintenance spending following the increase in the national motor fuels tax in 1983. Subsequently, federal aid to the states increased because of the rising costs of social programs that are largely or completely funded by the national government, especially medical care for the poor, which is discussed in Chapter 13. National welfare reform legislation signed shortly before the 1996 presidential election resulted in the states' being asked to take over new responsibilities for health benefits for the poor and to emphasize job placements instead of cash assistance as the focus of welfare programs.[16] At the same time, the national government passed along funding to help support public assistance programs. However, critics of state policy processes have continued to chide Texas officials for not taking full advantage of national programs and even

being willing to sacrifice considerable federal funds to avoid spending a smaller amount of state funds, a situation exemplified in 2011 when the legislature passed and the governor signed a request to the federal government to provide health funds as block grants and to cap the amount. Also, some federal funds have been made available to help meet the requirements of post-9/11 homeland security and to help create jobs and improve infrastructure with economic stimulus funds. Altogether, the states and localities agree that costs of meeting the many federal mandates have exceeded the revenues provided. Nationally, the fiscal relationship between the national government and the states is seen as "fractured," indeed "at an all-time low."[17]

Borrowing

Governments, like private citizens, borrow money for various reasons. Political expediency is one. Borrowing allows new programs to be implemented and existing ones to be extended without increasing taxes. A second reason is that borrowing allows future beneficiaries of a state service to pay for that service. Students who live in residence halls, for example, help pay off the bonds used to finance those halls through their room fees.

State government indebtedness is highly restricted in Texas, however. The framers of the state constitution strongly believed in "pay-as-you-go" government. A four-fifths vote of the legislature is needed to approve emergency borrowing, and the state's debt ceiling originally was limited to $200,000. A series of amendments has altered the constitution to allow the issuance of state bonds for specific programs, particularly land for veterans, university buildings, student loans, parks, prisons, and water development. In FY 2008, outstanding state indebtedness was $33.3 billion. Although this figure was the eighth highest absolute level of indebtedness among the fifty states, Texas was ranked fiftieth in terms of per capita state indebtedness.[18]

Other Nontax Sources

Because taxes are unpopular in Texas and elsewhere, government inevitably looks to nontax revenue sources whenever possible. The prospective budget deficits that began in 1985 have resulted in a pattern of raising money by increasing fees for almost everything, looking to gambling as a source of public revenue, and even manipulating state pension funds. An excellent example is college tuition, a type of **user fee**—that is, a sum paid in direct exchange for service.

Although current students may find this fact hard to believe, senior college tuition was only $4 per credit hour in 1984, plus about that much more in fees. Tuition and fees have risen steadily since 1984, as a reflection of both inflation and state policymakers' desire for students to pay a higher proportion of the costs of their own education. In 2004 boards of regents were given discretion to set tuition locally, and the governing boards took advantage of their new authority and raised tuition sharply. As a result, tuition and fees combined at state universities is now 100 times the old $4 rate. Tuition is much higher for students in graduate and professional schools and for out-of-state students. Each community college district sets its own rate because two-year colleges are financially supported not only by state revenues, but also by local taxes. Most community/junior colleges charge about 15 percent of the senior institution tuition.

Other fees—for everything from driver's licenses and car inspections to water permits, from personal automobile tags to day-care center operator licenses—have

continued to increase. Fines for various legal infractions have risen. Even the cost of fishing licenses has gone up.

Other nontax sources of state revenue include the interest on bank deposits, proceeds from investments, and sales and leases of public lands. Having a surplus increases investment income. The doldrums of the oil industry decrease income from land leases; higher prices encourage exploration and thus more leasing of land.

The 1987 legislature proposed a constitutional amendment, approved by the voters in November of that year, that permitted parimutuel betting on horse races and, in three counties, on dog races on a local-option basis. By 1991, however, track betting had contributed virtually nothing to state coffers because the state's share of the proceeds—5 percent—was so high that track developers declined the opportunity to invest. Even though the 1991 legislature lowered the state's share to a graduated rate beginning at 1 percent, first-class tracks have been slow in coming and not very successful financially.

After four years of proposals and debate, the state legislature placed a state lottery on the November 1991 ballot. Voters approved the lottery, which began in summer 1992. Since then, whether the revenues were to be dedicated to education has been an issue. The 1997 legislature did dedicate the revenues, but moved other funds that had previously been earmarked for education back to the general fund. Administrative scandals and some falloff in betting have resulted in the lottery's not meeting revenue expectations. Consequently, in 2003, the legislature authorized the state's participation in the Mega Millions multistate lottery to try to improve revenues. Various schemes, such as legal slot machines, to expand gambling as a revenue source have not succeeded because of public objections.

Gas drilling in the Barnett Shale has become a profitable source of revenues for the state and for local governments, especially those in the northern part of the state.

AP Photo/Donna McWilliam.

Taxation

Taxes are the most familiar sources of governmental revenue and the most controversial. Since colonial days and James Otis's stirring phrase "no taxation without representation," citizens have sought justice in the tax system. The conservative heritage of Texas has not always made justice easy to find.

Taxes are collected for two principal reasons. *Revenue taxes*—for example, the general sales tax—are the major source of government income. They make it possible for government to carry out its programs. *Regulatory taxes*—for example, the taxes on tobacco and alcohol—were originally designed primarily to control the individuals and/or organizations subject to them and to either punish undesired behavior or reward desired behavior. However, they are also easier taxes to raise because any given regulatory tax affects only part of the population, and other citizens are willing to support the increase.

Although our discussion focuses on **tax equity** (fairness), another great concern with the Texas tax system is the lack of elasticity, which was discussed earlier in this chapter as one of the key factors resulting in periodic **revenue shortfalls**—insufficient funds to cover spending. A system based so heavily on sales and excise taxes runs into problems when the economy sours because the lower and middle classes, on whom such taxes depend, curtail their spending. With that curtailment comes a tailing off of tax revenues tied to consumer spending.

The tax policies of individual states reflect their economic resources, their political climates, and their dominant interest groups. Forty-three of the fifty states levy a personal income tax, although in two, the income tax is limited to interest and dividends. Forty-five states levy a corporate income tax. Texas has no personal income tax and, instead of a true corporate income tax, levies a complex business franchise (margins) tax that is based on the gross receipts of the business minus either the cost of goods sold or the total personnel costs—the individual business decides which each year. Smaller businesses with gross receipts under $1,000,000 are exempt. The franchise tax has been altered several times in recent legislative sessions to broaden the base and produce more revenue, most recently in the third called session of 2006,[19] but the 2009 legislature gave 40,000 additional small businesses an exemption from the fee. The state of Washington levies a similar tax. The margins tax produces about $10 billion each biennium less than it was forecasted to yield in 2006.

Texas relies heavily on the general sales tax and other forms of sales taxes, such as the one paid at the pump for motor fuels. The result is a disproportionately high taxpaying burden on poor and middle-income taxpayers and an unevenness of the tax burden among different types of businesses. Each revenue shortfall brings with it debate over the need for a broader and more elastic tax system, but the state's traditionalistic/individualistic political culture is readily apparent in the usual results of these discussions—namely, finding ways to reduce the property tax and increase general and selective sales taxes, which both individuals and businesses pay. Even in 2011 when the state faced a $27 billion shortfall, the only tax measures discussed were passing a sales tax exemption on luxury yachts and what proved to be a complicated measure that would tax sales if the only state presence of an Internet company was a warehouse.

Discussions about taxation, whether at the national, state, or local level, are seldom objective. One's own political philosophy and tax status inevitably color one's comments on the subject. Indeed, when government talks about taxes, its

noble-sounding phrases such as "the public interest" do not always ring true. Today's citizens are sophisticated enough to realize that extensive campaigning, heated debates, and vigorous lobbying have formed our tax policies and that the public interest usually has been construed so as to benefit the influential. One of the least successful aspects of American democracy is the tax system, which at both the national and state levels tends to favor those who are better off. Modern-day proposals to eliminate the federal income tax and move to a system of a very large (over 20 percent) national sales tax exemplify how tax systems can be made to benefit the wealthy, because such schemes include taxes on clothing, cars, and washing machines, but not on the purchase of stocks, bonds, or real estate investment trusts.

Texas professes fiscal conservatism and practices that philosophy by limiting state and local debt and by operating on a pay-as-you-go basis. The state budget reflects the political conservatism of Texas in its taxing and spending practices. An analysis of who pays, who does not pay, and who benefits from Texas taxes reveals not only the political and economic philosophy behind taxation in the state, but also which special interest groups most influence the legislature.

LONE STAR MEDIA

How to Spend Money in a Fiscal Crisis

Schools were forced to dismiss teachers. Many college students could no longer get state financial aid. The old, the very young, the poor were left with fewer services than before. So what did the Eighty-second Texas Legislature choose to spend the state's money for during FY 2012–2013? Media, of course. While the amount of dollars is relatively small—around $16 million—when the total budget is considered, spending money to lure television and movie makers to Texas was a controversial topic during the legislative session when draconian budget cuts would result in closing nursing homes and reducing aid to crippled children.

Supporters of the bill pointed out that previous appropriations to attract TV and film had been successful, resulting in thousands of full-time jobs and high-profile projects such as TNT's remake of the long-running (1978–1991) nighttime Texas soap opera *Dallas*. They argued that the state had to spend enough to make the producers want to return to Texas for more projects.

Probably even more important to the state than movies and TV in general is Friday night high school football (itself the theme of a Fox dramatic show), the archetypical Texas form of entertainment. In 2007, the state had instituted a mandatory steroid testing program, which had identified very few cases of steroid use among high school athletes in spite of the $3 million spent on testing each year. In 2011, the legislature agreed the program was ineffective, but decided it should continue to receive $650,000 a year.

SOURCE: Aman Batheja, "Texas Budget Crunch? State Spends Millions to Lure Film, TV," *Fort Worth Star-Telegram*, April 4, 2011, online edition at http://www.mcclatchydc.com/2011/04/04/v-print/111502/texas-budget-crunch-state-spends.html; Robert T. Garrett, "Despite Tight Budget, Texas Lawmakers Pay for More Steroid Tests," *Dallas Morning News*, June 2, 2011, online edition at http://www.dallasnews.com/news/politics/texas-legislature/headlines/20110601-despite-tight-budget-texas-lawmakers-pay-for-more-steroid-tests.ece.

The Tax Burden in Texas

Texas has prided itself on being a low-tax state, and both George W. Bush and Rick Perry had legislative agendas that pushed tax relief—a popular short-term approach during a boom economy. Perry then pressed hard for no new taxes during serious budget shortfalls. Texas ranks forty-seventh in per capita state tax revenue, and forty-fifth in the percentage of personal income paid in state taxes.[20] The state ranks second in federal corporate income taxes and third in individual income taxes paid,[21] measures not only of business activity in the state (Big Oil is a major factor) and sizable personal wealth held by a minority of Texans, but also of the population size of the state and of the fact that the state has no personal income tax so that only a portion of the general sales tax can be used to offset the federal income tax whenever Congress authorizes such deductions.

One irony of the Texas tax situation is that the state does not fare well under many federal grant formulas that include tax effort—the tax burden already borne by citizens—as a criterion. The state does least well on matching grants for social services and welfare. Although Texas ranked third in individual and second in corporate income taxes paid, the state was ranked only forty-second in terms of per capita federal spending. In short, Texans contribute more in federal taxes to get back a dollar in federal grants than residents of most other states.

The tax burden discussion also raises two other issues. The first is ability to pay, and the second is whether individuals and businesses both really pay.

Ability to Pay

A matter of some importance to taxpayers is whether the tax system is progressive or regressive. **Progressive taxation** is characterized by a rate that increases as the object taxed—property, income, or goods purchased—grows larger or gains in value. As noted earlier, progressive taxation is based on ability to pay. The best-known example is the federal income tax, which progresses from relatively low rates for those with small incomes to increasingly higher rates for those with larger incomes. However, loopholes in the federal tax laws and ceilings on special taxes, such as Social Security, still result in a proportionately heavier tax burden for the middle class than for the wealthy.

Although technically a tax system that involves a higher rate with a declining base, **regressive taxation** has come to refer to a system in which lower-income earners spend larger percentages of their incomes on commodities subject to flat tax rates. The best example of Texas's reliance on regressive taxes is the general retail sales tax, which provides almost one-third of total state revenue and 56 percent of the tax revenue. The general sales tax is assessed at 6.25 percent on a wide variety of goods and services at the time of sale, regardless of the income or wealth of the purchaser. Municipalities also can levy a 1 percent additional tax, as can mass transit districts and county economic development districts. Municipalities can also add sales tax percentages of a half percent each for economic development and in lieu of reduced property taxes. The result is that most Texans pay a sales tax of 8.25 percent.

The additional selective sales (excise) taxes—those levied on tobacco products, alcoholic beverages, and motor fuels, for example—also are regressive. The $20,000-a-year clerk and the $200,000-a-year executive who drive the same distance to work pay the same 20-cent-a-gallon tax on gasoline, but who is better able to bear the tax burden? Figure 12-3 shows the major taxes in Texas.

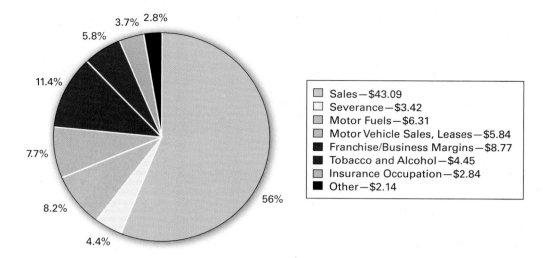

FIGURE 12-3 Estimated State Tax Collections by Major Tax, 2012–2013 Biennium, in Percentages (in Billions)*

SOURCE: "State Revenue . . . All Funds, Excluding Trust Funds," *Biennial Revenue Estimate, 2012–2013 Biennium* (Austin: Texas State Comptroller of Public Accounts, 2011), 41.

*TOTAL: $76.86 billion. All numbers are rounded.

The Institute on Taxation and Economic Policy, a Washington, D.C.–based nonprofit organization that studies state and national finance, reported in 2009 that in Texas, the poorest citizens pay about 8 percent of their income in sales taxes. The richest pay less than 2 percent.[22] The gap, while large, has narrowed somewhat since the 1990s. Also, Texas, unlike some states, does not yet tax "lifeline items"—food purchased at a grocery store, prescription medicines, and work clothes—and has a tax holiday to make it easier for parents to purchase school clothing for children.

At this stage, Texas cannot claim to have a progressive tax system. The restructuring of the corporation franchise tax in 2006 produced greater equity in business taxes and closed the loopholes that allowed major corporations to escape paying the tax, but the legislature also has authorized more exemptions in subsequent years. Nevertheless, the state has passed a constitutional amendment making institution of a personal income tax very difficult. Yet, a fair tax system is a value associated with democratic government. Many observers believe that a progressive income tax would be fairer than the general sales tax and could replace all or part of it. But the state's conservatism and the dominance of business lobbies in the state government have thus far precluded the adoption of a progressive tax policy. Moreover, in the early years of the twenty-first century, resentment against the U.S. Internal Revenue Service and the federal income tax has carried over into state politics and has made tax reform virtually impossible.

Taxes Paid by Individuals

A number of taxes are levied directly against individuals, for example, the inheritance tax, collected at the time beneficiaries inherit estates; the motor fuels tax, paid each time a motorist buys gasoline; and the ad valorem property tax, collected on real property, buildings, and land by local governments. (The state ad valorem

property tax was abolished by a 1982 constitutional amendment, but the property tax remains a mainstay for local governments.) Businesses also pay the motor fuels tax and local property taxes, of course, but by increasing prices they let their customers pick up the tab.

Some authorities would include all sales taxes in the category of taxes paid by individuals, on the assumption that businesses pass them on to the consumer just as they do local ad valorem and state vehicle registration taxes—whether that is the intention of the law or not. There are two types of individual sales taxes:

1. The *general sales tax* is a broadly based tax that is collected on most goods and services and must be paid by the consumer. It is illegal for a business to absorb the tax—for example, as a promotional device. This familiar tax was first adopted in Texas in 1961, with a 2 percent rate. Nationally, Mississippi was the first state to have a sales tax, but twenty-nine other states adopted the tax during the Great Depression of the 1930s. Originally, many exemptions existed, but these have become fewer and fewer with each legislative session except for an expansion of sales tax holidays that allow Texans to purchase school clothes and other items without paying a sales tax. Indeed, the tax is now paid on many services (lawn maintenance, for example), as well as goods (hamburgers, jeans).

2. *Selective sales taxes* (excise taxes) are levied on only a few items, comparatively speaking, and consumers are often unaware that they are paying them. These taxes are included in the price of the item and may not even be computed separately. Tobacco products, alcoholic beverages—tobacco and alcohol taxes are sometimes called "sin taxes"—automobiles, gasoline, rental of hotel rooms, and the admission price for amusements (movies, plays, nightclubs, sporting events) are among the items taxed in this category.

General and selective sales taxes account for almost four-fifths of the state's tax revenue. Business initially pays about half of these taxes before recouping them in their pricing.

Taxes Levied on Businesses

Taxes levied on businesses in Texas produce considerable revenue for the state, but are often regulatory in nature. One example is the *severance taxes* levied on natural resources, such as crude oil, natural gas, and sulfur that are severed (removed) from the earth. Their removal, of course, depletes irreplaceable resources, and part of the tax revenue is dedicated to conservation programs and to the regulation of production; thirty other states have similar taxes. Severance taxes once were the backbone of the state's revenue system. They have declined for almost three decades in spite of increases in the price of oil and the burgeoning natural gas drilling operations. They are expected to yield only 4.4 percent of the tax revenue for FY 2012–2013.

The major Texas business tax today is the *franchise tax*, which is also known as the *margins* tax and the *business activity* tax. It is assessed against corporations, partnerships, business trusts, professional associations, business associations, joint ventures, holding companies, and other legal entities. Excluded are sole proprietorships and general partnerships. This tax is a revenue tax that

reflects the cost of doing business in the state. Some people regard it as a type of corporate income tax because the business pays taxes based on its gross receipts. This tax was overhauled substantially in 1991, 2006, and 2009 to make it fairer. It originally emphasized taxes only on capital-intensive businesses, such as manufacturing, and collected little from labor-intensive businesses, such as computer software firms, financial institutions, and even the big downtown law firms. The 1991 version also left a loophole that let big corporations such as Dell, Inc. (the computer company) declare themselves to be partnerships and thus not covered by the tax. The more comprehensive version of the tax is expected to provide at least 11.4 percent of the tax revenue for FY 2012–2013.

In addition to the franchise tax, there are special *gross receipts taxes* levied on specific businesses, most notably utilities. Among other taxes levied directly on businesses in Texas is the *insurance premium tax,* levied on gross premiums collected by insurance companies. Miscellaneous *special taxes and fees* for such varied activities as chartering a corporation, brewing alcoholic beverages, and selling real estate also exist. Whenever possible, businesses pass these taxes along to consumers in the form of higher prices. Together, they account for about 6.5 percent of the state's tax revenue.

Because it is difficult to determine exactly what business taxes are passed on to consumers, one can only guess at who pays. Roughly 56.8 percent of the state's income comes from nontax sources. Of the revenue that comes from taxes, businesses directly pay at least 20 percent of the total. However, many taxes are paid by both individuals and businesses, making it difficult to assess what proportion of the taxes businesses and individuals actually pay. Examples of these latter taxes include those on motor fuels, motor vehicle sales and rentals, and utilities. Texas businesses actually contribute a higher percentage of state revenues than businesses nationally contribute to federal revenues. The federal corporate income tax, for example, produces slightly less than 8 percent of the national government's revenue. The most significant federal revenue sources are the personal income tax and the Social Security and Medicare taxes.

Who Benefits?

To address the question of who benefits from taxation policies, we must consider the kinds of services the government provides. Nothing would seem more equitable than a tax structure resulting in an exact ratio between taxes paid and benefits received, and in Texas, some taxes are levied with exactly that philosophy in mind. The motor fuels tax, 20 cents per gallon on gasoline and diesel fuel, is paid by those who use motor vehicles, and three-fourths of the revenues from this tax are spent on maintaining and building highways and roads. The remainder goes to public schools. However, the example points out a problem with the "benefit theory" of revenue. People who do not own automobiles and who do not buy gasoline also benefit from those big trucks hauling goods to market over state highways. The owners of an ambulance that transports an accident victim to a hospital buy the gasoline, but may benefit far less from it than do the victim and her or his family and friends.

Furthermore, we must consider not only *who* benefits, but *when* they benefit. For example, an entire economy is aided by educating children now, but it will not realize the benefit—or lack of benefit—of today's educational investment until today's children enter the workforce fifteen years from now.

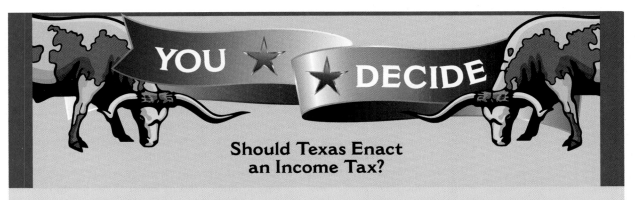

YOU ★ ★ DECIDE

Should Texas Enact an Income Tax?

Texas is one of seven states without a personal income tax. Should the Texas legislature enact an income tax?

PRO	CON
▲ The legislature should modernize the state tax structure and include an income tax because:	▼ The legislature should not consider an income tax because:
▲ The present tax system is regressive; an income tax could make it less so.	▼ The tax would require a constitutional amendment except under a very limited circumstance. It would be impossible to get a majority from voters.
▲ An income tax would make billions of new dollars available for state services.	▼ Texas does okay except when the economy is in a real slump.
▲ Legislative sessions would be less chaotic because the revenue stream would be more flexible.	▼ It is fair for poor people to pay a higher percentage of their income in taxes because they demand more government services.
▲ The tax system would be fairer because it would be based on ability to pay.	▼ People can control how much they pay in sales taxes by how much they spend.
▲ The state would probably receive more federal funds because it could meet the "tax effort" test better.	▼ Texas needs to attract new businesses; a corporate income tax would drive away business.

One of the "sin taxes" collected by the state is on tobacco. This tax is based on the philosophy that those who subject their bodies to the damaging effects of tobacco may be discouraged from doing so and thus benefit if they have to pay more money for the privilege. Although the percentage of smokers is declining, the decline is not particularly due to this tax, which has become, in effect, a use tax. Those who smoke receive no special benefits from revenues from this tax, which are used for schools, parks, and general government functions. To

conform to the benefit theory of taxation, the revenue from the tobacco tax would need to be spent primarily for cancer research, the treatment of lung diseases, and other programs related to the effects of smoking.

A strict benefit philosophy would have a disastrous effect on low-income citizens. For example, if all taxes were assessed on a pay-benefit basis, then the poorest citizens could not afford to educate their children, a situation that would only entrap them further in the cycle of minimal education, low-paying jobs, and marginal incomes. The extremely wealthy, on the other hand, could have their own police forces, four-lane roads to their weekend farms, and college classrooms with five-to-one student-teacher ratios. Society would hardly benefit from such a situation. Clearly, trying to apply a benefit theory of taxation, like all issues in taxation, is very difficult.

Contemporary Issues

The history of economic and fiscal policy provides important background. However, new issues also confront state policymakers.

Perspectives from the Past

For a half-century, Texas relied on oil and gas production taxes as the major source of state revenue, with most of these being paid by out-of-state purchasers. How good were the good old days? "Texas went from 1971 to 1984 . . . without an increase in state tax rates, or new taxes" while the population was growing 42 percent.[23] After the world oil market crashed, Texans were ill prepared to develop a responsible and responsive revenue policy to provide funds for state services. The boom and bust cycle became the fiscal way of life in Texas.

What's Next?

Texas will be no different from other governments in its need to find adequate and equitable revenue sources to support the services needed by a rapidly growing citizenry and to make up for periodic revenue shortfalls that have a major effect on all states. One strategy that the state will pursue is *performance evaluation and management,* including cutbacks to funding that are recommended in the biennial Texas Performance Review (TPR) and in human service spending. The importance of the Texas Performance Review can only grow. The TPR originated with John Sharp when he was comptroller and was pursued relentlessly by his successor, Carole Keeton Strayhorn. Strayhorn's approach, coupled with her refusal to certify the budget, led the 2003–2004 legislature to reduce her powers and grant the performance review authority to the Legislative Budget Board. The performance evaluation/cutback approach is grounded in a national movement to "reinvent government."[24] This demand emerged from strategic planning and quality management movements in the private sector as sluggish industries had to downsize—or in the new terminology, "rightsize." In Texas, it has also been used to accomplish a political agenda, for example, in trying to force universities to divert attention from research to degree production.

Performance reviews speak not only to "smaller," but also to "smarter." Periodically, *Governing* magazine examines management and/or fiscal policies in the states. The magazine published a fifty-state report on taxation early in 2003. The report began with the observation that "The vast majority of state

tax systems are inadequate for the task of funding a 21st-century government."[25] A top rating was four stars. Texas got one star on the adequacy of its revenue, one on the fairness of the system to taxpayers, but three on management of the system. In 2005, *Governing* graded the states again to see how they had weathered national economic downtrends and responded to state needs.[26] Those ratings gave Texas an overall grade of "B." In 2008, the Pew Center on the States graded the states, giving Texas these marks: "B" on money (finance, budget, for example); "B" on people (workforce, employee retention, for example); "B" on infrastructure (capital planning, maintenance, for example); and "A–" on information (strategic direction, managing for performance, for example).[27] In deference to the struggles of states with the recession and slow recovery, neither *Governing* nor the Pew Center had released a new report by 2011.

Another strategy that all states and the national government will use is **privatizing.** Two examples are the private prisons that now serve the state—the state contracts them for services—and the increasing rate of tuition and fees paid by college students. The first is direct private provision of service; the second is passing along the cost to private citizens rather than burdening the revenue system.

A third strategy is to *change the revenue structure* to avert the revenue shortfalls that plagued the state in the 1980s and early 2000s. Change would focus on making the system more elastic and better able to fund state services consistently. The major change to date is the restructuring of the corporate franchise/margins tax discussed earlier in this chapter. The dominant issue of the 1997 and 2005–2006 legislative sessions was revenue restructuring to lower school property taxes, but the lower property taxes did not stem entirely from a new revenue system. Instead, the difference between the revenues formerly raised by the school districts and what they raise now was to be made up by state surpluses, with uncertainties about what happens when there is not a surplus.[28] The Eighty-second Legislature in 2011 found that uncertainty meant massive cuts.

Another aspect of revenue structure is the competition among governments for tax sources. National and state governments both tax motor fuels, tobacco, and alcohol, for example, and both levels of government keep increasing tax rates. Both the state and local governments have general sales taxes. The upshot is that the combined tax rates begin to vex citizens after a while. Ironically, cuts in federal income tax rates since the 1980s enhance the state income tax as a logical new source of state revenue.

For tax restructuring to occur, state politics and citizen attitudes would have to change. Businesses, including partnerships, would have to accept some sort of business activity tax that functions as a true corporate income tax, whatever it is called. Ultimately, private citizens would have to be willing to accept a personal income tax. Businesses had to accept major changes in business taxes in 1991 and 2006, with the result that business taxes are broader and fairer than in the past, but the revenue is inadequate to fund state services. However, the mere advocacy of a personal income tax is a sure ticket out of office.

Democratic theory recognizes the equality of the citizenry, and many people think that a revenue system that extracts more from people the poorer they are seriously compromises equality. Since 1991, business has paid a greater share of taxes, but as previously noted, the tax system in Texas is still regressive, placing a proportionately heavier burden on those with the lowest incomes. The reality is that without an income tax, the state will always have difficulty meeting its revenue needs in anything other than a booming economy. Historically, Texas

Liberals like Ben Sargent compared the legislature's persistent refusal to raise taxes to meet the state's budget crisis to Emperor Nero's fiddling while Rome burned in A.D. 64.

Courtesy of Ben Sargent.

attracted businesses because they found a favorable tax structure in the state. However, the experience of other states with economic development indicates that many modern industries are also concerned about the stability of state services. Such stability is difficult in the absence of a flexible tax structure.

The difficulty of revenue restructuring is illustrated by the 1997 legislature's failed debate over tax reform. Similar frustration occurred in the failure of the legislature to address school finance problems in the 2003 regular session or the fruitless special session of April 2004, postponing the solution until the last moment in a 2006 special session. The Ben Sargent cartoon compares legislative inertia in the face of inadequate funding for state services to Nero's playing his fiddle while Rome burned.

Where Does the Money Go?

Occasionally, an argument is heard in the state's legislative chambers that reflects serious concern about budgeting a particular program—who will benefit from it, whether it is needed by society, and how it will be financed. More generally, however, whether funds are allocated for a proposed program depends on which interests favor it and how powerful they are, who and how powerful the opposition is, and what the results are of compromises and coalitions between these and "swing vote" groups. The political viewpoints of the legislators, the governor, and the state bureaucracy also have an impact on budgetary decisions. In short, decisions about spending public money, like decisions about whom and what to tax, are not made objectively. Rather, they are the result of the complex relationships among the hundreds of political actors who participate in the

state's governmental system. The biases of the political system are thus reflected in the biases of state spending. Rather than developing coherent public policy and seeking ways to fund programs and services, Texas allows the budget to determine policy priorities.

This section outlines the stages in the budgetary process and then describes the state's major expenditures.

Action without Vision

Vision without action is a daydream. Action without vision is a nightmare.

—Japanese proverb

The Eighty-second Legislature (2011–2012) changed the face of Texas politics, but perhaps not for the better. The $27 billion shortfall was enormous—the worst in the country—in a state that ranked toward the bottom in most state services already and that was growing in population. The solution was slash-and-burn. By 2011, accounting tricks such as delayed payments, early tax collections, political ruses such as castigating the federal government while using federal funds to balance the budget, and pure braggadocio about the fiscal health of the state left the state in considerable trouble. It had to cover a deficit for the FY 2011 budget and had inadequate revenues just to continue services as before in the wake of a significant population growth.

The basic problem was simply that a state that traditionally underfunded state services refused to identify new revenues. The inadequacy of the revised business activity tax that was developed as part of the solution to funding public schools in the 2006 session made the situation worse. The 2006 school finance bills were highlighted by bipartisanship, a desire to find a solution to a major problem (unequal funding of public schools coupled with a desire to cut property taxes), and the willingness to pass complex legislation to address the problem, but legislators had ignored the comptroller's warnings that the revenue would be inadequate and that forcing schools to reduce property taxes would cause problems later. Indeed, the tax, until modified, will always yield about $10 billion less than promised when it was passed

Historically, pragmatic legislators ironed out compromises during budget crises. No one got everything he or she wanted, but virtually everyone got something. Even undisputed conservatives were willing to vote for needed revenue measures. However, the twenty-first century has seen a different kind of legislator—suburban, given to the "not in my backyard approach," and much more ideological than in the days of mainly rural legislators. The traditional team approach has yielded to the individual members, who in turn are just as subject to all the instant communication devices as anyone else; that is, their constituents constantly tell them to vote "no." This point is important: however much one might prefer not to see Texas on the bottom of critical state service rankings, the people elected these legislators and this governor, and a majority of the people got what they asked for. The 2011 representatives elected by relatively wealthy Anglos voted to cut funding for public schools that will largely be attended by relatively poor Mexican Americans.

Moreover, the governor was more powerful than one would expect from history or the state constitution because of his long service and complete control of the state

(continued)

(continued)

bureaucracy. He was pressing for a complete victory of a balanced budget achieved with no new revenue to sell to national Republicans in his quest for a presidential nomination. He and his Tea Party sympathizers did not even want to use the Rainy Day (emergency) Fund to address the needs of the state, although the national audience the governor sought expressed curiosity about a state with billions in the bank that was firing teachers and closing nursing homes and Texas representatives were catching criticism at home from teachers and parents.

The battleground was H.B. 1, the House version of the budget. The Legislative Budget Board noted that if it were enacted as originally proposed, this bill would cost 335,000 jobs, a $19 billion decline in the state economy, and a similar drop in state revenue. The primary targets for cuts were public schools, higher education, and Medicaid, including nursing homes. While the Senate got a few concessions, the FY 2012–2013 appropriations bill was austere. The essence was "no new revenue regardless of population growth or public needs."

There is no right or wrong in political beliefs, and in Texas, the most conservative of views have long prevailed. The problem with the appropriations act for FY 2012–2013 is that it epitomizes the Japanese proverb stated earlier. *It is action without vision.* There were legislators in both houses who saw the consequences, but not enough of them. For the first time, public school funding, though slightly increased, was inadequate to continue programs that already existed. If the schools have large classes and other inadequate classroom situations, the youth will not be well prepared for jobs. Texas does not need to create more minimum-wage/below-the-poverty-line jobs. The hardest-hit victims of the college cuts have been students who were depending on state grants to finance their education; the road out of low-paying jobs is now blocked for them. On the medical side, the state has now gone after nursing homes with old folks and again after poor children. Ultimately, hospital emergency rooms—already subject to Medicaid and Medicare cuts—will bear the brunt of those cuts. These targets of budget slashing reflect the disaster of action without vision.

Sources: Robert T. Garrett, "Budget Would Slash Funds to Schools, Colleges, Medicaid," *Dallas Morning News*, January 19, 2011, 1A, 12A; Chris Tomlinson, "State Budget Crisis? Depends Who You Ask," *Denton Record-Chronicle*, January 17, 2011; Lori Taylor, "Digging in the Wrong Places," *Dallas Morning News*, February 6, 2011, 6P; "Dewhurst Says Education, Medicaid Rates Can Be Saved," *Dallas Morning News*, March 26, 2011; Ryan Holeywell, "How Bad Is It?" *Governing*, May 2011, 26–30; Dave Mann and Abby Rapoport, "Lege by the Numbers," and "Graphic Act," *Texas Observer*, May 6, 2011, 19, and June 17, 2011, 8–13, respectively; Paula Burka, "Capitol Affair," *Texas Monthly*, July 2011, 12–13; Paul Burka and Kate Blakeslee with Katherine Stevens, "The Best & Worst Legislators," *Texas Monthly*, July 2011, 78–93, 178–183; and Chris Tomlinson, "Views Differ on Texas Budget," *Denton Record-Chronicle*, June 25, 2011, 2A.

Planning and Preparation

The budgetary process consists of three stages: planning and preparation, authorization and appropriation, and execution (spending). Budget planning and the preparation of the proposed budget are functions of the chief executive in the national government and in forty-four states, but Texas has a **dual-budgeting system.** The constitution makes the legislature responsible for the state budget. The legislature is aided in this task by the Legislative Budget Board (LBB) and its staff, which prepare a draft budget. Four senators and four representatives

Although businesses spent years finding ways to avoid the old corporate franchise tax, basically saying "tax anybody but me," in 2006, the state's businesses agreed to a broad-based business activity tax to fund public schools. It has proved inadequate.

Courtesy of Ben Sargent.

compose the LBB, which is co-chaired by the lieutenant governor and the speaker of the House. Figure 12-4 depicts the workings of the LBB.

Modern governors have understood the importance of the budget as a political tool, and so, with the aid of the Budget, Planning, and Policy Division, the governor also prepares a budget. This duplicate effort is wasteful, but it does allow different political perspectives on state spending to be heard. In 2003, the legislature took a most unusual approach to budgeting by involving the governor as an equal participant with legislators themselves. By 2007, legislators were trying to find ways around gubernatorial vetoes once again. In 2011, Perry's long tenure and newly elected ultraconservative legislators who shared his philosophy resulted in the budget he wanted.

The two budgets agree in one respect: Both tend to be *incremental*—that is, both propose percentage increases or decreases for existing programs and the addition of new programs by way of feasibility studies and pilot programs. The recent emphasis on performance may at least give lawmakers a better picture of the real priorities of state agencies and how costs relate to benefits to the state.

Budget planning ordinarily begins in the spring of the even-numbered year before the year in which the legislature meets in regular session. Since 1992, strategic planning has been integrated with budgeting so that the LBB, the governor's office, and the agencies have a compressed time period for preparing budget proposals. State agencies submit their requests for the next biennium on forms prepared jointly by the governor's and the LBB's staffs. Then, at joint hearings, the two staffs try to obtain sufficient information from agency representatives about agency needs to make adequate evaluations of the requests from the agencies. These hearings are usually held in the early fall and are the

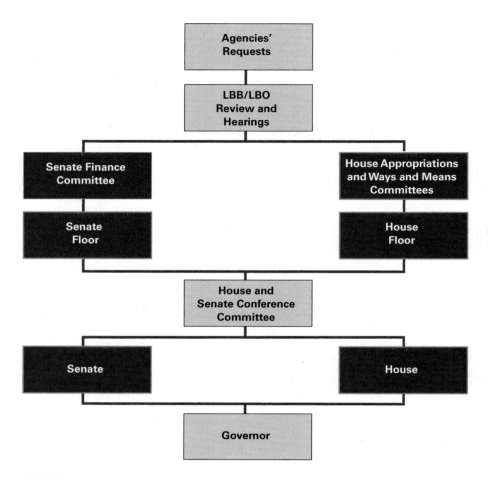

FIGURE 12-4 Role of the Legislative Budget Board (LBB) and Legislative Budget Office (LBO) in the Texas Budget Process

final joint effort of the two staffs. At this time, individuals and outside groups—the state's dominant interest groups—also provide input. Each staff then prepares a set of budget recommendations that reflects the priorities of its office. When completed, each document is almost two inches thick and provides summary information, as well as an agency-by-agency breakdown by specific budget categories. Both are submitted to the appropriate legislative committees for consideration.

Both budgets outline state expenditures for a two-year period. Completed in time for the opening of the legislature in January of one year (for example, 2013), they must project state spending through August two years later (2015), regardless of any changes in the economic outlook that may take place during that thirty-two-month period. Consequently, shifts in the funding of state programs may be needed. Certainly, when we realize that the constitutional directive for biennial legislative sessions means that the funding of state programs must be planned almost three years in advance, we more easily understand why the state budget planners lean toward incrementalism rather than rationalism.

Authorization and Appropriations

The authorization and appropriation stage consists of the authorization of programs to be provided by the state and the passage of a bill appropriating money—the state budget. The House Ways and Means (revenues), House Appropriations (spending), and Senate Finance (both revenues and spending) committees are the key legislative players. Agency representatives, the governor's staff, interest-group representatives, and private citizens testify on behalf of the particular agency or program of concern to them. There is considerable forming and reforming of coalitions as legislators, lobbyists, and committee members bargain, compromise, trade votes, and generally endeavor to obtain as much for "their side" as possible.

Past campaign contributions begin to pay off at this stage, and the relative power of different interest groups is reflected in the state budget. For example, political campaigns frequently include a call to "get tough on crime" and to build more prisons; in turn, prisons are typically well funded. The four main teachers' groups in the state expend considerable effort in trying to influence legislators, and schoolteachers usually get raises, albeit often small ones, though in 2011–2012, some got pink slips instead. The success of the business lobby is the most problematic. In 1995, business got virtually everything it wanted. In 1997, business buried the tax bill it did not want, but also found itself on the receiving end of a lot of negative legislation. In 1999, business got some tax breaks and the ability to shop for competitive electric rates. In 2003, the business lobby was so dominant that the visitors' gallery where corporate lobbyists sat while legislators were meeting was dubbed "the owner's box." In 2006, the business lobby accepted new taxes in order to fund public schools, and, in terms of fiscal policy, was virtually left alone in 2007 and 2009, except for additional franchise fee exemptions. In 2011, business mainly got more protection from lawsuits and greater highway funding.

The authorization and appropriation stage is a lengthy one, and the Appropriations and Finance committees submit their reports—the two versions of the appropriations bill—near the end of the session. Speaker Pete Laney and Lieutenant Governor Bob Bullock improved the process considerably, beginning in 1993, when they insisted on adequate time for review of the proposed state spending plan. The two versions are never identical; so, a ten-member conference committee composed of an equal number of senators and representatives carefully selected by the presiding officers must develop a single conference report on the budget, including adequate revenue measures to fund the proposed spending. The revenue stipulation is because Texas has a balanced-budget provision that requires the state comptroller to certify that expected revenues are sufficient to fund expenditures. The two houses must accept or reject the report as it stands. Usually, this approval comes fairly late in the session, often at the proverbial "eleventh hour" (in 2011, during a special session). The approved appropriations bill then goes to the governor for signature.

The governor has a very powerful weapon, the line-item veto, which allows the striking of individual items from the appropriations bill if he or she disagrees with the spending provision. However, the governor cannot add to the budget or restore funding for a pet project that the legislature rejected. Throughout this chapter, the reader will see slightly different dollar totals reflected in various tables and charts because the information was based on different documents, chiefly revenue estimates and the conference report on the appropriations act, with the governor still having the possibility of vetoes.

Execution/Spending

The actual disbursement of the state's income is rather technical and less interesting as a political process. It includes such details as shifting money into various funds, issuing state warrants and paychecks, internal auditing of expenditures by agency accountants, and external auditing by the state auditor's staff to ensure the legality of expenditures.

The major political issue involving budget execution has been efforts by several governors to gain greater control over spending between legislative sessions. In 1980 and 1981, voters defeated constitutional amendments that would have increased the governor's authority. The 1987 special legislative session resulted in some increase in the governor's authority to slow down expenditures. In 1991, the legislature not only empowered the LBB to move money from one agency to another agency based on performance, but also created a new tripartite body—the governor, the lieutenant governor, and the speaker—to deal with spending and reallocation.

A second political issue in budget execution concerns auditing. The state auditor, a legislative appointee, monitors state agencies and for many years has issued management letters directing agencies both to abandon and to implement different management practices. In 1988, Attorney General Jim Mattox issued an attorney general's advisory opinion that a legislative appointee could not constitutionally tell an executive agency head how to run the agency. However, with new powers granted in the tidal wave of performance-oriented reforms in 1991, the state auditor is now mandated to perform management audits.

Because the services delivered through state budget expenditures are of more interest to the average citizen than the technicalities of how the budget is executed, this section emphasizes a summary of spending on major state services. Figure 12-5 shows that health and human services plus education account for almost

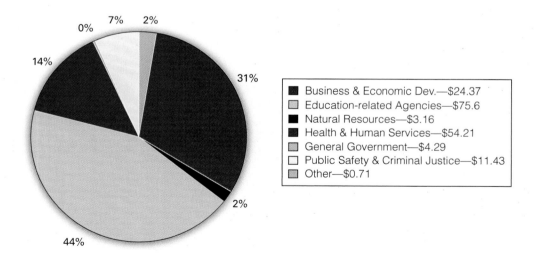

FIGURE 12-5 Texas State Spending by Function, 2012–2013 Biennium, in Percentages (in billions)*

SOURCE: *Conference Committee Report, H.B. 1, General Appropriations Bill,* 3rd printing (Austin: Legislative Budget Board, June 2011), 14.

*TOTAL: $172.3 billion. All numbers are rounded.

three-fourths of the FY 2012–2013 Texas budget of $172.3 billion (before the line-item vetoes). Many of the program areas that are summarized here as objects of expenditure are discussed throughout the book as significant political issues.

Education

For FY 2012–2013, 43.9 percent of the state budget was slated for public schools and higher education. About 70 percent of the education budget of $75.6 billion was for elementary and secondary schools in the state's 1,033 independent school districts and for state schools for the deaf and visually impaired. The state provides textbooks as well as special services, such as programs for disabled children and vocational courses, the State of Texas Assessment of Academic Readiness (STARR™) achievement tests, school buses, operating costs, and teacher salaries. The state does not pay the total costs of public education, however. Local school districts share the cost and also are responsible for buildings and other school facilities. Those that can afford it provide supplements to attract the best teachers, buy additional library books, develop athletic programs, and offer students enrichment opportunities.

As was summarized in Chapter 10, financial equality is the dominant issue affecting public schools. As of 2006, Texas ranked forty-fourth among the states in combined state and local per capita spending for public education.[29] Table 12-2 shows how the fifteen most populous states spend their money for various major categories of state services and allows a comparison of Texas with the other fourteen states, as well as providing the ranking for Texas among all fifty states. The figures are on a per capita basis—that is, dollars expended per person. In overall education expenditures Texas ranked thirteenth among the fifteen most-populated states and forty-fourth among all fifty states for education expenditures of all types.

Cartoonist Ben Sargent summarized the 2011 legislative session by pointing out that the legislature's solution to a major revenue shortfall was to slash the budget and ignore the implications for the future of the state.

Courtesy of Ben Sargent.

TABLE 12-2

Per Capita State Government Expenditures for Selected Functions, Fifteen Most Populous States, 2007, in Order of Overall Per Capita Expenditures

State	Total	Education	Highways	Hospitals	Public Welfare	All Other
New York	$7,790	$1,909	$219	$237	$2,399	$3,026
Massachusetts	6,809	1,648	268	78	1,885	2,930
New Jersey	6,481	1,718	302	226	1,375	2,860
California	6,421	2,001	251	172	1,548	2,449
Ohio	5,768	1,716	303	171	1,425	2,153
Washington	5,756	2,020	429	248	1,083	1,976
Pennsylvania	5,499	1,470	482	203	1,542	1,802
Michigan	5,447	2,131	279	205	1,263	1,569
North Carolina	4,868	1,830	332	152	1,214	1,340
Virginia	4,778	1,713	342	330	907	1,486
Illinois	4,624	1,197	366	74	1,214	1,773
Arizona	4,460	1,442	310	11	1,141	1,556
Georgia	4,394	1,636	526	77	1,017	1,138
Florida	3,999	1,223	377	38	953	1,408
Texas	**3,801**	**1,443**	**341**	**138**	**866**	**1,013**
50-state Average	5,426	1,709	342	160	1,306	1,909
Texas as % of Average and Ranking	**70%** **50**	**84.4%** **44**	**99.6%** **28**	**86%** **24**	**66.4%** **48**	**53%** **50**

NOTE: Numbers are rounded.

SOURCE: *Fiscal Size Up, 2010–11*, 54, based on U.S. Bureau of the Census Data.

The other large slice of the education dollar pie, about $20.3 billion, supports higher education: the operations of general academic institutions and community colleges, the technical college system, health science centers, and extension programs, plus retirement systems and debt payments on buildings. For both junior and senior colleges, a formula based on such factors as semester credit hours determines the basic level of state support, with the formula funding supplemented by special program funding and affected by performance norms originally adopted in 1992. One positive piece of legislation in 1997 was the creation of a greatly simplified funding formula. The community/junior colleges also are supported by local districts. In 2003, the legislature deregulated university tuition, thereby permitting the institutions to begin charging whatever they needed to charge in 2004. Local tuition and fees account for a sizable portion of campus funding and were a matter of considerable debate during the 2007 and 2009 sessions. One comparative measure of higher education in Texas is that

the state ranks thirty-first in the number of persons age twenty-five or older who hold a bachelor's degree. Another measure is that, of all students enrolled in higher education, in Texas, 88.1 percent are in public institutions, considerably above the national ranking of 76.8 percent. The remaining part of the education budget covers insurance, retirement, and various administrative expenses.

Health and Human Services

Some $54.4 billion—31.4 percent of the budget—is allocated for human services programs, including welfare, unemployment compensation, employment services, workers' compensation, services for special groups such as the blind and the elderly, and health programs such as mental health and retardation programs, children's health insurance, treatment of substance abuse, contagious-disease control, and treatment for catastrophic illnesses such as AIDS, cancer, and kidney failure. About 60 percent of the funding comes from the national government. Chapter 13 will discuss the welfare system.

Although expenditures for health and human services are the second largest segment of the state budget, Texas ranked forty-eighth among the fifty states in per capita expenditures for welfare services and twenty-fourth in hospital services. The state's rankings fluctuate because Texas has a tendency to cut social services first when the budget is tight. Indeed, the FY 2012–2013 budget covers only eighteen months of Medicaid expenses. Texas spending in most budget categories has been losing ground to per capita spending in other states during the early years of the twenty-first century.

Business and Economic Development

Texas's expenditures for business and economic development for FY 2012–2013 are $24.4 billion, or 14.1 percent of the total budget. This category includes transportation, economic development to promote the state's economy, the efforts of the Housing and Community Affairs Department on behalf of local governments, and employment and training services. Just under one-half of the expenditures in this category comes from federal funds, particularly highway matching funds to maintain and upgrade the 3,233 miles of federal interstate highways in Texas. In 1977, the legislature capped highway expenditures, with the result that the state has many poorly maintained roads and not enough highways. Despite the budget shortfall, the 2011 legislature increased spending in this area (see Chapter 14 for a fuller discussion). Texas ranks twenty-eighth

Truth in Government

The $27 billion starting deficit in 2011 was partly overcome by a late infusion of sales taxes and federal education dollars. The really controversial aspect of reducing the deficit to $23 billion was the misuse of dedicated funds in two ways. Instead of allocating their full share of funds to programs such as parks and helping poor people pay utility bills, $4.1 billion was either diverted or held back.

Source: Robert T. Garrett, "Budget Sits on Set-Aside Money," *Dallas Morning News*, July 4, 2011, 1A–2A.

among the states in per capita spending on highways. Rankings are not available for other services in this category.

Other Major Expenditures

The next largest category of expenditures is public safety, at just over $11.4 billion, or 6.6 percent of the total budget. This category includes law enforcement, prisons, and related programs. The remainder of the budget, less than a billion dollars, accounts for 4 percent of state expenditures. Services, programs, and agencies in this category include general government—the legislature, the judiciary, the governor, and various management offices—as well as parks, natural resources, and regulatory agencies. This category also includes set-asides of any surplus for future expenditures.

Summary

Economic conditions, the political climate, and power plays are all part of the game of generating revenues for state government and determining how that income will be spent. Both taxing and spending are usually incremental, with major changes rarely occurring. However, the state's boom-and-bust economy over the past thirty years has meant more tax and fee increases than usual and less budget growth. That "downer" scenario has periodically reversed itself when the economy is in the boom part of the cycle, such as FY 2008–2009, when both revenue and spending decisions were attributable to a robust economy, but that period was followed by the budget decisions for FY 2010–2011 and FY 2012–2013 that reflected a deep recession.

In comparing Texas with other states, we find that the combined state and local tax burden is relatively low, with Texas ranked in the bottom fifth of all states. These rankings are based only on taxes, not total revenues. We also note the significant absence of any personal or corporate income tax, although business has been asked to pay a larger share of the tax burden through the revamped, but inadequate, franchise tax. The fundamental difference in the Texas revenue system from that of many other states is the disproportionate burden borne by the poorest citizens. This regressive system raises serious questions about how democratic the tax system is in the state.

Democracies are also responsive to the citizenry. The state's spending may not meet the needs of all its citizens, particularly when one considers that it ranks in the bottom five of all states in its per capita spending for education, welfare, and general services, and only slightly better for highways, for which the federal government pays a large portion, and hospitals. However, Texas spending does match voter priorities, and the budget drives policy choices.

The Texas budget process differs procedurally from the ones used by most other states. Those differences include the dual-budgeting system, the extraordinary dominance of the presiding officers in the appropriations process, and the virtually absolute veto power of the governor as a result of the short legislative session.

Important aspects of state finance in Texas are as follows:

1. The reliance on taxes paid directly or indirectly by the individual

2. The reliance on regressive taxes such as the sales tax as a major revenue source for the state

3. The restrictions on borrowing

4. The importance of federal funds in the state budget

5. The extent to which the budgetary process is dominated by the legislature and to which the legislature in turn is dominated by the presiding officers

6. The obvious need for diversified revenue sources

7. The seemingly endless problem of school finance

The largest expenditure category is education, followed by health and human services, business and economic development, public safety and criminal justice, and "other," which includes everything else. Critical issues affecting some of these state service areas are discussed in the next two chapters and in earlier chapters.

Glossary Terms

block grants

categorical grants-in-aid

dual-budgeting system

elasticity

fiscal years

general revenue sharing

inflation

privatizing

progressive taxation

regressive taxation

revenue shortfalls

tax equity

user fee

13

The face of Texas public education is changing. In the 2010–2011 academic year, Latino children became a majority of students in Texas public schools.

Mario Villafuerte/Getty Images.

Public Policy—People

Here's a forecast of the hot policy issues facing legislatures . . . planning for emergencies, closing the energy gap, tax and spending limits, defining "public use," funding education, examining immigrant rights, GPS for sex offenders, dealing with real ID [authentic documents], contemplating stem cell research, and it's a campaign year.

NICOLE CASAL MOORE, *STATE LEGISLATURES*, JANUARY 2006

Educate and inform the whole mass of the people . . . they are the only sure reliance for the preservation of our liberty.

THOMAS JEFFERSON

OBJECTIVES

After reading this chapter, you should be able to

Define the meaning of public policy.

Understand the issue of federal mandates.

Identify and discuss the major social welfare and health care policies of the state.

Understand the redistributive nature of those programs.

Be introduced to the major issues of public education for the state.

Understand a number of issues facing higher education in state institutions.

INTRODUCTION

Public policy is where government comes face-to-face with citizens. The things that government does, or chooses not to do, affect all of us as we live our daily lives. Like all other states, Texas faces important public issues that need to be addressed to regulate the health, safety, and welfare of its citizens. The issues that the legislature addresses during its session constitute the state policy agenda. The choices elected officials make to solve **public policy** problems establish priorities for programs that benefit the public. Because the choices involve billions of dollars and often deal with conflicting values of citizens, people even argue, sometimes intensely, about whether government should address some problems at all. Consequently, many controversial issues confront state policymakers, leading to impassioned democratic debate.

In Texas, the backdrop of a traditionalistic/individualistic political culture that runs headlong into a newer moralistic culture among a vocal minority in the state often makes the disagreements over public policy issues sharp. Also, even when people agree that a particular problem needs to be addressed, they may disagree about the best way to deal with it. Furthermore, the fiscal health of the state can complicate the policy agenda considerably. The state never has enough money to fund all the desired programs at the same time, and so state finance itself becomes a major policy issue.

The development of public policy begins when decision makers identify a problem that needs to be addressed. When an influential public official, such as the governor or a legislator (see especially Chapters 6 and 7), recommends a government policy to deal with a problem, it is placed on the policy agenda, and the debates just mentioned may ensue. Often, gubernatorial and legislative viewpoints conflict. For example, in 2009, the legislature passed a bipartisan bill that would have provided full-day pre-kindergarten programs for high-risk Texas children. Governor Perry, without having objected to the bill during the session, vetoed it, explaining that the money appropriated for the program might be better used to expand existing programs.[1]

Similarly, interest groups and lobbyists often place items on the agenda by making known the priorities they think the state should set. These individuals and groups work through elected officials, the bureaucracy, and the media, but they are especially vigorous in pursuing legislative support for their policy emphases.

Another avenue for setting the policy agenda is through the *intergovernmental* system—the complex relationships among federal, state, and local governments—and through the *intragovernmental* system—the relationships that cut across the different branches of government. Often, these relationships result in a **mandate,** a term that refers to an action of one government or branch of government that requires another government to act in a certain way. National standards such as those required by the No Child Left Behind program in education that must be implemented by state and local governments is one major example. Intergovernmental and intragovernmental mandates help policymakers identify and define issues even when they would prefer to ignore them. Mandates are often burdensome to the lower level of government, which is required to act even though it receives no funding to help implement the new program. Nationally, the fiscal impact on the states from federal mandates for FY 2004–2007 was over $100 billion, and the National Conference of State Legislatures commented on the poor shape of American federalism.[2]

Mandates have several possible sources. These include the courts, administrative regulations, legislation, and/or highly publicized shifts in national priorities. For example, changes in Texas public school finance began in 1973 with a federal court order and continued with a 1987 state court order to provide a more equitable and "efficient" system of funding public schools.[3] The issue was not settled until 2006. Similarly, the state prison system was tied up in a long-running court suit that began in 1971, with the federal courts not relinquishing supervision until 2002.[4] The suit stemmed from historic problems, such as overcrowding, abuse of prisoners, and poor health care facilities.

The welfare system in Texas is a product of the state's emphasis on efficiency, national budget cutting, changing national priorities, and state efforts to gain administrative approval from the federal bureaucracy, as well as the traditionalistic/individualistic political culture. All states are struggling to provide adequate welfare and health care services in the midst of federal changes.

Another illustration of how public policy gets set is the intragovernmental example of state-assisted higher education in Texas. Like the Department of Human Services, a public university is a state agency. In 1997, the legislature enacted rules governing a number of business procedures universities had used to generate revenue, thus giving explicit instructions to executive branch agencies. The legislature also dictated diversity goals and called for greater excellence in higher education, but in doing so, it indirectly mandated that colleges and universities raise tuition sharply to generate funds to achieve curriculum, diversity, and excellence targets. By the first decade of the twenty-first century, many legislators, ruing the increasing cost of education for the students, began to question the tuition rates that had been raised in part because of regulations that the legislature had imposed on universities. In 2011, Governor Rick Perry called for a policy that would roll back the costs of higher education and ultimately make a university education available for a total cost of $10,000.[5]

Although mandates cause difficulties, they are but one of many issues that contribute to society's problems. Urbanization, industrialization, inflation, economic downturns, depletion of natural resources, the world oil market, citizen

demand, and the curtailment of federal funds to state and local governments are among other factors that cause difficulties. With new issues rising frequently, including the continuing growth of the Texas population, the policy agenda is constantly evolving.

This chapter provides a summary of Texas policies regarding the lives of citizens. Discussion of issues surrounding natural resources and the environment will follow in Chapter 14. For want of a better term, we refer to this chapter as dealing with "people policies," or policies having to do with the regulation of the health, welfare, and education of the citizens of the state. From the very beginning of our nation's history, these have been state functions. Of course, as time has gone by, the responsibilities of states have grown dramatically, both because of the expectations of citizens and because of the growth of technologies. In rural cultures, governments were often far away and lacking in resources, while urbanization has created the situation where citizens are always in close proximity to government services. In the period before World War II, medical care was much more primitive and citizens had fewer expectations regarding care; but with the development of antibiotics and modern medical screening technologies, both costs and expectations have increased. As the nation's economy has diversified and more and more jobs have come to require education as a prerequisite for employment, so too have pressures grown on the educational system. Finally, as governments have grown in complexity, the partnerships among national, state, and local governments have often been convoluted and difficult to understand

Some of these issues, such as poverty, health, and welfare, are favorites of progressives and liberals. Others have traditionally been of greater interest to conservatives, but are becoming more important for everyone. Still others, such as education, create widespread concern. The reader who keeps track of what the governor requests and what the legislature does every two years can get an idea of which political forces are dominant at any given time. Certainly, state policymakers find it more to their liking to deal with economic issues, which fit the conservative culture of the state, than with social issues, which they often address only by trying to "reform" current policies and practices that deal with social problems or by trying to gain "accountability" through slashing revenues.

Readers are also reminded that for all the issues, the cast of characters is constantly changing. It includes elected officials—the governor and other state executives, legislators, and judges, as well as their national counterparts—plus bureaucrats, representatives of various general and special interest groups, the media, local governments, business, and industry. In addition, public opinion changes as interpretations of any given situation become known.

The issues the state chooses to address and how state policymakers attempt to solve public problems permit another examination of how democratic the Texas political system is. Do policymakers try to deal with a wide variety of issues affecting all citizens? Or do they mainly look at issues placed on the agenda by political elites? Can they solve contemporary problems in the context of a conservative political culture when many of the issues stem from the needs of the "have-nots" of society, who traditionally have been supported by liberals? Do they consider alternative viewpoints? Can their policies be implemented effectively, or are they merely "smoke and mirrors" that only seem to address the problem?

Overall, Texas, when compared with other states, tends to rank toward the bottom in many service areas (see also Chapter 12). Also, the state is sometimes

slow to respond to issues such as adult health care, failures of electric dereg-ulation, and campaign finance.[6] However, state officials cannot proceed at a pace faster than that at which the public is willing to move and to fund. One of the awkward aspects of democracy is that following majority opinion does not always lead to wise or swift policy decisions.

Poverty, Welfare, and Health Care

The most basic of human needs are food, clothing, shelter, and health care. The basic question is whether the state should provide extensive services in these areas or be a "low-service state." Conservative agendas dominated national and state politics from the mid-1990s until the election of Barack Obama as presi-dent in 2008, and they have long shaped Texas politics. In short, for reasons that were discussed throughout this book, the viewpoints of individuals in upper-income brackets often dominate public policy, and the predominant tradition-alistic/individualistic political culture underlies this approach to politics. These political facts of life are particularly important when we examine the issues of poverty and welfare.

Whenever the government attempts to improve the quality of life for the poor, it is producing **redistributive public policy**[7]—that is, policy that redistrib-utes wealth from those who have the most to those who have the least. Inevitably, then, poverty, welfare, and health care politics produces strong emotions and sharp political divisions. In Texas, as elsewhere, some policymakers and ordinary citizens think that poor people could be more effective at helping themselves through job training, education, and looking for work. Even when compassion exists for those too ill or infirm to work, it does not spill over into sympathy for individuals deemed to be shirkers. Other people think that people are poor because they have never been given an opportunity to have a good education or relevant job training. Without question, the reasons for poverty are many. The task at hand is to determine how the state of Texas addresses poverty issues.

Any state's role in combating poverty and seeing to the welfare of its citi-zens is a mix of both state policy and federal programs. Because of changes in national policy, Texas, which has traditionally relied on federal funds for its welfare programs, has had to make changes in its own welfare system.

Poverty in Texas

The **poverty threshold** for a family of three in the lower 48 states was $18,530 for fiscal year 2011, while it is somewhat higher in Alaska and Hawaii.[8] This guideline is often stated for a family of three because a typical poor family con-sists of a mother and two children; an additional family member increases the line by $3,820.

Poverty statistics are census based and are reported after general popula-tion figures are made available. Thus, there is some lag time between the current year and the most recent year for which comparative statistics are available. The *Texas Fact Book 2010* includes data for 2007–2008. It reports that Texans had the highest percentage of citizens not covered by health insurance and the third highest percentage living in poverty. The per capita personal median income in Texas in 2008 was $38,575, leading to a ranking of twenty-third in

the country.[9] Ironically, even though Texas is a leader in the number of new jobs created annually, many of those jobs are low paying.

The National Center for Children in Poverty at Columbia University reports that 24 percent of all Texas children live in poverty—that is, the household income is below the poverty guideline—and another 24 percent are low-income, that is, their family income is less than 200 percent of the poverty threshold. At more than 48 percent living in poverty or low-income households, this exceeds the national average of 42 percent.[10] Seventeen of the 100 poorest counties in the United States are in Texas, including nine—Starr, Maverick, Willacy, Hudspeth, Presidio, La Salle, Dimmit, Hidalgo, and Zavala—in the twenty-five very poorest.[11] The per capita income in Starr County was only $7,069, less than a quarter of that for the state as a whole. Slight shifts in the various poverty rankings occur from year to year, but Texas rarely varies its relative position by more than one place.

Statistics for Medicaid (the program that provides health insurance for the poorest individuals) enlighten the poverty figures. Over 71 percent of the recipients of Medicaid are children; three-quarters of them live in households where at least one parent works. Seventeen percent of all Texas children receive Medicaid, but estimates are that another 1.4 million are not covered by any insurance program.[12] Rural south and southwest Texas and the ghettos and *barrios* of the largest cities have the highest number of poor people.

One question that arises when the stark numbers of Texas poverty are stated is "what about the homeless?" Neither the state nor the national government has a very accurate measure of the number of homeless people because the homeless are a mix of people who sometimes have work, sometimes do not, and include a substantial number of mentally ill people. When adequate help is provided, the majority of homeless move into housing and find a job, according to the U.S. Bureau of the Census.[13] The bureau conducted a large-scale study of homeless persons and providers of services to the homeless in 1995 and 1996, and estimated almost 2 million homeless persons nationwide. It determined that "overall the homeless were deeply impoverished and most were ill." Two-thirds had some type of chronic illness, with more than half of these beset with mental illness. According to the Texas Homeless Network, more than 265,000 Texans will experience homelessness during 2009. This research indicates that on any given day in Texas, there are more than 79,000 people who are experiencing homelessness.[14] More than a quarter of the homeless have a childhood history of living in an institution or being in foster care. Given the population size of Texas and the entrenched poverty in some parts of the state, one can safely assume a sizable homeless population.[15]

The Players and the Major Programs

HB 2292 passed by the legislature in 2003 resulted in a major reorganization of health, welfare, and social services in Texas. Twelve health and human services agencies were consolidated into four departments that are part of a large, umbrella agency known as the Health and Human Services Commission. Here are the super-departments, which split up and reassigned services offered by their predecessors:

- **Department of State Health Services (DSHS), which includes broad-based health services, health care information, mental health, and alcohol and drug abuse programs**

- **Department of Aging and Disability Services (DADS), which includes services for mentally challenged and community care, nursing home, and aging services**

- **Department of Family and Protection Services (DFPS), which includes child and adult protective services and childcare regulatory services**

- **Department of Assistive and Rehabilitative Services (DARS), which includes rehabilitation, services for the blind and visually impaired, services for the deaf and hard of hearing, and early childhood intervention**

Each of these departments is headed by a commissioner who reports to the executive commissioner of health and human services, who in turn reports to the governor. A nine-member Health and Human Services Council assists the executive commissioner in policy development. In addition, the Health and Human Services Commission determines eligibility for and administers a number of significant programs that cut across the departments. These programs include accreditation, welfare, Medicaid/CHIP, and nutrition, among others. Employment services and benefits are handled through the Texas Workforce Commission.

To help assist those in poverty, state governments participate in two kinds of programs, in each case in a cooperative way with the national government. The two kinds of programs are income assistance programs and health care programs. What makes assessing these programs at the state level alone difficult is that the programs are funded with high percentages of federal money, but are largely administered by state authorities.

More interestingly, the mix of costs and coverage of these kinds of programs has changed dramatically over the last two decades. Twenty years ago, the primary program for income assistance for families was a categorical grant

In this cartoon, Ben Sargent poses a "pro-life" dilemma. Though Texans tend to favor a "pro-life" position on abortion, the state has low levels of funding, compared to other states, on social services and education.

Courtesy of Ben Sargent.

called Aid to Families with Dependent Children (AFDC) and allowed families to receive benefits in an open-ended way as long as they could prove need. In 1996, AFDC was replaced by a block grant program called Temporary Assistance for Needy Families, a program allowing more flexibility at the state level in paying out benefits and capping the number of years a family can receive benefits at five years. As a result of this and other changes, income assistance "welfare" programs have been, relatively speaking, on the decline.

At the same time, both the advances in medical problems that can be treated and the costs of treating them have increased dramatically. Those increasing costs have meant that lower percentages of Americans have access to private health insurance and even middle-income families often lack health coverage. Indeed, because of the costs of health care coverage and hospitalization, nearly anyone lacking health care coverage is medically indigent. In Texas, the health care crisis is particularly acute, with Texas ranking worst in the nation with 24.4 percent of its population lacking health insurance as of 2007 and with the third-highest teenage birthrate in the country.[16]

How dramatic is the shift? In 2011, the Texas Department of Health and Human Services provided assistance to 109,862 clients a month through the TANF program. TANF cost $142 million in Texas general revenue funds and $916.2 million in federal funds, a large dollar amount, but a fraction of the health care costs. Health care dwarfed the traditional welfare program, with 2,900,000 acute-care Medicaid patients receiving assistance each month at a cost of $16.3 billion in Texas general revenue funds and $45 billion in all funds (including federal) for the Medicaid program. Even the much smaller **Children's Health Insurance Program (CHIP)** cost roughly twice what TANF did at $624.2 million in Texas general revenue funds and $2 billion in all funds.[17]

Against this background, then, the national debate on health care reform has especially important consequences in Texas. Because none of these health or welfare programs are solely the responsibility of the state, the outcome of congressional action on health care may dramatically transform the state role in that area.

Medicaid is the program in the United States used to provide health care assistance for the needy in society. Before the 1960s, the provision of health care for the needy was almost entirely borne at the state and local level, with county governments often having the lion's share of the responsibility. Beginning with the passage of Medicaid in 1965, the role of the national government increased dramatically and responsibility for administration centralized from county governments to the state, as the financial figures just cited demonstrate. Medicaid's principal programs are for children, the aged, the blind and disabled, and maternity care.

The CHIP mentioned earlier was originally passed by the national government in 1997 and provides for medical assistance for children even from families at above the official poverty level. With so many families without medical insurance, there was a priority given to making sure children had adequate health coverage. As Texas faced financial constraints in the early 2000s, the state restricted eligibility to the CHIP as a cost-saving device. In 2009, the legislature failed to expand coverage of the CHIP that would have provided assistance to 80,000 children.[18] However, the session did see some advances, with increased availability of physicians in rural areas, increased funding for nursing education, and protections for consumers hit with high fees when they consult "out-of-network" physicians.[19] Limited resources in the 2011 session precluded discussion of any expansion of benefits.

The national Social Security Administration provides direct case assistance for aged, disabled, and blind Texans through the Supplemental Security Income (SSI) program, and the U.S. Department of Health and Human Services channels funds to the consolidated Texas Health and Human Services Commission (HHSC) for the **Temporary Assistance to Needy Families (TANF)** program. TANF is a program for families with needy children under age eighteen who have been deprived of financial support because of the absence, disability, unemployment, or underemployment of both parents. The U.S. Department of Agriculture administers the **Food Stamp Program,** passing dollars through the HHSC.

All of these programs are designed to work with one another so that a person eligible to receive help from one program is *sometimes* eligible to receive help from one or more of the others, although the formulas determining eligibility vary with each program. Even though most states supplement these programs, Texas historically has chosen to provide "bare bones" programs. Figure 13-1 illustrates trends in the receipt of Food Stamps and Temporary Assistance to Needy Families (TANF) over the time frame of 1990 until 2011. Over that time, assistance from TANF has declined and Food Stamp reliance, though fluctuating a bit, has increased. Even if families receive all of the Medicaid, food stamp, and TANF assistance that is available from the Texas government, they will fall far short of the poverty line. As a relatively low-service state, these data have not changed significantly over the last few years. Figure 13-1 shows the fluctuating dependence of many Texans on various forms of assistance during the first decade of the twenty-first century.

Other social services include daycare, foster homes, energy assistance for low-income persons (to help with heating bills), child protective services, and job training. Changing federal and state policy, economic conditions, and population changes contribute to the variations in the numbers from year to year, but overall the numbers indicate that Texas does not do a particularly good job in helping poor people. Texas for years has ranked in the bottom quarter of states with regard to social services. It is a state of contrasts between rich and poor,

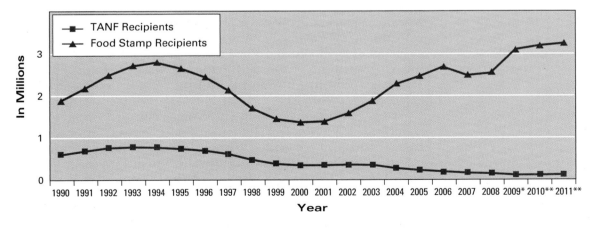

FIGURE 13-1 TANF and Food Stamp Caseloads Fiscal Years 1990–2011.

*Estimated.
**TANF target established in the General Appropriations Act 2010–11 Biennium. Food stamp recipients are estimated.

SOURCE: *Fiscal Size-Up, 2010–2011* (Austin: Legislative Budget Board, 2009), 203.

and although the stereotype of Texas is a state filled with rich oil tycoons, the state has large pockets of poverty and is perennially in the lower half of states in the nation in average per capita income.[20] Complicating this picture is the fact that Texas is now a state with a majority of ethnic minorities, a fact that adds political fuel to the debate over social policy.

Another related service is unemployment compensation—that is, payments to unemployed workers. This program is one that cuts across programs affecting business and those affecting the poor. It is administered by the Texas Workforce Commission, which also assists individuals in finding jobs and keeps records of employment in the state. Unemployment compensation is a joint federal-state effort. The basic funding method is a tax on wages paid by employers, plus any surcharge needed to make the system fiscally sound, and reimbursements from governmental units for any unemployment benefits drawn by their former employees. If a state has its own unemployment compensation program and an agency to administer it, the employers can charge off most of the tax on their federal tax returns. If the federal government administers the program directly, employers cannot take advantage of the tax write-off. In Texas, unemployment benefits vary according to previous wage and disability status. For FY 2008, the maximum unemployment benefit was $415 (the disabled received about twice that amount). Benefits are payable for a period up to twenty-six weeks, except when the federal government extends the period as it usually does during periods of prolonged unemployment.

The 2009 session confronted one of the modern complications of federalism, the fiscal relationships between national and state governments. When Congress passed the economic stimulus package, it provided for increased coverage for unemployment compensation in difficult times, but insisted that coverage be broader than current Texas law allowed.[21] Accordingly, in order to gain access to millions of national government dollars, Texas had to provide coverage for workers not previously covered. Before reversing course and accepting the federal money, Governor Perry briefly considered not accepting national money because after the package has expired, Texas might be obligated to pay more for unemployment compensation in the future.

Workers' compensation is a program to provide medical, income, death, and burial benefits for workers who are injured, become ill, or are killed on the job. The program has existed largely in its present form since 1917. The procedures and especially the costs of the program affect businesses of all sizes, from the local "Making the Cut" lawn-mowing service to the giant Exxon-Mobil Corporation, which is headquartered in Irving. Texas is unique among the states in allowing employers to choose whether to provide workers' compensation, although public employers and employers who accept a public construction contract must provide workers' compensation. Employers who are not participants in the program must notify both the Texas Workers' Compensation Commission and all employees. These employers have a number of options as alternatives to the workers' compensation program, including private insurance and setting aside reserve funds ("self-insurance").

Generally, Texas has a history of having laws that are not as protective of workers' rights as other states. In addition to having a "right-to-work" provision, prohibiting union membership as a condition for employment, the workers' compensation laws have generally had rather high costs with low worker benefits. Texas has not been unique in its workers' compensation problems.[22] In 1991, the "workers' comp" laws were changed to provide mandatory safety programs,

fraud, self-insurance, and a source of revenue for the insurance fund. Yet, evolving a workable workers' compensation program has not been an easy task.

After the state lowered workers' compensation costs to business in 1994, organized labor brought a court challenge to the system, complaining that the lowered costs were directly at the expense of workers and their benefits. In 1995, the Texas Supreme Court ruled against the workers. By late 1996, not only was the system solvent, but also the workers' compensation fund had become a big moneymaker. Even after the payouts to workers, the fund rebated $600 million to insurance companies. In 2003, Texas businesses received a bonus in the form of new limits on workers' compensation medical costs coupled with a prohibition against the use of pre-injury waivers of liability in lieu of workers' compensation coverage. Individual workers' benefits were enhanced at the same time. Benefits are based on the statewide average weekly wage, which is the maximum that the program will pay. For 2011, the maximum is $766.

Recent Policy Developments

Early in the 1990s, many states, including Texas, had addressed the issue of welfare reform, all of them with emphasis on converting welfare to workfare, forcing "deadbeat" dads and moms to provide child support, and employing modern electronics to aid in tracking those in the welfare system. In 1996, Congress passed and President Bill Clinton signed the Personal Responsibility and Work Opportunity Reconciliation Act, otherwise known as welfare reform. Fundamentally, this legislation followed the lead of the states in getting people off welfare and onto payrolls.

The *workfare* approach carried with it not only such positive values as helping welfare recipients regain their self-esteem by becoming better trained and gainfully employed, and freeing up money for other programs, but also such negatives as more rules and regulations. The federal reform allowed five years of welfare support, but the time clock begins to tick from the first date a recipient receives a check even though the person might have extensive training to undergo. Texas provides for only three years of assistance, although the average time on welfare is less than two years. The federal requirement is that the individual be working within two years, without the flexibility of the earlier Texas plan that includes job training, parenting or life skills training, and education or literacy training within the definition of work.[23]

The New "Down and Out"

The recession of 2001–2003 produced some strange side effects. Social service agencies in counties heavily populated by previously high-salaried individuals in the telecommunications industry—Collin County, for example—were receiving requests for financial assistance for out-of-work telecommunications executives and engineers. Caseworkers reported in the spring of 2003 that some of the applicants needed a "reality check." Unwilling to let go of their big houses, expensive cars, or club memberships, they were applying for assistance to continue their upscale lifestyle. They were not successful.

In their concern for reducing welfare fraud, putting people to work, and generally moving one step away from Big Government, the politicians initially failed to address the fundamental reality of welfare reform—namely, that the legislation forces single mothers of dependent children to go to work and may deprive their children of health care coverage through Medicaid. Because workfare means that their children will be either left alone all day or placed in daycare, this consequence would seem to contradict the much-touted "family values" espoused by many politicians. Less parental care is also likely to have the further consequences of more juvenile crime, poorer school performance, and thus, paradoxically, even more welfare dependency.

Welfare reform illustrates how complex social issues are. In trying to fix one set of problems, it is all too easy to create another set. The health care aspect of the problem was addressed in the federal Balanced Budget Act of 1997, which created the Children's Health Insurance Program for low-income children. Childcare has proved more elusive and is heavily dependent on local non-profit and community programs. In fact, the administration of President George W. Bush preferred faith-based programs to solve many social problems, including childcare. (Faith-based programs are those provided by churches and other religious organizations rather than by public agencies.)

The 1996 federal act created a "cafeteria-style" welfare system for the states, with each state receiving a block grant for welfare support, which it could apportion among programs that the state judged as having the highest priority. Proportionately less money now flows from Washington, and the states are allowed under the national legislation to slash their own welfare payments by 20 percent with no loss of federal funds.

Because budget surpluses in 1999 and 2001 allowed the state to fund social services, the legislature softened eligibility requirements and broadened some programs in those years. But with a faltering economy producing fewer tax revenues and more need for social services, by 2003, social service funding once again became a focal point of the legislative session. Medicaid expenses nationally were growing 7 to 8 percent a year, a major problem for Texas and many other states that were already facing deficits. State officials across the country found themselves having to decide among many well-deserving programs, such as health care, higher education, highways, and high schools.[24] The opening ploy of the Texas legislative session was a House plan to deal with the budget shortfall via massive cuts in social services; part of this strategy was to pare back social services that House conservatives detested. That plan was unfeasible not only because it lacked Senate support, but also because cutting state services meant cutting federal dollars. Nevertheless, the combination of revenue shortfalls coupled with an unwillingness to raise taxes led to significant cuts, even though the cuts were not as deep as the House wanted.

The Seventy-ninth Legislature in 2005 moved to shore up the health and human services programs somewhat. Financial supplements were made to cover Medicaid and the CHIP costs, and the application and operations aspects of these programs were modified, although to the great confusion of clients. Some of the people cut from services in 2003 were restored to the rolls in 2005 and even more in 2007. However, as mentioned, the CHIP was not expanded in the 2011 session, even with more than 1 million needy children still left without health care.

Governor Rick Perry also tried to intervene in health matters when he issued an executive order in 2007 requiring all sixth-grade girls to receive the vaccine for the human papillomavirus (HPV), which causes sexually transmitted disease and

Texas has high levels of poverty, and large numbers of citizens who need health care for their children, challenging programs such as the Children's Health Insurance Program. Texas is also visited from time to time by hurricanes, such as Hurricane Ike. The citizens pictured here are in need of basic necessities in the wake of the hurricane, testing the capacities of social programs in the state.

(Top) © AP Photo/ Eric Gay.

(Bottom) © Peter Turnley/ Corbis.

may cause cancer. The public and the legislature rejected his plan, but his action became a controversy in the 2012 race for the Republican presidential nomination.

In the face of large budget deficits in a state with a balanced budget amendment, Governor Perry suggested in late 2010 that Texas might simply opt out of Medicaid. At one point he even called it a "Ponzi scheme." However, because of the formulas where nearly two out of three dollars spent on Medicaid come from the federal government and the reality that nearly 3 million Texans require Medicaid assistance each month, the abstract thought of cutting state spending by slashing Medicaid never received serious consideration during the 2011 legislative

session. Nevertheless, the challenges of funding Medicaid remained a major issue, and when the session ended, only eighteen months of Medicaid had been funded in the two-year budget passed by the legislature. In spite of Texas's "Rainy Day Fund" reserves that can serve as a fallback for funding Medicaid, it appeared the year 2012 might yet be a challenge in the full funding of the Medicaid program.[25]

Analysis

The off-again/on-again support for social services results in muddled signals. One reading is that despite a set of elected officials even more conservative than those of the past, the state has developed a social conscience with regard to the needy. An alternative interpretation is that the state is mainly interested in money—finding ways not to spend state dollars on the poor and finding ways to get a bigger piece of the federal welfare pie. Beyond dispute is the fact that Texas has a welfare problem that is tied to social divisions that rest on ethnic conflicts and struggles between the haves and the have-nots.

A combination of stringent qualifications for recipients and a booming economy resulted in one effect desired by state and federal welfare reformers—namely, a drop in the number of aid recipients. The recession beginning in 2008, however, put increased pressure on health care benefits.

Texas, like other states, often does not spend all the money to which it is entitled by federal programs. According to *State Legislatures* magazine, the states with the highest poverty rates, including Texas, were spending less than 69 percent of their allotted funds. The states as a whole were spending only 76 percent of their block grant funds. This publication, which is published by the National Conference of State Legislatures, points out two important facts about the underspending. First, those individuals who remain on welfare will be very difficult to place in jobs for reasons such as domestic violence, little training, lack of transportation, and lack of childcare. Second, innovative states—Arizona, Colorado, Florida, Maine, Michigan, New York, Washington—used the funds not spent on TANF recipients to provide a variety of solutions to hard-core unemployment and chronic welfareism. One of the reasons for the sparring between Comptroller Carole Keeton Strayhorn and Governor Rick Perry and the legislative leadership in 2003–2004 was Strayhorn's frequent criticism that Texas was leaving federal money on the table to avoid spending state money.

Several factors make it likely that social services will be a perennial issue in Texas politics. First, the economy swings between boom and bust, and when the economy is sluggish, the number of aid recipients increases at the same time that the state is less able to pay for the services. Second, the state's immigration rate is among the highest in the country, and many of the immigrants, especially those who are illegal, lack essential job skills. They often constitute the working poor, especially because they are willing to work for inferior wages.[26] Third, disparities between rich and poor seem to be growing, and that difference is exacerbated by a rapidly growing elderly population with more women than men.[27] National tax policy intensified the phenomenon of the rich getting richer and the poor getting poorer. Fourth, the conservatism of Texans became more evident early in the 2000s, though the election of 2008 saw a bit of moderating in the legislature. One lingering issue in state politics is "the race to the bottom" phenomenon. In short, states would naturally find it advantageous if those who were neediest—in poverty, mentally disabled, and elderly, for example—would move elsewhere. Of course, no one would ever make such an argument explicitly, but the financial calculus is unarguable. As a result, states have incentives to limit their assistance of those in poverty.

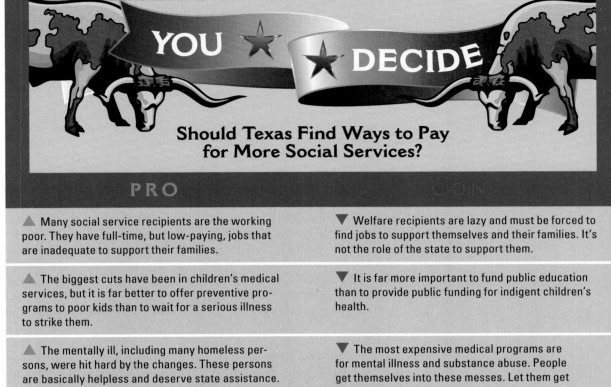

YOU ★ ★ DECIDE

Should Texas Find Ways to Pay for More Social Services?

PRO	CON
▲ Many social service recipients are the working poor. They have full-time, but low-paying, jobs that are inadequate to support their families.	▼ Welfare recipients are lazy and must be forced to find jobs to support themselves and their families. It's not the role of the state to support them.
▲ The biggest cuts have been in children's medical services, but it is far better to offer preventive programs to poor kids than to wait for a serious illness to strike them.	▼ It is far more important to fund public education than to provide public funding for indigent children's health.
▲ The mentally ill, including many homeless persons, were hit hard by the changes. These persons are basically helpless and deserve state assistance.	▼ The most expensive medical programs are for mental illness and substance abuse. People get themselves into these messes. Let them get themselves out.
▲ When good jobs are scarce and families are having a hard time making it economically, the state should provide even more social services, not fewer.	▼ Citizens cannot afford to pay more state taxes and fees to support poor people. If public programs exist, they should be funded entirely by the federal government.
▲ Human resources are the most important resources of all. It's good public policy to invest in them.	▼ Privatization is a highly desirable public policy. If people need help, they should ask local charities.

Education Policy

In many ways, the hopes and aspirations of American democracy are played out most centrally in the public schools. The founding fathers envisioned a society of educated citizens who could participate in informed discourse about their society and government and make informed choices in choosing their representatives in government, as the quote from Thomas Jefferson at the beginning of the chapter illustrates. Although public education in the United States as we now know it did not begin to develop until after the Civil War, it fits well with the aspirations of the Founders. As public education developed, it became far more

than just a venue to teach "reading, writing, and arithmetic," and took on other societal functions as well, including political and societal socialization, and the provision of equal opportunity to succeed.

A major example of the social agenda came with the forced integration of schools beginning in the 1950s with the U.S. Supreme Court case of *Brown v. Board of Education*. However admirable the goal of fulfilling the requirements of the U.S. Constitution's Fourteenth Amendment was, it illustrates the multiple goals of public education. (Discussion of issues of desegregation and equity in education can be found in Chapter 10.) Because of these varied goals, there has often been conflict in how to run a public-school system.

One of the central functions of state and local governments is public education. In every state in the country, including Texas, the largest single expenditure of government is for public education. The cost is borne by both state and local government, with the largest portion being spent by local schools. In Texas, the system is complex, with some of the responsibilities for public education residing at the state level and others at the local level. The state has Local Independent School Boards that hire teachers, build school buildings, and make judgments about allocations of resources in their own local areas. But Texas also has a State Board of Education that makes broader decisions about what is required to gain an education in Texas and to graduate from a Texas high school. The interaction between these two levels, along with the national government, makes for ongoing political struggles.

Until 1965, funding public education was almost exclusively the province of state and local governments (Texas school boards for local independent districts are discussed in Chapter 11.) It was one of the few areas of government policy that could be called exclusively a state and local function. The passage of the 1965 Elementary and Secondary Education Act was an attempt to bolster education and to focus especially on creating equal education opportunity for students in disadvantaged economic areas. The passage of the No Child Left Behind Act of 2001 (NCLB) expanded federal involvement in education by establishing requirements for annual testing of students in core subject areas, mandating the hiring of "highly qualified teachers," and allowing students in low-quality schools to transfer to more successful ones. This act has changed public education dramatically, though it has not been accompanied by funding necessary to accomplish its ambitious goals.[28]

Even with the federal programs, education programs are funded more than 90 percent by state and local funds, as discussed in Chapter 12. Passage of NCLB has made the purposes of public education seem even more complex, with competition among state, local, and national governments over controlling the nature and responsibility of public education. As a result of this competition, schools often seek to accomplish many different goals simultaneously.

In Texas, the conduct of education has met with mixed results. Without question, many graduates of Texas public schools are successful, and a number of schools and school districts are "exemplary." At the same time, Texas has had a number of notable challenges and has not always successfully met them. The Texas public school system is a large one, serving 4,847,844 students in the 2009–2010 school year. With the overall population growth in Texas, the public school system continues to grow, averaging 1.9 percent growth each year over the first decade of the twenty-first century, a rate nearly three times the growth of public schools nationwide.

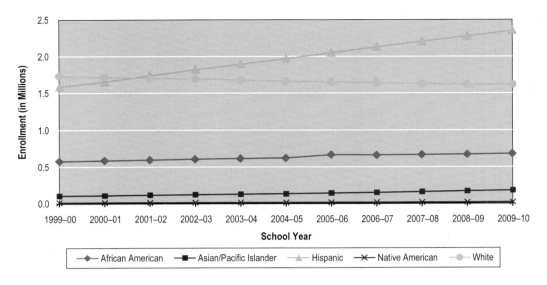

FIGURE 13-2 Enrollment by Ethnicity, Texas Public Schools, 1999–2000 through 2009–2010.

SOURCE: Enrollment in Texas Schools, 2009–2010, Division of Accountability, Texas Education Agency, September 2010, p. 6.

The population of the Texas system is diverse. Most of the growth in the public school population has been among minority students and the economically disadvantaged. The number of economically disadvantaged students continues to grow within every ethnic group. By the 2009–2010 year, the number of economically disadvantaged students had risen to 2,853,177, or 58.9 percent of all students.[29] The growth of the Latino student population is especially noteworthy, making up an absolute majority of public school students by the 2010–2011 academic year (see Figure 13-2). More than 800,000 Texas students have limited proficiency in the English language.[30]

With the hyper-growth rates in schools and the challenges of ethnic and economic diversity, come another set of challenges, maintaining a high quality of public education. In terms of educational attainment, Texas ranks dead last among states, with 79.6 percent of its population holding high school degrees, compared with an 85 percent average nationally.[31]

Education Reform

The history of modern education reform in Texas begins with the "No Pass, No Play" reforms of the mid-1980s. Under Governor Mark White, there was an emerging pressure to institute new standards to encourage high quality in education. A 1983 U.S. Department of Education study, *A Nation at Risk,* had found that the national education system had numerous deficiencies. White appointed a committee, with Ross Perot as a prominent member, to study the problem of education in Texas. What emerged from that committee was a recommendation for sweeping educational reform, including its most controversial recommendation that athletes not be able to participate in extracurricular programs if they were not passing all of their classes. Many reforms were instituted in 1984, including higher attendance standards, a longer school year, and incentives for excellent teachers.

The 1984 reforms were but a first pass at educational reform that has been ongoing since. The most dominant of the reforms involves assessment standards for all students. The Texas Assessment of Knowledge and Skills (TAKS) test became a ubiquitous feature of Texas education with a great deal of effort in public schools being exerted to help each school meet performance goals. Clearly, the tests ensured that covered curricula would be examined, though some critics suggested that the effort amounted to "teaching to the test" rather than pushing gifted students to hone their critical academic skills.

During the 2011 legislative session, TAKS was replaced with a new evaluation tool called STAAR (State of Texas Assessment of Academic Readiness). The new exams are designed to be more rigorous than their predecessors and are intended to encourage both academic performance and growth. The promise of STAAR is surely challenged by the major reduction in school financing passed by the legislature in 2011 with possible results of fewer teachers and larger class sizes. STAAR also promises to be controversial, for it proposes more days for standardized testing than under TAKS.[32]

Nontraditional Education Proposals

To enhance the quality of education, critics of the education system argue that three innovations might help. The first is the idea of **school vouchers,** a policy that would allow families who send their students to private schools to receive a tax deduction to cover a part of private school tuition. Proponents of school vouchers argue that the system would create competition between private and public schools and give incentives for public schools to increase the quality of their offerings. They also feel that the tax adjustments would constitute a net savings for the state government, since students who attend private schools do not expend public funds. Vouchers have never been instituted in Texas because

Texas has encountered a number of problems in education in the past several years. Particularly in the 2011 session of the Texas Legislature, the funding of public schools was vastly curtailed. Critics charged that the health of the Texas economy would be challenged because of reduced funding.

Courtesy of Ben Sargent.

opponents have successfully claimed that a voucher system would result in top students abandoning the public schools, making it more difficult to maintain a healthy academic environment in the public schools. They further point out that even tax credits would not make private schools accessible to poor families and would give tax breaks to wealthy families who would perhaps send their children to private schools even without public assistance.

A second nontraditional idea has met with much more success: **charter schools** public schools set up to have a unique academic interest. The schools are begun from scratch and are founded, proponents argue, to provide competition that will encourage standard public schools to improve their performance. The legislature first approved the founding of charter schools during the 1995 legislative session and has added authorizations over time until approximately 500 charter schools existed during the 2009–2010 academic year. Charter schools have met with mixed success, and it remains unclear whether they can foster a more generalized improvement in public education. The failure rates for charter schools over the fifteen-year history of them have hovered around one-third, so challenges remain.[33]

The third innovation is the growth of **home schooling** in Texas. In recent years, a growing number of families have chosen to educate their children in a

LONE STAR MEDIA

New Media Reduce the Role of Texas Schoolbook Adoptions Nationwide

Since the early 1960s, Texas has had a large role in determining the nature of textbooks used in the public schools. In 1961, a couple who lived in Longview, Texas, Mel and Norma Gabler, founded an organization called Educational Research Analysts. This organization, founded as a "Conservative Christian Organization," began to read textbooks across all disciplines of the school curriculum to make sure that the topics in the texts were consistent with traditional family values as defined by the Gablers. The Gablers then, often successfully, would lobby textbook publishers to make changes in their books so that the Gablers would not oppose their adoption in the state of Texas. Because the Texas market was so large, opposition from the Gablers might jeopardize the success of school texts nationally. Importantly, if textbook publishers did not conform to the Gablers' requests, the Gablers would oppose allowing them to be used in Texas public schools. There too they were often successful. The Gablers continued their quest as long as they lived, with Norma being the last to die in 2007.

Modern technology and the accessibility of the Internet as a source have diminished the role of textbooks in the educational process and have lessened the ability of one group to affect the information at hand for students. Publishers have downplayed the impact of Texas schoolbook adoption on national markets going forward, arguing that it is now easier and less expensive to tailor textbooks to specific states and requirements using modern technology. As a result, though the Gablers' organization lives on, its influence is likely to diminish over time.

SOURCES: Joe Holley, "Norma Gabler: Conservative Texan Influenced Textbooks Nationwide," *Washington Post*, August 2, 2007; Michael Birnbaum, "Historians Speak Out Against Texas Textbook Changes," *Washington Post*, March 18, 2010.

home environment rather than in public schools. In 1994, the Texas Supreme Court upheld a lower court decision that ruled that home schooling was protected just as private schooling was, making home schooling a viable option for education. Requiring education in public schools "deprived the home school parents of equal protection under the law," since their private schools in the home were unfairly discriminated against "on the sole basis of location in the home."[34] Recent estimates are that as many as 300,000 Texas students are being educated at home.

Texas Textbooks and Curricula

Texas is unique in some of the roles that are played by the State Board of Education (SBOE), an elected body with fifteen members. In Texas, school textbooks must be approved by the Texas Education Agency, overseen by the SBOE, to make certain that materials approved for classroom use cover the entire curriculum of an assigned course. Such a requirement is not entirely unusual in the United States, but the Texas process is perhaps the most politicized one in the country. It is so politicized because of two factors—the conservative nature of the SBOE and the population of Texas. Conservatism has led to charges by some that the process, rather than screening for academic excellence, has become a method

Prayer and Football

One of the issues that has been a constant source of conflict in public education has been the separation of church and state in publicly funded schools. Since 1962, a formally approved prayer has been banned in public schools, and since 1973, the standard has been that there cannot be an "excessive entanglement" between church and state.

Of course, there is an old joke that says that as long as there are exams in school, there will also be prayers in school. This joke underscores the reality that private, silent prayers are clearly allowed in schools.

And, in recent years, the U.S. Supreme Court has been supportive of "gather around the pole" activities where religious students may gather before school each day and say a group prayer as long as the activity is voluntary and public employees do not help lead the activity.

But what about prayers at public school football games?

In 2000, the U.S. Supreme Court heard a case coming out of the Santa Fe Independent School District in Texas concerning whether an "overtly Christian" prayer could be said before the beginning of a football came. In a 6–3 decision, the Supreme Court ruled that game prayers were public speech authorized by a government policy and taking place on government property at government-sponsored school-related events and therefore were not "private" speech. Since many students are required to attend football games, including pep squads, cheerleaders, dance teams, and the band in addition to the players, such prayers violated the separation of church and state and were ruled unconstitutional.

Source: *Santa Fe Independent School District v. Doe*, 530 U.S. 290 (2000).

of guiding curricula to match the conservative agenda of state board members. The size of the Texas adoption has forced textbook companies, in turn, to seek approval in Texas before they finish their textbooks. Once approved in the Texas market, those textbooks are distributed to states nationally. As a result, the Texas process has a major impact not just in Texas but nationwide.

The most recent example of the textbook adoption process came in the adoption of social studies standards by the SBOE in 2010. While the state board has traditionally set basic curricula requirements for high school graduation, they have not normally been involved in the day-to-day matters of what teachers cover in the classroom. In 2010, however, they made numerous changes to the social science curriculum. The curriculum played down the role of Thomas Jefferson among the founding fathers, questioned the separation of church and state as a central constitutional principle, and claimed that Communist infiltration of the U.S. government happened and constituted a real threat during the Cold War.[35]

The passage of the new curriculum came to counteract what members of the SBOE saw as a "liberal bias" among academics who write the books and classroom teachers. They wanted to show conservatism and Republican political philosophies in a better light, and the changes passed with a party-line vote, the ten Republicans supporting the changes and the five Democrats opposing them. A conservative leader on the SBOE said that the only purpose was to "add balance" to the curriculum because "Academia is skewed too far to the left." In contrast, a Democrat on the board argued that the mission was nothing less than an attempt at "rewriting history." "The social conservatives have perverted accurate history to fulfill their own agenda."[36]

Texas Higher Education

Texas is fortunate to have a number of community colleges, four-year colleges, and major research institutions to encourage students to attain education beyond high school graduation. The institutions of higher learning vary from open admission community colleges—which are open to anyone holding a high school diploma or a GED and which have relatively low tuition fees—to highly selective research universities with higher tuition rates. In 2008, 1,144,327 Texans were attending state institutions of higher learning.[37] Unlike elementary and secondary education, higher education is not provided to all students free of charge. As a result, there is a great deal of class bias involved in educational opportunity beyond the high school level, though through scholarships and other government programs, that bias can be mitigated.

From the beginning of the state, there were funds set aside to ensure the creation and maintenance of state universities. The Permanent University Fund (PUF) stems from land set aside to build university campuses, granted to the state university system in the 1876 Constitution. Originally thought to be barren land with little value, the land proved to have huge oil deposits under it and has been, as a result, a continuing source of revenue for Texas higher education. As of August 2007, the PUF owned 2,100,000 acres of land (with a value of $1.9 billion) and additional assets of $11.7 billion.[38] The funds are limited to the University of Texas and Texas A&M university systems and can be used only for capital investments (land acquisition, building construction and maintenance, capital equipment and library resources, for example), but they have been a huge boon to higher education in Texas from the beginning.

For many years, Texas was known nationally for its low tuition. One of the authors of this book fondly remembers his tuition and fees bill for a full semester in 1972 coming to a grand total of $88.50. But in recent years, as the state has sought to find ways to increase revenue streams and lower its financial responsibilities for higher education, tuition has increased rapidly. Tuition was once the same at all state universities, but in recent years, the legislature allowed for variations among different campuses. Fees have always been variable from one school to the next. Beginning in 2003, the legislature authorized universities to set their own tuitions, though they were limited in the amount they could raise tuition in any given year. Tuitions went up by more than an average of 80 percent over the balance of the decade as universities sought to find resources to maintain their programs.

By 2011, there was great concern that college education was slipping from the grasp of low-income students, and Governor Perry proposed that universities come up with a $10,000 degree that would include all tuition, fees, and textbooks. Such a degree would almost certainly entail community college education for two years, online courses, and use of Internet sources instead of textbook material.[39] Supporters of this proposal pointed out that it would make college education more accessible to the average citizen, but many educators were skeptical that the proposal could be accomplished without significantly reducing the rigor and quality of a university degree. Some observers thought Governor Perry's secondary motive was to challenge the high cost of university research at the state's research-oriented universities.

In addition to cost, another issue affecting universities has to do with giving access to members of ethnic minorities. In the latter half of the twentieth century, universities began to seek diversity in their student populations, bowing both to the political climate in the United States following the civil rights era and to the notion that diversity is a virtue unto itself, exposing students to people unlike themselves in some ways. Admissions programs that take race, gender, and ethnicity into account are known as **affirmative action** programs. Affirmative action was a controversial idea from its inception, with supporters arguing that it was necessary to make up for historical patterns of discrimination and detractors arguing that merit, rather than race and ethnicity, should determine college admission.

In 1996, in the case of *Hopwood v. Texas*,[40] arising from the University of Texas School of Law, the Fifth Circuit Court of Appeals in New Orleans ruled that race could not be used as a criterion for admission. Following that decision, the Texas attorney general ruled more broadly that affirmative action could not be used in any institution of higher learning. In response, the Texas Legislature passed a law in 1997 requiring the University of Texas and Texas A&M to admit anyone who finished in the top 10 percent of his or her high school class into their schools. The "ten percent rule," as it was called, was designed to give access to students who graduated from urban minority schools to ensure that diversity would remain at state universities. In 2009, the legislature effectively changed that rule to an eight percent rule, a rule that took effect for the 2011 academic year.

Meanwhile, the U.S. Supreme Court decided the case of *Grutter v. Bollinger*, coming out of the University of Michigan Law School, in 2003. In the *Grutter* case, the Court ruled that race could be considered, along with a number of other factors, in a holistic admissions process for universities.[41] Though Texas still is not a state that uses aggressive affirmative action rules, it has opened up the admissions process to consider race a bit in the last few years.

Analysis

Texas public education, both at the elementary/secondary education level and the university level, has met with mixed results. Without question, Texas has some of the finest public schools in the country. But Texas also has some of the biggest challenges. The state ranks well below average among states in school funding and much higher than average in high school dropout rates. And even among those students who graduate, SAT score averages trail the national norms.

Although there is much to be happy with in Texas education, without question a continuation of current trends will not be sufficient to remain competitive nationally in the twenty-first century. The cuts in education spending during the 2011 legislative session, while necessary to balance the state budget, were not a promising sign.

Conclusion

The state has shown stinginess in trying to mitigate poverty, a cavalier approach toward the environment, and even an inconsistent policy toward business, fostering big business but not always considering smaller businesses or the importance of **infrastructure** such as highways. In each of the issues examined in this chapter, powerful interests dominate the outcome, and the average citizen's perspective is not always considered. When judged by standards of democratic theory, Texas often falters. However, there are signs of improvement—creating a consolidated environmental agency with real clout, for example, though even that agency has come under criticism for not enforcing laws vigorously. Moreover, solutions to major state problems are often compounded and confounded by the inter- and intragovernmental nature of public policy.

The resolution of each issue is important to the future of Texas, and each is linked not only to the others discussed here, but also to other significant issues that are not outlined in this chapter. Without addressing the considerable poverty of the state, Texas may find it difficult to resolve other policy issues, such as economic diversification and sound public education. But without economic growth and the infrastructure to support it, finding jobs for those with limited skills will be impossible. Moreover, abject poverty tends to foster crime. Education has long been seen as the key to the proverbial better future. However, Texas has allowed its higher education system to lag behind that of the nation as a whole, and its economic future depends on catching up. Everyone needs clean water, air, and land, and environmental quality also is tied to the need for economic diversity to avoid further expansion of high-pollution industries.

None of these issues is new. All are costly to deal with—so much so that solving one problem may worsen another. Many hold the possibility of legal action by individuals favoring or opposing a particular course of action.

Summary

Texas policymakers have dealt with all the issues described in this chapter to some extent, but problems remain on the public policy agenda.

1. The Texas economy regularly cycles through the highs of booms and the lows of busts. The revenue implications of these cycles were discussed in the previous chapter. This chapter has indicated that such shifts result in varying periods of

attention on business development. The legacy of the traditionalistic/individualistic political culture is a tendency to try to fulfill the wishes of the business community even if state services go unfunded.

2. Human services, which present many challenges, have gone through fundamental changes recently in Texas and elsewhere. Transformation of the welfare system into a workfare system is a national priority with which Texans can agree. However, the change in philosophy and the reduction in federal social spending are both boon and bane to Texas. While welfare programs have declined, health care programs have mushroomed, with those programs being the focal point of state human resource funding in the near future. In addition, the state probably will continue to have one of the highest proportions of poor people in the country for the foreseeable future, and also will continue to use cuts in social programs as a way to balance the budget in lean financial times.

3. Challenges in public education in Texas remain. The state has some excellent schools, but the funding of public schools remains lower than the national average, while the need for high-quality education in an ever-increasingly technological world is self-evident. If Texas is to be competitive for attracting new business into the state in the years to come, a well-educated workforce will be required.

4. The need for quality education is made difficult to meet by the changing demographics of the state. With the majority of schoolchildren in Texas now being Latino, and many of them having English as a second language (if they speak English at all), the challenges of education become even more apparent. Moreover, with many children of minority status living in poverty, educational opportunity lags.

5. In higher education, the largest challenge is allowing access to education among low-income students. Tuition continues to rise while incomes do not. Governor Perry proposed a $10,000 college degree during his 2011 State of the State Address as a way to address this issue of accessibility. However, many observers think that this aspiration is unreasonable. Nevertheless, it certainly acknowledges the problem and sets the stage for consideration of ways to allow more Texans to receive a college education.

The issues discussed in this chapter affect all citizens, albeit in different ways. They bring to mind the haves and have-nots of our society, disparities among ethnic groups, and even problems of mortgaging our children's future by failing to address current problems.

Glossary Terms

affirmative action

charter schools

Children's Health Insurance Program (CHIP)

Food Stamp Program

home schooling

infrastructure

mandate

Medicaid

poverty threshold

public policy

redistributive public policy

school vouchers

Temporary Assistance to Needy Families (TANF)

workers' compensation

14

Public Policy—Resources

Oil was the most important Texas energy source of the twentieth century. Wind may become the most important Texas energy source of the twenty-first century.

W. Scott/Shutterstock.com.

One hundred years ago, Texans were carrying guns and fighting over water. Not much has changed.

PETE LANEY, SPEAKER OF THE TEXAS HOUSE OF REPRESENTATIVES,
TO THE MEMBERSHIP OF THE HOUSE, DURING THE 1990S

Mephistopheles (the Devil):
. . . if through life you'll go with me
In that case I'll agree . . .
I'll be your servant, be your slave!
Faust:
And what in turn am I to do for you?

"FAUST," EPIC POEM BY JOHANN WOLFGANG VON GOETHE,
GERMAN WRITER/NATURALIST, 1830S

Build it, and they will come.

DISEMBODIED VOICE TO KEVIN COSTNER'S CHARACTER,
IN THE 1989 FILM *FIELD OF DREAMS*

OBJECTIVES

After reading this chapter, you should be able to

Describe the political conflict over water likely to increase in frequency in Texas, and discuss the reasons why.

Display an understanding of the metaphorical term "Faustian bargain," and explain why it applies to the making of energy policy.

Give at least one advantage, and at least one disadvantage, for each potential source of energy for society.

List three themes that are important in Texas energy politics, and explain how each example offered in the text illustrates the theme.

Explain what historical themes in Texas environmental politics are illustrated by the stories of Glenn Shankle and TCEQ, and by ligustrum and the "noxious invasive plant" list.

Describe the most critical areas of air and water pollution in Texas.

Discuss concerns about and strategies for dealing with the dependency of Texans on vehicles using the internal combustion engine.

INTRODUCTION

It is in the nature of textbook-writing that the subject matter of this book has been about circumstances and events that will be in the past by the time students read about them. But the real value of any government textbook lies in its ability to enable its readers to understand their present circumstances so that they can, by acting, have an effect upon the future. The purpose of Chapters 13 and 14 is to apply the understanding of Texas politics supplied in the first twelve chapters to policy problems that are troublesome now and will continue to challenge Texans in the future. Chapter 13 examined "people" policies, whereas this chapter focuses on "resource" policies. In both, the context provided in the first twelve chapters is brought into play in the analysis of making and implementing Texas public policy.

Political scientists have spent many decades studying the inputs (citizen votes, public opinion, lobbying, media accounts), the processes (debates, legislative votes, calculations, hearings), and outputs (laws, rules, budget expenditures) of government, and have come up with a variety of "models," or systematic explanations, of how and why government produces the laws and actions that it does. One of the major conclusions of that literature is that there is not one single model that explains all types of policy outputs, or even how any one type of policy is handled from one policymaking episode to another. Therefore, we do not have a simple set of arguments to help us explain why Texas government produces one type of policy as

opposed to another. In general, in these two chapters we are applying the sorts of explanations that we have used in earlier chapters of the book—the interaction of ideology and interests, the way the fragmented state system of institutions functions, and the maneuvering of Texas politicians within the larger context of American federalism. In addition, however, we will be bringing in some approaches that are more specific to the policymaking literature, particularly the analysis of economic costs-versus-benefits, and the portrayal of trade-offs of advantages and disadvantages more broadly defined.

Water Supply

For many people there is no mystery about where water comes from—turn on the tap in the kitchen or the bathroom, and out it flows. And it is easy, amidst the many economic, political, and personal troubles of daily life, to never realize that water supply is one of the most worrisome problems facing Texas. Indeed, while such high-profile problems as terrorism may never actually harm Texas, water supply is a difficulty that is absolutely certain to pose major challenges in the near future.

West of the **hundredth meridian** of latitude—the imaginary line that forms the eastern boundary of Texas's panhandle and extends south, crossing the Rio Grande not far northwest of Laredo—average rainfall drops off to fewer than twenty inches a year, making agriculture impossible without irrigation.[1] But the averages are not reliable indications of how much precipitation might fall at any place at any time, for Texas rainfall is notoriously fickle. Thus, at least parts of the state experienced droughts in 1996, 1998–2000, 2003, 2005–2006, 2007–2009, 2010, and more than 98 percent of the state was too dry in 2011.[2] Meanwhile, floods devastated Austin in 1981, the entire state in 1991, Dallas–Fort Worth in 1995, Del Rio in 1998 and again in 2010, Abilene in 2000, Houston in 2001, Midland in 2005, and El Paso in 2006.[3] In Texas, during any given year, it is almost possible to predict with confidence that there will be too much water or not enough.

Adding to the dangerous swings of nature is the further difficulty that Caddo Lake, on the border with Louisiana, is the only natural lake in the state. Texans, historically, have had to build reservoirs if they wanted to ensure a steady water supply, and, in fact, have already constructed several hundred. But the "easy dam sites" (that is, the places where it is relatively inexpensive to build a dam) are all taken by now, the state's water-storage capacity is not growing, and meanwhile the demand for water continues to increase as the population expands.

There is now available for human use, in an average year in Texas, 17 million acre-feet of water from surface and underground sources (an **acre-foot** is the amount sufficient to cover an acre of land to a foot deep, or 325,851.4 gallons). But if the projections made by water professionals are accurate, at present usage rates the state will need an additional 9 million acre-feet by 2060.[4] So the question will become more urgent for Texans every year: are we going to get more water from somewhere, or are we going to use the supply we have more efficiently? If the population continues to grow, there is no third option.

Meanwhile, as the quotation from House Speaker Pete Laney at the beginning of this chapter illustrates, Texas has already experienced a variety of political

conflicts over water. As the squeeze between water demand and water availability gets tighter, there are bound to be more frequent and more intense squabbles. These conflicts will be of several kinds.

Urban Dwellers versus Farmers

One type of conflict that is certain to become more common can be termed "cities versus farmers." In the Western states, typically 70 to 80 percent of the water is used by agriculture for irrigating crops, but as urban populations grow, they demand more and more of the available liquid. Projections are that by 2040, Texas cities will use more water than Texas farmers.[5] Because the cities can afford to pay more for water than agricultural interests, they will inevitably crowd farmers out of the water market, unless farmers use their political influence to thwart the cities' desires. The situation faced by the Lower Colorado River Authority (LCRA) in 2009 illustrates the sort of problems that will grow more numerous in the future.[6]

Although Texas water law, in general, favors landowners' use of the water on and under their property, if the state owns reservoirs, then the state and its institutions decide who gets what, and how much it will cost. The LCRA is a nonprofit utility established by the legislature in 1934 to govern the downstream half of the Colorado River, which rises in the Llano Estacado near the New Mexico line northwest of Lubbock, and flows 800 miles southeast to the Gulf. The LCRA manages drinking-water supply, makes electricity, tries to prevent floods, and governs wastewater for the Austin metropolitan area and many smaller cities along the river.

Outside the urban areas, however, rice farmers in Matagorda, Colorado, and Wharton counties take a great deal of water, because growers flood the field to kill weeds. In 2009, the LCRA provided 370,000 acre-feet of water from Lakes Travis and Buchanan to about 350 rice growers, and a further 70,000 acre-feet from the run of the Colorado river, at a price of $5.39 an acre-foot. Meanwhile, the LCRA was charging urban businesses $138.00 an acre-foot. If the utility had charged farmers what it charged the nonagricultural businesses for water, the farmers would have been unable to afford the expense and would have gone out of business.

In other words, as a matter of policy the LCRA was subsidizing agriculture at the expense of nonagricultural businesses. The subsidies could not be justified by the fear that if rice farmers disappeared, Texans would have no rice to eat. Many countries produce rice, and importing it is easy. Instead, the subsidies were based on an assumption that is rarely spoken—agriculture is such a wholesome activity that it should be supported by nonagricultural interests even if it is uneconomical.

But such assumptions tend to break down when water becomes scarce, as it did during the summer of 2009. Faced with a serious drought, leading to rapidly falling lake levels, the people who govern the LCRA realized that they would soon not have enough water to satisfy the desires of farmers, urban businesses, and homeowners. The LCRA therefore had to make a choice among the various claimants. In the late summer it announced that if the drought continued, it would cut off water to the rice farmers. Naturally, that news was greeted with approval by urban interests and consternation by agricultural interests.

Heavy autumn rains refilled the lakes, and defused the 2009 crisis. But the day of reckoning for water users in central Texas has only been postponed. The next drought that hits the area will see a still greater population and still more businesses demanding to have their thirsts quenched. Given the exploding number of urbanites, and the small number of farmers, the farmers face a future

in which they can no longer depend on enough water to sustain their rice crops. The politics of the next drought may include the elimination of one of Texas's traditional ways of life.

Private Property Rights versus State Regulation

The conflict described above dealt with *surface* water—the kind available in rivers and lakes. There are also disagreements about *underground* water—the kind that may have been enclosed in natural subsurface reservoirs, called "aquifers," for many thousands of years. Although water is pretty much the same stuff no matter where it is found, the law and politics of underground water in Texas are not quite the same as the law and politics of surface water.

For more than a century, Texas has relied on two contradictory principles for dealing with questions of the management of underground water.[7] The first principle, a legal doctrine known as the **Rule of Capture**, favors private ownership and use of such water. It holds that groundwater is more-or-less absolutely owned and controlled by the person who owns the surface land over the water. A landowner can pump all the water under his land that he desires, even if his neighbor's well runs dry, and even if the state has an interest in protecting underground water for future generations. The Rule of Capture, of course, is consistent with Texas's traditional emphasis upon private property rights. The second principle, however, which is embodied in a series of laws passed by the legislature over the past several decades, recognizes that there is a public interest in the management of the state's underground water resources. The laws have established the Texas Water Development Board (TWDB) to try to coordinate the 98 locally controlled groundwater conservation districts, and in a loose sort of way given them all the authority to plan the drawdown of water to make it last as long as possible.

Meanwhile, for decades farmers in the Panhandle and High Plains have pumped water from the Ogallala Aquifer, one of the several underground reservoirs that nature has maintained for ages under the surface of Texas land, to irrigate their corn, sorghum, and wheat fields. The pumping has now severely depleted the aquifer in some places, and left it sorely in need of protective regulation. In some counties, two-thirds of the original groundwater is gone, and the TWDB predicts that only one-third of the original Texas portion of the Ogallala will remain by 2060.

Nevertheless, what is good for Texans as a whole, and in the long run, may go against the interests of individual Texans in the short run. In Hemphill County in the northeastern corner of the Panhandle, for example, in 2009, the people on the local water development board voted to slow the pumping of water from the Ogallala. Meanwhile, in Roberts County just to the west, the local water development board was encouraging much faster depletion of the groundwater. The result would have to be that land in Hemphill County that bordered Roberts County would be drained, as its groundwater was sucked to the west to fill the vacuum as the Roberts County water was pumped away.

In the meantime, oil and gas tycoon T. Boone Pickens had extended his interests into the "water mining" business, buying the rights to underground Panhandle water in the hope of selling it soon to the thirsty, growing Dallas–Ft. Worth metro area cities. One of Pickens's Mesa Water company purchases was the legal right to half of the underground water in a ranch in Hemphill County. In 2010, Mesa Water and the rancher, George Arrington, sued the Texas Water Development Board claiming that Hemphill County could not

legally set a different pumping rate than the surrounding counties, because, in doing so, it would condemn the owners of underground water rights to seeing the value of their property lessened each year, as their assets invisibly migrated over the county line to the west. In the words of the lawsuit, the policy adopted in Hemphill County would "result in groundwater flowing from peripheral areas of Hemphill County to adjoining counties in amounts up to 18,000 acre/feet per year," which would mean that "Plaintiffs own groundwater in the areas that will be drained. This fact has caused a taking of Plaintiffs' groundwater and a diminution in the present fair market value of Plaintiffs' Hemphill County groundwater rights."

But the members of the Hemphill County Water Conservation District were not about to agree that they lacked the authority to set rules for pumping levels that differed from those permitted by all the counties around them. "The Conservation Amendment to the Texas Constitution," their lawyers wrote in response to the claims of Pickens's lawyers, "establishes that conservation of natural resources, including groundwater, is not only a public responsibility, but a public duty." Moreover, addressing the larger philosophical issue, they argued that "Petitioners' constitutional arguments, taken to their logical next steps," would paralyze the local regulatory agencies and, in effect, destroy public management of underground water resources.[8]

The lawsuit brings up a dilemma that Texans do not often face squarely: which should prevail, an individual's direct economic interest, or the indirect interests of all citizens, in the present and the future, when the two come into conflict? For most of their history, Texans have assumed that there was no conflict, and that if individuals were left free to pursue their personal goals, everyone would benefit. But as water becomes scarcer, lawsuits and political struggles of the kind occurring now in Hemphill County will become more common and widespread. Texans may have to rethink their basic philosophy of life and government.

Economic Development versus Environment

A further problem created by Texans' growing need for the ungrowing resource of water is that it is not just human beings who need the liquid of life. Other creatures in the environment must have a certain amount of water to sustain them. When growing human populations demand more and ever more of the resource, sooner or later there comes a moment when people have to decide whether to allow other species to live, which will mean that humans have to either use less, or go on consuming more, which will mean that other species may cease to exist.

In California in 2007, for example, a federal court held that the state's agribusiness in the San Joaquin Valley was taking so much water that it was about to make some indigenous fish, including the delta smelt and the chinook salmon, extinct. The court ordered that water that had been intended to irrigate crops in the southern part of the valley must instead be left in the rivers. As a result, the smelt and the salmon are (barely) holding on, but much of the farmland in the southern valley has turned into a dust bowl.[9]

Water conflicts are not yet as bad in Texas as they are in California, but the writing is on the wall. A warning for the future can be seen in the recent conflict over water for whooping cranes.[10] These are large ("tall enough to peck your eyes out," as they are sometimes charmingly described) migratory birds that winter on the Gulf Coast near Aransas Pass, feeding and nesting in the **estuary** formed by the entrance of the Guadalupe River into San Antonio Bay. The cranes are

Endangered whooping cranes are vulnerable to water use by humans far upstream from their home on the coast.

TOM UHLENBROCK/MCT/Landov.

one of those kinds of organisms that conservationists call "charismatic species," types of animals (tigers, grizzly bears, bald eagles, monarch butterflies) and plants (redwoods, bluebonnets) that involve people emotionally. Threats to charismatic species can energize the public to become interested in saving those species and, by extension, their whole habitats. They therefore have an effect upon public policy.

Such is the case with whooping cranes. The birds, which originally numbered in the many hundreds of thousands, had, by 1937, been reduced by the onslaught of human civilization to a total of 15 in Texas and 6 in Louisiana. In that year the federal government established the Aransas National Wildlife Refuge on the coast, to protect the birds during their winter breeding sojourn in Texas. In 1967 the birds were listed as endangered, and in 1973 the federal Endangered Species Act created a series of legal protections for all listed species. Partly because of the Act's shielding of such species from the threat of economic development, and partly because of the nurturing efforts of scientists and environmentalists, the crane population began to recover. By the first decade of the twenty-first century, the birds numbered about 240 individuals.

Enter the **Texas Commission on Environmental Quality (TCEQ)**. This state agency's mission is to strive to "protect our state's human and natural resources consistent with sustainable economic development."[11] The fact that there may sometimes be a conflict between environmental protection and economic development is not something that the people of TCEQ are prepared to admit. The agency is responsible for issuing air and water operating permits to businesses operating in Texas. Readers of preceding chapters in this book will not be surprised to learn that businesses that desire a permit are able to bring intense pressure to bear on the agency through political channels. In other words, science and the public interest are not the only concerns that determine TCEQ policy.[12] As a result, TCEQ has authorized so many permits for businesses to use Texas surface water that in years of scarcity many of the rivers come close to going dry.

The fall of 2008 and winter of 2009 saw insufficient rainfall in much of the southern half of Texas. By late winter, environmentalists noted with alarm that 23 whooping cranes, or 8.5 percent of the entire flock, had died during the previous few months. Although there is some attrition in the bird population every

winter, this seemed to be a large and dangerous fluctuation. Scientists studying the cause of the die-off came to the conclusions that, because TCEQ had okayed so many permits for so many businesses to withdraw water from the Guadalupe River, the drought had caused freshwater amounts in San Antonio Bay to fall steeply. Blue crabs living in the Bay, which depend upon a certain mixture of fresh- and saltwater ("brackishness," in the vocabulary of those who talk about water), had found their environment too salty, and had either died in large numbers or moved somewhere else along the coast. The cranes, dependent upon the crabs for food, had discovered the pantry going bare. Without enough food to go around, an unusually large number of the cranes had either died of starvation or, weakened by malnutrition, succumbed to disease.

When accused of having favored economic development over environmental protection, and thus of having caused stress on the crane population, TCEQ, in effect, answered that the problem was the drought, not its own policies. Environmentalists, of course, pointed out that Texas had endured occasional droughts for many thousands of years, and yet the whooping cranes had thrived. It was only when a (foreseeable) dry year had coincided with TCEQ's unrestrained granting of water-withdrawal permits that the recovery of the cranes was threatened. Naturally, TCEQ refused to agree that it shared any blame for the plight of the cranes.

People in the area around San Antonio Bay reacted to this problem by organizing and founding the Aransas Project, a coalition of citizens, organizations, and local businesses "who want," according to its Web site, "responsible water management of the Guadalupe River basin." In March 2010, the Aransas Project filed suit in federal court, charging that TCEQ policies were in violation of the Endangered Species Act.[13] The plaintiffs asked the federal courts to force TCEQ to reduce the amount of water it permitted businesses to withdraw from the Guadalupe during low-rainfall years.

As this book went to press, the issues surrounding TCEQ's policies, and the larger issue of the conflict between an ever-growing population and economy, and an unexpandable supply of water for the environment, have not been resolved. But the Aransas Project lawsuit, like the Hemphill County lawsuit, has brought issues to the courts that Texas's democratic political system has usually tried to avoid. Whatever the specific decisions in such cases, the conflicts they represent and the philosophical dilemmas they pose will be with Texans for a long time. Soon the political system will be unable to continue avoiding such conflicts and dilemmas, and will have to face them squarely.

Interbasin Transfers and Dam-Building

If people keep moving to Texas and demanding more water, then one possibility is to bring in the essential liquid from outside. In humid East Texas, cities such as Houston and Texarkana will have little trouble supplying their needs for the foreseeable future. But as one moves from east to west across the state, annual rainfall drops by about five inches per 100 miles. Thus, Beaumont can count on an average of 56 inches a year, Dallas 35, Abilene 24, and El Paso 9.[14] Although, as already mentioned, averages are an unreliable guide to how much rain will fall in any particular year, still, they give a good indication of which cities can usually depend on having enough water, and which cities have to anticipate a difficult future. It is inevitable that the people in the dry cities will wonder about the feasibility of bringing in water from somewhere else.

There is a long history of ideas, ranging from the solidly practical to the remarkably fanciful, to import water from moister areas of the state and the country. During the 1960s, various politicians and business leaders sponsored the Texas Water Plan, a gigantic engineering project that would have diverted water from the Mississippi River below New Orleans to several Texas cities, including Dallas and Fort Worth, then continued on to water the high plains between Amarillo and Lubbock. In 1969, however, the state's voters, suspicious of its costs and the amount of energy that would be required to lift and transport enormous amounts of heavy liquid, vetoed the Texas Water Plan.[15] But schemes to manage and import water did not die with that particular boondoggle.

Until the 1980s, San Antonio relied upon the Edwards Aquifer, another underground reservoir of prehistoric water, to fulfill its municipal needs. But as its population began to grow beyond the abilities of the aquifer to supply those needs, the city administration planned to construct the Applewhite Reservoir on the Medina River. Nevertheless, in the early 1990s, the city's voters twice refused to authorize bond sales to pay for construction, and the project was abandoned. Then, during the drought of 1996, San Antonio and Corpus Christi began exploring ways of transporting water from the seven Colorado River lakes in central Texas southward to their residents. The Lower Colorado River Authority, along with the cities it served, including Austin, immediately raised a loud political hue and cry that other Texans were attempting to "steal our water." The conflict became so heated that journalists began to use the phrase "the war for the Colorado."[16] That particular incident subsided without a major inter-basin transfer. But San Antonio is still searching for a large, stable water supply. And that city's plight is an indicator of what the rest of the state will face just a little farther down the historical road.

Faced with the potential for more of this sort of struggle between those areas that have lots of people and little water and those that have enough water and few people, the state's politicians have attempted, within the confines of the Texan political culture, to meet the citizens' impending needs. In 2001, the legislature placed on the ballot a constitutional amendment expanding the authority of the Texas Water Development Board and providing additional bonding authority for the TWDB to help build water projects. It passed. In 2002, the TWDB published *Water for Texas—2002*, a three-volume, fifty-year plan for the development of water resources in the state. This plan was amended in 2006 to become the 2007 State Water Plan.[17] Meanwhile, in 2003, the legislature had passed seven water conservation bills, the most notable being those that created an ongoing task force to monitor and make recommendations about water conservation in the state, and that spelled out five- and ten-year requirements for water savings, including percentage reductions in the average daily water use per person.

In 2007, the legislature passed a law designed to speed the construction of new reservoirs. Among other provisions, it designated sites for the location of dams. There is no assurance, however, that the dams will actually be built. Farmers in East Texas resist having their land gobbled up and flooded so that the residents of cities farther west can water their lawns. (Indeed, during the summer, up to 65 percent of municipal water use can go to lawn-watering).[18] As San Antonio has already discovered, it is one thing to have a water plan, and another to overcome all the political conflicts that stand in the way of implementing the plan.

While citizens and government agencies dicker about dams, pipelines, and water rights, the state's population continues to grow and to demand more

water. In 2007, J. Kevin Ward, executive administrator of the TWDB, warned Texas's citizens that "The viable, readily available water resources are gone, and we're running out of water to develop." Ward forecast that by 2060, Texas would need to have invested a projected $178 billion for municipal drinking-water systems, $150 billion for sewer lines and plans, and $30 billion for water supply needs if its ever-expanding population was to live its customary civilized lifestyle.[19] And to finance those billions, of course, Texas government would have to tax the citizens, who show few signs of being willing to abandon their traditional opposition to paying higher levies for government services.

The future of Texas politics, therefore, promises to offer many intense conflicts over water supply. There will be arguments between eastern and western parts of the state, between cities and rural areas, between agriculture and industry, between sports groups (particularly fishing organizations) and developers, and possibly between Texans and residents of other states who have "excess" water Texas would like to import. The politics of water, like the rest of the state's politics, promises to be loud, colorful, and endlessly fascinating for observers of democracy.

Energy Supply

All life on Earth depends upon achieving access to energy. Plants get it from the Sun, while animals get it by eating plants, or eating other animals that eat plants. At this most basic level, humans are animals and need energy to survive. But civilization, too, over and above its biologically human component, requires a steady supply of energy. Building a skyscraper, or driving a car from Beaumont to El Paso, or manufacturing a cell phone, or distributing paper napkins to a fast-food chain, or an uncounted number of other activities, would never exist if abundant energy was not available to be put to use. Where the future energy supply is going to come from, and how much it will cost, therefore, are questions of vital interest to all Texans, whether they are aware of it or not.

Although energy, like water, is at its most basic just one thing—the ability to do work—within the practical context of the technology, economics, and politics of energy, it is split into a fantastic number of problems, controversies, and uncertainties. Even for the restricted area of one state, therefore, the general topic of energy supply is far too complex for a portion of one chapter in a textbook. Indeed, whole textbooks are devoted to just one aspect of the subject, from the economics of energy to the engineering of a single energy resource.[20] Consequently, this section will not be a comprehensive treatment of the subject. First, it will give a brief overview of the advantages and disadvantages of various sources of energy supply and, second, provide details on some aspects of energy politics in Texas.

Sources of Energy

The political problem of energy supply starts at a philosophical level. Some people believe that economic market forces should be permitted to "decide" how energy is to be supplied. That is, the choices of individual consumers, responding to price cues, and the investment decisions of businesses, also responding to prices, should determine what sources of energy are used. In general, we

have termed people who endorse this philosophy "conservatives." Other people think that public safety, or freedom from coercion by foreign governments, or protection of the environment should take precedence over economic efficiency, and that therefore government should regulate and subsidize energy markets. We have termed people who endorse this philosophy "liberals." Always, however, when considering philosophical arguments, people tend to be swayed by their personal interests, so public philosophies often become less important than private influence over decision makers.

When discussing energy policy, one of the great epic poems of Western literature often supplies a grand metaphor to help us understand the situation. In the 1830s the German poet Johann von Goethe wrote "Faust," the story of a man who, in order to gain knowledge, love, and power, sells his soul to the Devil. Thus Faust achieves all he wants in life, but is condemned (with the partial exception of a twist at the end) to suffer in Hell in the afterlife. Ever since, the notion that people can achieve desirable things, but only if they pay a terrible cost, has been known as a **Faustian bargain.** When it comes to energy policy, the notion of a Faustian bargain is a useful one, because every energy option promises to supply Americans and Texans with much of what we need for the good life, but only at a price that increasingly looks terrible, no matter which alternative we choose.

Because people's philosophies disagree and because interests taint political discussion, it is impossible to give a completely objective summary of the Faustian bargain inherent in each energy-supply option. But to the extent that the raucous public and scholarly arguments of the last century or so fall into clear patterns, the following account compiles the upsides and downsides of the main contenders for the title of "Texas's energy source of the future."

Oil

For Texas, the twentieth century was the century of oil. The great Spindletop strike of 1901 permitted the creation of an industry that made many Texans individually rich, supported thousands of ordinary workers and their families, and raised the state as a whole from an agricultural backwater floundering in the aftermath of Civil War to an industrial, urbanized giant. As was to be expected for an industry that was the backbone of the state's economy for many decades, the oil industry was extremely powerful in Texas politics. Texas officeholders both in Austin and Washington almost considered it their duty to nurture the industry and give its representatives what they asked for in the way of laws and regulations (or lack of regulations).[21]

The peak of Texas oil production, however, was reached in the early 1970s. Although the amount the state produces rises and falls with the price of oil on the world market, still, the overall direction is clearly downward. Meanwhile, other industries have risen to prominence in the economy. Texas still possesses just under a quarter of all U.S. reserves of crude oil, and is home to about 28 percent of all the country's producing wells, which provide about 22 percent of its national total. Refineries in the Houston area make up the largest refining complex in the country, and the nation's largest single refinery is in Baytown. Altogether, Texas's twenty-seven refineries located along the Gulf Coast process more than 4.7 million barrels of crude oil per day, and account for more than a quarter of the nation's refining capacity.[22] So although Texas's oil industry is not the dominant force in the state's economy and politics that it once was, it is now and will continue to be a major player.

One major advantage of oil as a source of energy is that it has been crucial for so long that the state, like the nation, possesses a wealth of infrastructure and institutions to utilize it. Millions of vehicles relying on internal combustion engines sit in garages and clog roads. Gas stations dot every city and sit on lonely stretches of highway. Pipelines and refineries already exist. Moreover, of course, every time someone buys a gasoline-burning vehicle in one of the other forty-nine states, the purchase helps to create jobs for Texans. The state's citizens are well aware that, in a sense, modern Texas was built by the oil industry.

Oil has other advantages, too. Because it is a liquid, it is relatively easy and inexpensive to transport (through pipelines). The means of extracting and refining it have been developing for more than a century, and many of the experts on the subject live and work in Texas. Furthermore, it is ideal for the form of transportation that Americans in general, and Texans in particular, find most congenial—individually owned automobiles. Other sources of energy are easily used in such forms of transportation as trains and streetcars, but only oil has so far been manufactured into a convenient vehicle fuel. For this combination of reasons, oil has the greatest advantage of all: it is relatively cheap.

Oil will thus continue to be a very important source of energy for decades to come. But over the last forty years or so, the world has learned that reliance on oil contains more than one Faustian downside. When the Organization of Petroleum Exporting Countries (OPEC) doubled the price in 1973, and at the same time Saudi Arabia shut in its wells to protest the support the United States had given to Israel within the international community, the double whammy threw all industrial economies into chaotic recession. Although Texans, who often worked for some facet of the industry, continued to cherish it, suddenly oil no longer seemed cheap and convenient to citizens of most other states. The prospect of another supply disruption—which in fact became a reality during the Iranian revolution of 1979—turned out to be a specter that has haunted the nation's consumers and policymakers ever since.

But the nation's ever-greater dependence on a fuel that, as luck would have it, is mainly found in politically unstable regions of the Middle East, South America, and Africa, and in Russia, which has its own uses for its resources, is not the only major downside to oil. Beginning in the 1980s, scientists began to raise an alarm that burning fossil fuels, and in particular oil, was releasing so much carbon dioxide into the air that the accumulating chemical in the upper atmosphere was blocking the "bounce" of the sun's rays back into space, thus creating a "**greenhouse effect**" that was causing the Earth's climate to warm. Over the last quarter-century, as higher average world temperatures have caused ice sheets in Greenland and Antarctica to begin melting, thus dumping enormous amounts of water into the oceans, sea levels have started to rise. Some coastal cities are already in danger of flooding during high tide, some low-lying island countries in the Pacific Ocean are in danger of vanishing beneath the waves, and various other possibly catastrophic changes have alarmed citizens and policymakers in almost every country.[23] As a result, there is an anxious worldwide movement to try to eliminate the burning of fossil fuels and thus find a substitute for oil in every economy. The major downside of the use of oil for energy, then, may be that it is causing the end of civilization as the industrial world has known it for more than a century.

But oil has other environmental problems that, though smaller than global warming, are nevertheless serious. The act of drilling for and producing, then transporting, oil introduces many opportunities for environmental degradation. When a well is producing, there is danger that the oil—which is poisonous to all

life—will find its way out of a broken casing and into the underground water supply. When companies are trying to get more oil out of an old well, they often inject water, sand, and chemicals under pressure into the ground, hoping to force more of the valuable liquid to and up the well bore. It appears that sometimes the chemicals they use for this "hydraulic fracturing," or "**fracking**," contain toxic substances.[24] (There will be more discussion of fracking in the sections on natural gas, and on protecting the environment.) Moreover, as the easy-to-find-and-produce fields dry up, oil companies are inspired to look for the "black gold" in places that are harder to reach, and more environmentally sensitive. Especially relevant to Texas, companies have for decades been drilling in ever-deeper water in the Gulf of Mexico. In April 2010, a drilling platform named the Deepwater Horizon, operated by BP (British Petroleum) in 5,000 feet of water, blew up, killing eleven workers and precipitating a huge oil spill—50,000 barrels a day—that continued into September, fouling beaches and devastating the fishing business in Louisiana, Alabama, Mississippi, and Florida. The federal government estimated that about 5 million barrels flowed into the Gulf in five months, making it the largest oil spill in history.[25] The fact that the toxic plume of oil spared Texas was irrelevant to the fact that the disaster illustrated the terrible potential for environmental destruction inherent in the production of oil.

The price of oil in a technical, short-term sense, then, is still low compared to the prices of other usable forms of energy. But the "price" in a broad, difficult-to-define, long-term sense is so high that there are major efforts being conducted, on the world stage, within the United States, and in Texas itself, to find a way to make a transition away from oil (and the other fossil fuels) toward a different energy base. Because a great many people in Texas still find employment in searching for, producing, transporting, and retail sales of oil, this effort within the state is more complicated and conflicted than it is in other states and countries that are not so dependent upon production of the black liquid.

Natural Gas

A close cousin to liquid oil, and always found in the same underground reservoirs, petroleum in a gaseous state was for decades of little value. Towns located near oil fields began, during the 1920s, to use natural gas for lighting and heat, but because it was so hard to gather and transport, there was almost no other market for it. (In this textbook, "natural gas" refers to the stuff that comes out of the ground and is burned directly for fuel, as distinct from "gasoline," which is refined oil, and used as fuel for automobiles.) As a result, when producers brought up the worthless gas with the precious oil, they usually burned it at the wellhead—an action known as "flaring." In the early decades of the twentieth century, citizens living near major oil fields could read a newspaper outside at night because of the light supplied by the hundreds of natural gas flares that lit up the sky.[26]

Functioning as the protector of the state's natural resources, the Railroad Commission outlawed flaring in 1947, and after that producers began to find markets for their gas in the suburbs that sprang up around large cities—especially in the West and South—during the post–World War Two economic boom. By the middle 1950s, people in the business were searching for, and producing, natural gas in its own right, independently of any oil that might also be in the reservoir. Since that era there have been periodic booms and downtimes in the gas industry, but the fuel as a whole is a major energy source for the country

as a whole, and for Texas in particular. The state produces roughly 30 percent of the nation's total, and accounts for nearly 20 percent of its consumption.[27] The natural gas production tax officially supplied 0.8 percent of state revenue in fiscal year 2010, along with oil's 1.2 percent, but those figures greatly underestimate petroleum's contribution because they do not take account of the countless people who are directly or indirectly employed in the industry, and contribute to sales taxes every time they buy something within the state boundaries.[28]

The advantages and disadvantages of natural gas as an energy source are similar to those for oil, although there are also some important differences. Table 14-1 displays estimates by the federal Department of Energy (DOE) about the costs of generating electricity in hypothetical plants to be built that would come online in 2016. Such estimates are always to be regarded with skepticism, partly because they rely on guesses about future fuel costs that may prove to be wildly unrealistic, and partly because they do not take into account such indirect costs as the price to a nation of health care that may be needed because of the pumping of pollutants into the air and water. Nevertheless, they give a good indication of the sorts of considerations that Texas policymakers must think about when they are trying to decide on public policy toward energy supply. The table shows that natural gas is, in general, an inexpensive source of electric power. (The DOE economists did not include the costs of oil-generated power in their calculations, presumably because, although power plants can be built that burn oil, they never are these days, for a variety of reasons.) Gas vies with coal for the title of cheapest source of fuel for electric utilities. Moreover, natural gas is a far cleaner source of energy than is coal. Although it produces greenhouse gases and other pollutants, gas emits many fewer noxious chemicals per unit of energy produced than coal.[29]

TABLE 14-1

Estimated Cost of New Electrical Generation by Resource, 2016

Energy Source	Cost per Kilowatt-Hour
Conventional coal	$.10
Advanced coal	.11
Natural gas fired—	
Conventional combined cycle	.08
Advanced combined cycle with carbon capture and sequestration	.11
Advanced nuclear	.12
Wind	.15
Solar photovoltaic	.40
Geothermal	.16
Hydroelectric	.12

NOTE: "Advanced" in the table refers to technologies that produce less pollution.

SOURCE: Energy Information Administration, *Annual Energy Outlook 2010*, December 2009 (DOE/EIA—0383 [2009]).

Further, during the 1990s, advances in the technology of producing natural (more fracking) gas opened up a vast reservoir that underlies the area around Ft. Worth, the Barnett Shale.[30] By 2011 this field had become the largest in Texas and was on its way to becoming the most productive in the country. With this new supply, and others on the horizon, the future supply of natural gas in the United States looks secure. In other words, unlike the supply of oil, the supply of gas does not depend on the stability of international politics and the vagaries of international markets. Even more appealing to Texas politicians, the fact that the future supply will come out of the state means that their own policies will govern the industry, not the policies of a federal government they generally mistrust. All this makes gas an attractive choice for the future of Texas energy.

But natural gas is not exempt from the Faustian bargain. It is extremely explosive, and always a danger whether it is being used by a single homeowner or a giant industrial complex. Leaking pipes, inexpertly attached fittings, corroded metal casings, earthquake-ruptured containment vessels, careless smoking,

Tragedy Can Be the Cost of Progress

In 1930 the supergiant East Texas Field, containing six billion barrels of oil and a huge amount of natural gas, was discovered in Rusk County, about 110 miles southeast of Dallas and in the general vicinity of Kilgore. Coming along just as the Great Depression was tightening its grip on the country, the field caused an economic boom and changed the area forever.

Among the changes brought in by the development of the field was one that would have tragic consequences. Because the natural gas that was produced along with the oil was of so little value, the oil producers often ran it in pipelines to some vicinity where it could be burned. They permitted just about anyone to siphon off this residue, or "green gas," for whatever heat and light they could get out of it.

In early 1937 the public school in New London, a small town 12 miles south of Kilgore, engaged some plumbers to run a pipeline from the Parade Gasoline Company's green gas line into the school. Apparently the fixtures connecting the various pipes together under the school were poorly attached, and leaked gas into the basement of the building. Natural gas is odorless and colorless, so no one detected the leak.

On March 18, someone struck a spark in the basement and the school exploded, killing 298 students, teachers, and staff. It was the worst disaster in the history of American education.

Texas state political institutions responded to the tragedy with several laws. The most important was the one that required any company producing natural gas to inject it with "thiols," foul-smelling chemicals that quickly alert people to the presence of natural gas in their area.

The presence of an identifying malodorant in natural gas has undoubtedly warned countless people of a problem, and averted many other tragedies. But nothing can be done to render gas less explosive, and so it remains a very dangerous choice as a source of energy.

Sources: Archie P. McDonald, "New London School Explosion," Texas Escapes online magazine, www .texasescapes.com; "March 18, 1937: Natural Gas Explosion Kills Schoolchildren in Texas," from *This Day in History* on the Web site www.history.com; and Wikipedia.

terrorist bombs, and many other avoidable but inevitable occurrences can lead to instant destruction and tragedy wherever natural gas is being used. Although various foul-smelling chemicals are now added to gas as it is produced to alert people if there should be a leak (see the box entitled "Tragedy Can Be the Cost of Progress"), still, every year there are fatal explosions. In September 2010, a natural gas pipeline underneath a residential neighborhood in San Bruno, California, burst and ignited, killing eight people and destroying forty homes. Three months later, a gas leak caused a blast in a furniture store in Wayne, Michigan, killing two. In January 2011, another pipeline break in a residential neighborhood of Philadelphia triggered an explosion that killed one person and injured six. A month later, five people were killed when a cast-iron pipeline installed during the 1920s ruptured and blew up in Allentown, Pennsylvania.[31] And the danger is not only to small buildings. In March 2005, there was a massive detonation in BP's Texas City refinery that killed 15 and injured 170.[32]

Moreover, although natural gas is cleaner than oil and much cleaner than coal as a fuel for electric power plants, it is still a hydrocarbon that releases greenhouse gases and other pollutants when burned. And like oil, its production from the ground can be filthy unless it is handled with great concern for the environment. Residents living near the 15,000 wells drilled in the Barnett Shale over the past decade, for example, have registered many complaints about air and water pollution with federal and state regulators.[33] An investigation of documents produced by the federal Environmental Protection Agency and the Texas Commission on Environmental Quality by the *Dallas Morning News* reported that they "reveal a pattern of emissions of toxic compounds, often including cancer-causing benzene, from Barnett Shale facilities."[34]

So natural gas, like oil, is in many ways an unsatisfactory source of energy for Texas.

Coal

Coal was the energy source of the nineteenth century, the substance that fueled the industrial revolution in the United States.[35] It heated houses, powered factories, and made the railroad—the keystone technology of that time, as the computer is the keystone technology of our time—possible. Now, as Table 14-1 illustrates, coal is still an important source of power because it is cheap. It is cheap to mine (unless one takes into account the lives lost in the process), cheap to transport (although not as cheap as oil and gas), and cheap to burn. Part of its cheapness is based on the fact that it does not explode like natural gas or melt down and release radioactivity like uranium. Furthermore, Americans who rely on burning coal for their energy need never worry about having their supply disrupted by a hostile foreign government. Within the borders of the United States lies enough coal to power the country for centuries.[36] Because it is inexpensive and abundant, coal is used to power more than 44 percent of the country's electricity generation.[37]

Nevertheless, coal's advantages are balanced by its very serious drawbacks. From 1990 to 2009, 765 miners died in accidents in the United States, an average of 38 a year.[38] Meanwhile, about 700 were expiring each year from pneumoconiosis, or "black lung disease," which is caused by years of breathing coal dust in the mines.[39] If, instead of bringing up the coal from underground, companies instead choose to "strip mine," or remove the land over the coal with dynamite and bulldozers, what they gain in safety for their workers is lost in terms of the destruction of the ecosystem. As one article on strip mining in *Time* magazine

put it, in an area that has been strip mined, "Huge piles of gray debris . . . stand like gravestones over land so scarred and acidic only rodents can live there."[40]

But coal has an even worse impact on the environment when it is burned. It is by far the most polluting fuel. According to the Union of Concerned Scientists, a typical coal-burning power plant generates, in a year's operation, 3,700,000 tons of carbon dioxide (CO_2), the major gas that is causing global warming, 10,000 tons of sulfur dioxide (SO_2), which causes acid rain, 10,200 tons of nitrogen oxide (NO_2), which causes smog, 170 pounds of mercury, 225 pounds of arsenic, 114 pounds of lead, and a variety of types of other noxious stuff in smaller quantities.[41] Various kinds of technology can be installed into boilers and onto smokestacks to clean these pollutants out of the factory's discharge before they reach the atmosphere, but all of them are expensive and raise the cost of coal-fired power. To make coal cleaner, therefore, is to progressively erase the reason people choose coal in the first place.

Almost all of the coal mined in Texas is lignite, the lowest grade (that is, the type with the lowest yield of energy per ton burned). All of it is consumed within the state, generally by utilities that mine it and burn it onsite. Lignite's virtue is that, compared to other types of coal, it is relatively low in sulfur. It is still a major emitter of greenhouse gases, however. But Texas's appetite for coal is larger than its internal supply, so it imports many tons each year from mines in Wyoming. Despite its image as a state that relies on petroleum, Texas consumes more coal than any of the other forty-nine states, and according to the federal Energy Information Administration, "its emissions of carbon dioxide and sulfur dioxide are among the highest in the nation."[42]

In other words, embracing coal as a favored energy source is no way out of the Faustian bargain for Texans.

Nuclear Power

Of all the possible sources of energy, nuclear power is the one that offers a Faustian bargain in the starkest terms. For "atomic energy," as it used to be called, offers both the most tempting possibility for virtually unlimited clean power, and the most worrisome potential to exact a hellish price.

Nuclear power is not a viable option for fueling individual automobiles. Its value lies in its ability to produce vast quantities of electricity. Theoretically, at some point in the hypothetical future, that electricity could supply charging stations for millions of electric cars, thus freeing the United States from all dependence on oil. For the near-term, however, nuclear power is an alternative for public utilities and the types of work that electricity does in modern American life.

Nuclear power works by boiling water, indirectly, with a controlled amount of heat from atomic fission reactors. The steam is then used to rotate turbines that produce electricity. The two nuclear plants in Texas, Comanche Peak, south of Ft. Worth, and the South Texas Nuclear Project, west of Houston, supply about 10 percent of the state's electricity.[43] The other 102 U.S. reactors produce about a fifth of the country's electric generation.[44]

As Table 14-1 illustrates, nuclear power is now almost as inexpensive as natural gas and coal. Nuclear advocates argue that if the licensing process for new reactors could be streamlined and some of the political impediments to operation could be removed, nuclear power would become even cheaper.[45]

The relative cheapness of nuclear power, however, is less attractive than some of its other attributes. It does not release greenhouse gases into the atmosphere because it does not burn anything to produce heat. It therefore does not

contribute to global warming, or to any sort of air pollution. Nuclear plants do cause "thermal pollution" because the water used to cool their reactors itself becomes heated in the process. If water is drawn from, say, an estuary on the coastline, the organisms in that estuary are adapted to living at certain temperatures, and then hot water from a nuclear plant is dumped back into the ocean, the ecosystem will suffer grievously. This difficulty, however, can be overcome by allowing the water to sit in cooling ponds for a specified time, and the problem, at any rate, is not nearly as severe as the environmental stresses that nuclear power avoids. As a result, pro-nuclear advocates often argue that nuclear power is the environmentally responsible choice.[46]

Unlike the situation with, oil, the supply of nuclear power can be made stable. The uranium fuel is entirely available from mines within the United States, so that there is no potential for supply disruptions because of the vagaries of international politics.[47]

Nuclear power is therefore clean, affordable, and strategically secure. Its downside lies more in the realm of potential than in the realm of actual reality. But that potential is so grim that it gives many good citizens grave doubts about the wisdom of pursuing, or even continuing, the development of the energy source.

The first problem with nuclear power lies in the potential for a catastrophic accident. The temperature of the radioactive rods must be carefully controlled. Too little heat, and they will fail to accomplish their goal of producing steam. Too much heat, and they will literally melt each other and the factory in which they are housed. The danger is not that there could be a nuclear bomb–type explosion, but that a meltdown would allow large amounts of radioactivity to be released into the atmosphere, thus causing very severe health problems for the people living downwind. Given the human propensity to make mistakes, if enough people are engaged with enough technological complexity in enough nuclear power plants, the probability would seem to be very high that errors will be made, and that some of those errors will be bad enough to lead to a meltdown.

Cartoonist Michael Ramirez satirizes the probable result if humans rejected the Faustian bargain and refused to make choices among energy sources: civilization would die and humans would have to go back to living in caves.

By permission of Michael Ramirez and Creators Syndicate, Inc.

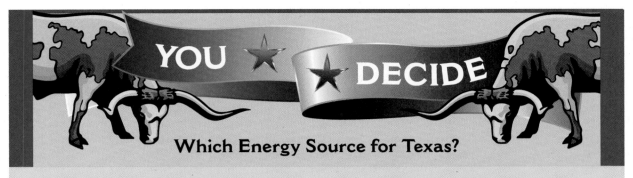

YOU ★ ★ DECIDE

Which Energy Source for Texas?

Every potential source of energy has something to recommend it. Every potential source has a serious downside. But policymakers cannot simply note that no choice is perfect and go on to something else. They have to decide among alternatives, all of which are costly in some way.

Pretend that you are a Texas official. Which energy choice would you endorse? You should probably start by ranking the various strengths and weaknesses of each energy source in terms of your own values. What is most important to you? Price? Safety? Environmental protection? What is next most important? And so forth.

There is a large lesson to be learned from this exercise: governing is hard.

ENERGY SOURCE	ADVANTAGES	DISADVANTAGES
Coal	Abundant in United States Nonexplosive Comparatively inexpensive	Dangerous to mine underground; environmentally destructive to strip mine Very polluting, including production of greenhouse gases
Hydropower	Cheap No pollution of any kind	Only available where large rivers flow out of mountains (i.e., not in Texas) Cannot be used to power individual transportation Dams block migrating fish, damage riparian ecosystems
Natural Gas	Abundant in United States, especially in Texas Compared to oil, relatively less polluting Transportation infrastructure already in place	Highly explosive Produces greenhouse gases Prices are notoriously volatile
Nuclear Power	Abundant in United States Does not produce greenhouse gases Does not produce air or water pollution	Potential to be very dangerous to produce Problem of disposal of dangerous radioactive wastes Produces thermal pollution of cooling water Good for producing electricity, but not for fueling individual transportation
Oil	Infrastructure in place Relatively inexpensive Good for fueling individual transportation	Major producers are often unstable or hostile politically, leading to possibility of supply disruption Produces greenhouse gases Potential for environmentally disastrous spills Even without a spill, production can be highly polluting to groundwater

(continued)

(continued)		
Renewables (solar, wind)	Except for manufacture of equipment, nonpolluting; especially do not produce greenhouse gases Do not rely on foreign supply Inexhaustible long-run supply	Expensive Infrastructure not in place Unreliable short-run supply (when sun doesn't shine or wind doesn't blow) Onshore and offshore wind turbines kill birds; offshore turbines disrupt fish migrations
Conservation (Efficiency)	No dependence on foreign sources Large long-run cost savings No additional pollution	Requires coordinating the behavior of millions of people over a long period, either through command-and-control mechanisms or prices Reliance on prices can be very hard on poor people; reliance on command-and-control risks creating evasion, black markets, shortages, unintended consequences

Sources: See chapter endnotes numbers 19 through 61.

In fact, this is what happened in the world's worst nuclear accident, at Chernobyl, a city in the Ukraine, then a republic of the Soviet Union, in 1986. The reactor itself was badly designed, and operators were not well trained. When a power spike occurred, plant workers inadvertently worsened the problem with their actions. There was a series of explosions caused by steam pressure buildup in the reactor, exposing its inner components and draining all the cooling water out of the plant. The fuel rods were then exposed to the air, and ignited, sending a plume of radioactive fallout over the Western Soviet Union and much of northern and western Europe. Fifty people were killed directly by the explosions and radiation sickness. Estimates of the number of people killed indirectly by radioactive contamination of air and water vary widely, from 4,000 to almost a million.[48] Even at the lower estimate, this incident has brought home forcefully, to people around the world, the dangers inherent in badly managed nuclear power and has affected public opinion in many countries by making people quite wary of this energy source.

As this book was being written, another nuclear catastrophe was unfolding in Japan, where a massive 9.0 Richter-scale earthquake and its accompanying tsunami severely damaged several nuclear reactors on that country's northeastern coast. With the cooling systems knocked offline, Japanese officials were scrambling to pour enough seawater over the reactors to prevent the fuel from melting through the containment shielding and creating another Chernobyl-type disaster. The accident was potentially so catastrophic that it caused the governments of several nuclear-dependent countries to reconsider the safety of their own reactors.[49]

Nuclear advocates argue that both the Ukrainian and the Japanese experiences are not directly relevant to the United States in general or Texas in particular, because our reactors are better designed, or because our reactor operators are better trained, or because (specifically relevant to Texas power plants) the geological setting (with a very low probability of an earthquake) of our plants makes the Japanese comparison inappropriate.[50] They point out that in the only

serious accident at a civilian installation in this country's history, at Three-Mile Island in Pennsylvania in 1979, no one was killed or injured and only a tiny amount of radioactivity was released into the air. Furthermore, they maintain that improvements have been made in the design of American reactors and in the procedures for operating them since 1979, so that another accident is very unlikely.

But these arguments come from experts, and ordinary citizens often do not possess the expertise to evaluate the conclusions. They do not have the education to enable them to judge the persuasiveness of technical arguments. But anyone could evaluate the televised images coming out of Japan during the spring of 2011, in which helicopters were frantically trying to drop loads of seawater onto damaged reactors, hoping to avoid a catastrophic meltdown. Such scenes have a powerful emotional impact, and stay in the memory for a long time. There is therefore a strong dose of skepticism in public opinion about the safety of nuclear power.

The second problem with nuclear power is the puzzle of what to do with the radioactive waste.[51] The power plants produce electricity with enriched-uranium fuel rods. After some years of service, the rods are no longer useful and must be discarded, but they remain radioactive, and therefore dangerous to human and all other life, for about 10,000 years. Since the 1960s the federal government has been trying to find a permanent place to put the spent rods so that they will not leak radioactivity into the environment, and especially the groundwater. Since 1983 the federal Department of Energy has spent more than $10 billion on research into ways to dispose of fuel. It has considered shooting it into outer space, sinking it to the bottom of the ocean, or finding ways to recycle it.

Researchers have concluded that it is technically possible to seal the rods in steel canisters and bury them in geologically stable areas of the country. But this technical solution always comes up against a political consideration, the NIMBY syndrome (for "Not in my backyard"). Everyone wants to find a solution to the problem of nuclear waste, but nobody wants it buried near them. Once the word *radiation* is used in public discussion, citizens react with fear and rejection. Surveys reveal that Americans would rather live near a chemical-waste landfill, an oil refinery, or a pesticide plant than near a nuclear waste depository.

Thus, when George W. Bush was president of the United States, he was engaged in finding a place for the country to store its spent nuclear fuel rods. In 2002 Congress passed a law, which Bush signed, allocating the waste to a site at Yucca Mountain in the state of Nevada. The decision was ironic, because during the previous decade, when Bush had been governor of Texas, he had strenuously opposed siting the waste in his own state. Thus do politicians try to deal with the challenge of nuclear waste disposal by making it someone else's problem.

At any rate, the Yucca Mountain disposal site soon became mired in political opposition from local politicians and environmentalist groups in Nevada and Washington, D.C., as well as unfavorable court decisions. The fact that Harry Reid, the Democratic party leader in the U.S. Senate, represented Nevada made these obstructionist efforts all the more effective. By 2009 the idea of storing spent wastes in Yucca Mountain had effectively been abandoned, and the Obama administration did not appear to be searching for an alternative. Meanwhile, more than 89,000 tons of nuclear waste have been sitting in "temporary" above-ground storage facilities in thirty-nine states, a number that has been growing at the rate of 2,000 tons a year.

Thus, although the serious long-run problem of nuclear waste disposal may have a technical solution, its political aspects appear to be insoluble. Added to the crucial difficulty of the potential for a catastrophic accident, these two downsides of nuclear power are so severe that for many people they overbalance the otherwise great advantages of relying on nuclear power as an energy source. For much of the public, the price of that particular Faustian bargain is too high.

Renewables

The term *renewables* is applied to sources of energy that appear to come directly from Nature, without much intervention by human technology, specifically, power from wind and the sun. (The possibility of power from geothermal sources and from hydropower exists in some states, but these forms of energy will not be discussed here because they are not relevant to the future of Texas.) In both wind and solar energy, the Faustian bargain is reversed from the way it structures the social choices of oil, natural gas, coal, and nuclear power. In those sources, the direct price is low, but the "by-product price" in terms of pollution, danger, or both, is very high. In regard to wind and solar power, the by-product price is relatively low, but the direct price is high. As Table 14-1 illustrates, the cost of wind-generated electricity is roughly a quarter-again to a third-again higher than the nonrenewable sources, while the cost of solar power is as much as four times higher. If Texas is going to stop relying on the conventional four power sources and "go renewable" in the future, therefore, Texans are going to have to pay a good deal more for their electricity.

Of the renewables, the cheaper, and therefore the more realistic short-term alternative, is wind. In fact, Texas farmers in the drier areas have been using windmills to pump water for their livestock since the nineteenth century. Currently there are more than 2,000 large wind turbines in West Texas alone, as anyone who drives along Interstate Highway 10 between Van Horn and Ozona can attest. Texas leads all other states in wind-power generation capacity, and utilities are building new mills all the time.[52] Utilities are signing up to purchase electricity from wind turbines for a variety of reasons, including subsidies and mandates from both the federal and state governments, improved technology, and concerns about possible federal laws that would penalize the sorts of carbon emissions that are produced when burning fossil fuels.[53] Nevertheless, wind provides only about 1 percent of Texas's electrical generation power, and the projections are for that proportion to rise only very slowly over the next few years.[54]

Moreover, although the wind is free, operating a gigantic field of enormous spinning propellers exacts various kinds of costs. "Metal fatigue" tends to set in after a certain amount of time, so the rotors have to be frequently tested for weakness. If they do fail, they can split and be hurled away from the mill, crashing into other mills and creating damage that is expensive to repair. Further, windmills frequently have fatal consequences for birds migrating through the field of rapidly rotating propellers, a problem that will increase as the wind becomes more important as a source of power. Less obviously but just as stressful for wildlife, wind turbines situated offshore can disrupt the path of migrating fish.[55]

Solar power is the environmentalists' dream, the application of science that would directly harness sunlight to provide an energy source that is limitless and clean. But the technology to convert sunlight into electricity, while it has existed for decades and is steadily being improved, remains complicated and expensive.[56] The expense comes from the fact that while the sun's power

is direct and simple, the means to turn it into something usable by humans is labyrinthine. To generate enough power to make it worth a public utility's time and investment, either acres of land must be covered with photovoltaic cells that use chemicals to change sunlight into electric current (cells that themselves are the end product of a long manufacturing process that requires much energy input and several exotic minerals) or tens of thousands of specially fabricated mirrors must be precisely arranged so that they focus sunlight on a single point—a container in which water is boiled to turn turbines. In either case, the equipment must be constantly maintained. Dirty cells and mirrors do not function well, so they must be frequently polished.[57] It is also possible for individual homeowners to install solar-collecting equipment on their roofs, but again, the equipment is so expensive that it may take decades for the owners to save enough on the "free" availability of sunlight to make the whole transaction economical.[58]

Furthermore, wind and solar energy share the considerable disadvantage that the supply is highly capricious—the wind may not blow for days, and the sun does not shine at night or on cloudy days. Therefore, both utilities and homeowners must have backup energy-supply systems ready to kick in when the renewable source is not available. These systems, of course, add to the expense.

For those societies and individuals who are willing to pay more—sometimes much more—for a supply of clean power, renewables are an attractive choice. But for societies and individuals who are attempting to optimize the energy return on their investments, the large-scale utilization of power from wind and energy will be, for the foreseeable future, an unrealistic ambition.

Efficiency

The more efficient use of resources would seem to be a way to avoid having to choose among the various unpleasant alternatives offered by diverse energy options. The value of increasing efficiency is easy to understand for automobiles. A late-model car with a hybrid engine may deliver an average of 45 miles per gallon, whereas an aging SUV gas-guzzler might achieve only 15 mpg. The hybrid is therefore three times more efficient than the SUV, and will use one-third the gasoline if driven the same number of miles. Scholars have calculated that if all U.S. autos could be made to offer at least 35 mpg, the nation would save millions of barrels of imported oil each year, and each consumer would, after a certain number of years, save thousands of dollars on gasoline.[59] The same principle holds for every energy-using machine and appliance. More efficient refrigerators, more efficient light bulbs, more efficient air conditioners and heaters, and so forth, could save the nation enough energy to make the problems of environmental pollution, climate change, dependence on international supply, and potential meltdowns very much less severe than they are now.

Energy efficiency, however, is a desirable *end*. The problem lies in deciding what *means* to adopt to achieve the end. There are two basic options. In the first, governments, state or federal, could rely on pricing, usually through targeted taxes, to persuade consumers and investors to change their behavior. For decades, for example, some economists have recommended taxing gasoline at much higher rates, thus changing consumer behavior across a wide spectrum of American life. If gasoline cost six or eight dollars a gallon, this reasoning goes, consumers would get rid of their old gas-guzzling vehicles, buy more fuel-efficient

cars, make fewer and shorter trips to the store, support public-policy initiatives to construct public transportation instead of more highways, and so on. Similarly, if taxation would double or triple the cost of electricity, consumers would demand more efficient appliances and use those they already owned less. In fact, history has demonstrated that when international events have caused gasoline costs to spike, smaller, more-fuel-efficient cars have become more popular with consumers.[60] Thus, vast changes in public behavior, resulting in large reductions in the use of energy, could be achieved if governments were willing to tax energy use.

But both the moral and political objections to using tax policy to change mass behavior are formidable. Morally, the sorts of taxes that would discourage energy use are the types of levies—sales taxes—that are "regressive taxes" (see Chapter 12) that hit harder as people live farther down the income ladder. That is, hiking energy taxes would be hard on the middle class and very hard on the poor. (This principle, of course, applies equally to the problem of water supply. Higher utility taxes would induce people to use less water, but the wealth-drain would hit the poor most painfully.)

Politically, the fact is that people resent taxes, and resent gasoline taxes especially. Many public opinion surveys since 1973 have demonstrated that citizens in general vociferously oppose higher gasoline taxes, and are willing to punish any politician who supports them.[61] Therefore, while in economic theory higher gasoline and electricity taxes are the best strategy for creating an energy-efficient society, in political reality there is no immediate prospect that politicians who have to face the voters will ever institute such taxes as public policy.

The second possible strategy for making American, and Texan, society more energy-efficient would consist of various command-and-control policies, as well as sundry types of subsidies for doing what the government wants done. The federal government, for example, has mandated in its Corporate Average Fuel Efficiency (CAFE) policy the average number of miles per gallon, for each car company, that all the vehicles produced and sold in the United States must have. As of 2011, the standard was 27.5 mpg for automobiles, and 22.2 for light trucks, vans, and sports-utility vehicles.[62]

But there are serious problems with command-and-control policies, also. Suppose people resist acting in the ways the government is telling them to act; then what? Suppose, to continue the CAFE example, people do not buy the more fuel-efficient vehicles that would save the country many barrels of oil. What is the government to do? Should the government penalize car companies because consumers do not prefer the models the government wants them to prefer? Should the government penalize the consumers? If so, how? Such questions, if answered in the affirmative, would involve the government in a great deal of micro-managing of the economy, an activity that is certain to be unpopular with both business and consumers.

When such considerations are taken into account, the tendency of most politicians is to refuse to intervene to make companies and citizens behave in a way that uses energy more efficiently. But that neglect guarantees that the question of efficiency will be handled by the price system or not at all.

In practice, neglect has been the dominant—although not the only—strategy practiced by both U.S. and Texas politicians when faced with the challenge of making energy policy. As a result, the nation and the state have drifted toward greater and greater reliance on imported oil, and greater and greater emissions of greenhouse gases.

The Politics of Energy in Texas

Although the politics of energy in Texas is magnificently complicated, some themes stand out. The first is "Texas versus the federal government."

As our discussion of the fight between Texas politicians and the federal Environmental Protection Agency in Chapter 1 illustrated, there is at the present time a ferocious determination among Texans to handle the resources within their state in their own way. But this determination is not new. It is, in fact, almost a tradition for Texans to fight federal agencies over energy policy.

For example, from the 1930s to the 1950s there was a continuous, shrill controversy over control of oil drilling in the offshore areas of the several coasts of the United States.[63] The federal government, like the government of every other nation with a seacoast, claimed jurisdiction to grant drilling rights to petroleum companies, and collect royalty payments if oil was discovered, in the ocean waters along its shoreline. The states bordering the various oceans, however—California on the Pacific, Texas, Louisiana, and Florida on the Gulf, Virginia on the Atlantic—insisted that they had jurisdiction out three miles from land, or, in the case of Texas and Florida, the "historical boundaries" that reached ten miles from shore. At stake was the determination of which government would collect the possibly huge royalty checks if large oil fields were discovered within those underwater areas. When Republican Dwight Eisenhower ran for the presidency in 1952, he promised to back a national law that would grant jurisdiction over the Tidelands to the states. His pledge was one of the reasons that Texans broke with their traditional allegiance to the Democratic Party that year (see Chapter 4). After Eisenhower was elected, he honored his promise and backed the Submerged Lands Act, which gave Texas, among other coastal states, title to the oil rights within ten miles of land. Thus, the way Texas is skirmishing today with the federal government over regulation of air pollution is merely a continuation of a conflict with a long history, a conflict that is sure to continue in new forms into the future.

A second theme that is common in the politics of Texas energy is "pseudo laissez faire." As discussed in Chapters 1 and 4, the semiofficial conservative ideology of the majority of Texans exalts the unregulated marketplace and disdains government interference in business decisions. Yet many of the same conservative politicians who present themselves as small-government conservatives are happy to use tax money to subsidize and promote businesses they think are good for the state's economy.

For example, the state's subsidies and other encouragements for solar and wind power by electric utilities would not have been predicted by someone familiar with Texans' professed devotion to free-market, nongovernment policies. Indeed, Governor Perry is fond of repeating the philosophical position—this one from a speech on May 27, 2010—that "government's main job is to establish a positive climate for business development then get the heck out of the way so visionary leaders can do what they do best—generate innovative products and create jobs."[64] Yet Perry, perhaps surprisingly, has been a strong advocate of subsidizing renewable energy.

In 1999, when Perry was Lieutenant Governor, the legislature passed, and Governor George W. Bush signed, a law to encourage the development of renewable energy.[65] The law established a complicated but workable system of rules that mandated electric utilities to steadily increase the proportion of their energy production that comes from renewable sources. The rules were to be enforced by

the Electric Reliability Council of Texas (ERCOT). To compensate utilities for the expense of adding wind and solar capacity, the law, in effect, exempted the part of their business devoted to renewable energy from the state's franchise tax (Texas's version of the corporate income tax; see Chapter 12). By thus depriving itself of income to encourage business to do something it would not do in the free market, the state is indirectly subsidizing the building of wind and solar capacity by private industry. In 2005 and again in 2009, as Governor, Perry sponsored additional laws continuing and expanding the state's sponsorship of renewable power. As Perry's Web site put it in 2011, "The Governor has made diversifying the energy mix of Texas's electricity one of his major priorities, and renewable energy . . . plays a key role in that diversification."

In other words, the Governor and the state legislature, though dominated by people who call themselves conservatives, have engaged in making energy policy that, under other circumstances, they might very well denounce as "socialism," and label both un-American and un-Texan. True free-market conservatives, watching this exercise in pseudo laissez faire, have not been fooled. "The growth of windpower capacity in Texas is not the result of consumer choice and natural economics but mandates from the Texas legislature," complained Robert Bryce, a libertarian energy journalist, in 2009.[66] Exactly why such strong conservatives as Governor Perry and the members of the Texas legislature have been willing to contradict their own ideology is a question that has not been researched. Readers of this textbook might suspect that the answer could have something to do with the influence of utility corporation lobbyists. But there is no evidence either way, so the conclusion must be that the making of energy policy in Texas is a good deal more complicated and unpredictable than it may at first appear.

A third theme in Texas energy policy is the "politics of regulation and deregulation." That theme was much in the public's view after a serious cold snap in February 2011 caused a number of electricity-generating plants to fail.[67] ERCOT, which has the authority to direct electricity in a crisis, decreed that "rolling blackouts," in which various citizens around the state would be deprived of their power for six hours, would go into effect until the state's generating capacity was restored. Tens of thousands of homes therefore went dark and cold for part of a day, and one man in Houston evidently died when his oxygen machine shut off. The blackouts caused a citizen outcry, sparked investigation by the legislature, and brought up the question of whether ERCOT directly, and the state government indirectly, could have prevented the problem.

All public utilities function under some sort of government regulation. Normally, public regulators permit utilities to charge more to their customers than they would be able to charge if they were under competition in a free market. In return for being able to charge more, regulators require that utilities keep a good deal of backup capacity. That is, utilities must have bigger plants, and more plants, than they need most of the time, so that under unusual circumstances, when there is a spike in the demand for electricity, the utilities can meet the demand. Further, authorities prevent competition in the utilities market, forbidding consumers to "shop around" for power from utilities that can offer cheaper electricity because they have invested in less backup generating capacity. In effect, the public authorities allow utilities to charge monopoly prices in return for making them invest in a large amount of surplus generating capacity that will sit idle most of the time. This policy is in line with modern liberal ideology: because competition in a free market forces companies to focus on

short-run profits and neglect long-run potential problems, government must regulate in order to make everyone focus on the long-run public interest.

In 1999, however, Texas partially deregulated its public utilities. Government authorities no longer required utilities to keep a certain amount of backup capacity. Instead, they permitted consumers to shop around for service from electric utilities, and permitted the utilities to decide how much investment, if any, they would put into backup generating capacity. This policy, of course, unlike the policy of subsidizing renewable energy, is in line with conservative economic ideology: government should get out of the way and let companies decide about investments, and consumers decide about purchases, within the free market. Faced with a new regulatory environment, consumers began to switch their public utilities in search of lower rates, and utility companies began to shed their excess capacity, becoming smaller so that they could compete by offering lower rates to consumers.

When the unusually cold winter of 2011 caused Texans to turn up their electric heaters all over the state, then, utilities did not have enough spare generating capacity and the whole system threatened to crash. ERCOT therefore had to step in and decree the rolling blackouts.

The electricity supply problem of 2011 illustrates with unusual clarity the real-life consequences of ideological differences. Conservatives say that government should let free markets determine the supply and price of energy, and the result will be good for both business and consumers. Liberals say that only government regulation can ensure that long-run considerations, rather than the short-run pursuit of profit, enter into the investment calculations of business and the buying calculations of consumers. In Texas, conservative ideology and conservative policies are dominant. Therefore, Texans enjoy an unusual amount of freedom in their energy markets, but they are subject to occasional crises like the blackouts of 2011. When it comes to electricity supply, Texans have chosen liberty over security.

Protecting the Environment

To discuss the environment is to discuss energy, since the mining and burning of fossil fuels are among the most serious causes of environmental problems. But it is also to discuss transportation, because the purpose of much energy use is to permit automobiles and trucks to function. And it is to discuss water, because that liquid is one of the most important components of the human environment. Therefore, to focus on the environment, which is the subject of this section, is to engage in a certain amount of repetition.

NIMBY and YBNIIMP

As we have emphasized in this book, the United States, and each of its individual states, is a democracy, which means that The People are the source of legitimate authority. But democracy faces an ironic difficulty, because when it comes to energy policy, The People are sometimes part of the problem. Specifically, when queried about their views on energy in public opinion surveys, citizens often express contradictory and sometimes absurd attitudes toward the various possible policies that government could pursue. When it comes to energy, therefore,

governments cannot always give The People what they want, because what The People say they want does not make sense.

On the one hand, consistently, over several decades, at least two-thirds of Americans answer on the affirmative when they are asked if they consider themselves to be "environmentalists." Question number one in Table 14-2 illustrates the stability of citizens' positive attitude toward environmentalism. In addition, roughly nine-and-a-half million citizens belong to a pro-environment interest group such as the Sierra Club, Environmental Defense Fund, Friends of the Earth, Greenpeace, or any of the more specialized organizations.[68] It would seem, then, that there is a very strong base in public opinion for government policy to protect the environment.

TABLE 14-2

U.S. Public Opinion about Environmentalism, 2000–2010

1. Gallup Polls, 2000 and 2009:

   What is your relationship to the environmental movement?

	Active/Sympathetic	Neutral/Unsympathetic
2000	71%	28%
2009	70	28

2. Ipsos/McClatchy Poll, 2009:

   What if a cap-and-trade program [which would hopefully lower carbon emissions by industry] significantly lowered greenhouse gases but raised your monthly electrical bill by $25 a month?

Support	Oppose	Unsure
43%	55%	2%

3. ABC News/Washington Post/Stanford University Poll, 2007:

   For each of the following, please tell me whether you favor or oppose it as a way for the federal government to try to reduce future global warming.

	Favor	Oppose	Unsure
Increase taxes on electricity so people will use less of it.	20%	79%	1%
Increase taxes on gasoline so people either drive less or buy cars that use less gas.	32%	67%	0%

4. CNN/Opinion Research Corporation Poll, 2010:

   With which of these statements about the environment and the economy do you most agree? Protection of the environment should be given priority, even at the risk of economic growth. Or, economic growth should be given priority, even if the environment suffers to some extent.

Give Environment Priority	Give Economy Priority	Both	Unsure
45%	51%	3%	1%

NOTE: The response "Both" in question 4 was not in the prompt; it was volunteered.

SOURCES: Question number one from www.gallup.com/poll/27256/state-environmentalism-us.aspx; questions two, three, and four compiled at the Web site Pollingreport, www.pollingreport.com/enviro.htm.

On the other hand, the seemingly solid majority in favor of environmental protection melts away as soon as hypothetical policies are mentioned that might cause Americans to suffer inconvenience. As questions 2, 3, and 4 in Table 14-2 illustrate, majorities are only willing to support the idea of pro-environmental policies as long as those policies do not restrict economic growth or require them to pay higher taxes.

It would seem, therefore, that when it comes to environmental protection, there is a special case of the NIMBY syndrome. This one might be called the YBNIIMP syndrome, for "Yes, But Not If I Must Pay." Environmental protection policy must be made within the paradox that such policies are popular in general but will be unpopular if there are specific costs attached that citizens perceive as falling on themselves. The opinion poll results in Table 14-2 are for U.S. citizens. Given the historical hostility that Texans have shown to paying taxes, however, it is a safe bet that they also will show a variation of the YBNIIMP syndrome when asked to judge environmental policies.

Texas and Environmental Protection

Furthermore, that customary opposition to taxes has, historically, combined with various other aspects of Texas culture to make environmental protection an uphill climb. Texas's traditionalist-individualist culture, described in Chapter 1, places an emphasis on private, short-run exploitation of nature. Such legal doctrines as the Rule of Capture, described earlier in this chapter, officially reinforce the attitude that public interests should not interfere with private gain. The historical result has been that, well into the second half of the twentieth century, Texans were free to exploit and despoil their environment. As Tai Kreidler wrote in his recent survey of the relationship of Texans to their environment, "Hunting game to extinction occurred frequently. . . . The east Texas black bear . . . vanished from the landscape . . . herons and snowy egrets were nearly wiped out. . . . In the 1950s . . . 'indiscriminate clear cutting' [of forests began]. . . . After cutting the larger trees, lumber crews bulldozed the remainder, eliminating any possibility for old forest regrowth. . . . The expedient way in which the natural environment was used seemed to indicate that Texans believed the land and resources were inexhaustible."[69]

The awareness that resources are in fact limited, and that government action is needed to protect land, water, air, plants, and animals for the present and future public, advanced only slowly in Texas, and against grudging resistance. During the 1930s the Railroad Commission began to make rules to try to stop pollution of land and water, above- and below-ground, by the oil and gas industries. The state first put into place quality standards for municipal water systems in 1945. In 1951 the Department of Health performed the first air-quality study. Two years later the legislature created the Texas Water Pollution Advisory Council, the first state agency with the direct responsibility to deal with pollution. In 1993 the legislature combined a variety of programs and agencies charged with protecting the environment into the Texas Natural Resources Conservation Commission (TNRCC) and gave it general responsibility for managing air, water, and waste programs. In 2002 TNRCC was reorganized, given slightly different responsibilities, and had its name changed to the Texas Commission on Environmental Quality (TCEQ). Officially, therefore, Texas now recognizes the need to protect the environment, and has a set of government agencies with authority to enforce laws that advance their mission.

Distinctive but Not Unique

Although the laws creating Texas's environmental protection agencies are in many ways similar to those in other states, and those passed by the federal government, in one important way they are different. Texas is one of fifteen states that explicitly commands its environmental regulatory agencies to take economic trade-offs—that is, the cost of regulation—into account when regulating air, water, and waste pollution. As a result, those agencies' mission statements differ in tone from those of the other states and the national government. The Texas Commission on Environmental Quality mission statement, for example, tells the reader that the agency "strives to protect our state's human and natural resources consistent with sustainable economic development."

On the one hand, critics argue that such language encourages TCEQ and other state agencies to sacrifice environmental cleanliness when that goal comes into conflict with the need to make money. "What they think is better for the environment seems to be to do as little as possible," as one environmentalist put it. On the other hand, defenders of that sort of approach to environmental regulation argue that it is simply sensible government to take into account the costs of what one is doing. "Ignoring the cost of regulation is not good public policy," is the way one free-market advocate summarized the point of view.

Source: Asher Price, "Business Climate," *Austin American-Statesman*, April 3, 2011, D1.

Public Policy and Private Interests

Although Texas now has a set of laws and institutions charged with protecting the environment, a principle discussed in Chapter 1, *private influence over public policy*, is powerfully relevant to TCEQ, the Railroad Commission, the Parks and Wildlife Department, and the other such state administrative agencies. Through interest groups and personal contacts (Chapter 3), through campaign contributions and the party system (Chapter 4), and through indirect pressure exerted through legislators (Chapter 7), people who will make more money if the government does not interfere with their plans to exploit nature have a powerful incentive to try to corrupt the system. In addition, old-fashioned, pre-industrial legal doctrines such as the Rule of Capture often give private individuals an advantage over government servants trying to protect the public interest. These two tendencies do not always combine to thwart efforts to protect the environment. But modern environmental politics in Texas is always an ongoing struggle in which the environment is not necessarily the winner.

One of the ways that private interests routinely make it easy for themselves to influence public policy in Washington, D.C., has become so common that political scientists have given it an informal name: the "revolving door."[70] As we discussed in Chapter 3, the name refers to the practice of wealthy special interests hiring government regulators as executives or lobbyists once they have

finished their stint as members of the agency that is responsible for regulating that industry. Staff members, and the commissioners themselves, of the Federal Communications Commission who retire from the commission are often quickly hired by the National Association of Broadcasters, for example. When it comes to the federal government, the revolving door has been much investigated, and every few years studies become available relating what percentage of people who left a given set of government agencies are now working for the business they used to regulate. In state politics, however, scholars have not given a great deal of attention to the phenomenon. There are no statistics on how many regulators leave Texas agencies and are then immediately hired by the industry they used to oversee. The only thing available is a set of examples, such as the following.

Although there is no solution, as yet, to the problem of disposal of high-level nuclear waste, there is a storage site, in Andrews County in Texas (along the New Mexico border), that has been approved for storage of low-level waste. "Low-level" means less radioactive, and therefore less dangerous, and for fewer years. Low-level waste is still a threat to groundwater if it is handled carelessly, however. Therefore, the Dallas-based company that wanted to deposit it at the site, Waste Control Specialists, needed both a special law from the legislature and a permit from TCEQ. After years of lobbying and many dollars in campaign contributions, Waste Control Specialists received its law from the legislature in 2003. Its permit application then went to the Commission's technical staff in its Radioactive Materials Division. That division employs the engineers and geologists, supposedly insulated from political concerns, who are charged with determining whether the waste might be a threat to the environment.

Much to the consternation of Waste Control Specialists, and, apparently, the Commissioners, these scientists concluded that, in fact, the waste was a threat to the groundwater under the high plains. They recommended that the permit be denied. But in 2007, the Commissioners, ignoring the experts on their own staff, granted the permit anyway. Outraged at this apparent indifference to the public health and environmental interest, and insult to their professional integrity, three of the scientists resigned.

The legal department of TCEQ then sent around a memo to the remaining scientific employees, addressing the question of whether it was unethical for them to continue working on a project they considered to be an ecological threat. The legal department's answer: "No, it is not unethical for a TCEQ professional to work on an application that is not in their opinion protective of human health or the environment." And just in case there was any remaining doubt, the memo continued, "Insubordination is expressly prohibited."

At this point, the obvious question to ask is, why did the Commissioners disregard their own staff recommendation and grant the permit? A possible answer arrived a year and a half after the permit was granted. In the middle of 2008, TCEQ Executive Director Glenn Shankle retired from the agency. In early 2009, he accepted a job as a lobbyist for Waste Control Specialists, which was to pay him at least $100,000 a year.[71]

There is no way to know how much use of the "revolving door" enables private interests whose goals clash with the public interest to corrupt the functioning of the state agencies charged with protecting the Texas environment. All that can be said, on the basis of such examples as TCEQ, is that it does happen.

Alien Invaders!

Although some people might find them cute, feral hogs are very destructive and expensive for Texas farmers.

© Fred LaBounty/Alamy.

Protection of the environment is a government policy area with many different facets because it encompasses many different kinds of problems. One particular challenge in Texas is the prevalence of non-native species, many of which are harmful to native species. Typically, a plant or animal is brought to this country or this state by a person with a specific plan for it, but it escapes into the wild (although sometimes it is deliberately released). Afterward, because it is now free of the predators that kept its numbers in check in its native land or water, it multiplies at a fantastic rate and becomes a serious problem.

There is a large number of **invasive species** with which Texas government is trying to deal. Just one example from each category will give an idea of the problem.

Plants: Hydrilla (*Hydrilla verticullata* in scientific terminology) is a freshwater plant, native to the Old World, that was brought to Florida during the 1960s by a fish fancier for his aquarium, escaped into the natural water supply, and began to spread over the country. By the 1980s it was a problem in Texas lakes. It multiplies at a rapid rate, forming mats on the water surface that sometimes cover most of it extent, crowding out native plants and making human activities, such as boating and fishing, impossible. It has choked the surface of Caddo, Bastrop, and other lakes, and has become an expensive headache for local governments and the Department of Parks and Wildlife.

Insects: Fire ants (*Solenopsis invicta*) arrived in the United States at the port of Mobile, Alabama, from South America during the 1930s as stowaways on a cargo ship. They have since spread west to California and north until they have encountered seriously cold winters, which means that they have infested every county of Texas. They attack in hordes when their nest is disturbed, and bite painfully, leaving a sore that hurts and itches for days. They are so voracious that they have put many smaller ground-dwelling animals, such as the horned lizard (the state reptile) and quail, at risk of extinction. Ranchers spend many millions each year trying to protect their cattle, and especially the calves, from their ravages. The ants are also attracted to electric fields, so that they invade boxes of wiring, chewing through the insulation and causing the system to short out. As a result, they have become the leading cause of traffic-light failure in Texas.

Mammals: Feral hogs (*Sus scrofa*) are the descendants of domesticated Eurasion pigs that were brought to Mexico by the Spaniards in the sixteenth century, escaped into

(continued)

(continued)

the wild, and prospered. They have been in Texas since the 1680s. They are not related to Texas's native wild pig, the javelina or peccary (*Tayassu tajacu*). Feral hogs are large, intelligent, adaptive, prolific, and extremely destructive. They eat crops and tear up ground while rooting for tubers and insects, destroy fences, and spread disease. Because they breed so fast, killing almost all the hogs in a given area is not enough; they will soon repopulate the landscape. The state Department of Agriculture estimates that hogs cause more than $400 million worth of damage each year.

Birds: Several hundred European starlings (*Sturnus vulgaris*) were released in Central Park, New York City, in 1890 by the members of the American Acclimatization Society, in what now seems like a bizarrely wrongheaded plan to introduce all the birds mentioned in Shakespeare's works to the New World. (The Bard dropped this particular species into *Henry IV*, Part I). They now number somewhere in the neighborhood of 200 million on the continent, which means that there are millions in Texas. Starlings are a medium-sized bird, iridescent purple-green in summer and brown in winter. In Texas, they take over the homes of such cavity-nesting species as purple martins, bluebirds, and woodpeckers, expelling the occupants, thus placing stress on the native avian population.

Texas governmental agencies at all levels, and private individuals all over the state, are forced to spend time, money, and mental energy to deal with the ever-present threat of invasive species.

It is no consolation that Texas itself may have been the source of species that have invaded other places. For example, the prickly pear cactus (several species in the *Opuntia* genus), native to Texas and other parts of North America, is an invasive species in Australia, where it is considered a noxious weed. Authorities in the province of Queensland are fighting the prickly pear with herbicides and a moth whose larvae eat the plant, but the battle is not won and the costs are already considerable.

As world trade and tourism increase, it is likely that Texas authorities will find themselves dealing with more expensive campaigns against alien invaders.

SOURCES: Steve Campbell, "State on Rocky Ground in Fight against Non-Native Plants," *Austin American-Statesman*, January 22, 2011, B5; Mike Leggett, "Never-Ending Battle with Feral Hogs Takes to the Air," *Austin American-Statesman*, January 27, 2011, C3; Bill Bryson, *In a Sunburned Country* (New York: Broadway Books, 2001), 138; Web sites www.texasinvasives.org, www.scientificamerican.com, and www.agr.state.tx.us/, plus Wikipedia and personal experience.

The revolving door, however, is not the only force with which honest regulation must contend. Even if they don't hire former regulators, interest groups who make money by engaging in activities damaging to the Texas environment can still flex lobbying muscles that influence public policy.

For example, the state Agriculture Department and the Parks and Wildlife Department each keep a list of harmful invasive species (see the box entitled "Alien Invaders!"). The sale or ownership of any plant on the list is generally punishable as a misdemeanor. But the list does not include every non-native species, nor even every species that the two agencies consider a threat to the ecosystem. For some species, there is an economic demand, and the desire of some consumers for a pretty plant outweighs the judgment of scientists that the plant is harmful to the Texas environment.

A case in point is ligustrum (*Ligustrum japonica*), also known as privet, an evergreen shrub from Japan and Korea that is popular with some Texas gardeners because it is hardy, dense with foliage, fast-growing, and, to some people's taste, attractive.[72] Despite its desirable qualities, botanists say that ligustrum harms the environment by crowding out native plants, intercepting sunlight in the air so that natives cannot grow on the ground, thereby leaving the earth bare and subject to erosion after rains. The Lady Bird Johnson Wildlife Center has therefore identified this shrub as harmful to the state's ecosystem. The two state agencies charged with protecting the native ecosystem would like to place it on the "noxious invasive plant" list.

Nevertheless, ligustrum is not listed, and is unlikely to be. There is money to be made. Because some homeowner-gardeners like it, nurseries stock it, and it can be purchased at Home Depot and Lowe's. As a consequence, groups that speak for the interests of the people who sell ligustrum are actively influencing politicians to keep the state agencies charged with protecting the state's ecosystem from doing their job. "We want to make sure the general public knows that just because someone says it's invasive, they shouldn't not purchase it," Jim Reaves, director of legislative and regulator affairs for the Texas Nursery and Landscape Association told a reporter for the *Austin American-Statesman*. "We've got people in our industry who have been growing the plants for years and years."

During the 2010 election cycle, the landscape and nursery industry gave a total of $238,018 in campaign contributions to strategically placed politicians. The number-one recipient was Agriculture Commissioner Todd Staples, whose re-election organization was enriched by $63,000. Other elected officials who received money from the group are state Senators Glenn Hegar (R-Katy) and Troy Fraser (R-Abilene), who each received $2,000. (Fraser was chair of the Senate Committee on Natural Resources during the 2011 legislature.) Also accepting contributions were Representatives Don Haycock (R-Killeen), who garnered $1,000, and Yvonne Gonzalez-Toureilles (D-Atascosa), who accepted $2,000 (but failed in her bid for re-election anyway).

Once in office, politicians typically do not forget their contributors. In the 2005 legislature, for example, landscapers (who call themselves, ironically, "the green industry") supported successful efforts to prohibit cities and counties from barring the planting, sale, or distribution of such noxious or invasive plants as ligustrum. As in the past, so probably in the future: Most likely Texas government agencies will be able to get serious about eradicating only the invasive species that have no economic constituency.

The Problems Continue

Meanwhile, according to standards from the federal government, Texas is deficient in a number of measures of environmental health. As the map in Figure 14-1 illustrates, many of the state's urban counties, including those where Houston, Dallas, San Antonio, Austin, Fort Worth, El Paso, Beaumont–Port Arthur, and Texarkana are located, are classified as "nonattainment" or "near nonattainment areas" by the federal Environmental Protection Agency, meaning that their air contains too much of one or more of the pollutants the EPA measures. Thus, people living in those areas are breathing some or all of the following: ozone, carbon monoxide, nitrogen dioxide, sulfur dioxide, particulate matter, or lead.[73]

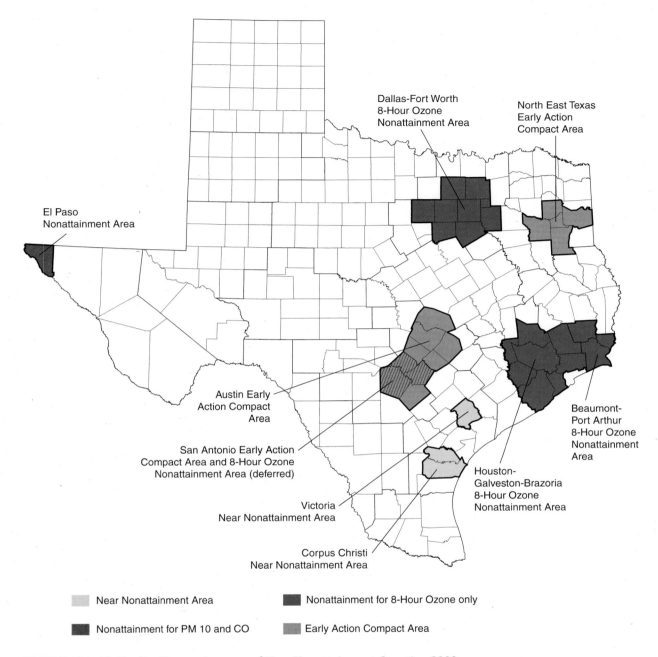

FIGURE 14-1 Air Quality Nonattainment and Near Nonattainment Counties, 2009

SOURCE: © *2002–2011 Texas Commission on Environmental Quality.*

The news is not much better for water. Although Texas does not seem to have the dirtiest rivers in the country—Indiana has achieved that dubious distinction—or the single filthiest waterway—the Ohio River wins the anti-prize—it still experiences enough pollution to place it fourth among the states in total volume of toxic discharges. And individual state waterways rank among

the most polluted in the country. The Houston ship channel, although it is only fifty miles long, ranks fifteenth among American waterways for such discharges—almost three million pounds of various contaminants in 2007. The Brazos River, which runs through Abilene, Waco, and College Station, ranks first among all rivers for receiving discharges of lead, fourth for release of reproductive toxicants (which cause adverse effects on the male and female reproductive system), thirteenth for discharges of cancer-causing chemicals, and fourteenth for releases of developmental toxicants (which damage fetuses and young children). The Sabine River, which forms part of the boundary between Texas and Louisiana, places eleventh for developmental toxicants and ninth for reproductive toxicants.[74]

Within the maneuvering and arguing of institutions, interest groups, ideologies, media, activists, and wealthy individuals, Texas politicians deal with threats to air, water, land, and the environment in general. During the 2011 legislature, a variety of proposals were on the table.

One that passed was a bill to require energy companies to post, on a Web site (www.FracFocus.org), the chemicals that they inject underground when fracking rock to produce natural gas. The bill had been considerably weakened from the one desired by environmentalist groups (for one thing, it exempted chemicals that the companies considered to be "trade secrets'), and it was given to the industry-friendly Railroad Commission to be implemented, which introduced many opportunities for further weakening. Still, it provided public interest groups with the potential for gathering useful information and spotting threats to the public's health.[75]

A measure that failed to pass was the combination of two bills that were intended to create funding for the state water plan. If the bills had been enacted, as many as twenty-six new above-ground reservoirs might have been constructed, costing as much as $27 billion. But the state's desperate budget situation doomed all such large, expensive projects, and implementation of the water plan was put on the shelf until the next legislative session.[76] Two other measures that became victims of the legislature's short session time and preoccupation with the budget were the "Sunset" bills (see Chapter 8) for the Public Utility Commission and the Railroad Commission. Both agencies were to be re-reviewed in the two years between legislative sessions, and brought up for scrutiny again in 2013.[77]

In Case the Bluegills Are Blue

The media frequently report strange and dangerous items found in waterways, including everything from industrial chemicals to birth control pills. In 2004, a Baylor University scientist found concentrations of Prozac, a medicine used to treat clinical depression, in bluegills, a type of fish living in Dallas's Pecan Creek near a water treatment plant.

Source: "Fish Pharm Redux," *Fly Rod & Reel*, March 2004, 14.

LONE STAR MEDIA
Exposé or Propaganda?

The subjects of energy supply and environmental protection come together in the process of drilling for natural gas. Although gas is considered one of the "cleaner" sources of power because it gives off fewer pollutants than coal or oil when burned, the process of producing it is by no means sanitary. In recent decades, as companies have learned how to engage in "hydraulic fracturing"—"fracking" in industry lingo—they have opened up vast numbers of reservoirs that were previously unproduceable because their geology was "tight." In a tight formation, there are no passageways between the millions of small chambers containing gas, so it will not flow to a well bore. In the fracking process, water mixed with various chemicals is forced down the well and out into the formation, where it shatters the rock, opening up many tiny passageways through which the gas flows. Fracking has opened up bonanzas of natural gas in the Marcellus Shale of Pennsylvania and the Barnett Shale of Texas, among other locations.

But the boom in natural gas drilling has not escaped accusations of environmental degradation. In particular, a documentary film entitled *Gasland*, made by Josh Fox and released in 2010, has garnered a great deal of publicity and brought up the questions: Is this film an honest depiction of greedy companies and compliant politicians victimizing helpless citizens, producing a mother lode of gas while poisoning land and water—or is it a deceptive bit of media manipulation, using fraudulent "facts" and unfair insinuations? Is it dramatic visual journalism or shameless propaganda? The controversy over the nature of *Gasland* especially has centered on its most dramatic scene, in which a resident in a gas-drilling area turns on the tap to let water run into his kitchen sink, and then lights the water on fire. Could fracking be so polluting that it renders water flammable? The documentary also makes other, only-slightly-less-frightening allegations, such as that the chemicals that the frackers inject underground are toxic to humans and other creatures.

The film had already won a number of awards, including a Special Jury Prize at the Sundance Film Festival in early 2011, when it was nominated for an Academy Award in the "Best Documentary" category. Apparently feeling that the dangers of giving extra publicity to the film were less than the dangers of allowing its accusations to go unchallenged, Lee Fuller, executive director of an industry-sponsored group named Energy in Depth, wrote a letter to the Academy, asking that it be withdrawn from consideration for the Oscar. Charging that the film was an "expression of stylized fiction" with "errors, inconsistencies and outright falsehoods," Fuller asked the Academy to take "remedial action"—in other words, to withdraw the documentary from Oscar consideration.

The Academy refused the request to disqualify *Gasland*, but in the end the Oscar went to another documentary, *Inside Job*, about the great banking crash of 2008. There is no way to tell, of course, if the gas industry's efforts had an effect on the outcome.

To see scenes from *Gasland*, log onto YouTube. To order the film or to learn about the controversy, simply type its name into a search engine. To access a highly critical article on a Web site sponsored by America's Natural Gas Alliance, "The Truth About 'Gasland,'" go to http://anga.us/learn-the-facts/the-truth-about-gasland.

SOURCES: Michael Rubinkam, "Industry Tried to Get 'Gasland' Disqualified," *Denton Record Chronicle*, February 26, 2011, A4; and the above-named Web sites.

Transportation

It may seem odd that transportation is included in a discussion of resources, because the action of moving something or somebody from one place to another may seem like a different topic than the power used to do the moving. But transportation, like communication, is an activity that humans use to further their economy, and is therefore a resource. Furthermore, like water, energy, and the environment, transportation is not just a personal subject, but is at least partly governed by public policy.

Moreover, transportation as a topic partially overlaps with both energy and environment, because it consumes energy and produces pollutants. To discuss it, therefore, once again requires some duplication with earlier sections of this chapter.

From the beginning of civilization, the most common form of transportation above mere human or animal muscle-power was to move a cart or box on wheels over some kind of road. From early in the twentieth century, the most popular form of transportation in the United States, and certainly in Texas, was to power the "box" with an internal combustion engine, a machine known as an automobile.

Texas is still an area in which most of the transporting is done with a box powered by an internal combustion engine, although some of those machines are now called trucks, sports-utility vehicles, pickups, and other, more exotic names. Such vehicles have the great appeal that they allow individual people to go where they please on their own schedule. Partly because of the freedom and romance this sort of transportation evokes, and partly because a huge complex of industries has grown up that is dependent upon a continuation of national driving habits, the momentum of our transportation choices of the past is very great today.

The Costs of the Internal Combustion Engine

Nevertheless, for some time now automobile transportation has been seen to have very great costs that were not obvious when it became part of the national culture. For most of the last century, cars and trucks killed more than 40,000 Americans each year on the highways, about 6.5 million in all. Only in the last few years has the combination of seat belts, air bags (both of them mandated by the federal government), and tough anti-drunk-driving laws begun to bring the death toll down to the still-horrendous total of 32,708 in 2010. Over and above the deaths, all the accidents suffered on American roads since 1900 have been estimated to have cost the nation about $230 billion. In Texas in 2009, there were 59,164 road accidents and 3,089 deaths. Not a single day of the year went by without at least one Texan dying in an accident on the state's roads.[78]

But the direct costs of car culture are only the most measurable of the problems created by the internal combustion engine. There are many indirect consequences that are extremely expensive, although hard to measure. Texas has 79,696 miles of pavement, from interstate highways to park roads, and that number does not include the amount of asphalt in parking lots, because no one keeps track of that number.[79] Each square foot of pavement is one square foot into which rain cannot soak, and on which vegetation cannot grow. The more paved roads, therefore, the less surface area for water to enter and replenish

Automobiles have always symbolized personal freedom to Americans in general and Texans in particular. When they become too numerous and concentrated, however, they stop being the servants of people, and become their masters. When that happens, they can become the symbol of servitude rather than of freedom.

Courtesy of Ben Sargent.

aquifers and springs, and the less room for plants to clean the air. Furthermore, the air needs cleaning, because the more than 20 million vehicles in Texas spew out roughly 200 million tons of carbon dioxide each year, plus huge amounts of other noxious gases.[80]

The pollution, of course, tends to be concentrated in the cities, rather than spread evenly over the state. During the 1990s scientists working for the Natural Resources Defense Council calculated the number of cardiopulmonary deaths attributable to a particular kind of air pollution in each Texas city per 100,000 population. Bringing each estimate up to date, and disregarding, for the sake of simplicity, other kinds of air pollution deaths, it is possible to make a very rough estimate of how many residents in each city were killed in 2010 by the air they had been breathing.[81] The results are thus:

Amarillo: 15
Corpus Christi: 126
Dallas: 328
El Paso: 182
Houston: 672
Laredo: 74
San Antonio: 306
Wichita Falls: 36

Not all these deaths, of course, were directly caused by automobile exhaust. Some percentage of the pollution inhaled by the unfortunate victims in each city was the result of industrial pollution. It is impossible to disentangle the contribution to any individual death by one cause or another. Nevertheless, these figures indicate in a very general way the important fact that Texans are being killed by air pollution, much of which is caused by tailpipe gases.

On top of this pollution is the fact that vehicle exhaust is a major cause of global warming. Put starkly, the internal combustion engine is both killing individual Texans and altering the climate of the planet.

Added to these serious problems are the costs of traffic congestion. In 2010 the Texas Transportation Institute estimated that Houston had the fourth-worst congestion problem in the country (behind Chicago, Washington, D.C., and Los Angeles). According to the Institute's calculations, the typical Houston commuter had been delayed 58 hours by traffic jams in 2009, which caused him or her to waste 52 gallons of gasoline and spend an extra $1,322 in fuel and lost time. Dallas–Ft. Worth–Arlington was the sixth-worst among very large cities (48 hours, 38 gallons, and $1,077), while Austin was fifth among large cities (39, 32, and $882). San Antonio had been comparatively easy to get around in, ranking only seventeenth among large cities, but even there the average commuter had spent 30 hours waiting, burned 28 extra gallons of fuel, and spent $663 unnecessarily.[82]

In short, reliance on the internal combustion engine to move millions of people imposes steep costs on society and the environment. For this reason, concerned citizens and government officials have for some time been looking for ways to either create a different means of transportation or mitigate the costs associated with the automobile.

Which Way Transportation Policy?

At all levels of government, policymakers have a choice between three basic strategies for addressing transportation issues. They can build more roads, force cars to become cleaner and safer, or make available alternative forms of transportation.

No matter which strategy government officials, activist citizens, and transportation scholars prefer, they are certain to come up against the YBNIIMP syndrome. All potential strategies cost money. Citizens want solutions to transportation difficulties, but they do not want to pay for them.

Strategy Number One: Build More Roads

Anticipating what was obviously the wave of the future, in 1917 the legislature created the Texas Highway Department to pave, build, and maintain the state's roads.[83] It also set the state's vehicular speed limit at 25 miles per hour and, in 1923, authorized its first gasoline tax, one cent a gallon. The agency would be reorganized and renamed several times, and both the speed limit and gas tax raised repeatedly. It is now known as the Texas Department of Transportation, or TxDOT, the speed limit is now 80 mph on some country highways, and the gas tax is now twenty cents a gallon. But the politics of transportation have not changed much in nine decades.

As its original name suggests, the mind-set at TxDOT has always been to build roads. The people at the agency have traditionally tended to think in terms of accommodating the needs of the internal combustion engine. As journalist Griffin Smith wrote in his critique of the Highway Department mentality in 1974, the training of the agency's employees, and their socialization within its organizational culture, "have given Texas an established Highway Department bureaucracy of transportation professionals who think only roads . . . [whose] outlooks are routinely predisposed to favor highway transportation over rail mass transit and other modes." Further, since 1917 there has been a complex

of interest groups in place—oil companies, cement-asphalt-and-tire dealers, bus and truck companies, road-building contractors, among others—who have had economic interests in building more roads, and who have organized and lobbied the legislature in favor of using state money for roads as opposed to other forms of transportation. Finally, there has been, as Smith put it, "the postwar (meaning after World War II) infatuation of Texans themselves with the private automobile—a passion for individual mobility that scarred most forms of 'public transportation' with a vulgar social stigma."

Even though various public interest group spokespeople and policy scholars, as far back as the 1960s, were urging that public money be spent to try to move Texans in the faster, cleaner forms of transportation—high-speed trains, subways, monorails, and so on—that were in use in cities of the American Northeast and other countries in Europe and Asia, the state's mind-set was resolutely oriented toward the internal combustion engine. It was not until the 1980s that some Texas politicians, especially the mayors of large cities, began to think in a serious way about the need to provide alternate means of getting their constituents to work.

Gasoline taxes have traditionally paid for new roads in Texas. But in recent decades such taxes have proven inadequate to finance the repairing of all the state's highways and the building of new ones. Further, federal funds for such purposes are falling victim to the national government's budget problems. The logical solution to the problem of building more roads with less available tax money is to build toll roads, raising money to finance road-building bonds by making motorists pay to use the highways. But it turns out that Texans detest the idea of traveling on pay-as-you-drive roads almost as much as they dislike the idea of paying taxes. Nevertheless, with gasoline tax revenue stagnant, a variety of interests and arguments have been backing the construction of toll roads, and slowly, against loud opposition, the state has been building them. As of 2011, there were 87 miles of such roads functioning in Texas, with ongoing planning for more.[84]

The conflict created by the felt need of some people and interests to build more roads colliding with the determination of many Texans neither to pay higher taxes nor to pay road tolls is illustrated by the massive debacle of the Trans-Texas Corridor (TTC) during the first decade of the twenty-first century.[85] In 2002, Governor Rick Perry unveiled his plan to build 4,000 miles of multiuse highways across Texas from the Mexican border into neighboring states of the north and east. The feasibility of the plan was based on a complicated set of new laws, including changes to the state's power of "eminent domain" (the authority to take private land for public purposes) and power to borrow money through bonds, which had been approved by a tiny percentage of the public in a referendum in 2001. Another enabling amendment was approved in 2003 by a similarly modest slice of the public. To build the highways, the state would have had to take over about 584,000 acres—900 square miles—of mostly rural property for rights-of-way. Perry had already lined up a number of foreign corporations—from Spain and Australia—to construct the roads. The price tag would have been somewhere in the neighborhood of $200 billion, and would have been paid, ultimately, by tolls on drivers using the roads. The state's Department of Transportation, under a Commission of Perry appointees, was to administer the whole giant scheme.

Nevertheless, although plans for the Trans-Texas Corridor were well along by the time its reality hit the consciousness of ordinary Texans, the deal was still

not quite done. And as the public realized that a large amount of farmland was going to be seized and paved, that millions of Texans were going to be paying tolls and paying off bonds for decades, and that the politicians had tried to sneak the deal under their radar, the state's citizens exploded with rage. Phrases such as "The Toll Road to Serfdom," "The Great Texas Land Grab," and "Highway Hucksters" quickly became part of ordinary conversation. Grassroots anti-TTC organizations sprang up combining, in their infuriated membership, anticorporate liberals with pro-private-property conservatives. Activists of both major political parties discovered that the only thing they had in common was a hatred of the TTC.

Politicians began to run for cover. In early 2009, TxDOT's executive director Amadeo Saenz declared that the agency would take no further action on the TTC. In July 2010, the Federal Highway Administration issued a "no action" decision on the plan, thus formally killing the project.

Strangely enough, neither Governor Perry nor any other elected politician paid a price for sponsoring the Trans-Texas Corridor. Instead, public and political wrath turned on TxDOT. The 2008 sunset report on the agency (see Chapter 8) stated that "An obvious distrust characterizes the legislature's and the public's recent relations with the Department" and suggested that it might be abolished. Instead, the legislature ordered another, special sunset review in four years.

The particular conflict over the Trans-Texas Corridor might be over. But the desire of many Texas interests to build more roads, and the desire of many Texans citizens not to pay taxes or tolls, will continue.

Strategy Number Two: Make Cars Cleaner and Safer

The federal government has been the leader in making vehicles both cleaner and safer. In terms of cleaning the air, Congress passed a law in 1975 mandating that all cars and light trucks must have a certain Corporate Average Fuel Economy (CAFE). That is, the average miles per gallon of all vehicles of a given type sold by the company must be above a certain floor. At the present time, the CAFE rule for automobiles is 27.5 mpg, and for light trucks, 22.2.[86] In terms of safety, in 1977 the Department of Transportation issued a rule that by 1983 all vehicles sold must feature seat belts. Similarly, air bags were made mandatory in 1994.[87]

A few states, notably California, have made independent efforts to provide that all the vehicles sold within their borders are as pollution-free as is practical. In 1990 California passed the first of what has come to be known as its "Clean Cars" laws. Together, these laws provide rebates to consumers who purchase low-emission vehicles, impose various penalties on cars that are heavy emitters of global-warming gases, and provide a variety of other incentives (such as specially designated parking spaces) for cleaner vehicles. As of 2011, Arizona, Connecticut, Maine, Maryland, Massachusetts, New Hampshire, New Jersey, New Mexico, New York, Oregon, Pennsylvania, Rhode Island, Vermont, and Washington have followed California in adopting some or all of its Clean Car policies. In regard to safety, most states impose mandatory seat-belt-wearing laws on drivers and passengers, and all have adopted some kind of rules to discourage drunk driving.[88]

Texas has not been at the forefront of efforts to make cars cleaner and safer. The state is one of about thirty that requires its motorists to get their vehicles inspected once a year. Like most other states, it has laws mandating seat-belt use and punishing drunk driving.[89] But it does nothing bold or imaginative to deal with any of the costs associated with the automobile. It is no California.

A Technological Fix?

For decades, the fantasy of everyone who worries about the filthy nature of automotive exhaust has been a car that produces no noxious emissions. The only even slightly practical way to realize such a dream is to build a vehicle that runs on electric power from a battery, one that is so useful yet cheap that consumers will want to buy it. Although such cars would not be "zero emissions" in the large sense—because the manufacture of the vehicle itself and its battery require power, which must come from a utility that probably burns fossil fuel, and because the electricity to recharge the battery also must originate in a utility—on overall balance, such cars would be much cleaner than the vehicles with internal combustion engines that they would replace.

For many years, practical electric vehicles, an ideal sought by both independent inventors and huge car companies during much of the twentieth century, tended to have a fatal drawback. They could not travel very far—generally about 40 miles—without needing to be recharged. Because commuters were leery about trusting their trip to and from work each day to a vehicle that might well run out of juice on the way home, none of these cars appealed to consumers.

In 2010, however, the Chevrolet Volt and the Nissan Leaf came onto the market. According to the information put out by the companies, the Leaf will get about 100 miles on a single battery charge. The Volt's battery will only provide enough power to send it 40 miles, but the Volt features a backup gasoline engine to fuel the car to the next charging station. These features are evidently enough to allay the fears of consumers, and both cars have stirred great interest. Encouraged by many federal government incentives—including a $7,500 tax credit and a $3,000 home-charging unit—about 20,000 Americans, and 1,000 Texans, reserved cars from the first year's run of production.

The arrival of the Volt and Leaf will not automatically solve the problem of automobile pollution. Among other potential problems, the nation still has to build an infrastructure of charging stations comparable to the net of gas stations it has now. Furthermore, the vehicles are expensive for small cars. The Volt, for example, will cost $32,780 after the tax credits. According to one set of calculations, if gasoline averages $3 per gallon, a Volt owner would have to drive the car for 32 years to break even on the cost, and 13 years if the price of gas rose to $5 a gallon. Pro-electric advocates hope that the price of the vehicles will come down with time, as consumers buy them and the technology evolves, but that development is not guaranteed.

Nevertheless, the fact that these vehicles are available, and that at least some governments are supporting their use, gives hope that part of the downside of the automobile may be eliminated through the mechanism of the market, without government having to annoy citizens with coercive rules.

Sources: "With Nissan Leaf, Perks Keep Coming," *Austin American-Statesman,* October 23, 2010, E1; Brian Sloboda and Andrew Cotter, "Driveway Revolution," *Colorado Country Life,* March 2011, 14; "No Fueling: All-Electric Vehicle Now Hums Along Austin Streets," *Austin American-Statesman,* March 25, 2011, B7.

Strategy Number Three: Create Alternatives to Transportation by Automobile, and Persuade People to Use Them

In 1993 one group of scholars calculated that, under moderate assumptions of population growth, by 2020 each Lone Star motorist would have to reduce his or her driving by 37.5 percent in order to avoid worsening the already unclean air in the state's cities.[90] Nothing that has happened since 1993 has tended to make the prediction seem inaccurate. The prospect of seeing the air above the state's large cities become unbreathable has so alarmed their leaders that for some time they have been trying to find alternatives to the automobile. The most popular alternative is rail travel.

There are two types of rail transportation under discussion, high-speed heavy-rail between cities, and light-rail within cities. Here we will discuss only one, the within-city alternative. **Light-rail metropolitan transit**—in which commuters get to work via subway, monorail, streetcars, or some other variation on the theme—is popular with urban planners partly because of studies that conclude that one person riding light-rails instead of driving a car for one year reduces hydrocarbon emissions by 9 pounds, nitrogen oxide emissions by 5 pounds, and carbon monoxide emissions by 62.5 pounds.[91] Light-rail also holds out the promise of lessening traffic congestion, relieving the city administration of supplying more parking downtown, and being more helpful than a bus system to poor citizens who do not own a car, although these expectations are controversial. But the promise of the alternate form of mass transit is so appealing that many city leaders have loaned their money and prestige to efforts to persuade Texans, notorious for their love of automobiles and pickups, to support the construction of light-rail systems.

Progress has been slow, however, and not always satisfactory. The Dallas Area Rapid Transit (DART) authority began operating the first light-rail system in the American Southwest in 1996. Houston's MetroRail began running the first, eight-mile leg of its system in 2004. In 2009, Austin Capital Metro began offering commuter train service between the small town of Leander and the city's downtown convention center on a route that had the cost-saving virtue of running on an existing thirty-two-mile freight line. Other Texas cities—San Antonio, for example—have not opted for light-rail, relying instead on improved bus service. All the light-rail systems have experienced problems with cost overruns, lower-than-projected ridership, management blunders, and a variety of other disappointments.[92]

Public transportation advocates argue that the problems are just growing pains, and that the kinks will be ironed out as time and experience progress. But many other observers differ, arguing that mass transit is inherently unsuited to the Lone Star State's cities.

Houston's light-rail system can be seen as an example of the problems common to all such transportation efforts in Southern and Western cities, which typically, having grown up with the automobile, have very low densities. In the older, pre-auto-age cities such as those in the Northeast and Europe, any mass transit system is within the reach of very many potential riders per mile. In Houston, however, the city is so spread out, with people and buildings so far apart, that there are many fewer potential riders per mile. For example, New York City is almost exactly half as large, geographically, as Houston (305 square miles to 602), but contains almost four times as many

Advocates of light-rail transit, such as this one in Houston, hope that Texans can be persuaded to leave their cars at home and "take the train" to work.

© Stephen Finn/Alamy.

people (8.2 million to 2.1 million). In New York, therefore, there are eight times as many potential riders per square mile as there are in Houston. Since a new mile of track, and a new station, cost roughly the same in both cities, it is inevitable that Houston can expect fewer riders, and therefore fewer dollars in fares, per mile.

All urban transit systems run at a financial loss, and must be subsidized by tax money. But Houston's transit deficit must be systematically much greater than New York's. Yet the Bayou City is in tax-averse Texas, so its prospects of help from the state government are much worse than those of the Big Apple. It therefore faces a much more daunting funding situation.

Given this difficult fiscal reality, Houston's city leaders apparently decided that they had to cut corners. Whereas most light-rail systems avoid running on city streets (using monorails, subways, or tracks that in other ways somehow stay out of the way of vehicular traffic), Houston's politicians endorsed a plan that would run the trains down the already-congested avenues and boulevards. The result should have been foreseen, but wasn't. During the first test month before the line was opened to commuters in 2004, MetroRail trains collided with five passenger cars. The first year there were 62 accidents. Between 2004 and 2010, there were a total of 313 collisions between trains and automobiles or trucks. Houstonians took to mocking MetroRail with the nicknames "A Streetcar Named Disaster" (after a famous play by Tennessee Williams, *A Streetcar Named Desire*) and "Wham-Bam-Tram." MetroRail leaders blamed the auto drivers for these accidents, accusing them of running red lights or failing to look before turning left.[93] No doubt these observations were accurate, but they were also beside the point. The cheap design of the system, from the beginning, ensured that the trains would be frequently crashing into cars. Moreover, even in the absence of accidents, the presence of additional large metal machines moving among and alongside automobiles has only increased congestion on the city's streets.

The fact that Houston's transit leaders were not unusually foolish in trying to skimp on the financing of their system was made obvious in Austin in 2011. City leaders, very much wanting to extend light-rail over the downtown area

and to the airport, but apparently intimidated by the potential cost, unveiled a plan that reproduced Houston's fundamentally flawed strategy. They announced a new system in which almost half of the 16.5-mile route would run in the middle of surface streets—an even higher percentage than the light-rail system in Houston.[94]

Trying to escape from the tyranny of the automobile, yet fated to work within the low-density of Texas cities, proponents of light-rail systems have apparently adopted the philosophy expressed in an iconic line from the 1989 movie *Field of Dreams:* "Build it, and they will come."[95] Pro-rail advocates argue that once fully functioning, efficient, cheap mass transit systems are in place, urban Texans will change their commuting habits in the short run, and their living habits in the long run. As citizen behavior evolves, Texas cities will become denser, which will make for more financially viable public transit, which will lead to better service, which will cause still more modifications of citizen behavior, and so on in a virtuous spiral. Whether such a vision is a realistic blueprint for the future of Texas cities, or whether it is as much a fantasy as the movie that spawned its slogan, is a question to be considered in additional editions of this textbook.

Summary

In this chapter we continued the discussion of public policy in Texas that we began in Chapter 13. We examined the policy choices available to Texas government, and the way its political system is already dealing with some of them, in regard to water supply, energy supply, protection of the environment, and transportation.

The first subject was water supply. Our major theme in this section was the growing conflict between the static amount of water available for human use and the rising Texas population. We examined three conflicts over Texas water likely to be especially important in the future: urban dwellers versus farmers, the environment versus development, and source areas versus destination areas in relation to the issue of interbasin transfers.

The next subject was energy supply. Our major theme in this section was the lack of a perfect energy-supply choice against a backdrop of difficult, and sometimes painful trade-offs among factors like price, safety, volume of supply, availability of infrastructure, strategic security, and environmental impact. Expanding on the theme of difficult trade-offs, we looked briefly at the possibility of Texans using oil, natural gas, coal, nuclear power, wind, solar, and conservation as their "energy source of the future." We also discussed a few of the recent decisions made within the Texas political system on these issues.

We then turned to the subject of environmental protection. Our major theme in this section was the long-term conflict between the state's cultural tendency to emphasize economic development rather than environmental protection, and the more recent desire of many Texans to preserve and enhance the state's ecosystem. With that conflict as a backdrop, we explored some recent environmental issues and the way they have been handled by the state's political institutions.

Transportation was the final subject. Our major theme in this section was the various policy strategies that the state could follow when dealing with problems created by Texans' historical reliance on the internal combustion engine. We identified, and expanded upon, three possible strategies for addressing the issue: build more

roads, make cars cleaner and safer, and create alternatives to the automobile, then persuade people to use them. While examining these strategies, we discussed some examples of how the state's political system has dealt with transportation problems in the past and how it is addressing them in the present.

Glossary Terms

acre-foot

estuary

Faustian bargain

fracking

greenhouse effect

hundredth meridian

invasive species

light-rail metropolitan transit

Rule of Capture

Texas Commission on Environmental Quality (TCEQ)

CHAPTER 1

1. Much of this account draws on material in *The Texas Almanac 1964–1965* (Dallas: A. H. Belo, 1963), 35–54; *The Texas Almanac 1986–1987* (Dallas: A. H. Belo, 1985), 163–224; *The Texas Almanac 1992–1993* (Dallas: A. H. Belo, 1991), 27–54; and other footnoted material.

2. Alwyn Barr, *Black Texans: A History of African Americans in Texas 1528–1995* (Norman: University of Oklahoma Press, 1996), 17.

3. David Montejano, *Anglos and Mexicans in the Making of Texas 1836–1986* (Austin: University of Texas Press, 1986), 54, 58; Louis L'Amour, *North to the Rails* (New York: Bantam Books, 1971).

4. Jonathan W. Singer, *Broken Trusts: The Texas Attorney General versus the Oil Industry, 1889–1909* (College Station: Texas A&M, 2002), 5.

5. Barr, *Black Texans,* op. cit., 134–135; Montejano, *Anglos and Mexicans,* op. cit., 143–144.

6. "Texas a Net Loser from Falling Oil Prices, Economist Reports," *Energy Studies,* vol. 11, no. 5 (May/June 1986), 1 (newsletter of the Center for Energy Studies at the University of Texas at Austin).

7. Robbie Morganfield, "Texas Passes NY," *Houston Chronicle,* December 28, 1994, 1A.

8. Calculated from tables on page 14 of *Crime in Texas 1992* (Austin: Texas Department of Public Safety, 1993).

9. Duwadi Megh, "Study: No. 2 'Cyberstate' Texas Lost the Most Jobs in Tech Bust," *Austin American-Statesman,* June 26, 2002, D1.

10. "Ike's Insurance Bill Is Highest in State History," *San Antonio Express-News,* January 31, 2010, B6.

11. David Shieh, "Major Storm on Coast Could Have Big Financial Impact Statewide," *Austin American-Statesman,* June 16, 2008, A1; Kelley Shannon, "Texas's Ike Insurance Tab Rising Rapidly," *Austin American-Statesman,* September 25, 2008, D1; Char Miller, "Ike's Wake," *Texas Observer,* October 3, 2008, 11.

12. Asher Price, "Hurricane Alters Debate on Coastal Construction," *Austin American-Statesman,* September 23, 2008, A1.

13. Meghan Ashford-Grooms, "Texas's Jobless Rate Outpaced Nation's in 18-Month Period," *Austin American-Statesman,* October 7, 2010, B1.

14. The information in this discussion comes from the following sources, all in the *Austin American-Statesman*: Ramit Plushnick-Masti, "Perry to Obama: Halt EPA Takeover," May 29, 2010, B1; Asher Price, "EPA Re-Airs 1990s Debate," May 31, 2010, A1; Asher Price, "Abbott Files Legal Challenge to EPA Pollution Decision," June 15, 2010, B1; Ramit Plushnick-Masti, "EPA Voids 16-Year-Old Air Permit Program," July 1, 2010, A1.

15. Information in the following account comes from Michael Graczyk, "Parole Board Refuses to Stop Man's Execution," *Austin American-Statesman,* August 14, 2002, B6; Susan Ferriss, "Execution Leads Fox to Scrap Trip," *Austin American-Statesman,* August 15, 2002, A1; Toby Sterling, "World Court: U.S. Must Stay 3 Executions," *Austin American-Statesman,* February 6, 2003, F1; Linda Greenhouse, "Treaty Doesn't Give Foreign Defendants Special Status in U.S. Courts, Justices Rule," *New York Times,* June 20, 2006, A15.

16. The following discussion is based on Daniel J. Elazar, *American Federalism: A View from the States,* 3rd ed. (New York: Harper & Row, 1984), 109–173; Ira Sharkansky, "The Utility of Elazar's Political Culture: A Research Note," in Daniel J. Elazar and Joseph Zikmund II, eds., *The Ecology of American Political Culture: Readings* (New York: Thomas Y. Crowell, 1975), 247–262; and Robert L. Savage, "The Distribution and Development of Policy Values in the American States," in ibid., 263–286, and Appendices A, B, and C. For evidence that the Texas political culture continues to persist as originally described, see Paul Brace, Kevin Arceneaux, Martin Johnson, and Stacy G. Ulbig, "Does State Political Ideology Change Over Time?" *Political Research Quarterly,* vol. 57, no. 4 (December 2004), 529–540, esp. 534.
17. Sharkansky, "Utility," op. cit., 252.
18. For a description and evaluation of social Darwinism in American culture, see Carl N. Degler, *In Search of Human Nature: The Decline and Revival of Social Darwinism in American Social Thought* (New York: Oxford University, 1991), and David F. Prindle, *The Paradox of Democratic Capitalism: Politics and Economics in American Thought* (Baltimore: Johns Hopkins University, 2006), 107–122.
19. Kathleen O'Leary Morgan and Scott Morgan, *State Rankings 2010: A Statistical View of America* (Washington, D.C.: CQ Press, 2010), 525, 546.
20. Erik Eckholm, "Report: Poverty Hits 1 in 7," *Austin American-Statesman*, September 17, 2010, A1.
21. Top states for business, July 9, 2007, from CNBC Web site, www.cnbc.com, accessed December 2, 2010.
22. David Hendricks, "Texas Ranks High for Small Business Health," *San Antonio Express-News*, February 6, 2010, C1.
23. The CED's state rankings and a discussion of how they were created can be found on its Web site, www.cfed.org/search, and put in "Texas Rankings." All states that made the honor roll in 2002 also made it in 2007.
24. Alicia A. Caldwell, "Census: More Than Half of Texans Are Minorities," *Austin American- Statesman,* August 11, 2005, B1.
25. Jay Root, "Census Data Shows Huge Hispanic Growth in Texas," Associated Press Report, February 17, 2011.
26. Steve Murdock, Steve White, Md. Nazrul Hoque, Beverly Pecotte, Xuihong You, and Jennifer Balkan, *The New Texas Challenge: Population Change and the Future of Texas* (College Station: Texas A&M, 2003), 7; *Latinos in Texas: A Socio-Demographic Profile* (Austin: Tomas Rivera Center, 1995), 66, 84, 111.

CHAPTER 2

1. Martha Derthick, in "American Federalism: Half-Full or Half-Empty," *Brookings Review*, Winter 2000, 24–27, examines the status of federal-state relations at the beginning of the twenty-first century.
2. See www.constitution.legis.state.tx.us/ for the complete text of the Texas Constitution.
3. Texas was governed by Mexico from 1821 to 1836. Beginning in 1824, the Mexican Congress, acting under the Mexican Constitution, joined Texas and Coahuila, with Saltillo as the capital. That arrangement prevailed until independence in 1836. Thus, Texas was also governed by a seventh constitution, albeit as a colony, not as an independent nation or a state.
4. See, for example, Fred Gantt Jr., *The Chief Executive in Texas: A Study in Gubernatorial Leadership* (Austin: University of Texas Press, 1964), 24.
5. The Jacksonians supported slavery and the brutal treatment of Native Americans.
6. Jim B. Pearson, Ben Procter, and William B. Conroy, *Texas, The Land and Its People*, 3rd ed. (Dallas: Hendrick-Long, 1987), 400–405; *The Texas Almanac*, 1996–1997 (Dallas: *Dallas Morning News*, 1996), 499.
7. Historical perspectives are based on remarks of John W. Mauer, "State Constitutions in a

Time of Crisis: The Case of the Constitution of 1876," Symposium on the Texas Constitution, sponsored by the University of Texas Law School and the *Texas Law Review*, October 7, 1989.

8. The Grange originated in Minnesota in the 1860s in protest to farmers' grievances about low prices and the actions of big business—namely, the railroads and the grain companies—with which they had to deal. The organization reached its peak of power and membership in the 1870s.

9. Wilbourn E. Benton, *Texas Politics: Constraints and Opportunities* (Chicago: Nelson-Hall, 1984), 51.

10. Because of its length, the entire Texas Constitution is rarely reproduced. However, the *Texas Almanac* included the full text with all amendments until the 2000–2001 edition, and continues to summarize proposed amendments and to track their passage. As previously noted, the complete document can be found online at www.constitution.legis.state.tx.us/.

11. A full discussion of poorly organized sections and provisions in conflict with federal law can be found in *Reorganized Texas Constitution without Substantive Change* (Austin: Texas Advisory Commission on Intergovernmental Relations, 1977).

12. The Alabama Constitution had approximately 365,000 words as of 2010. This and other comparative information can be found in *The Book of the States, 2010 Edition*, vol. 42 (Lexington, Ky.: Council of State Governments, 2010), 11.

13. The definitive study of the Texas Constitution is Janice C. May, *The Texas State Constitution, A Reference Guide* (Westport, Conn.: Greenwood Publishing Group, 1996), and *The Texas State Constitution* (New York: Oxford University, 2011).

14. Article I, Section 4 stipulates acknowledgment of the existence of a Supreme Being as a test for public office; however, this provision is not enforced because it violates the U.S. Constitution.

15. As long as citizens were legally perceived to be citizens of the state first and of the nation second, state guarantees were vital. In recent years, state courts have begun to reassert themselves as protectors of rights because the federal courts have begun to be less assertive in their own decisions.

16. See, for example, David Westphal, "Homeland Security Plan Spurs Liberties Concerns," *Sacramento Bee*, August 9, 2002; "Numbers," *Time* magazine, December 23, 2002, 21; and "USA Patriot Act," *Wikipedia, the Free Encyclopedia*, posted at http://en.wikipedia.org/wiki/Patriot_act, February 1, 2006.

17. Article XV specifies the grounds for impeachment of judges, but not for the impeachment of executive officers; only the power to impeach the latter is given.

18. Thad Beyle, *Gubernatorial Power: The Institutional Power Ratings of the Governors of the 50 States*, January 31, 2011, available at www.unc.edu/-beyle/gubnewpwr.html. For historical perspective, see also Beyle, "The Governors," in Virginia Gray, Russell L. Hanson, and Herbert Jacob, *Politics in the American States*, 7th ed. (Washington, D.C.: CQ Press, 1999), 210–211. Beyle's chapter is the basis for other comments about ranking. In the 4th edition of Virginia Gray, Herbert Jacob, and Kenneth N. Vines, eds., *Politics in the American States* (essentially an earlier edition of the 1999 book), Beyle rated the Texas governor in the weakest six in formal powers. See also Thomas R. Dye and Susan McManus, *Politics in States and Communities,* 13th ed. (New York: Pearson Longman, 2008), especially Chapter 7.

19. Even with all the modern cases dealing with the rights of the criminally accused, no national prohibition exists on the state's right to appeal in criminal cases. See *Palko* v. *Connecticut,* 302 U.S. 319 (1937), for the Supreme Court's position on the issue. Texas allowed no appeal by the state until 1987.

20. Contrary to popular opinion, a justice of the peace without legal training cannot become a judge on a superior (appeals) court. Qualifications for these courts include ten years as a practicing lawyer or a combination of ten years of legal practice and judicial service.

21. Some years ago, *Forbes* magazine reported that Texas and Alabama have the most expensive judicial elections in the country. With major amounts of money—as much as $2 million for a Texas Supreme Court seat—on the line, vote-getting skills become especially important. See Laura Casteneda, "D.C. Worst, Utah Best on Litigious List," *Dallas Morning News*, January 3, 1994, 1D, 4D.

22. Although many small school districts have consolidated, Texas continues to be among the national leaders in the number of special districts. The state had 3,381 special districts when the most recent Census of Governments was taken in 2007, almost three times the number of municipalities.

23. The National Municipal (now Civic) League of Cities State Constitutional Studies Project last produced its *Model State Constitution*, 6th ed., in 1968 (New York: National Civic League). Web searches reveal a variety of other "models," all of which seem to be partisan versions of constitutions from states where constitutional revision has been active.

24. For example, a majority of states, including Alabama, New York, Pennsylvania, South Carolina, and Texas, do not have a provision allowing citizens to initiate a constitutional amendment. California, Illinois, Michigan, and Montana are among the eighteen states that provide for the citizen initiative. *The Book of the States, 2010,* 15.

25. A detailed analysis of the 1975 document is available in George Braden, *Citizen's Guide to the Proposed Constitution* (Houston: Institute of Urban Studies, University of Houston, 1975). The University of Houston served as a research and information center during the revision efforts and published numerous reports beginning in 1973.

Scholars from across the state were involved in the Houston research. One, Janice C. May, published a book-length study, *Texas Constitutional Revision Experience in the 70s* (Austin: Sterling Swift, 1975). A summary of the general literature on the revision efforts and of voting behavior can be found in John E. Bebout, "The Meaning of the Vote on the Proposed Texas Constitution, 1975," *Public Affairs Comment*, vol. 24 (February 1978), 1–9, published by the Lyndon B. Johnson School of Public Affairs at the University of Texas at Austin.

26. Draft resolution and "Comparison of Current and Proposed Constitutions" provided by the office of Senator John Montford, January 1992.

27. Sam Attlesey, "Texas Constitution Outlasts Plan for Rewrite," *Dallas Morning News*, April 25, 1999, 54A.

28. See, for example, "Member Update: Texas Constitutional Revision," *The Texas Voter* 40 (Winter 2005), insert, and Heber Taylor, "It's Time to Draft a New Texas Constitution," *Galveston County Daily News* (November 9, 2005), originally available at http://galvestondailynews.com/story.lasso?ewed52df9eea56de051ec.

CHAPTER 3

1. Texans for Public Justice, "Loan-Shark-Financed Campaigns Threaten Payday Loan Reform," March 2011, 2–3, from www.tpj.org; Jim Hawkins, "Opportunity Missed in Texas's Payday Lending Law," *Houston Chronicle,* June 1, 2011, from Web site.

2. Articles in the *Austin American-Statesman* are the sources for this discussion of the telecommunications conflict: "Cable Industry Sues Again over Law," January 28, 2006, F2; Bruce Meyerson, "Sprint Joining Cable Providers to Battle SBC," November 3, 2005, B1; Claudia Grisales, "SBC Asks to Provide TV to San Antonio," October 11, 2005, D1; "Cable Firms Sue to Stop Telecom Law," September 9, 2005, C1; "Perry Approves

Changes to Telecom Laws," September 8, 2005, C2; Bruce Mehlman and Larry Irving, "On Telecom, Texas Is Set to Bring on Competition," August 31, 2005, A13; Tim Morstad and Gus Cardenas, "Texas Needs to Stand Up to Big Phone Companies," August 18, 2005, A13; Claudia Grisales, "Phone Lobby Spent Big to Outmaneuver Cable Rivals," August 18, 2005, A1; Claudia Grisales, "Phone Companies Gain TV Win," July 18, 2005, B1; Phil King, "On Telecom, Legislature Lost a Chance to Help Consumers," June 30, 2005, A13; Jaime Martinez, "Bill Would Only Widen Digital Divide in Texas," May 17, 2005, A13; Claudia Grisales, "Legislative Battle over Television Looms," May 7, 2005, A1; Claudia Grisales, "Ad War Erupts in Fight over Telecom Reform," April 28, 2005, D1; Gary Chapman, "To Ensure Texas' Future, We Must Rewrite the Rules on Telecom," March 5, 2005, A15.

3. Anthony J. Nownes, Clive S. Thomas, and Ronald Hrebenar, "Interest Groups in the States," in Virginia Gray and Russell L. Hanson, eds., *Politics in the American States: A Comparative Analysis*, 9th ed. (Washington, D.C.: CQ Press, 2008), 117.

4. Testimony of Robert J. Hunter before the Committee on Commerce, Science, and Transportation of the U.S. Senate, October 22, 2003, available on the Web site of the Consumer Federation of America, www.consumerfed.org/, accessed September 22, 2006.

5. Elyse Gilmore Yates, "Insure Integrity in the Insurance Industry," *Texas Observer*, February 8, 1991, 11.

6. Diane Renzulli and the Center for Public Integrity, *Capitol Offenders: How Private Interests Govern Our States* (Washington, D.C.: Public Integrity Books, 2002), 105.

7. Bruce Hight, "Runaway Rates Have Consumers Seeing Red," *Austin American-Statesman,* September 1, 2002, H2; Shonda Novak, "Consumer Groups Call for Regulation of Home Insurers," *Austin American-Statesman*, September 7, 2002, G1.

8. Carlos Guerra, "Insurance Money Trail," *Austin American-Statesman*, August 7, 2002, A11.

9. Ibid.; Shonda Novak, "Insurers Ordered to Retool Pricing," *Austin American-Statesman*, August 14, 2002, A1.

10. Dave Harmon, "Insurers Face New Scrutiny under Law," *Austin American-Statesman*, June 11, 2003, B1; Shonda Novak, "Insurers Ordered to Slash Rates," *Austin American-Statesman*, August 9, 2003, A1; Shonda Novak, "Insurers Must Cut Rates," *Austin American-Statesman*, September 13, 2003, F1.

11. Terrence Stutz, "State Tops in Cost of Home Insurance," *Austin American-Statesman*, November 17, 2010, B7; W. Gardner Selby, "Despite Changes, Home Insurance Priciest in Texas," *Austin American-Statesman*, April 24, 2007, A1.

12. Saul Elbein, "Like a Bad Neighbor," *Texas Observer*, June 11, 2010, 10; Melissa Del Bosque and Dave Mann, "Status Woe," *Texas Observer*, June 26, 2009, 26; Terrence Stutz, "State Farm Loses Another Round in Fight over Refunds," *Austin American-Statesman*, April 12, 2011, B5.

13. Nownes, et al., "Interest Groups in the States," op. cit., 121.

14. From the Texas Ethics Commission Web site, www.ethics.state.tx.us/.

15. Texans for Public Justice, "Austin's Oldest Profession: Texas' Top Lobby Clients and Those Who Serve Them," May 2010, http://www.tpj.org/2010/05/recession-hits-austins-oldest.html.

16. Dave McNeely, "After Agitating Cyclists, Senator Revises Bike Bill," *Austin American-Statesman*," March 29, 2001, B1; and state legislative Web site, www.capitol.state.tx.us/.

17. "Ex-Lawmaker Helps Push Through Budget Provision as Lobbyist," *Austin American-Statesman* , May 1, 2007, B5; Texas Ethics Commission Web site, www.ethics.state.tx.us.

18. Paul Burka, "Is the Legislature for Sale? *Texas Monthly*, February 1991, 118.

19. James A. Garcia, "Lobbying Group Subsidiary Will Gather Insurance Data," *Austin American-Statesman*, August 27, 1996, B1; information updated by authors on April 25, 2011.

20. Laylan Copelin, "Ethics Legislation Passes in Overtime," *Austin American-Statesman*, June 2, 2003, 1.

21. Nownes, et al., "Interest Groups in the States," op. cit., 117.

22. "History in the Making," *PR Newswire*, June 2, 2003, 1.

23. Dick Weekley, "Texas Ranks 'Best in the Nation' in Tort Liability Index, but Report Shows More Reforms Are Needed," on Web site of Texans for Lawsuit Reform, http://www.tortereform.com/node/355, and information from Pacific Research Institute, www.pacificresearch.org; both sites accessed September 23, 2006.

24. Source: Texas Ethics Commission campaign contribution report for 2010, from Web site www.ethics.state.tx.us/.

25. Tom Craddick, "Reining in a Civil Justice System Gone Wild," *Austin American-Statesman*, August 29, 2003, A15; Jake Bernstein and Dave Mann, "The Rise of the Machine," *Texas Observer*, August 29, 2003, 8.

26. Wayne Slater, "'Loser Pays' Pays Plenty," *Dallas Morning News*, March 29, 2011, A1.

27. Capitol Confidential, "Texas Leads the Way with 'Loser Pays' Reform; Blow to Trial Lobby," http://biggovernment.com/capitolconfidential, May 24, 2011.

28. The information in this section is based on Mary Flood, "Doctors Orders: Medical Lobby Becomes a Powerhouse in Austin," *The Wall Street Journal*, May 19, 1999, T1; Osler McCarthy, "Doctor, Lawyer Groups Bury the Hatchet," *Austin American-Statesman*, February 28, 1999, J1; Laylan Copelin, "Influence Is Name of Game for an Army of Lobbyists," *Austin American-Statesman*, January 12, 2003, E3; "Texas Docs Led by Old Political Hand," *Modern Healthcare*, April 21, 2003, 32; R. G. Ratcliffe, "Perry Signs Prompt Pay Legislation," *Houston Chronicle*, June 18, 2003, A17; David Pasztor, "Doctors' Lobbying Stirs Concern," *Austin American-Statesman*, September 2, 2003, B1; news release, Texans for Public Justice, "Prop. 12 Proponents Gave $5.3 Million to Perry, Dewhurst and Lawmakers in 2002," August 29, 2003, 2; Jason Embry, "Top-Spending PACs Backed by Lawyers, Businesses, Parties," *Austin American-Statesman*, January 26, 2009, B1; Texas Ethics Commission records, from its Web site.

29. "Memo to TMA Members after New Tax Bill Passed," on TMA Web site, www.texmed.org/, accessed September 24, 2006.

30. From the TMA's Web site, "Liability Reforms Bring More Care, More Doctors to Texans; TMA Survey Confirms: Prop 12 Was Good for Texas."

31. Basic sources for this section on the TTLA are Charles P. Elliott, Jr., "The Texas Trial Lawyers Association: Interest Group under Siege," in Anthony Champagne and Edward J. Harpham, eds., *Texas Politics: A Reader* (New York: W.W. Norton, 1997), 162–176; Terry Maxon, "Lawyers Top Doctors in Fund Raising for Prop. 12," *Dallas Morning News*, August 21, 2003, D1; David Pasztor, "Prop. 12 Fight Has Silenced Lawyers," *Austin American-Statesman*, September 4, 2003, A1.

32. Ross Ramsey, "Poll: Texas Voters Just Don't Like Trial Lawyers," *Texas Tribune*, September 27, 2010, accessed online.

33. Laylan Copelin and David Pasztor, "Limits on Damages Narrowly Approved," *Austin American-Statesman*, September 14, 2003, A1; Jake Bernstein, "Bustin' Labels," *Texas Observer*, September 26, 2003, 6.

34. Source for both campaign contribution and lobbying expenditures is the TEC Web site; on Steve Mostyn: Brandi Grissom, Ross Ramsey, Emily Ramshaw, and Jay Root, "Updated: Windstorm Negotiations Fail," *Texas Tribune*, May 30, 2011, from Web site.

35. See notes 26 and 27.

36. Basic sources for the section on the Christian Right are: William Martin, *With God on Our Side: The Rise of the Religious Right in America* (New York: Broadway Books, 1996); Chuck Lindell, "Pulpit to Polls Movement Gathers Steam," *Austin American-Statesman*, March 6, 1994, A1; Paul Burka, "The Disloyal Opposition," *Texas Monthly*, December 1998, 117; Molly Ivins, "State Board of Obfuscation," *Austin American-Statesman*, November 3, 1999, A17; Matt Curry, "In Texas, Appealing to Churchgoers Is an Integral Part of Campaigning," Associated Press news release, July 24, 2002, 1.

37. DeLay quoted in Jim Lobe, "Another Toxic Texan Rises to the Top," Inter Press Service news release, November 16, 2002, 2.

38. This summary of the Christian Right in the 2007 legislature is based on information in Emily Ramshaw, "Fruitful Year for Christian Right," *Dallas Morning News*, May 17, 2007, A1.

39. Jason Embry, "Role of Social Issues Seen in Sonogram Vote," *Austin American-Statesman*, March 8, 2011, B1.

40. Abby Rapaport, "Christian Conservatives Lose Former SBOE Chair," *Texas Tribune*, March 3, 2011, from Web site; Dave Mann, "Schooled," *Texas Observer*, April 30, 2010, 3.

41. Andrew Kaspar, "In Austin, Union Label Hard to See," *Austin American-Statesman*, March 6, 2011, D1; U.S. Department of Labor, Bureau of Labor Statistics Web site, www.bls.gov/news.release/union2.nr0.htm, accessed April 30, 2011.

42. Basic information on LULAC comes from: Benjamin Marquez, *LULAC: The Evolution of a Mexican-American Political Organization* (Austin: University of Texas, 1993); Lori Rodriguez, "LULAC Turning Puerto Rican," *Houston Chronicle*, July 9, 1994, A25; James E. Garcia, "Latino Politics: Up to LULAC to Reform or Be Left Behind," *Houston Chronicle*, September 9, 1999, OUTLOOK, 1; Lori Rodriguez, "LULAC's Leaders Speech at Convention First Ever," *Houston Chronicle*, July 11, 2002, A1; Lori Rodriguez, "LULAC Role Evolves, but Equity Still Focus," *Houston Chronicle*, July 23, 2002, A1; Amber Novak, "Up in Smoke," *Texas Observer*, May 23, 2003, 4; Scripps Howard Austin Bureau, "LULAC Sponsors Students' Trip to Austin to Oppose School Cuts," *Corpus Christi Caller-Times*, May 4, 2003, C4; "LULAC Questions GOP Tax Plan," *La Prensa San Diego*, May 23, 2003, Online Edition, 1; Meena Thiruvengadam, "CAFTA Proves Divisive for LULAC Chapters," *San Antonio Express-News*, July 8, 2005, B8.

43. Krissah Williams and Jonathon Weisman, "Latino Groups Play Key Role on Hill; Virtual Veto Power in Immigration Debate," *The Washington Post*, May 16, 2007, A04; and entry on bill in Wikipedia, accessed October 18, 2008.

44. Gary Scharrer, "SBOE Standards for Social Studies Appealed to Feds," *Houston Chronicle*, December 20, 2010, from Web site.

45. Gary Scharrer, "GOP Leaders Endorse Revision of History Curriculum Standards," *San Antonio Express-News*, March 16, 2011, from Web site.

46. Nownes, et al., "Interest Groups in the States," op. cit., 117.

47. Kathleen O'Leary Morgan and Scott Morgan, *State Rankings 2010: A Statistical View of America* (Washington, D.C.: CQ Press, 2010), 142, 125.

48. Hartman quoted in Jenine Zeleznik, "Lobbyists Warn Texas Teachers about Upcoming Special Session," *The Monitor*, September 10, 2003, 1.

49. Whiteker quoted in Jason Embry and Robert Elder, "Fed Up, Pro-Education Candidates Step Up," *Austin American-Statesman*, October 23, 2005, A1.

50. Christiopher Smith Gonzalez, "Session's End Creates Graveyard of Dead Legislation," *Texas Tribune* Web site, May 31, 2011; "Stout Resistance Slows, Then Stops an Awful School Finance Bill; Special Session Could be Called," from Texas Federation of Teachers Web site, May 31, 2011.

CHAPTER 4

1. The customary assignment of liberals to the left side of the political spectrum and conservatives to the right side derives from the seating of parties in the French Parliament. Royalists, Gaullists, and others of a conservative persuasion always sit to the right of the center aisle, while socialists, communists, and others of more "progressive" persuasion sit to the left.

2. From the Gallup Poll, conducted nationwide on February 3, 2010, Web site accessed December 18, 2010: gallup.com/poll/125066/State-States.aspx.

3. Robert S. Erickson, Gerald C. Wright Jr., and John McIver, "Political Parties, Public Opinion, and State Policy in the United States," *American Political Science Review,* vol. 83, no. 6 (September 1989), 729–750, especially 737.

4. John R. Alford, Carolyn Funk, and John Hibbing, "Are Political Orientations Genetically Transmitted?" *American Political Science Review,* vol. 99, no. 2 (May 2005), 153–167.

5. Douglas E. Foley, *Learning Capitalist Culture: Deep in the Heart of Tejas* (Philadelphia: University of Pennsylvania Press, 1990), 110.

6. Quoted in Molly Ivins, "Political Writing—A State of Lazy Journalism," *Texas Humanist,* November–December 1984, 14–15.

7. Angle quoted in Josh Berthume, "The Twittering Class: Can Social Media Transform Politics—and Reboot Texas Republicans?" *Texas Observer*, June 12, 2009, 13.

8. Culberson quoted in ibid, 16.

9. Gladwell quoted in Frank Rich, "Facebook Politicians Are Not Your Friends," *New York Times,* October 9, 2010, downloaded from Web site.

10. Ibid.

11. Robert Quigley, "Reshaping Journalism," *Austin American-Statesman*, April 25, 2010, F1.

12. Poll taken by the University of Texas/*Texas Tribune,* under the direction of Professor Daron Shaw, from October 11 to 19, 2010, from Web site http://texaspolitics.laits.utexas.edu/11_8_9.html, accessed October 3, 2011.

13. Dave McNeely, "Party Politics in the Precincts," *Austin American-Statesman,* March 4, 2000, A15.

14. Molly Ivins, "Texas Elephants Look to Ostracize the RINOs," *Austin American-Statesman,* June 12, 2002, A17; Jake Bernstein, "Elephant Wars," *Texas Observer,* July 5, 2002, 16.

15. 2006 Republican state platform, page 12.

16. Gerald C. Wright and Brian Schaffner, "The Influence of Party: Evidence from the State Legislatures," *American Political Science Review,* vol. 96, no. 2 (June 2002), 376–377.

17. Dave McNeely, "Bipartisanship: The Road Not Taken in '03," *Austin American-Statesman,* January 4, 2004, H1.

18. Sean Theriault, "Party Polarization in the U.S. Congress: Member Replacement and Member Adaptation," *Party Politics,* vol. 12, July 2006, 483–503.

19. Dave McNeely, "For Incumbent Democrats, Some Heads Are Starting to Roll," *Austin American-Statesman,* March 10, 2004, A12; Ken Herman, "Wilson Pays Price for Siding with GOP," *Austin American-Statesman,* March 11, 2004, A1.

20. Laurie Goodstein, "Issuing Rebuke, Judge Rejects Teaching of Intelligent Design," *New York Times*, December 21, 2005, A1; W. Gardner Selby, "Perry: Add Intelligent Design to Classes," *Austin American-Statesman*, January 6, 2006, A1.

21. "Populist Party Platform," in Michael B. Levy, ed., *Political Thought in America: An Anthology* (Chicago: Dorsey Press, 1988), 356–359.

CHAPTER 5

1. "White primary" laws and rules prevented voting in primary elections by anyone who was not Caucasian. Although the Fifteenth Amendment to the U.S. Constitution, passed in 1870, guaranteed the right of all citizens

of any race to vote in general elections, it did not apply to primaries. The poll tax law required a citizen to pay a tax months in advance of election day in order to register. Unless registered, citizens were not legally qualified to vote. Poor people, of whom many were minority citizens, were often unable to pay the tax and thus became ineligible to vote. The U.S. Supreme Court invalidated Texas's white primary law in 1944 in *Smith v. Allwright*, 321 U.S. 649. The Twenty-fourth Amendment to the Constitution, adopted in 1964, forbid the poll tax in federal elections. Under threat of federal action, Texas repealed its state poll tax law in 1966 by amendment of its constitution. The state legislature, however, adopted a severe registration law that was, in effect, a poll tax under another name. A federal court struck down this law in *Beare v. Smith*, 321 F. Supp. 1100 (1971).

2. *Beare v. Smith*, 321 F. Supp. 1100 (1971).

3. Erik Eckholm, "Report: Poverty Hits 1 in 7," *Austin American-Statesman*, September 17, 2010, A1.

4. U.S. Census Bureau, statistical tables on voter turnout in 2004, 2006, and 2008 elections, available at www.census.gov.

5. We are grateful to Daron Shaw of the Government Department of the University of Texas at Austin for sharing these data with us. They are culled from three polls conducted by the Government Department under Shaw's direction during 2008.

6. 2010 election spending from the *Texas Tribune* Web site, www.texastribune.org/library/data/2010-general-election-cost-per-vote.

7. Laylin Copelin and David Elliott, "Williams Outspending Richards 2-1," *Austin American-Statesman*, October 30, 1990, A1; Colleen McCain Wilson, "For Sanchez, More Wasn't Better," *Dallas Morning News*, November 7, 2002, A1.

8. Wilson, "More Wasn't Better," ibid.; Laylan Copelin, "Costs Soar in Race to Be Governor," *Austin American-Statesman*, October 29, 2002, B1; Wayne Slater and Pete Slover, "For Sanchez, Perry, the Well Isn't Dry Yet," *Dallas Morning News*, October 13, 2002, A1; Pete Slover, "Political Checks and Balances," *Dallas Morning News*, January 16, 2003, A1.

9. Keith E. Hamm and Gary F. Moncrief, "Legislative Politics in the States," in Virginia Gray and Russell L. Hanson, eds., *Politics in the American States: A Comparative Analysis*, 9th ed. (Washington, D.C.: Congressional Quarterly, 2008), 165–166.

10. Texans for Public Justice, *Keeping Texas Weird: The Bankrolling of the 2006 Gubernatorial Race*, September, 2006, accessed on TPJ's Web site on October 2, 2006, www.tpj.org/.

11. Laylan Copelin, "Few Fans of Campaign Changes," *Austin American-Statesman*, April 22, 2007, B1.

12. Glenn quoted in Roger H. Davidson, Walter J. Oleszek, and Frances E. Lee, *Congress and Its Members*, 11th ed. (Washington, D.C.: CQ Press, 2008), 72.

13. Mike Ward, "65% of Politicians in Poll Favor Public Favor Public Financing of Campaigns," *Austin American-Statesman*, March 11, 1990, B8.

14. Quoted in Jeff South and Jerry White, "Computer Network Tracks Politicians' Funds," *Austin American-Statesman*, August 16, 1993, B1.

15. "Perry Fined $1,500 for Missing Info," *Austin American-Statesman*, March 24, 2011, B3; Laylan Copelin, "Ethics Panel Fines Legislator over Campaign Spending," *Austin American-Statesman*, November 7, 2008, B5; Laylan Copelin, "Ethics Commission Quietly Disciplines State's Politicians," *Austin American-Statesman*, June 19, 2008, B1.

16. Julia Malone, "Campaigns Take Low Road," *Austin American-Statesman*, October 26, 2006, A7.

17. Kim Fridkin Kahn and Patrick Kenney, "Do Negative Campaigns Mobilize or Suppress Turnout? Clarifying the Relationship Between Negativity and Participation," *American Political Science Review*, vol. 93, no. 4 (December 1999): 877–889; Stephen D.

Ansolabehere, Shanto Iyengar, and Adam Simon, "Replicating Experiments Using Aggregate and Survey Data: The Case of Negative Advertising and Turnout," ibid., 901–909.

18. Gary R. Orren and Nelson W. Polsby, *Media and Momentum: The New Hampshire Primary and Nomination Politics* (Chatham, N.J.: Chatham House, 1987).

19. The Texas Secretary of State oversees the activities of the county clerks in relation to primary elections. The rules are so numerous and complicated that the SOS's office holds regular seminars to educate the clerks about their responsibilities. See www.sos.state.tx.us/search/index.jsp, accessed on April 5, 2009.

20. From the Texas Secretary of State Web site, www.sos.state.tx.us/elections/candidates/guide/demorrep.shtml, accessed February 11, 2011.

21. David Pasztor, "Millions Pour into Proposition 12 Fight," *Austin American-Statesman*, September 6, 2003, A1; Laylin Copelin and David Pasztor, "Limits on Damages Narrowly Approved," *Austin American-Statesman*, September 14, 2003, A1.

22. "Votes Are In, and Two-Thirds of Those in Texas Came Early," *Dallas Morning News*, November 12, 2008, A3.

23. "Judge Says Perry Took Ruling Out of Context in Ad," *Austin American-Statesman*, July 31, 2002, B3; Molly Ivins, "The Summer of Our Discontent," *Denton Record-Chronicle*, August 10, 2002, A6.

24. Ken Herman, "Perry Uses DEA Murder in New TV Ad," *Austin American-Statesman*, October 26, 2002, B1.

25. Jeff Zeleny and Megan Thee, "Exit Polling Shows Independents, Citing War, Favored Democrats," *New York Times*, November 8, 2006, A1.

26. "Watkins: A New Day in Dallas County," www.WFAA.com, accessed November 8, 2006; Dan Felstein and Chase Davis, "Warning for GOP in Harris County," *Houston Chronicle*, November 9, 2006, A1;

Thomas Korosec, "Democrats Turn Dallas County a Shade of Blue," *Houston Chronicle*, November 9, 2006, B4.

27. W. Gardner Selby, "Though Democrats Made Gains, Looks Like GOP Has Hold on State," *Austin American-Statesman*, November 6, 2008, B1; "Democrats Enjoy Big Wins in Administrative, Judicial Races," *Dallas Morning News*, November 6, 2008, A17.

28. Jay Root, "The Texas Governor's Race," in Larry Sabato, ed., *Pendulum Swing* (Boston: Longman, 2011), 389-394; W. Gardner Selby, "Perry: Add 'Intelligent Design' to Classes," *Austin American-Statesman*, January 6, 2006; "How the Candidates Stack up on Issues," *Austin American-Statesman*, October 17, 2010, E1.

29. Ken Herman, "Perry Is Again Asking Voters: A Killer or Me?" *Austin American-Statesman*, October 27, 2010, A8.

30. We are grateful to Professor Richard Murray of the University of Houston Political Science Department for supplying us with these voter turnout figures.

31. Bob Moser, "Viva Los Republicanos," *Texas Observer*, December 10, 2010, 19; Dave Mann, "Knock, Knock, Who's There?" *Texas Observer*, August 6, 2010, 13.

CHAPTER 6

1. The U.S. Constitution provides for a maximum of one representative for each 30,000 people. If no ceiling were statutorily set and this limit were actually attained, the U.S. House of Representatives would have about 10,292 members. The Texas Constitution sets a maximum membership of 150 in the House, although it allows one representative for each 15,000 citizens within that limit. If legislators represented only 15,000 constituents, the Texas House would have more than 1,676 members.

2. Information on the legislatures of other states has been summarized from *The Book of the States, 2010*, vol. 42 (Lexington, Ky.: Council of State Governments, 2010), 85–174.

3. See Dawson Bell, "Reducing Rancor in Michigan," *State Legislatures*, December 1999, 22–24, especially the sidebar analyzing term limits on p. 23; and Stanley M. Caress, et al., "Effect of Term Limits on the Election of Minority State Legislators," *State and Local Government Review*, vol. 35 (Fall 2003), 183–195.

4. According to census count for 2010, Texas has a population of 25,145,561 persons. Dividing that figure by 31 for senatorial districts yields the ideal district size of 811,147; dividing by 150 for representatives, the figure is 167,637. Obviously, citizens move in and out of districts, so the numbers are not exact, and they change as the population increases.

5. A county was entitled to a maximum of seven representatives unless its population exceeded 700,000; then one additional representative could be districted for each additional 100,000 in population.

6. 369 U.S. 186 (1962).

7. 377 U.S. 533 (1964).

8. A multimember district is one in which two or more representatives are elected by all the people in that district. All the representatives represent all the people of the district. Multimember districts tend to reduce considerably the ability of ethnic minorities to win elections, and the citizens tend not to be sure which representative is truly theirs.

9. See Steven Bickerstaff, "Legislative and Congressional Reapportionment in Texas: A Historical Perspective," *Public Affairs Comment*, vol. 37 (Winter 1991), 1–13, for a good review of early redistricting developments.

10. See Kathleen A. Bratton, Kerry L. Haynie, and Beth Reingold, "Gender, Race, Ethnicity and Representation: The Changing Landscape of Legislative Diversity," in *The Book of the States, 2008*, 73–79; and Arturo Vega, "Gender and Ethnicity Effects on the Legislative Behavior and Substantive Representation of the Texas Legislature," *Texas Journal of Political Studies*, vol. 19 (Spring/Summer 1997), 1–21.

11. See, for example, *Shaw v. Reno* (509 U.S. 630, 1993), which dealt with standards of racial equality in redistricting; and *Hunt v. Cromartie* (526 U.S. 541, 1999), which resulted in a requirement that overt racial gerrymandering had to be present to overturn district lines.

12. A good account of the Republican feuding can be found in Patricia Kilday Hart, "Party Poopers II," *Texas Monthly*, December 2001, 60, 62, 64.

13. The media in Texas ran the 2003 redistricting story as a front-page/lead item for weeks. A few of the more useful sources are these: Pete Slover and Matt Stiles, "Majority of AWOL Lawmakers Where You'd Least Expect: Oklahoma," and Christy Hoppe and Gromer Jeffers, Jr., "Angry Over Redistricting, State Reps Deny Quorum," run as companion pieces under the banner "Democrats Disappear," *Dallas Morning News*, May 13, 2003, 1A, 11A; Patricia Kilday Hart, "The Unkindest Cut," *Texas Monthly*, October 2003, 44–52; Lee Hockstader, "Caught in the Crossfire," *Washington Post Weekly Edition*, October 6–12, 2003, 14.

14. For background, see "Redrawn Map Looking Good for Incumbents," *Austin American-Statesman,* April 14, 2011, B-1, B-3; Michael E. Young and Ryan McNeill, "Hispanics Drive Texas' Growth," *Dallas Morning News*, February 18, 2011, 1A, 19A; "Young, Diverse, Divided Texas," *Dallas Morning News*, January 30, 2011, 1A, 27A. See also, on the politics of redistricting, Ken Herman, "Redistricting: The Process of One Person, One Vote, One Giant Mess," *Austin American-Statesman*, April 26, 2011, A3; and Jay Root, "Minority, GOP Power Shape New Texas House District Map," *Austin American-Statesman*, April 29, 2011, B3.

15. See, for example, Robert T. Garrett, "Uncivil Politics Causes Concern," *Dallas Morning News*, May 11, 2011, 1A–2A.

16. Comparative data come from *The Book of the States, 2010*, 113–116. For background information, see Karen Hansen, "Legislative

Pay: Baseball It Ain't," *State Legislatures*, July/August 1997, 20–26; "Legislator Pay Inches Up," *State Legislatures*, May 1999, 5; and "State Legislators' Salaries Down 6%," *PA Times*, March 2007, 1, 10.

17. Morgan Cullen, "The Changing Face of State Legislatures," *State Legislatures*, July/August 2009, 21.

18. See Legislative Reference Library, "Membership Statistics for 82nd Legislature, available at http://www.lrl.state.tx.us/sessions/sessionSnapshot.cfm?legSession=82-0 on May 11, 2011; "What Is the Median Age in Texas?", http://wiki.answers.com/Q/What_is_the_median_age_of_Texas.

19. Karen Brooks, "Lawmakers Plan to Put More Religion in Your Life," *Dallas Morning News*, April 22, 2007; and Karen Brooks and Staci Hupp, "House: Allow Religion in School," *Dallas Morning News*, May 1, 2007, 1A, 2A.

20. See expenditures for all state offices at http://www.followthemoney.org/database/state_over view.phtml?s=TX&y=2010.

21. See Emily Ramshaw, "Do Campaign Funds Bankroll a Cushy Lifestyle?" *Dallas Morning News*, December 17, 2006, 1A, 13A.

22. See, for example, Paul Burka, "Uncivil Union," *Texas Monthly*, June 2005, 8, 10, 12; and Christy Hoppe, "Whose Political Style Will Win in Austin?" *Dallas Morning News*, May 20, 2005, 1A, 8A.

23. Paul Burka, "A Giant Void," *Texas Monthly*, January 2004, 14–16; see also "Bye-bye, Big Guys," *Dallas Morning News*, March 7, 2004, 1H, 6H.

24. See Dave McNeely and Jim Henderson, *Bob Bullock: God Bless Texas* (Austin: University of Texas Press, 2008), for a very readable account of Bullock's domination in the Texas Senate, and Bill Hobby, with Sarah Tiede, *How Things Really Work: Lessons from a Life in Politics* (Austin: Dolpha Briscoe Center for American History, University of Texas, 2010), for insights into a more civilized era of Texas politics.

25. See H. Gardner Selby, "A Natural Long Shot," *Austin American-Statesman*, February 22, 2008, A1, A8–A9; and Paul Burka, "Hello, My Name Is Regular Joe," *Texas Monthly*, April 2009, 128–131, 226–227, 232.

26. Jason Embry, "Was Straus Wrong Target for Activists?" *Austin American-Statesman*, May 3, 2011, B1, B4; and Jay Root, "GOP Supermajority Makes Its Mark," *Denton Record-Chronicle*, April 10, 2011, 3A.

27. In the U.S. Congress, seniority is more narrowly defined as continuous service on a committee. The congressional reforms of the 1970s modified the selection of committee chairpersons to allow some departure from the practice that the most senior member of the committee who is a member of the majority party always serves as chair. Seniority is more important in the U.S. Senate than in the U.S. House of Representatives.

28. Karl T. Kurtz, "Custodians of American Democracy," *State Legislatures*, July–August 2006, 28–35.

29. An excellent account of the nastiness of the legislature in 2003 can be found in Paul Burka, "Ruthless People," *Texas Monthly*, December 2003, 14–18.

30. See http://www.lrl.state.tx.us/sessions/billStatistics.cfm to see a statistical summary of bills and resolutions introduced, passed, and vetoed in recent legislative sessions.

31. Ken Herman, "See If You Can Follow the Rules in the Texas Senate," *Austin American-Statesman*, May 5, 2011, A10.

32. The Legislative Reference Library provides detailed information about the legislative process in Texas at http://www.lrl.state.tx.us/citizenResources/LegProcess.html.

33. The lack of public support for the legislature is not unique to Texas or to state legislatures. See "The Poor Public Attitude toward the Legislature," *State Legislatures*, April 1995, 5; John R. Hibbing and Elizabeth Theiss-Morse, *Congress as Public Enemy: Attitudes Toward American Political Institutions* (Cambridge: Cambridge University Press, 1995).

34. Garry Boulard, "The Great Divide," *State Legislatures*, February 2011, 22–25.

35. Alexander Heard, ed., *State Legislatures in American Politics* (Englewood Cliffs, N.J.: Prentice Hall, 1966), 3.

36. Christopher Z. Mooney concludes that Texas defies the national pattern that states with large populations and a high degree of heterogeneity tend to be more professionalized than small, more homogeneous states. See "The Political Economy of State Legislative Professionalism," Paper presented at the Annual Meeting of the Southwestern Political Science Association, March 19–21, 1992, Austin. Mooney examined thirty years of measurements of the professionalism of legislative bodies in "Measuring U.S. State Legislative Professionalism: An Evaluation of Five Indices," *State and Local Government Review*, vol. 26 (Spring 1994), 70–78. This article is a methodological note, but a table showing the fifty states indicates that Texas did not fare well on professionalism measures. The situation has not changed.

37. The *Texas Observer* analysis is published in June and the *Texas Monthly* rankings in July following the regular legislative session.

38. Paul Burka and Patricia Kilday Hart, "The Best and Worst Legislators," *Texas Monthly*, July 2009, accessed at http://www.texasmonthly.com/2009-07-01/feature2.php on May 20, 2011.

39. Dave Mann, "By the Numbers," *Texas Observer*, May 20, 2011, 14.

CHAPTER 7

1. Two exceptions to this tradition were (1) Richard Coke, the first governor under the 1876 Constitution, who served only one term; and (2) Ross S. Sterling, who was not re-elected in 1932. James E. Ferguson was re-elected in 1916, but was impeached and removed from office in 1917. His wife, Miriam A. Ferguson, was later elected twice to nonconsecutive terms.

2. The constitution does spell out the grounds for removing judges, however. Other officials subject to impeachment include the lieutenant governor, the attorney general, the commissioner of the General Land Office, the comptroller, and appellate court judges. The grounds stipulated for impeachment of judges include partiality, oppression, official misconduct, incompetence, negligence, and failure to conduct the business of the court. See Fred Gantt Jr., *The Chief Executive in Texas* (Austin: University of Texas, 1964), 123. Ferguson was impeached and convicted for mishandling public funds, conduct brought to light because funds for the University of Texas were involved.

3. Andrew Knapp, "Governors' Salaries Range from $1 to $206,500," May 21, 2007, http://govpro.com/issue_20070101/gov_imp_66568/, accessed May 20, 2009.

4. "Texas Taxpayers Footing Big Bill for Gov. Rick Perry's Temporary Home," *Dallas Morning News*, May 17, 2010.

5. Ibid., 154.

6. The Web site of the Texas governor (www.governor.state.tx.us/divisions) provides an up-to-date list of the various divisions of the governor's office.

7. Thad L. Beyle, "Being Governor," *The State of the States* (Washington, D.C.: CQ Press, 1996), 77–107, discusses how governors might be evaluated, including the index developed by the National Governors Association.

8. Brian McCall, *The Power of the Texas Governor* (Austin: University of Texas Press, 2009), 72–77.

9. An interesting assessment of the Clements years can be found in George Bayoud and James Huffines, "25 Years Later: Clements' Texas Legacy Stands Tall," *Austin American-Statesman*, November 6, 2003, A15.

10. For an excellent look at the career of Ann Richards, see Jan Reid, "Ann: An Appreciation," *Texas Monthly*, November 2006, 177–179, 278–280.

11. Term taken from a Richards's biography with that title. Mark Shropshire and Frank Schaeffer, *The Thorny Rose of Texas: An Intimate Portrait of Governor Ann Richards* (Birch Lane Press, 1994).

12. As of 2007, Texas claimed four former U.S. presidents—Dwight Eisenhower, who was born in the state; Lyndon Johnson, who was a lifelong resident; George H. W. Bush, who moved to Texas during an oil boom when he was a businessman, not a politician; and most recently, former President George W. Bush.

13. McCall, p. 126.

14. "The Big Winners and Losers of 1999: The Governor Had a Banner Year, While Local Education Lost Out," *Wall Street Journal*, December 29, 1999, T1.

15. Laylan Copelin and Jason Embry, "Lawmakers Rising Against Perry Policies," *Austin American-Statesman*, March 18, 2007, A1; see also Arnold Garcia, Jr., "Commentary: After a Series of Political Setbacks, Perry's Skidding on the Ice," *Austin American-Statesman,* March 11, 2007, H3.

16. W. Gardner Selby and Jason Embry, "Governor Says Texas Is One State That Could Leave Union, Though He's Not Pushing It," *Austin American Statesman,* April 17, 2009; *Texas v. White*, 74 U.S. 700 (1869).

17. See the following bills passed in 2003: HB 2292, regular session; HB 7, third called session; and SB 2, third called session.

18. SB 2, Article 7, third called session, Seventy-eighth Legislature, exempts river authorities, junior college districts, agencies headed by one or more statewide elected officials, agencies with a majority of board members not requiring Senate confirmation, and agencies reporting to one or more elected officials. Purely local boards are also exempted.

19. This practice is most common with the licensing and examining boards in various health care fields.

20. See Paul Burka, "Behind the Lines: Altered State," *Texas Monthly*, July 2003, 6, 10, 12.

21. E. Lee Bernick, "Special Sessions: What Manner of Gubernatorial Power?" *State and Local Government Review* 26 (Spring 1994), 79–88, reports that special sessions tend to be cyclical and somewhat responsive to national events that force the states to enact new legislation. Bernick studied special sessions in all fifty states for 1959 through 1989.

22. Unlike the president, the governor does not have a "pocket veto." The governor must send a veto message to block a bill; laying a bill aside without a signature results in the bill's becoming law, even if the legislature adjourns.

23. Congress granted the U.S. president the item veto in 1996; the president used the power eighty-two times before the U.S. Supreme Court declared it unconstitutional in 1998.

24. Pat Thompson and Steven R. Boyd, "Use of the Item Veto in Texas, 1940–1990," *State and Local Government Review* 26 (Winter 1994), 38–45, provide perspective on the history of the item veto.

25. Dave Michaels and Robert T. Garrett, "Obama Wants to Speed Outflow of Stimulus Funds," *Dallas Morning News,* June 9, 2009.

26. James McGregor Burns, *Leadership* (New York: Harper & Row, 1978), 42–45.

27. See, for example, Paul Burka, "So Far, So Bad," *Texas Monthly*, May 2003, 6, 10, 12.

CHAPTER 8

1. The numbers in this paragraph are based on an actual count of entries in Appendix A, *Fiscal Size-Up, 2010–2011 Biennium* (Austin: Legislative Budget Board, December 2009).

2. See Josh Goodman, "The Second Best Job in the State," *Governing* (April 2009), 34–39.

3. See, for example, Grover Starling, *Managing the Public Sector,* 5th ed. (Fort Worth: Harcourt Brace, 1998), Chapter 7.

4. See "Bureaucracy" in *From Max Weber: Essays in Sociology*, translated, edited, and with an introduction by H. H. Gerth and C. Wright Mills (New York: Oxford, 1946), 196–244.

5. Emmette S. Redford, *Democracy in the Administrative State* (New York: Oxford, 1969), 3.

6. An excellent study of bureaucratic power at the national level is Francis Rourke, *Bureaucracy, Politics, and Public Policy*, 4th ed. (Boston: Little, Brown, 1986). Rourke's framework is adopted here.

7. Paul Appleby, *Big Democracy* (New York: Alfred A. Knopf, 1945), 7.

8. *Report to the 82nd Legislature* (Austin: Sunset Advisory Commission, February 2011), 3, 193–195, 204–205; *Guide to the Sunset Process* (Austin: Sunset Advisory Commission, December 2009), 11–12; and *General Information* on the Sunset Commission Web site at http://www.sunset.state.tx.us/faq.htm.

9. See Alan J. Bojorquez, "New Open Government Legislation," *Texas Town & City*, October 1999, 11–14.

10. Kelley Shannon, "Tinkering with the Sunshine," *Dallas Morning News*, April 11, 2011, 1A–2A.

CHAPTER 9

1. Quoted in Donald Dale Jackson, *Judges* (New York: Atheneum, 1974), 7.

2. "Gin, 'Barbed' Cases Make Morrison Fun," University of Texas *Daily Texan,* February 19, 1964, 1.

3. Dietz quoted in Arnold Garcia, Jr., "Do You Know Who Your Judges Are? Maybe You Should Find Out," *Austin American-Statesman,* September 14, 2002, A11.

4. Jackson, *Judges,* op. cit., 98.

5. Most of the information in this discussion comes from Bruce Hight, "Justices Bickering over Abortion Law," *Austin American-Statesman,* June 23, 2000, B1; the court case is *In re Jane Doe,* No. 00-0024 (Tex. Sup. Ct., June 22, 2000); on Owen's confirmation, see John Council and T. R. Goldman, "Senate Showdown Ends with Owen Confirmation," *Texas Lawyer*, vol. 20, no. 13, May 30, 2005, 5.

6. Texas Attorney General's Office Web site, www.oag.state.tx.us/, accessed June 15, 2011.

7. *Hopwood v. State of Texas* (78 F.3d 932, 5th Cir. 1996).

8. Attorney General's Letter Opinion 97-001, February 5, 1997.

9. Attorney General's Letter Opinion JC-107, September 3, 1999; Juan B. Elizondo, Jr., "Cornyn Rescinds Hopwood Opinion," *Austin American-Statesman,* October 12, 1999, A1.

10. *Grutter v. Bollinger et al.*, 539 U.S. 306 (2003); *Gratz et al. v. Bollinger et al.*, 539 U.S. 244 (2003).

11. Statistics from State Bar of Texas Web site: www.texasbar.com/, accessed June 15, 2011.

12. *Justice at the Crossroads: Court Improvements in Texas* (Austin: Chief Justice's Task Force for Court Improvement, 1972), 11.

13. *Texas Courts: A Study by the Texas Research League,* Report Two: "The Texas Judiciary: A Proposal for Structural-Functional Reform" (Austin: Texas Research League, 1991), xi.

14. *Annual Report for the Texas Judicial System, Fiscal Year 2010* (Austin: Office of Court Administration, 2010), 13, 14, and passim.

15. *Crime in Texas 2009* (Austin: Department of Public Safety, 2010), 53.

16. *Crime in Texas 1992* (Austin: Department of Public Safety, Crime Records Division, 1993), 14.

17. *Crime in Texas 2009* (Austin: Texas Department of Public Safety, 2010), 66.

18. "Prison Count 2010: State Population Declines for the First Time in 38 Years," Issue Brief, Pew Center on the States, April 2010, 3–4.

19. *Texas Crime, Texas Justice* (Austin: Comptroller's Office, 1994), 51.

20. Bruce Fein and Burt Neuborne, "Why Should We Care about Independent and Accountable Judges?" *Journal of the American Judicature Society,* vol. 84, no. 2 (September/October 2000).

21. Henry R. Glick, "Courts: Politics and the Judicial Process," in Virginia Gray and Russell L. Hanson, eds., *Politics in the American States: A Comparative Analysis*, 8th ed. (Washington, D.C.: Congressional Quarterly, 2004), 239.

22. Judge Eileen F. O'Neill, "Judicial Lottery Snakes-Eyes for Texas," *Houston Chronicle*, November 20, 1994, C1.

23. David J. Willis, "Separate Myth, Fact on the Judicial Process," *Houston Chronicle*, February 5, 1995, C1.

24. Glick, "Courts," op. cit., 249.

25. Wynne quoted in Michele Mittelstadt, "Political Money Eroding Trust in Judicial System," *Dallas Morning News*, February 22, 2002, A6.

26. David B. Rottman and Roy A. Schotland, "2004 Judicial Elections," in *The Book of the States*, vol. 37 (Lexington, Ky.: Council of State Governments, 2005), 305–308.

27. Texans for Public Justice, *Lowering the Bar*, available on the TPJ Web site: www.tpj.org/index.jsp.

28. TPJ Web site, ibid.

29. Adam Liptak and Janet T. Roberts, "Campaign Cash Mirrors a High Court's Rulings," *New York Times*, October 1, 2006, A1.

30. Mike Ward, "High Court Justice Leaves Case Involving Campaign Solicitor," *Austin American-Statesman*, April 13, 1996, B6.

31. Connie Mabin, "Suit Fails to Change Judicial Elections," *Austin American-Statesman*, September 28, 2000, B1.

32. Michele Mittlestadt, "Political Money Eroding Trust in Judicial System," *Dallas Morning News*, February 22, 2002, A6.

33. Debbie Nathan, "Wheel of Misfortune," *Texas Observer*, October 1, 1999, 22.

34. The Spangenberg Group, *A Study of Representation in Capital Murder Cases in Texas* (Austin: State Bar of Texas, Committee on Legal Representation for Those on Death Row, 1993), 157, 163.

35. Jeff South, "Inequality Found in Sentencing," *Austin American-Statesman*, September 4, 1993, A1.

36. David Pasztor, "Death Penalty Law Not Being Followed, Study Finds," *Austin American-Statesman*, October 29, 2003, B1; National Public Radio report, October 29, 2003.

37. From the Texas Department of Criminal Justice Web site: http://www.deathpenaltyinfo.org/state_by_state, accessed January 15, 2007.

38. Ralph Blumenthal, "Texas Judge Draws Outcry for Allowing an Execution," *New York Times*, October 25, 2007; Christy Hoppe, "Judge Sharon Keller Reprimanded for Conduct Related to 2007 Stay of Execution Filing," *Dallas Morning News*, July 16, 2010.

39. Robert Tanner, "Time to Mend Justice?" *Austin American-Statesman*, April 29, 2007, G1.

40. "Inmate Freed After DNA Mix-Up," *Austin American-Statesman*, March 13, 2003, B2.

41. Robert Tharp, "Freedom Isn't Easy for Wrongly Convicted Man," *Austin American-Statesman*, August 5, 2006, D7; "Perry Pardons Man Wrongly Convicted," *Austin American-Statesman*, December 21, 2006, B3.

42. Information about the case of Cameron Todd Willingham comes from David Grann, "Trial by Fire: Did Texas Execute an Innocent Man?," *New Yorker*, September 7, 2009; Bob Ray Sanders, "Texas Forensic Science Commission Members Shine Light into Some Dark Places," *Fort Worth Star Telegram*, September 21, 2010.

CHAPTER 10

1. *Gitlow v. New York*, 268 U.S. 652 (1925).

2. *Texas v. Johnson*, 491 U.S. 397 (1989).

3. Erik Rodriguez and Tony Plohetski, "Demonstrations Begin Peacefully, End in Arrests," *Austin American-Statesman*, March 21, 2003, B1.

4. *McCreary County v. ACLU*, 545 U.S. 844 (2005).

5. *New Braunfels v. Waldschmidt*, 109 Tex. 302 (1918).

6. *Ireland v. Bible Baptist Church*, 480 S.W.2d 467 (1972).

7. *Reynolds v. Rayborn,* 116 S.W.2d 836 (1938).

8. *Engel v. Vitale,* 370 U.S. 421 (1962).

9. *Abington School District v. Schempp* and *Murray v. Catlett,* 374 U.S. 203 (1963).

10. In 1995, the Gallup Poll reported that 71 percent of Americans responded that they would favor a constitutional amendment that would permit prayers in public schools. Although that exact question containing the word "amendment" has not been asked again, large majorities regularly say that they support the idea of Judeo-Christian displays in public institutions; for example, in 2001, 66 percent favored prayers in public schools; see *The Gallup Poll: Public Opinion for 1995 and 2001* (Wilmington, Del.: Scholarly Resources), 50, 107. In 2005, 76 percent of the American public supported the display of plaques featuring the Ten Commandments in county courthouses; see the Associated Press, "Split Rulings on Ten Commandment Displays," www.msnbc.com for June 27, 2005.

11. Kim Sue Lia Perkes, "Survey: Texans Support Prayers in Public Schools," *Austin American-Statesman,* November 21, 1999, B1.

12. Susan Weddington, "A Referendum on Tradition," *Austin American-Statesman,* March 3, 2000; John Cornyn, "Free Speech Means a Right to Prayer," *Austin American-Statesman,* March 31, 2000; Paul Mulshine, "Whose Religion?" *Austin American-Statesman,* April 4, 2000, A1.

13. David Jackson, "High Court Rejects Pre-Game Prayer," *Dallas Morning News,* June 30, 2000, A1.

14. Lorenzo Sadun, "New Texas Pledge Creates More Divides Among States," *Austin American-Statesman,* August 30, 2003, A21.

15. Jim Vertuno, "House Votes to Put 'Under God' in Texas Pledge," *Houston Chronicle,* May 4, 2007.

16. *Croft v. Perry,* No. 09-10347 (Ct. App., 5th Cir., October 13, 2010).

17. *Texas Crime Rates, 1960-2009,* http://www.disastercenter.com/crime/txcrime.htm, accessed July 4, 2011.

18. Number of justifiable homicides from Handgun Control Web site, www.bradycampaign.org, accessed September 12, 2006; estimate of protective use from Dye, *Public Policy* op. cit., 73.

19. Much of this discussion of arguments over the Second Amendment is based on information in Robert J. Spitzer, *The Politics of Gun Control* (Chatham, N.J.: Chatham House, 1995).

20. Jack Manfuso, "Poll: Most Texans Back Gun Limits," *Austin American-Statesman,* June 30, 2000, B3.

21. Rick Green, "The Real Story of the Second Amendment," *Austin American-Statesman,* April 10, 2000, A9.

22. *District of Columbia v. Heller,* 554 U.S. 570 (2008); *McDonald v. Chicago,* 561 U.S. ___, 130 S. Ct. 3020 (2010).

23. Virginia Gray ranks Texas as the forty-fifth most conservative (that is, most permissive of private gun ownership) among the states; see "The Socioeconomic and Political Context of States," in Virginia Gray and Russell L. Hanson, eds., *Politics in the American States: A Comparative Analysis,* 8th ed. (Washington, D.C.: Congressional Quarterly, 2004), 4, Table 1.1.

24. Robert W. Gee, "Gun-Rights Advocates Brace for Battle," *Austin American-Statesman,* August 30, 2002, B1; Michele Kay, "New Concealed Handgun Law Reverses Limits," *Austin American-Statesman,* June 21, 2003, B1.

25. "Governor Signs Off on Self-Defense Law," *Austin American-Statesman,* March 28, 2007, A11; Jeff Wentworth and Patrick Rose, "Criticism of Gun Bill Was Way Off-Target," *Austin American-Statesman,* March 28, 2007, A11.

26. *Roe v. Wade,* 410 U.S. 113 (1973).

27. Texas Department of State Health Services, http://www.dshs.state.tx.us/chs/vstat/latest/nabort.shtm, accessed June 28, 2011.

28. Suzanne Gamboa, "Most Favor Abortion Notice Bill," *Austin American-Statesman,* March 3, 1997, B1; Mike Norman, "Texas Pre-Abortion

Sonogram Bill Short on Details," *Fort Worth StarTelegram,* June 17, 2011.

29. David Pasztor, "Senate Passes Bill That Defines a Fetus as an Individual," *Austin American-Statesman,* May 23, 2003, A1; Melissa Ludwig, "Law on Abortion Stayed for Now," *Austin American-Statesman,* August 5, 2003, B1; Rachel Proctor, "Your Right to Not Much," *Texas Observer,* August 20, 2003, 4.

30. Kelley Shannon, "Execute Doctors for Abortions? Some Say It Could Happen," *Austin American-Statesman*, August 30, 2005, B3; Jason Embry, "Texas Abortion Law under Scrutiny," *Austin American-Statesman*, July 13, 2006, A1.

31. Attorney General of Texas, Opinion Number GA-0501, January 24, 2007; we are grateful to Charlotte Harper of the AG's office for clarifying the meaning of this opinion for us.

32. *Brown v. Board of Education of Topeka,* 347 U.S. 483 (1954).

33. Joel Anderson, "Judge Ends School Desegregation in Dallas," *Austin American-Statesman,* June 6, 2003, B3.

34. Kent Fischer, "Public School, Private Club," *Dallas Morning News*, November 18, 2006, A1.

35. *Edgewood Independent School System v. Kirby,* 777 S.W.2d 391 (Tex. 1989).

36. Kenneth K. Wong, "The Politics of Education," in Grey and Hanson, *Politics in the American States,* op. cit., 368.

37. "Wealthy Make More Donations, Study Finds," *Dallas Morning News,* April 15, 2004, A3.

38. Jason Embry, "School Tax System Unconstitutional," *Austin American-Statesman*, November 23, 2005, A1; Maeve Reston, "Taxpayers' Lawsuit Challenges State's School-Finance System," *Austin American-Statesman,* April 6, 2001, B5; Alberta Phillips, "School Finance Gives Robin Hood Bad Name," *Austin American-Statesman*, April 27, 2001, A15.

39. Jason Embry and Corrie MacLaggan, "It's Finished: All of School Finance Plan Goes to Perry," *Austin American-Statesman,* May 16, 2006, A1; Christy Hoppe, "School 'Fix' Plan: Is It Sufficient?" *Dallas Morning News*, May 13, 2006, A1.

40. Most of the information in this account comes from Michael Berryhill, "Prisoner's Dilemma," *New Republic,* December 27, 1999, 18–23.

41. Information on the Tulia case is based on Adam Liptak, "Texas Cases Challenged over Officer's Testimony," *New York Times,* March 18, 2003, A20; Nate Blakeslee, "Free at Last?" *Texas Observer,* April 25, 2003, 10; David Pasztor, "In Infamous Tulia, 13 to Walk Free Today," *Austin American-Statesman,* June 16, A1; David Pasztor, "DA Faces State Bar Inquiry in Tulia Case," *Austin American-Statesman,* August 2, 2003, B1; Editorial, "District Attorney in Tulia Case Should Be Held Accountable," *Austin American-Statesman,* December 29, 2004, A10.

42. Pasztor, "Infamous Tulia," ibid.

43. David Pasztor, "Amarillo to Pay $5 Million to 45 in Tulia Case," *Austin American-Statesman*, March 12, 2004, A1; Alan Bean, "A Letter from Tulia," *Texas Observer*, February 18, 2005, 29.

44. *Legal Responsibility and Authority of Correctional Officers* (College Park, Md.: American Correctional Association, 1975), 5.

45. See, for example, Frank S. Malone, *Correctional Law Digest 1977* (Toledo, Ohio: University of Toledo, 1978).

46. Frank S. Kemmerer, *William Wayne Justice* (Austin: University of Texas, 1991), 145–149; *Morales v. Turman,* 326 F. Supp. 577 (1971), 38; *Ruiz v. Estelle,* 666 F.2d 854 (1982); one of the authors of this text made several visits to the TDC units during the period of litigation and can personally attest the accuracy of many of Ruiz's charges; see also Steve J. Martin and Sheldon Ekland-Olson, *Texas Prisons: The Walls Came Tumbling Down* (Austin: Texas Monthly Press, 1987); "Inside America's Toughest Prison," *Newsweek,* October 6, 1986, 48–61.

47. Mike Ward, "After 30 Years, Ruiz Is Ready for Case's Close," *Austin American-Statesman,*

June 12, 2002, A1; Ed Timms, "30-Year Texas Prison Battle Ends," *Dallas Morning News*, June 9, 2002, A1.

48. *The Book of the States 2006* (Lexington, Ky.: Council of State Governments, 2006), 537–538.

49. Ken Anderson, *Crime in Texas: Your Complete Guide to the Criminal Justice System* (Austin: University of Texas, 1997), 73.

50. *Furman v. Georgia,* 408 U.S. 238 (1972).

51. *Gardner v. Florida,* 430 U.S. 349 (1977); *Woodson v. North Carolina,* 428 U.S. 289 (1976); our summary of these death penalty rules is based on J. W. Peltason, *Understanding the Constitution,* 8th ed. (New York: Holt, Rinehart & Winston, 1979), 185.

52. www.deathpenaltyinfo.org/number-executions-state-and-region-1976, accessed July 1, 2011.

53. Robert Tharp, "Is Death Penalty Losing Capital?" *Dallas Morning News*, December 30, 2005, A1.

54. Mike Ward, "Life Without Parole Among 600 Laws Signed by Governor," *Austin American-Statesman*, June 18, 2005, A15.

55. Alberta Phillips, "We Must Draw the Line at Executing Juvenile Offenders," *Austin American-Statesman,* September 1, 2002, H3.

56. Alfred P. Carlton, Jr. (president of the ABA), "Executing Juveniles Demeans Our Justice System," *Austin American-Statesman,* August 27, 2002, A9; David Pasztor, "Global Review of Death Penalty," *Austin American-Statesman,* October 28, 2003, A1.

57. Mike Ward, "High Court Spares Juvenile Offenders," *Austin American-Statesman*, March 2, 2005, A1; the case is *Roper v. Simmons,* 543 U.S. 551, 125 S. Ct. 1183, 161 L. Ed. 2d 1 (2005).

58. Dave Montgomery, "Texas Court Dismisses Reprimand Against Judge," *Fort Worth Star Telegram*, October 12, 2010.

59. Diane Jennings, "Keller Hearing Set for San Antonio," *Dallas Morning News,* June 18, 2009.

60. David Pasztor, "House Passes Bitterly Fought Tort Reform Bill," *Austin American-Statesman,* March 29, 2003.

61. Howard Marcus and Bruce Malone, "2003 Reforms Helping Doctors Do Their Work," *Austin American-Statesman*, April 10, 2006, A9; Jon Opelt, "Contrary to What Study Says, Malpractice Lawsuits Drive Costs," *Austin American-Statesman*, March 18, 2005, A15.

62. Alex Winslow, "The Human Toll of 'Tort Reform,'" *Austin American-Statesman*, April 12, 2006, A11; Bernard Black, Charles Silver, David Hyman, and William Sage, "Hunting Down the Facts on Medical Malpractice," *Austin American-Statesman*, March 14, 2005, A9.

63. Bill Hammond, "New Era of Pro-Business Leadership Is Good for Texas," *Austin American-Statesman*, April 15, 2003, A11.

64. Mimi Swartz, "Hurt? Injured? Need a Lawyer? Too Bad!" *Texas Monthly*, November 2005, 258.

CHAPTER 11

1. Discussion of county government in Texas relies in part on Robert E. Norwood and Sabrina Strawn, *Texas County Government: Let the People Choose* (Austin: Texas Research League, 1984). This monograph is the most extensive work available on the subject.

2. See *County Quickfacts* at http://quickfacts.census.gov/qfd/states/48000.html. Click on Texas, and then enter the county of interest.

3. Although one often sees commissioners court written as *commissioners'* with an apostrophe, Chapter 81 of the *Texas Local Government Code* is explicit in the lack of an apostrophe.

4. Norwood and Strawn, op. cit., 157.

5. Bell County Judge John Garth, in a conversation with one of the authors on February 21, 1991.

6. Travis County Judge Bill Aleshire in "Elected County Officials—Unlike City—Actually Run Government," *Austin American-Statesman*, September 26, 1996, A15.

7. Robert Elder, Jr., and Brad Reagan, "Rural Counties Try to Stay One Step Ahead of Growth," *Wall Street Journal*, July 12, 2000, T1, T3.

8. Richard Oppel (editor of the paper), "Time to Ask Right Questions about County Government," *Austin American-Statesman*, September 22, 1996, E3; and Richard Evans, Liz Sumter, and Wayne Branscom, "County Governments Need More Power to Manage Growth," *Austin American-Statesman*, April 5, 2009, originally available at http://www.statesman.com/search/content/editorial/stories/04/05/0405judges_edit.html.

9. Provisions for how both home-rule and general-law municipalities can organize are found in Chapters 9 and 21–26 of the *Texas Local Government Code*. An extensive look at the concept of home rule both in Texas and nationally can be found in Dale Krane, ed., *Home Rule in America* (Washington, D.C.: CQ Press, 2000).

10. See Victor S. DeSantis and Tari Renner, "City Government Structures: An Attempt at Clarification," *State and Local Government Review*, vol. 14 (Spring 2002), 95–104.

11. Texas *Almanac, 2010–2011* (Denton: Texas State Historical Association, 2010), 500–510, by count. The method of calculation may result in slight counting errors. Additional information on forms of government is available from http://webapps.icma.org/WhosWho/index.cfm?fuseaction=R, "Who's Who: Recognized Local Governments," a directory accessible only by members of the International City/County Management Association.

12. A thorough look at modern council-manager government can be found in John Nalbandian and George Frederickson, eds., *The Future of Local Government Administration: The Hansell Symposium* (Washington, D.C.: International City/County Management Association, 2002); in the monthly issues of *PM: Public Management*, published by ICMA; and the work of James H. Svara, for example, "Conflict and Cooperation in Elected-Administrative Relations in Large Council-Manager Cities," *State and Local Government Review*, vol. 31 (Fall 1999), 173–189.

13. Bill Hansell, "Evolution and Change Characterize Council-Manager Government," *PM: Public Management* (August 2000), 20.

14. See Robert B. Boynton, "City Councils: Their Roles in the Legislative System," *Municipal Year Book 1976* (Washington, D.C.: International City Management Association, 1976), 67–77, for a detailed discussion on the characteristics of the two models.

15. See Jane Mobley, "Politician or Professional? The Debate over Who Should Run Our Cities Continues," *Governing*, February 1988, 41–48, for an excellent discussion of the advantages and disadvantages of mayors versus city managers as executive officers of cities.

16. See *Model City Charter*, 8th ed. (Denver: National Civic League, 2003).

17. See *Texas Local Government Code*, Chapters 22–25.

18. See, for example, Robert B. Boynton, "City Councils: Their Role in the Legislative System"; Tari Renner and Victor S. DeSantis, "Contemporary Patterns in Municipal Government Structures," *Municipal Year Book 1993* (Washington, D.C.: International City/County Management Association, 1993), 57–68; Daniel R. Morgan and Robert E. England, *Managing Urban America*, 4th ed. (Chatham, N.J.: Chatham House, 1996), 58–80.

19. John Nalbandian discusses local representation in "Tenets of Contemporary Professionalism in Local Government," in George W. Fredrickson, *Ideal and Practice in Council-Manager Government* (Washington, D.C.: International City/County Management Association, 1985), 157–171.

20. Reese Dunklin and Brooks Egerton, "'Designer Districts' Benefit Developers," *Dallas Morning News*, July 3, 2001, 1A, 12A.

21. Peggy Heinkel-Wolfe, "Two Voters to Decide Taxing District," *Denton Record-Chronicle*, October 3, 2010, 1A; and "A Funeral with No Mourners," *Denton Record-Chronicle*, February 17, 2011, 4A.

22. See Jennifer Peebles, "Growing Governments: How 'Special Districts' Spread across Texas with Limited Oversight and Accountability—but with Plenty of Power to Tax," *Texas Watchdog*, available February 15, 2011 at http://www.texaswatchdog.org/2011/02/growing-governments-how-special-districts-spread-across-Texas-power-to-tax/1297796531.story. *Texas Watchdog* investigates abuses of transparency in government.

23. Elizabeth Kellar, "5 Mega Issues Drive Local Changes," *PM: Public Management* (January/February 2011), 6–11.

24. See, for example, Edward C. Olson and Laurence Jones, "Change in Hispanic Representation on Texas City Councils between 1980–1993," *Texas Journal of Political Studies*, vol. 18 (Fall/Winter 1996), 53–74; Laurence F. Jones, Edward C. Olson, and Delbert A. Taebel, "Change in African-American Representation on Texas City Councils: 1980–1993," *Texas Journal of Political Studies*, vol. 18 (Spring/Summer 1996), 57–78.

CHAPTER 12

1. Bob Bland, "Why Worry about Local Government Finances," *Academic Matters*, a joint newsletter of the International City/County Management Association and the National Association of Schools of Public Affairs and Administration, June 2011, available at http://icma.org/en/article/101240/why_worry_about_local_government_finances?pub=2&issue=&utc_source=academic+matters&utc_medium=email&utc_campaign=. Although the article emphasizes local government, the point pertains to state government as well.

2. *Fiscal Size-Up, 2010-11 Biennium* (Austin: Legislative Budget Board, 2009), 9, available online at http://www.lbb.state.tx.us/Fiscal_Size-up/Fiscal%20Size-up%202010-11.pdf. *Fiscal Size-Up* is an excellent source of information about Texas state finance, and is published about six months after the close of each regular session of the Texas legislature.

3. Wayne King, "Despite Success, Sun Belt Oil Patch Is Finding It's Not Immune to Recession," *New York Times,* June 9, 1981, 11.

4. See, for example, "Employment in Texas by Industry," *Texas Almanac* (Denton, Texas State Historical Association, 2010), 507.

5. "States Listed by GDP," *Wikipedia*, available at http://en.wikipedia.org/wiki/List_of_U.S._states_by_GDP on June 2, 2011.

6. "U.S. Equivalents: Comparing U.S. States with Countries," *The Economist*, available at http://www.economist.com/blogs/dailychart/2011/01/us_equivalents on June 2, 2011.

7. "Mining Industry Top States by Percentage of State Economy," *EconPost* available at http://econpost.com/industry/mining-industry-top-states-percentage-state-economy on June 20, 2011.

8. Angela Shah, "Texans' Confidence in Economy Erodes," *Dallas Morning News,* March 17, 2003, 1D, 3D; "No Job Growth Seen," *Dallas Morning News,* March 7, 2003, 1D, 11D; Jonathan Weisman, "Jobs Gone for Good," *Washington Post National Weekly Edition,* September 15–21, 2003, 65; and Greg Schneider, "Another Kind of Homeland Security," *Washington Post National Weekly Edition,* February 9–15, 2004, 18–19.

9. Angela Shah, "Texas Ranked No. 1 for Corporate Locales," *Dallas Morning News*, March 3, 2006, 1D, 5D.

10. Angela Shah, "Texas Jobless Rate Dips to 4.1%," *Dallas Morning News*, June 16, 2007, 1D; Brendan Case, "18% of Jobs Linked to Trade," *Dallas Morning News*, May 18, 2007, 3D; "Top Global Cities," *Dallas Morning News*, March 27, 2007, 3D; and Bob Moos, "Texas Leaps to No. 2 as Place to Retire," *Dallas Morning News*, May 29, 2007, 1D, 6D.

11. "Private Sector Wages," *Texas Observer*, October 15, 2010, 3. See also Brendan Case and Troy Oxford, "Charting the Recession's Depth," *Dallas Morning* News, March 15, 2010, 1D.

12. "Movin' on Down," *Texas Observer*, June 3, 2011, 16. See also Robert T. Garrett and Brendan Case, "Much of Job Growth in Low-Wage Positions," *Dallas Morning News*, August 21, 2011, 1A, 32A.

13. See Brendan Case and Troy Oxford, "Punched in the Payroll," *Dallas Morning News*, February 14, 2011, 1D; Case and Oxford, "Working Better in Texas," *Dallas Morning News*, April 4, 2011, 1D; Paul W. Taylor, "Lone Star Vocation," *Governing*, April 2011, 8.

14. Kelly Kristof, "10 Best and Worst States to Make a Living," *CBS Money Watch*, posted April 12, 2011, at http://keatho .wordpress.com/2011/04/17/10-best-and-worst-states-to-make-a-living/; Mark J. Perry, "Most Favorable, Least Favorable Business Climates," *A View from Corporate America*, accessed on the Carpe Diem blog site on June 3, 2011, at http://mjperry.blogspot .com/2008/07/most-favorable-least-favorable-business.html; and Kail Padgiff, "2011 State Business Tax Climate Index, Eighth Edition," Tax Foundation, posted October 26, 2010, at http://www.taxfoundation.org/research/ show/22658.html.

15. Brendan Case and Collin Eaton, "School Cuts Are Risky Business, Executives Say," *Dallas Morning News*, June 3, 2011, 1A, 5A. See also "Education," *Texas on the Brink* (Austin: Texas Legislative Study Group, 2011), 3, posted February 13, 2011, at http://texaslsg .org/texasonthebrink/?page_id=27.

16. See, for example, Carl Tubbesing and Sheri Steisel, "Answers to Your Welfare Worries," *State Legislatures,* January 1997, 12–19; Rob Gurwitt, "Cracking the Casework Culture," *Governing*, March 1997, 27–30; and William McKenzie, "Texas Tries to Pick Up the Federal Burden," *Dallas Morning News,* May 20, 1997, 13A.

17. Carl Tubbesing and Vic Miller, "Our Fractured Fiscal System," *State Legislatures*, April 2007, 26–28, quotation on p. 26.

18. *Book of the States, 2010 Edition,* vol. 42 (Lexington, Ky.: Council of State Governments, 2010), 440; and *Texas Fact Book, 2010* (Austin: Legislative Budget Board, 2010), 23.

19. See H.B. 3, Seventy-ninth Legislature, Third Called Session; and Dave McNeely, "Texas-Style Tax Cut," *State Legislatures*, April 2007, 22–25.

20. See the information on the Web site of the Tax Foundation, specifically "State and Local Tax Burdens, All States, One Year, 1997–2009," at http://www.taxfoundation .org/taxdata/show/336.html; and *Texas Fact Book, 2010,* 23.

21. *Texas Fact Book, 2010* (Austin: Legislative Budget Board, 2010), 20, is the source for the impact of the comparative data on federal taxing and spending.

22. Carl Davis, et al., *Who Pays? A Distributional Analysis of the Tax Systems in All 50 States* (Washington, D.C.: Institute on Taxation and Economic Policy, 2009), 102–103, available at http://www.itepnet.org/whopays3.pdf.

23. "Bullock's Tax Speech Serves as a Warning for State," *Austin American-Statesman,* January 27, 1991, A8.

24. See, for example, David Osborne and Ted Gaebler, *Reinventing Government* (Reading, Mass.: Addison-Wesley, 1992), especially Chapter 5, "Results-Oriented Government"; Jonathan Walters, "The Cult of Total Quality," *Governing,* May 1992, 38–41; and the many reports stemming from the Texas Performance Review and the National Performance Review. See also Julia Melkers

and Katherine Willoughby, "The State of the States: Performance-Based Budgeting Requirements in 47 Out of 50," *Public Administration Review,* vol. 58 (January/February 1998), 66–73.

25. Katherine Barrett, Richard Greene, Michele Mariani, and Anya Sostek, "The Way We Tax: A 50-State Report," originally available at www.governing.com/archive/2003/feb/8p3intro.txt, quotation on p. 1; and "Texas," from the *Grading the States Summary, 2008,* by the Pew Center on the States at http://www.pewcenteronthestates.org/states_card.aspx?abrv=TX.

26. Katherine Barrett and Richard Greene, with Zach Patton and J. Michael Keeling, "Grading the States '05: The Year of Living Dangerously," *Governing,* available at http://governing.com/gpp/2005/intro.htm. From this overview section, one can examine the report cards of the individual states.

27. "Texas," from *2008 Grading the States Summary*, published by the Pew Center on the States at http://www.pewcenteronthestates.org/states_card.aspx?abrv=TX.

28. Dave McNeely, "Texas-Style Tax Cut," *State Legislatures*, April 2007, 22–26.

29. Comparative data are drawn from "Texas at a Glance," *Texas Fact Book, 2010*, 17–23, and from *Fiscal Size-Up, 2010-11,* 54.

CHAPTER 13

1. Alan Greenblatt, "Federalism in the Age of Obama, *State Legislatures*, July–August 2010, 26–28.

2. See Carl Tubbesing and Vic Miller, "Our Fractured Fiscal System," *State Legislatures*, April 2007, 26; and William T. Pound, "Federalism at a Crossroads," *State Legislatures*, June 2006, 18–19.

3. *San Antonio Independent School District, et al. v. Rodriguez*, 411 U.S. 1 (1973), and *William Kirby, et al. v. Edgewood Independent School District, et al.*, 777 S.W.2d 391 (1989), are the appellate court opinions.

4. *Ruiz v. Estelle*, 666 F.2d 854 (1982) and 650 F.2d 555 (5th Cir. 1981).

5. Ralph K. M. Haurwitz, "Agency Backs Perry's $10,000 Degree Plan," *Austin American-Statesman*, April 27, 2011.

6. See, for example, David Pasztor, "Low-Hanging Fruit," *Texas Observer*, January 26, 2007, 8–10, 20–21, for critical issues that the state legislature may continue to dodge.

7. See, for example, the policy discussion of Randall B. Ripley and Grace A. Franklin, *Congress, the Bureaucracy, and Public Policy*, 5th ed. (Monterey, Calif.: Brooks/Cole, 1991), Chapters 1 and 6.

8. See the U.S. Department of Health and Human Services guidelines at http://aspe.hhs.gov/poverty/11poverty.shtml.

9. See *Texas Fact Book, 2010,* at http://www.lbb.state.tx.us/Fact_Book/Texas_FactBook_2010.pdf, p. 30.

10. See the National Center for Children in Poverty Web site at http://www.nccp.org/profiles/.

11. Statistics derived from U.S. Census Bureau data and U.S. Department of Commerce.

12. *Fiscal Size-Up, 2010–2011* (Austin: Legislative Budget Board, 2009), 111; *Texas Medicaid in Perspective* (Austin: Texas Health and Human Services Commission, 2007), 1–1; and "The Cost of Doing Nothing," *Texas Observer*, June 15, 2007, 3.

13. "Study Provides Look at Homeless," *Dallas Morning News*, December 8, 1999, 3A. See also Joel Stein, "The Real Face of Homelessness," *Time*, January 20, 2003, 52–57; and Wendy Cole and Richard Corliss, "No Place Like Home," *Time*, January 20, 2003, 58–61.

14. Eric Samuels and Greg Fiero, Texas Balance of State 2010 Summary Report, Texas Homeless, Network, 2010, p. 2. Accessed at http://www.thn.org/kb/balance-of-state-continuum-of-care/texas-bos-point-in-time-materials-for-2011-surveycount/.

15. See "Census Finds Drop in Dallas' Homeless," *Dallas Morning News*, April 17, 2007, 1B, 8B, for a look at homeless issues in one metropolitan center.

16. *Texas Fact Book, 2010,* 20.

17. *Texas Fact Book, 2010,* 52.

18. Peggy Fikac, "The Texas Legislature: Governor Says Session's Task Is Set in Stone," *Houston Chronicle*, June 29, 2009.

19. Dianna Hunt, "Healthcare Leaders Say Their Industry Did Fairly Well in the Recent Session," *Fort Worth Star Telegram,* June 29, 2009, C1.

20. Suzannah Gonzales and Corrie MacLaggan, "Texas Is Fifth-Poorest State, Data Show," *Austin American-Statesman*, August 30, 2006, B1; recent census data place Texas as the twenty-first-poorest state: http://www.census.gov/statab/ranks/rank29.html.

21. Kate Alexander, "To Get Stimulus Money, Texas Must Ease Rules on Unemployment Benefits," *Austin American-Statesman*, February 26, 2009.

22. Brenda Trolin, in "Can Workers' Comp Work?" *State Legislatures,* May 1992, 33–37, examines the problems and attempted solutions in various states, with Texas being prominently mentioned in the report.

23. "Welfare Reform, Part Two: A Kinder, Gentler Plan for Texas," *Texas Government News*, September 23, 1996, 2. For an excellent explanation of the federal legislation and its consequences, see Carl Tubbesing and Sheri Steisel, "Answers to Your Welfare Worries," *State Legislatures*, January 1997, 12–19.

24. Scott Pattison, executive director of the National Association of State Budget Officers, in a joint meeting of two standing panels of the National Academy of Public Administration meeting on "Social Equity Implications of Local, State, and Federal Fiscal Challenges," held in Washington, D.C., Raleigh, N.C., and across the country via conference telephone on June 13, 2003.

25. Mitchell Schnurman, "Don't Opt Out of Medicaid," *Fort Worth Star Telegram,* November 21, 2010.

26. See Daniel Gross, "Reeled In," *Dallas Morning News*, February 4, 2007, 1P, 5P.

27. Bob Moos, "The Gender Gap Endures, Even in Retirement," *Dallas Morning News*, June 18, 2006, 1A, 10A.

28. Kenneth K. Wong, "The Politics of Education," in Virginia Gray and Russell L. Hanson, *Politics in the American States* (Washington, D.C.: CQ Press, 2008), 352.

29. Texas Education Agency, *Enrollment in Texas Public Schools, 2009–2010,* September 2010, ix.

30. Jason Embry, "Hispanics Now Make Up a Majority of Texas School Population," *Austin American-Statesman*, March 23, 2011.

31. *Statistical Abstract of the United States, 2011*, http://www.census.gov/compendia/statab/cats/education/educational_attainment.html, accessed July 13, 2011.

32. Sue Armstrong, "Texas School Districts Reaching Point at Which They Can't Do More with Less," *Fort Worth Star Telegram*, March 12, 2011.

33. Nancy Frank, *Charter Schools: Experiments in Reform, an Update* (Austin: Texas Legislative Budget Board, 1995); Kenneth K. Wong and Francis X. Shen, "Politics of State-Led Reform in Education: Market Competition and Electoral Dynamics," *Education Policy* vol. 16, 161–192; Shirley Jenkins, "Metro Academy Was Caught in a 'Vicious Cycle,' State Says," *Fort Worth Star Telegram*, July 25, 2011.

34. *TEA, et al. v. Leeper, et al.,* No. D-2022 (Tex. Sup. Ct. 1994).

35. Michael Birnbaum, "Historians Speak Out About Proposed Texas Textbook Changes," *Washington Post,* March 18, 2010.

36. James C. McKinley, Jr. "Texas Conservatives Win Curriculum Change," *New York Times*, March 12, 2010.

37. *Texas Fact Book, 2010,* 54.

38. Permanent University Fund, Texas Senate, http://www.senate.state.tx.us/75r/senate/commit/c535/20080625/062508_THECB_HEAF_PUF_Overview.pdf, accessed July 14, 2011.

39. Ralph K. M. Haurwitz, "Higher Education Agency Embraces Perry's $10,000 Degree," *Austin American-Statesman,* April 27, 2011.

40. *Hopwood v. Texas,* 78 F.3d 932 (5th Cir. 1996).

41. *Grutter v. Bollinger,* 539 U.S. 306 (2003).

CHAPTER 14

1. Wallace Stegner, *Beyond the Hundredth Meridian: John Wesley Powell and the Second Opening of the West* (Penguin: New York, 1954), 214.

2. Christopher Conte, "Dry Spell," *Governing,* March 2003, 20–24; Stephanie Wang, "Drought Hits State Hard," *Austin American-Statesman,* January 23, 2009, A1; Chad Thomas, "East Texas Drought Threatens Agriculture," *Austin American-Statesman,* June 7, 2010, B4; Asher Price, "La Nina-Fueled Drought Worsens; Little Relief Is Expected in April," *Austin American-Statesman,* March 26, 2011, A1.

3. Jonathan Burnett, *Flash Floods in Texas* (College Station: Texas A&M University Press, 2008), 304–308; Jorge Vargas, "More Border Residents Flee as Flooding Worsens," *Austin American- Statesman,* July 8, 2010, B1.

4. Kathleen Hartnet White, "Water Supply," accessed at Texas Public Policy Foundation Web site, December 30, 2009.

5. Joe Nick Patoski, "Playing by the Rule," *Texas Observer,* June 25, 2010, 11.

6. This account is based on information in the following: Asher Price, "Rice Farmers Brace for Dry Days," *Austin American-Statesman,* October 14, 2009, A1; Editorial, "Rice Farmers May Be up a Creek," *Austin American-Statesman,* November 16, 2009; LCRA Web site.

7. The information in this section is based on Forrest Wilder, "Cash Flow," *Texas Observer,* September 3, 2010, 13; Joe Nick Patoski, "Playing by the Rule," *Texas Observer,* June 25, 2010, 10.

8. *Mesa Water, L. P. and G&J Ranch, Inc. v. Texas Water Development Board* documents;

we are grateful to Cole Camp, Assistant Manager of the Panhandle Groundwater Conservation District, for supplying us with documents pertaining to this lawsuit.

9. Dan Bacher, "Judge Upholds Pumping Limits to Protect Delta Smelt," Alternet, http://blogs.alternet.org/speakeasy/2010/02/11/1419/; "San Joaquin Dust Bowl Blamed on Water Fight," http://abcnews.go.com/Business/wirestory?id=12397809.

10. Information on this subject comes from Asher Price, "Whooping Cranes Are Subject of Likely Suit," *Austin American-Statesman,* December 9, 2009, B1; the Web site of the Aransas Project, http://thearansasproject.org/; Forrest Wilder, "Whooping Cranes Rock the System," *Texas Observer,* March 30, 2010.

11. Mission statement from the TCEQ Web site, March 7, 2011.

12. For an illustrative example, see "The Science of Squelching," *Texas Observer,* February 5, 2010, 3.

13. *Aransas Project v. Shaw, et al,* filed March 10, 2010; as of August 2011, when this book went press, no decision had been issued in this case.

14. Rainfall statistics from http://web2.airmail.net/danb1/annualrainfall.htm.

15. Marc Reisner, *Cadillac Desert: The American West and Its Disappearing Water* (New York: Penguin, 1993), 443–446.

16. Helen Thorpe, "The War for the Colorado," *Texas Monthly,* May 1997, 98.

17. *2007 State Water Plan* is available at http://www.twdb.state.tx.us/wrpi/swp/swp.asp.

18. *Texas: The State of Flowing Water,* documentary film broadcast on KLRU, Austin, February 12, 2009.

19. Jim Watts, "Official: We're Running Out of Water Legacy," and "State Needs to Step Up," *The Bond Buyer,* February 14, 2007, 27.

20. For example: Robert J. Duffy, *Nuclear Politics in America: A History and Theory of Government Regulation* (Lawrence: University Press of Kansas, 1997).

21. Robert Engler, *The Politics of Oil: Private Power and Democratic Directions* (Chicago: University of Chicago Press, 1961); Robert Engler, *The Brotherhood of Oil: Energy Policy and the Public Interest* (Chicago: University of Chicago Press, 1977); David F. Prindle, *Petroleum Politics and the Texas Railroad Commission* (Austin: University of Texas Press, 1981).

22. U.S. Energy Information Administration—State/Territory Energy Profiles—Texas, www.eia.gov/cfapps/state/state_energy_profiles.cfm?sid=TX, accessed March 15, 2011.

23. John Collins Rudolf, "Polar Ice Loss Is Accelerating, Scientists Say," www.nytimes.com, March 3, 2011, from http://green.blogs.nytimes.com/2011/03/11/polar-ice/loss/is-accelerating-scientists-say/?hp; Geoffrey Lean, "Disappearing World: Global Warming Claims Tropical Island," *The Independent*, Web site accessed March 25, 2011: www.independent.co.uk/environment/climate-change/disappearing-world-global-warming-claims-tropical-island-429764.html.

24. Matthew Daly, "Report: Firms Put Diesel into Ground Without Approval," *Austin American-Statesman*, February 1, 2011, A4.

25. "Gulf of Mexico Oil Spill (2010)," *New York Times*, accessed at Web site, March 16, 2011.

26. Prindle, *Texas Railroad Commission,* op. cit., pp. 55–59.

27. Energy Information Administration, op. cit.

28. Comptroller's Web site, http://www.window.state.tx.us/taxbud/revenue.html, accessed March 16, 2011.

29. www.epa.gov/cleanenergy/energy-and-you/affect/natural-gas.html.

30. Elizabeth Souder, "Push for Coal-Fired Power Cools Down," *Dallas Morning News*, January 19, 2011, D1; Asher Price, "Dewhurst Turns to Natural Gas to Replace Coal-Fueled Plants," *Austin American-Statesman*, January 30, 2011, D1; Daniel Yergin, "Stepping on the Gas," *Wall Street Journal*, April 2, 2011, from Web site.

31. Katherine Q. Seelye, "Blast Kills 5 in Pennsylvania," *New York Times*, February 10, 2011.

32. Tom Price and T. J. Aulds, "What Went Wrong: Oil Refinery Disaster," *Popular Mechanics*, published in July 2005 issue; accessed through Web site.

33. Mike Lee, "EPA Still Working on Barnett Shale Air Pollution Problem, Agency Says," *Fort Worth Star-Telegram*, May 11, 2010.

34. Randy Lee Loftis, "Most Barnett Shale Facilities Release Emissions," *Dallas Morning-News*, April 11, 2010.

35. Clark E. Cochran, Lawrence C. Mayer, T. R Carr, N. Joseph Cayer, Mark J. McKenzie, and Laura R. Peck, *American Public Policy: An Introduction*, 10th ed. (Boston: Cengage, 2012), 110.

36. B. Guy Peters, *American Public Policy: Promise and Performance*, 8th ed. (Washington, D.C.: CQ Press, 2010), 363.

37. Rotman, "Praying for an Energy Miracle," op. cit., 49.

38. "Coal Mining Deaths in U.S., 1990–2009," http://frankwarner.typepad.com/free_frank_warner/2006/01/us_coal_mining.html.

39. Brenda Wilson, "The Quiet Deaths Outside the Coal Mines," April 6, 2010, from the National Public Radio Web site, www.npr.org/templates/story/story.php?storyId=126021059.

40. "Environment: The Price of Strip Mining," *Time*, March 22, 1971, accessed from Web site: www.time.com/time/magazine/article/0,9171,904921,00.html.

41. From the Union of Concerned Scientists Web site: www.ucsusa.org/clean_energy/coalvswind.CO2c.html.

42. Energy Information Administration, op. cit.

43. Ibid.

44. Rotman, "Praying for an Energy Miracle," op. cit., 49.

45. Samuel McCracken, *The War Against the Atom: The Overwhelming Case for Nuclear Power—and Against the Groups and Individuals Who Continue to Fight It* (New York: Basic Books, 1982), 171; Thomas R. Dye,

Understanding Public Policy, 13th ed. (Boston: Longman, 2011), 224–225.

46. John M. Sutton, "Nuclear Energy? Yes, It's Worth Considering," *Austin American-Statesman*, February 26, 2011, A13; see also the Web site of Professor Bernard L. Cohen: http://www.phyast.pitt.edu/~blc/.

47. A great deal of information regarding the world's supply of uranium, broken down by countries, is available at: http://www.world-nuclear.org/info/reactors.html, accessed March 25, 2011.

48. Wikipedia on Chernobyl.

49. Robert Mackey, "March 17 Updates on Japan's Nuclear Crisis and Earthquake Aftermath," *New York Times*, March 17, 2001, and James Kantor and Judy Dempsey, "Germany Shuts Down 7 Plants as Europe Plans Safety Tests," *New York Times*, March 15, 2011, both accessed on Web site, www.nytimes.com, March 25, 2011; Shino Yuasa and Jeff Donn, "Japan Fears Core Breach," *Austin American-Statesman*, March 26, 2011, A1.

50. George Monbiot, "Why Fukushima Made Me Stop Worrying and Love Nuclear Power," *The Guardian*, www.guardian.co.uk, published March 21, 2011, accessed March 25, 2011; John Horgan, "The Scientific Curmudgeon—Holding Firm on Nuclear Power," *The Stute*, March 25, 2011, http://media.www.thestute.com, accessed March 25, 2011.

51. Information in this section comes from the following sources: Gary Taubes, "Whose Nuclear Waste?," *Technology Review*, vol. 105, no. 1 (January/February 2002), 60–67; Bob Keefe, "Nuclear Plant Waste Disposal Is a Mountain-Size Problem," *Austin American-Statesman*, January 27, 2002, A5; Bob Keefe, "Nuclear Waste Consolidation Plan Angers Nevadans," *Austin American-Statesman*, January 27, 2002, A6; Eric Pianin, "Bush Approves Nuclear Waste Site," *Austin American-Statesman*, February 16, 2002, A11; Matthew L. Wald, "Court Ruling Could Stall Nuclear Power Efforts," *Austin American*-Statesman, July 10, 2004, A7; "Future Dim for Long-Planned Nuclear Dump," *Austin American-Statesman*, March 6, 2009, A7.

52. Energy Information Administration, op. cit.

53. Texas Comptroller of Public Accounts, "Window on State Government: Texas Energy Quick Facts," www.window.state.tx.us/finances/captrade/tx_energy_quickfacts.html, accessed March 19, 2011.

54. Robert Bryce, "Texas Wind Power: Reality vs. Hype," MasterResource: a free-market energy blog, August 24, 2009: www.masterresource.org.

55. Ted Williams, "Wind Power Could Kill Millions of Birds per Year by 2030," www.flyrodreel.com/blogs/tedwilliams/2011/february/power-could-millions-birds; Ted Williams, "Wind Advisory," *Fly Rod and Reel*, January/February 2006.

56. Rotman, "Praying for an Energy Miracle," op. cit.

57. Ibid.

58. Severin Borenstein, "The Market Value and Cost of Solar Photovoltaic Electricity Production," Center for the Study of Energy Markets, Working Paper #176, January 2008, from www.ucei.berkeley.edu/PDF/csemwp176.pdf, accessed March 25, 2011.

59. There are many such calculations, each using a slightly different set of assumptions; for example, see Roger Lippman's table of calculations at igc.org (accessed March 25, 2011).

60. Peters, *American Public Policy*, op. cit., 360.

61. Michael E. Kraft and Scott R. Furlong, *Public Policy: Politics, Analysis, and Alternatives*, 3rd ed. (Washington, D.C.: CQ Press, 2010), 371–373; "Poll: Americans Worried but Reject Higher Taxes to Fix Bridges," August 9, 2007, from CNN, http://articles.cnn.com/2007-08-09/politics/bridges.poll, accessed March 26, 2011; "Poll: Majority of Americans Oppose Gas Tax, New Energy Taxes in Wake of Gulf Oil Spill," Institute for Energy Research, July 7, 2010, http://www.instituteforenergyresearch.org/2010/07/07/poll-majority-of-americans-oppose-gas-tax-new-energy-taxes-in-wake-of-gulf-oil-spill/, accessed October 2, 2011.

62. Dye, *Understanding Public Policy*, op. cit., 223.

63. Engler, *Politics of Oil*, op. cit., 86–95, 391–394.

64. From http://governor.state.tx.us/news/speech/14686/.

65. Information in this discussion comes from the following sources: www.nationalwind.com/texas.wind.facts, accessed March 27, 2011; "Expansion of Renewable Energy," Office of the Governor Web site, www.governor.state.tx.us/priorities/infrastructure/energy/expansion-of-renewable-energy; Lisa Chavarria, "Wind Power: Prospective Issues," *Texas Bar Journal* (October 2005), 832–841.

66. Robert Bryce, "Texas Wind Power: Reality vs. Hype," August 24, 2009, from www.masterresource.org/2009/08/texas-wind-power-the-numbers-versus-the-hype.

67. Information in this section comes from Brett Perlman, "Blackouts Raise Lots of Questions About Electricity Industry," *Austin American-Statesman*, February 10, 2011, A8; Ross Baldick, "ERCOT and the Historic Failure of Electric Generators," *Austin American- Statesman*, February 23, 2011, A6; Forrest Wilder, "Rolling Profits," *Texas Observer*, March 11, 2011, 2; Kate Galbraith, "Has Electric Deregulation Helped or Hurt Texans?," *Texas Tribune,* July 12, 2010, www.texastribune.org.

68. Peters, *American Public Policy*, op. cit., 373, 375.

69. Tai Kreidler, "Lone Star Landscape: Texans and Their Environment," in John W. Storey and Mary L. Kelley, eds., *Twentieth-Century Texas: A Social and Cultural History* (Denton: University of North Texas Press, 2008), 389, 393, 395.

70. See William T. Bianco and David T. Canon, *American Politics Today*, 2nd ed. (New York: W. W. Norton, 2011), 320.

71. Forrest Wilder, "The Science of Squelching," *Texas Observer*, February 5, 2010, 3; Web site of Senator Elliott Shapleigh, http://shapleigh.org/news/2992, accessed March 28, 2011;

Forrest Wilder, "Radioactive Gifts," *Texas Observer*, April 8, 2001, 2.

72. Information on the ligustrum is from Asher Price, "While Some Remove Invasive Plants, Others Sell Them," *Austin American-Statesman*, March 12, 2011, A1; and Web sites: for Texas Invasives, www.texasinvasives.org, and the campaign finance records of the Texas Ethics Commission, www.ethics.state.tx.us/main/search.htm.

73. Information from the Comptroller's Office: www.window.state.tx.us/specialrpt/tif/energy.html.

74. Tony Dutzik, "Wasting Our Waterways: Toxic Industrial Pollution and the Unfulfilled Promise of the Clean Water Act" (Austin: Environment Texas Research and Policy Center, 2009), 9–16.

75. Tom Fowler, "New Fracturing Disclosure Rules May Take Awhile," *Houston Chronicle*, May 31, 2011, accessed on the Web site of the *Texas Tribune*, June 1, 2011.

76. Matthew Tresaugue, "Despite Drought, Water Plan Dies," *Houston Chronicle*, May 24, 2011, from Web site.

77. Tim Eaton, "PUC Sunset Bill Falls," http://www.statesman.com/blogs/content/shared-gen/blogs/austin/politics/entries/2011/05/24/puc_sunset_falls.html?cxntfid=blogs_postcards, May 24, 2011; Enrique Rangel, "Chisum Looks Ahead to Railroad Commission," *Texas Tribune,* from Web site, May 31, 2011.

78. From Car-Accidents.com, Wikipedia, and the Texas Department of Transportation Web sites.

79. From TexasHighwayMan.com.

80. Calculated from information in Matthew Philips, "The CO_2 State," *Newsweek*, February 28, 2008, from Web site.

81. We took the estimates for number of cardiopulmonary deaths per 100,000 population attributable to particulate air pollution made for the years 1990–1994 in each city, available at www.nrdc.org/air/pollution/bt/Tx.asp; we updated population figures based on either the 2010 census or the nearest estimate in

time, divided 100,000 into the population, and then multiplied by the rate estimated by the NRDC.

82. Texas Transportation Institute, "2010 Annual Urban Mobility Report," Table 1, http://mobility.tamu.edu/files/2011/09/national-table_1.pdf.

83. Information on the politics of road building comes from the following sources: Texas Department of Transportation Web site, www.dot.state.tx.us/; Griffin Smith, "The Highway Establishment and How It Grew and Grew and Grew," in David F. Prindle, ed., *Texas Monthly's Political Reader*, 3rd ed. (Austin: Texas Monthly Press, 1985), 69–80.

84. Ben Wear, "Privately Run Toll Roads Back in Fast Lane," *Austin American-Statesman*, March 24, 2011, A1; "Window on State Government," Comptroller's Office report, www.window.state.tx.us/specialrpt/tif/transportation.html.

85. Information on the Trans-Texas Corridor from Eileen Welsome, "The Highwayman," *Texas Observer*, December 14, 2006 (from Web site); "Trans-Texas Corridor News," Web site: http://transtexascorridor.blogspot.com/; Web site of TxDOT, op. cit.; 2008 Sunset Advisory Commission Staff Report on TxDOT, available at http://www.sunset.state.tx.us/82ndreports/txdot/chart81.pdf.

86. www.nhtsa.gov/cars/rules/cafe/overview.htm.

87. http://en.wikipedia.org/wiki/Seat_belt#History.

88. Elizabeth Ridlington and Rob Sargent, "State Clean Cars Program: An Effective Way to Slash Global Warming Pollution (Boston: National Association of State PIRGs, no date), Available at http://cdn.publicinterestnetwork.org/assets/0e e8f393c41c52c551b6f3585fb816d4/US-State-Clean-Cars-Program.pdf; www.climatechoices.org/ca/solutions/solutions_discount.html; www.foe.org/transportation/clean-cars-campaign.

89. www.ghsa.org/html/stateinfo/bystate/tx.html.

90. Leon F. Bouvier and Dudley L. Poston, Jr., *Thirty Million Texans?* (Washington, D.C.: Center for Immigration Studies, 1993), 87.

91. Thomas A. Garrett, "Light-Rail Transit in America: Policy Issues and Prospects for Economic Development," Federal Reserve Banks of St. Louis, 2004, 9.

92. Bill King, "The Emperor's New Light Rail: Metro Expansion Plan Rests on Myths and Falsehoods," *Houston Chronicle*, March 20, 2010, from Web site; Garrett, "Light-Rail Transit," op. cit., 7 (on DART); Ben Wear, "Plan to Put Trains in Car Lanes on Half of Route Is Unusual," *Austin American-Statesman*, April 4, 2011, B1.

93. Phil Magness, "A Streetcar Named Disaster," *Houston Chronicle*, March 7, 2004, from Web site; Wendy Siegle, "Houston Trains to Houston Drivers: We Are Bigger and Heavier Than You," KUHF, January 19, 2011, from Web site, http://transportationnation.org/2011/01/19/houston-trains-to-houston-drivers-we-are-bigger-and-heavier-than-you/; Rosanna Ruiz, "Move It! Left Turns Blamed in Light Rail Collisions," *Houston Chronicle*, November 23, 2008, from Web site.

94. Ben Wear, "Plan to Put Trains in Car Lanes on Half of Route Is Unusual," *Austin American-Statesman,* April 4, 2011, B1.

95. The line does in fact appear in public debate about Houston's light-rail line. The phrase is used by kjb434 in the exchanges of October 21, 2010 at http://swamplot.com/metro-light-rail-construction-slows-to-a-crawl/2010-10-21/.

Glossary

A

acre-foot   The amount of water sufficient to cover an acre of land to a foot deep, or 325,851.4 gallons (Chapter 14).

administrative discretion   The freedom that administrators (bureaucrats) have in implementing and interpreting laws (Chapter 8).

ad valorem property tax   A tax based on the value of real property, and in some cases, the contents of structures, assessed at some cents per $100 of valuation (Chapter 11).

affirmative action   Admissions program that takes race, gender, and ethnicity into account to attempt to make up for past patterns of discrimination (Chapter 13).

appellate jurisdiction   The authority of a court to hear cases sent to it on appeal from a lower court. Appellate courts review only the legal issues involved and not the factual record of the case (Chapter 9).

appointment and removal powers   The governor's constitutional and statutory authority to hire and fire people employed by the state (Chapter 7).

at-large elections   Elections in which each candidate for any given public office must run jurisdictionwide—in the entire city, county, or state—when several similar positions are being filled (Chapters 9 and 11).

attorney general's advisory opinion   A legal opinion as to the constitutionality of legislative proposals (bills), rules, procedures, and statutes (laws) (Chapter 9).

B

bicameral   For a legislative body, divided into two chambers or houses (Chapter 6).

biennial   Two years. Thus, a biennial legislative session occurs every other year, and a biennial budget is one that directs spending for two years (Chapter 6).

bill   A proposed law written on a piece of paper and submitted to a legislature (Chapter 6).

Bill of Rights   The first ten amendments to the U.S. Constitution. The Texas Bill of Rights, included as Article I in the Texas Constitution, resembles the national Bill of Rights. Generally speaking, bills of rights are sections of constitutions that list the civil rights and liberties of the citizens and place restrictions on the powers of government (Chapter 2).

block grants   Federal funds that can be used for a broad range of programs; the state or local government recipient can determine specific uses within broad guidelines (Chapter 12).

bureaucracy   A type of organization that is characterized by hierarchy, specialization, fixed and official rules, and relative freedom from outside control (Chapter 8).

C

campaign   The activities of candidates and parties in the period of time before an election that try to persuade citizens to vote for them (Chapter 5).

capital punishment   The execution of a convicted criminal, normally imposed only on murderers (Chapter 10).

casework   A legislator's doing favors for constituents, such as troubleshooting or solving a problem (Chapter 6).

categorical grants-in-aid   Federal funds that can be used only for specific purposes (Chapter 12).

charter schools   Special public schools set up to provide unique educational opportunities for students who attend them (Chapter 13).

checks and balances   An arrangement whereby each branch of government has some power to limit the actions of other branches (Chapter 2).

Children's Health Insurance Program (CHIP)   A federal-state cooperative block grant program that provides health care assistance to uninsured children from low-income families (Chapter 13).

civil jurisdiction   The authority of courts that handle noncriminal cases, such as those dealing with divorce, personal injury, taxes, and debts (Chapter 9).

civil liberties   Individual freedoms such as speech, press, religion, and assembly. The protection of these liberties is essential to a vital democratic society. Generally, the protection of civil liberties requires forbidding government to take certain actions (Chapter 10).

civil rights   The constitutional claims all citizens have to fair and equal treatment under the law. Among the most important civil rights are the ability to vote in honest elections, to run for and serve in public office, and to be afforded a fair trial presided over by an impartial judge if accused of a crime. Civil rights refer to actions that government must take in order to ensure equal citizenship for everyone (Chapter 10).

civil service system   A personnel system in a government administrative agency in which employees are hired, fired, and promoted by the agency, rather than by elected politicians outside the agency. Individuals generally are hired and promoted through some sort of written examination. There are often restrictive rules that make firing an individual employee difficult. Often called the "merit system" (Chapter 8).

clientele group   An interest group that benefits from or is regulated by an administrative agency (Chapter 8).

closed primary   A primary in which only voters who are registered members of that party may participate (Chapter 5).

coalition   A group of interests and individuals supporting a party or a candidate for office (Chapter 4).

commissioners court   The administrative and legislative body of a county; in Texas, it has four elected members and is presided over by an elected county judge (Chapter 11).

concurrent jurisdiction   The authority of two or more different types of courts to hear the same type of case (Chapter 9).

conference committee   A temporary joint committee of both houses of a legislature in which representatives attempt to reconcile the differences in two versions of a bill (Chapter 6).

conservatism   A political ideology that, in general, opposes government regulation of economic life and supports government regulation of personal life (Chapters 1 and 4).

constituent function   The power of a legislative body to propose constitutional amendments and, in the case of a state legislature, to ratify amendments to the national constitution (Chapter 6).

constitution   The basic law of a state or nation that takes precedence over all other laws and actions of the government (Chapter 2).

constitutional amendment   A change in a constitution that is approved by both the legislative body, and, in Texas, the voters. National constitutional amendments are not approved directly by voters (Chapter 2).

constitutional revision   Making major changes in a constitution, often including the writing of an entirely new document (Chapter 2).

co-optation   The process by which industries and their interest groups come to dominate administrative agencies that were originally established to regulate the industry's activities (Chapter 3).

Court of Criminal Appeals   The highest state appeals court with criminal jurisdiction (Chapter 9).

criminal jurisdiction   The authority of courts that handle offenses punishable by fines, imprisonment, public service, or death. These offenses include murder, rape, assault, theft, embezzlement, fraud, drunken driving, speeding, and other acts that have been defined as criminal by the state legislature or municipal authorities (Chapter 9).

D

democracy   The form of government based on the theory that the legitimacy of any government must come from the free participation of its citizens (Chapter 1).

district elections   Elections in which a polity is divided into geographical areas; candidates for public office must run in one small area rather than in the whole polity; each district usually sends one representative. Also called single-member district elections (Chapter 9).

district system   A system in which a candidate is required to live in the particular geographic area in which he or she runs for office (Chapter 11).

dual-budgeting system   A system in which both the executive branch and the legislative branch prepare separate budget documents (Chapter 12).

E

elasticity   The flexibility and breadth of the tax system so that state revenues are not seriously disrupted even if one segment of the economy is troubled (Chapter 12).

Equal Protection Clause   The passage in the Fourteenth Amendment to the U.S. Constitution that guarantees all citizens the same rights as all other citizens; originally (1868) intended to guarantee equality under the law to the newly freed slaves, but has since been expanded to other realms (Chapter 5).

estuary   An ecological system created by a freshwater river flowing into a saltwater sea or lake; a transition zone that is saltier than the river but less salty than the sea, and in which salinity varies with the tides and the amount of river water flowing in at various seasons (Chapter 14).

exclusive jurisdiction   The sole authority of one court over a given type of case (Chapter 9).

F

faction   A group of citizens within a political party who differ on some important issues from the members of other groups within the same party (Chapter 4).

Faustian bargain   A metaphorical term applied to human choices in which the potential benefits are great, but the potential price—monetary or otherwise—may be even greater; taken from the epic poem "Faust" by the German poet Goethe, in which Faust sells his soul to the Devil in return for money, power, knowledge, and love (Chapter 14).

federal system   A system of government that provides for a division and sharing of powers between a national government and state or regional governments (Chapter 1).

felony   A major crime, punishable by at least a year in prison upon conviction. Capital felonies may involve the death penalty (Chapter 9).

filibuster   An effort to kill a bill in a legislature by unlimited debate; it is possible in the Texas and U.S. Senates, but not in the Houses of Representatives (Chapter 6).

fiscal year   The budget year for a government or a corporation; it may not coincide with a calendar year. In Texas, the state fiscal year runs September 1 through August 31. Municipal fiscal years run October 1 through September 31, the same as the federal fiscal year (Chapters 6 and 12).

Food Stamp Program   A federal-state cooperative block grant program to provide food-purchasing assistance to low-income families (Chapter 13).

formal qualifications   Qualifications specified by law for holding public office (Chapter 6).

fracking   Petroleum industry shorthand term for "hydraulic fracturing," in which water and chemicals are forced at high pressure into rock formations to break up the rocks, thus permitting the oil and/or gas to flow to a well bore more easily (Chapter 14).

G

general election   An election in which voters choose government officeholders (Chapter 5).

general laws   Statutes that pertain to all municipalities that do not have home-rule status (Chapter 11).

general revenue sharing   A federal program that allowed state and local governments great

flexibility in the use of federal funds. It expired in 1986 (Chapter 12).

gerrymandering   The practice of drawing electoral districts in such a way as to advantage one party or one faction (Chapters 6 and 11).

grand jury   A legal body of twelve or more individuals convened at the county seat. The grand jury considers evidence submitted by prosecutors and determines whether there is sufficient evidence to indict those accused of crimes (Chapter 9).

greenhouse effect   A consequence of the buildup of certain gases in the atmosphere that trap the sun's rays, thus causing a warming of the Earth's climate (Chapter 14).

H

hierarchy   Levels of authority in an organization, with the maximum authority on top (Chapter 8).

home rule   The ability of cities with populations of 5,000 or more to organize themselves as they wish within the constitution and laws of Texas (Chapters 2 and 11).

home schooling   The decision, allowed under Texas law, for families to educate their children at home instead of in public schools (Chapter 13).

hundredth meridian   The imaginary line of longitude that runs north-south down the eastern side of the Texas Panhandle, and continues to cross the Rio Grande near Laredo; the traditional beginning of the "The West" in the United States, because west of the line average rainfall drops below twenty inches a year (Chapter 14).

I

ideology   A system of beliefs and values about the nature of the good life and the good society, and the part to be played by government in achieving them (Chapter 4).

impeachment   The process of formally accusing an official of improper behavior in office. It is followed by a trial, and if the official is convicted, he or she is removed from office (Chapter 7).

impresario   In general, a promoter or organizer of an event; in the context of Texas history, a person who brought groups of settlers to Texas when it was Spanish or Mexican territory (Chapter 1).

incorporation   A historical activity by the U.S. Supreme Court that makes the protections of citizen rights established in the Constitution applicable to state and local governments (Chapter 2).

indictment   An official accusation that a person or organization has committed a crime, normally issued by a grand jury, and normally involving felonies rather than misdemeanors (Chapter 9).

individualistic political culture   The culture, historically dominant in the middle tier of American states, in which citizens understand the state and nation as marketplaces in which people strive to better their personal welfare, citizen participation is encouraged as a means of individual achievement, and government activity is encouraged when it attempts to create private opportunity and discouraged when it attempts to redistribute wealth (Chapter 1).

inflation   A rise in the general price level, which is the same thing as a fall in the value of the dollar (Chapter 12).

infrastructure   The costly government investments in physical, nonhuman resources such as highways, bridges, water lines, and sewer systems; these make possible economic growth and a reasonable quality of life (Chapter 13).

interest   Something of value or some personal characteristic that people share and that is affected by government activity; interests are important both because they form the basis of interest groups and because parties attempt to form many interests into an electoral coalition (Chapter 4).

interest group   A number of people who are organized to defend an interest they share or wish to promote; the interest can be narrow (rice-growers, for example) or broad (consumers, for example) (Chapter 3).

intergovernmental transfers   Money granted to a lower-level of government by a higher-level of government for a specific use, for example, welfare dollars that are passed to the county from the state and the national governments (Chapter 11).

invasive species   Plants and animals that have been introduced into Texas in recent times, and which often cause environmental problems (Chapter 14).

item veto   The governor's constitutional power to strike out individual items in an appropriations bill (Chapter 6).

J

judge   A public official who presides over a court (Chapter 9).

judiciary   A collective term referring to the system of courts and its judges and other personnel (Chapter 9).

juvenile courts   Special state courts that handle accused offenders under the age of seventeen (Chapter 9).

L

laissez faire   A French phrase loosely meaning "leave it alone." It refers to the philosophy that values free markets and opposes government regulation of the economy (Chapter 1).

legislative oversight   The legislature's supervision of the activities of state administrative agencies. Increasingly, the emphasis of oversight is on increasing efficiency and cutting back management—doing more with less (Chapter 6).

legitimacy   People's belief that their government is morally just and that therefore they are obligated to obey it (Chapter 1).

liberalism   A political ideology that, in general, supports government regulation of economic life and opposes government regulation of personal life (Chapters 1 and 4).

light-rail metropolitan transit   Public transportation on small-gauge railroad lines, used within rather than between cities (Chapter 14).

lobby   To try to influence government policy through face-to-face contact (Chapter 3).

lobbyist   A person who attempts to influence government policy through face-to-face contact (Chapter 3).

M

mandate   Action that the national government requires state and local governments to take or that the state requires cities, counties, and special districts to take (Chapters 11 and 13).

Medicaid   A jointly funded federal-state program to provide medical care to low-income families (Chapter 13).

message power   The governor's means of formally establishing his or her priorities for legislative action by communicating with the legislature (Chapter 7).

misdemeanor   A small or moderate crime, punishable by fines or, at maximum, a year in jail (Chapter 9).

moralistic political culture   The culture, dominant in the northern tier of American states, in which citizens understand the state and the nation as commonwealths designed to further the shared interests of everyone, citizen participation is a widely shared value, and governmental activism on behalf of the common good is encouraged (Chapter 1).

N

NIMBY   "Not In My Back Yard," a semi satirical term referring to the fact that people often want waste products (in this case, nuclear waste) disposed of but not near to where they live (Chapter 14).

nonpartisan elections   Elections in which candidates bear no party label such as Republican or Democrat (Chapter 11).

O

one-party system   A state that is dominated by a single political party, characterized by an absence of party competition, inadequate debate of public policy, low voter turnout, and usually conservative public policy (Chapter 4).

open primary   A primary in which all registered voters may participate, whether or not they are registered members of the party holding the primary (Chapter 5).

original jurisdiction   The authority to hear a case first, usually in a trial (Chapter 9).

original trial courts   Courts having the authority to consider and decide both criminal and civil cases in the first instance, as distinguished from appellate courts (Chapter 9).

P

permanent party organization   The small, fixed organization that handles the routine business of a political party (Chapter 4).

place system   A form of at-large election in which all candidates are elected citywide, but the seats on the council are designated Place One, and so forth, and each candidate runs only against others who have filed for the same place (Chapter 11).

plea bargain   The process in which an accused person agrees to plead guilty to a lesser crime and receives a lighter sentence. He or she avoids having to stand trial on a more serious charge, and the state saves the time and expense of a trial (Chapter 9).

plural executive   A system of organizing the executive branch that includes the direct election of multiple executives, thereby weakening the chief executive, the governor. Related concepts include disintegration and fragmentation (Chapters 2 and 7).

plutocratic   A term used to describe a government in which policy is made for the benefit of a few rich interests working behind the scenes; that is, government for the wealthy (Chapter 3).

political action committee (PAC)   A group formed by a corporation, trade association, labor union, or other organization or individual for the purpose of collecting money and then contributing that money to one or more political candidates or causes (Chapter 3).

political culture   A shared framework of values, beliefs, and habits of behavior with regard to government and politics within which a particular political system functions (Chapter 1).

political interest group   A private organization that attempts to influence politicians—and through them public policy—to the advantage of the organization (Chapter 3).

political party   An organization devoted to winning public office in elections, and thus exercising control over public policy (Chapter 4).

political socialization   The process by which we learn information, values, attitudes, and habits of behavior about politics and government (Chapter 4).

populism   The political belief or mass movement based on faith in the wisdom and virtue of the common people, and on the conviction that they are being cheated by elites (Chapter 4).

populist   Someone who believes in the rights, wisdom, and issues of the common people, and that those people should be protected from exploitation by corporations, rich people, and government (Chapter 7).

poverty threshold   The level of income below which a family is officially considered to be poor. It is established annually as the basis for determining eligibility for a variety of social programs. Also called the federal poverty line (Chapter 13).

primary election   An election held within a party to nominate candidates for the general election or choose delegates to a presidential nominating convention; also known as *primary* and *direct primary* (Chapter 5).

privately funded campaign   A system in which candidates and parties must rely on private citizens to voluntarily donate money to their campaign chests; except partially at the presidential level and for some offices in some states, this is the system used in the United States (Chapter 5).

privatizing   Turning over public programs to the private sector to implement. For example, municipalities often contract with private waste management companies to dispose of solid waste. The state has contracted with a private firm to operate some Texas prisons (Chapters 6 and 12).

progressive taxation   A tax system based on ability to pay that requires wealthy people to pay taxes at a higher rate than poor ones (Chapter 12).

pseudo laissez faire   A phrase referring to the tendency of entrepreneurs to oppose government involvement in the economy at the general philosophical level, but to seek government assistance for their particular business (Chapters 1 and 4).

publicly funded campaign   A system in which the government pays for the candidates' campaign expenses, either directly or through parties. This system is not used in the United States, except partially at the presidential level and for some offices in some states (Chapter 5).

public policy The overall purpose behind individual governmental decisions and programs. It is the result of public officials' setting of priorities by creating the budget, making official decisions, and passing laws (Chapter 13).

R

realignment A change in the standing decision to support one party or another by a significant proportion of the electorate, resulting in a change in which party has a "normal" majority on election day (Chapter 4).

reapportionment To reallocate legislative seats by adding seats to areas with heavy population growth and taking away seats from areas without growth (Chapter 6).

redistributive public policy Laws and government decisions that have the effect of taking wealth, power, and other resources from some citizens and giving those resources to others. Examples would be the graduated income tax and affirmative action programs (Chapter 13).

redistricting The designation of geographic areas that are nearly equal in population for the purpose of electing legislators—national, state, and local (Chapter 6).

regressive tax A flat-rate tax that is not based on ability to pay; as a consequence, the poorer the payer of the tax, the larger the percentage of income that goes to the tax (Chapter 12).

revenue bonds Government debt that is sold to private investors and paid off by the revenue produced from services such as water sales (Chapter 11).

revenue shortfall A situation in which state revenues are not expected to be adequate to fund programs and services at current levels (Chapter 12).

revolving door A name given by political scientists to the process in which government regulatory agencies hire their personnel from within the industry being regulated; after they leave the agency, employees are typically hired once more by the regulated industry (Chapter 3).

Rule of Capture A legal principle, inherited from Great Britain but still important in Texas, in which a private landowner is given absolute authority over the underground water underneath his or her property (Chapter 14).

S

school vouchers A policy that would allow families who send their students to private schools to receive a tax deduction to cover a part of private school tuition. This has not been enacted in Texas (Chapter 13).

secular A term that means "apart from religion." Public policies must serve a secular, as opposed to a religious, purpose to avoid establishing a religion (Chapter 10).

seniority In a legislative body, the amount of time spent in continuous service in one house or committee (Chapter 6).

separation of powers A phrase often used to describe the U.S. political system; it refers to the assigning of specific powers to individual branches (or departments, in Texas) of government. In reality, the powers of the branches overlap, so that "separate institutions sharing powers" would be a more accurate description of the U.S. system (Chapter 2).

session power The governor's constitutional authority to call the legislature into special session and to set the agenda of topics to be considered in that session (Chapter 7).

single-member district A designated geographic area from which only one representative is elected (Chapter 6).

social Darwinism A philosophy, drawn from the biological theory of evolution, that holds that the rich are superior people and deserve their wealth, while the poor are inferior and deserve their poverty (Chapter 1).

spoils system Appointing people to government jobs on the basis of whom they supported in the last election and how much money they contributed (Chapter 11).

stimulus funds To help in recovering from the recession of 2007–2009, the national government created a variety of funds to help both the private sector (banks, insurance companies, automobile industry) and the public sector (local law enforcement, additional school teachers) (Chapter 11).

suffrage　The legal right to vote in public elections (Chapter 5).

sunset review　The process by which the legislature reviews the performance of administrative agencies, and then renews, reorganizes, or eliminates them (Chapter 8).

Sunshine Law　A law that provides for public access to the records of administrative agencies (Chapter 8).

Supreme Court　The highest state appellate court with civil jurisdiction (Chapter 9).

T

tag　A means by which an individual senator can delay a committee hearing on a bill for at least forty-eight hours (Chapter 6).

tax equity　The inherent fairness of a tax. As the term is used in this book, ability to pay is a factor in fairness (Chapter 12).

Temporary Assistance for Needy Families (TANF)　A federal-state cooperative block grant program that provides cash assistance to indigent families with dependent children for a period of up to five years (Chapter 13).

temporary party organization　The organization formed to mobilize the party's potential electorate and win an election (Chapter 4).

Texas Commission on Environmental Quality (TCEQ)　The agency responsible for protecting the state's water, air, and land from pollution (Chapter 14).

third party　A minor political party that fails to achieve permanence but frequently influences the major parties and, through them, public policy (Chapter 4).

tort　A private or civil wrong or injury resulting from a breach of a legal duty that exists by reason of society's expectations about appropriate behavior, rather than a contract. The injured party sues the alleged offender in order to receive compensation for his or her losses (Chapter 10).

traditionalistic political culture　The culture, historically dominant in the southern tier of American states, in which citizens technically believe in democracy but do not encourage participation, and government activity is generally viewed with suspicion unless its purpose is to reinforce the power of elites (Chapter 1).

trial jury　Six to twelve persons who determine the legal guilt or innocence of defendants in a criminal trial or the liability of defendants in a civil trial (Chapter 9).

trickle-down theory　A theory of economic development that maintains that government should create a very favorable climate to attract business and industry, and that the prosperity thus created will trickle down to rank-and-file citizens (Chapter 1).

turnover　The proportion of the legislature that consists of first-term members because previous members retired, died, or were defeated at the polls (Chapter 6).

U

user fee　A fee for a specific governmental service charged to the person who benefits from the service; a greens fee at a municipal golf course and college tuition are both user fees (Chapters 11 and 12).

V

veto power　The governor's constitutional authority to prevent the implementation of laws enacted by the legislature. The item veto allows the governor to delete individual items from an appropriations bill (Chapter 7).

voter registration　The process used in every democracy to list the residents who are eligible to vote; it is necessary to prevent fraud, but also discourages turnout by erecting a barrier between the citizen and the simple act of voting (Chapter 5).

voter turnout The proportion of the eligible citizens who actually cast their ballots in an election (Chapter 5).

W

workers' compensation A program that provides medical, income, death, and burial benefits for workers who are injured, become ill, or are killed on the job (Chapter 13).

Y

YBNIIMP "Yes, But Not If I Must Pay," a semi satirical term referring to the fact that citizens often want government to take actions benefiting themselves, but do not want to pay for those actions with taxes, tolls, and so forth. (Chapter 14).

Index

Texas Politics